ULTIMATE SECURITY
COMBATING WEAPONS OF MASS DESTRUCTION

JANNE E. NOLAN, BERNARD I. FINEL, AND BRIAN D. FINLAY, *Editors*

A JOINT PROJECT OF
THE CENTURY FOUNDATION AND
GEORGETOWN UNIVERSITY

THE CENTURY FOUNDATION PRESS　　　◆　　　NEW YORK

The Century Foundation sponsors and supervises timely analyses of economic policy, foreign affairs, and domestic political issues. Not-for-profit and nonpartisan, it was founded in 1919 and endowed by Edward A. Filene.

Library of Congress Cataloging-in-Publication Data

Ultimate security : combating weapons of mass destruction / Janne E. Nolan, Bernard I. Finel, and Brian D. Finlay, editors.
   p. cm.
Includes bibliographical references (p.   ) and index.
  ISBN 0-87078-478-1 (alk. paper)
 1. United States--Military policy. 2. Nuclear weapons--United States.
3. Nuclear nonproliferation. 4. Weapons of mass destruction. 5. World politics--1995-2005. I. Nolan, Janne E. II. Finel, Bernard I. III. Finlay, Brian D.
IV. Title.
UA23.U1142 2003
327.1'747'0973--dc22

2003020991

Cover design and illustration by Claude Goodwin.
Manufactured in the United States of America.

FOREWORD

For at least several decades, the United States has exceeded all other nations in its spending on developing and acquiring new weapons of war. Indeed, one of the strongest current political taboos inhibits any position other than total support for the notion that this nation should maintain its present global preeminence in military power. America believes in doing what it takes to sustain a technological edge over any potential enemies. This nation also believes that other countries, recognizing that our military establishment is intended only for defensive purposes, should not seek to compete with or follow our example when it comes to weapons spending or research.

It is true that the United States has voluntarily eschewed some categories of weapons, notably chemical and biological agents of destruction, while urging other nations to do so as well. And when it comes to the most destructive category of all, nuclear weapons, we have, with mixed success, long followed a strategy of attempting to reduce existing nuclear arsenals and prevent their spread to other nations. Unfortunately, it is unlikely that the task will get any easier soon.

Two trends have intensified concerns about the spread of chemical, biological, and nuclear weapons, the so-called weapons of mass destruction (WMD). First, the science and technology that make possible the development and deployment of such weapons is inevitably becoming more and more accessible. In fact, the pace and spread of scientific knowledge and the dissemination of technology accompanying the globalization of commerce can affect the ease with which nations can acquire these weapons themselves. Second, while the collapse of the Soviet Union eliminated the principal threat of global mass destruction, the more chaotic political situation in many parts of the world following the cold war has created new tensions, threats, and, as September 11 demonstrated, even attacks. The notion of terrorists, especially, in possession of weapons of mass destruction is a nightmare that haunts both policymakers and average citizens. As we are learning, sometimes to our horror, the end of the bipolar conflict between the communists and the West has released a variety of hostile forces whose main purpose is to make a point by killing as many people as possible.

In that context, this volume, representing some of the newest and best thinking about nonproliferation issues, could not be more timely. For The Century Foundation, it is the latest in a long series of foreign policy studies we have supported since the end of the cold war, including Robert Art's *A Grand Strategy for America*, Henry Nau's *At Home Abroad: Identity and Power in American Foreign Policy*, Walter Russell Mead's *Special Providence: American Foreign Policy and How It Changed the World*, and William Durch's *Constructing Regional Security: The Role of Arms Transfers, Arms Control, and Reassurance*. Some of our publications have focused on critical hot spots, including Karl Meyer's *The Dust of Empire: The Race for Mastery in the Asian Heartland*; Selig Harrison's *Korean Endgame: A Strategy for Reunification and U.S. Disengagement*; Barnett Rubin's *Blood on the Doorstep: The Politics of Preventive Action*; and a number of white papers, including Stephen Sestanovich's "At Odds with Iran and Iraq: Can the United States and Russia Resolve Their Differences?"; "Establishing a Stable Democratic Constitutional Structure in Iraq: Some Basic Considerations," a guide prepared by the Public International Law & Policy Group and The Century Foundation; and Richard Kauzlarich's "Time for Change? U.S. Policy in the Transcaucasus."

Perhaps the most important message in this collection of essays is that, beginning in 2000, military options were growing in importance as a component of nonproliferation policy, sometimes at the expense of more nuanced diplomatic and economic instruments. One strong supporting piece of evidence for this conclusion is the war against Iraq. The authors of this volume did not know, writing their final chapters in late 2002 and early 2003, that the American government would respond to the proliferation challenge so dramatically with an imperative for a military invasion of one country thought apparently to harbor an arsenal of weapons of mass destruction. No one welcomes the ongoing empirical demonstration of how limited in effectiveness and decisiveness such an imbalanced policy has proved to be.

The book is divided into three parts. In the first, the editors of the volume give a comprehensive and insightful picture of the current nonproliferation terrain and the most important changes in recent history and approach by the American government. Then, Amy Zegart describes the structure and approach that have dominated American arms control and disarmament efforts over time, focusing especially on the persistence of organizational weakness, as well as the failure to develop a coherent national plan to guide policy and action.

The second part of the volume discusses a number of critical issues that will confront any American government trying to come to terms with the increasing danger of the spread of weapons of mass destruction. Joseph Cirincione gives an overview as well as some significant details on the efforts to achieve nonproliferation through multinational agreements, and Robert S. Litwak provides a thoughtful analysis of the role of force as well as a mechanism for restraining countries that might be attracted to developing weapons of mass destruction. David A. Kay, currently special adviser for strategy in Iraq, looks back to the experiences of the Persian Gulf War prior to the recent conflict and uses the lessons learned to point to the current disarmament challenges in Iraq. Rose Gottemoeller examines the continuing efforts to stem the proliferation of weapons of mass destruction from the former Soviet Union and looks ahead at the possibility of developing non-force-related inducements that would make a more successful nonproliferation regime. Jessica Stern outlines the limits and needs of nonproliferation policy in the currently highly relevant area of terrorist threats, especially bioterrorism.

This section then turns to the tensions between globalization and commercial imperatives and the spread of technology that can provide further vital information for those who would develop weapons of mass destruction. William W. Keller indicates that the military assistance and sales of conventional arms by Western nations sometimes unintentionally helps countries acquire weapons of mass destruction. Joanna Spear's essay has a special focus on NATO and U.S. nonproliferation policy. She explains in terms comprehensible to a layman that the strategic culture of the Western alliance is important in determining what sort of global nonproliferation policy is possible and would be effective over time.

The last part of the book pulls together the recommendations and conclusions implied by the other chapters. Taken together, these three sections provide evidence of both American success and folly in recent decades. Perhaps more important, they indicate how, going forward, America's closest allies, especially in NATO, can work together to create a more successful nonproliferation strategy.

On behalf of the authors and The Century Foundation, I want to thank the MacArthur Foundation, especially Jonathan Fanton, Kennette Benedict, and Renee DeNevers. It also is important to note that this volume was the result of a joint venture with Georgetown University.

Special thanks are due to Janne Nolan and Brian Finlay, who guided the project since its inception during their time on the staff of The Century Foundation, and to Bernard Finel of Georgetown University.

Richard C. Leone, President
The Century Foundation
September 2003

CONTENTS

ACKNOWLEDGMENTS

Preparing a volume of essays is very much a collaborative effort. The volume would of course not have been possible without the contributions of the authors of the essays who were writing at a time when world events mandated seemingly constant updating of their materials. The editors extend sincere gratitude to these individuals both for the excellence of their contributions and their enduring commitment to this project. We also are very grateful for the generous support received from the John D. and Catherine T. MacArthur Foundation and the W. Alton Jones Foundation, particularly George Perkovich.

The editors are grateful to Georgetown University and to The Century Foundation for sponsoring this effort. Special thanks are owed to Professor Michael Brown, Director of the Center for Peace and Security Studies, and Ambassador Robert Gallucci, Dean of the School of Foreign Service, at Georgetown University. The president and senior leadership of Georgetown also deserve credit for encouraging policy-related research under its auspices.

At The Century Foundation, the editors would like to thank the President of the Foundation, Richard Leone, and Senior Vice President Carol Starmack, whose painstaking attention to detail allowed this project to move forward. Rob Wiygul of the Washington office was extremely helpful in the early stages of preparing the volume, as was Steven Greenfield of the Foundation's New York office, who edited the final manuscript. Beverly Goldberg, Vice President and Director of Publications, provided support and encouragement throughout.

PART ONE
INTRODUCTION

INTRODUCTION
THE TRANSFORMATION OF AMERICA'S NONPROLIFERATION POLICY

Janne E. Nolan, Bernard I. Finel, and Brian D. Finlay

The proliferation of weapons of mass destruction and other advanced military technologies has emergedas the preeminent security concern for the United States since the end of the twentieth century. This was pointedly demonstrated in early spring 2003 by the U.S.-led invasion of Iraq, which embraced the twin objectives of destroying Saddam Hussein's military arsenal and toppling his regime. In North Korea, Pyongyang's nuclear saber rattling and illicit missile technology exports are newly testing the diplomatic skill and military resolve of the administration of George W. Bush. Elsewhere, the continued acquisition of nuclear technologies by Iran from Russia, the intensifying nuclear rivalry between India and Pakistan, the prospect of China as a nuclear "peer competitor," and the looming threat of terrorists acquiring weapons of mass destruction (WMD) have heightened the urgency of finding workable strategies to counteract proliferation.

The perception of the weapons proliferation threat has undergone radical change over the past decade. Overcoming the challenges posed by regional powers acquiring nuclear, biological, or chemical weapons now forms the core of American force planning and military strategy. This was highlighted in the official articulation of security priorities, the "National Security Strategy of the United States of America" of 2002, which famously asserts the American right to use "preemptive" force unilaterally against hostile regimes pursuing the acquisition of WMD. To emphasize the point, the Bush administration issued a subsequent document entitled "A National Security Strategy to Combat Weapons of Mass Destruction."[1]

The elevation of nonproliferation to a central security preoccupation represents a major transformation of American policy, both conceptually and institutionally. Since the 1960s, proliferation traditionally has not been an important issue for the Pentagon or the intelligence community. Overshadowed by the U.S.-Soviet military rivalry, the diffusion of weapons to smaller powers was of relatively marginal concern for national security. Nonproliferation policy was confined largely to the diplomatic activities of the Department of State, agencies with predominantly technical man-dates like the Department of Energy, or multinational bodies like the United Nations or specialized missions such as the International Atomic Energy Agency, tasked with monitoring international efforts to restrict the trade in proscribed technologies.

Such institutional alignments reflected the prevailing view that coun-tries with fledgling military capabilities, dwarfed many times over by America's vast technological superiority, were not likely to pose a risk to U.S. interests of the kind that warranted special preparations. This view allowed for relatively laissez-faire and often commercially driven ratio-nales to promote the trade in arms and military technologies between developed and developing countries throughout the late twentieth century. An international agreement to restrict the spread of ballistic missiles tech-nologies—the Missile Technology Control Regime—was implemented in the late 1980s, but the impetus stemmed from the association of these systems with nuclear operations.

Spurred by the progressive internationalization and commercializa-tion of technology trade in the late twentieth century, military contracts and assistance programs issuing from the developed to the developing world encouraged the growth of regional arsenals in many of the states that are posing concerns today. As the technical capacity of smaller states improved, augmented by the diminished ability of industrial countries' governments to restrict technology exports in a increasingly globalized trading system, many beneficiaries of great-power largesse—including North Korea, Pakistan, Iraq, and China—also became producers of weapons and military components.

In the last decade of the twentieth century, and particularly after the Iraqi use of indigenously modified Scud missiles against coalition countries during the 1991 Persian Gulf War, concerns about "rogue states," global terrorism, and the widening diffusion of illicit technologies gave rise to a new security logic. Reflected in new policies for "homeland security," counterproliferation, or a strategy of preemption to destroy facilities in countries seeking to acquire WMD, American policymakers repositioned proliferation as a strategic issue of the highest order. The terrorist attacks on American territory on September 11, 2001, sparked a fundamental reordering of budgetary and institutional alignments to combat global weapons diffusion, leading to a second war against Iraq in 2003.

Security reasoning during the cold war posited that any sign of imbalance between the rival superpowers' forces presaged dangerous instabilities, requiring immediate steps to guard against the perception that either side was gaining a military advantage. Modernization programs and new deployments of both nuclear and advanced conventional weapons were accelerated accordingly, even when both sides already possessed tens of thousands of operational nuclear systems.

Current thinking has reversed this calculus, suggesting that the "asymmetry" of small states' arsenals actually exacerbates the threat to Western interests. By this logic, a state or substate group possessing only a handful of rudimentary weapons could stymie the ability of the larger powers to protect their interests or to project force. Emerging powers with asymmetrical forces are regarded as a particular menace because they are considered to be lawless and inherently belligerent, unconstrained by the codes of conduct that pertained through the five decades of superpower military rivalry. For such an "undeterrable" state, traditional instruments of dissuasion cannot be expected to check aggressive ambitions.

The fear that a growing number of states and terrorist organizations are bent on waging anti-Western campaigns has catalyzed the United States to develop and deploy a wide range of new countermeasures to protect American territory and overseas installations, from missile defenses guarding against "rogue" attacks to long-range, precision strike forces designed to destroy suspect military installations around the world. Intelligence resources and operations have been reoriented to detect and interrupt the trade in illicit technologies and materiel, which increasingly is being conducted by industrial mercenaries or commercial brokers who seek to profit from the violent ambitions of subversive movements or "outlier" states.

Government organizations designed to manage domestic affairs also are becoming involved in preparations to respond to potential violence from abroad. Law enforcement officers, health care providers, and newly formed local emergency response agencies are urgently training to contend with attacks against Americans.[2] Federal and state health departments are stockpiling antibiotics and vaccines to respond to outbreaks of disease that could result from bioterrorism.[3] The Department of Commerce is reevaluating export control policies for certain commercial technologies, and even the Environmental Protection Agency is considering ways to contend with new threats against the physical environment.

Well before the most recent war against Iraq, the United States was criticized by both allies and adversaries for what some believe to be an undue preoccupation with military force to counter proliferation—at the expense of other kinds of international engagement. The disputes waged in the United Nations Security Council and among NATO members about the necessity for and legitimacy of military intervention in Iraq in 2003 revealed fundamental differences between the United States and the majority of other countries about the management of the proliferation threat, in Iraq and globally.

What accounts for the distinct character of American policy? What is the basis for the prevailing definition of proliferation in the United States, and is it borne out by empirical reality? What else might account for the increase in the salience of proliferation in military calculations? How and why did the fear of "rogue" state aggression and domestic terrorism become so central to U.S. defense planning even before September 11, 2001? What events, agencies, or individuals have been the most influential in driving this shift in priorities? And, most important, are American institutions and policies likely to be effective in redressing these threats?

This volume gathers together eight prominent scholars and practitioners to examine how the U.S. government has organized to contend with the proliferation phenomenon in the post–cold war environment. Looking at the interplay between domestic and global trends, the chapters that follow present narrative analyses of how various aspects of proliferation are being handled in the United States, including the integration of nonproliferation objectives into military planning, coercive approaches to prevent technology diffusion, and the role of international cooperation.

THE ROLE OF DOMESTIC ORGANIZATION

In the first chapter, Amy Zegart, an assistant professor of policy studies at UCLA and author of the prizewinning study of organizational influences on policy formulation *Flawed by Design: The Evolution of the CIA, JCS, and NSC*, traces the evolution of the policymaking apparatus for nonproliferation in the United States. Zegart draws on historical cases of policy innovations— including the establishment of the Arms Control and Disarmament Agency in 1961 and organizational reform efforts in the late 1990s with respect to nonproliferation—to identify the difficulties of adapting existing governmental structures for new challenges. These difficulties derive in part from the crosscutting nature of the proliferation problem, which blurs jurisdictional and institutional lines. Zegart explains how the self-interest of those who work to establish new policy mechanisms, the dynamics of the bureaucratic process itself, and the nature of American democracy act together to create organizational flaws that are extremely resistant to change.

The continuing inability of presidents and their administrations to achieve genuine and effective innovations in nonproliferation, Zegart argues persuasively, derives in large measure from the resilience of established agencies, which are inclined to promote parochial rather than national or international objectives. The disjuncture between the fluid nature of proliferation challenges and the static nature of organizations has left the U.S. government poorly equipped to deal with new contingencies because these require the coordination of multiple agencies with distinct agendas. Zegart examines the implications of institutional inertia for future policy innovations and provides recommendations for reform.

The next chapter provides the international dimension of organizations involved in nonproliferation. This and the subsequent five chapters, which present case studies of specific policy instruments, further illustrate how hindrances to policymaking and to formulating effective responses to new security challenges can arise from suboptimal organizational alignments. Understanding such dynamics adds an essential dimension to the examination of current nonproliferation policy debates.

THE INTERNATIONAL NONPROLIFERATION REGIME

Joseph Cirincione, director of the nonproliferation programs at the Carnegie Endowment for International Peace, presents a comprehensive overview of international organizations—the systems and agreements that have been established to regulate WMD commerce and to dissuade states from acquiring such weapons. He reviews the development of the international norms, treaties, and other arrangements that together make up the global nonproliferation regime. His chapter traces the evolution of the regime from World War II to the post–cold war era. Cirincione argues that, despite recent rhetoric seeking to downplay the importance of or even disregard existing arrangements, efforts to constrain proliferation necessarily will continue to rely on the network of instruments that prohibit or severely hinder states' access to critical military resources and materiel.

As enshrined in the 1968 Treaty on the Non-Proliferation of Nuclear Weapons, the regime emphasizes a strategy of technology denial. The success of this strategy and of the overall global nonproliferation regime admittedly has ebbed and flowed over the past six decades. Judging from the empirical record, however, it has on balance been positive. Compared to the dire prognostications of the 1960s suggesting that dozens of states would acquire nuclear arsenals before the end of the twentieth century, the relatively limited number of new nuclear countries is an indication that the regime, however imperfect, has worked. The vast majority of states that have the technical capacity to develop weapons of mass destruction—particularly nuclear forces—have not done so. On the contrary, the record of nuclear forbearance and deliberate abandonment of fledgling nuclear programs is far more extensive than the list of states that have established programs or that harbor nuclear ambitions.

Cirincione cautions that the assertion by many Bush administration officials that this highly articulated set of arrangements could readily be replaced with new instruments is imprudent. Over the long run, global multilateral cooperation has provided a solid return on national investments, particularly in those instances in which American leadership has been brought to bear to secure desired objectives. The involvement and support of presidents has proved especially important, both to forge domestic consensus on behalf of nonproliferation goals and to demonstrate American commitment internationally.

THE ASCENDANCE OF COUNTERPROLIFERATION

The five chapters that follow examine a number of alternative approaches to the management of proliferation that have emerged over the past decade. These include the heightened emphasis on the use of coercive instruments, such as military force and trade sanctions, to target adversarial states and stem the global trade in illicit technologies; the first attempt at "coercive disarmament" undertaken after the Persian Gulf War in 1991 and the lessons that can be drawn from it for future nonproliferation policy; the systematic efforts of the United States and other advanced countries to employ cooperative incentives and programs to prevent the diffusion of dangerous technologies and materials, particularly from countries formerly part of the Soviet Union; the renewed attention that is being given to the threat of biological terrorism, a particularly dangerous phenomenon that is severely testing the ability of governments to contain it; and the continued spread of conventional and dual-use weapons technologies, which, by contrast with other forms of proliferation, has received far less attention from governments around the world. Each of these chapters draws on the direct experiences of the authors in policy formulation, providing both a historical and a prescriptive context for framing future options.

In Chapter 3, Robert Litwak, director of international programs at the Wilson Center and a former National Security Council director for nonproliferation and export controls, analyzes the implications of the heightened prominence accorded to the military components of American nonproliferation policy after the Persian Gulf War and September 11, leading up to the armed intervention against Iraq in 2003. Building on policies adopted by its predecessor, the Bush administration embraced a much more ambitious set of policy instruments to target states seeking to acquire weapons of mass destruction. The recent war against Iraq can be seen as the result of a culmination of decisions over the past decade that drove American policy to a greater reliance on force to achieve nonproliferation objectives. Radical changes in the international environment beginning in the early 1990s had already reshaped American leaders' perception of how to deal with the proliferation threat. The reorientation of the Pentagon's missions and budgets to counterproliferation in the Clinton administration, however, had encountered considerable opposition in the executive branch and the Congress. There has been no serious questioning in the Bush administration, however, and the momentum toward a military-based counterproliferation strategy has accelerated accordingly.

The decision to emphasize force as the most reliable instrument to prevent states' acquiring weapons of mass destruction has not necessarily had the effect that leaders hoped to achieve. Even in the wake of the defeat of the repressive Ba'athist regime in Iraq, threats to American interests worldwide continue to rise, not least from what remains of al Qaeda and other anti-Western, fundamentalist Islamic movements. Whether and to what degree terrorists and their sponsors have been either dissuaded from or galvanized in their quest to attack Western interests after the Iraq war remains to be seen.

Still, it is not necessarily the case that the use of force has to undercut broader efforts to elicit international cooperation. Litwak argues that the threat of or actual use of military measures can be part of a continuum of nonproliferation instruments that features economic sanctions and export controls as well as financial incentives, multilateral treaties, and diplomacy. At the same time, undue emphasis on military measures can compete with other, potentially more effective instruments, and it can generate confidence that is misplaced if designated objectives in reality cannot be redressed by coercive means alone. The contemplated use of force not only to deter the use of weapons of mass destruction but also to stop their acquisition, for example, represents a form of "mission creep" that is fraught with operational difficulties.

Contrary to conventional wisdom, the use of force is no less problematic nor is it necessarily more decisive as a nonproliferation instrument than the encumbrances of multilateral diplomacy. Unanticipated complications and uncertainties can arise in military operations—ranging from the lack of precise intelligence to guide "surgical strikes" against suspected WMD sites to adverse political consequences engendered by accidental attacks on civilian installations. It is neither politically prudent nor likely to be effective to undertake military measures other than as a last resort, Litwak concludes, and then only after a full assessment of the potential costs and benefits.

COERCIVE DISARMAMENT
LESSONS FROM IRAQ

Following the first Persian Gulf War, the international community expressed astonishment over the discovery of the scope and sophistication of Iraq's covert nuclear, chemical, and biological weapons programs. Iraq's military advancement was almost entirely the product of technology imports and technical assistance programs from the West throughout the previous decade—a tribute to the lack of international attention paid to Saddam Hussein's military ambitions until the invasion of Kuwait.

In Chapter 4, former chief nuclear weapons inspector for the United Nations in Iraq and currently special adviser to the Central Intelligence Agency David Kay analyzes the lessons that can be drawn from the experiences of the United Nations Special Commission on Iraq (UNSCOM) in the 1990s. The inspections undertaken following the 1991 Gulf War, under the mandate of the United Nations Security Council, represented the first international effort to impose coercive disarmament and full transparency in a state that had clandestine programs to develop weapons of mass destruction. This is a case study of another policy innovation—"involuntary nonproliferation"—which has received a lot of attention as a result of the decision to wage a second war against Iraq.

The success of the inspections regime of the 1990s is disputed in the policy community. The inspections were terminated in 1998, prior to the completion of the disarmament mission, as a result of Iraqi intransigence and political controversies involving participating governments and the leadership of the United Nations. Kay concludes, however, that this approach to nonproliferation is not necessarily sui generis and that the tools and verification mechanisms that UNSCOM had begun to develop could be made to work in other contingencies, such as the search to uncover weapons programs in Iraq today. To do so successfully, however, would require clear political commitment of the participating countries to support and sustain the effort, as well as more robust channels for mediating disputes, which will inevitably arise. Both of these were severely lacking in the first instance.

As an object lesson for future initiatives to detect and eliminate weapons installations in Iraq and elsewhere, the UNSCOM example highlights the vital importance of codified inspection measures to achieve successful disarmament. Military strikes and the defeat of an adversary on the battlefield proved to be a necessary precondition to allow the inspection regime to gain access to the country's weapons installations in 1991. It was rigorous and exhaustive inspections, augmented by critical intelligence provided by defectors and others with direct knowledge of the covert programs, however, that led to the successful destruction and dismantlement of suspect sites. As the United States takes steps to rebuild Iraqi political and economic infrastructure under a new regime after the 2003 war, the successes and missteps of this disarmament experiment need to be taken into account.

COOPERATIVE DISARMAMENT
THE CASE OF THE FORMER SOVIET UNION

With the collapse of the Soviet Union in the early 1990s, the threat of sudden proliferation of weapons technologies and sensitive materiel from installations throughout this vast region constituted an unprecedented challenge. The deterioration of security protecting the Soviet arsenal presented seemingly insoluble dilemmas for a state system that had long relied on strict, authoritarian controls to police the activities of its population. The sheer number and geographical distribution of high-risk installations in and of themselves proved daunting.

In 1990, for example, more than 11,000 strategic warheads were scattered across four newly independent states, none of which had the experience to establish stable central governments in the short term at least. An estimated 21,000 tactical nuclear weapons, similarly, were held in an undisclosed number of locations spread throughout the former Soviet Union.[4] Although estimates vary, Russia also is believed to have produced as much as 1,350 metric tons of highly enriched uranium and plutonium during the cold war, all of which needed to be protected against theft or other forms of compromise.[5] And thousands of Russian nuclear and biological weapons scientists faced the prospect of economic dispossession in the face of a disintegrating Soviet military establishment, giving them compelling incentives to migrate to countries that would pay for their expertise.[6]

This new security threat impelled American policymakers to take urgent steps to secure and contain the vast resources of the decaying Soviet weapons infrastructure. The proliferation implications of this case were not only wholly different in character from those in Iraq and elsewhere but also orders of magnitude more dangerous to regional and global security. In Chapter 6, Rose Gottemoeller, a senior associate at the Carnegie Endowment for International Peace and a former deputy undersecretary of energy, examines how threat reduction initiatives and inducements were developed to mitigate the risks of massive, spontaneous proliferation from Russia and the other successor states. The commitment of significant resources and technical assistance to help a former adversary to achieve a secure and stable order has been an extraordinary demonstration of American will and ingenuity.

Gottemoeller argues that the overall impact of these initiatives on global nonproliferation has been significant. A myriad of cooperative weapons dismantlement and stockpile security programs have stemmed what otherwise would undoubtedly have been a massive outflow of weapons and materiel onto the global market. The Cooperative Threat Reduction Program alone has deactivated more than 13,000 warheads, eliminated 1,473 missile silos, cut up 167 strategic bombers, and destroyed 728 submarine-based ballistic missile launchers.[7]

Nonproliferation initiatives also have been marked by an unusually high degree of intergovernmental coordination involving more than a dozen agencies just within the United States. This has had the salutary effect of increasing the scope and level of governmental attention to the importance of cooperative measures to combat the spread of weapons and technology. While still severely underfunded relative to the scope of the remaining challenges, these initiatives have received the support of influential members of Congress and have managed to overcome multiple domestic political obstacles. As Gottemoeller concludes, the success of programs in the former Soviet Union suggests there are genuine opportunities to apply these kinds of nonproliferation techniques and incentives to other regions. This experience demonstrates that cooperative approaches to disarmament can work when there is a mutuality of interests and sustained bureaucratic attention.

THE THREAT OF BIOLOGICAL WEAPONS
A SPECIAL CASE

Jessica Stern, a widely published author and terrorism specialist at Harvard University who also is a former National Security Council official, examines the rising threat of biological terrorism. The perception of this threat has been magnified recently by the deliberate dissemination of anthrax in the United States by a still unidentified terrorist.

The inherent nature of biological agents, many of which can be replicated in mass quantities with relatively little technical sophistication, creates particular difficulties for governments seeking to control their diffusion. Traditional mechanisms used to constrain the trade in dangerous technologies, such as security classification, restrictions on exports, or recognized verification schemes, have little relevance for products that are almost entirely within the domain of the commercial sector. Stern makes the case for a comprehensive overhaul of existing policies and legal restrictions to elicit the cooperation and direct involvement of private technology firms in designing regulatory measures.

Aside from the physical risks that certain kinds of biological weapons carry for unprotected populations, the threat of biological attack also has pronounced psychological effects on the public mind. This complicates the task of governments in issuing warnings or helping the public to prepare for possible contingencies. Biological agents, more than other kinds of weapons, tap into deep-seated human fears of invisible threats and random poisoning. Stern notes that the psychological dimension makes the management of biological terrorism especially tricky, and different policy approaches run the risk of provoking either inadequate or disproportionate responses to perceived threats.

GLOBALIZATION AND MILITARY COMMERCE

Echoing themes regarding private commerce and the limits of government control presented in the chapter by Stern, William Keller examines the impact of a globalizing economic order on the international trade in arms and conventional weapons technologies. The traditional locus of military trade regulation has been governments, working unilaterally or as part of export cartels to restrict the flow of goods to specific countries. The restrictions on trade from West to East codified in the Coordinating Committee (COCOM) during the cold war, for example, were regarded as a vital instrument of containment against the Soviet Union.

In the current environment, governments can no longer ensure control over the disposition of technology, even within their own borders. Powerful secular trends are transforming the foundations of sovereignty, with major implications for international commerce. Worldwide integration of production facilities and distribution networks, the rapid pace of technological innovation, and the commercialization of advanced military technologies are vitiating traditional state supremacy and undercutting countries' ability to monitor military exports and imports.

In the interest of remaining economically competitive, states have had to acknowledge the increasing futility of protectionist instruments for an ever-longer list of commodities, including advanced technologies that are useful for developing weapons. A growing number of multinational corporations are producing military or dual-use items, and even the United States relies on overseas suppliers for vital defense components. With virtual, real-time communications, firms operating in any number of places can supply critical technologies and materiel on a global basis, leading to the ever-widening dissemination not just of weapon systems but design expertise and production technologies.

COOPERATING WITH ALLIES

The succeeding chapter provides an overview of current nonproliferation policies from the standpoint of the European allies. Allied cooperation to combat global proliferation is examined in light of the transatlantic stresses that have emerged over differences about policies perceived to reflect an excessive American preoccupation with the use of force. Joanna Spear, a senior lecturer at the University of London, discusses the way in which different political cultures and institutional alignments in several European states account for divergences with the United States over threat perceptions and preferred policy instruments. Despite the conflicts marking the debate prior to the U.S.-led military intervention in Iraq in 2003, however, Washington has had to adapt to and accommodate the demands of cooperation and coordination with allies, and in some cases with competitors such as China, in order to devise effective policies.

Spear scrutinizes the nonproliferation dialogue among Western governments and concludes that the United States has structural impediments that interfere with its ability to communicate effectively with its allies about nonproliferation objectives. As a result of the decision to assign greater authority for nonproliferation to the Pentagon, the United States has used NATO as the preferred route for engaging other states. The European allies, however, continue to generate and execute nonproliferation policy through their foreign ministries. As a result, many American initiatives have been ill coordinated with those of overseas partners or misconstrued, impeded by the lack of strong relationships between officials representing the two sides. This gap continues to widen and threatens to undermine worldwide acceptance of American approaches in the future. As long as the reasons for policy differences remain poorly understood, Spear argues, the prospects for mounting an effective international strategy to stem weapons of mass destruction are discouraging.

TOWARD A NEW NONPROLIFERATION PARADIGM

In conclusion, the editors provide an overview of the new challenges in nonproliferation policy and offer some recommendations for reforms. Because the transformation of threat perceptions and accompanying policy responses discussed here has occurred at both the international and domestic levels, many of the recommendations concern the need to harmonize the various approaches adopted by the United States, its allies, and others during the past decade. As the problems of proliferation increasingly become merged with the threat of international terrorism, moreover, it becomes clear that a genuine global partnership is essential to prevent catastrophic security developments. It is hoped that this analysis proves useful to the policymakers who are grappling with these dilemmas on a daily basis, as well as to scholars and students now and in the future.

1

THE ORGANIZATION AND ARCHITECTURE OF NONPROLIFERATION UNDERSTANDING THE REGIME

Amy B. Zegart

The importance and broad scope of disarmament matters require continuing presidential attention. The complex interrelationships between disarmament activities, foreign affairs, and national security also require that close working-level coordination and cooperation be established between the new agency [I propose] and . . . other agencies.

. . . [S]tudies and consultations have inescapably pointed to the conclusion that a new effort . . . will be necessary . . .

—John F. Kennedy, June 29, 1961[1]

The nation lacks a comprehensive policy and plan to meet the threat posed by the proliferation of weapons of mass destruction.

The President must lead efforts to combat proliferation and direct immediate steps to make those efforts more coherent, consistent, and effective.

—Deutch Commission Report, July 14, 1999[2]

Few would dispute that the September 11 terrorist attacks lend new urgency to halting the spread and use of weapons of mass destruction (WMD).[3] Although most experts believe Osama bin Laden does not have such weapons, the preponderance of evidence suggests that al Qaeda and other terrorist organizations have tried and may in the future succeed.[4] Today there is enough fissile material in Russia to build 60,000 nuclear warheads, and much of it is poorly secured. Rudimentary instructions for building a nuclear bomb can be found on the Internet.[5] Biological and chemical agents are even easier to obtain and, as the recent anthrax mail cases demonstrate, not as difficult to deploy as scientists previously believed. The threat of a WMD attack on American soil appears to be more serious and more imminent than it has at any time since the height of the cold war.

How well prepared is the United States to combat the proliferation and use of weapons of mass destruction? How effectively have U.S. nonproliferation organizations adapted to the end of the cold war and the emergence of new WMD threats such as transnational terrorism?

This chapter takes snapshots of two time periods: John F. Kennedy's efforts to reform how nonproliferation policy was administered in 1960–61 and a series of government studies examining nonproliferation organization in 1999–2001, ten years after the end of the cold war. Juxtaposing these pictures reveals something disturbing: in nonproliferation policy, the United States has never gotten the organizational basics right. This is not to suggest that the apparatus of nonproliferation has remained entirely static over time. There have been some significant changes in the nonproliferation architecture, most notably the 1997 merger of the State Department and the Arms Control and Disarmament Agency (ACDA)[6] and the consolidation of nonproliferation programs in the Department of Defense in 1993 and 1997.[7] However, these changes mask more significant continuities. For forty years U.S. nonproliferation efforts have been hampered by the same two organizational problems: poor day-to-day policy coordination and the near total absence of mechanisms to ensure long-term policy coherence. Policymakers have been well aware of these deficiencies but have been unable to rectify them.

Why have these fundamental organizational weaknesses persisted for so long? Conventional wisdom suggests that organizational problems arise when presidents do not have the will or power to set clear priorities and "knock bureaucratic heads together." According to this view, poor individual leadership leads to poor system performance. By contrast, this chapter, following a survey of the Kennedy reforms and the more recent initiatives directed at reorganization, makes a case that organizational problems are rooted in four enduring realities that span presidencies: the structure of American democracy; the self-interest of officials and politicians; the dynamics of bureaucratic operations; and the nature of nonproliferation policy. These four characteristics impede good design of policymaking networks and processes at the outset and erect high barriers to subsequent reform. They explain why all presidents have faced the same kinds of organizational problems and have achieved the same limited results.

The chapter concludes with a discussion of the implications of this stasis, offering some thoughts about how, and how much, policymakers can improve nonproliferation policy organization in the future. Subsequent chapters in this volume provide more detailed case studies of an evolving nonproliferation policy through the 1990s, ranging from cooperative regime building as described by Joseph Cirincione to the more coercive actions described by Robert Litwak. Each chapter can be viewed through the model of defective organization building described here.

At the outset, it is worth underscoring that nonproliferation policy refers to the full spectrum of government initiatives related to WMD threats: preventing the further spread of chemical, nuclear, and biological weapons and their means of delivery; rolling back existing programs; deterring and defending against an attack; and managing the consequences of WMD use. Each of these issue areas is extremely complex. For example, it is one thing to discourage states from developing and intensifying their existing WMD arsenals (the vertical proliferation problem) and quite another to prevent other states or terrorist groups from acquiring these weapons in the first place (the horizontal proliferation problem). Even narrower topics such as treaty compliance have spawned vast literatures.[8] In such a rich and multifaceted policy domain, generalization can be difficult.

But it also can be worth the effort. When policy areas are particularly complicated, cutting to core problems and explaining them in generalizable ways become all the more important. The challenge is to identify fundamental policymaking deficiencies and constraints whose amelioration could prepare the ground for dramatic and widespread advances across the full range of WMD challenges.

THE PERSISTENCE OF ORGANIZATIONAL WEAKNESSES: TWO SNAPSHOTS IN TIME

On September 26, 1961, John F. Kennedy signed legislation creating the ACDA. The passage of the Arms Control and Disarmament Act was the most extensive reorganization of nonproliferation activities since World

War II. For Kennedy, the legislation improving U.S. arms control capabilities capped six months of intensive work by his administration and delivered on one of his central presidential campaign pledges. Nearly forty years later, as ACDA closed its doors, another reform movement was brewing. It focused more on a broad range of WMD proliferation issues and less on the specifics of U.S.-Soviet arms control and worldwide disarmament. It took shape as a disjointed assortment of studies and proposals—including four blue-ribbon commissions,[9] one Senate study,[10] an Energy Department task force,[11] and fifteen General Accounting Office (GAO) reports[12]—rather than a well-organized presidential initiative. It was more bipartisan and yet less overtly successful. Despite these differences, the reform movement of 1999–2001 bore one eerie similarity to its Kennedy-era predecessor. It faced the same enemy. The critical organizational difficulties it addressed were precisely the same ones Kennedy had tried, and failed, to fix nearly four decades earlier.

These problems can be classified into two distinct categories: policy coordination and programmatic coherence (see Figure 1.1).[13]

Put simply, policy coordination has to do with making sure the proverbial left hand knows what the right hand is doing. It involves managing the day-to-day formulation and execution of specific policies by specific agencies. At its essence, policy coordination involves immediate or near-term decisions that are specific in nature—whether to impose sanctions against Iraq, whether to conduct additional tests for a national missile defense system. Policy coordination guards against interagency miscommunication, missteps, and, to a degree, deliberate opposition between bureaus with interests at stake. It also helps ensure that policies are developed and implemented in a timely manner. In short, getting policy coordination right means ensuring that government agencies can follow the well-worn medical adage "do no harm."

How do we know good policy coordination when we see it? Unfortunately, there is no absolute, objective measure of success.[14] However, there are three indicators that, when taken together, provide a useful gauge of effectiveness. First, when policy coordination falters, agencies become more likely to undermine one another, either unwittingly or intentionally. In that case, contradictory positions from different parts of the bureaucracy become apparent. In the most serious cases, these differences can lead to public policy reversals. Second, poor coordination can more readily lead to cumbersome policy development and implementation. Third, terminology provides a good measure of difficulties: when critical words and ideas mean different things to different agencies, it is fair to

Figure 1.1: Fundamental Organizational Deficiencies and Indicators

	Policy Coordination	Programmatic Coherence
Characteristics	◆ Specific policy decision Should the United States sanction Iraq?) ◆ Immediate term (this week/this year) ◆ Primarily manages bureaucratic missteps	◆ Comprehensive approach to policy area (What should U.S. nonproliferation policy be?) ◆ Long term (5–20 years) ◆ Primarily manages bureaucratic rivalry, opposition
Indicators	1. Contradictory policies 2. Cumbersome policymaking process 3. Conflicting terminology	1. Policy as "hanging threads" 2. No high-level focal point 3. Little or no integrated planning and budgeting

assume that coordination is not at its best. An effective organization might be expected to experience some of these problems some of the time, but they should be rare and should be confined to relatively minor issues.

Programmatic coherence differs from policy coordination in several respects. It entails developing multidimensional long-term strategies and providing the necessary resources to pursue them. Whereas policy coordination helps answer the question of whether to impose sanctions against Iraq, programmatic coherence addresses the broader issues of what America's sanctions policy should be, how it should relate to other strands of nonproliferation policy such as international treaty regimes and responses to the actual use of weapons of mass destruction, and how to best invest American resources and organizational capabilities to achieve overarching program objectives several years out. By nature, programmatic debates invite greater bureaucratic rivalry. They have higher stakes, involve more encompassing questions, and take a longer view. Thus, successful programmatic coherence mutes or manages bureaucratic opposition.

Three critical indicators suggest when programmatic coherence falters. First, there is the absence of a clear, overarching strategy. Instead of strands in a woven fabric, individual policies resemble hanging threads. Agency programs appear to operate in isolation or even at cross-purposes rather than in concert. Second, there is no effective focal point—a high-level office or person below the president that brings together the various instruments of the departments and agencies concerned. Finally, there is little in the way of integrated planning or budgeting to ensure resources are well matched against priorities. The more prevalent these programmatic coherence problems are, and the more frequently they appear during times of urgency, the less probable the organization will achieve its objectives.

POLICY COORDINATION PROBLEMS
THEN AND NOW

During the 1950s, it became clear that coordination problems were widespread. In 1957, the Disarmament Subcommittee of the Senate Foreign Relations Committee found that different U.S. agencies were undercutting each others' positions when dealing with foreign powers.[15] As Senator Hubert Humphrey later noted, in one instance the Department of Defense and the Budget Bureau announced unilateral force cuts while the State Department was trying to negotiate force reductions with the Soviets. In another, the Defense Department closed some military bases at the same time the State Department was resisting base closure in a disarmament agreement.[16] These missteps were only likely to get worse. By 1961, nonproliferation policy involved at least nineteen major executive branch agencies and departments.[17]

Delay also became a major issue. At the 1960 ten-nation disarmament talks, for example, U.S. representative Frederick Eaton could not initially convey the U.S. position to American allies because the Defense and State departments had not yet resolved their differences. Henry Cabot Lodge, Jr., who served from 1953 to 1960 as the U.S. ambassador to the United Nations and who participated in numerous arms control talks during that period, gave direct testimony about the dangers of the cumbersome policymaking process. Appearing before the Senate Foreign Relations Committee during the 1961 ACDA debate, Lodge remarked, "The executive branch of the U.S. Government is not organized as it should be for big, bold strokes in foreign relations." He went on, "All too frequently, under the present system, it takes too much time to get a U.S. position on any subject involving more than one department. . . ." Although Lodge declined to provide examples in the committee's public sessions,[18] he did underscore that the Soviet Union had gained advantage by moving much faster than the Americans, "with all of the advantages of secrecy and surprise." Lodge emphatically reiterated his position toward the end of his statement: "As one who has been on the receiving end for almost 8 years, I know that it is indispensable for the U.S. representative to be in a position to make counterproposals promptly. . . ."[19]

John F. Kennedy was less diplomatic. On the 1960 presidential campaign trail, then-Senator Kennedy told a New Hampshire audience that U.S. arms control negotiators "have been wholly unprepared to either seize the disarmament initiative or promptly respond when the Russians . . . did seize the initiative." He went on to list examples in rapid fire, noting that the United States had not been prepared to respond Soviet disarmament proposals in 1955 or in 1959 and that American delegates to the 1958 Surprise Attack Conference were "ill-staffed, ill-prepared and ill-advised."[20] Kennedy was not exaggerating. When the Soviet Union accepted the American proposal for a Surprise Attack Conference in September 1958, the United States had no prepared position or even a team in place to develop one. Ad hoc working groups of private citizens and various agency officials were pulled together at the eleventh hour to draft a technical position. The head of the American delegation, William Foster, was a private lawyer with no experience in disarmament negotiations.[21]

Policy coordination weaknesses appear to have gotten worse with time. In large part, this can be attributed to the rising salience and complexity of nonproliferation issues. From 1961 to 1999, as the scope of nonproliferation policy expanded and assumed greater prominence, the number of agencies involved in various aspects of safeguarding against weapons of mass destruction ballooned from nineteen to nearly a hundred. In WMD counterterrorism alone, federal government efforts are currently spread across forty-five agencies that include the Centers for Disease Control and Prevention and the National Institutes of Health, organizations that have never before played a critical role in national security policymaking.[22] Congress's own fragmentation has increased as well, with executive branch nonproliferation organizations now reporting to more than twenty House and Senate oversight committees or subcommittees. More organizations have meant less coordination. As Senator Arlen Specter put it, when it comes to nonproliferation policy, "the federal government is a mess. Nobody's in charge."[23]

Specter's remark reflected the consensus of his colleagues at the Deutch Commission. A bipartisan, blue-ribbon panel chaired by former Central Intelligence Agency director John Deutch, the commission spent more than a year performing a comprehensive assessment of the administering of U.S. nonproliferation policy and recommending specific changes. Its July 1999 report was unequivocal: the U.S. government was poorly prepared for combating the spread of weapons of mass destruction. Specifically, the commission found precisely the kind of policy confusion and delay that hindered policymaking in the 1950s. Echoing Lodge's comments, the report noted, "When a new problem involves . . . the development of a coordinated response from several agencies, the process is cumbersome and slow. . . ."[24] According to the commission, all too often disputes that should have been resolved quickly at lower levels had to be resolved slowly at higher levels, by deputy secretaries or cabinet-level officials.

The Nunn-Lugar Cooperative Threat Reduction program provides perhaps the most telling example of these coordination problems. Launched in early 1992, Nunn-Lugar was a bold plan to provide American assistance in reducing and controlling weapons of mass destruction in the former Soviet republics. By all accounts, the program has been a resounding success. More than 5,500 nuclear weapons designed to destroy the United States have been dismantled, and three Soviet successor states— Ukraine, Kazakhstan, and Belarus—have become nuclear-free.[25]

Even so, the program has faced serious obstacles and encountered significant delay not only from opponents but from well-meaning supporters within the executive branch. For example, the Deutch Commission was struck by the lengthy planning and difficulties involved in getting the necessary resources for Operation Auburn Endeavor, a 1998 mission that removed five kilograms of highly enriched uranium from Georgia in the Caucasus.[26] Decisionmakers confirmed the commission's findings. In their general account of the Nunn-Lugar program, Deputy Secretary of Defense William J. Perry and Assistant Secretary of Defense Ashton B. Carter pointedly criticized the organizational problems they encountered:

> . . . it was difficult to shake the grip of the old-style arms control bureaucracy. Officials used to the glacial pace of arms control during the Cold War sought endlessly to form "interagency nego- tiating teams" and send them to foreign capitals, rather than sending the engineers and technical specialists who were essential to action on the ground. These and other well-intentioned "helpers" around Washington's other agencies and the White House needed to be discouraged from impeding the program. . . .[27]

Another high-level administration official put the situation a bit more colorfully. "If you want to buy some weapons shit from Kazakhstan, it takes two years of NSC interagency meetings before we can do anything."[28]

The difficulties of the Nunn-Lugar program and the more general findings of the Deutch Commission have been well supported. Since 1999, as mentioned previously, other commissions, studies, numerous GAO reports, an Energy Department task force, and a score of congressional hearings have examined various aspects of how nonproliferation policy is formulated.[29] All of them have found major, fundamental coordination problems. One recent GAO report revealed that federal, state, and local governments had no clear chain of command for dealing with a WMD ter- rorist incident.[30] In April 2001, Senate Judiciary Committee hearings remarked that the Department of Health and Human Services was trying to create a national vaccine stockpile that failed to match intelligence estimates about the most likely chemical and biological agents that ter- rorists would use.[31] The Gilmore Panel, an expert commission that was created by Congress to assess American capabilities for contending with a WMD terrorist attack, found in December 1999 that agencies failed to use common definitions in their terrorism response plans. Critical terms such as "weapon of mass destruction," "terrorism," and "mass casualties" meant different things—and triggered different responses—in different agencies.[32] In January 2001, the Energy Department's Russia Task Force found that, even within a single department, nonproliferation efforts were not working in concert; according to the task force's *Report Card on Nonproliferation Programs with Russia,* the Energy Department had no mechanism to ensure that technologies developed in one nuclear waste cleanup program would be shared with others.[33]

While these examples suggest problems lurking in the wings, press reports have been quick to register more public coordination snafus as well. Perhaps the best known of these occurred in March 2001, when President Bush reversed his own secretary of state on nonproliferation policy toward North Korea. Just one day after Secretary Colin Powell had publicly indicated the administration planned to continue ballistic missile control discussions with Pyongyang, the president put the talks on hold.

In sum, policy coordination problems have been pervasive and fairly serious since the Eisenhower administration. In the 1950s, two of the three problem indicators—contradictory policies and cumbersome policymaking—manifested themselves on several occasions, most critically, with regard to arms control agreements with the Soviet Union. Foreign policy episodes in the 1990s revealed continuing coordination problems, from unclear chains of command to public policy reversals on North Korea to contradictory definitions of "weapons of mass destruction." Ironically, the same kinds of difficulties plaguing ill-prepared arms control negotiating teams in the 1950s led to burdensome delays in removing nuclear weapons from Soviet successor states forty years later.

Programmatic Coherence Problems Then and Now

Programmatic coherence problems evident at the height of the cold war also persisted throughout the century. The first and most obvious of these problems has been the generally disjointed nature of nonproliferation policy—what I term "policy as hanging threads." In his 1960 presidential campaign, Kennedy gave a major speech that hit on just this theme, though he used a different metaphor. "The most gaping hole in American foreign policy today is our lack of a concrete plan for disarmament," he declared. Using the speech to propose a new U.S. Arms Control Research Institute (what later became the ACDA), Kennedy delivered a blistering attack of the Eisenhower administration, saying that it had failed to develop any clear or comprehensive approach to superpower disarmament issues. "No issue . . . is of more vital concern to this Nation than disarmament," Kennedy maintained, "and yet this Nation has no consistent, convincing disarmament policy." Political rhetoric aside, Kennedy's speech pinpointed the cross-cutting nature of the policy challenge. "A new agency is not enough," he plainly admitted. The objective was to implement the agency's recommendations "at the highest levels" and to manage "the resistance likely to arise" in the State and Defense departments, the Atomic Energy Commission, and other agencies involved in disarmament policy.[34] In short, Kennedy's speech called for greater programmatic coherence, for a comprehensive, long-term approach to disarmament that could integrate the parochial perspectives and differing outlooks of the various departments and agencies. Nelson Rockefeller, the governor of New York and a dark horse candidate for the Republican presidential nomination, issued a similar call on July 8: "We must establish within our government at the highest level a fully staffed agency to inspire and to coordinate all activities bearing upon arms control and inspection. Such an agency— both pressing research and coordinating departmental actions—should be directly responsible to the President, or to the First Secretary of the government whenever such an office is created."[35]

In the election, with Vice President Richard Nixon as the likely Republican presidential candidate, both Kennedy and Rockefeller certainly stood to gain by criticizing the Eisenhower administration's organization for arms control and disarmament. Yet two events suggest that these criticisms were not far off the mark. The first was the incumbent's response. On September 9, Eisenhower's secretary of state, Christian Herter, announced the creation of the United States Disarmament Administration (USDA). The agency was housed within the State Department. It was charged with reconciling the divergent views of various agencies involved in disarmament policy and with providing a more substantial research program to support negotiation efforts. Although the USDA's creation served to blunt campaign criticism, and although the agency soon lapsed in the new administration, evidence suggests that Herter and others acted out of a serious concern for improving government organization in this policy area.

Kennedy's follow-through after the election provides even more compelling evidence of the sincerity of his criticisms. One of the new president's first actions was to appoint John J. McCloy as his special disarmament adviser. McCloy, a well-respected Republican, a defense advocate, and adviser to several past presidents, was charged with making specific

recommendations about disarmament policy and organization of the policymaking apparatus. As Arthur Schlesinger observed, Kennedy's choice
of McCloy was a classic and shrewd political maneuver to lay the necessary
political groundwork for instituting change.[36] McCloy, for his part, lost
no time. Within six months, he had consulted extensively with relevant
cabinet departments and agencies and had drafted a bill for the new
ACDA that was introduced to Congress. The president, in his transmittal letter of June 29, 1961, for that bill, reiterated his campaign themes. In
particular, he focused on the need for a nonproliferation system that would
bring together all of the relevant policy and agency pieces. "Peace cannot
be brought about by concentrating solely on measures to eliminate
weapons," he wrote. Instead, Kennedy's nonproliferation concept sought
to be wide-ranging, "tak[ing] into account the national security, our foreign
policy, the relationships of this country to international peacekeeping
agencies . . . and our domestic, economic, and other policies."[37] In fact,
Kennedy's letter devoted more attention to policy integration than anything else.

The second problem that Kennedy and other reformers sought to
address in 1960–61 was closely related to the first: nobody seemed to be in
charge. There was no executive branch agency or senior official responsible for developing an overarching nonproliferation strategy or for ensuring
that all of the departments and agencies were working in concert. In the
1950s, criticism mounted that Eisenhower was not actively crafting or
directing the U.S. disarmament effort, nor did he ever empower another
high-level official to do the job in his stead. In 1957 Benjamin Cohen, a
former U.S. representative to the United Nations Disarmament
Commission, emphasized the costs of failing to provide sustained, high-
level programmatic attention. Cohen testified in a congressional hearing:
". . . since you can't have disarmament without the cooperation of the
Defense Department and the State Department . . . whoever is in charge
of disarmament must be in a relationship to the President that he can
bring the matters to the President's attention and get a decision rather
than merely taking the lowest common denominator of agreement
between the State Department and the Defense Department."[38]

Former atomic energy commissioner Thomas E. Murray painted an
even more vivid picture of what occurs when there is no focal point. "When
we come right down to it," he wrote in 1960, "it is not easy to say precisely
who makes atomic energy policy in the United States or how it is made."
Even on basic policy decisions, he added, government consisted of a "tor-
tuous maze" filled with agencies that tried to dilute or modify proposals.[39]

Kennedy picked up on this theme. His March 1960 disarmament campaign speech called for a new arms control agency to be "under the immediate direction of the President" in order to "coordinate . . . and follow through on the research, development, and policy planning needed for a workable disarmament program." Such an agency would act as a "clearinghouse." It would be the "one responsible organization—guided and directed by the White House" on which hopes for peace would be centered.[40] Rockefeller stressed the same point, insisting that the new agency be "directly responsible to the President" in order to exert the necessary guidance and leverage over the policy process.[41] Although in the end Kennedy's ACDA did not have sufficient high-level authority or direct presidential access to play the role he envisioned, as will be seen in more detail later in this chapter, the 1961 bill transmittal to Congress reiterated his desire to create a "focal point at the highest level of government for the consideration of disarmament matters."[42]

The final issue bedeviling programmatic coherence had to do with resource planning and allocation. In 1961, when the Senate Foreign Relations Committee held its ACDA hearings, there was no coordinated or unified budget for nonproliferation activities in the U.S. government. In fact, there was no list or official record of which agencies performed what functions. Senator Hubert Humphrey succeeded in amassing the organizational information but not the budgetary data. In presenting his findings to the committee, Humphrey euphemistically remarked, "We are trying to determine the total amount of money involved, but it is somewhat difficult." His frustration soon emerged. "I believe the people of the United States are entitled to know how much the Federal Government is spending—how and where—in this field, subject of course to national security regulations."[43] Humphrey's request was more than just an accounting issue. It was a matter of determining the appropriate level of resources necessary for combating a problem and of matching those resources to the right programs. The absence of any budget for proliferation-related activities either within individual cabinet departments or across them made it extraordinarily difficult to do these tasks well.

All three of these problems still plague nonproliferation policy. From 1999 to 2001, every single government study and report that dealt with proliferation found no vision or strategic plan. For example, the Hart-Rudman Commission, which conducted the most comprehensive review of U.S. national security organization in the past fifty years, found the "most troublesome" problem to be "a lack of an overarching strategic framework guiding U.S. national security policymaking and resource allocation."[44] Of particular concern to the commission was the absence of a strategy to defend the U.S. homeland from a conventional or WMD attack: "One of this Commission's most important conclusions . . . was that attacks against American citizens on American soil . . . are likely over the next quarter century. . . . The United States, however, *is very poorly organized to design and implement any comprehensive strategy to protect the homeland.*"[45]

The Gilmore Panel on WMD terrorism concurred. Its 2000 report to Congress and the president bluntly stated, "The United States has no coherent, functional national strategy for combating terrorism." Instead, the panel found that U.S. counterterrorism strategy amounted to little more than a "loosely coupled" set of executive branch plans, programs, and policy statements joined by ad hoc initiatives created by activist members of Congress.[46]

Examining the full scope of nonproliferation policy, the Deutch Commission also found loose pieces rather than a broad strategy. "We do not have a comprehensive approach to combating the proliferation of weapons of mass destruction," its report concluded.[47] The core problem was organizational, not conceptual. The commission noted, "It is not difficult to identify the key elements of an effective government response" and then proceeded to list them. Critical among them was the ability to develop "coordinated and consistent government-wide strategies," to integrate agency perspectives and programs, and to delineate clearly responsibilities among the departments and agencies.[48] Like Kennedy, the Deutch Commission found that the various agencies, when left to their own devices, tended to approach nonproliferation policy with too parochial a perspective:

> Today . . . both diplomatic and military efforts to combat proliferation too narrowly confine the range of tools they employ and the goals they seek. In the case of the Defense Department-led efforts, there is a natural focus on military instruments to respond to the potential threats of weapons of mass destruction. State Department-led efforts, by contrast, naturally focus on formal diplomatic tools. . . . A set of effective strategies reflecting today's proliferation challenges must go further than this.[49]

Not even the September 11 terrorist attacks against the World Trade Center and Pentagon spurred reorganization for the sake of programmatic coherence. As one GAO director testified on November 14, 2001, "We agree with the views expressed by the Deutch Commission and the Baker-Cutler Task Force that a missing element from the current U.S. government implementation of nonproliferation programs is an integrated strategic plan."[50] Nearly forty years after Kennedy's assessment, these panels once again cited the critical need for a new mechanism to harmonize the different voices amid the nonproliferation bureaucracy.

The studies and reports also mirrored Kennedy's criticism of the Eisenhower administration; in particular, the Deutch Commission highlighted the need for greater presidential leadership and for the designation of a single, high-level official or agency under the president's direction to manage nonproliferation policy. Its report concluded:

> With no one specifically in charge of all proliferation-related efforts, no one is ultimately accountable to the President and to Congress. Thus, the present system lets agencies protect their perceived institutional interests rather than fully contributing to an overall plan for achieving broader objectives. Blame can be deflected and diffused to other participants in the interagency process. Such diffuse responsibility invites inefficiency and ineffectiveness, and avoids accountability.[51]

In fact, it appears that even within specific areas, nonproliferation policy suffered from the same problem. In U.S.-Russian arms control programs, for example, the Energy Department task force called for a new office to synchronize objectives, programs, and budgets. In the area of WMD counterterrorism, the Hart-Rudman Commission, the Gilmore Panel, and the GAO all called for establishing a high-level focal point in the interest of effective management.[52] As the Gilmore Panel put it, "The organization of the Federal Government's programs for combating [WMD] terrorism is fragmented, uncoordinated, and politically unaccountable."[53] Since September 11, the Bush administration has attempted to fill this hole, creating an Office of Homeland Security based in the White House and a new cabinet Department of Homeland Security that brings together twenty-two different agencies, including the Immigration and Naturalization Service, the Coast Guard, the Customs Service, and the Federal Emergency Management Agency. Although the new department is expected to consolidate and improve U.S. border security operations (the department's border and transportation security division houses 90 percent of it employees and accounts for two-thirds of its budget),[54] its ability to integrate American counterterrorism policy more generally remains much in doubt.

The Deutch Commission found no progress on Senator Humphrey's demand for a unified executive branch nonproliferation budget, or even for a budget system that tracked nonproliferation-related expenditures within cabinet departments and agencies. The implications appeared far more serious than even Humphrey had imagined: "The success of any campaign depends on the resources available to wage it, and on the ways in which these resources are brought to bear. Currently, however, no one decides what level of resources should be devoted to proliferation-related efforts, there is no overall plan for how those resources should be allocated and no consistent evaluation of the effectiveness of these expenditures."[55] The commission found that, lacking central administrative guidance, individual agencies and congressional committees and subcommittees had no way to allocate funds in the right places with maximum effect. The result: redundancy in some areas of nonproliferation policy and critical inattention to others.[56]

SUMMARY

The snapshots from 1960–61 and 1999–2001 reveal persistent weaknesses in the organization of nonproliferation policy. In both periods, reformers found that bureaucratic agencies inadvertently and sometimes deliberately worked at cross-purposes. In the arms control talks of the 1950s, State Department negotiating teams were undercut by the Department of Defense and other agencies on more than one occasion. Moreover, U.S. arms control efforts were usually ad hoc, poorly supported, and inefficient. Without a comprehensive disarmament strategy or the administrative capabilities to support it, the United States was left scrambling to respond to Soviet proposals. In the Senate Foreign Relations Committee hearings of 1961, Kennedy adviser McCloy admitted he was surprised that Washington had fared as well as it had in bilateral talks with Moscow. McCloy made it clear that he believed American success had come despite, not because of, government organization.[57]

Although a great deal has changed since McCloy's testimony, the basic organizational weaknesses he described have not. The same problems of policy confusion and delay still hinder U.S. nonproliferation efforts. In March 2001, President Bush found himself reversing his own secretary of state on North Korea policy. And even one of the Pentagon's greatest successes, the Nunn-Lugar program, took a tremendous effort on the part of high-ranking officials to get off the ground. Like the arms control talks of the 1950s, the end result proved a success but the process did not.

Lingering problems entrenched in the bureaucratic structure made it much tougher and more protracted than it should have been to deal with one of the gravest threats to American national security since the cold war.

Even more serious has been the persistence of failures in programmatic coherence over the past four decades. When John F. Kennedy campaigned for president in 1960, he saw fundamental deficiencies in the U.S. government's organization for disarmament and arms control. In a policy area where Kennedy described the threat as a "nuclear sword of Damocles, hanging by the slenderest of threads," these problems loomed large.[58]

According to more recent commission reports, studies, and testimony, the U.S. government still lacks a long-term, comprehensive approach to deal with the proliferation of weapons of mass destruction. It still lacks a clear mechanism, in the Deutch Commission's words, to "orchestrate the entire spectrum" of U.S. policy perspectives, programs, and tools.[59] And it still lacks a planning and budgeting system that would enable policymakers to come up with informed judgments about how best to spend American resources in a field of responsibility that crosses so many agency lines. The Soviet Union's "nuclear sword of Damocles" may no longer hang precariously overhead, but transnational terrorism has taken its place. In short, it appears that fundamental organizational deficiencies in nonproliferation decisionmaking have had long lives. The unanswered question is why.

Explaining Organizational Continuity

Despite his best efforts, Kennedy failed to overcome the weaknesses he identified on the campaign trail. The president succeeded in passing legislation that established a new ACDA, but the agency was never able to perform the job it was meant to do. It was hobbled from birth.[60] Things only grew worse as time passed. Existing organizational arrangements proved exceptionally resistant to reform, and Kennedy's actions ultimately cast a long shadow through history; we are still living with the deficiencies they created and entrenched.

No doubt presidential leadership—the ability and willingness of various presidents to set policy priorities and to carry out those priorities—explains part of this historical pattern. It should come as no surprise that when the president gives an issue low priority, when chief presidential advisers disagree about policy emphases, or when the president himself is weak, bureaucratic rivalries and organizational problems become more pronounced. Indeed, nonproliferation policy priorities are often hard to determine and even harder to maintain as circumstances change. Should India be sanctioned for its nuclear program or supported as the world's largest democracy and a potential counterweight to China? Should Pakistan's nuclear program be forgotten if it continues providing assistance in the war against terrorism? For presidents, answering these kinds of questions means balancing difficult options and expending political capital, two things most presidents try to avoid. But avoidance only makes organizational problems worse. According to those who stress the primacy of presidential leadership, the more presidents set the agenda, the more they establish clear policy goals and use the power of their office to support them, the better nonproliferation organizations will perform.

Although this explanation captures an important part of reality, it appears better suited to explaining changes in organizational effectiveness than the persistence of organizational problems over time. Why? Because of the nature of its independent variable, presidential leadership. As presidential scholars have long argued, different presidents bring different capabilities and policy preferences to the job.[61] If presidential leadership really were a major determinant of organizational effectiveness, then these natural differences between presidents should have led to some significant fluctuation in problems relating to the application of nonproliferation policy over time.

But the two snapshots of nonproliferation organization do not indicate such variation. Indeed, one of the most striking findings is the similarity of organizational problems—both in type and magnitude—from the Kennedy to the Bush administrations. While it is certainly possible that some significant variation occurred between these two points in time, it seems highly unlikely. Changes to bureaucracy are hard to make and even harder to undo.[62]

Even a generous interpretation of the presidential leadership story appears unsatisfying. Let us assume for a moment that the cogency of U.S. nonproliferation strategy has suffered because all presidents since Kennedy failed to exercise the kind of leadership necessary to get the organizational basics right. In that case, presidential leadership appears to be an intervening variable, not an independent one. The real question begging to be answered is: Why did so many presidents in such different circumstances behave in similar ways? What underlying forces were so strong as to keep presidents from addressing these fundamental problems during and after the cold war?

As these questions suggest, identifying the root causes of longstanding organizational problems requires taking a step back, focusing less on the leadership of specific presidents and more on the enduring realities that all presidents face. Four other conditions and developments, taken together, provide a more general explanation for the nagging persistence of organizational problems in nonproliferation policy.

The first of these is the structure of American democracy. Put simply, the U.S. political system erects serious obstacles to creating effective bureaucratic organizations at the outset and to reforming them down the road. This is because the framers of the Constitution, who were intent on preventing the kind of oppressive government they faced in Europe, deliberately divided power between the branches. Over time, political norms and informal rules (such as the congressional committee system and the filibuster) have been grafted onto this formal constitutional structure in ways that make any kind of legislative change an uphill battle. For nonproliferation organizations, all of this means that opponents have numerous opportunities to kill or hobble fatally any new agency or arrangement.[63] Moreover, the worst problems are the least likely to get fixed because fundamental organizational reform usually requires new legislation.

Second, the structure of American democracy shapes the incentives and capabilities of different political players in ways that exacerbate all of these problems. Presidents, as the only nationally elected officials, have good reasons to consider issues like organizational effectiveness that have nationwide impact, but they lack the capabilities to get what they need. As Richard Neustadt pointed out more than thirty years ago, presidents are weak.[64] Although they can win big at times, presidents must choose their battles with care because they have little time, few formal powers, and limited political capital. In addition, substantive policy issues almost always rank higher on the president's priority list than the more arcane issues of bureaucratic functionality. When the choice is between passing a tax cut or redesigning the nonproliferation architecture, little wonder presidents choose to put organizational reform on the back burner.

Legislators have very different incentives and interests. If legislators want to win reelection, then they must cater to local interests ahead of national ones. Foreign policy in general and foreign policy organizations in particular do not sit high on the congressional agenda. In addition, members of Congress care about maintaining the power of the institution. Generally, this means that senators and representatives prefer executive arrangements that diffuse authority and capacities. The more different agencies in the executive branch, the more power bases can accrue in the legislature to oversee them. As one former senior official put it, "The Hill will not grant you rationality. Why? Because they have people up there . . . who have their own power bases that they don't want to give up."[65]

Bureaucrats, finally, have their own interests and powerful weapons to pursue them. Although presidents rely on their executive agencies to get things done, bureaucrats have other ideas, obligations, aims, and constituencies that conflict with those of the Oval Office. Nowhere is bureaucratic self-interest more at play than in the design of competing agencies. While most domestic policy areas are fairly discrete, in foreign policy agencies are tightly connected; one agency's work invariably affects what another does. In such a complex web, the battle for power and autonomy is zero-sum. No agency wants to yield authority or discretion to another.

On the whole, the interests and motives of politicians and officials suggest that presidents are unlikely to seek thoroughgoing organizational change, and, when they do, they are unlikely to succeed. With so many pressing issues, so little time, and so much benefit attached to policy success rather than organizational reform, presidents have little reason to take on the fight. Legislators and bureaucrats are a big part of the calculation. The average member of Congress pays no serious attention to foreign policy agency design because he or she knows it packs no punch at the polls. Even worse, senators and representatives know that reorganizing the executive branch means upsetting the applecart of congressional committee jurisdiction. Bureaucrats are even more formidable opponents. They have powerful incentives to care about the design and operation of agencies outside their own and to protect their own autonomy, jurisdiction, and influence, even at times at the expense of good policymaking.

The third enduring reality that helps explain the continuity of organizational problems is most straightforward: bureaucratic arrangements almost always get harder to change with time. The longer any single organization lives, the more entrenched its existence, routines, norms, and relationships become. Perhaps even more important, the more interconnected agencies become, the harder it is for the entire system to adapt. Nobel laureate Herbert Simon illustrated the point with a human evolution analogy.

> . . . designing each organ to adapt to changing requirements will be much easier if the design of any one organ has little effect on the efficiency of the others; if the heart can be designed without redesigning the lungs, for instance. With a higher degree of dependence, the continued "favorability" of any change in one organ will depend on what changes occur in the other organs at the same time or in the future.[66]

As Simon suggests, the more organizations there are and the more tightly coupled they become, the more difficult it is for the entire system to revamp. Adapting to shifting circumstances becomes exponentially more difficult because success requires so many changes in so many places.

Fourth, the nature of nonproliferation policy works against effective organization. As noted earlier, this policy arena is highly complex. It spans a wider array of domestic and international issues, requires a more varied kit of policy tools, and involves a bigger and more and diverse field of government officials than most other foreign policy problems. Although foreign and domestic policies have become increasingly intertwined, non-proliferation policy requires vastly different domestic and international components. Under the nonproliferation rubric, policy problems range from inspecting American cattle at home to inspecting weapons programs abroad, from securing U.S. airports to securing Russian fissile material, from training local health care workers in bioterrorism response to training special operations forces in cave-to-cave combat.

Nonproliferation policy also stretches across more, and more disparate, agency lines than most other policy areas. While no foreign policy issue is simple, most foreign policy problems—NATO expansion, the North American Free Trade Agreement, Sino-American relations, for instance—require coordinating diplomatic, military, and economic concerns among a relatively small set of agencies that have a long history of working together. Nonproliferation policy, by contrast, currently involves ninety-six organizations at the federal level alone. These agencies, which range from the Russian Plutonium Disposition Program to the Food and Drug Administration to the Immigration and Naturalization Service, include many that have not traditionally worked together.[67]

Complicating the picture even further, nonproliferation involves a particularly high degree of uncertainty between policies and outcomes. In some foreign policy issues, the relationship is fairly straightforward: in the 1994 Mexican peso crisis, for example, it became clear that U.S. intervention helped restore Mexican financial stability. Similarly, deploying U.S. Navy ships to the Taiwan Straits in 1958 succeeded in easing military hostilities between China and Taiwan. To be sure, most issues involve more murky connections between policies and outcomes. The extent to which U.S. sanctions helped end South African apartheid or containment contributed to the Soviet Union's demise fit this category. However, two aspects of nonproliferation policy place it at the extreme end of the uncertainty spectrum: proliferators deliberately seek to hide their activities, and nonproliferation success is, by definition, a nonevent—the absence of the spread or use of weapons of mass destruction. In these conditions, the challenge is not just to select an appropriate course of action. It is more fundamental: defining and determining the scope of the policy problem itself.

All of these characteristics spell bad news for nonproliferation strategy designers. The multifaceted nature of the policy area means there are more components to integrate, more varied strands to weave together. The large number and diverse set of agencies involved in nonproliferation policy means there are more moving parts in a bureaucratic machine that has developed no natural way of making them run together. The tenuous correlation between policies and outcomes makes it particularly difficult to define policy problems or to evaluate the effectiveness of discrete approaches. With so many policy facets, so many bureaucratic players, and so much uncertainty, nonproliferation policy by its very nature stacks the deck against organizational effectiveness.

In sum, the structure of American democracy, the rational self-interest of politicians, the basic principles of bureaucratic division of labor, and the nature of nonproliferation policy all suggest that effective organizational design will be elusive. In the best of circumstances, legislation will be difficult to pass. Crippling compromises will be an inevitable part of the policymaking process. Bureaucrats will be poised for battle. Legislators will be focused on reelection and on maintaining their own committee power. The policy area will remain crowded, complex, and murky. And fundamental reform will grow more difficult by the day.

ORGANIZATIONAL DEFICIENCIES REVISITED

Kennedy's creation of ACDA and the subsequent history of the nonproliferation policymaking process reflect the constraints described above. Two findings stand out. First, Kennedy and his successors have been loath to tackle organizational reform, for the same reasons. In fact, Kennedy backed away from establishing the ACDA even though he held a deep personal interest in the subject and made it one of his central foreign policy campaign issues. In July 1961, the president decided not to place the ACDA legislation on his "must list" of legislative priorities and told his disarmament adviser, John McCloy, that the bill would have to be passed without strong administration support.[68] According to McCloy, the president had become convinced that congressional opposition would kill the bill, a defeat he could not accept so early in his administration.[69] It took an extensive lobbying effort by

McCloy and Senator Humphrey to convince Kennedy to change his mind.[70]

No president after Kennedy has undertaken an extensive reform of nonproliferation policy organization, even though most have been aware of the ongoing problems. Nixon, Ford, Carter, and Reagan all chose to establish informal, temporary, alternative negotiating channels and interagency processes rather than overhaul the existing arms control system established by Kennedy. Even the Clinton administration, which elevated nonproliferation policy to unprecedented importance, declared a national state of emergency concerning weapons of mass destruction, and contributed to the Deutch Commission's study, did not implement a single one of the commission's recommendations for thoroughgoing reform. As one official explained, the administration "didn't want to fight the fight" with Congress, particularly in an election year and as it would entail more centralization in the White House, which "Congress always despises."[71] Other commission recommendations have suffered similar fates. Between 1999 and 2001, the Hart-Rudman Commission, the Gilmore Panel, the National Commission on Terrorism, and a five-year GAO analysis all highlighted the urgent need for organizational reform in the realm of WMD counterterrorism. Before September 11, however, none of the major recommendations from these commissions were adopted. Although some organizational changes, most notably the creation of the White House Office of Homeland Security and the Department of Homeland Security, have appeared since then, they have not yet resolved the fundamental problems with policy coordination and programmatic coherence that Kennedy first identified.

Second, even in the rare instance when a president chose to initiate reform, his efforts were thwarted by exactly the forces one would expect. Tracing the ACDA bill's development from Kennedy's original formulation to final passage reveals that, in each phase of the process, the proposed agency grew weaker and further removed from the president's vision.

In the beginning, Kennedy made it clear that he sought a powerful, independent agency that reported directly to him. The "U.S. Arms Control Research Institute" he proposed during the campaign was, as noted above, to be "under the immediate direction of the President." Although he emphasized that the new agency would not infringe on the prerogatives of any existing agencies, it was designed to do much more than provide technical research to other departments and agencies. It was meant to take a vigorous, lead role in policy development and planning.[72]

But that is not what the president got. Bureaucrats had the first crack at the bill. As Duncan Clarke writes in his history of the agency, "Virtually every department had some reason to object to ACDA's establishment."[73] McCloy agreed. From January to June of 1961, he shuttled between the State Department, the Joint Chiefs of Staff, the Atomic Energy Commission, the National Aeronautics and Space Administration, and other institutions in an effort to fashion a bill acceptable to all sides. "It was like walking through mud up to the knees," McCloy said later. "No one was too anxious to have this thing."[74]

The end result showed the ramifications of this executive branch wrangling and congressional compromise. Four changes are noteworthy. First, whereas Kennedy's original proposal gave the ACDA director direct presidential access by making him the "principal adviser to the President on disarmament matters,"[75] the final piece of legislation made the director the principal adviser to both the secretary of state and the president.[76] Second, while Kennedy's bill provided the agency head would work "under the direction" of the president and the secretary of state,[77] the actual statute mandated that the director operate under the guidance of the secretary alone.[78] Third, whereas Kennedy's bill charged the director with developing "suitable procedures to assume coopera-tion, coordination, and a continuing exchange of information among affected Government agencies," subject to presidential approval and consultation with other agencies,[79] the legislation vested coordination authority in the president alone.[80] Finally, the statute removed entirely a section that insisted all government agencies keep each other fully informed of "policy decisions, activities, statements, studies, research and other matters . . . which affect disarmament matters."[81] In its final incarnation, the Arms Control and Disarmament Act succeeded in weakening the most important sources of power for the new agency: its direct relationship to the president and its authority to coordinate the activities of the other agencies.

Reforming the nonproliferation architecture appears to have gotten only more difficult over time. The proliferation of agencies involved with nonproliferation as well as congressional oversight committees and subcommittees has created more parts to coordinate, more voices to har-monize, and more roadblocks to success. With so many more stakehold-ers in the current system, reform must cover more ground in order to be successful. It must redraw more bureaucratic and congressional bound-aries, and it must redistribute power from a wider range of places to reap results.

CONCLUSION

Many critics argue that U.S. foreign policy agencies are poorly equipped to meet the new challenges of the post–cold war world. They are only half right. The truth is that most foreign policy agencies were never well designed to handle the old challenges of the cold war. In the nonproliferation field, policymakers have found serious organizational weaknesses for more than four decades. From Kennedy to Bush, policymaking has suffered from poor coordination and weak programmatic coherence. Departments and agencies have undercut or contradicted one another. Responses to changing developments and needs have been slow and ponderous. Policies to handle proliferation have lacked an overarching strategy or plan. There has been no high-level office or person in charge to weave the threads of all the departments and agencies engaged in combating weapons of mass destruction into a single fabric. No budgetary mechanism has existed to help prioritize, track, or evaluate program effectiveness.

These organizational problems have been so enduring because their causes are so deeply embedded in the structure of American democracy, in human nature, in the design of bureaucratic organizations, and in the nature of nonproliferation policy. In the United States, the political system makes any kind of reform difficult to achieve and ensures that even successful change will include crippling compromises. Self-interest guarantees that almost all presidents will avoid tackling systematic reorganization because bureaucrats and Congress will resist it. Instead, presidents will do what they can under the radar screen, creating new capabilities and organizations informally. In the end, this may only make matters worse. As the nonproliferation policy apparatus grows larger and more complex, reform will have to be that much more sweeping to produce results.

What is to be done?

Although this analysis does not offer cause for celebration, it does suggest two cautionary observations about how to maximize the chances for successful organizational reform.

First, given the complex and well-entrenched sources of dysfunction in nonproliferation policy, the windows of opportunity for organizational reform will be few and fleeting. From the cold war until September 11, in fact, prospects for reform appeared slim. Despite the importance of nonproliferation, not a single president after Kennedy opted to push for bold changes. Initially, the World Trade Center and Pentagon attacks, coupled with the sudden menace of anthrax sent through the mail and growing public awareness of al Qaeda's interest in weapons of mass destruction, raised the possibility of organizational revamping in nonproliferation policy. Indeed, for many Americans today there is no danger more frightening than the specter of terrorists armed with nuclear, chemical, or biological weapons. Only such a high level of public awareness and concern can provide the necessary political impetus for the president to advance reform proposals. Even then, public awareness and concern usually will not be enough because the reform stars align only briefly, because organizational restructuring is inherently difficult to achieve, and because there are always numerous areas in need of improvement that compete for the president's attention and support. This can be seen clearly in the case of September 11, in which George W. Bush chose to use the considerable political support generated by the terrorist attacks to create a new Department of Homeland Security and to conduct war in Iraq rather than to deal with serious and well-known deficiencies in areas such as nonproliferation policy or intelligence coordination. Despite the president's record-high approval ratings, his two priority initiatives did not come quickly, easily, or cheaply. Had Republicans not gained seats in the 2002 midterm election, the Homeland Security Department bill might well have remained deadlocked in Congress. And the war in Iraq has exacted a substantial political price in terms of American relationships abroad.

To improve the chances of success in such an environment, reformers need to be able to recognize these windows of opportunity when they arise and be prepared to exploit them quickly, before competing priorities drain the president's surge in political capital. In practical terms, this "hurry up and wait" approach means working to develop serious, detailed reform plans and enlist the support of influential political officials well in advance of crises and maintaining the capability to deploy a rapid-reaction reform team that can work with administration officials and legislators once the opportunity arises. The September 11 window may now be closed. However, the unfortunate likelihood of future terrorist attacks against Americans and the continuing spread of weapons of mass destruction suggest that reformers will have further occasions to tackle critical organizational problems in U.S. nonproliferation organization in the not too distant future. The key is to start now.

Second, organizational reformers should resist the temptation to focus narrowly on the immediate problems at hand; instead, they should concentrate on the fundamentals. The history of nonproliferation suggests that organizational basics—ensuring day-to-day coordination and long-term programmatic coherence—are the hardest problems to remedy but once resolved may have the greatest potential leverage across a range of complex and unforeseen policy challenges. If nonproliferation organizations are managed to coordinate their daily work, if they are working in concert to support a national strategy, and if their programs are evaluated and measured against a common standard, then any future WMD problem can be tackled more effectively. When all of the parts in a car engine are running together, the car can move in any direction.

Organizational reform should start by dealing with programmatic coherence: developing an integrated national nonproliferation strategy, creating a high-level focal point to coordinate efforts throughout the bureaucracy, and establishing a cross-agency budgeting process to match resources against priorities. A government-wide strategic plan need not be created out of whole cloth. Essential elements of it already exist within individual agencies. What is lacking, however, is an overarching perspective that considers the best mix of policy programs and how that mix can be sustained or changed over time.

Establishing effective leadership is more challenging but equally important. The core problem here is not that the U.S. government lacks the necessary capabilities, ideas, or manpower for nonproliferation policy. It is that the bureaucracy has grown unwieldy and has no central coordinating mechanism. It has become a body without a brain. To be sure, experts will continue to disagree about the best organizational solution to this problem—whether, for example, to locate a hub within the existing National Security Council staff structure or to devise a new cabinet agency. In the end what matters most is that some new office or position be created, that it be elevated to the highest level of government—with direct access to the Oval Office—and that it be clearly vested with the personal trust and authority of the president. Kennedy's best intentions for ACDA went awry because he failed to endow the organization with the direct access and presidential authority it needed to keep other bureaucratic players in line.

Finally, as the old adage goes, you cannot manage what you cannot measure. Setting up a budget that spans nonproliferation agencies will enable the new central coordinator to determine priorities, to evaluate more clearly costs and benefits of competing programs, and to send clear marching orders to the rest of the bureaucracy.

The task is difficult, but the stakes are high. Presidents cannot manage nonproliferation policy by themselves. They have too many obligations and too little time. Even the best-intentioned president does not have the resources to ensure personally that vaccine stockpiles match intelligence estimates of biohazard risk, that policy innovations get off the ground, or that programs are well integrated in support of a comprehensive strategy. These tasks require organizational capabilities. In nonproliferation policy, organizational reform may not be a panacea, but it is the right place to start.

PART TWO
EXPLORING THE TOOLS OF NONPROLIFERATION

2

ADDRESSING PROLIFERATION THROUGH MULTILATERAL AGREEMENT
SUCCESS AND FAILURE IN THE NONPROLIFERATION REGIME

Joseph Cirincione

There is a great and pervasive fear that some nation or some group will use a nuclear, biological, or chemical weapon in the United States, killing hundreds or hundreds of thousands of people. Many feel the danger of such an attack is increasing. What was once the precoccupation of a small group of proliferation specialists has now become a shared concern across a broad spectrum of military leaders, defense and intelligence officials, political leaders, journalists, and the general public. The spread of weapons of mass destruction is widely regarded today as the most urgent national security threat. A recent report on proliferation from the U.S. Department of Defense, for example, begins: "In virtually every corner of the globe, the United States and its allies face a growing threat from the proliferation and possible use of nuclear, biological, and chemical (NBC) weapons and their deliver systems. . . . We have become increasingly concerned in recent years that NBC weapons, delivery systems and technology may all be 'for sale' to the highest bidder."[1]

The sense of urgency is not new. Since the first atomic bomb destroyed the first city, efforts to stop the spread of these weapons have had a curious schizoid character of pessimistic threat assessments coupled with optimistic proposals for developing either military or diplomatic counters.

Military measures include policies to deter attacks by assured devastating counterattacks, weapons to seek out and destroy the threats before attacks can be launched, and defenses either to intercept attacking weapons or to reduce the casualties from attacks. Diplomatic efforts encompass negotiated treaties and agreements to reduce or ban weapons and restrict technologies, confidence-building measures to reduce instability, international summits and meetings to promote common security, and sanctions to enforce compliance with international norms.

Nonproliferation efforts have had, like the stock market, their bull and bear years. It has often been difficult to predict when one cycle would end and the other begin. The failures can be so dramatic that investors lose faith and flee for other, safer positions. The history of the past fifty-seven years, however, shows that, over the long run, the nonproliferation regime has provided a solid return on national investments.

While the negotiated, verifiable arms control process has lost favor within the White House, it is useful to note that the multilateral nonproliferation regime has been a key—though perhaps not exclusive—tool in limiting the spread of nuclear weapons, materiel, and expertise. The development of international norms, regimes, laws, and organizations to address nuclear nonproliferation has gone far to restrict the number of states possessing offensive nuclear capabilities.

This chapter begins by tracing the evolution of the nonproliferation regime from post–World War II to post–September 11. Next, it evaluates the utility of negotiated multilateral agreements in contending with the proliferation of weapons of mass destruction. The chapter considers the interplay between domestic and international politics that has colored the formation, successes, and failures of the nonproliferation regime. It also considers two recent case studies that demonstrate how that regime has adapted since the end of the cold war as the United States and the international community have sought to manage proliferation challenges.

In the Beginning
America Organizes for the Atomic Threat

The Allies had defeated the fascist dictators. Millions had lost their lives in the epic battles. Millions more were homeless in the ruined cities of Asia and Europe. But in January 1946, the existence of even a few atomic bombs so alarmed the new United Nations General Assembly that it ordered its

Atomic Energy Commission (AEC) to "make specific proposals . . . for the elimination from national armaments of atomic weapons and of all other major weapons adaptable to mass destruction."[2]

The United States, the dominant force in the United Nations, enjoyed a nuclear monopoly but realized it would not last. As Henry Sokolski points out, strategic thinking was then informed by two premises about nuclear weapons:[3] first, that "there can be no adequate military defense"[4] against nuclear weapons (as a joint Allied declaration stated in November 1945); and, second, that threats of retaliation would not prevent a devastating nuclear first strike by a determined adversary.

In June 1946 Bernard Baruch, the United States representative to the AEC, presented the American plan:

> We are here to make a choice between the quick and the dead. . . . Science has torn from nature a secret so vast in its potentialities that our minds cower from the terror it creates. Yet terror is not enough to inhibit the use of the atomic bomb. . . . We must provide the mechanism to assure that atomic energy is used for peaceful purposes and preclude its use in war.[5]

The Baruch plan proposed the creation of an international agency that would alone possess the knowledge and control of all atomic energy activities "potentially dangerous to world security" and the power to control, inspect, and license all other atomic activities. The United States, he said, would stop its production of atomic bombs once the regime was in place and would then eliminate all existing bombs.

Cold war ambitions and suspicions both within the U.S. government and in Moscow stifled the Baruch plan, while the allure of atomic power soon spread nuclear technology to other states.[6] During the late 1940s and early 1950s, witnesses promised congressional committees that atomic-powered planes and cars would soon be a reality and that nuclear power would make electricity so cheap it would no longer be metered.

By December 1953, when President Dwight Eisenhower stepped to the podium at the United Nations, the United States had conducted forty-two nuclear tests, had developed hydrogen bombs with explosive power equal to millions of tons of TNT (compared to the equivalent of 12,000 tons of TNT represented by the bomb dropped on Hiroshima), and was equipping each of its military services with nuclear weapons for a wide range of missions. But the Soviet Union also was now testing and deploying nuclear weapons, as was the United Kingdom (with U.S. help).

Eisenhower warned that, "the knowledge now possessed by several nations will eventually be shared by others— possibly all others."[7] While countries were already beginning to build warning and defensive systems against nuclear air attack, he cautioned, "Let no one think that the expenditure of vast sums for weapons and systems of defense can guarantee absolute safety for the cities and citizens of any nation. The awful arithmetic of the atomic bomb does not permit any such easy solution."[8]

Eisenhower proposed the creation of the International Atomic Energy Agency (IAEA) to promote the peaceful uses of atomic energy while the world's nuclear powers "began to diminish the potential destructive power of the world's atomic stockpiles." By the time the IAEA opened for membership in 1956, the disarmament components of the original vision were gone, but the promotion of atomic energy remained, though coupled with regulations and inspections to ensure that its assistance "is not used in such a way to further any military purpose." In 1960, France exploded its first nuclear weapon, and other industrial nations were exploring their nuclear options.

This led Senator John Kennedy to criticize then Vice President Richard Nixon in their third presidential debate in October 1960 for not doing enough to end nuclear testing and stop the spread of nuclear weapons. "There are indications, because of new inventions," he said, "that ten, fifteen or twenty nations will have a nuclear capacity—including Red China—by the end of the presidential office in 1964."[9]

As president, Kennedy proposed in 1961 a plan that included all the elements that negotiators pursue today as part of the international non-proliferation regime (see Box 2.1): a comprehensive nuclear test ban; a ban on the production of fissionable materiels for use in weapons; the placement of all weapons materials under international safeguards; a ban on the transfer of nuclear weapons, their materials, or their technology; and deep reductions in existing nuclear weapons and their delivery vehicles, with the goal of eventually eliminating them. "The weapons of war must be abolished," he said, "before they abolish us."[10]

THE REGIME EMERGES
EXTENDING NONPROLIFERATION THROUGH
INTERNATIONAL ORGANIZATION

Kennedy's plan was negotiated successfully by his successor, Lyndon Johnson, and signed into law by President Richard Nixon. The Treaty on the Non-Proliferation of Nuclear Weapons, popularly known as the Non-Proliferation

Box 2.1: What Are Weapons of Mass Destruction?

Nuclear Weapons

A nuclear weapon is a device in which most or all of the explosive energy is derived from fission or a combination of fission and fusion processes. Such explosions cause catastrophic damage, attributable to both the high temperatures and ground shocks produced by the initial blast and the lasting residual radiation. Nuclear fission weapons produce energy by splitting the nucleus of an atom, usually highly enriched uranium or plutonium, into two or more parts by bombarding it with neutrons. Each nucleus that is split releases energy as well as additional neutrons that bombard proximate nuclei and sustain a chain reaction. Fission bombs, such as those dropped on Hiroshima and Nagasaki, are the easiest to make and provide the catalyst for more complex thermonuclear explosions. In such weapons a fission explosion creates the high temperatures necessary to join light isotopes of hydrogen, usually deuterium and tritium, which similarly liberate energy and neutrons. Most modern nuclear weapons use a combination of the two processes, called "boosting," to maintain high yields in smaller bombs.

Biological Weapons

Biological weapons intentionally disseminate infectious diseases and conditions that would otherwise appear only naturally or not at all. Such agents can be divided into bacterial agents (such as those that cause anthrax), viruses (such as smallpox), rickettsia (such as Q fever), chlamydia, fungi, and toxins (such as ricin). Features that influence their potential for use as weapons include infectivity, virulence, toxicity, pathogenicity, incubation period, transmissibility, lethality, and stability. Genetic engineering profoundly magnified the threat from biological weapons. Agents that are extremely harmful in nature can be modified to increase virulence, production rate per cell, and survivability under environmental stress, as well as to mask their presence from immune-based detectors. As most agents are living organisms, their natural replication after dissemination increases the potential impact of strike, making such weapons even more attractive. Any country possessing a pharmaceutical or food storage infrastructure already has an inherent stabilization and preservation system for biological agents. Aerosol delivery is optimal, while explosive delivery also is effective but to a lesser degree because of the possibility for inactivation of the organism owing to heat from the blast.

Continued on page 52

Box 2.1: What Are Weapons of Mass Destruction? (cont.)

Chemical Weapons

Chemical weapons use the toxic properties, as opposed to the explosive properties, of chemical substances to produce physical or physiological effects on an enemy. Classic chemical weapons, such as chlorine and phosgene, were employed during World War I and consisted primarily of commercial chemicals used as choking and blood agents, which caused respiratory damage and asphyxiation. Blistering agents such as mustard gas and lewisite, which cause painful burns necessitating medical attention even in low doses, marked the advent of the first chemical weapons to yield a significant military effect. Mustard gas, owing to its low cost and ability to produce resource-debilitating casualties, has been a popular weapon and was used to inflict numerous casualties during the Iran-Iraq War.

Nerve gases, or anticholinesterase agents, were discovered by the Germans in the 1930s and represent the beginning of modern chemical warfare. Such agents block an enzyme in the body that is essential for nervous system function, causing loss of muscle control, respiratory failure, and eventually death. These gases, all liquids at room temperature, are lethal far more quickly and in far lower quantities than classic agents and are effective either when inhaled or when absorbed through the skin. Nerve gases can be classified as either G-agents (sarin) or V-agents (VX), both of which are exceedingly volatile and toxic. Other types of chemical weapons include mental and physical incapacitants (such as BZ) and binary systems that combine two agents to form a poisonous gas, both of which have undergone limited military development. Chemical weapons can be delivered through bombs, rockets, artillery shells, spray tanks, and missile warheads, which generally use an explosion to expel an internal agent laterally.

Sources: U.S. Department of State, "Biological Weapons Convention," n.d., available online at www.state.gov/www/global/arms/treaties/bwc1.html; Federation of American Scientists, "Biological Weapons," Washington, D.C., updated October 21, 1998, available online at www.fas.org/nuke/intro/bw/intro.htm; Carey Sublette, "Frequently Asked Questions about Nuclear Weapons," MILNET Mirror, available online at http://www.milnet.com/milnet/nukeweap/ August 9, 2001; Federation of American Scientists, "Chemical Weapons—Introduction," Washington, D.C., updated October 21, 1998, available online at www.fas.org/nuke/intro/cw/intro.htm; Federation of American Scientists, "Nuclear Weapon Design," Washington, D.C., updated October 21, 1998, available online at www.fas.org/nuke/intro/nuke/design.htm; Joseph Cirincione with Jon B. Wolfsthal and Miriam Rajkumar, *Deadly Arsenals: Tracking Weapons of Mass Destruction* (Washington, D.C.: Carnegie Endowment for International Peace, 2002), pp. 57–66.

Treaty or NPT, entered into force in 1970 with almost one hundred nations as original signatories. It remains the centerpiece of today's regime.

Nixon criticized the treaty while campaigning in 1968 but signed it with relish in a Rose Garden ceremony. "Let us trust that we will look back," he said, "and say that this was one of the first and major steps in that process in which the nations of the world moved from a period of confrontation to a period of negotiation and a period of lasting peace."[11]

The treaty has become a mainstay of the international security system, enjoying near universal acceptance, with almost every nation in the world a member of the treaty regime. One hundred and eighty-two nations have pledged never to acquire nuclear weapons; in addition, the five nuclear powers recognized by the treaty are all members and have declared their willingness to reduce and eventually eliminate their arsenals. "The basic purpose of the NPT was to provide another choice," explains George Bunn, a principal member of the NPT negotiating team, "to establish a common nonproliferation norm that would assure cooperating nuclear weapon 'have-not' countries that if they did not acquire nuclear weapons, their neighbors and rivals would not do so either."[12]

The treaty, of course, did not emerge in a diplomatic vacuum. It is part and parcel of the political and military balance of power and alliance systems of the late twentieth century. Alliance security arrangements, including the promise that the United States would extend a "nuclear umbrella" over Europe and Japan, undoubtedly made it easier for several industrial nations to abandon their nuclear weapons programs. The Soviet Union simply enforced nonproliferation on its alliance system. The United States, too, was not averse to using strong-arm tactics to compel, for example, Taiwan and South Korea to abandon nuclear weapons research. In many developing nations, nuclear ambitions ran into the formidable financial and technological obstacles to both nuclear power and weapon development.

At a time when there is increasing interest in unilateral approaches to security arrangements, it is important to point out that financial and technical challenges and power relations within alliances were not in themselves sufficient barriers to proliferation. These concerns were present in the 1960s as well as the 1970s. But before the signing of the NPT, proliferation was on the rise; afterward, it was on the decline. The critical importance of the NPT is that it provided the international legal mechanism and established the global diplomatic norm that gave nations a clear path to a nonnuclear future.

Moreover, it is a path that is encouraged and enforced by the dominant political and military powers. The NPT and other treaties do not exist apart from or in opposition to alliance arrangements; rather, they embody those arrangements. The nonproliferation regime is thus much more than pieces of paper. It is a series of agreements that, like the Magna Carta or the Declaration of Independence, capture the political reality of the time and are enforced by the collective political will of the participants.

David Fischer, a historian of the nonproliferation regime, wrote in 1992:

> A broadly shared perception that one's national interest is better served by not possessing nuclear weapons is thus the foundation of the international non-proliferation regime. [T]he former Axis nations had no choice in the matter but since then their enforced renunciation has become firmly embedded in national policy. In some cases renunciation presupposed that the USA would shield them with her nuclear umbrella but even that link has now lost most of its relevance. In many small developing countries nuclear abstention may simply reflect technical inability. But in several countries the decision to forego nuclear weapons came after pro-longed internal debate as in Sweden, Switzerland, Belgium, Yugoslavia, Turkey, Egypt, and Spain. Even in Australia there were once powerful voices in favor of nuclear weapons.[13]

THE REGIME EVOLVES
EXPANDING THE MULTILATERAL WEB

The success of the NPT and improving relations with the Soviet Union encouraged other nonproliferation efforts. In addition to the NPT, President Nixon also negotiated or initiated many of the other corner-stones of today's international control regimes. To implement controls over the export of nuclear-weapons-related materials and equipment, Nixon established the NPT Exporters Committee (known as the Zangger Committee) that set the first major agreement on uniform regulation of nuclear exports by actual or potential nuclear suppliers. He negotiated and implemented the Anti-Ballistic Missile Treaty limiting defensive armaments and the companion Strategic Arms Limitation Treaty (SALT) limiting offensive arms, both signed in May 1972.

Nixon also announced in 1969 that the United States would unilat-erally and unconditionally renounce biological weapons. He ordered the destruction of the considerable U.S. weapons stockpile in that category and the conversion of all production facilities for peaceful purposes. He reversed fifty years of U.S. reluctance and sought ratification of the 1925 Geneva Protocol prohibiting the use in war of biological and chemical weapons (subsequently ratified under President Gerald Ford). The president successfully negotiated the Biological and Toxin Weapons Convention (BTWC), signed in 1972 and ratified by the Senate in 1974, prohibiting the development, production, stockpiling, acquisition, and transfer of biological weapons.

President Ronald Reagan followed a first term characterized by defense budget increases, new nuclear weapons programs, and, most famously, the Strategic Defense Initiative (SDI) with a flurry of arms control agreements. He had campaigned against President Jimmy Carter's SALT II treaty, but in office he largely observed its limits. He went further by negotiating and signing the landmark Intermediate-Range Nuclear Forces Treaty (INF) in 1987, requiring the destruction of all 2,700 U.S.and Soviet missiles and their launchers with ranges between 500 and 5,500 kilometers (a treaty some argue should be globalized to prohibit all missiles of this range anywhere in the world). That same year, Reagan initiated the Missile Technology Control Regime (MTCR), the first effort to control the spread of ballistic missile technology. He also negotiated the first strategic treaty that actually reduced (rather than limited) deployed strategic nuclear forces.

President George H. W. Bush signed Reagan's Strategic Arms Reduction Treaty (START) in 1991 and kept the momentum going by negotiating and signing in January 1993 the START II treaty, the most sweeping arms reduction pact in history. President Bush also negotiated and signed the Chemical Weapons Convention (CWC) prohibiting the development, production, acquisition, stockpiling, transfer, or use of chemical weapons. Perhaps setting a model for future reductions, in 1991 Bush announced that the United States would unilaterally withdraw all of its land- and sea-launched tactical nuclear weapons and would dismantle all of its land- and many of its sea-based tactical systems. The president also took the initiative to end the twenty-four-hour alert status of the U.S. bomber force and brought a substantial portion of the land-based missile force off of hair-trigger alert readiness to launch within fifteen minutes. Two weeks later, President Mikhail Gorbachev reciprocated with similar tactical withdrawals and ordered the de-alerting of 503 Soviet intercontinental ballistic missiles.

Though the arms limitation campaign was begun by Eisenhower, inspired by Kennedy, and pushed by Johnson, the major diplomatic lifting was actually done by Presidents Nixon, Reagan, and Bush, who either negotiated or brought into force almost all the instruments that make up the interlocking network of treaties and arrangements we refer to as the nonproliferation regime. President Bill Clinton added the Agreed Framework with North Korea that froze that nation's nascent nuclear program; won Senate ratification of Bush's START II treaty and chemical weapons ban; helped denuclearize Belarus, Kazakstan, and Ukraine; won the permanent extension of the NPT in 1995; and negotiated and signed the long-sought Comprehensive Nuclear Test Ban Treaty (CTBT), still awaiting entry into force. Over time, the nonproliferation regime emerged as a living organism capable of evolving to meet new challenges. The resulting skein of agreements described in Table 2.1 served to prevent the widespread diffusion of weapons, technology, and know-how.

NUCLEAR FORECASTS

Since the signing of the NPT in 1968, the treaty regime has greatly restricted—though not completely prevented—the spread of weapons of mass destruction. As noted above, President Kennedy worried in the early 1960s that while only the United States, the Soviet Union, the United Kingdom, and France then possessed nuclear weapons, by the middle of the decade, fifteen or twenty nations could obtain them. The concern was not that Third World countries would acquire the bomb but rather that the advanced industrial nations would—particularly Japan and Germany. Italy, Sweden, and other European nations were actively pursuing nuclear weapons programs. Neutral Sweden was then developing plans to build a hundred nuclear weapons to equip its air force, army, and navy.

Twenty years after Kennedy's warning only China (with Soviet help) had openly joined the ranks of the new nuclear nations, while India had exploded a so-called peaceful nuclear device and Israel was building a secret nuclear arsenal. All the other nations that had studied nuclear programs in the 1950 and 1960s had abandoned their pursuits. The treaty regime failed, however, to constrain the nuclear arms race between the two superpowers in the 1960s and 1970s, sometimes known as "vertical proliferation." Soviet strategic nuclear warheads tripled, from more than 1,800 warheads in 1968 to 5,800-plus in 1978, while U.S. strategic weapons increased from about 9,000 to 14,000 during the same ten years.

TABLE 2.1: MAJOR ELEMENTS OF THE NONPROLIFERATION REGIME

TITLE	DATE	NO. OF PARTICIPANTS	DESCRIPTION
Treaty on the Nonproliferation of Nuclear Weapons (NPT)	Entered into force in 1970	188 signatories	Under the treaty, the five "nuclear weapons" states commit to pursue general and complete disarmament, while the remaining "nonnuclear weapons" states agree to forgo developing or acquiring nuclear weapons.
Chemical Weapons Convention (CWC)	Entered into force on Apr. 29, 1997	152 members; 172 signatories	The treaty prohibits the production, stockpiling, acquisition, and transfer of chemical weapons.
Biological and Toxin Weapons Convention (BTWC)	Entered into force on Mar. 26, 1975	146 member states;170 signatories	The treaty prohibits the development, production, stockpiling, acquisition, and transfer of pathogens or toxins in weapons systems or other means of delivery.
Comprehensive Test Ban Treaty (CTBT)	Opened for signature Sept. 24, 1996	101 ratifications; 167 members	The treaty prohibits nuclear test explosions of any size and establishes a rigorous global verification system to detect violations.
Missile Technology Control Regime (MTCR)	Announced on Apr. 16, 1987	33 participants	This is an informal export control arrangement, designed to regulate the spread of ballistic and cruise missiles capable of delivering a 500-kilogram payload 300 kilometers or more.
Agreed Framework	Signed on Oct. 21, 1994		In exchange for North Korea halting and agreeing to dismantle its nuclear program, a U.S.-led coalition agreed to supply North Korea with two light-water reactors.

Source: Joseph Cirincione with Jon B. Wolfsthal and Miriam Rajkumar, *Deadly Arsenals: Tracking Weapons of Mass Destruction* (Washington: Carnegie Endowment for International Peace, 2002), p. 34.

This enormous increase in the number of nuclear weapons in just two nations dominated both military thinking and diplomatic efforts in these years. Depending on where one lived, either the United States or the Soviet Union, or both, were blamed for the problem, but in any case the greatest nuclear danger was generally regarded as the "nuclear arms race," not proliferation.

At the beginning of the 1980s, however, proliferation experts were again ringing alarm bells about the possible spread of weapons to other nations. The regime was failing, experts warned, not just with the superpowers but among new nuclear nations. Kennedy's problems were now regarded as relatively minor compared with the new decade's challenges. Lewis Dunn wrote in a 1982 Twentieth Century Fund study: "The relative stability of the early decades of the nuclear age—when the United States' monopoly on the bomb was lost but the spread of nuclear weapons was slow and limited—may be ending. We are now entering a much more dangerous stage of proliferation, in which possession of the bomb by countries in conflict-prone regions is not only possible but probable and the threat of actual use of nuclear weapons is growing."[14]

Dunn's study listed eighteen developing nations that had either the capability or the ambition to build nuclear weapons. In addition to Yugoslavia in Europe, the list included, in Africa: Libya, Egypt, Nigeria, and South Africa; in the Americas: Argentina, Brazil, Chile, and Mexico; and, in Asia: Syria, Iraq, Saudi Arabia, Iran, Israel, Pakistan, India, Taiwan, and South Korea. "The conditions that checked the scope and pace of [the first wave of] proliferation have eroded," he warned. "For many nations, the technical barriers to acquisition of nuclear weapons are easier to overcome. The disincentives to 'going nuclear' are becoming less compelling and often are only dimly perceived." Still, Dunn argued that "traditional nonproliferation policies designed to slow the pace and contain the scope of proliferation must remain at the core of U.S. strategy."[15]

At the beginning of the 1990s, Leonard Spector listed eleven "emerging nuclear weapons nations." The pattern of "slow, steady expansion of nuclear weapon capabilities in the developing world" was continuing in the new decade, he warned, in Israel, India, Pakistan, and South Africa (now de facto nuclear weapons states) as well as Libya, Brazil, Argentina, Iraq, Iran, North Korea, and Taiwan.[16]

Spector highlighted an important new trend: the emergence of "potential nuclear powers with deeply ingrained hostilities toward the United States."[17] In his hindsight, the proliferation of the previous decades seemed almost benign, as it involved almost exclusively nations that, "if not always friends of the United States, were at least not openly antagonistic to American interests."

ASSESSING AN EVOLVING REGIME

Looking back over the past half century, two observations about proliferation assessments seem clear: the future always seemed more terrifying than the past, and the pessimistic projections of experts proved wrong. This is not to say that proliferation was not and is not a serious problem or that it was wrong for the experts to develop worst-case scenarios. Indeed, the expert warnings may have helped motivate policies that reduced proliferation. If a few crises had developed just a little differently, we might today be analyzing a world that had experienced further use of nuclear weapons, perhaps many nuclear weapons. The threats concerning biological weapons, although greatly reduced from the days when both superpowers stockpiled and prepared to use thousands of such weapons, are still uncertain. But the fact remains that, although nuclear, biological, and chemical arsenals in the United States and the Soviet Union grew to grotesque levels and the technology of these weapons has become increasingly accessible, the world was not devastated by a thermonuclear war, and no one has used a biological weapon. The number of prospective nuclear nations has shrunk dramatically over the past twenty years, not increased; there are thousands fewer ballistic missiles in the world today than fifteen years ago; and there are far fewer countries possessing any weapons of mass destruction than there were twenty, thirty, or forty years ago.

We may not have been quick, but neither are we dead. Moreover, the international norm has been firmly established that countries should not, under any circumstances, possess or use either biological or chemical weapons. The vast majority of nations fully comply with these treaties; violators are pressured to fall into line. Global expectations are that the existing stockpiles of nuclear weapons will be greatly reduced, even if their eventual elimination seems a distant hope.

The experts' warning lists were accurate at the time, but since 1964, only three nations have overcome the substantial diplomatic and technical barriers to acquisition of nuclear weapons. Today there are still only five nuclear weapons states recognized by the NPT that enjoy special legal right and privileges. Listed in order of the size of their nuclear arsenals, they are Russia, the United States, China, France, and the United Kingdom. This picture remained remarkably stable until 1998, when India and Pakistan both detonated nuclear devices and declared their intentions to deploy nuclear weapons. Though neither is believed to have done so yet, India is probably capable of deploying tens of weapons over the next few years, as is Pakistan. Israel is widely believed to have as many as one hundred nuclear weapons but neither acknowledges nor denies their existence. Neither India, Pakistan, nor Israel is a member of the NPT.

Apart from these eight (see Table 2.2), only two other counties are believed to be pursuing nuclear weapon programs. North Korea may have accumulated enough material to construct two weapons but agreed in 1994 to freeze its plutonium production program. This arrangement largely collapsed in 2003. North Korea announced its withdrawal from the NPT and may become the world's ninth nuclear nation. Iran is believed to be slowly pursuing nuclear and missile programs, and disclosure of large-scale uranium facilities in late 2002 raised fears that Iran could follow North Korea's lead and withdraw from the NPT after developing its nuclear infrastructure. Finally, United Nations inspectors destroyed Iraq's nuclear program after the Persian Gulf War, but the Bush administration claim that Iraq had reconstituted its program and that new UN inspections could not stop it led directly to the 2003 Iraq war. With the overthrow of the regime of Saddam Hussein, Iraq is unlikely to pursue any new programs for many years.

That is, few of the twenty or so nations that fueled Kennedy's concern actually acquired nuclear weapons, and just three of Dunn's list of eighteen

TABLE 2.2: WORLD NUCLEAR ARSENALS

Russia	20,000
United States	10,700
China	410
France	348
United Kingdom	185
Israel	98–172 suspected
India	50–90
Pakistan	3–50

Source: Joseph Cirincione with Jon B. Wolfsthal and Miriam Rajkumar, *Deadly Arsenals: Tracking Weapons of Mass Destruction* (Washington, D.C.: Carnegie Endowment for International Peace, 2002), p. 43.

or Spector's list of eleven have nuclear weapons today, with only North Korea and Iran still on everyone's nuclear watch list.

In the meantime, several major countries abandoned nuclear programs, including Argentina and Brazil, and four others relinquished their nuclear weapons to join the NPT as nonnuclear nations. Ukraine, Belarus, and Kazakstan, thanks to the skillful diplomacy of senior officials in both the Bush and Clinton administrations, gave up the thousands of nuclear weapons they had acquired from the breakup of the Soviet Union. South Africa, on the eve of its transition to majority rule, destroyed the six nuclear weapons the apartheid regime had secretly constructed. The new South African government could have retained these weapons and the program, but Nelson Mandela concluded that South Africa's security was better served in a nuclear-free Africa than in one with several nuclear nations—exactly the logic that inspired the original members of the NPT decades earlier. Africa is one of several areas of the world that have established nuclear-weapon-free zones prohibiting the use or possession of such weapons anywhere.[18]

The discussion has focused on nuclear proliferation, but adding chemical and biological weapons to the equation does not alter the overall assessment. According to Thomas W. Graham's analysis of proliferation threats:

> The multiple proliferation threats of weapons of mass destruction, ballistic and cruise missiles, and covert or terrorist delivered chemical, biological, radiological and nuclear weapons in the first decade of the 21st century are finite (at most 17 countries or approximately a dozen and half countries, out of roughly 190 in the world); acute proliferation threats are far *smaller* in scope (3 to 7 countries) and perhaps smaller in complexity than the U.S. experienced during the Cold War; there is little or no current evidence that these combined proliferation threats are growing, let alone expanding uncontrollably as some officials and influential experts have stated over the past two administrations. In fact, most of the evidence suggests that contemporary multiple proliferation threats are shrinking in terms of number of countries involved.[19]

"Multilateral and bilateral nuclear non-proliferation efforts have been a remarkably successful threat reduction policy especially given the limited financial and cabinet level leadership resources devoted to this task,"

Graham concludes.[20] "The nuclear non-proliferation battles that were fought and won over the last four decades were much more difficult, in my opinion, than current national security challenges to deal with the *multiple proliferation threats* of today."[21] The most difficult threat, he believes, and many agree, is the proliferation problem presented by the thousands of nuclear weapons, tons of nuclear materials, and thousands of unemployed scientists in Russia. But even that challenge can be "solved" with an investment of approximately $30 billion given wise U.S. leadership and Russian cooperation, according to the January 2001 "Report Card on the Department of Energy's Programs with Russia," written by a commission chaired by Lloyd Cutler and Howard Baker.

This is a stunning record of success. But can it hold? Are international conditions so different today that the regime can no longer work? Or did these nonproliferation victories have little or nothing to do with treaties at all?

TWENTY-FIRST-CENTURY PROLIFERATION

Some argue that, now that superpower conflict is over, we confront a fundamentally different proliferation problem. The old policies and strategies must change, they believe, to deal with "a world of terror and missiles and madmen," as George W. Bush said during the 2000 campaign.[22]

Few would deny that the regime has helped prevent the larger, industrial nations from acquiring or using nuclear, chemical, or biological weapons and has reduced or eliminated existing stockpiles. The argument today is about whether the holdouts can be brought into the regime or whether it is hopeless to think that such nations will share the same values as those expressed by the regime's founders. Others contend that the military challenges facing the United States are so demanding that it ought not be restrained by multilateral arrangements that might stop it from taking actions necessary to thwart new dangers.

Modern-day arms control treaties, in this view, are worse than no treaties at all. They only promote complacency, lulling America into a false sense of security. While the West disarms, several non-Western nations—what Charles Krauthammer calls "Weapon States"—are striving to acquire and deploy nuclear, chemical, and biological weapons and ballistic missiles. Samuel Huntington believes that while the West naively "promotes nonproliferation as a universal norm and nonproliferation treaties and inspections as means of realizing that norm," non-Western nations "assert their right to acquire and to deploy whatever weapons they think necessary for their security," seeing weapons of mass destruction "as the potential equalizer of superior Western conventional power."[23]

The 1998 nuclear tests in South Asia seemed to confirm this view. "Only effective missile defense, not unenforceable arms control treaties," Senate Majority Leader Trent Lott stated after the tests, "will break the offensive arms race in Asia and provide incentives to address security concerns without a nuclear response."[24]

These arguments have a point, for the nonproliferation norm has never been universally recognized. As noted above, several key nations have stayed out of the regime; others are nominally in it but are strongly suspected of cheating on their obligations; and skeptics within many nations, not just the United States, criticize what they believe is the idealistic approach in trying to prevent proliferation through meaningless treaties. As one Indian advocate told me during a conference, "Arms control treaties only control the arms that no one wants any longer."

Testifying before the Senate Foreign Relations Committee in October 1999 in opposition to the ratification of the Comprehensive Test Ban Treaty, Jeane Kirkpatrick summarized the case against the treaty regime:

> With rogue states developing the capacity to attack our cities and our population . . . Americans and their allies are more vulnerable than we have ever been. Mr. Chairman, the threat to America, its cities and populations is here and now. It has expanded dramatically, not only because of systematic Chinese theft of America's most important military secrets and because of the inadequate U.S. policies governing the safekeeping and transfer of technology, but also because several countries who are signatories of the Nuclear Non-Proliferation Treaty have violated their commitments under the Treaty.
>
> China is not a signatory of the NPT. Russia is. So are Iran, Iraq and Libya. North Korea, India and Pakistan are not [sic. China and North Korea are signatories]. Obviously, whether or not a government has signed the NPT has little impact on its behavior with regard to proliferation. . . .
>
> That is the critical point concerning the arms control approach to national security. We cannot rely on this treaty to

prevent the countries that are actually or potentially hostile to us from acquiring and testing nuclear arsenals and ballistic missiles. The evidence is clear.[25]

THE HARD CASES
THE CHEATERS AND THE ABSTAINERS

From the expansive threat list of the past forty years, the roster of problem nations is down to a few hard cases. But whether or not these cases can be resolved will determine whether we are nearing the end of decades of diplomatic effort or the beginning of a new wave of proliferation. It is worth looking briefly at two of the toughest: North Korea and India.

North Korea, like Iraq and Iran, represents the danger that a nation will express its overt commitment to prohibitions on weapons of mass destruction, only to acquire them covertly. Each of the three is a member of the NPT. Iraq and North Korea have clearly violated their treaty commitments; Iran is suspected of violations.

The nuclear tests in India and Pakistan in early 1998 presented another type of challenge to the regime, that of established states outside the regime openly developing nuclear weapons capability. India, Pakistan, and Israel are the only countries in the world remaining apart from the NPT regime. Though neither India nor Pakistan has yet deployed any nuclear weapons, they have declared their intentions to do so. Although Israel officially maintains a policy of nuclear ambiguity, it is widely believed to have several dozen operational weapons. As long as these nuclear arsenals remain, regional rivalries may lead other nations to re-examine their own nuclear options, prompting a collapse of the regime at least in spirit if not substance.

NORTH KOREA

North Korea's pursuit of nuclear weapons posed the most serious challenge to the international nonproliferation regime in the early and mid-1990s. North Korea's considerable plutonium production capabilities may have, according to the CIA, generated enough plutonium for one or two nuclear weapons during the late 1980s and early 1990s. Moreover, North Korea was building a nuclear complex capable of producing dozens of weapons a year and enough surplus yield to export weapons-grade plutonium to other states. This combination of events would have undercut the basis for conventional deterrence in Korea and potentially destabilized the entire system of nuclear restraints.

North Korea's nuclear program was frozen and would have been, according to the terms of the 1994 Agreed Framework, eventually dismantled in exchange for an internationally led project to built two modern light-water reactors. While these reactors also produce plutonium, North Korea lacks the facilities to extract plutonium from the fuel used in them. Furthermore, the plutonium produced in light-water reactors is less attractive for use in weapons.

Critics maintain that the nonproliferation regime failed in the case of North Korea since that nation was able to produce plutonium for nuclear weapons and was then able to blackmail the United States and other countries into providing the North with modern nuclear reactor technology. These detractors complain that the treaty framework should have prevented North Korea from producing and extracting the plutonium in the first place and that the desire to preserve the regime led to the completion of a counterproductive agreement to trade North Korea's current nuclear complex for two new reactors.

This view dominated the policy process when the Bush administration came into office in 2001. While Secretary of State Colin Powell favored continuing the approach developed by the Clinton administration, he lost out to regime critics. President Bush froze any dialogue with North Korea for the first eighteen months of his administration, then adopted a policy aimed at eliminating the regime entirely rather than trying to erase its nuclear capabilities. Many of the same officials who favored the war with Iraq argue for military strikes in Korea. Former chairman of the Defense Policy Council Richard Perle, for example, says, "I don't think anyone can exclude a kind of surgical strike that we saw in 1981 when the Israelis destroyed the Osirik reactor [in Iraq]."[26]

To be sure, North Korea violated its commitments under the NPT and did not comply with its obligations to the IAEA to make a full and accurate accounting of its past nuclear activities. This is completely unacceptable. However, the regime's instruments were critical in the 1990s to identifying and finding a path to remedy North Korea's past violations. The case of North Korea, which is laid out in the following paragraphs, demonstrates the value of the nonproliferation norm embodied in the NPT and the worth of the treaty mechanisms if they are fully supported by member states.

North Korea joined the NPT in 1985 (under pressure from the Soviet Union), a move that obligated it not to pursue the production or development of nuclear weapons and to negotiate and comply with a safeguards agreement with the IAEA within eighteen months. North Korea clearly violated the NPT during the late 1980s by operating unsafeguarded nuclear facilities and for failing to disclose fully its nuclear materials and facilities once it finally signed a safeguards agreement with the IAEA in 1992.[27] The concern is that North Korea may have produced enough plutonium for one or two nuclear weapons and has not yet produced a satisfactory accounting for this plutonium.

North Korea's membership in the NPT and its alleged violation of it gave the United States the international support it needed to intervene and negotiate the agreement that froze the North's program until 2003. Without this agreement, Pyongyang might have produced enough plutonium in these years for hundreds of nuclear weapons. North Korean operation of an unsafeguarded, plutonium-producing reactor, however, was public knowledge in 1989, and the U.S. government may have known even earlier about the North's activities. It was not until the IAEA began its statutory effort to verify the accuracy of North Korea's NPT/IAEA safeguard declaration in 1992 that the scope of North Korea's plutonium program became an issue of international attention. Without the treaty and the IAEA, and the international attention to Pyongyang's activities these regime tools brought, North Korea might have progressed much further than it did in its pursuit of nuclear weapons materials. It also is important to keep in mind that even a fully NPT-compliant North Korea would have been allowed to operate its nuclear facilities and extract weapon-usable amounts of plutonium, though this would have taken place under safeguards. While the right of countries to produce weapons-usable materials within the treaty regime has been cited as a shortcoming, this is an issue that can be applied to many more countries than North Korea.

The case of North Korea also marked a major turning point for the regime, coming as it did so close to the end of the Gulf War and the revelations of what Iraq was able to do under the nose of IAEA inspectors. The increased backing for the IAEA, in terms of both political support and access to intelligence information, greatly strengthened its ability to identify and draw attention to safeguard violations. The North Korean example seems to reinforce the argument that, with sufficient international political, technical, and financial support, the instruments provided by the treaties and arrangements of the nonproliferation regime can at least restrain (and very possibly prevent) the acquisition of nuclear weapons even in the case of a nation determined to acquire them.

The disclosure in late 2002 that North Korea had secretly pursued a separate uranium enrichment facility raised another violation of the NPT—and a new challenge. The hard-line approach of the Bush administration was answered by a similarly hard-line approach from the Korean dictator, including the announced withdrawal from the NPT and the restarting of plutonium production and reprocessing. Even as North Korea threatened to become the world's first plutonium Wal-Mart, the crisis was deferred during the second Persian Gulf War, and by mid-2003 it had yet to be resolved.

THE SOUTH ASIAN DILEMMA

From the beginning of the nuclear age, Indian leaders have argued strongly for complete nuclear disarmament. But their vision clashed sharply with that of the United States and the Soviet Union in the 1960s. India's primary objection to the regime created by the NPT is that it is discriminatory, what New Delhi called "nuclear apartheid." Over the years, the lack of commitment beyond rhetoric of the five nuclear powers to their pledge in Article VI of the NPT to eliminate their nuclear arsenals has only reinforced this perception of the regime. K. Subrahmanyam, the head of India's National Security Advisory Board, says a "reciprocity of obligations" was critical for India, which is why it opposed the "imposition of a discriminating treaty dividing the countries of the world into five privileged ones and the rest."[28] When the NPT first entered into force, India had been independent for only twenty years, and the option to pursue nuclear weapons became embedded in the determination to guard the country's sovereignty.

George Perkovich, author of *India and the Bomb*, maintains that the momentum toward the May 1998 tests began in 1995 with the indefinite extension of the NPT and picked up with India's inability to stop the CTBT in 1996. With the lack of any concrete commitment toward disarmament either in 1995 or 1996, Indian strategists saw these developments, along with the NATO doctrine reaffirming the first use of nuclear weapons in providing for Europe's security, as a means of cynically continuing the prevailing power system, in which India did not play a part. For such strategists, the regime only served to legitimize nuclear weapons in the hands of a privileged few. It made those predis-posed to developing the bomb determined not to stumble into a nuclear straitjacket.

India's former foreign minister, Jaswant Singh, has said that the tests "achieved the objectives of giving India additional strategic space and autonomy."[29] Many pronuclear Indian analysts and policymakers firmly believe that power and due respect grow out of the nuclear-armed warhead of a long-range missile. Ironically, improved U.S.-Indian relations since the tests only convince them that they are right.

Perkovich argues that India's tests destroyed the illusion that there is no relation between nuclear disarmament and nonproliferation. For India, he says, nuclear policy was in part a narrative on equity. Domestic politics in nuclear-aspiring states tie nonproliferation to progress in creating the right environment for nuclear disarmament. Nuclear aspirants can be nudged toward rolling back their programs only in a world where such weapons no longer hold any currency and do not form a part of military strategy. In this light, as long as the powerful states do not practice what they preach, others will be tempted to emulate them in order to gain recog-nition and power.[30]

Perkovich acknowledges that "unproliferation" is not a politically tenable policy for the immediate future and avers that, particularly in democracies, the acquisition of nuclear weapons so changes domestic pol-itics that the removal of the original reasons to go nuclear is insufficient to roll back the program.[31]

India's testing moratorium and its impressive record on export con-trols make its policies currently consistent with both the NPT and the CTBT as a nuclear weapons state. It also has shown relative restraint in missile development and deployment. Since its testing, the short-range Prithvi missile has been relocated away from the border with Pakistan, and there have been only a few tests of the medium-range Agni missile. The ruling Bharatiya Janata Party has resisted domestic pressure to resume nuclear testing and to carry out frequent missile testing. The government has evinced a subtle shift in its hitherto implacable attitude toward the nonproliferation regime. Foreign Minister Singh emphasized that "India's policies have been consistent with the key provisions of the NPT that apply to nuclear states."[32] Indian strategists have begun to argue that the NPT regime should be revised to accommodate India's new status. While reconciling South Asian nuclear programs with the NPT—or constructing a parallel regime—is difficult, the new Indian attitude recognizes the power and utility of the regime and its norms.

THE FUTURE OF THE MULTILATERAL NONPROLIFERATION REGIME

Scholars draw varying conclusions from history. Stanford professor Scott Sagan summarizes the three major theories about why states decide to build or not to build nuclear weapons:

> "The security model," according to which states build nuclear weapons to increase national security against foreign threats, especially nuclear threats; "the domestic politics model," which envisions nuclear weapons as political tools used to advance parochial domestic and bureaucratic interests; and "the norms model," under which nuclear weapons decisions are made because weapons acquisition, or restraint in weapons development, provides an important normative symbol of state's modernity and identity.[33]

Leading conservative analysts today favor the "security model" or variants of it. They share a profound pessimism about the future viability of the regime's core instruments. This tendency has merged with an ideological predisposition against multilateral arrangements. Arms control, environmental accords, and international courts are anathema. Multilateral arrangements weaken America like "Gulliver in the land of Lilliputians, stretched out, unable to move, because he has been tied down by a whole host of threads," warned Senator Jeff Sessions during the test ban treaty debate in October 1999.

It may not be necessary, however, to resolve core ideological differences in order to reach agreement on practical policy issues. Sagan points out,

> For policymakers, the existence of three different reasons why states develop nuclear weapons suggests that no single policy can ameliorate all future problems. Fortunately, some of the policy recommendations derived from the models are quite compatible: for example, many of the diplomatic tools suggested by the domestic politics model, which attempts to reduce the power of individual parochial interests in favor of nuclear weapons, would not interfere with simultaneous efforts to address states' security concerns. Similarly, efforts to enhance the international status of some non-nuclear states need not either undercut deterrence or promote pro-nuclear advocates in those countries.[34]

Today, the world faces two types of proliferation threats, characterized previously as the cheaters and the abstainers: the danger that several developing nations could acquire nuclear weapons; the concern that the three non-NPT nations will retain or even expand their nuclear arsenals. Either threat could lead directly to the breakdown of the nonproliferation regime and the acquisition of nuclear weapons by several industrialized, hitherto abstaining, nations.

The case of Japan illustrates the dangers. The sudden doubling of Asian nuclear weapons states in 1998 caught Tokyo by surprise. Many Japanese were then disturbed by how quickly the world accepted India and Pakistan's de facto status. This was not the bargain the Japanese agreed to when—after lengthy internal debate—they joined the NPT in 1976. North Korea's launch of a medium-range Taepo-dong missile in August 1998 further agitated the Japanese public and political leaders, stirring new debates about Japan's military and nuclear policies. "Japan must be like NATO countries," said Vice Defense Minister Shingo Nishimura. "We must have the military power and the legal authority to act on it. We ought to have aircraft carriers, long-range missiles, long-range bombers. We should even have the atomic bomb."[35] Nishimura was forced to resign over his comment, but he is not alone in his sentiment, nor is South Asia the only new concern.

If, for whatever reason, tensions rise and nuclear weapons deployments increase in Asia, Japan may well come to believe that its security is best served not by the U.S. nuclear umbrella but by building its own arsenal. Japan's withdrawal from the NPT would almost certainly trigger the collapse of the treaty. Some in Asia might decide quickly to follow Japan's lead, others would hedge their bets and begin nuclear weapons research, and Iran and Iraq, among others, would likely openly accelerate their programs.

This is why many believe it is absolutely critical that the political and diplomatic deterrents to the spread of weapons of mass destruction remain powerful. "Unless Japan sees clear efforts toward reducing the role of nuclear weapons in international affairs," concludes Princeton scholar Kent Calder, "it may be increasingly prone to either manipulate its shadow nuclear standing diplomatically or, in an extremity, go nuclear."[36]

Even the NATO allies, who have long benefited from the protections offered by the U.S. nuclear umbrella, look to the treaty regime and the decrease of nuclear weapons as fundamental to their national security policies. According to the joint statement of the ministers of the North Atlantic Council:

The proliferation of nuclear, biological and chemical (NBC) weapons and their means of delivery continues to be a matter of serious concern for the Alliance as it poses risks to international and regional security and can pose a direct military threat to Allies' populations, territory and forces. The principal non-proliferation goal of the Alliance and its members remains unchanged: to prevent proliferation from occurring, or, should it occur, to reverse it through diplomatic means. In this context we continue to place great importance on non-proliferation and export control regimes, international arms control and disarmament as means to prevent proliferation. . . . The Nuclear Non-Proliferation Treaty (NPT) is the cornerstone of the nuclear non-proliferation regime and the essential foundation for the pursuit of nuclear disarmament.[37]

How can the history of success and failure in the regime and its lessons for decisionmakers be translated into a policy agenda? Senator Richard G. Lugar (R-Ind.) recently summarized the basic framework that today guides most proliferation experts and officials in the United States and Europe:

There are four main lines of defense against weapons of mass destruction and ballistic missile threats. Individually, each is insufficient; together, they help to form the policy fabric of an integrated "defense in depth":

- The first is prevention and entails activities at the source such as the Nunn-Lugar/Cooperative Threat Reduction program—a program that has deactivated over 5,500 nuclear warheads and engaged efforts to stop the spread of weapons of mass destruction and associated knowledge.

- The second is deterrence and interdiction and involves efforts to stem the flow of illicit trade in these weapons and materials at foreign and domestic borders.

- The third line of defense is crisis and consequence management and involves greater efforts at domestic preparedness such as the Nunn-Lugar-Domenici program which has supplied more than 100 American cities with the training to deal with the consequences, should such threats turn into hostile acts.

- The fourth line of defense must include limited missile defenses against the growing ballistic missile capabilities of so-called rogue states.[38]

The interlocking set of treaties and agreements to reduce and prevent the threat from weapons of mass destruction, policy specialists believe, remains a highly effective (and cost-effective) defense. Even when this line is breached, as it has been, it seems highly unlikely that the country violating or spurning the relevant treaties would use its weapons because of the threat of devastating retaliation. The United States alone has the ability to destroy any opponent with its overwhelming conventional armed forces. These views do not exclude active defensive systems. While effective missile defenses outside the atmosphere seem impractical—because they could be overwhelmed by lightweight decoys and other countermeasures—defenses against short-range Scuds and Scud derivatives may prove practical and could be deployed to protect troops and defended areas.

Active diplomacy has a very good chance of reducing or preventing the threat that North Korea will produce or export advanced missile systems or nuclear weapons. With their nation impoverished and isolated, North Korean leaders seem willing, even eager, to negotiate a halt to Pyongyang's missile development and to implement agreements to end its nascent nuclear weapons program in exchange for diplomatic recognition and a nonaggression treaty with the United States. Even as North Korea advanced step by step to unfreeze its plutonium production capabilities and declared its right to have nuclear weapons during 2003 it stated that its entire program was up for negotiation. The Bush administration, deeply divided internally over whether to negotiate a verifiable end to the Korean program or pursue regime change or preemptive military action, remains thus far unable to fashion a coherent response to the North Korean challenge.

Similarly, Western experts on Iran are much more sanguine about that nation's capabilities and intentions regarding weapons of mass destruction than some of the worst-case scenarios indicate. Iran looks as though it is aggressively constructing facilities for manufacturing and reprocessing reactor fuel that also could be used to create material for nuclear weapons. But the government does not yet appear to have decided to develop these weapons. The U.S. goal, argues Geoffrey Kemp of the Nixon Center, should now be "to try to convince Iran that it has more to gain from walking away from the decision to cross the nuclear threshold."[39]

The risks of mishandling Iran are huge, says Kemp, and the military strikes against the new nuclear facilities some now urge are highly risky and uncertain of success. Therefore, "we should focus on the political and diplomatic options" and "rely on the more traditional approach of working with our friends and partners to contain Iranian behavior."[40]

If reform elements continue to make progress internally and if the United States could convince other nations to eliminate their remaining assistance to Tehran's missile and nuclear programs, Iran could once again become a regional power with friendly relations with the United States. Ending North Korea's missile development assistance would in itself cripple Iran's program, greatly reducing any near-term danger that Tehran could develop a long-range missile.

In many ways, South Asia represents the most difficult challenge for the nonproliferation regime. Even here, though, as indicated above, there remains the possibility that treaties and agreements could be constructed that parallel the NPT regime while taking into account the particularities of the South Asian situation.

A great deal depends on U.S. policy choices. While some demonize the United States, it remains the one nation in the world with the resources, status, and leadership capable of galvanizing international nonproliferation efforts. Here liberals and conservatives should agree. Analyst James Ceasar observes, "For other nations, multilateralism means choosing to engage in an action; for the United States it means assuming the primary responsibility in any major engagement. . . . The whole system depends on the national resolve of the United States."[41]

Without doubt, the Bush administration has assumed this primary responsibility for military enagagments and in selected diplomatic efforts, but it has abandoned the traditional U.S. leadership in multilateral negotiations. With the military success of the operations in Afghanistan and Iraq, the administration may feel ad hoc arrangements will suffice. However, Henry Sokolski contends, "I think it's fair to say the burden is on those who would tear down the traditional arms control regime to show how they would achieve the same goals by other means."[42] With the jury still out on the effectiveness and necessity of the war in Iraq, the administration has not developed a convincing strategic framework to replace the treaties it shuns.

Historically, domestic and international pressures have combined to impel the United States—and other nations—toward negotiated agreements. Many problems, be they uprooting terrorist networks or restricting missile technology, are too large for any one nation, even one as powerful as the United States, to solve alone. Despite the heated rhetoric of some administration officials, it may well be that the powerful moderating mechanisms inherent in the U.S. foreign policy process, realistic appraisals of the continuing importance and successes of international nonproliferation agreements, the substantial problems involved in reconstituting Iraq after the war, and the influence and preferences of U.S. allies will combine to develop new approaches that could sustain and even expand the arms control regime in the new decade.

3

NONPROLIFERATION AND THE USE OF FORCE

Robert S. Litwak

Under what conditions, if any short of war, should the United States employ its military capabilities against a state possessing or acquiring weapons of mass destruction (WMD)?[1] After a bitterly contentious debate in the UN Security Council, the United States went to war against Iraq in March 2003 without an international mandate to achieve Iraqi WMD disarmament. In the aftermath of that conflict, the Bush administration faced immediate and looming nuclear crises with North Korea and Iran. In addressing these and other postwar nonproliferation challenges, U.S. officials must grapple with a persisting policy tension: the reality that attaining the capability to attack an adversary's unconventional weapons in time of war creates a military option as well for contingencies falling short of full-scale hostilities. This analysis will consider military capabilities and their use as part of the continuum of nonproliferation instruments that ranges from economic sanctions and export controls to multilateral treaties and diplomacy.

Traditional nonproliferation focused on multilateral, noncoercive policy instruments. The Treaty on the Non-Proliferation of Nuclear Weapons (NPT) is the embodiment of this conception of nonproliferation—a "grand bargain" under which states agree to forgo the pursuit of nuclear weapons in return for technological assistance from the established nuclear powers and a commitment to gradual disarmament by those powers. This approach remained dominant as long as the proliferation problem was centered on advanced industrialized or industrializing countries with a significant stake in regional security. However, as the cold war was ending, the U.S. government became increasingly concerned with the danger posed by so-called rogue states. This category lumped together a disparate group of states (whose core members were Iraq, Iran, and North Korea) with significant differences in their domestic situations and international behavior but whose ruling regimes were perceived as potentially irrational and undeterrable. Not surprisingly, as the rogue state rubric gained currency so did the interest in more coercive forms of nonproliferation. The Reagan administration actively debated the use of force against Libyan chemical weapons capabilities. Subsequently, the focus on forceful means of dissuasion was enhanced by the discovery of a massive WMD complex in Iraq following the first Persian Gulf War in 1991.

This chapter examines the rise of the concept of counterproliferation, as forceful nonproliferation is sometimes called. In particular, it examines whether counterproliferation is feasible and effective—a topic also considered by David Kay in his chapter in this volume—as well as the implications for policy coordination and programmatic coherence. While it is possible to incorporate forceful counterproliferation into a sensible approach to nonproliferation, the number of cases in which counterproliferation is appropriate is quite small. The use of force gained heightened policy prominence following the unprecedented September 11 terrorist attacks when the Bush administration, in its September 2002 National Security Strategy document, elevated military preemption to official U.S. doctrine to forestall WMD acquisition or use by a hostile state or terrorist group.[2]

In this transformed international environment, the challenge for policymakers is to develop situation-specific strategies, employing the appropriate instruments of coercion and inducement along the aforementioned continuum of choice on the basis of sound analysis of the states or organizations provoking concern.[3] The development of a repertoire of targeted nonproliferation strategies that takes into account each state's particular circumstances should be informed by relevant historical experience across a broader spectrum. Historical cases in which force has been seriously contemplated or actually used against proliferators are few (a telling fact in itself) and have been highly context-specific. An examination of these sui generis cases will not yield any deterministic laws of state behavior. But this historical record does suggest the general criteria—political, military, legal—by which decisionmakers, when confronted with a particular case, may assess the efficacy of force as an instrument of nonproliferation policy.

The first section of the chapter traces the increased prominence given coercive nonproliferation in U.S. policy under the twin impact of the end of the cold war and the first Persian Gulf War,[4] which triggered a change in the perception of the nonproliferation threat. An equally important determinant of U.S. policy was the organizational imperative of the Department of Defense to reorient its mission and budget for the perceived requirements of this new era. This section also considers military preemption against rogue states and terrorist groups, which the Bush administration, as noted, made official U.S. doctrine following the September 11 terrorist attacks.

The second section examines five cases in which force against a proliferator was used or seriously considered by the United States (with the exception of one instance involving Israel, which is included nonetheless because of its precedent-setting importance): the Chinese nuclear program, 1963–64; the Israeli bombing of Iraq's Osiraq nuclear reactor in June 1981; the 1991 Gulf War against Iraq and the enforcement of UN Security Council disarmament resolutions in its aftermath; the North Korean nuclear crisis of 1993–94; and the bombing of a suspected chemical weapons factory in Sudan in August 1998.[5] Employing Alexander George's method of structured, focused comparison, each brief case summary addresses a common set of questions under three categories.[6] The first is the character of the proliferation threat precipitating the decision to use force or not: is the threat imminent; is the assessment based on sound intelligence; and can the target state be persuaded or deterred from acquiring or using this WMD capability? The second category relates to the politico-military context: is the mission militarily feasible; have nonmilitary alternatives been exhausted; is the nonproliferation issue linked to another issue or embedded in a broader policy context; and does the proposed action have multilateral support, or will it be undertaken unilaterally? The third category is the assessed consequences of the use of force: will the target state retaliate directly or indirectly against the United States or its allies; could the action trigger a broader conflict, a "catalytic" war; could the attack have unacceptable collateral damage, either to the environment or in civilian casualties; are there costs to inaction (for example, the potential for coercive diplomacy by a WMD-armed proliferator)?[7]

Based on these case study findings, the third section examines the criteria and conditions influencing decisionmaking about the use of force, as well as the impact of U.S. counterproliferation policy on target state behavior and motivations. The fourth and concluding section addresses policy implications, the renewed prominence of counterproliferation, and the challenge of multilateralism—that is, the possibility of making coercive measures consistent with traditional arms control and nonproliferation efforts. This chapter aims not to make a normative statement about the use of force but rather to identify and flesh out the key issues underlying those criteria to improve the quality of debate on the role of force in nonproliferation policy.

THE RISE OF COUNTERPROLIFERATION

The first use of force to prevent proliferation occurred prior to the nuclear age, when commandos and allied aircraft bombed the German heavy-water factory in Nazi-occupied Norway in 1943. More than half a century and a cold war later, this issue remains perhaps the most contentious of those pertaining to nonproliferation. In the 1990s, the United States used or considered the use of force against unconventional weapons capabilities in three instances: Iraq, North Korea, and Sudan, when the Clinton administration attacked a site suspected of producing chemical weapons in Khartoum as part of a larger counterterrorism strike in retaliation for the truck bombings of the American embassies in Kenya and Tanzania by terrorists linked to Osama bin Laden. These episodes reflected the new prominence of coercive nonproliferation in U.S. policy—a development symbolized by the Pentagon's 1993 Defense Counterproliferation Initiative (CPI), which, notwithstanding its initiators' protestations to the contrary, aroused concern overseas that the United States was prepared to use force against hostile proliferators preemptively and unilaterally. Critics viewed the Defense CPI as motivated by a bureaucratic interest in mobilizing support for congressional funding of a new post–cold war mission for the department.

The charting of recent American security strategy has been strongly influenced by the fact that the end of the cold war coincided with a hot war in the Persian Gulf. The global challenge posed by the Soviet Union was supplanted by a concern about the "Iraqs of the future," radical Third World states threatening regional stability. In the area of nonproliferation and arms control, this conjunction has had implications both beneficial and worrisome. On the one hand, the transformation of the U.S.-Soviet relationship made possible rapid progress in terms of "vertical" proliferation to reduce substantially each side's strategic nuclear arsenals. On the other hand, the first Gulf War and its aftermath revealed the staggering magnitude of Iraq's WMD programs, thus highlighting the problem of "horizontal" proliferation. Indeed, the Gulf War culminated a decade of increasing international concern about the spread of unconventional weapons to aspiring regional powers. Iraq was but the most egregious example of this trend because its acquisition of WMD capabilities was linked to an expansionist foreign policy. During the Iran-Iraq war (1980–88), Saddam Hussein's regime flouted international norms of warfare through its indiscriminate missile attacks on Iranian cities and, most grievously, its battlefield employment of chemical weapons. The United States failed to condemn these acts (which in 1988 included the use of chemical weapons against Iraq's own Kurdish population) vigorously because of the Reagan administration's tilt toward Iraq in the war against revolutionary Iran and its commitment to an engagement strategy in hopes of moderating Baghdad's behavior.

But Iraq was not the only potential proliferator of concern. CIA director William Webster revealed in 1989 that ten countries were developing biological weapons and fifteen would be capable of producing ballistic missiles by 2000, while in his September 1989 UN speech President George H. W. Bush stated that more than twenty nations possessed chemical weapons or the capability to produce them.[8] Political scientist Michael Klare, tracing the rise of what he refers to as the American "Rogue Doctrine," notes that by the late 1980s, U.S. officials began to link the WMD and terrorism issues in the context of certain Third World states. In his January 1989 Senate confirmation hearings, Secretary of State-designate James Baker explicitly did so, stating that "chemical warhead and ballistic missiles have fallen into the hands of governments with proven records of aggression and terrorism."[9] During the Reagan-Bush years, external behavior flouting international norms (regional aggression, state sponsorship of terrorism, and the pursuit of WMD capabilities) came to define "outlaw" status.[10] After the Iraqi invasion of Kuwait in August 1990, opinion polls indicated that among the various rationales the first Bush administration offered for the use of force (energy security, moral and legal norms against interstate aggression) the one that resonated most with the American public was concern over a nuclear-armed Iraq.[11]

The recasting of the nonproliferation policy agenda at the end of the cold war was notable in two respects. First, the traditional, primary focus on nuclear weapons was broadened to "weapons of mass destruction," incorporating biological and chemical capabilities and their means of delivery (both ballistic and cruise missiles).[12] Second, along with heightened concern about horizontal proliferation and the demand side, the political turmoil in the Soviet successor states posed an enormous challenge to the nonproliferation regime's ability to constrain the supply side, consisting of sensitive technologies and highly trained, financially destitute experts. The key condition that has altered the traditional nonproliferation equation has been the increased availability of fissile material, which had previously been the major technological brake on an aspiring nuclear proliferator. After the first Persian Gulf War, UNSCOM (the United Nations Special Commission) inspectors discovered that the Iraqi regime possessed a plausible nuclear bomb design and had spent some $10 billion on a nuclear infrastructure to produce highly enriched uranium (HEU) for a weapon.[13]

The first authoritative statement of the Clinton administration's emerging rogue state policy was made by National Security Adviser Anthony Lake in a spring 1994 *Foreign Affairs* article. In "Confronting Backlash States," Lake argued that "as the sole superpower, the United States has a special responsibility to neutralize, contain, and through selective pressure, perhaps eventually transform these backlash states into constructive members of the international community." Specifically citing North Korea, Iran, Iraq, Libya, and Cuba, he asserted that these regimes— with their authoritarian ruling cliques, their "aggressive and defiant" behavior, and their pursuit of WMD capabilities—made clear their "recalcitrant commitment to remain on the wrong side of history."[14] Secretary of State Madeleine Albright further elevated the rogue state concept to official status: "Dealing with the rogue states is one of the challenges of our time . . . because they are there with the sole purpose of destroying the system." She argued that rogue states constituted one of four distinct categories of countries in the post–cold war international system (the other three being advanced industrial states, emerging democracies, and failed states).[15]

In tandem with this reorienting of the chief global threat from communism to rogue states, the Clinton administration elevated WMD proliferation as a policy priority and laid out an ambitious nonproliferation agenda in September 1993.[16] The Department of Defense conducted a bottom-up review to determine the necessary U.S. force structure for the post–cold war era. That review recommended a force structure some three-quarters the size of that existing at the end of the cold war, which was to be geared toward fighting two "major regional conflicts" with "rogue leaders set on regional domination through military aggression while simultaneously pursuing nuclear, biological, and chemical capabilities."[17] In December 1993, two months after the release of the bottom-up review, Secretary of Defense Les Aspin enunciated the Defense CPI at the National Academy of Sciences as a response to this new threat. He highlighted the specter of "a handful of nuclear devices in the hands of *rogue states* or even terrorists" and stated that "at the heart of the Defense Counterproliferation Initiative . . . is a drive to develop new military capabilities to deal with this new threat."[18]

The CPI included proposed changes in procurement (for example, improved nonnuclear munitions to target underground installations), intelligence gathering, and military doctrine. The declared objectives of U.S. counterproliferation doctrine ranged from deterring countries from acquiring and using weapons of mass destruction to protecting U.S. forces and allies from possible WMD use if deterrence failed and defeating an adversary armed with WMD. The CPI reflected the Defense Department's efforts to internalize the lessons of the first Gulf War, during which U.S. forces had been threatened by and, in turn, had targeted Iraqi unconventional capabilities. But it also was powerfully motivated by the department's organizational interest in integrating new missions deriving from the rogue state threat into its planning and budgeting with an eye to future hardware acquisitions and the deployment of existing resources. On the issue of force structure and budget, however, it is important to differentiate between the general, large-scale reorienting of U.S. forces from global containment to regional security—the strategy of fighting two regional conflicts called for in the bottom-up review—and the specific funding allocations related to counterproliferation. By 1998, the latter expenditures totaled around $6 billion, of which $4 billion was for air and missile defense.[19]

The public presentation of the Defense CPI generated considerable confusion and alarm over two interrelated issues. The first was the analytical and policy distinction between counterproliferation and nonproliferation. Confusion stemmed from a lack of clarity about whether the initiative was being advanced as a component of or an alternative to traditional nonproliferation policy. This question of programmatic coherence was resolved in February 1994, when the National Security Council (NSC) issued a memorandum of agreed definitions that characterized counterproliferation as "the activities of the Department of Defense across the full range of U.S. efforts to combat proliferation, including diplomacy, arms control, export controls, and intelligence collection and analysis, with particular responsibility for assuring that U.S. forces can be protected should they confront an adversary armed with weapons of mass destruction or missiles."[20] Both this NSC memorandum and the May 1994 report of the interagency Counterproliferation Program Review Committee, chaired by Deputy Secretary of Defense John Deutch, underscored that the initiative was firmly embedded within a comprehensive nonproliferation policy.[21] Despite this affirmation that military capabilities were part of the continuum of nonproliferation instruments, questions about counterproliferation have persisted because of the second critical issue raised by the CPI.

Secretary Aspin's December 1993 speech and the public rollout of the Defense CPI were widely interpreted overseas as auguring possible unilateral and preemptive American military strikes against suspected targets producing or housing WMD in the Third World.[22] Response to the initiative, of course, was not formulated in a political vacuum. Political perceptions of the CPI, particularly among foreign governments and research institutes, were shaped by rhetoric about America's role as the "the sole superpower" and calls by opponents of multilateralism for the United States to seize the "unipolar moment" and "unashamedly lay down the rules of world order and be prepared to enforce them."[23] Timing also affected perceptions. The launch of the CPI occurred as the 1993–94 nuclear crisis with North Korea was unfolding. During that period, several hard-line critics of the Clinton administration's handling of the crisis advocated military strikes against the North's nuclear facilities as the preferred alternative to diplomacy with this rogue state. Thus, the North Korean crisis raised the specter of preemptive unilateral military action while also reinforcing the perception that counterproliferation was being advanced as an alternative to traditional nonproliferation policy. Critics of the CPI argued that force should be used only as a last resort and that any such use should be authorized by the UN Security Council to give it legitimacy. Department of Defense officials attempted to assuage these concerns about the CPI. Assistant Secretary Ashton Carter, who had overall responsibility for the Pentagon's counterproliferation program, told the press that "this is not about preemption." But others acknowledged that military preemption might be undertaken if alternative nonproliferation instruments failed and if intelligence indicated an imminent threat against U.S. or allied troops in the field.[24]

Another increasingly prominent issue that fed into the controversy over counterproliferation during the 1990s was ballistic missile defense. A congressionally chartered commission, chaired by Donald Rumsfeld, currently secretary of defense, concluded in 1998 that previous CIA National Intelligence Estimates had been overly optimistic and that a rogue state could develop and deploy an intercontinental ballistic missile (ICBM) within as little as five years. In response to the Rumsfeld Commission and the August 1998 testing of a long-range missile by North Korea, President Clinton's secretary of defense, William Cohen, announced plans to accelerate the development of a national missile defense program to counter the "threat posed by

rogue nations."[25] In an earlier (April 1996) speech on nuclear nonproliferation, Cohen's predecessor as secretary of defense, William Perry, had spoken
about the "future threat that a rogue state, that may be impossible to deter,
will obtain ICBMs that can reach the United States."[26]

Secretary Perry's reference to "undeterrable" rogue states was striking,
as it suggested that states such as North Korea, Iran, and Iraq are prone to
irrational behavior and that reliance on the traditional rules of deterrence
may be inadequate.[27] The imputation of irrationality is highly questionable
as a basis for policy. As will be discussed later in the context of the impact
of coercive nonproliferation on target state behavior, the most recent
experience with Iraq during the 1991 Persian Gulf War strongly suggests
the contrary. However, because "rogue" carries the dubious connotation of
an essentially crazy leadership not susceptible to traditional deterrence, it
bolsters the rationale for ballistic missile defense to neutralize this "undeterrable" threat. Likewise, the assertion that rogue regimes are fundamentally irrational in character or "beyond the pale" (as Secretary of State
Warren Christopher said of Iran) reinforces the tendency to view counterproliferation as an alternative to nonproliferation. This crude assumption about rogue states implicitly supports the conclusion (embraced by
ideological opponents of arms control and nonproliferation) that diplomacy and other nonmilitary instruments will invariably prove futile in
forestalling proliferation.

The Clinton administration used the designation of rogue state to
justify politically hard-line policies (for example, the Iran-Libya
Sanctions Act) toward these hostile countries. But despite its apparent
utility for political mobilization, this approach also exposed significant
liabilities that eventually prompted a reassessment by the Clinton foreign
policy team. First, because the term "rogue state" has no standing in international law and is quintessentially political, its application was selective
and contradictory. Syria, a state that possesses weapons of mass destruction
and has sponsored terrorism, was omitted from the rogue list because of its
importance to the Middle East peace process. Cuba, however, which no
longer poses a real security threat, was occasionally included because
that played well to the Cuban émigré community. In addition, the
Clinton administration discovered that a term used to mobilize political
support for one policy could be turned against it on another, as when a
Republican critic called for the cancellation of a presidential visit to China
in 1998 because it was a rogue state.

Second, beyond its being a uniquely American political concept
applied unilaterally, the "rogue" designation led to strategic inflexibility. By

lumping together and demonizing a disparate group of countries, the Clinton administration was pushed toward a generic strategy of containment and isolation. In the nonproliferation realm, it undermined the administration's ability to employ noncoercive instruments. This constricting approach came up against hard political realities, first with North Korea in 1994, when the acute danger posed by the North's advanced nuclear weapons program necessitated negotiation, and then with Iran in 1997, after the election of a reformist president, Mohammad Khatami, created an opportunity for U.S. diplomacy to influence that country's political evolution, if only at the margins. Because any deviation from the comprehensive quarantining of rogue states was castigated as appeasement by hard-liners in Congress (witness the reaction to the U.S.-North Korean Agreed Framework of October 1994), the Clinton administration's scope for diplomatic action was sharply limited.[28] The increasingly evident liabilities of the rogue state approach led to the State Department's June 2000 announcement formally dropping the term from the U.S. diplomatic lexicon. The impetus behind the decision was the need to differentiate between cases—for example, distinguishing between Iran, where changed political circumstances offered new possibilities for progress, and Iraq, where the threat posed by Saddam Hussein required a continued policy of monitoring and isolation.

Shortly after assuming office, President Bush reversed the Clinton administration's move and resuscitated the rogue state terminology. In his first speech to Congress in February 2001, he warned of the threat from "rogue nations intent on developing weapons of mass destruction."[29] The revived rhetoric is primarily attributable to the Bush administration's efforts to mobilize political support for ballistic missile defense. The administration also has placed increased emphasis on counterproliferation and linked it to missile defense—a development symbolized by the creation of a "Proliferation Strategy, Counterproliferation and Homeland Defense" directorate within the NSC. As during the Clinton era, the deficiencies of the rogue state framework will likely undercut the Bush administration's ability to pursue differentiated policies toward the disparate group of states associated with this category and, in particular, to develop a repertoire of country-specific strategies incorporating noncoercive instruments as appropriate. Such a nuanced approach—making room for a limited dialogue under UN auspices with Iran regarding the Afghan crisis—became imperative in the wake of the September 11 attacks as the Bush administration worked to forge an international coalition against terrorism. Bush's aides, however, continued to highlight the threat posed by rogue states, citing it as a major rationale for the U.S. withdrawal from the Anti-Ballistic Missile Treaty. Pragmatically engaging on a contingent basis potentially reformable states while simultaneously characterizing them as essentially crazy regimes "beyond the pale" creates a persisting tension in U.S. policy.

In the decade after the cold war and Operation Desert Storm, the use of force as an instrument of nonproliferation policy became an issue of contention between the United States and both its key NATO allies and other UN Security Council members. Russia, China, and France opposed coercion to compel Iraqi compliance with the Security Council's disarmament resolutions but had no credible alternative approach. As Joanna Spear discusses in her chapter in this volume, within NATO, European members eschewed the term counterproliferation, believing that it connoted preemptive military action and could therefore seriously undermine multilateral nonproliferation efforts.[30] The policy tension evident in the American debate—that is, over military capabilities that officials would want in war but that create the potential for preemptive action against a hostile proliferator in contingencies short of war—was replicated within the Alliance.[31] In assessing U.S. nonproliferation policy during the 1990s, French expert Gilles Andréani observed: "Non-proliferation has always been a careful balancing act between international consensus-building . . . and the development of punitive and defensive options to protect one's security should non-proliferation fail on the other. [In American policy] one finds convincing signs of a gradual shift from the former to the latter. . . ."[32] This perception overseas has been reinforced by the Senate's rejection of the Comprehensive Test Ban Treaty, the 1998 air strikes in Sudan and Iraq, and the Bush administration's openly skeptical attitude toward multilateral treaties and renewed emphasis after the September 11 terrorist attacks on counterproliferation aimed at rogue states. U.S. allies have registered their opposition to preemptive military action undertaken without UN Security Council authorization. Following September 11, the Bush administration, pointing to the potentially horrific consequences of a terrorist attack, elevated preemption to official doctrine, justifying this move as an extension of the inherent right of any state to self-defense. Controversy continues over the conditions under which the United States would consider the preemptive use of force against a hostile state and whether such a counterproliferation policy would be pursued as a component of, or as an alternative to, traditional nonproliferation.

After the September 11 terrorist attacks, Secretary of State Colin Powell declared, "Not only is the Cold War over, the post–Cold War period

is also over."[33] Although the attacks did not alter the structure of international relations, they did usher in a new age of American vulnerability. The administration's previous security focus on rogue states and WMD proliferation, particularly in the context of missile defense, was broadened to encompass the new war on terrorism. Indeed, President Bush directly linked the proliferation and terrorism issues in a speech three months after the attacks, declaring that "rogue states are clearly the most likely sources of chemical and biological and nuclear weapons for terrorists."[34] In his January 2002 State of the Union address, the president referred obliquely to the necessity of preemptive military action in the post–September 11 era. He identified Iraq, Iran, and North Korea as an "axis of evil" and stated that his administration "will not stand by, as peril draws closer and closer. The United States of America will not permit the world's most dangerous regimes to threaten us with the world's most destructive weapons."[35] The controversy generated by the "axis of evil" speech quickly prompted the Bush administration to declare that military action was not imminent against any of these countries, and that the United States would continue to employ the full range of nonproliferation instruments to keep them in check. Secretary Powell affirmed that the administration would fulfill American obligations under the Agreed Framework with North Korea and was open to dialogue with Iran. Proponents of the "axis of evil" formulation argued that tough rhetoric—"speaking truth to power"—would compel these countries' improved behavior. Critics feared that it would effectively preclude policy differentiation toward three states of very distinct natures.

Speaking at West Point on June 1, 2002, President Bush explicitly made the case for preemptive action, citing the mass-casualty consequences of a WMD attack on American soil and the unique political character of the rogue regimes and terrorist groups whose activity defied traditional deterrence and containment strategies. "Deterrence," he contended, "means nothing against shadowy terrorist networks with no nations or citizens to defend. Containment is not possible when unbalanced dictators with weapons of mass destruction can deliver those weapons on missiles or secretly provide them to terrorist allies."[36] Building on that speech, the White House's "National Security Strategy of the United States of America," published in September of the same year, codified a major strand of what some have referred to as the Bush Doctrine. The document declared: "To forestall . . . hostile acts, by our adversaries, the United States will, if necessary, act preemptively. . . . The purpose of our actions will always be to eliminate a specific threat to our allies. . . . The reasons for actions will be clear, the force measured, and the cause just."[37]

The Bush administration's public rollout of the new National Security Strategy precipitated considerable criticism and confusion, particularly about four critical issues.[38] The first is the policy tension at the core of the document. Different sections offer contrasting answers to the question, Is preemption a revolutionary new idea for U.S. foreign policy in the age of global terrorism? Or is it simply a traditional instrument of self-defense in the American panoply that is now receiving greater emphasis in the transformed, post–September 11 context? Initial press reports declaring the death of deterrence and containment, and the administration's preference for muscular counterproliferation over multilateral nonproliferation treaties, gave rise to the view that preemption is indeed a revolution in U.S. strategy. Administration officials have attempted to allay concerns, particularly with America's most important European allies, over this interpretation. Powell assured the Senate Foreign Relations Committee:

> [W]e have not abandoned containment, we have not abandoned deterrence. . . . We haven't abandoned these time-honored methods of using our national power. . . . [But, because of the new terrorist threat] that does not respond to theories of containment . . . a doctrine of preemption, or an element of preemption in our strategy is appropriate. . . . [S]o see it as an elevation of one of the many tools that we've always had, but don't see it as a new doctrine that excludes or eliminates all the other tools of national security. . . .[39]

Notwithstanding efforts by the Bush administration to defuse the flap over preemption, this policy debate persists, as does its derivative: whether counterproliferation will be pursued as an alternative to or as a complement to traditional nonproliferation policy.

A second thorny issue arising from the National Security Strategy is the international precedent set by an American preemption doctrine. Critics hold that preemption, particularly when the threat is not demonstrably imminent, undermines a fundamental norm of global governance. If the United States exercises this unilateral military option, it gives license to other states to do the same. (A possible preemptive military strike by India on Pakistan's nuclear facilities, for example, is frequently mentioned.) Some observers hold that this new U.S. policy is troubling not only in its own nature but also could prompt states that feel particularly menaced, such as Pakistan or Iran, to act precipitately in order to pre-empt the potential preemptor.[40]

A third line of criticism of the National Security Strategy is the continued conflation of the terrorism and proliferation agendas.[41] The preemptive use of force against a terrorist group like al Qaeda enjoys broad international legitimacy because such an organization presents a clear danger. That international consensus breaks down over the possibility of a military strike against a state to prevent proliferation, even a state regarded by Washington as a "rogue" or member of an "axis of evil." A related issue—the potential transfer of WMD capabilities from rogue states to terrorists—remains contentious. Some terrorism experts question whether the incentive for transfer exists, arguing that the certainty of devastating retaliation by the United States would be a powerful deterrent. The Bush administration questions whether deterrence can forestall this possibility and in the National Security Strategy document regards it as a major danger. During the heated debate leading up to the second Persian Gulf War, the administration claimed that it had evidence of links between Saddam Hussein's regime and al Qaeda, though it did not allege direct Iraqi complicity in the September 11 attacks.

Finally, some questioned the utility of promulgating a general doctrine of preemption when military action was envisaged only toward a single state—Iraq. The administration was making the specific case for intervention there because of Hussein's eleven-year record of noncompliance with UN Security Council resolutions mandating that country's WMD disarmament while simultaneously framing that proposed military action as the first application of the new U.S. preemption strategy.

CASES

The preceding discussion on the development of counterproliferation policy provides a necessary context for the specific case histories summarized in this section. These cases focus on specific instances, strikingly few in number, in which military force was either used or seriously contemplated as an instrument of nonproliferation policy. Their purpose is not to provide a detailed history but rather to permit the drawing of policy-relevant generalizations about the criteria and conditions governing the use of force as a nonproliferation policy instrument.

CHINA'S NUCLEAR PROGRAM, 1963–64

Recently, declassified documents from the U.S. National Archives indicate that the Kennedy administration seriously explored the feasibility of a preemptive military strike on China's nascent nuclear capability in the early 1960s.[42] Although the issue received less public attention than the ongoing crises in Southeast Asia and Berlin, the administration viewed China's prospective acquisition of nuclear weapons as a major threat to U.S. national security. Significant gaps in U.S. intelligence about China's nuclear program existed despite the availability of some U-2 and CORONA satellite imagery. But on the basis of available evidence, CIA National Intelligence Estimates concluded that China would be able to test an atomic device during the 1963–65 period. This assessment precipitated the Kennedy administration's moves in 1963 to explore preventive military options and even to enlist Soviet cooperation in (or acquiescence to) such an action against China's nuclear infrastructure. Underlying President Kennedy's militant position on the Chinese nuclear program was the perception of Mao's China as fundamentally more dangerous and irresponsible than the Soviet Union (with which terms of "peaceful coexistence," as Nikita Khrushchev put it, could be negotiated).[43]

With Kennedy's encouragement, U.S. officials initiated contingency planning for air strikes on Chinese nuclear facilities, and the possibility of a covert operation by Republic of China (Taiwan) commandos also was broached. Soviet officials rebuffed the Kennedy administration's diplomatic feelers about a coordinated approach to the Chinese nuclear threat. As this planning process unfolded, State Department analysts questioned the underlying premise that China's acquisition of nuclear weapons would have an "intolerable" impact on U.S. security. By October 1963, a hundred-page study by State Department expert Robert Johnson offered a less alarming view. Johnson argued that a nuclear-armed China would not fundamentally change the balance of power in Asia and could be deterred from aggression by overwhelming U.S. conventional and nuclear superiority. He viewed the Chinese program as being primarily motivated by a desire to deter an attack on China itself and that the Mao regime was unlikely to alter its risk-adverse military policy.[44] The Kennedy assassination and Lyndon Johnson's accession to the presidency effectively ended the U.S. debate on preemption. President Johnson rejected "unprovoked" military action against China—a decision plausibly attributed to a less alarmist view of China's nuclear program, an aversion to any military action that could escalate the Vietnam War, and the desire to bolster his image as the peace candidate in the 1964 electoral campaign against the hawkish Barry Goldwater.[45]

ISRAELI RAID ON IRAQ'S OSIRAQ NUCLEAR REACTOR, JUNE 1981

On June 7, 1981, a squadron of Israeli F-15s and F-16s surreptitiously traversed Jordanian and Saudi Arabian air space to bomb Iraq's French-made, Osiris-type reactor near Baghdad. Since the 1970s, Israel had closely monitored Iraq's concerted efforts to obtain nuclear technology. Under a 1974 bilateral nuclear cooperation agreement with France, Iraq had proposed the purchase of a 500MW gas-graphite reactor, which would have produced large quantities of plutonium, ideal for a nuclear weapons program. The French balked at this request, offering a 70MW research reactor as an alternative. The Baghdad regime's acceptance of this option over a more capable but proliferation-resistant light-water reactor was indicative of Iraq's primary interest in acquiring fissile material rather than producing energy.[46]

Prime Minister Menachem Begin viewed the prospect of a nuclear-armed Iraq under Saddam Hussein as an existential threat to Israel. Labor Party leader Shimon Peres reportedly cautioned Begin against military action, arguing that Israel would be diplomatically isolated and that the intelligence was inadequate. In early spring 1981, Mossad, Israel's intelligence service, predicted the Iraqi reactor could go into operation as early as July. For Begin, a window of opportunity existed before the nuclear fuel (the bulk of which had not yet arrived from France) was loaded into the reactor. In tandem with this intelligence estimate, a key influence on Begin's decisionmaking was Israel's scheduled parliamentary elections at the end of June. Begin feared that if Labor defeated his Likud Party, Peres would attempt to address the Iraqi nuclear threat diplomatically through the French and would never authorize a preventive strike on Osiraq.[47]

In the wake of the preemptive Israeli air strike on the Osiraq facility, international reaction was sharply critical. Rejecting Israel's claim of anticipatory self-defense, the UN Security Council condemned the attack as "a clear violation of the Charter of the United Nations and the norms of international conduct."[48] A decade later, only after UNSCOM inspectors discovered the magnitude of Saddam Hussein's covert nuclear weapons program, the Israeli assessment of Iraqi intentions was validated. Though a tactical success, the efficacy of the 1981 air strike remains an issue of debate, with proponents arguing that it bought time (not an inconsequential goal in nonproliferation policy), while skeptics observe that it did not deter Iraq from acquiring nuclear weapons and may even have further motivated the Hussein regime.

THE FIRST PERSIAN GULF WAR AND OPERATION DESERT FOX

As part of Operation Desert Storm in January–February 1991, U.S. and allied aircraft targeted Iraq's unconventional weapons and missiles in order to protect coalition forces and to prevent their use against other countries in the region (most notably Israel). These missions were not conducted to roll back proliferation per se but rather were an extension of war. Their legal basis derived from the pertinent UN Security Council resolutions authorizing the use of force to reverse Iraqi aggression in Kuwait. During the air war, coalition aircraft registered approximately 970 strikes against suspected nuclear, biological, and chemical weapons sites. An additional 1,500 missions were aimed at suppressing Iraq's Scud missile force.[49]

UN Security Council Resolution 687 codified the cease-fire terms of the first Persian Gulf War in early 1991. That resolution created the United Nations Special Commission to oversee the destruction of any weapons of mass destruction that survived the conflict and to establish a verification system to ensure long-term compliance. The magnitude of the Iraqi WMD program, as it became known after 1991 through UNSCOM inspections, was striking both in its breadth and depth. UNSCOM and International Atomic Energy Agency (IAEA) officials uncovered efforts by Iraqi scientists to use the full range of uranium enrichment techniques to produce fissile material for nuclear weapons. In May 1994, UNSCOM announced that over a two-year period all known Iraqi chemical munitions, agents, and precursors had been destroyed; this encompassed more than 27,000 chemical-filled bombs, rockets, and artillery shells, 30 chemical warheads for Scud missiles, 500 tons of mustard and nerve agents, and thousands of tons of precursor chemicals. UNSCOM inspections also revealed an extensive Iraqi program to produce and weaponize biological agents. After the defection of Hussein Kamel, czar of Iraq's WMD programs, to Jordan in August 1995, the Baghdad regime finally admitted to producing 90,000 liters of botulinum toxin and 8,300 liters of anthrax and developing the capability to deliver these biological weapons by Scud missiles and aerial bombs. A particularly disturbing aspect of the Iraqi biological weapons program was that some of the pertinent technologies (ostensibly acquired by the Iraqis for legitimate agricultural and biomedical purposes) were not on export control lists. Thus, for example, Iraq was able to procure tons of biological growth medium, an amount that went far beyond any legitimate civilian use, for weapons purposes.[50]

UNSCOM's startling revelations about the magnitude of Iraqi WMD capabilities that had survived Desert Storm, as well as the assessment provided by the Department of Defense's own *Gulf War Air Power Survey*, highlighted the limited effectiveness of the U.S. air campaign. These findings underscored the critical importance of extensive intelligence for targeting unconventional weapons and the ability of a determined proliferator to make such capabilities less vulnerable to attack through deception and mobility, a finding echoed by David Kay in his more detailed chapter on the Iraq confrontation in this volume. For example, UNSCOM inspectors revealed the existence of twenty-one nuclear-related facilities in Iraq, whereas the prewar target list included only two such sites. The survey analysts concluded that the air campaign no more than "inconvenienced" Iraq's nuclear weapons program and that the actual destruction of any mobile Scud missiles by fixed-wing coalition aircraft could not be confirmed.[51]

During the post–Gulf War period, the United States and Britain employed instruments of coercive nonproliferation—economic sanctions and the threats of force—to try to compel Iraq's compliance with Security Council Resolution 687. Declining international support for economic sanctions and the opposition of Russia, China, and France on the UN Security Council to the use of force to enforce Resolution 687 emboldened Saddam Hussein to engage in brinkmanship by defying UNSCOM. He linked his own fate to the survivability of Iraq's WMD capabilities by placing them under the control of his presidential guard, the Special Security Organization, headed by his son, Qusay. Thus, any U.S. military strike on Iraq's WMD capabilities would be, in effect, an attack on Saddam Hussein personally. Indeed, UNSCOM officials believe that Special Security Organization units shuttled Iraq's WMD assets around Saddam Hussein's network of presidential palaces to defeat the UN's inspection regime.[52] A senior UNSCOM official referred to this tactic as Iraq's "philosophy of concealment through mobility."

In 1998, a series of crises over Iraqi noncompliance and noncooperation with UNSCOM led to four days of sustained air attacks by the United States and Britain. The air campaign, code-named Operation Desert Fox, relied heavily on cruise missiles and was the most extensive use of force against Iraq since the end of the Gulf War in 1991. During the four-day air campaign, Secretaries Albright and Cohen and National Security Adviser Samuel Berger declared that the U.S. commitment to use force against Iraq was open-ended. But to what purpose? At the outset of Operation Desert Fox, Secretary Cohen stated that the goal was to degrade Iraq's WMD capabilities and "not to destabilize the regime."[53] The Clinton administration was caught politically between domestic critics, who wanted more sustained air attacks aimed at undermining Saddam Hussein, and UN Security Council members, who were reflexively opposed to the use of force and sought only Iraq's compliance with Security Council Resolution 687.

When Operation Desert Fox concluded, U.S. and British forces had flown more than three hundred combat sorties and fired more than four hundred cruise missiles at Iraqi targets. In early January 1999, General Henry H. Shelton, chairman of the Joint Chiefs of Staff, reported to Congress that the raids had inflicted more damage than originally estimated. The raids destroyed or severely damaged twelve missile production sites and eleven command-and-control facilities. But, in a striking admission, U.S. and British planners did not target chemical and biological weapons facilities out of fear that such attacks might release deadly toxins into the atmosphere and produce unacceptable civilian casualties.[54]

NORTH KOREA'S NUCLEAR PROGRAM, 1993–94

Former secretary of defense William Perry has called the 1993–94 North Korean nuclear crisis the most dangerous episode of the post–cold war era.[55] In U.S. contingency planning during that crisis, the Clinton administration examined the option of military strikes on the North's advanced nuclear facilities. The Democratic People's Republic of Korea, as the North officially called itself, possessed an operational 5MW graphite-moderated reactor and a reprocessing facility for spent nuclear fuel at Yongbyon and had begun construction of two additional 50MW and 200MW nuclear reactors. The CIA estimated that the regime of Kim Il Sung could have extracted as much as twelve kilograms of plutonium from fuel rods, enough for two bombs, when the Yongbyon reactor was shut down. A January 1993 request from the IAEA for a "special inspection" of suspect sites, which North Korea was obliged to grant as an NPT signatory, was the immediate precipitant of the crisis. The regime rejected the request and threatened to withdraw from the NPT in March 1993, a move that prompted calls on Capitol Hill and by press commentators for a tough American counteraction, including the consideration of military options.

The row over IAEA inspections took a significant escalatory turn in April 1994 when North Korea announced its intention to shut down the Yongbyon reactor to remove spent fuel containing sufficient plutonium for an additional four or five bombs. In June 1994, the IAEA referred the matter to the UN Security Council, and the United States moved to strengthen its defenses in South Korea in anticipation of a diplomatic campaign to impose economic sanctions on the North. The Kim Il Sung regime responded with defiance, declaring that sanctions would be tantamount to a declaration of war. The Clinton administration adopted the sanctions strategy after considering—and rejecting—the alternative of military preemption. Secretary Perry explained the rationale behind this decision to forgo the option that hard-liners outside the administration, including some former senior Bush administration officials, were advocating:

> By May [1994] the negotiations between North Korea and the IAEA had broken down . . . [and] we were faced with the highly dangerous prospect that North Korea would have five or six nuclear bombs. . . . I asked General [John] Shalikashvili [chairman of the Joint Chiefs of Staff] . . . for an update of a contingency plan, which had been requested earlier, for destroying key components at the reactor site with a military attack. . . . The plan was impressive. . . . However, both General Shalikashvili and I had concluded that such an attack was very likely to incite the North Koreans to launch a military attack on South Korea.[56]

The significant possibility that a preemptive attack on the Yongbyon nuclear facilities would have a catalytic effect, triggering a general war on the Korean peninsula, removed the military option from consideration. In addition to the danger of inadvertent escalation, incomplete intelligence gave U.S. policymakers no assurance that air strikes would hit all the pertinent targets at Yongbyon or that this military action would eliminate the North Korean nuclear threat if some illicit reprocessing of spent fuel to extract plutonium had occurred during the earlier reactor shutdowns. In mid-June, as the Clinton administration prepared to push for UN Security Council sanctions, the crisis was defused during former president Jimmy Carter's controversial trip to Pyongyang, which resulted in Kim Il Sung's pledge to "freeze" activity at the Yongbyon site. The Carter mission broke the impasse and led to intensive bilateral negotiations that culminated in the U.S.-DPRK [Democratic People's Republic of Korea] Agreed Framework of October 1994. Under the terms of the nuclear agreement, castigated as appeasement by congressional and other hard-liners who rejected diplomatic engagement with this "rogue" state, North Korea agreed to freeze and eventually dismantle its Yongbyon facilities in return for two "proliferation-resistant" 1,000 MW light water reactors provided by a U.S.-led international consortium, the Korean Peninsula Energy Development Organization (KEDO), created for that purpose.

COUNTERPROLIFERATION AND COUNTERTERRORISM IN SUDAN, AUGUST 1998

On August 20, 1998, U.S. cruise missiles destroyed the al Shifa pharmaceutical plant in Khartoum, which the Clinton administration charged was producing a precursor chemical for VX nerve gas and was linked to the terrorist Osama bin Laden. The Sudan attack came thirteen days after the bombing of the U.S. embassies in Kenya and Tanzania, which killed a dozen Americans and hundreds of foreign nationals. U.S. officials had linked the embassy bombings to the bin Laden network. This counterproliferation mission was conducted as part of a broader counterterrorism operation, code-named Infinite Reach, involving a simultaneous cruise missile strike on bin Laden's base camp in Afghanistan.[57] The raids also provoked domestic political controversy, with critics charging that President Clinton had taken this dramatic action to deflect attention from the scandal that later led to his impeachment. Clinton told congressional leaders that "these strikes were a necessary and proportionate response to the imminent threat of further terrorist attacks. . . ." State Department officials did not publicly justify the attacks in terms of U.S. nonproliferation policy but rather argued that their legal basis was the right of self-defense under Chapter VII, Article 51 of the UN Charter.

National Security Adviser Berger defended the intelligence on which the Sudanese strike was based, declaring to the White House press corps that "with respect to the so-called pharmaceutical factory in Khartoum . . . we know with great certainty" about its role in chemical weapons production.[58] Secretary of Defense Cohen stated at a Pentagon briefing that Osama bin Laden "had an interest in acquiring chemical weapons . . . and that this facility produces the precursors [for] VX."[59]

In the aftermath of the raid, press reports called into question the Clinton administration's evidence regarding the plant and its links to bin Laden. U.S. officials acknowledged that the al Shifa plant may have been producing "legitimate pharmaceuticals" and provided further details of the intelligence underlying the strike—most notably, the revelation that a covertly obtained soil sample from the plant's vicinity had contained traces of Empta, the VX precursor chemical. Some experts criticized the CIA's analysis of the soil sample, claiming that it did not meet the standards of the agency monitoring the Chemical Weapons Convention.[60] Others suggested that an agricultural insecticide could have been mistaken for the precursor.[61] Rejecting these reports and questions about the legitimacy of the attack on the al Shifa plant, Berger insisted, "I have even more certainty about this that I did at the time we struck it. . . ." But the persistence of these questions diplomatically isolated the United States (with even British officials privately expressing "dismay and anger").[62] Additional information about the August 1998 cruise missile strike was revealed during the 2001 embassy bombings trial in New York, when one defendant provided "partial, but nonetheless striking corroboration of the Clinton administration's 1998 claim that al-Qaeda was involved in producing chemical weapons in Khartoum."[63]

CRITERIA, CONDITIONS, AND CONSEQUENCES

On the basis of the case summaries, this section examines the criteria and conditions governing the use of force as an instrument of nonproliferation policy as well as the impact of coercive nonproliferation on the motivations and behavior of the target states. Though one can develop general propositions about both the use and limitations of force based on historical experience, specific decisions by policymakers will be highly context-dependent and will be contingent on accurate target state assessment analysis.

CHARACTER OF THE THREAT

The United States may have a general interest in preventing proliferation and supporting the "international nonproliferation regime," but it does not regard all would-be proliferators as threats to American security. The perception of threat derives from both capabilities and intentions, not just the former. U.S. administrations distinguish between new and de facto nuclear proliferators—Israel, India, and Pakistan—that challenge an important international norm but do not directly threaten the United

States and those countries designated as "rogue" that do pose such a secu-rity threat. Thus, the cases in which the United States would actually contemplate the use of force involve a subset of countries that are pursu-ing the acquisition of WMD capabilities and those that have hostile inten-tions. Those states can be termed "hostile proliferators."[64]

Judgment about intentions is the threshold issue regarding the use or consideration of the use of force. Although hostile intent is a necessary condition, it alone is not sufficient to precipitate action. It is the con-junction of hostile intent and the capability to act on it that would prompt U.S. decisionmakers to consider the use of force. Sound intelligence must indicate that the threat is imminent—either that WMD will be used or that an important technological barrier will be crossed. For example, a major determinant of Prime Minister Begin's decision to authorize the Osiraq raid in June 1981 was intelligence that the nuclear reactor was on the verge of becoming operational. Likewise, the immediate precipitant of the North Korean nuclear crisis in spring 1994 was the shutdown of its nuclear reactor without IAEA supervision and the danger that the North would then remove spent fuel from the reactor core and reprocess it to extract fissile material for its nuclear weapons program.

An additional important issue relating to target state analysis is whether deterrence can forestall the threat posed by a hostile proliferator. In this context, the imputation of irrationality or recklessness can be an important determinant. A major motivating force underlying President Kennedy's militancy about China's nuclear program was his perception of Mao's regime as fundamentally irresponsible. Begin viewed Saddam Hussein as a latter-day Hitler and, continuing the analogy, his nuclear program as the potential instrument of a new Final Solution against the Jewish state; this analysis largely drove the Israeli decision to conduct a preemptive air strike.

In the post–cold war era, the assertion that rogue states may be unde-terrable has led to an increased policy emphasis on coercive nonprolifer-ation and "homeland defense." This imputation of irrationality, however, is a questionable premise on which to base policy. The experience with Iraq during the first Persian Gulf War points to the contrary. Saddam Hussein may have been ruthlessly expansionist, but he did not act irra-tionally. When Secretary of State James Baker met Foreign Minister Tariq Aziz in January 1991 just prior to the outbreak of hostilities, he reportedly told the Iraqi, "God forbid . . . chemical weapons are used against our forces—the American people would demand revenge, and we have the means to implement this."[65] The Iraqi leadership told UN officials in 1995 that they interpreted Baker's statement as a threat to retaliate with nuclear weapons if Iraq used chemical or other unconventional weapons against American and coalition forces.[66] The crudeness of the rogue state formulation obscures the importance of strategic culture in shaping a target state's worldview and calculus of decisionmaking. That the logic underlying a target state's behavior is not readily apparent to outsiders does not make that regime irrational. The analytical challenge is to "unlock the strategic personality" of the target state and to develop an approach that corresponds.[67] Such analysis is the prerequisite for determining whether the use of force is appropriate or not in a particular context.

Politico-Military Context

After the threshold determination about threat characterization, several considerations affect decisionmaking about the use of force. In addition to reliable strategic intelligence about a hostile proliferator's motivations and intentions, painstaking tactical intelligence is necessary to determine whether or not a military option is even feasible. The challenge of obtaining this information and translating it into effective military action was highlighted by the 1991 Gulf War experience and the postconflict revelations by UNSCOM about the magnitude of Iraqi WMD capabilities and missiles that had escaped detection and destruction. In the 1994 North Korean crisis, incomplete intelligence gave Clinton administration officials no assurance that all pertinent nuclear-related targets could be destroyed through air strikes.

Military action is not just an issue of feasibility, however; it also depends on the political context. Because international norms insist that force be an instrument of last resort, nonmilitary options should be exhausted before considering military instruments. Convincing others, most notably the UN Security Council, that all nonmilitary alternatives have been exhausted will be vital to have any chance of gaining multilateral support for the use of force. As discussed earlier, the rogue state approach politically hinders the ability of U.S. policymakers to pursue such alternative strategies—in particular, diplomatic initiatives incorporating incentives (for example, the U.S.-DPRK Agreed Framework) that hard-liners will invariably label appeasement.

The case summaries indicate that counterproliferation missions can be subsumed in a broader political context in which nonproliferation itself plays a subordinate policy role. The 1998 strike on the Sudanese factory was piggybacked onto a counterterrorism mission. The 1991 air campaign against Iraq's WMD capabilities was conducted in the course of a war authorized by the UN Security Council to expel Iraqi forces from Kuwait. In the North Korean case, the implementation of the Agreed Framework and related proposals concerning the North's ballistic missile program are embedded in the fabric of a North-South Korean rapprochement and efforts to engineer a "soft landing" for the North Korean economy and society.

A final issue affecting the politico-military context is the legal basis for the proposed use of force. In 1992, the UN Security Council recognized the proliferation of weapons of mass destruction as a threat to international peace covered under Chapter VII of the UN Charter. The unilateral exercise of force against a proliferator has been justified by the United States, following the August 1998 cruise missile strike on the Sudanese plant, and by Israel, after the June 1981 Osiraq strike, as the exercise of their right of self-defense under Chapter VII, Article 51. But the right of self-defense under Article 51 has been narrowly interpreted by the international community to reject the assertion of anticipatory self-defense except in the face of imminent peril—meaning that the threat of an armed attack must be "instant, overwhelming and leaving no choice of means, and no moment of deliberation."[68] In international law, imminence cannot simply be inferred from suspect activity at a possible WMD-related facility in apparent contravention of nonproliferation norms. In light of these legal constraints, former IAEA official David Fischer concludes, "It would be impossible to institutionalize, at the global or regional level, the right of any state individually to take measures of forcible counterproliferation in time of peace."[69]

Even when Chapter VII authorization has been granted by the Security Council, members will balk when specific permission is not requested in a particular instance. For example, during Operation Desert Fox, other UN Security Council members criticized the United States and Britain for not going back to that body for authorization before launching the air campaign. The U.S. and British governments argued that they were acting under existing Security Council Resolution 687 authorization in the face of Iraq's "material breach" of the cease-fire resolution.

These legal criteria establish a very high bar for the use of force even when the target state's WMD capability and imminently hostile intent have been affirmed. Indeed, a working consensus with U.S. allies is likely to be highly difficult to secure. As political scientist Stephen M. Walt soberly concludes regarding such prospects, "Not only are democratic states generally disinclined to fight preventive wars, but allies are likely to face different levels of risk and will probably disagree about the level of threat and the probability of success."[70] The problem is even more formidable in the UN Security Council, which has sole power to authorize the use of force to address threats to peace short of imminent war but in which action can be blocked by any of five vetoes. This political dynamic was strikingly evident in UN Security Council deliberations over Iraq during the twelve-year period between the end of the first Persian Gulf War in 1991 and the most recent conflict. Contending perspectives among the permanent members—notably the United States and Britain versus France and Russia—over the state of Iraqi WMD capabilities, the continued efficacy of inspections, and the imminence of the threat produced a sharp split over the use of force.

CONSEQUENCES

A third set of criteria and conditions governing the use of force focuses on the consequences of its employment. In considering the use of force against a hostile proliferator, a primary concern must be the capability for the target state to retaliate. Depending on the scope of the WMD program and the solidity of the intelligence, a policymaker could not discount the possibility that a hostile proliferator might lash out with any surviving unconventional capability against a U.S. ally or forces in that regional theater. Some of the measures supported through the Department of Defense's Defense CPI (for example, protective suits) could limit the potential damage, but a significant possibility of WMD retaliation still would be a major constraint on bringing force to bear against a hostile proliferator. In two cases where force was employed—Iraq in 1981 and Sudan in 1998—neither Israel nor the United States feared WMD retaliation by the target state.

During the North Korean crisis, the fear of escalation—the possibility that a counterproliferation strike on the North's nuclear infrastructure would provoke all-out war on the Korean Peninsula—was a key determinant of U.S. policy. This overriding concern prompted the Clinton administration to pursue alternative, nonmilitary approaches—initially economic sanctions in the UN, later, bilateral negotiations leading to the U.S.-DPRK Agreed Framework.

Additionally, the desire to limit collateral damage both to the environment and to the civilian population has tempered the resort to force. To avoid an environmental catastrophe the Israelis struck the Osiraq reactor before its HEU fuel had been loaded into the core and the facility was operational. Likewise, during Operation Desert Fox, the United States and Britain abstained from striking chemical and biological sites for fear of releasing dangerous toxins into the atmosphere. In the Sudan operation, the Joint Chiefs of Staff took a second building off the Khartoum target list because they believed the intelligence about its connection to chemical weapons production was weak and that a cruise missile attack would result in significant civilian casualties. Most tellingly, in Afghanistan, when its forces were engaged in active military operations in autumn 2001, the United States reportedly eschewed bombing suspect al Qaeda biological and chemical weapons development sites out of concern about the accuracy of intelligence and the release of deadly toxins.[71] Collateral damage from strikes against weapons of mass destruction is an ever-present consideration that elected officials in democratic societies will need to take into account and is a constraint on the use of force against a hostile proliferator. This problem may be mitigated, however, by the advent of a new generation of so-called agent-defeat warheads specifically designed to destroy chemical and biological agents while minimizing collateral damage.[72]

U.S. counterproliferation capabilities are unlikely to deter a would-be proliferator from acquiring weapons of mass destruction. Their security, domestic political, and normative motivations are deep-seated and powerful; counterproliferation capabilities do not alter them.[73] Particularly in light of the cases discussed above, the likely impact of U.S. counterproliferation activity will be to drive target state programs further underground. The history of Saddam Hussein's WMD program is dramatic testimony to the ability of a determined proliferator to develop a massive covert program. If counterproliferation capabilities will not forestall WMD acquisition, what about deterring actual use by a hostile proliferator? The threat potential could cut both ways. On the one hand, preparedness measures such as protective biochemical suits could convince a target state that it has nothing to gain militarily from WMD use. On the other hand, its regime might resort to WMD use if it believed that it was on the verge of being overthrown by external forces. During the 1991 Persian Gulf War, Iraq forward-deployed chemical munitions, and the question of whether Saddam Hussein predelegated authority to commanders to use unconventional weapons under certain conditions remains unresolved. An Iraqi official subsequently asserted that Baghdad would only have used its WMD capabilities in retaliation to such use by coalition forces.[74] But given the primacy of regime security to Hussein, the continuation of the war into Iraq—a much-discussed "march on Baghdad"—also could plausibly have precipitated Iraqi WMD use against the U.S.-led coalition. And yet, when that very scenario unfolded in April 2003 as U.S. forces approached Baghdad, Hussein's forces did not use chemical weapons. This remains one of many open questions about the second Persian Gulf War.

A senior U.S. official who participated in the negotiation of the U.S.-DPRK Agreed Framework argues that the North Koreans did not distinguish between a narrow U.S. counterproliferation option against the North's nuclear facilities and general war. That fear of general war may have influenced Kim Il Sung's decision to pursue the diplomatic course after the Carter mission in mid-June 1994. Some analysts maintain that coercive instruments—economic sanctions and the prospect of application of military force—were a key determinant of the Pyongyang regime's ultimate decision to accept the Agreed Framework.[75]

IMPLICATIONS FOR POLICY

The current debate over the use of force as an instrument of nonproliferation policy now revolves around the Bush administration's preemption strategy. In his 2002 State of the Union address, President Bush labeled Iraq, Iran, and North Korea as an axis of evil and warned that his administration would not remain idle in response to such perceived threats as these countries represented. In the new age of vulnerability ushered in by the September 11 terrorist attacks, preemption is being called a "matter of common sense" in the words of the new "National Security Strategy of the United States of America." But even in this era of heightened risk historical experience offers relevant insights for policymakers into the conditions governing the use of force to forestall proliferation.

The cases in which the United States would consider the use of force involves the small group of states with both hostile intent and the capability to absorb proliferation technology. Sound target-state analysis based upon accurate intelligence is essential in assessing intentions and the imminence of military threat. The determination of intentions—understanding a regime's "strategic personality," or how history and political culture influence its worldview and actions—in turn governs what type of preventive strategy, if any, would be effective. The threshold concerns that responsible policymakers must address before the application of force are formidable: whether the case involves a "hostile proliferator," whether the intelligence is adequate, whether the threat is imminent, and whether the risks and anticipated collateral damage are acceptable, among others. For this reason, preemption should be a rarely invoked option and should not be general doctrine.

The analysis of cases involving the use of force reveals that counterproliferation is not the definitive policy instrument that some would wish. Indeed, force is no less problematic and uncertain in terms of yielding desired outcomes than its nonmilitary alternatives. Proponents of preemption often cite the 1981 Israeli raid on Iraq's Osiraq nuclear facility as a model to be emulated. But the Osiraq case, far from being a paradigm, was a rare instance in which all the conditions for success were present: specific and highly accurate intelligence; negligible risk of collateral damage or retaliation. More often in history, the utility of force has been affected by major constraints: the possibility of triggering full-scale war (North Korea, 1994); uncertain and contentious intelligence (Sudan, 1998); the threat of unacceptable collateral damage to the population and environment (Iraq, 1998).[76] Moreover, the benefits of a counterproliferation strike may prove ephemeral if such action results in driving the development of weapons of mass destruction underground—witness Saddam Hussein's concerted efforts to reconstitute his nuclear program after 1981. In short, force is not a silver bullet.

Successful prevention strategies will forestall the need for preemption. The instances in which force has been considered or used for nonproliferation purposes, including the second Persian Gulf War, have been *preventive* rather than preemptive because in none was actual WMD use imminent. Prevention strategies employ the full array of nonproliferation tools, including multilateral treaties, export controls, and economic coercion. For example, U.S. assurances of security given to threatened allies in Taiwan and South Korea have resulted in nonproliferation success stories. The depth of the administration's commitment to nonmilitary restraints on proliferation is further called into question by the gap between the magnitude of the problem (the prime instance is "loose nukes" in the former Soviet Union) and the inadequacy of the financial resources devoted to it. The National Security Strategy document perfunctorily acknowledges the contribution of nonmilitary instruments, but the Bush administration appears at best ambivalent about the efficacy of those instruments in contending with the proliferation hard cases it has lumped under the axis of evil rubric. In his June 2002 West Point speech, President Bush declared, "We cannot put our faith in the word of tyrants who solemnly sign nonproliferation treaties and then systematically break them."

Under what conditions, short of war, would policymakers still resort to the use of force? One such condition would be if conflict with a WMD-armed adversary directly threatened the United States. In that circumstance, the preemptive use of force could be considered the initiation of a war that was inevitable. Former secretary of defense William Perry told the Senate Foreign Relations Committee in July 2001 that the United States should issue a policy "that we will attack the [missile] launch sites of any nation that threatens to attack the US with nuclear or biological weapons."[77] A second contingency identified since September 11 that would precipitate U.S. military action is if a hostile proliferator were to transfer WMD capabilities to a nonstate terrorist group. The Bush administration has increasingly explicitly linked the dangers of terrorism and proliferation. In his 2002 State of the Union address, Bush admonished, "In the war against terror, one of the worst things that can possibly happen is al Qaeda-like organizations becoming allied and operationally attuned to nations which have weapons of mass destruction."[78] During the debate over military action against Iraq, U.S. officials specifically cautioned of the danger that Saddam Hussein might transfer WMD capabilities to al Qaeda. Similar concern has been expressed with respect to North Korea, which has threatened to export nuclear materials. While the plausibility of a WMD transfer scenario is much debated, the United States can step up deterrence against it by making explicit that conclusive evidence of any such move by a hostile proliferator would trigger an immediate American military response with the objective of regime change.

Because of strong international sentiment against the use of force, multilateral support, especially within the UN Security Council, will be exceedingly difficult to secure. In no instance has Security Council authorization for the use of force been granted explicitly to prevent proliferation. The increased emphasis by the United States on unilateral preemption is fueled, in part, by the belief that the UN Security Council has failed to meet the global security responsibilities originally envisioned for it and that international law, such as the Article 51 proscription against anticipatory defense, is woefully outdated. The speech President Bush gave on Iraq on September 12 at the United Nations attempted to place the onus back on the Security Council to enforce its own resolutions so as not to become an ineffectual, latter-day League of Nations.[79]

A major issue arising from the war in Iraq is whether a dialogue among the UN Security Council's permanent members, as well as within the international community more broadly, can lead to a consensus on rules governing the use of force. The persisting dilemma in this problematic area of international law is how to develop general rules that permit military action under some circumstances but not under others. Because the requisite political consensus for change among the major powers simply does not exist, proposals to codify updated rules on the use of force are premature. Nonetheless, on the specific issue of preemption, a significant interim step in bridging the contentious policy gap between the United States and other countries would be an exchange of views on security to bring greater analytical and political clarity to the concept of imminence, which is the key determinant of preemptive action. Laying out intelligible and transparent criteria of "imminent threat" could provide a basis for collective action, whether by the Security Council or, if that were not possible, by an ad hoc coalition. These security discussions should encompass the full range of pertinent considerations, such as whether the target state has used unconventional weapons in the past, is in current violation of Security Council resolutions, or has manifested hostile intentions. Agreement on the meaning of imminence also could assist policymakers in recognizing and confronting *incipient* threats, for which nonmilitary instruments might still be effective as part of a prevention strategy. An international security dialogue that achieved some consensus on preemption could reduce the need for the United States—or other nations—to resort to preemptive, unilateral action. Such a security conference appears unlikely in the aftermath of the acrimonious Security Council debate in 2002–2003 over the use of force to coerce Iraqi WMD disarmament. The refusal to grant a UN seal of approval led the Bush administration to decide to go to war with a "coalition of the willing," brushing aside questions of an international mandate. The postwar controversy over U.S. and British intelligence regarding Saddam Hussein's WMD programs, which furnished the rationale for military action, will make it that much harder to mount a compelling case for multilateral action in the future. Multilateralism offers political legitimacy but constrains America's freedom of action—a constraint some regard as unacceptable after September 11. In facing nonproliferation crises after the war in Iraq, notably with North Korea and Iran, the challenge for American policymakers is how the United States might tend to its national interests without calling into question its commitment to the norms of international order.

4

IRAQ AND U.S. NONPROLIFERATION POLICY

David A. Kay

NOTE: Subsequent to submitting his contribution to this volume, David Kay was appointed by the director of central intelligence to serve as the special adviser for strategy in Iraq. In this capacity, he is managing the effort to track and destroy weapons of mass destruction that may remain in Iraq after the recent war to topple Saddam Hussein. His chapter, which is focused on the lessons learned from the experiences of weapons inspections and dismantlement in Iraq after the 1991 Persian Gulf War, provides essential and unique insights for the current challenges of Iraqi disarmament. It was completed before the outbreak of hostilities in late winter/spring of 2003.

—The Editors

Whereas previous chapters in this volume have examined a wide range of nonproliferation and counterproliferation initiatives, this chapter focuses on a particular case, Iraq. More than any other case, Iraq demonstrates both the potential successes and the limitations of "involuntary nonproliferation." In the wake of Iraq's firing Scud missiles and using poison gas against its own people in the Persian Gulf War, measures to dismantle the country's nuclear, biological, and chemical capabilities were mandated by UN Security Council resolution, and thus U.S. nonproliferation efforts were in this instance supported by a set of tools that were unprecedented in their coerciveness and invasiveness. Though the

United Nations Special Commission on Iraq (UNSCOM) destroyed vast quantities of Iraq nuclear and nonnuclear materials by the time this invasive inspection regime was dismantled through Iraqi intransigence in 1998, pessimists wondered whether anything had been achieved other than to delay Iraqi plans to rebuild its capacity for making weapons of mass destruction. The Bush administration's plans to use force in support of "regime change" in Iraq remain hotly contested.

After sketching the struggles with Iraq that dramatically transformed U.S. and international nonproliferation policy from largely passive cooperation to far-reaching and aggressive interventionism, this chapter examines the policy's successes and analyze UNSCOM's inability to roll back Iraq's program for the development of weapons of mass destruction (WMD) in its entirety. Finally, it assesses the potential for future exercises in coercive, involuntary nonproliferation. Successful coercive nonproliferation will require the development of specialized tools and organizations capable of sustaining efforts for an extended period of time.

Since the dawn of the nuclear age the United States had resorted to a range of methods—some more assertive than others—to try to limit additional states gaining access to nuclear weapons. Initial efforts focused on unilateral controls on nuclear technology and diplomatic pressure on would-be proliferators. The North Atlantic Treaty Organization (NATO) and similar mutual security arrangements provided guarantees that, in effect, promised the protection of the U.S. nuclear umbrella to our allies and, it was hoped, alleviated the pressure on them to develop their own nuclear forces. With the entry into force in March 1970 of the Treaty on the Non-Proliferation of Nuclear Weapons (NPT), an expanded web of measures was put in place that attempted to meld incentives—such as access to peaceful nuclear technology and a promise that the existing nuclear powers would eventually dismantle their own nuclear forces— with measures to provide assurance against cheating through international inspections. The initial steps, taken well before the signing of the NPT, were not universally successful. Most of the failures, however, seemed inevitable. It was no surprise that the United Kingdom, the Soviet Union, France, Israel, and China pushed ahead with their nuclear ambitions regardless of American nonproliferation strictures.

Although there were some outright failures subsequently—India and Pakistan most notably—as Joseph Cirincione has suggested in an earlier chapter, these cooperative nonproliferation efforts yielded some remarkable successes. At one time or the other it looked altogether possible that Canada, Sweden, Switzerland, Italy, the Federal Republic of Germany,

Japan, South Korea, and Taiwan might develop nuclear weapons. Several of these states did, in fact, gain a capacity to produce nuclear weapons. In every case, however, the panoply of voluntary nonproliferation policies crafted by the United States managed to bring these programs to a halt.

It is against this context of largely successful voluntary nonproliferation measures that Iraq stands in sharp contrast.[1] Voluntary measures to ensure nonproliferation were discarded in Iraq in the aftermath of the 1991 Gulf War. UN Security Council Resolution 687 (April 3, 1991), the cease-fire resolution that ended the war, required that all chemical and biological weapons, nuclear weapons material, and ballistic missiles with a range greater than 150 kilometers be identified and destroyed, removed, or rendered harmless. The resolution also directed that this same process should apply to all subsystems or components and any research, development, support, or manufacturing facilities for such nuclear material or prohibited weapons and that Iraq's undertaking not to use, develop, construct, or acquire such weapons in the future should be the subject of an ongoing monitoring system.[2] To achieve these aims a new international body, UNSCOM, operating under the authority of the UN Security Council, was created. By December 1998, when all UNSCOM inspections were halted by Iraq, there had been more than nine hundred inspections and monitoring visits carried out by UN teams.

The nonproliferation process being attempted in Iraq might better be termed coercive disarmament and verification. In the first place, the arms limitations were being imposed rather than being a cooperative undertaking. Second, Iraq's continual resistance to compliance and its active attempts to deceive became so prevalent that the disarmament and verification measures used had to be extremely extensive and intrusive. Third, and as a result of the previous two concerns, there is much uncertainty as to the extent of success of the disarmament of Iraq's offensive capabilites, while confidence in the lasting impact of the reversal has decreased with time since monitoring teams were removed.[3]

It is worth considering briefly the coercive nature of the attempt to deprive Iraq of its WMD capacity. Iraq had suffered stunning losses in the hundred hours between the onset of the ground phase of the Gulf War on February 24, 1991, and its conclusion on February 28.[4] Iraq faced the unpalatable choice of accepting a dictated cease-fire that included agreeing to surrender its chemical, biological, and nuclear weapons, its long-range missiles, and its production capabilities or accepting the certainty that the U.S.-led coalition would take Baghdad and destroy the country's political leadership.

Hussein's regime traded a grudging, and temporary, acceptance of its own disarmament for political survival. Once the imminent military threat to the regime's survival was removed, however, Iraq's willingness to cooperate in the reversal of its WMD capability also disappeared. For example, Iraq's first letter on April 6, 1991, to the president of the Security Council began with seven pages of objections to Security Council Resolution 687 and then concluded with a one-sentence statement that it had "no choice but to accept this resolution."[5] The cease-fire resolution required Iraq to submit a complete listing of the quantities and location of its prohibited weapons and their production systems, and it was this declaration that served as the basis for their destruction. It became apparent soon after the Iraqi declaration was submitted on April 18 that full disclosure was not forthcoming. The declaration acknowledged approximately 10,000 nerve gas shells, 1,000 tons of nerve and mustard gas, 1,500 chemical weapon bombs and shells, and 52 Scud missiles with 30 chemical and 23 conventional high-explosive warheads, but it denied that Iraq had any biological or nuclear materials subject to the cease-fire prohibitions. Within three months the UN inspectors had already found four times more chemical weapons than Iraq had declared—46,000 chemical shells as compared with the 11,500 specified and 3,000 tons of chemical agents as compared with the stated 650 tons.

Within two months of the Iraqi declaration, a previously unknown nuclear program was uncovered by inspectors despite unrelenting obstructions. By October 1991, only seven months after the Iraqi declaration, more than 100,000 chemical shells had been found by inspectors—almost ten times the specified number. The process of hiding, cheating, and deception did not stop in 1991. In 1995, a biological weapons program was discovered along with further evidence of Scuds and continuing efforts to perfect chemical, biological, and nuclear weapons and missiles to deliver them. On June 11, 1997, Rolf Ekeus, head of UNSCOM, reported to the Security Council on four recent efforts by Iraq to obstruct inspection teams that prevented them from carrying out their duties. On arrival in Baghdad on June 21, the deputy head of UNSCOM, Charles Duelfer, declared, "We are convinced there are prohibited things which Iraq is concealing."[6]

The difference between cooperative and coercive nonproliferation is perhaps most clearly signaled by inspections having begun in Iraq on the basis of false and incomplete declarations of the quantities and locations of prohibited weapons and materials and a clear statement by the government of Iraq that it found the inspections inequitable and was submitting to them because it had no other choice. In the case of voluntary nonproliferation agreements, the arguments as to desirability and coverage of arms control arrangements always preceded their entry into force, whereas in the case of a coercive rollback, in Iraq there was never a genuine accord on the elimination of prohibited weapons systems.

THE METHODS OF INSPECTIONS

While the lack of a consensual basis for coercive nonproliferation stands in stark contrast to other arms control arrangements, that is not the only difference. Inspection techniques have always been among the hardest details to negotiate in a voluntary inspection regime, with all sides concerned that agreed methods be limited in scope and capable of only revealing information on the narrow items being offered up for inspection. In coercive circumstances such as in Iraq, where the purpose is to remove whole categories of weapons capabilities in the face of resistance, techniques that have broad capabilities to indicate prohibited activities and are difficult to foil become extremely useful. Many of the techniques, approaches, and equipment used in Iraq had never been used for voluntary nonproliferation or traditional arms control. These included:

GO ANYPLACE, ANYTIME, WITH ANYONE. Traditional arms control inspections have been based generally on agreed lists of inspection sites or procedures that ensure significant advance notice of inspections. The nuclear inspections in Iraq, in fact, started on the same basis, with Iraqi authorities being given twenty-four to forty-eight hours' notice of inspection locations. It was only after Iraq repeatedly responded by moving material or denying entry to sites that resort was made to inspections without prior notice to the Iraqis of locations. Such zero-notice inspections became the key to unraveling critical elements of Iraq's arsenal of weapons of mass destruction.

As Iraq's efforts to shield its prohibited weapons became more extreme, the list of sites subjected to inspection had to grow apace. Inspections covered such unusual places as a chicken farm, cemeteries, a hospital for amputees, a women's college dormitory, government ministries, presidential "palaces," private residences, and museums.

The range of inspection personnel used in Iraq also has far exceeded anything seen in voluntary arms control. Technical inspection experts were drawn from universities, industry, national laboratories, and intelligence organizations, in addition to national militaries and diplomatic corps, the traditional bastions of arms inspectors. The technical array of expertise required in Iraq extended across a wide spectrum of biological, chemical, nuclear, and missile fields and even to those experienced in detecting and untangling maneuvers of deception.

UNRESTRICTED ACCESS TO INSPECTION EQUIPMENT. Traditional, on-site arms control inspections have always been based on carefully negotiated agreement as to the tools that inspectors may use, how they are to be employed, and the right of the inspected state to examine such equipment before it is used. Iraq was a significant exception, with inspectors having the right to bring in whatever equipment they felt was required for the task regardless of Iraqi objections. This right became an essential element of UNSCOM's operations as Iraq resorted to large-scale deceit to hide its WMD capacity.

UNRESTRICTED RIGHT TO AERIAL PHOTOGRAPHY AND HELI-COPTER FLIGHTS OVER IRAQ. Only in an adversarial arms control situation would one find inspectors demanding the right of unrestricted movement and observation throughout the airspace of a target country. Yet it was just such flights in Iraq that produced some of the most startling discoveries.

UNLIMITED AUTHORITY TO CONDUCT ENVIRONMENTAL MEA-SUREMENTS AND SAMPLING. A major advance over previous arms control arrangements was the ability to use sophisticated environmental sampling techniques in Iraq. The first evidence of Iraq's clandestine nuclear program was found through the use of such sampling. And many sites where Iraq denied weapons work had taken place were confirmed to be part of its weapons complex through environmental monitoring. Serving the need to understand the full extent of Iraq's production of chemical and biological weapons, the tools of environmental measurement and sampling provided compelling proof of Iraq's continued efforts to conceal the true extent of this program.

USE OF NATIONALLY SUPPLIED INFORMATION. Multilateral arms control regimes have operated on the basis of information supplied to the regime by the states being inspected. Nationally generated information often played an important role in shaping a treaty and in determining what was to be covered, but seldom was such information directly available to the inspectors subsequently implementing the treaties.[7] In the case of UNSCOM, nothing has been more important than access to timely national intelligence of an unprecedented quality and volume. Inspections in Iraq saw extensive sharing of nationally supplied technical knowledge and procedures: data collection techniques and analytical capabilities were put at the service of UNSCOM; experienced information analysts were assigned to provide full-time backstopping to the inspection effort; and even a U-2 aircraft with sensors was leased by the United States to the United Nations.

THE ACCOMPLISHMENTS OF COERCIVE NONPROLIFERATION

UNSCOM, and the attempt at coercive nonproliferation, finally passed into history on December 17, 1999, when the UN Security Council approved a new organization, the United Nations Monitoring, Verification and Inspection Commission (UNMOVIC), to replace UNSCOM.[8] UNSCOM actually died a year earlier, on December 16, 1998, when the United States launched Operation Desert Fox, an air strike on Iraq, a day after UNSCOM chairman Richard Butler issued a report declaring that Iraq had failed to live up to its promise to restore full cooperation with UNSCOM in disarming it. UNSCOM's inspections in Iraq, which, in the face of Iraqi opposition, had been only sporadic for the previous two years, finally ceased altogether in December 1998.[9] UNMOVIC, as of mid-2001, has still not undertaken a single inspection in Iraq, and Iraq remains defiant in its statements that it will no longer accept UN efforts to disarm it forcibly.

UNSCOM's most lasting accomplishment as the first agent of coercive nonproliferation will probably not be the Iraqi weapons that were destroyed, though substantial progress was made. Nor will it be the demonstration that the United Nations can, on occasion, break through its diplomatic arthritis and undertake a truly innovative operation. More important in the long run is that UNSCOM has provided convincing evidence of how easily a state with dedication and money can construct a broad capability spanning all types of weapons of mass destruction while managing to maintain its status as a member in good standing of the voluntary nonproliferation system and how difficult it is to remove this capability in the face of determined opposition. A great debt is owed to UNSCOM for the renewed attention that has been paid to proliferation during the past ten years and the substantial efforts that have gone into attempting to improve on the leaky pre–Gulf War regimes that allowed and, in some cases, even aided the Iraqi weapons buildup.

THE SOURCES OF SUCCESS

The UNSCOM-directed effort from 1991 to 1998 accomplished a great deal, even though it failed to achieve the intended objective of eliminating Iraq's WMD capabilities. Identifying the reasons that this undertaking achieved what it did should be of interest not only to those concerned with the coercive reversal of proliferation, although one should never forget the essentially involuntary character of the inspection process. It may well be that if we better understood the roots of UNSCOM's successes some lessons could be drawn as to how to improve the more numerous voluntary nonproliferation efforts.

First, UNSCOM had one central advantage: a single clear focus. It was tasked to find and then destroy, remove, or render harmless Iraq's weapons of mass destruction. It had no responsibilities for the postwar reconstruction of Iraq, humanitarian relief, or the promotion of the peaceful side of nuclear, chemical, or biological technology. Multinational bureaucracies are difficult organizations for outsiders to understand. It is almost equally difficult for insiders to keep them focused on attainable and pragmatic objectives. They are impossible to run with mixed or conflicting objectives. Policy coordination is thus at a premium. UNSCOM was able, for a period of time, to dodge this particular bullet, and that made a tremendous difference.

Second, the United Nations did something in creating UNSCOM that it had never done before. UNSCOM was made a subsidiary organ of the Security Council and was not to be subordinate to or dependent on the secretary-general or the UN Secretariat. UNSCOM reported directly to the Security Council, free of all the internal political pressures and compromises that render most UN reports senseless and make direct action impossible. This arrangement also made it possible to mount a field operation largely free of the morass of rules that hobble most UN missions. From little things—the first cipher lock on a UN office and the first reasonably secure communications system—to much more consequential actions—requesting and using national intelligence information and availing itself of aerial reconnaissance resources—UNSCOM used its freedom from the UN bureaucracy to respond effectively to an unprecedented challenge.

Equally important, the Security Council recognized that the success or failure of UNSCOM would be viewed as its own success or failure. Particularly when compared to how situations such as Bosnia were handled, the Security Council, in the case of UNSCOM, was remarkably consistent in maintaining a unity of purpose up until 1996–97. By 1996, the Gulf War was becoming for many Security Council members a matter of history, not an ongoing problem. Attention was turning to future trade and investment opportunities, to the more traditional concerns of seeking political advantage over rivals, and to a renewal of Israeli-Palestinian conflict. Within the Secretariat, and particularly in the office of the secretary-general, there was a growing fatigue and unhappiness with the intrusive arms control approach. UNSCOM was seen as too prone to resort to confrontational methods that hindered the more traditional, and comfortable, activities of the United Nations aimed at aiding populations in distress.

Third, UNSCOM was blessed with what, by the standards of the UN system at least, was remarkably effective leadership. Rolf Ekeus, who was selected by the Security Council to chair UNSCOM, demonstrated during his six years the rarest of combinations of leadership qualities in the United Nations: integrity, stubbornness, ability to resist intimidation, personal courage, diplomatic prowess, and the capacity to inspire subordinates.[10]

Fourth, as well led as UNSCOM was, it benefited considerably from the incompetence and failures of Iraq. In the early years of UNSCOM, Iraq was the type of opponent of which one can usually only dream: overly centralized; brutal in a way that inspired more fear in its own supporters than in the inspectors; crude and incompetent in presenting its own case; cheating on all matters, large and small, so that it became viewed as universally untrustworthy; and unable to formulate and follow a coherent strategy. The pattern was set during the second inspection, when an UNSCOM team managed to catch and photograph Iraqis secretly trying to move large uranium enrichment equipment that Iraq had denied having in the first place.[11]

Fifth, as mentioned previously, UNSCOM had access to a vast range of inspection resources and techniques that had never before been used in nonproliferation efforts. These resources and procedures included national intelligence information, environmental monitoring technology, aerial reconnaissance, personnel drawn from national weapons programs, hand-held GPS devices, mobile satellite communications, real-time digital photography with direct transmission to New York, zero-notice inspections, detailed interviews with target-country officials, and document seizure.

While UNSCOM deserves credit for recognizing that it could not carry out its mission without the tools provided by national intelligence services, inadequate credit has been given to the handful of intelligence officials who were willing to break through the considerable barriers of distrust inculcated by their own countries' services with regard to sharing some of the crown jewels of their data collection systems with a diverse group of UN personnel. This was not done without considerable risk to their own careers, yet it was essential to making the first few UNSCOM inspections the striking successes that they were.

The post–Gulf War inspections carried out by UNSCOM, in fact, saw an unprecedented level of sharing of national intelligence information and techniques. Technical data was shared between individual country intelligence services and UN agencies beginning with the very first Iraqi inspection. While the U.S. intelligence community took the lead in assisting the United Nations, significant contributions were made by other coalition partners, particularly the United Kingdom. None of these resources and techniques was a panacea; without them, however, it would not have been possible eventually to unmask a program as well hidden as that of Iraq.

Nationally supplied intelligence allowed UNSCOM to perform better in the following five functional areas than any previous multilateral arms control arrangement.

1. Context setting: Outlining the Iraqi program to develop and acquire weapons of mass destruction, including identifying foreign suppliers and experts, Iraqi facilities and personnel associated with the program, probable milestones in the programs' development, and likely developmental, testing, and production routes taken by Iraq.

2. Shaping inspection objectives/questions: Helping specify and prioritize, from among the vast range of interesting possibilities that might be pursued by individual inspection missions, the objectives and questions that these missions should address.

3. Identification: Identifying specific inspection targets that should be pursued, the likely Iraqi concealment and security responses to such inspections, and possible counters for these.

4. Technical support: Providing data collection and analytical support, equipment, and personnel for the inspection effort and processing information brought back by inspectors or otherwise obtained.

5.   Critiquing/feedback: Continuing assessment of the progress of the inspection and long-term monitoring program and of Iraqi efforts to counter the inspections as a basis for suggesting improvements.

THE LIMITS OF SUCCESS

Despite the advances made by UNSCOM, it was far from perfect. When UNSCOM came to an end after seven and a half years of the most intrusive arms inspection regime ever to be imposed, significant uncertainty remained as to the true extent of the Iraqi weapons program. Astounding revelations—such as those concerning Iraq's biological weapons—continued to arise. Rolf Ekeus, speaking in Washington on June 10, 1997, as he was about to step down from his job, was asked to look ahead at the future of the Iraqi weapons programs and concluded that "this sweet, wonderful, fantastic power [that Iraq feels it gets from these weapons] is why Iraq will not give them up."[12]

UNSCOM suffered throughout its existence, but particularly in the early years, the organizational shortfalls one would expect in an agency that was thrown together with no advanced planning. The problems of policy coordination and programmatic coherence identified by Amy Zegart in her chapter in this volume were exemplified in the way UNSCOM was set up to function. Early inspections in the missile and biological areas were poorly organized and supported. The slowness of UNSCOM in fielding capable biological inspection teams directly contributed to Iraq's successful efforts to hide the true extent of this program. Operational security issues, even after several sharp warnings, were given too low a priority, and Iraq managed to monitor the International Atomic Energy Agency (IAEA) and UNSCOM communications and gain advance warning of upcoming inspections.[13]

UNSCOM also shared with the IAEA the all too ready desire to declare victory and proceed to less intrusive and politically more comfortable monitoring programs. The monitoring program itself was more dependent on Iraqi cooperation and good behavior than most realized at the time. One example is that UNSCOM installed only slightly more than one hundred video cameras to monitor strategic locations where Iraq was known to have produced critical components for its WMD program before the Gulf War. By comparison, large office complexes or shopping centers in the United States and Europe routinely have several hundred cameras to monitor activity. The advantages UNSCOM gained initially in being free of the UN Secretariat and the secretary-general eventually became liabilities as both became prime targets for Iraqi complaints about the coercive measures UNSCOM was using. Eventually the secretary-general, and the Secretariat as a whole, began to echo Iraq's complaints and worked actively to rein in UNSCOM. The tremendous advantage that UNSCOM gained by being able to focus solely on Iraq's weapons of mass destruction and not having to worry about the state of public health in Iraq, infant mortality, malnutrition, the education system, or similar matters made the agency a target in the eyes of the permanent UN bureaucracies that focus on precisely those issues.[14] UNSCOM, hearing in these complaints an echo of the Iraqi propaganda line, became widely blamed for the worsening living standards that the average Iraqi faced after the end of the Gulf War. In short, UNSCOM ultimately ran up against some ingrained organizational interests within the United Nations.

UNSCOM was able to accomplish a great deal because it was an arm of the Security Council, and the Council believed that the success of UNSCOM in disarming Iraq would lead to a larger role for itself. Unfortunately, the euphoria of the post–cold war world was ephemeral, and the separate national interests and rivalries broke apart the unity of support on the Security Council for disarming Iraq. Russia had more than $7 billion dollars in loans to Iraq that would not be repaid until inspections and sanctions came to an end. France had continuing commercial interests in Iraq, particularly in the reconstruction of the Iraqi oil industry. China had never been in favor of a strong Security Council that could intervene in regional disputes. Even the United States, by 1995, placed greater importance on other foreign policy issues, namely, the Middle East peace process and relations with Russia, and was unwilling to let UNSCOM's determination to pursue rigorously its mandate to disarm Iraq lead to crises that might sideline other important issues.

Intelligence sharing also became a major weakness as political support for disarming Iraq eroded. The process of sharing national information and collection capabilities with the international inspection teams in Iraq presented a unique set of problems. Many of the international inspection and support staff were from competing cold war alliances or neutral nations, including one person who had earlier in his career been identified in the press as a KGB officer operating in the United States. Even among those from NATO countries, very few of the permanent UN or IAEA staff had recent experience in their respective national security bureaucracies. The United Nations and IAEA had neither secure communications nor secure document reproduction and storage facilities. Not a single meeting room or office in New York or Vienna met the standards required by the United States and United Kingdom for holding discussions involving sensitive materials. There was a complete lack of "security culture" among the UN and IAEA staff, with neither organization providing even basic security orientation briefings for their staffs at headquarters or, more significantly, for those undertaking inspections. Probably most difficult of all, neither the UN nor IAEA bureaucracies had experience in collecting, assessing, or using sensitive information. Among other things, this meant that the international staff was largely ignorant of the sensitivities of those responsible for national intelligence to matters such as openly discussing sources and methods.

For their part, the national officials providing information were without significant experience in working with UN staff and failed to understand that much of their resistance to compartmentalization and security procedures is rooted in their identity as international civil servants not beholden to any country's government. The UN and IAEA both have as one of their core cultural values that distinctions among staff should not be made on the grounds of nationality—and this was generally held to even during the worst of the cold war days when few had any doubt that the loyalties of Soviet staff ran to Moscow, not to the UN Charter. The very concepts of compartmentalization and "need to know" do not have effective analogues in UN practice.

It understates the problem to say that stereotypes and misunderstandings abounded at the beginning of the Iraq inspections on both sides of this collaboration. That many of these difficulties abated for a while during the course of the inspections is the result of the dedication shown by all involved to the mission of unmasking and eliminating the Iraqi program for weapons of mass destruction and of the experience gained through this pioneering cooperation. Troubles and suspicions, however, remained. Within the United Nations and IAEA, to an extent not fully appreciated at the national level, the inspections in Iraq always existed on a unique and very tenuous base of support, subject to continual questioning both from staff and member states as to whether this type of operation was appropriate. In the lead-up to Desert Storm, there was a significant UN constituency for the view that the international organization's flag was only providing a cover for a U.S. military operation. This view gained strength after the war as sanctions began to make an impact on everyday life in Iraq, and many came to accept Iraq's propaganda that the inspections were only hurting the average Iraqi. With the erosion after 1996 of political support in the Security Council and Secretariat for Iraqi disarmament, these concerns over the extent to which UNSCOM was relying on collaboration with national intelligence outfits gained strength and provided ready ammunition to those that wanted to limit or end UNSCOM.[15]

Faced with Iraq's deception[16] and refusal to comply, what are the chances for success of any coercive nonproliferation system? The short answer is that the UNMOVIC system that was designed to succeed UNSCOM has very little chance of working if Saddam Hussein's regime continues its constant cheating and deception. UNSCOM did not directly detect the Iraqi efforts to develop new missiles, nor did it unearth the previously unknown biological weapons program. Both of these came to light as a result of the defection of two of Saddam's sons-in-law, and given their ultimate fate (they were killed on their return to Iraq), it would be unwise to count on a supply of equally knowledgeable but naively stupid defectors.

UNSCOM itself, before it passed out of existence, declared that confidence in the effectiveness and comprehensiveness of its long-term monitoring system depends on a full knowledge of Iraq's prohibited programs. Effective monitoring requires

> possession by the Commission of a full picture of Iraq's past programs and a full accounting of the facilities, equipment, items, and materials associated with those past programs, in conjunction with full knowledge of the disposition of dual-purpose items currently available to Iraq, the technologies acquired by Iraq in pursuing the past programs, and the supplier networks it established to acquire those elements of the programs that it could not acquire indigenously. . . . Clearly, knowing where to focus effort requires knowledge of what Iraq would have achieved in its past programs. . . . A necessary prerequisite for a comprehensive solution is that Iraq demonstrate a full openness and a manifest willingness to cooperate in all its dealings with the Special Commission.[17]

WHITHER COERCIVE NONPROLIFERATION?

It should now be clear to all that the Iraqi efforts to acquire nuclear, chemical, and biological weapons and missile delivery systems did not end with the Gulf War[18] and that UNSCOM and its successor, UNMOVIC, have not achieved the objectives established in UN Security Council Resolution 687 of eliminating Iraq's WMD capabilities and establishing an ongoing monitoring system that would detect any attempt to start new illegal weapons programs. Iraq freely and repeatedly—both before and after the

Gulf War—has broken international obligations that it accepted not to acquire weapons of mass destruction and has engaged in deceptive strat-agems to defeat international efforts to reveal and destroy such armaments. Even after a decade of the most coercive, intrusive arms inspection regime ever to be imposed on a country, Iraq continues to develop these weapons.

The failure of the international community to impose disarmament with a credible system of verification on Iraq raises fundamental questions about the utility of such an approach. Iraq should have been an easy case. It had invaded two of its neighbors, Iran and Kuwait, in the previous ten years. It had used chemical weapons in clear violation of international agreements, both against its own citizens and against Iranian soldiers. It was known to have carried out political assassinations abroad against its opponents. Its leader has a megalomania complex that invites derision.[19] And it had just lost a war at the hands of an international coalition that included most of its neighbors, leaving it with a devastated economy and military. It would be hard to imagine a regime in a less favorable situation for fending off international demands that it surrender its weapons of mass destruction. Why did the coalition and the United Nations ultimately falter?

The roots of this failure are both conceptual and operational. In hindsight, more may be learned about the future of forcible disarmament from the conceptual errors made by UNSCOM rather than those relating to the operational fulfillment of directives. Although the method used against Iraq to eliminate its WMD capabilities is based on the application of force, it has a strong—and usually overlooked—voluntary component, making the degree of cooperation that the state to be disarmed is expected to provide a pressing concern. Coercion is essentially about changing the other side's mind about the costs and benefits of a particular course of action, not about imposing an outcome militarily.

The cease-fire that ended the Persian Gulf War envisaged that Iraq would provide UNSCOM and the IAEA with a complete list of all of its prohibited weapons, all associated development and manufacturing facilities, and the location of all of these. These would then be eliminated by UNSCOM, and a long-term monitoring system administered by the UN and the IAEA would ensure that Iraq did not rebuild weapons of mass destruction. This might have been an elegant solution to a war that ended with the aggressor still in possession of a vast arsenal of lethal weaponry, except that the required cooperation was not forthcoming from Saddam Hussein and his regime. As events have shown, Iraq successively filed with UNSCOM almost two dozen "full, final, and complete disclosures" of its prohibited weapons—and each one was shown by subsequent events to be false. Iraq's lack of compliance with the weapons inspection process has been the one constant throughout these past ten years.

Without Iraq's acquiescence and minimal cooperation in its own disarming, UNSCOM fell back on two vital tools: economic sanctions and reliance on intelligence supplied by national governments, principally the United States, to make its inspections effective. UNSCOM's mistake was to believe that either of these tools could be maintained for any considerable time in the face of determined Iraqi resistance. Saddam Hussein was easily able to game the system and manipulate perceptions regarding the impact of UN economic sanctions to his own advantage. Most of the world quickly came to believe that the economic sanctions were maintained at the insistence of the United States alone and that they were devastating to Iraqi children. Whether this was true was immaterial; the political effect was the same. Furthermore, normal commercial pressures soon made smuggling both lucrative and effective, and sanctions lost much of their ability to punish the regime. Those involved in securing access to national intelligence data for use in the inspections never viewed this as an activity that could long endure. Unfortunately, the norms, mores, and interests of the two communities (the intelligence services and UN officials) were too different to provide the basis of a stable relationship. In much of the world represented at the United Nations, the CIA is seen as the root of all evil, responsible for a wide range of evils ranging from coups, to drug smuggling, to AIDS. This is an article of faith, not a subject for dispassionate examination. It was apparent from the very beginning that if UNSCOM were dependent on nationally supplied intelligence for a long period of time, the political support in the United Nations for this information sharing would disappear.[20] An equal worry was that if this cooperation did continue for an extended duration, the national intelligence services would begin to use UNSCOM for their own purposes, which might well go beyond the agency's mandate. In short, UNSCOM faced delegitimization as a result of utilizing an essential tool—the intelligence reports it relied on member states to make available.

Absent the consent of the target state, the international community faces the stark choice of whether it will resume the use of force to compel compliance or will compromise—a debate that reportedly occupies the minds of many within the present Bush administration. Searching for historical precedent, in the case of post–World War I Germany, the evidence was unambiguous: German rearmament and remilitarization of the Rhineland was met by temporizing and acceptance, not by enforcement action. Initiatives to ensure Iraq's full cooperation were a mixture of carrots and sticks. The United Nations imposed economic sanctions and import restrictions that would be lifted when Iraq's disarmament was certified by UNSCOM. As sanctions failed to yield cooperation, Iraq's blocking of inspections and even an attempted assassination of former President Bush were met by limited military responses that were clearly below the threshold needed to enforce the will of the international community. In 1998, Iraq unilaterally ended the inspections. Economic sanctions have continued for a decade but pack less punch with each passing year as Iraq has developed a sophisticated sanction-busting strategy, and most of the world grew fatigued with the conflict and doubtful of their utility and moral justification. The tragedy of the terrorist attack on the World Trade Center has led some in the United States to push for a reexamination of the consequences of leaving Iraq free of inspections and with ineffectual economic sanctions in place. However, there is little evidence that other governments are willing to join a military effort to oust Saddam Hussein. An escalation of violence in Israel and the West Bank further complicates American calculations in pressing allies for a change of regime in Baghdad.[21]

Iraq's political will to maintain its weapons of mass destruction was undiminished and perhaps even increased by its Gulf War defeat. The regime was left in control and redeployed the scarce resources of Iraq toward the continued development of weapons of mass destruction. At best, UNSCOM disrupted and delayed Iraq's WMD program, but it did not eliminate Saddam Hussein's aspirations for such weapons or fundamentally reverse its technical capabilities to engineer them. Similar to the treatment of Germany in the interwar period, international actions have dealt with manifestations rather than fundamentals in Iraq. As world politics changed, new threats emerged elsewhere, economic opportunities beckoned in trading goods for Iraqi oil, and Iraq became more skillful in depicting the "unfairness" of the sanctions/inspection regime.

The record of this attempt to reverse a dangerous buildup of a belligerent's arms capabilities solely with the tools of coercive nonproliferation while neglecting the political process that led to proliferation is not encouraging. Buying time is only worthwhile if that time is invested in securing fundamental political change. In neither the case of interwar Germany nor of Iraq was that investment made. The consequences in Germany were World War II. The failure to couple an effective political strategy (in essence, finding a way to remove an uncooperative Iraqi regime) with the efforts of UNSCOM may similarly result in instability and conflict in the Persian Gulf.

It is always hazardous to attempt to predict what governments will do when faced with unpleasant tasks such as disarming a proliferator. It is probably equally foolish to believe that approaches to reversing proliferation that have proved unsuccessful will be abandoned simply because they have not worked in the past. Politics, more often than not, involves making choices among imperfect alternatives.

Even so, it seems unlikely that the UN system will try to adopt a model of coercive disarmament and verification. In the case of Iraq, this was not a role that the IAEA sought but rather one that it accepted only reluctantly. The compelling argument inside the IAEA secretariat and its board of governors was that the alternative to participating in this exercise in coercive disarmament was to let a new UN body, UNSCOM, intrude into the nuclear arena; this was seen as too close to organizational suicide for the IAEA to accept.[22] In the case of the United Nations, Secretary-General Kofi Annan has publicly expressed his unhappiness with "UNSCOM cowboys" and has sought to ensure that any future inspection efforts in Iraq respect the dignity and sovereignty of that state, conforming more closely to UN norms. UNMOVIC has given up seeking national intelligence information, and the providers of such information have ceased to offer it. Coercive disarmament, by its very nature, violates the autonomy of the state being disarmed and hence is an unnatural act for an international organization.

The experience with Iraq leaves the international community with a set of unhappy lessons: Voluntary arms control arrangements may fail to prevent or detect massive violations when the target state is clever and determined to subvert the accords. Military action may stop well short of removing the industrial and technical capabilities needed to support WMD programs and may leave untouched the political will that led a state to seek such capabilities. Finally, coercive disarmament and verification measures, even when backed by economic sanctions and access to national intelligence information, can fail when met by a regime firmly convinced its own interest requires that it maintain a WMD capability.

How will the international community use these lessons to shape future behavior to control proliferation? Certainly there is considerable room to improve voluntary arms control verification regimes. The IAEA safeguards system prior to the Persian Gulf War was surprisingly lax. This was not a secret, but member states did not believe that the threat of undetected proliferation was serious enough to bear the financial and political costs that would need to be incurred to correct these failures. The Iraq experience—and that of North Korea—has gone some way in revising this calculus, and IAEA safeguards are better today than before the Gulf War. Whether they are good enough to uncover clandestine proliferation remains uncertain.[23]

Steps also can be taken toward a more formidable military response to proliferation. Not surprisingly, analysis of the results of the Gulf War has yielded considerable activity in this area. The United States has invested heavily, under the rubric of counterproliferation, in improving its intelligence and offensive operations against WMD targets, and the present Bush administration has justified its national missile defense program on the grounds of responding to proliferation by so-called rogue states.

While there is vast room for improving the capabilities for coercive disarmament and verification operations, few such enhancements have been even proposed, much less taken. The reasons for this lack of action are fairly straightforward. First, coercive disarmament and verification only takes place when all other options have failed. To plan for failure is one of the most difficult of all bureaucratic actions, as it requires acknowledgment that approaches advocated by others may well bear the risk of disastrous consequences. This is not a message that those pressing for voluntary arms control or military action welcome. Second, coercive disarmament and verification has no organizational champions. Arms control bureaucracies and their private sector advocates lobby for more resources and attention. The military services and defense contractors are never short of glossy PowerPoint briefings on new weapon systems that claim to foil the most determined proliferator. The current debate over the necessity for nuclear weapons to use in defeating hardened and deeply buried targets is but one recent indication. One will search long and hard, however, for the vocal advocate of coercive disarmament equipped with a program of training and systems that could make this approach more effective. This despite the record showing that there is great room for improvement in the execution of coercive disarmament. In both cases where this approach has been tried, post–World War I Germany and Iraq, improvisation on the fly was the order of the day. With both operations, their effectiveness declined over time as support weakened and the inspected became smarter about evasion.

It seems far more likely that steps will be taken to refine arms control verification and to sharpen military counterproliferation responses than to hone the performance of future UNSCOM-type coercive disarmament and verification operations. One consequence will be that the next time the international community decides to take up arms to stop a proliferator, the pressure will be intense to "go to Baghdad"—that is, to carry on the conflict to the point of changing the target state's political leadership—rather than to end the conflict early and rely on multilateral coercive disarmament and verification to secure the destruction of WMD capabilities.[24] The unpleasant fact is that the failure of UNSCOM has probably ensured that future conflicts involving WMD proliferation will be more violent, will involve more casualties, and will be harder to terminate.

5

COOPERATIVE INDUCEMENTS
CRAFTING NEW TOOLS FOR NONPROLIFERATION

Rose Gottemoeller

Throughout the cold war, the Kremlin operated a highly effective security network around its nuclear arsenal and associated materials. With the collapse of the Soviet Union, that system, designed for a unitary state with a closed society and closed borders, faced realities that it was ill equipped to manage. In 1990, the Soviet military maintained an estimated 11,052 operational strategic weapons, with as many in reserve and an inactive stockpile. It was estimated that an additional 21,700 nonstrategic warheads existed. Complicating matters further, these weapons were, following the breakup, spread across four different states.[1] And warheads were only part of the problem. While precise estimates are difficult, even today the former Soviet states are thought to possess more than 1,500 tons of weapons-usable material, of which an estimated 700 tons is locked up within the Russian nuclear arsenal. The remaining material is maintained in a variety of other forms ranging from metal weapons components to impure scrap. These materials are stored in an estimated four hundred buildings at more than fifty sites. While 99 percent of the weapons-usable material is now located in Russia, civilian facilities in Belarus, Kazakhstan, Latvia, Ukraine, and Uzbekistan also have quantities of plutonium and highly enriched uranium (HEU) large enough to pose proliferation risks.[2] Financial pressures placed intense burdens on the ten so-called closed nuclear cities within the former

127

Soviet Union, where in excess of 100,000 trained nuclear weapons work-ers, including 3,000–5,000 highly skilled designers and engineers, faced an uncertain future.[3] In 1991, under the leadership of Senators Sam Nunn and Richard Lugar, the United States embarked on an ambitious program to assist Russia in the progressive downsizing of its enormous nuclear weapons arsenal amassed during the cold war. Ten years later, the original program and those that followed it have achieved impressive results: Belarus, Kazakhstan, and Ukraine returned nearly four thousand nuclear weapons to Russia; more than five thousand warheads have been deactivated and more than one thousand missiles and missile launchers have been destroyed; many weapon and material storage facilities have received security and safety enhancements; more than one hundred tons of HEU have been purchased from Russia; and there have been other ini-tiatives helping to provide Russian weapons scientists with employment in peaceful projects.

Within U.S. national security circles, the risk of nuclear prolifera-tion was seen as a dramatic new threat with the end of the cold war. The traditional strategy of denying would-be proliferators access to the pre-cursors of nuclear weapons, viewed in isolation, seemed an inadequate mechanism to ensure the nonproliferation of nuclear technology. Moreover, the collapse of the Soviet Union presented unforeseen chal-lenges to policymakers who had otherwise proved remarkably innovative in devising ingenious solutions to problems rooted in the legacy of the cold war.

This chapter examines in detail threat reduction initiatives and inducements as a mechanism for nonproliferation, considering first the accomplishments of the programs and the degree to which they have mapped out "routine" approaches that might be applied globally and to other functional areas. It will explore how the various nuclear threat reduction programs have transformed U.S. nonproliferation policy. It will then survey the barriers to such initiatives that have emerged both domestically and internationally, which have hobbled attempts at deep-er cooperation. Following a discussion of specific examples, the chapter considers some of the large policy issues that will have to be addressed before widening cooperative programs. It also explores what policy approaches might most successfully encourage the transfer of such pro-grams to other regions of the world. Although the chapter tends to emphasize the U.S.-Russian experience because the greatest volume of activity has taken place in the Russian Federation, examples from other countries are used as well.

THE TRANSFORMATION OF
NONPROLIFERATION POLICY

Cooperation inside the old Soviet nuclear and military complex has been pivotal in the broad transformation of nonproliferation policy in the past decade. The United States and the Russian Federation, together with other post–Soviet states, have worked together for two main purposes: to prevent the leakage of nuclear weapons, material, and know-how out of the old Soviet arsenal and to enable the steady elimination of strategic weapons platforms under the Strategic Arms Reduction Treaty (START), at a time when Russia and its neighbors could ill afford to sustain the process to meet treaty commitments on their own. In serving those purposes, the United States, Russia, and other countries involved have gained a bonus in that they now have extraordinarily detailed knowledge of how to handle jointly particular nuclear security problems and weapon system elimination techniques. The extent of cooperation in these areas would simply have been unthinkable a decade ago.[4]

Controversy has accompanied the cooperation, however, and has shaped it. From its first days, the program was buffeted by domestic political requirements. The earliest projects, for example, had a "buy American" provision that enabled them to gain support on Capitol Hill but engendered real hostility from the Russians. Moscow came to believe that the program was producing better results for U.S. private sector contractors than for Russian missile and nuclear sites. Moreover, there have been those in the U.S. Congress who from the outset have linked the programs to U.S. efforts to downsize and restructure its own cold war military complex. The United States has trouble enough bankrolling its own base closures and officer retraining programs, the argument goes. Why should it pay for the Russians to do so? If Americans pay for Russian downsizing, is that not just a hidden subsidy to their military modernization programs? They have scarce resources; why should they not be forced to spend them on closing bases rather than building new weapons?

In point of fact, the Russians had so few resources for defense spending in the first decade after the Soviet breakup that they neither downsized their weapons complex nor modernized it. The result was a slow implosion that yielded its own significant dangers, particularly as the physical infrastructure protecting nuclear weapons and materials crumbled. Whereas the Soviet Union had spent significant funds on maintaining the gates, guns, and guards at these facilities, later years saw the gates fall away and the guards descend into undisciplined behavior as the quality of their training and equipment collapsed. In the winter of 1998, for example, following the previous August's ruble crisis, guards at certain nuclear facilities refused to leave their guardhouses to patrol because they had no boots or winter clothing. Indeed, at some facilities they refused to come to work at all because the guardhouses were without heat or electricity.

The dangers to nuclear security inherent in the severe Russian economic crisis somewhat dampened early objections to the programs, but criticism of them has remained a constant feature of the annual budget cycle on Capitol Hill. Every year produces a crop of reports from Congress's General Accounting Office focusing on issues raised about the programs by congressmen, senators, and their staffs.[5]

In April 2002, the executive branch sought relief from congressional constraints on the programs by proposing a permanent waiver of the legislative requirement, enacted in the original language of Nunn-Lugar, that the president certify annually the Russians' intent to fulfill their commitments to arms control treaties. The Bush administration had hesitated to certify Russian performance in this regard, expressing concern that Moscow might be maintaining covert biological and chemical weapons programs. Thus far, Congress has not acquiesced to a permanent waiver. As Congressman Mac Thornberry said, "A blanket waiver removes some of the leverage we have to make sure Russia complies with the intended purposes of these funds."[6]

The constant congressional criticism has led to other restrictions on the programs. Since the mid-1990s, for example, the Department of Defense has been statutorily forbidden to engage in any defense conversion activities using U.S. government funds. It also has been prohibited from constructing officer housing or engaging in military retraining programs, these activities being a particular lightning rod for those in Congress dissatisfied with the process of base closure and officer retraining in the United States.[7] The programs have been most successful with Congress when they have made reference to the hard security needs of the United States. Hence the Department of Defense program to accelerate the elimination of nuclear launchers in the START I context has been couched as a way to diminish the strategic nuclear threat to the United States. At the same time, it is portrayed as being in the Russian national interest because it relieves Moscow of the cost burden of START-mandated eliminations at a time when the launchers might be close to posing an operational danger, contaminating their surroundings or even exploding if they remain in deployment. The program has come to be called Cooperative Threat Reduction—it responds to threats in a way that serves the interests of both countries.

There are, however, tensions in this approach. The Russians have from time to time objected to the notion that the crumbling of their nuclear weapons complex, which they are trying hard to shrink in an orderly way, is a threat. Threat reduction has had an impact as well at the negotiating table, for it has tended to relegate Russia to the role of an aid recipient, not a full partner.

The issue first surfaced in the late 1990s, when the Clinton administration obtained funds from Congress for an "Expanded Threat Reduction Initiative" (ETRI), and went to the Group of Eight (G-8) to gain additional resources for this program. The Russians, who are participants in the G-8, objected to the suggestion that there may somehow be an expanded threat, although the name referred to efforts to solicit contributions from a larger group of countries rather than a bigger threat. The Russians nevertheless strove to have the initiative's name adjusted to "Nonproliferation and Disarmament Cooperation Initiative" in the G-8 context.

In 2002, this problem was addressed more completely when the G-8 established the "Global Partnership against the Spread of Weapons and Materials of Mass Destruction." The focus here has been on engaging the G-8 countries equally in threat reduction cooperation, with each responsible for making a contribution to the ten-year effort. Russia has proudly proclaimed its intention, as a partner, to contribute $2 billion.

The threat reduction approach has succeeded best when the Russians have faced an actual security crisis in one of their nuclear installations. The Luch facility near Moscow, which produces and stores certain types of weapons-usable nuclear material, opened up for cooperation after several Luch employees were caught stealing small amounts plutonium in 1992. The incident was a wake-up call for the Ministry of Atomic Energy (MinAtom, for short) and led to an extensive and successful joint effort to upgrade physical security and personnel reliability at the facility.[8] Likewise, after an unbalanced young sailor rushed onto a nuclear submarine and took its crew hostage at gunpoint in 1997, the Russian Navy decided that it urgently needed to take steps to safeguard weapons facilities at submarine bases. This decision has resulted in a number of successful enhancements in the monitoring and protection of nuclear weapon facilities maintained by the navy.[9]

A country must have its eyes open to the dangers that can erupt if its nuclear facilities are subject to thievery from insiders or hostile penetration by terrorists, enemies, or madmen. As long as its leaders insist that there is no threat or, alternatively, that it can handle the threat alone, it will be unlikely to grant foreigners access to its most secret installations, the nuclear weapons production compounds and deployment ranges. The severe crisis that beset the country's nuclear complex after the Soviet Union's breakup was the eye-opener for Russians.

It is worth emphasizing that, for all its complaints and concerns, Congress actually steadily expanded the budget for such threat reduction programs throughout the 1990s. The original Department of Defense program was not a direct budget appropriation but simply congressional language giving the program the right to rechannel funds from other places in the defense budget—an approach that sorely affected its popularity with the rest of the Pentagon. By the mid-1990s, however, the program had proved itself sufficiently to acquire a direct budget appropriation, which has been steady at approximately $400 million per year over the past five years. These funds must be added to those of the Department of Energy, which saw its budget for threat reduction work rise to surpass $300 million in direct appropriations in fiscal year 2001. Likewise, the Department of State has been spending about $50 million per year on the International Science and Technology Center and other programs. When President Bush submitted his FY02 budget request, he cut Department of Energy programs by $100 million, but Congress acted to restore $70 million of that. Following the September 11 attacks, the Bush administration and Congress cooperated in a supplemental budget process that resulted in an FY02 budget of more than $1 billion for the Department of Energy programs alone. The department's budget for FY03 for these programs also exceeded $1 billion.[10]

Given this combination of intense scrutiny and strong budgetary support from Congress, what sort of success can be predicted for efforts to transform these bilateral programs into a new tool for nonproliferation policy worldwide? Will the United States have the political will to expand the experience beyond Russia and the newly independent (formerly Soviet) states to new countries of proliferation risk? Can U.S.-Russian collaboration in eliminating weapons of mass destruction be extended to developing new strategic cooperation between the two powers? Many specialists believe that the intimate knowledge developed through the process of American and Russian specialists working together will be easily accepted as a template for solving other nonproliferation problems. Others believe that there is a particular quality to the cooperation between the United States and the former Soviet states, born of the long-standing superpower relationship at the negotiating table and in treaty implementation settings, that is unique and cannot readily be translated to other regions and situations.

SETTING COMMON DEFINITIONS

While the joint work on nonproliferation often goes under the name Cooperative Threat Reduction (CTR), or the Nunn-Lugar program, it should be noted that CTR only refers to the START launcher eliminations and other projects undertaken by the Department of Defense in cooperation with the Russian Ministry of Defense, especially. A range of programs directed at the problems of the nuclear weapons complex, especially the protection and control of and accounting for nuclear-weapons-usable materials, are the responsibility of the U.S. Department of Energy and do not fall under the CTR heading. Likewise with the brain drain programs managed by the State Department, which are associated with the International Science and Technology Center in Moscow and the Ukrainian Science and Technology Center in Kiev. This chapter therefore uses the general term "threat reduction" when referring to the Defense, State, and Energy Department programs.

Also to be considered are related types of work that often fall under the "lab-to-lab" rubric. These are projects conducted in cooperation between the Department of Energy and Ministry of Atomic Energy weapons laboratories. Often begun as part of an effort to prevent a brain drain from the former Soviet weapons laboratories, they have grown in the past decade to serve broader purposes, such as engaging weapons scientists in the development of technologies that will enhance verification of arms control agreements (START; the Comprehensive Test Ban Treaty [CTBT]) or enabling monitoring of undertakings such as the Mayak fissile material storage facility.

THE HISTORY AND SCOPE OF THREAT REDUCTION

Threat reduction cooperation has provided a number of practical, workable solutions for proliferation and arms reduction problems, from launchers and deployment sites through warheads to nuclear material safekeeping and disposition. Since 1992, when the Nunn-Lugar program was first launched, the efforts have evolved into a full-spectrum approach that tries to wrestle with every phase of the arms reduction process.

LAUNCHER ELIMINATION

The initial focus of the CTR program was the problem of denuclearization of newly independent Ukraine, Kazakhstan, and Belarus, where nuclear weapons had remained after the breakup of the Soviet Union. This provides a good example of the high-profile political attention that the threat reduction initiatives have received from the U.S. executive branch. The most famous episode was in Ukraine, where Secretary of Defense William Perry personally presided, during several trips, over the removal and elimination of a missile deployment site, including destruction of silos. This process was followed by the remediation of the site and, eventually, its return to agriculture with a highly symbolic planting and harvest of sunflower seeds.

Symbolism aside, Perry's concern for the project was important to its continued momentum. The salience of the effort ensured that Ukraine and the United States worked together fairly quickly to develop the critical procedures, from contracting through the physical work with the launchers and silos. Even with this level of attention, however, many frustrations were encountered early on in wrestling with the bureaucratics on both sides and with the uncertain legal situation in Ukraine. In other countries where cooperative demilitarization of major weapons systems might be tried, similar situations could be encountered, which means that such projects would be difficult to get started without careful guidance by senior officials. Once past the initial shoals, however, the working-level routines become established, and steady progress becomes possible.

WARHEAD TRANSPORTATION

Ukraine also was an early example of cooperation in the transportation of warheads. Although the United States never was involved in actually handling or moving the approximately 1,900 warheads that eventually left Ukraine for elimination in Russia, it did provide railcars and related equipment to help facilitate the process and hasten its completion. In addition to this transportation assistance, warhead work has involved efforts by the departments of Defense and Energy to provide enhanced protection of, control of, and accounting for warheads at Ministry of Defense sites.

This work has encountered barriers in Russian unwillingness to allow the United States access to the warhead sites for audit and examination purposes. For instance, the U.S. government, as a condition of assistance, retains the right to examine the on-site use of equipment and materiel provided for warhead transportation projects. Because Moscow has so far been unwilling to provide for audits and examinations at warhead sites, this work has not yet gone forward. This kind of hesitation is likely to be encountered at highly secret facilities of any country where cooperative work is proposed, but the requirement is an important aspect of U.S. contracting procedure, especially so in countries where corruption may be a problem.

MATERIAL PROTECTION, CONTROL, AND ACCOUNTING

Although warhead protection was a difficult objective, the material protection, control, and accounting (MPC&A) programs have been picking up speed in recent years. Evidence of this can be found in the larger number of facilities that are now open to joint work. In 1993, when the program was first getting under way, it was impossible to work at sites under the purview of the Ministry of Atomic Energy or the Ministry of Defense. The first site where U.S. and Russian specialists collaborated to bring weapons-usable nuclear material under greater security was the Kurchatov Institute, a facility controlled by the Russian Academy of Sciences. Since that time, and partially in response to the Luch episode described above, access to sites has improved somewhat, and cooperative work is going on at more than thirty sites both inside and outside the Russian defense complex. The United States and Russia have worked out a fairly standard set of measures to improve the security of weapons-usable material at these sites. First, the two sides conduct a joint survey of the facility and decide what needs to be done on an urgent basis. They proceed immediately with these "quick fix" measures, which usually include rapid upgrades to the physical security of the site: perhaps cutting foliage away from the facility fence line, shoring up the fence itself, replacing wooden doors with metal ones, and placing bars over windows or bricking them up. After these urgent measures are completed, the team proceeds with longer-term efforts such as putting in electronic sensors and alarms, closed-circuit TV cameras, and personnel access control systems.

Once the physical security of the site is improved, the two parties begin to work on personnel training and the installation of equipment to improve material control and accounting. Often, facility managers are not sure exactly how much weapons-usable material is at the facility owing to the vagaries of Soviet-era accounting practices. One of the goals of the U.S.-Russian cooperation, therefore, has been to create a "nuclear material security culture" that embraces modern standards of accounting and control.

These steps by this time have become routinized and could easily be fashioned into "solution sets" for MPC&A problems in other countries. In this context, however, certain issues should be mentioned. Most prominent is the problem of sustainability—once the joint work is completed and the Americans depart, will the Russian team continue to maintain and operate the equipment and sustain high standards of protection, control, and accounting? This problem came to prominence after the 1998 ruble crash, when cash flow problems at some of the plants became so severe that they were unable to pay their electricity bills, and the electronic sensor systems installed cooperatively were simply turned off. The program has tackled this problem in several ways. First, a "fail-safe" approach has been instituted whereby, if an electronic system fails or is turned off, there is a default to a brute-force physical security measure. For example, electronic sensors on windows are backed up by metal window bars. Second, a greater number of Russian companies have been certified to maintain and replace the systems, and more and more Russian-designed and -built equipment for the projects is being used. If a facility needs a spare part, its procurement is hence much simpler than previously.

Ultimately, the Russians will be responsible for sustaining these improvements, and they will have to decide whether they are going to do so to a high international standard. This issue of what standard to pursue in material protection, control, and accounting is likely to crop up in other settings where nuclear material has been accumulated but international cooperation has been at a minimum.

FISSILE MATERIAL STORAGE

Another large-scale material protection project is the Mayak fissile material storage facility. Located in Ozersk in the South Urals, the Mayak site is being constructed through a Department of Defense-MinAtom joint project. Once completed, the facility will hold fifty metric tons of pluto-nium extracted from Russian nuclear weapons. If a second wing is built, the facility could hold more than one hundred tons. The substance will be placed in canisters and locked down in a highly secure vertical pipe stor-age system. Ultimately, it should be consigned to the plutonium disposition program, but it can remain in this storage site for an extended period of time.[11] One of the issues to be wrestled with in regard to the Mayak stor-age facility is the question of weapons origin. The Soviet Union and the Russian Federation produced many tons of plutonium over the years as a by-product of civilian energy generation. Although weapons-usable, it has never been part of the defense complex. Concerned that the Russian Federation might put this civilian-origin material in the facility and hold on to the material coming out of the weapons complex for future nuclear warhead production, Congress passed a law requiring that the material entering Mayak be certified as "weapons origin."

This requirement has produced some interesting technological solutions that will be discussed in greater detail below. The main point to be made here is that any nonproliferation work conducted interna-tionally with U.S. government funds will be subjected to close con-gressional scrutiny—often with exacting requirements. Although these stipulations are worthy, they can delay or complicate projects. They also point to the need for constant communication between the executive branch and Congress in order to try to take care of such concerns early. In the case of threat reduction cooperation, there are a number of knowl-edgeable congressional staff who can help to work through problems. However, a much larger number of members and staff are hostile to the programs or indifferent, which may pose a significant barrier to expand-ing U.S. government funding beyond its current emphasis on the former Soviet Union.

MATERIAL TRANSPORT AND DISPOSITION

Once the material is protected, the United States and its partners have often moved to further stages, such as preparing it for International Atomic Energy Agency (IAEA) safeguards or for transport to more secure sites or disposition facilities. Ultimately, of course, the goal is to get rid of the material rather than store it in weapons-usable form, but often it must be prepared for very long-term residence in a variety of facilities, some designed for that purpose, as with Mayak, and some not.

An excellent example of such work is the project undertaken at the Aktau chemical combine in Kazakhstan. Aktau was the site at which the Soviet Union produced advanced fuel for its nuclear submarine fleet. When the first U.S. team entered Aktau along with their Kazakhstani partners, they found approximately three hundred tons of spent and fresh fuel rods, which they estimated would contain three tons of ivory-grade plutonium highly suitable for weapons. The fuel rods were not difficult to move or lift; the team assessed that two men with a pickup truck could make off with a considerable number of them. The presence of the material was especially worrying because Aktau is a Caspian seaport town located about two hundred kilometers north of Iran. The Iranians, the team was aware, were preparing to open a consulate there.

The team rapidly undertook a project that upgraded the basic physical protection of the site. When that was completed, it proceeded to place the fuel rods in cans with highly radioactive waste material packed around them, which made the cans heavy and dangerous to move. When the cans were filled, they were locked down in the fuel pool at the site and placed under IAEA safeguards. The cans will eventually be transported to a more secure site within Kazakhstan, probably to be put into dry storage.

A similar project was undertaken for the North Korean fuel rods in its nuclear installation at Yongbyon. Under that effort, approximately 8,000 fuel rods were canned and locked down under IAEA safeguards. Unfortunately, once North Korea moved to withdraw from the Treaty on the Non-Proliferation of Nuclear Weapons (NPT) in early 2003, the fuel was removed from the canisters, and the North Koreans started to reprocess it. Nevertheless, this canning project demonstrates that threat reduction initiatives have already been implemented in a setting beyond the former Soviet Union.

Ultimately, drawing a lesson from the North Korean episode, the material must be permanently eliminated. The United States and Russia have already been working for nearly a decade to dispose of HEU from the former Soviet nuclear arsenal through the so-called highly enriched uranium deal. HEU as a weapons material has the advantage of being easily transformed into a saleable product, low-enriched uranium, which can be fabricated into civilian power plant fuel and sold on the open market. That is the concept that drove the HEU deal. HEU is down-blended to low-enriched uranium in Russia, transported to the United States, and sold, an elegantly enterprising solution to a proliferation problem, even if it has caused serious perturbations in the market for civilian fuel.[12]

Plutonium is much more difficult to dispose of in such a direct commercial way. For that reason, the United States and Russia have agreed to a strategy whereby some plutonium will be fabricated into mixed oxide fuel (MOX) and burned in commercial power plants. This effort will require government funding to implement since commercial power companies would be unlikely to alter their plants to burn MOX unless the project were supported by subsidy.

More recently, some ideas have emerged for involving commercial firms in the plutonium disposition effort or for storing the material for a long period of time, pending development of new types of plutonium reactors. These reactors, probably twenty years away from operation, would be "proliferation resistant" because they would not breed more plutonium in the process of consuming it as fuel. These ideas are worthy of study because the United States and Russia have had some difficulty in bringing other countries, particularly in the G-8, into the plutonium disposition arrangements, sometimes out of resistance to burning MOX, sometimes out of real or contrived political or budgetary constraints. Although public sector funding will continue to be needed, commercial involvement may take some of the pressure off government budgets.

Although no other country will have nearly the volume of material to eliminate that the United States and Russia do, the applicability of such disposition efforts to other countries is clear. For example, research reactors in other countries are often fueled by HEU and store small amounts of highly enriched uranium on-site. The United States already has an international program, the Reduced Enrichment for Research and Test Reactor initiative, designed to provide incentives to countries to convert their research reactors to low-enriched uranium and dispose of the HEU. Currently, Russia, the United States, and the IAEA are working together to launch a similar procedure for the sixteen Soviet-built research reactors outside of Russia, many of them in Eastern Europe. The 2002 withdrawal of HEU from the Vinca reactor in Yugoslavia back to Russia is an initial example of such an effort.

From protection of sites through transportation to elimination of both weapon systems and nuclear materials, the United States, Russia, and other countries in the region have, by necessity, created a number of workable "solution sets" to existing proliferation problems. Although practical difficulties remain in each category, they nevertheless have enough of an implementation history that their potential in other settings is clear. Less visible, however, has been the work that has been done to address pressing new problems, some of which also may be applicable to other regions.

Circumventing the Barriers to Cooperation

The United States and Russia have been working together on some challenging nonproliferation and arms control problems, often through lab-to-lab efforts. Certain collaborations were spurred by specific congressional requirements such as those demanding weapons-origin plutonium only at the Mayak storage facility. These projects have involved both technology and the development of cooperative methodologies or procedures.

In the Mayak case, technology has been at the forefront. The two countries have been working together to develop a sensor that would enable an inspector to determine that a container holds nuclear material that is of weapon origin but would not enable that person to determine the exact attributes of the weapon in question. Neither country is willing to give up that kind of information, which is the most highly secret weapon-design knowledge that either possesses. The two countries have already been able to demonstrate a sensor that can identify a number of attributes of material in a canister but would then give a monitor no more information than a red-light/green-light signal. If plutonium oxide were present in a can, for example, and that were one of the attributes indicating weapons origin, the monitor would receive a green-light signal.

Several attributes have to be used in such a case, along with careful procedures, such as testing the sensor against a control canister just prior to its use in an actual monitoring event. Nevertheless, U.S. and Russian experts have already been able to demonstrate this "information barrier technology" to their mutual satisfaction, and further sensor development is currently going forward in Russia. Joint technology development of this type may be very useful in future arms control undertakings where maintenance of secrets is justifiable and critical for the countries involved. Monitoring of warhead elimination, for example, is a challenge—one in which successful information barrier technology is likely to be important—that the United States and Russia have been contemplating in strategic arms reduction efforts.

Even absent new technologies, methodology and procedure refinement will be vital to future arms control and nonproliferation regimes as they move into challenging new territory. U.S. and Russian experts have been considering the application of existing technology to intriguing new problems. For instance, neither the United States nor Russia is likely to be willing to allow the routine presence of foreign inspectors in highly secret facilities such as warhead plants.

To resolve this problem, U.S. and Russian experts have been developing software that would allow an inspector to take a virtual tour of a facility such as a warhead plant even prior to setting foot in it. Inspectors can pinpoint precisely where they need to go and what they need to do and convey it to the other side in advance, to aid them in site preparation. In this way, the United States and Russia have begun to work out the conceptual steps that will have to be mutually agreed before either will be willing to proceed with inspections in highly sensitive facilities.

Multilateral projects have been undertaken as well. For example, the IAEA has been working with the United States and Russia to develop procedures that would enable the two countries to initiate IAEA monitoring procedures at facilities in their nuclear complexes. This work is being undertaken in preparation for the so-called Trilateral Initiative, an unprecedented U.S.-Russian-IAEA effort to implement safeguards on the territory of these two nuclear weapon states under the NPT.

CONSTRAINTS ON GENERALIZATION

Threat reduction and related activities have applications in other regional and policy settings. Difficulties in generalizing the principles and best practices derived from individual projects to other settings have already been mentioned. This section considers the more "umbrella" constraints that would apply across the board to any attempt to foster such cooperation beyond the former Soviet states. Some of them are related to the peculiar nature of the threat reduction approach; others are related to the state of policy development in a particular region. Both sets of limitations will have to be considered in any effort to expand the application of these methods to a broader set of nonproliferation problems.

RECIPROCITY ISSUES

The United States and Russia have now enjoyed nearly a decade of cooperation on Nunn-Lugar projects developed, among other things, to accelerate Russian launcher eliminations under the START I treaty. The

United States has become somewhat of an "industrial partner" in Russian START eliminations, gaining access and understanding beyond what would have been expected from the START verification regime alone.

This enhanced access has been both prudent and necessary in order to ensure that U.S. assistance to the Russian Federation has been wisely and properly spent. The right to conduct audits and examinations, as mentioned, is a critical requirement when the United States agrees to extend assistance to any country. U.S. engineering companies have taken on the role of prime contractor in many of these projects. Although the companies are private entities, their contracting requirements with the government have given a degree of transparency to the processes of launcher elimination at Russian facilities; furthermore, the very "routinization" of their presence at the facilities has in many cases grown into a close working relationship with their Russian counterparts.

Because of this tight working relationship on Russian START eliminations, the United States enjoys a somewhat higher level of confidence in what is going on in Russian facilities than Russia has enjoyed in U.S. facilities. It is not that Russian understanding of American START eliminations is inadequate: both sides continue to agree that the START verification techniques and procedures provide adequate assurance that eliminations have actually occurred.

The nature of the cooperation as assistance justifies this difference, but it also places a barrier in the way of more general application of the transparency techniques developed in the course of weapons elimination. As long as the United States is "paying to view" how its assistance is being used, there will be little justification for and considerable resistance to introducing the same techniques into U.S. settings. Congress, in particular, might object to such steps and might even pass measures to keep them in check. This is a particular obstacle to using the lessons learned from Nunn-Lugar in future START verification protocols or in future confidence-building and transparency regimes designed to complement accelerated unilateral reductions.

This difficulty will emerge in any country or region where the cooperation is associated with a U.S. assistance program. If the United States is wholly paying for the measures, such as a material protection, control, and accounting program, then an argument can be made, and frequently is in political forums such as Congress, that no reciprocity is due. However, this may be a hard sell for the countries involved, especially any that have complained in the past about the "discriminatory nature" of U.S. nonproliferation policy.

Several means might be developed to deal with the reciprocity issue, like fitting threat reduction measures into existing international cooperation, perhaps through the IAEA. The physical protection of nuclear materials is currently part of the IAEA's stable of activities, and such protective measures provide an example of the IAEA responsibilities that could perhaps be renewed and strengthened by drawing on the recent experience in the former Soviet Union. Another course might be to establish a number of demonstrations at U.S. facilities to which foreign partners might be invited and that might be used as training sites as the cooperation develops. This approach would clearly represent a change of profile for the U.S. facilities involved and would require that at least a portion of the sites be set aside for more simplified access by foreigners.

"LACK OF FIT" WITH EXISTING REGIMES

Since the nuclear testing in India and Pakistan in May 1998, the United States has been trying to work out effective policies toward these two countries without undermining the existing NPT regime. In the Clinton administration, Deputy Secretary of State Strobe Talbott engaged in a series of discussions that were aimed at halting the move toward weaponizing and making operational nuclear arms in the region. He also emphasized trying to get the two countries to sign the CTBT and begin negotiations on a Fissile Material Cutoff Treaty (FMCT).

While these diplomatic efforts had not yet borne fruit, Washington was extremely cautious about engaging the Indians or Pakistanis in activities bearing on the safety or security of their emerging nuclear forces. The concern was that certain types of cooperation would violate the NPT's prohibition on assisting nonnuclear states. Such activities, in other words, could create a de facto recognition of nuclear status for the two countries before the diplomatic process had extracted enough assurances from them about the limits that would be placed on further nuclear development.

By the final days of the Clinton administration, however, the diplomacy had not advanced significantly. The new Bush team embarked on its own efforts to resolve this problem, especially following the events of September 11. Whatever approach is considered, however, the intense regional enmities that led the two states to develop a nuclear strike capability in the first place constitute a barrier to an outside power like the United States trying to commence discussion of threat reduction-type activities with the Indians and Pakistanis. This barrier may be breached in several ways, but such solutions will require significant attention from the governments in all three capitals. One solution might be to consider a limited step, such as discussions of MPC&A in the framework of a discussion of best practices, beginning with exchanges of briefings between experts. Such an interaction might be begun without broaching the larger issue of non-NPT status, but because it would engage influential technical elites it also could pave the way for more fruitful discussion at higher levels.

For any approach, if the focus is on trying to make progress with threat reduction-type activities, they likely will have to be de-linked from broader issues of principle concerning the NPT regime. Such a tactic has actually proved quite effective in the U.S.-Russian context, where cooperation on Nunn-Lugar projects has been regarded as in the wider national security interest of both countries. Taking this perspective, threat reduction has therefore been treated separately from issues of concern between Washington and Moscow, such as the expansion of NATO and the bombing of Kosovo. In even the most difficult periods, talks about nuclear security have been permitted to continue and have not been considered to compromise other principles.

COLLISION WITH LARGER POLITICAL PROBLEMS

Where threat reduction cooperation is not established, however, larger political problems can have a profound impact on its development. An example of this is the collision in the late 1990s between efforts to establish material protection, control, and accounting cooperation with China and the concerns that arose in Washington about the possibility of illicit technology transfers, first involving satellites, then warhead design information. The warhead case, involving an alleged Chinese spy at a U.S. nuclear weapons laboratory, stopped cooperation between U.S. and Chinese laboratories in a decisive way. U.S. and Chinese lab-to-lab cooperation on material protection had begun very slowly, guided by caution on both sides.[13] The American side had been concerned to ensure that the cooperation stayed in step with wider U.S. nonproliferation policy as well as with extensive guidelines on security matters, and it instituted a special interagency review process to that end. The Chinese side, historically cautious about conveying evidence of a nuclear complex less well developed than that of the United States and Russia, was resistant on general principle. However, in 1997 and 1998, the two sides slowly developed a project involving a demonstration of MPC&A technologies and procedures. This demonstration took place at an institute in Beijing in the summer of 1998, and the two sides widely assessed it to be a positive experience. Incipient cooperative activity in fact resulted in an invitation to the U.S. team to visit the Chinese nuclear complex city of Minyiang. It was among the first Western delegations to visit the city. As a result of the success of the demonstration, the two sides began preparing new projects for collaboration.

Cooperation was quickly halted on the heels of allegations in Washington in late 1998 and 1999 that U.S. weapons laboratory personnel had been involved in passing secrets regarding warhead production to the Chinese. This spy scandal created a barrier to further lab-to-lab activity at the same time that it was becoming a larger political problem between the United States and China.[14] One can imagine any number of political problems, such as the bombing of the Chinese embassy in Belgrade, that could have halted the cooperation during this period. Unlike the Russian case, which, as mentioned, is deemed to be in the national security interest of both countries, threat reduction cooperation with China was at a fledgling stage. Both countries were tentative about the program, and neither was willing to defend its benefits to national security in a crisis.

Unless the partners in the cooperation believe that it has a mutual national security benefit, such as resolving a "loose nukes" problem, larger issues of concern are likely to continue to interrupt progress episodically. Incorporating threat reduction into already established regimes, as the United States and Russia did with the START elimination efforts, may be one way to insulate it from the vicissitudes of bilateral relations. Another way may be to ensure that, while the cooperation has ongoing guidance from government officials involved at a working level, it also gains high-level blessing, perhaps in a summit context. It seems clear, however, that the breakup of the Soviet nuclear arsenal created a particularly urgent security rationale for international cooperation that will probably not be relevant in other settings. Stable cooperation, therefore, is likely to require both attention from on high and bureaucratic commitment at a lower level.

Demand for Quick Fixes, Quick Results

In response to congressional demands that there be clear metrics of success for the programs and clear exit strategies, that is, a definition of when and how the goals of the programs will be accomplished so that U.S.

involvement can end, those cooperative programs that support projects producing concrete results within a short time period have enjoyed a larger share of the threat reduction budget. Programs devoted to the elimination of weapons or to securing nuclear material have thus tended to prosper, while programs focused on less clearly definable problems have grown slowly or have been subject to budget cuts. Nowhere has this been more clear than in the contrast between the Department of Energy's MPC&A program and the same department's brain drain programs, the Initiatives for Proliferation Prevention and the Nuclear Cities Initiative.

Between fiscal year 1999 and 2001, for example, the MPC&A program grew from an $135 million annual budget to $173 million. In FY02 Congress rewarded it with a $190 million appropriation, despite a cut the Bush administration requested that would have brought the program back to $138 million. With the supplemental funding that came after September 11, the total FY02 appropriation for MPC&A eventually reached $293 million.

The "brain drain" programs have had to chart a much rockier budget path. In contrast to MPC&A, for example, the Initiatives for Proliferation Prevention program has hovered below $25 million, with a small rise from $22.5 million in FY99 to $24.5 million in FY01. The Nuclear Cities Initiative, which was the subject of critical General Accounting Office (GAO) reports in FY00 and FY01, experienced more fluctuating budgetary fortunes. From $7.5 million in FY00, it went to $27.5 million in FY01 and then was cut to $6 million in the FY02 Bush budget request, following a second critical GAO report.[15] The final FY02 spending plan, including the supplemental appropriation, combined the two programs into a single budget line, the "Russian Transition Initiatives." The resulting budget was $57 million for both programs.

The Nuclear Cities Initiative, like the Initiatives for Proliferation Prevention, fell victim to criticism that its goals were ill defined and that it had neither clear benchmarks for success nor clearly defined contingency plans for wrapping up a project if it were determined to be ineffective. Both programs strive to ensure that nuclear weapon scientists and engineers do not become tempted to sell their knowledge and talents to countries for which proliferation is a serious concern—a difficult mission because it is tough to prove that a scientist kept safely at work in his Russian nuclear city might otherwise have moved to Iraq.[16] From the earliest days of Cooperative Threat Reduction, however, working on the human element in the breakup of the Soviet nuclear arsenal has been a consistent program goal, despite its unpopularity in Congress.

Both the Nuclear Cities Initiative and the Initiatives for Proliferation Prevention program have taken steps to improve their management, clarify the goals they seek to achieve, and describe their exit strategies. In the case of the latter, this has amounted to focusing unequivocally on projects that have commercialization potential and bringing in Western companies from the outset as coinvestors. If a project does not "graduate" to commercial status within a defined period of time, it loses its program support.

The Nuclear Cities Initiative has begun to focus squarely on the goal of shutting down nuclear warhead facilities in the Russian Federation and ensuring that scientists and engineers who lose their jobs in the weapons complex find viable nondefense employment. In that sense, the Nuclear Cities Initiative is different from the brain drain programs that have gone before it. Both Initiatives for Proliferation Prevention and the International Science and Technology Center, which is managed by the Department of State, are programs that have focused on keeping scientists at work within their weapons research and production facilities. Even if they move eventually into commercial projects, those projects are sited in weapons laboratories and plants, where they remain under the management control of the directors of those facilities. The directors naturally prefer programs that keep their nuclear weapons specialists in place in case of future necessity.

The Nuclear Cities Initiative, by contrast, is the first of the brain drain programs aiming to accelerate the shutdown of nuclear weapons facilities and to develop employment options for specialists who are leaving the nuclear complex for good. As such, it is less well liked by Russian nuclear managers. Nevertheless, the Ministry of Atomic Energy is committed to the program. As Lev Ryabev, then first deputy minister of atomic energy, said in a speech in Atlanta in March 2001, "it is the logical end of the nuclear arms reduction process," moving the workforce out and transforming the facilities to nonmilitary work.[17]

The brain drain programs are examples of threat reduction efforts that do not lend themselves to easily attainable results, as can be achieved quickly in the elimination of individual weapon platforms. A similar problem affects those projects that require long periods for lead time, construction, or other implementation. For example, in the North Korean case, certain nonproliferation goals, such as canning the plutonium fuel rods at the Yongbyon reactor to prevent further reprocessing, were accomplished in a fairly straightforward way, with little scrutiny or criticism from the U.S. Congress. By contrast, the long-term, large-scale effort to prevent further production of plutonium by replacing the plutonium-generating reactors with light-water reactors faced constant struggle, with a troubled budget process on Capitol Hill and regular difficulties with the foreign partners in the project. Even before the discovery of a uranium enrichment program in North Korea, the Bush administration had raised doubts about the future of the program.

In any country, a project requiring years of funding will be scrutinized sharply and will experience ups and downs in the budget process. It seems clear that projects that accomplish quick results will be supported more easily in the U.S. political system than those that demand years of investment and commitment, and this has clear implications for attempts to replicate the threat reduction experience elsewhere. This balance between quick results and long-term commitment should be weighed carefully as programs are developed to expand such cooperation to new countries or regions.

CONCLUSIONS
OPPORTUNITIES FOR ESTABLISHING THREAT REDUCTION AS A TOOL OF NONPROLIFERATION

While the discussion in this chapter has highlighted the difficulties of transferring the lessons learned and best practices in threat reduction in the former Soviet context to other situations, there are important potential gains to be considered despite the problems involved. All of them require careful work and will be complicated to implement, both bureaucratically and in a larger policy sense. Nevertheless, they may represent real opportunities to advance U.S. policy goals.

SPUR INNOVATION IN THE STRATEGIC RELATIONSHIP

The United States and Russia are developing a revamped framework for strategic cooperation, which will involve a new relationship between nuclear offense and defense and much closer cooperation to maintain that relationship than was possible during the cold war. To highlight the notion of cooperation, the emphasis in U.S.-Russian efforts to present the framework has been on joint partnership and mutual interests rather than assistance.

The threat reduction programs have long embraced this philosophy, and so their experience can serve as a spur to innovation in the strategic relationship. Both the Department of Energy and the Department of Defense have developed industrial partnerships with Russian companies for work inside the Russian missile, submarine, and nuclear facilities. From this cooperation, both sides have learned about the technical and engineering practices of the other and have become accustomed to resolving differences in a mutually satisfactory and effective way. The results of these joint undertakings can inform and facilitate the development of a revised framework for strategic cooperation. In fact, one might argue that the new framework already exists in the guise of threat reduction. The key is to fuse the pragmatic experience with the larger strategic and policy issues. The threat reduction model shows ways to build confidence and mutual interest in missile defense technology development and deployment. Russia and the United States should be able to establish industrial partnerships in at least some areas of the missile defense arena similar to those that have flourished in the realm of threat reduction. In short, the precedent for technology cooperation is well established and needs only be taken into a new, more "strategic" policy environment.

ADVANCE TENTATIVE ENGAGEMENT

Beyond the U.S.-Russian strategic relationship, threat reduction cooperation can be used to engage countries in other regions, countries that have been trying to establish dialogue but have only been able to proceed in a tentative manner. An example of this is U.S. efforts to establish a dialogue on a FMCT with India and Pakistan. The many issues surrounding an FMCT negotiation will be difficult to resolve, but the countries involved may find it in their interest to engage in a preliminary discussion of cooperation on material protection, control, and accounting methods, technologies, and procedures. These discussions could proceed without any reference committing the parties to an FMCT negotiation. However, they would facilitate arriving at a common understanding of the goals of a production cutoff as well as some of the standards that would have to be maintained throughout its implementation.

If the preliminary discussions proceed in a satisfactory manner, then the participants may decide to continue with demonstrations of MPC&A equipment and procedures. The United States would most likely conduct such activities in separate tracks with India and Pakistan, although it is possible that some could take place on a trilateral basis. Trilateral action may have to begin as a "second-track" affair, without formal government participation. Indeed, such collaboration would be so new and so sensitive for all of the governments involved that even a bilateral undertaking might have to begin on a second-track basis. In that case, the governments should be involved in planning and oversight, in order to judge when or if to shift to first-track (government-to-government) cooperation.

INVOLVE THREAT REDUCTION PARTNERS

In certain cases, Washington might find it difficult to be involved in threat reduction cooperation directly because of long-standing tensions or outright distrust of the United States. With these countries, an American administration might consider engaging other partners to launch the cooperation and to resolve questions that may arise. For example, Ukraine and Kazakhstan have been eager to share their experience with threat reduction cooperation and the nonproliferation regime with countries that have been cautious about engaging with the United States and with the nonproliferation regime overall. In South Asia, for example, they may be effective in introducing the technologies and procedures of material protection, control, and accounting to a skeptical India and Pakistan. Ukraine, with its significant nuclear power industry, might link up well with India, while Kazakhstan, which has shared Central Asian security concerns with Pakistan, might be most effective there.

Russia has the most extensive threat reduction program and the widest international diplomatic experience. If the United States and Russia could develop a closely coordinated strategy for extending threat reduction cooperation to other countries, it could be a productive partnership. The two would essentially be joining forces to convey the methods and benefits of this type of cooperation and could help to shape progress if it were thought appropriate to incorporate cooperation more formally into a multilateral framework such as the IAEA. Such a partnership, however, would require a great deal of work to develop a sound consensus on what aspects of their shared experience are transferable to other settings. It also would require more generally a stable and positive relationship between the two countries to enable close interaction and diplomatic coordination. The latter is probably more difficult to achieve.

For that reason, even if Russia and the United States cannot enter into full-scale partnership on extending threat reduction cooperation to other countries, it is important that they continue to expand the cooperation into new substantive areas. For example, the development of new sensor technologies to monitor warhead elimination described earlier is the kind of joint work that will lead to true innovation in arms control verification proceedings in coming years. Thus, the two countries should continue jointly to "push the envelope" with regard to this and other new technological challenges. Such cooperation can be done in a low-key way, on the level of technical dialogue, undisturbed by the fluctuations in the larger political environment. Regardless of profile, though, it will generate important benefits for both countries, whether they are working closely together or holding each other at arm's length.

SEEK NEW ADVOCATES BEYOND THE PROBLEM CASES

In considering how most effectively to transmit the threat reduction experience to other parts of the world, looking beyond the proliferation "problem cases" may be the best way to proceed. The United States should work to widen international understanding of the benefits that have accrued from threat reduction cooperation and should try to engage other countries in projects that would solidify their understanding of such programs. In the Reduced Enrichment for Research and Test Reactors (RERTR) program, the United States is already assisting countries around the world in converting such reactors to low-enriched uranium fuel. These projects often involve issues of material protection, control, and accounting as well.

The United States, perhaps in cooperation with Russia, which also is seeking to convert to lower-enrichment research reactors that it built, might bolster these efforts by incorporating lessons learned from past experience, communicating them in international forums such as that which could be provided by the IAEA. In this way, a country such as South Africa, which is considering shifting its reactors to take lower-enriched fuel, could study what has been accomplished in the U.S.-Russian context and might be willing not only to participate but also to become an advocate in broader nonproliferation policy circles.

At a minimum, the United States, Russia, and the other countries that have been involved in the programs thus far might engage the IAEA in an extended dialogue about the results of their threat reduction initiatives, in order to encourage more international attention to these problems and the solutions that have been developed for them. The IAEA, of course, has both lengthy experience and broad responsibilities with regard to safeguards and protection, control, and accounting of nonweapon material around the world. The threat reduction programs that have been conducted over the past decade in the former Soviet Union have been closely tied to IAEA standards, for projects have often been a prelude to IAEA safeguards being introduced at a particular site. Involving the IAEA in threat reduction efforts also could help develop advocacy for such cooperation in the international community, even among IAEA member states such as Iran that normally have little contact with the United States.

There are important opportunities for replicating the threat reduction programs that have been implemented on former Soviet territory over the past decade, but it is important to consider the limits as well. In the first instance, the United States would have to undertake an accounting of the lessons learned from the experience, extracting the benefits and at least considering how to temper the problems. Such an effort would require sustained attention from the executive branch and overall support from the president.

Furthermore, the United States could probably not accomplish such a transfer unilaterally. At a minimum, a positive attitude from Russia will be necessary to attract other countries to the methods and technologies of the cooperation. If the overall U.S.-Russian relationship is in a persistent state of negativity or indifference, then it will be difficult to work up international enthusiasm for broader threat reduction activities beyond the borders of the former Soviet Union.

Equally important will be domestic support for such programs, especially on Capitol Hill. Given the on-again, off-again nature of the budget process for the existing threat reduction programs, it will not be easy to establish new budgetary authority for work in countries beyond the former Soviet Union. However, the struggle against terrorism, and especially against terrorism involving weapons of mass destruction, may provide the needed impetus for progress in this area. Difficulties will be eased if other countries in addition to the United States are willing to make real contributions to such programs. That is why the G-8 Global Partnership is such an important development.

Despite the obstacles, the threat reduction cooperation of the past decade has had many positive results. It has proved just how innovative joint work can be in securing, monitoring, and decommissioning weapons of mass destruction, spurred by necessity and national security interests. In this way, threat reduction has the potential to reinvigorate international efforts to secure nuclear materials under the NPT and beyond.

What we are seeing, in essence, is the emergence of an important new tool of nonproliferation policy. This tool has great promise, but it will need to be honed and then carefully applied in order to achieve the kind of progress witnessed in the past decade with Russia and its neighbors. The United States will not be able to recapitulate its experiences of threat reduction in the former Soviet Union in exactly the same way when dealing with new countries. However, the procedures, techniques, and working relationships established will be useful models to employ in conjunction with other partners in this arena.

6

MODIFYING NONPROLIFERATION POLICY TO MEET THE TERRORIST THREAT
CONTROLLING BIOLOGICAL WEAPONS AGENTS

Jessica Stern

Concerns about the proliferation of technologies for weapons of mass destruction were exacerbated in the mid- to late-1990s by the recognition that it was not only states that could acquire such weapons but subnational groups—including terrorists.[1] Security experts and the media began to note that the United States, with its open society and traditions of free commerce and communication, could be particularly vulnerable to terrorist infiltration.[2] The spread of nuclear weapons may have remained the predominant preoccupation of the U.S. government, but as the decade evolved there was a growing appreciation of the risks of other unconventional materials, such as chemical and biological agents.

Galvanized by the attack on the Tokyo subway by the Aum Shinrikyo cult using poisonous chemicals in 1995, the fear of domestic terrorism grew steadily in the United States. Seven days after the September 11 attacks on the World Trade Center and the Pentagon, anthrax spores were spread through the U.S. mail, making clear that fears of biological attacks were not unfounded. By the end of that year, anthrax-contaminated letters had infected eighteen people and caused five fatalities.[3]

Although the anthrax attacks resulted in relatively few casualties, the overall level of awareness and precautions taken by the American public in response to the attacks increased.[4] This is especially the case in the areas that were directly affected, including parts of Florida, New York, New Jersey, Maryland, and Washington, D.C.[5]

The economic and social disruptions that resulted were far more significant than the level of direct physical harm. The delivery of mail in various parts of the country was stopped or slowed for weeks or months. Federal office buildings were closed either in response to a spate of terrorist warnings or because of actual contamination, as in the case of the Hart Senate Office Building, which had to be evacuated for four months and reopened only after extensive decontamination. Some ten thousand people along the East Coast, actually or potentially exposed to virulent anthrax spores, were prescribed prophylactic antibiotics.

The government's investigations into the source of the anthrax attacks demonstrated serious shortcomings in its ability to respond to or prevent domestic terrorist incidents. Remarkably, officials possessed only limited knowledge about the effects of biological agents, and there were gaps in intelligence coverage of potential sources of biological and chemical threats. The intelligence community as a whole had severely underestimated the threat of domestic terrorism, particularly attacks using low-technology delivery systems such as the mail service.

Both official and public analysis of the likeliest source of terrorist threats had long focused on the migration of scientists trained in the development and production of advanced weapons from the former Soviet Union to countries such as Iraq. The most acute threat to American territory, in turn, was widely perceived in Washington to be the use of ballistic missiles by a so-called rogue state. The 1998 Rumsfeld Commission report, which became the gold standard in Washington for evaluating the missile threat and which continues to define U.S. defense planning, concluded that "concerted efforts by a number of overtly or potentially hostile nations to acquire ballistic missiles with biological or nuclear payloads pose a growing threat to the United States, its deployed forces and its friends and allies. These newer, developing threats in North Korea, Iran, and Iraq are in addition to those still posed by the existing ballistic missile arsenals of Russia and China, nations with which we are not now in conflict but which remain in uncertain transitions."[6] Even after September 11 and the anthrax scares, moreover, Bush administration officials continued to be fixated on Iraq as the primary counterterrorist target, notwithstanding that the strain of anthrax used in the United States is widely believed to have originated in an American laboratory.[7]

The degree to which the United States was unprepared for a domestic biological attack was highlighted some months before the anthrax scares. In a report conducted by the Canadian Department of National Defense and transmitted to the U.S. government in advance of the anthrax incidents, findings showed that even dry anthrax spores could diffuse and pose serious risks to individuals who opened an envelope containing dangerous spores in an office setting.[8] Belatedly, it was reported that American officials appeared surprised by this revelation.

In reality, the diffusion of anthrax through contaminated mail proved even more effective than was anticipated. Anthrax spores were found throughout mail-handling facilities that had processed infected letters. Subsequent evidence showed extensive cross-contamination from the original letters to other mail, and it is actually this phenomenon that is believed to have caused two of the American fatalities.

There was much confusion among health officials about how to treat infected individuals as well as uncertainty about the availability of certain antibiotics or even how to gauge how many inhaled spores were likely to cause infection. Physicians discovered that the mechanism of infection remained poorly understood.[9] The FBI was forced to admit to Congress that it had no idea how many American laboratories had access to the strain of anthrax used.[10] More than a year into the investigation, no suspect or group had been named in connection to any of the mailed anthrax spores. Although the government appears to suspect that the attack strain of *Bacillus anthracis* originated in a U.S. Army research facility, investigators claim they are unable to determine how the individual or group responsible for the attacks acquired the strain or what quantity might remain at large.[11]

The anthrax attacks also exposed loopholes in the laws governing possession of biological agents. Prior to the passage of legislation prepared in response to the anthrax attacks, it was not illegal to possess biological warfare agents per se. The onus was on the government to prove beyond a reasonable doubt that the individual intended to use the agent as a weapon.[12] The USA Patriot Act (Unifying and Strengthening America by Providing Appropriate Tools Required to Intercept and Obstruct Terrorism), written and passed in the immediate aftermath of the attacks, criminalized the possession of biological agents except for medical purposes or "bona fide" research. It also prohibited "restricted persons," as defined in the act, from working with them, raising concerns in the scientific community that research on infectious disease could be hampered.[13]

Additionally, in December 2001 both the House and Senate passed versions of the Bioterrorism Preparedness Act. The legislation is intended to sharpen the ability of the federal government to respond to a bioterrorist attack by enhancing detection capabilities following an attack, by investing more in disease surveillance systems and public health laboratories, by refining techniques to treat the victims of an attack, and by improving hospitals' as well as state and local authorities' capacity for responding to bioterrorist attacks. The bill also expands pharmaceutical stockpiles and accelerates the development of new treatments, including a smallpox vaccine.[14]

Perhaps most important, the anthrax attacks revealed the extent to which biological weapons induce disproportionate fear. The terrorist strikes on September 11 killed an estimated three thousand.[15] The anthrax attacks killed five people and changed the way American citizens view the mail service. Perhaps because of the difficulty of assessing risk, anxiety about future attacks is rising. A number of surveys indicate that the public considers chemical and biological terrorism to be among the gravest threats to Americans. Although the anthrax attacks resulted in relatively few casualties, at least one poll suggested that public concern about biological terrorism had increased.[16]

Americans are increasingly unwilling to accept involuntary risks. They demand cleaner water, tougher air pollution standards, better treatment for disease, and safer cars. The effects of the national risk-reduction campaigns are mixed, however, because remedies for one danger often create new ones. This concept is most familiar in medicine, where pharmaceuticals prescribed to fight one disease may increase the incidence of others. Doctors, regulators, and ordinary citizens make risk trade-offs every day. Sometimes it takes years before the adverse consequences of risk-reduction strategies become known. As policymakers scramble to strengthen existing measures to minimize the possibility of future biological attacks, they may be prone to choosing remedies that substitute new risks for old ones in the same population, transfer risks to new populations, or create new risks in new populations.[17]

What happens in such trade-offs when the target risk (the one the remedy is designed to reduce) evokes disproportionate fears? The literature provides few answers. But Americans' reaction to nuclear power provides some clues.[18] The countervailing dangers of relying on carbon fuels—air pollution and global warming—may turn out to be far more dangerous for human health than the target risk. Yet, widespread fear of radiation has made it difficult to increase reliance on nuclear power. Experience with nuclear power suggests that decisionmakers should be particularly careful when dealing with target risks that induce dread among the populace since there is a danger of choosing policies whose costs exceed their benefits. For example, it remains to be seen if the extensive use of antibiotics in response to the anthrax attacks caused drug resistance and vulnerability to other diseases.

As the other chapters in this volume suggest, grappling with these risk issues will be complicated by the organizational divisions within the U.S. government. Even with the creation of the Department of Homeland Security, the agencies dealing with biological weapons remain scattered. Indeed, because so many first responders are likely to appear at the local and state government level, action by the federal government is insufficient to solve these problems. This chapter focuses on one remedy—legal controls on the possession of biological weapons agents. It begins by assessing the real and the popularly perceived risk of biological terrorism. It turns next to considering current U.S. laws regulating possession of biological agents and the changes that are being proposed to reduce the possibility of a future biological attack. These changes will be viewed in the context of the general shift in the nature of nonproliferation policy in the United States. It is important to recognize that some of the policy prescriptions offered to address nonproliferation concerns—especially solutions proposed in response to biological terrorism—could introduce countervailing risks in an area related to counterterrorism but regulated by different policy agencies: the effort to fight emerging and reemerging infectious disease.

It is difficult to design risk-reduction strategies that do not create countervailing dangers. But sometimes it is possible to develop "risk-superior" policies, which provide an equivalent level of benefit while minimizing countervailing dangers, or even "dual-use" remedies, which simultaneously address two problems.[19] Dual-use strategies for risk reduction offer win-win solutions. These include pursuing medical countermeasures that will improve the public health infrastructure, regardless of whether major biological attacks ever occur; expanding epidemiological surveillance for human, animal, and plant diseases; and increasing compliance with Centers for Disease Control (CDC) regulations regarding "reportable" diseases. In weighing the trade-offs inherent in nonproliferation and antiterrorism laws, it is important to consider the welfare not only of Americans but of citizens of other countries. Policy proposals for reducing the threat of biological terrorism may entail countervailing risks that are borne disproportionately by the world's poorest populations, especially in Africa, raising questions of distributional equity. Since materials for the production of biological weapons can be found around the globe, domestic proposals are unlikely to be effective unless combined with wider cooperative efforts.

Combating biological terrorism must be at the top of our national security agenda, but it is important to develop strategies that are prudent, not paranoid. Effective policy design requires understanding the concept of dreaded risks and checking the temptation to try to regulate away these evils without considering the possibilities for unintended, adverse consequences.

UNDERSTANDING THE RESPONSE TO TERROR
WHAT ARE DREADED RISKS?

For more than a quarter century, psychologists and risk analysts have sought to identify the attributes of risks that frighten people. They have found that fear is disproportionately evoked by certain characteristics such as involuntary exposure, unfamiliarity, invisibility or by instances when victims may not realize they were exposed or the effects are delayed, when the mechanism of harm is poorly understood, or when long-term effects or the number of people likely to be affected is difficult to predict.[20] In contrast, when risky activities are perceived as voluntary or familiar and the subject feels—perhaps wrongly—that he or she is in control, danger is likely to be underappreciated.[21] On average, more than one hundred Americans die in car accidents on a daily basis.[22] And yet, because the risk is largely voluntary and drivers feel the illusion of control, most Americans blithely expose themselves to it.[23] Biological terrorism is unusual in that it possesses all of the characteristics that psychologists have shown to be conducive to dread.

Analysts also have shown that spectacular risks are especially feared.[24] The media tend to focus on dramatic events: tornadoes, fires, drowning, homicides, and accidents. People tend to fear terrorism more than ordinary crime. Because Belfast is considered a "terrorist" city, many people consider it to be more dangerous than Washington, D.C., although there are far more murders per capita in Washington than in Belfast.[25] We feel a gut-level fear of terrorism and are prone to trying to eradicate the risk entirely, with little regard to associated costs.[26]

Spectacular terrorist attacks—those featuring biological agents prominent among them—are now commonplace in literature and film, becoming part of the collective imagination. It is the popular fear of terrorism that has, in part, driven U.S. military strategy to respond to what some believe to be an exaggerated threat. The terrorist strikes of September 11 and the anthrax attacks that followed made clear that the threat is real. The images of the World Trade Center buildings collapsing and of confused and weary officials vacillating in the wake of the anthrax strikes will long remain in the collective national psyche. Studies show that people tend to magnify the likelihood of events that are easy to imagine or recall.[27] Psychiatrists believe that persons who had traumatic experiences in the past or who suffer with depression may find it more difficult to cope with the events of September 11 and may develop post-traumatic stress disorder.[28] The Environmental Protection Agency (EPA) observes that people ignore hazards that seem routine, like indoor air pollution, but fear those that are "high profile," like hazardous waste sites, that actually pose lower aggregate risks to human health.

Most of us rely on rules of thumb in calculating risks. Rather than carefully weighing pros and cons, we use heuristic devices. Supreme Court Justice Stephen Breyer explains, "We simplify radically; we reason with the help of a few readily understandable examples; we categorize (events and other people) in simple ways that tend to create binary choices—yes/no, friend/foe, eat/abstain, safe/dangerous, act/do not act—and may reflect deeply rooted aversions, such as fear of poisons."[29]

An additional complication is introduced because it is impossible to get a handle on the likelihood of future terrorist attacks, especially the prospect for terrorists to deploy biological weapons. Most analysts assume that terrorists have been held back from using germs in the past, for the most part, by a combination of moral and political constraints. But political constraints are likely to be less relevant for multinational groups, such as al Qaeda and its associates, unless global surveillance is intensified and international law is strengthened. Lethal attacks are becoming more large scale. Production and dissemination technologies for biological agents are rapidly improving. And the weapons themselves are proliferating, becoming accessible to state sponsors of terrorism.

DISGUST AND HORROR

Unlike the threats associated with conventional weapons attacks, terrorism using biological and in some cases radiological weapons is particularly troubling to the human psyche. In *The Anatomy of Disgust*, William Miller explains that horror is "fear-imbued" disgust; it is a subset of disgust for which "no distancing or evasive strategies exist that are not themselves utterly contaminating."[30]

What makes horror so horrifying is that, unlike fear, which presents a viable strategy—run—horror denies flight as an option. Because the threatening thing is disgusting, one does not want to strike it, touch it, or grapple with it. Because it is frequently something that has already gotten inside of you or takes you over and possesses you, there is no distinct "other" to fight anyway.[31]

Diseases penetrate us and inhabit us. We cannot physically remove them like a sword or a bullet; we cannot escape being defiled. In the aftermath of a conventional bombing campaign, we can run from collapsing structures; we know immediately whether we have escaped. When biological agents spread or radiological isotopes are dispersed, we may not know whether we have been poisoned, and we may not be able to escape no matter how fast we run.

Unlike conventional weapons, pathogens are ingested. They contaminate the air we breathe, the water we drink, the food we eat. Ingestion and nourishment—essential to life—become linked to defilement and death. Evil and disgust go hand in hand: what is evil or cruel disgusts us; what disgusts us may seem tainted with evil. Whether one subscribes to the notion of natural law or to the social construct of evil, the same emotions of dread and indignation often are evoked in the presence of evil. But indignation, Miller posits, is inadequate in the face of evil.[32]

The idea of involuntary exposure is inherently fear inducing. Nearly 40 percent of those queried in a recent study agreed with the statement, "If a person is exposed to a chemical that can cause cancer in humans, then that person will probably get cancer some day."[33] The question provided no specifics about the magnitude of exposure. When the question referred to a specific quantity ("an extremely small amount"), 80 percent of respondents disagreed with the statement that the person exposed would "probably get cancer some day."[34] While the authors of the study conclude that inferences about chemical exposure relate to "the pragmatics of language interpretation," the study also reveals that the idea of exposure in itself evokes dread, especially when specifics are not provided, as would likely be the case in the event of a biological attack.[35]

HORROR OF DISEASE

Part of our fear of biological weapons attacks is related to disease and contagion. What makes bioterror particularly frightening, disgusting, and infuriating is the idea that someone would deliberately contaminate us and that we in turn might contaminate others.

Epidemic disease has by orders of magnitude killed more people than war. Fear is a reasonable response to the threat. But people tend to fear unusual diseases more than well-known, more common killers. Malaria, an ancient disease, kills a million people a year worldwide. Marburg, discovered in 1967, has only killed ten people; Ebola has killed 891 since its discovery in 1976.[36] Yet it is Ebola and Marburg that have inspired terrifying books and movies. We respond to the likelihood of death in the event the disease is contracted (the unusual aspect of Ebola) rather than the compound—and low—probability of both contracting the disease and succumbing to its effects.[37] The pneumonic plague that broke out in Surat, in India's Gujarat state, in 1994 caused widespread panic. Hundreds of thousands of people reportedly fled in panic, including 80 percent of the city's private doctors. Outside experts estimated that there were fewer than one hundred cases of pneumonic plague in Surat and fewer than one hundred cases of bubonic plague in Beed, in the neighboring state of Maharashtra, but the disease is estimated to have cost India $2 billion because of its impact on tourism and on exports.[38] Biological terrorism could involve diseases that have come to seem exotic, especially in industrialized societies, increasing their hold on our imagination and heightening dread.

CAN SCIENCE REDUCE RISKS AND FEARS?

In 1957, the National Association of Science Writers surveyed American views of science. Nearly 90 percent of those polled believed that the world was "better off because of science."[39] Eighty-eight percent believed that science was "the main reason for our rapid progress," and 90 percent felt there were no negative consequences of science.[40] In the 1970s, technological optimism began to erode. A series of environmental disasters, most notably the nuclear power plant accidents at Three Mile Island and Chernobyl, contributed to the public's loss of faith. In a series of polls in the 1980s, in stark contrast to the 1957 survey, a fourth or more of those surveyed believed that technology would do more harm than good to the human race or that its risks outweighed its benefits.[41] Philosopher of science Kristin S. Shrader-Frechette argues that scientists have contributed to the public's loss of faith in their work; by presenting "their own educated (but controversial) guesses as science, they can jeopardize the credibility of science. The result can be the anti-science sentiment that is widespread today."[42] In this light, it is perhaps not surprising that Europeans distrust the government scientists who are telling them that the outbreak of bovine spongiform encephalopathy (mad cow disease) is now under control or that the risk of contracting new variant Creutzfeldt-Jakob disease, which is fatal to humans, is minimal.[43]

A particularly frightening aspect of biological warfare or terrorism is that it may be difficult to distinguish it from a natural outbreak of disease. Although making such a determination proceeds more rapidly than in the past, suspicions and fears still have plenty of opportunity to develop.[44] Sometimes people mistakenly attribute the effects of biological weapons to disease. Conversely, they sometimes blame sabotage for naturally occurring epidemics.

When West Nile encephalitis was first diagnosed in New York in the summer of 1999, CIA officials reportedly speculated that the virus, which had never been seen in the Western Hemisphere, might have been deliberately introduced.[45] Ultimately, the CDC concluded that the outbreak was not deliberate. But the difficulty of identifying the virus and its origin—which was exacerbated by the lack of communication between public health officials and the veterinary community—illustrates the complexity of distinguishing a biological weapons incident from a natural occurrence of disease. This difficulty will increase as urbanization, crowding, travel, poverty, and misuse of antibiotics continue to increase the incidence of infectious diseases once thought to be under control.[46]

On the rare occasions when biological weapons have been used or accidentally released, scientists and government officials often first assumed natural epidemics. For instance, the Soviet Union insisted that the 1979 anthrax outbreak in the closed city of Sverdlovsk, during which at least sixty-six people died, was caused by infected meat. American experts initially accepted the Soviet explanation. Following the collapse of the Soviet Union, a team of American academic investigators proved that the deaths were caused by an aerosol emission from a local military facility.[47] When 751 people in Oregon became infected with salmonella in 1984, public health authorities never suspected biological terrorism. A year later, an unrelated law enforcement investigation revealed that a cult headed by Bhagwan Shree Rajneesh had deliberately spread pathogens causing the disease.[48] And when Robert Stevens, an avid outdoorsman and a photo editor for the supermarket tabloid the *Sun*, was found to have contracted anthrax, Florida state health officials initially attributed the source of the disease to a naturally occurring strain of the bacteria found in some soils.[49] Faced with just a single case of inhalation anthrax, the

CDC investigated only natural sources of infection for two days—before discovering anthrax spores in the American Media building mailroom.

These uncertainties, taken together, suggest that policymakers have been and will continue to be susceptible to rushing to develop counter-measures to a perceived threat, without first assessing countervailing dangers. They may feel politically vulnerable, knowing how their constituents would react if, after a biological weapons attack, preparations were shown to be inadequate. They also may overestimate the risk of panic. Social psychologists have shown that people tend to see others as overly emotional and to attribute their reactions to their personalities while judging themselves to be rational and flexible.[50] The purpose of this assessment is not to suggest that people should not fear terrorism, or that policymakers ought not seek to reduce risks, but to point out that fear can influence our ability to assess accurately risk trade-offs, especially between mundane (but common) and spectacular risks to human health.

CAN THE RISK OF BIOTERRORISM BE ASSESSED?

It is not possible—even for governments—to assess the risk of biological terrorism accurately. The costs of doing so—in terms of both money and violations of civil liberties—would be unacceptably high. Unlike, for example, assessments of the risk of smoking cigarettes, there are no actuarial data that would enable experts to develop informed, quantitative judgments of the likelihood and likely impact of biological weapons attacks. Biological agents have rarely been used in the past and never on a massive scale.[51] Data on terrorist crimes—even those involving conventional weapons—are notoriously bad. Terrorists do not advertise their capabilities and intentions, and experts have a hard time predicting their likely response to government actions, evolving technologies, and changes in the world situation. Moreover, the effects of the weapons themselves are unpredictable, depending on the virulence of the strain, technique of dissemination, vulnerability of the victims, weather conditions, and terrain.

Nonetheless, it is necessary to attempt a qualitative risk assessment. On the supply side, several states known to have sponsored terrorism have made improvements in their unconventional arsenals. Iraq in particular was discovered to have produced a wide variety of lethal biological agents.[52] The Soviet Union was discovered to have developed antibiotic-resistant pathogens for use as weapons. Troubling, too, were revelations

that the Soviet Union had produced several tons of smallpox and indications that both Iraq and North Korea may have acquired the virus as
well.[53] Smallpox, which killed some three hundred million people in the
twentieth century alone, is lethal to 30 percent of those it infects. It is
highly contagious. The only known prophylactic treatment is vaccina-
tion soon after exposure. Since 1980, when the World Health
Organization (WHO) certified that smallpox had been eradicated, few
countries have maintained vaccine stocks. In the event that smallpox
were deliberately or accidentally released, most of the world's population
would be vulnerable.[54]

On the demand side, several incidents that occurred prior to the lethal
anthrax mailings of 2001 made clear that terrorists continue to be interested
in acquiring and using weapons of mass destruction. Perhaps the most significant of these was Aum Shinrikyo's chemical attack on the Tokyo subway in 1995, killing twelve and sending thousands to hospitals.[55] The cult
also attempted to use biological weapons, apparently unsuccessfully. Osama
bin Laden, the accused mastermind of a series of spectacular terrorist crimes,
including the attacks on the World Trade Center and the Pentagon, was
reported to be interested in acquiring biological agents. The CIA alleged
that bin Laden's operatives had trained "to conduct attacks with toxic
chemicals or biological toxins."[56] In addition, Hamas, a Palestinian terrorist organization, is "pursuing a capability to conduct attacks with toxic
chemicals."[57] Iraq under Saddam Hussein repeatedly made menacing nois-
es about smuggling anthrax and other weapons of mass destruction into
Great Britain, in one case threatening to put anthrax in duty-free bottles of
alcohol, cosmetics, cigarette lighters, and perfume sprays.[58] Several antigovernment individuals and groups in America were found to have acquired
biological agents, revealing gaps in existing regulations regarding the sale or
possession of lethal or incapacitating biological agents.

Despite clear indications of eroding constraints, terrorists have yet
to employ biological agents to carry out mass-casualty attacks. Although
the perpetrator of the fall 2001 series of infectious mailings used a highly
refined powder, the letters sent identified the material as anthrax and
warned recipients to seek treatment, suggesting the sender did not intend
to kill people. Most incidents to date have involved readily available and
easily deployed, food-borne pathogens, resulting in relatively few casualties. This could change if a state chose to sponsor a biological attack or if
a group managed to secure assistance from former government scientists.
As aerosolization technologies continue to improve, high-casualty biological attacks will become easier to carry out.

Another troubling development is that terrorist groups have begun organizing themselves as networks or virtual networks rather than large organizations so as to evade detection. Domestic extremists in the United States are increasingly operating according to the principle of "leaderless resistance," which involves phantom cells or individuals carrying out actions on their own and not communicating directly with any central authority of the movement that inspires them.[59] In addition to making it more difficult for law enforcement authorities to monitor antigovernment activities, virtual networks enable individuals who are socially ill at ease to work together on a common cause, without having to meet face-to-face.[60] Similarly, international terrorist organizations are forming loose affiliations that function across national boundaries, making them harder to identify, penetrate, and stop.[61] Director of Central Intelligence George Tenet reports that Osama bin Laden's organization and other terrorist groups also have been placing increased emphasis on using surrogate groups to avoid detection.[62] It is difficult to predict how these groups will change their methods of operation in the wake of stepped-up U.S. efforts to find and eliminate terrorist networks around the world.

In response, government agencies have increased the frequency of exercises and preparations for responding to WMD attacks. These exercises have revealed that hospitals are likely quickly to exhaust their supply of antidotes and vaccine; "first responders" (police and firemen) are inadequately trained and likely to succumb themselves; and coordination among state, local, and federal officials is all but nonexistent.[63] Hospital laboratories are poorly prepared for biological crises. Secure communication links among doctors, veterinarians, and local and federal public health officials are yet to be established. The public health infrastructure is still inadequate for timely response and containment of outbreaks. Systems for ensuring that medication and personnel are disseminated appropriately are undeveloped. Moreover, the lack of fully coordinated global disease surveillance could obstruct early response to a bioterrorist attack.[64]

Despite the shock of what took place in fall 2001, the scholarly and analytic communities remain divided about the likelihood of catastrophic biological attacks. National security experts, who tend to focus on supply-side issues (proliferation), congregate in the pessimists' camp. The relative ease of growing certain pathogens has led some to conclude that mass-casualty attacks employing biological weapons are all but inevitable. Even in light of the events of 2001, the most pessimistic of these assessments fail to consider terrorists' practices (terrorists tend to stick with the same tactics) and historical precedents (biological agents have been used only rarely, and on a small scale). Terrorists who want to escalate to large-scale, open-air biological attacks would have to overcome several technical hurdles: acquiring the appropriate strain, growing it, and disseminating it as a respirable aerosol. Cultures can be acquired from a variety of sources, including nature and, reportedly, former Soviet laboratories trying to make ends meet.[65] The exception of the 2001 anthrax attacks, which used primitive means of delivering the agent (sending anthrax spores through the U.S. Postal Service), aside, even the wealthy Aum Shinrikyo cult seems to have been unable to take the first step toward carrying out a bioterror attack on a mass scale—the acquisition of a lethal strain. This has led some analysts to conclude that realization of the threat of bioterrorism on a catastrophic scale remains unlikely.

Scholars who focus on the demand side—looking at the terrorists themselves—tend to congregate in the optimists' camp.[66] But the optimists are likely to be wrong. Technologies for growing and aerosolizing biological agents are improving; terrorist attacks are becoming more lethal, suggesting that moral constraints against killing large numbers may be eroding; groups are emerging that have demonstrated or stated their interest in acquiring biological weapons; and former Soviet biologists' financial difficulties may eventually persuade at least one such scientist to sell his or her weapons expertise. Even a single scientist trained to create respirable aerosols could significantly advance a weapons development program. Moreover, according to some definitions, terrorism involves deliberately targeting noncombatants to influence a population through fear.[67] Whether the perpetrator is an individual, a group, or a state would in any case make little difference to the victims of a biological attack.[68]

By now, a number of analysts, such as Joshua Lederberg, have carried out qualitative risk assessments, and a consensus seems to be emerging about several threat characteristics.[69] Experts agree that the probability of biological attacks is inversely correlated with their severity, with the most likely attacks resulting in low numbers of casualties. Hoaxes, resulting in no physical harm, are likely to continue to predominate. Hoaxes require no expertise and no money on the part of the perpetrator, but they nevertheless can impose heavy costs. The city of Los Angeles estimated that to respond to a series of threats it received around the new year in 1999 cost $1.5 million.[70] The probability of attacks resulting in tens of thousands or even more deaths is low. But the consequences, especially if governments do not prepare for such eventualities, are potentially devastating.[71] This characterization of risk and damage, which is based on the kinds of attacks terrorists have carried out so far, the kinds of technologies they can easily acquire, and interviews with members of contemporary terrorist groups, is subject to margins of error, notwithstanding its qualitative nature. But the critical point is that an assessment that the likelihood of the kind of mass-casualty attack that Lederberg warns about is extremely low still results in a threat with high expected costs.

THE LAW REGARDING POSSESSION OF BIOLOGICAL AGENTS

Three kinds of provisions cover possession of biological weapons: international law, domestic law, and federal regulations governing shipping of pathogens. The 1925 Geneva Convention forbids the use of bacteriological agents. Similarly, the 1972 Biological and Toxin Weapons Convention (BTWC) prohibits states from developing, producing, acquiring, retaining, or transferring biological agents, toxins, or delivery systems for use as a weapon. The United States deposited its instrument of ratification in 1975.

The BTWC was written at a time when biological weapons were considered of marginal utility on the battlefield. Unlike the much later Treaty on the Non-Proliferation of Nuclear Weapons (NPT) and the Chemical Weapons Convention (CWC), the BTWC has no routine or challenge inspection protocol and no requirement to declare facilities that could be used to produce biological agents. Thus, there is no mechanism for investigating suspicious outbreaks of disease, such as the anthrax epidemic that occurred in Sverdlovsk, which President Boris Yeltsin subsequently admitted was caused by an accidental release from an illegal biological weapons facility.[72] Moreover, the treaty was written to apply to states, not subnational groups or individuals.

Advances in biotechnology have made biological weapons far more practical, to the degree that the likelihood for small groups or even individuals to acquire them must be taken more seriously. Advanced fermenters make it easier to optimize growth of microorganisms, and new technologies for coating and aerosolizing microorganisms make dissemination less challenging. Although it is unlikely that individuals or small groups could carry out major biological weapons attacks without assistance from experts trained in state programs, they might be capable of launching smaller-scale strikes. The drafters of the BTWC did not envisage these advances. Nor did they have a full awareness of the Soviet Union's massive program or foresee the potential for a brain drain when that state broke apart. The treaty does little to counter these new threats. Philip Heymann, Matthew Meselson, Julian Perry-Robinson, and others have proposed a convention to prohibit biological and chemical weapons under international criminal law, but the prospects of its quick adoption are not encouraging.[73]

The Bush administration, in pulling out of the process to negotiate a compliance and transparency protocol for the treaty in July 2001, cited two reasons: national security (the protection of military secrets) and the economic importance of industrial proprietary knowledge. Even prior to that retreat, the United States was engaged in secret activities that veered close to BTWC violation.[74] Treaty signatories routinely declare the scope and nature of their defensive programs. Following the 2001 anthrax attacks, the FBI had considerable difficulty finding out from the military and other branches of government exactly what the United States was doing with virulent strains of anthrax and where.[75] In this instance, secret defense programs were in conflict with civilian safety and investigation processes that could lead to the arrest of the person or persons threatening the nation with deadly germs via the U.S. mail.

CDC REGULATIONS

The Antiterrorism and Effective Death Penalty Act, enacted on April 24, 1996, required the Department of Health and Human Services to regulate the transfer of "select agents." The Centers for Disease Control and Prevention came up with a list of twenty-four microbial pathogens and twelve toxins that, if transferred to another facility, would require registration.[76]

The regulations applied only to those who acquire the specified agents through a self-disclosed transaction with a legitimate supplier. They did not apply to organizations or individuals that isolate threat agents from nature, acquire them surreptitiously though informal transactions, or shipped or received them prior to April 15, 1997, the date that CDC issued the regulations. Animal and plant pathogens were not covered. According to CDC, there also are compliance problems with the new rules: only 120 out of an estimated 300 university, government, and commercial labs that the CDC expected to register had actually done so in 1999. When individuals request to be registered to receive select agents, law enforcement personnel are not informed.[77] As Congressman Fred

Upton of Michigan observed, the focus of the rule on "transfers, rather than possession, probably encourages such non-compliance; since it would be difficult for an enforcement agency to demonstrate that a possessor violated any transfer rules, unless the possessor is actually caught in the specific act of transferring or receiving."[78] Furthermore, "a vast majority of academic institutions report they have no centralized inventory. They don't know what they have."[79]

In 1999, the Department of Justice tried to fix some of these problems. The Clinton administration issued a statement in May 1999 indicating that it planned to criminalize the unauthorized possession of listed biological agents and would require background or security checks for all persons working with these agents in laboratories.[80] The Justice Department reported that initially it suggested prohibiting all foreign scientists from working with listed threat agents. Later it proposed limiting access to scientists from countries that are members of NATO.[81] Congress also became interested in improving security and safety standards for dangerous biological agents. As Congressman Tom Bliley of Virginia explained, "we permit anyone in this country—including felons, foreign nations from sensitive countries and members of extremists [sic] groups—to lawfully possess even the most deadly biological agents, including anthrax, the plague, and the Ebola virus. They don't even have to notify or register with any federal agency or gain government approval to possess them. . . . Simply put, if the FBI can't prove their intent to [use] the agents as a weapon, current law can't touch these people, despite the real threat their possession may pose to public health and safety."[82] These problems were addressed in the USA Patriot Act and the Bioterrorism and Preparedness Response Act.

LAWS REGULATING POSSESSION

Parties to the BTWC are required to adopt legislation making it illegal for individuals to possess biological agents for purposes prohibited by the convention. Congress fulfilled this requirement in the Biological Weapons Act of 1989. Title 18, Section 175, brings U.S. law into conformity with the terms of the BTWC described earlier. It also forbids persons from knowingly helping a foreign state or any organization to obtain biological weapons or their means of delivery and prohibits attempting, threatening, or conspiring to do the same. A loophole in the law, which allowed individuals to possess biological agents for purported peaceful purposes, was closed with an amendment making it illegal to possess "any biological agent, toxin, or delivery system of a type or in a quantity that, under the circumstances, is not reasonably justified by a prophylactic, protective, bona fide research, or other peaceful purpose."[83] But an apparent loophole still stands: Who is the arbiter of what constitutes bona fide research?[84]

The law also prohibits restricted persons from possessing, transporting, or shipping select agents. A "restricted person" is defined as an individual who is under indictment for a crime punishable by imprisonment for a term exceeding one year; has been convicted in any course of a crime punishable by imprisonment for a term exceeding one year; is a fugitive from justice; is an unlawful user of controlled substances; is an illegal alien or an alien from a state the State Department has designated as a sponsor of terrorism; has been adjudged a mental defective, has been committed to a mental institution, or has been discharged dishonorably from the armed services.[85]

COUNTERVAILING RISKS IN CONTROLLING ACCESS TO PATHOGENS

The arguments for controlling access to pathogens are clear. What are the costs and benefits of doing so, and what countervailing risks might be introduced? Is there any indication that emotional responses to the threat have influenced authorities to go too far?

The first consideration is the list of restricted persons. Individuals known to have acquired biological agents in the past for questionable purposes might not have been captured under the list's guidance. Larry Harris, a neo-Nazi who bought three vials of *Yersinia pestis,* the bacterium that causes plague, in 1995, purportedly for his own research, would have been allowed to work with listed agents under the new rules (although probably not at home). And if the FBI is correct in its belief that the person responsible for the 2001 anthrax mailings was a former government insider, that person, too, would probably have made the cut. At the same time, scientists with important skills could be barred from working with listed agents now. There are undoubtedly highly talented scientists who have spent time in mental hospitals, for example.

Some policymakers would like to see the regulations controlling access to pathogens and related information tightened. The International Traffic in Arms Regulations (ITAR) regulates export of items on the munitions list. If a project falls under ITAR, an export license is required before information can be shared with foreign nationals, including scientists and students. Design, development, engineering, and manufacture of defense articles (including chemical and biological agents) come under a provision called "defense services," which are controlled for export.[86] "ITAR is comprehensive, complex, time-consuming, and often inconsistent," and, in the experience of the Massachusetts Institute of Technology, it often requires legal interpretation, explains Eugene Skolnikoff.[87] He expects that "it is only a matter of time before ITAR will be extended" to biological research that could be construed as having military applications.[88]

Another consideration is the identity of the regulatory agency and those running it. Who will ensure that scientists working in the labs in question are properly certified? Foreigners constitute 25–30 percent of graduate students working in microbiology research laboratories. CDC strongly objects to the idea of becoming the biological equivalent of the Nuclear Regulatory Commission. Turning it into a law enforcement agency could impede its scientists' ability to collaborate with foreign and domestic researchers on improving disease prevention, surveillance, and response. Many scientists have voiced concerns that the regulations will impose heavy costs on the "good guys" with little effect on "bad guys."

Consider further that all threat agents listed by the CDC occur in nature.[89] Ebola is endemic in Africa. Multidrug-resistant tuberculosis is spreading rapidly through Russian prisons. No matter how tight the controls on laboratory research, determined terrorists could attempt to isolate these agents from sick persons' blood or from the soil in the case of germs like anthrax. The Aum Shinrikyo cult traveled to Zaire in search of Ebola, with the aim of using it as a biological weapon.

Still another concern is that cultures of threat agents also are available from collections outside the United States. The purpose of these collections is to facilitate medical research. Hospitals use them to check the accuracy of diagnostic methods and instruments. Pharmaceutical companies need them to test the effectiveness of vaccines and other medical countermeasures. Universities use them in basic research. Until recently, cell culture collections routinely sent samples to any country that requested them in the belief that they were promoting public health. For example, during the 1980s, the Commerce Department approved exports of *Bacillus anthracis*, the organism that causes anthrax, and *Clostridium botulinum*, the organism producing botulinum toxin, from the American Type Culture Collection.[90] The CDC sent Iraq cultures of West Nile virus.[91] Because of growing concern about biological weapons proliferation, in

February 1989 the Commerce Department banned export of pathogen cultures to Iraq, Iran, Libya, and Syria.

The Australia Group, thirty-two countries plus the European Commission, lists twenty-four biological agents and eleven toxins that it urges members to restrict, but the list is not legally binding.[92] And most countries around the world are not members. There are more than fifteen hundred cell culture collections worldwide, according to the *New York Times*.[93] The World Federation for Culture Collections, the largest international association for cell cultures, reports 472 members in sixty-two countries.[94] After the CDC required shippers and receivers to register prior to transfer of select agents, Raymond Cypess, the head of the American Type Culture Collection, urged the World Federation for Culture Collections to back similar rules. His proposal was rejected, however.[95] Culture collections and whole laboratories may be susceptible to theft. And because of the difficulty of detecting freeze-dried pathogens, the ability of the U.S. Customs Service to stop illegal imports of small quantities, such as seed cultures, is minimal.[96] But the availability of threat agents from other sources does not necessarily imply that U.S. laboratories should neglect to make improvements in security, as long as the benefits exceed the costs.

Another consideration is that the new regulations could hamper research on disease organisms that occur naturally in some parts of the world but also are possible threat agents. There could be a rush to destroy legitimate seed stocks, as occurred in Iowa in the wake of the anthrax attacks. The new regulations will cause heartburn for university administrators and researchers, and there is a danger that they will decide to walk away from this kind of critically important research, warns Ronald Atlas, the president of the American Society of Microbiology.[97] CDC scientist Stephen Ostroff argues, "There is a need to expand research involving select agents, not to constrain it. We must bring the best and brightest minds to bear on the development of better vaccines, antiviral agents, antibiotics, and other therapies for exposure to, or illness from, biological agents. To do so, we need to ensure that restrictions on possession or handling of biological agents do not have a chilling effect on the willingness of scientists and research establishments to take part."[98]

The U.S. government and the international community are beginning to recognize disease in itself as a threat to global security. According to a recent National Intelligence Estimate, "new and reemerging infectious diseases will pose a rising global health threat that will complicate U.S. and global security over the next 20 years. These diseases will endanger U.S. citizens at home and abroad, threaten U.S. armed forces deployed overseas and exacerbate social and political instability in key countries and regions in which the United States has significant interests."[99]

This emerging consensus about the increasing importance of controlling infectious disease for human welfare and security suggests that limiting access to pathogens could entail risks to public health potentially far more significant than the threat such an action is designed to address. While deliberate dissemination of biological agents could conceivably kill millions of people, terrorists and states have generally avoided their use. Infectious disease, by contrast, is the leading cause of death in the world and the third leading cause of death in the United States. Every day, tens of thousands of people die from communicable diseases around the world.[100] Thus, in not allowing certain scientists access to listed pathogens, the government is making an implicit decision to counter a potential threat regardless of how it may introduce complications in the fight against a more immediate one—one that is already killing millions of people annually.

CONCLUSION

Studies of perceived risk show that fear is disproportionately evoked by certain risk characteristics. Biological agents are mysterious, unfamiliar, indiscriminate, uncontrollable, inequitable, and invisible. The effects of these weapons also are difficult to predict and poorly understood by science. They are physically disgusting as well, a trait associated with moral aversion. The media tend to highlight terrorist incidents, heightening dread and panic still further. We feel a gut-level fear and are prone to trying to eradicate the risk entirely, with little regard to costs. This fear can impair our ability to weigh different types of risk—their probabilities and consequences—against each other. Experience with nuclear power and competing fossil fuel sources that seem safer but generate more pollution suggests that decisionmakers should be particularly careful when dealing with risks that evoke disproportionate dread since there is a danger of responding by choosing policies whose costs exceed their benefits.

More strictly limiting access to pathogens is critical for minimizing the risk of future bioterrorist strikes, but only within certain bounds, taking into consideration the countervailing risks. Banning felons or foreigners from states that sponsor terrorism from working with listed agents in U.S. labs is probably a prudent measure, provided that exceptions can be made in case of emergency and that a certification system can be developed with minimal impact on research. But proposals to bar scientists from non-NATO countries or, worse still, all aliens, would present significant, offsetting dangers for public health worldwide.

A second, more immediate worry is the possibility that additional regulations could dampen researchers' enthusiasm for working on listed agents at a time when such research is required more than ever.

To minimize countervailing dangers, no further restrictions on laboratory personnel should be put in place without carefully consulting the scientific community. A system of incentives should be developed to ensure that laboratories do not abandon research on listed agents because of the added regulatory requirements. Laboratory directors and administrators should be briefed on the new rules and ought to be assured that the government will help them comply, in part by providing them financial assistance to do so.

"Dual-use" policy remedies have positive externalities for the developing world and for improving public health rather than the negative ones associated with banning foreigners' access to pathogens in U.S. labs. One such policy would be to improve public health and disease surveillance systems for human, animal, and plant diseases worldwide. Laboratories need to be built in the field, a system for transporting samples needs to be developed, and communication links among laboratories, national health ministries, WHO Collaborating Centers, hospitals, and private, voluntary organizations need to be established. The revolution in communications technologies must be applied to disease monitoring and control.[101] Without such a system in place, physicians will be hard-pressed to identify and respond to unusual infectious outbreaks, whatever their source.

Biological weapons, political scientist Leonard Cole observes, have always been seen as "inherently sneaky, unfair, abhorrent," for reasons that are hard to explain.[102] John Moon, a historian, describes the revulsion as deep, mysterious, and ultimately inescapable. It can be rationalized away; it cannot be exorcised.[103] As the technology for producing these weapons continues to refine and spread, those striving to prevent their use are in a race with those who would do us harm. Part of the race is technical—to develop better pharmaceuticals and diagnostics. And part of it involves devising better laws. But the all too overlooked challenge will be to ensure that the dread evoked by these weapons does not push us to take actions with unacceptably adverse effects on liberties or human health.

7

"GLOBALIZATION" AND NONPROLIFERATION
SECURITY AND TECHNOLOGY AT A CROSSROAD?

William W. Keller

American policy guiding technology trade faced a political crisis in 1999 when it was publicly revealed that U.S. firms had cooperated with the People's Republic of China on commercial satellite ventures, aiding China's strategic missile programs. The degree to which this was a deliberate violation and the relative importance of the transferred technology and know-how in advancing China's weapons expertise was much disputed. The incident nevertheless provoked intense congressional scrutiny of the Clinton administration's policies. Within months, a virulent partisan attack on policies guiding technology trade and collaboration was launched in Congress. Spearheaded by Congressman Chris Cox (R.-Calif.), a Republican-led study[1] charged the Clinton administration with being lax if not complicit in allowing sensitive technologies to spread to a potential adversary like China.

It has long been understood by policymakers and technology analysts that the U.S. export control process is not only cumbersome for American commerce but also quite inefficient in tracking the flow of weapons-related and dual-use technologies, significantly those that pose the greatest risks to global security. The sheer complexity of the governmental infrastructure for monitoring exports hinders America's ability both to promote legitimate business and to achieve nonproliferation objectives. Indeed, the administration of export controls encompasses more than a dozen agencies scattered across the departments of State, Defense, Commerce, and Treasury, among others, as well as the National Security Council in the White House.

The case of alleged transfer of missile technology to China is a microcosm of more fundamental policy dilemmas, particularly the progressive internationalization of technology markets and production and the growing convergence between military and commercial technologies. In combination, these two developments have transformed the challenge of regulating technology trade, making state-based export controls and other national regulatory instruments to stem the supply of technical expertise increasingly ineffectual. Export control regimes based on the premise that states can contain the spread of technology by imposing protectionist instruments at the national level have proved increasingly inadequate in a globalizing trading system.

This chapter examines various conceptions of globalization and then turns to how trends in international trade and investment are affecting the diffusion of weapons-related technologies. It then considers the systemic and practical challenges with which any technology control arrangement will have to contend to be effective in the twenty-first-century economic environment. The next section provides a set of recommendations about ways to create more workable nonproliferation regimes, emphasizing the critical contribution of private industry in helping governments to develop appropriate and enforceable standards of trade conduct and accountability. Finally, the chapter explores the inevitable trade-off between liberty and security in a world where technologies underlying weapons of mass destruction are potentially available to a wide range of states and substate organizations.

WHAT IS GLOBALIZATION?

Over the past decade or so, the term "globalization" has become a catchall characterization for twenty-first-century international society. The Internet is usually pointed to as the most conspicuous and ubiquitous manifestation of globalizing trends. A search of the World Wide Web in July 2003 yielded 1,750,000 pages that use the term "globalization," as well as 508,000 pages that reference both "globalization" and "security." Official

U.S. national security documents, similarly, offer abundant allusions to globalization, with a wide variety of rather vague definitions. In 1999, for example, a White House document defined the word in the following way: "Globalization—the process of accelerating economic, technological, cultural, and political integration—is bringing citizens from all continents closer together, allowing them to share ideas, goods, and information in an instant."[2] This basic definition was subsequently adapted in a Defense Science Board report, which referred to globalization as "the integration of the political, economic, and cultural activities of geographically and/or nationally separated peoples." This definition, in turn, is repeated in a report commissioned by Congress.[3]

In the administration of George W. Bush, a document outlining the U.S. national security strategy does not explicitly use the term "globalization" but rather assumes a world in which "the distinction between domestic and foreign affairs is diminishing" and terrorism is a "globalized" phenomenon.[4] In the view of this administration, the United States has a responsibility to eradicate global terrorism using, among other tactics, preventive military intervention to eliminate foreign terrorists. This was demonstrated in November 2002 by the Central Intelligence Agency in Yemen, employing a Predator unmanned aerial vehicle equipped with an AGM-114 Hellfire air-to-surface antitank missile.[5] Al Qaeda operative Qaed Senyan al-Harthi, also known as Abu Ali, and five other suspected associates were assassinated by remote control.

These definitions, assumptions, and derivations are based on sweeping assertions that are difficult to substantiate. It is not self-evident, for example, that a global culture is emerging, in light of the numerous instances of ongoing inter- and intrastate conflict and international terrorism. The post–cold war era proclamations of a "new world order" yielded quickly to the harsh facts of ethnic cleansing, genocide, religious strife, and sporadic terrorism. Claims about the effects of globalization on society or the international system often turn out to be more rhetoric than reality. Advanced communications have certainly contributed to the volume of information about global events and allowed for the emergence of genuinely transnational phenomena. But this cannot yet be described as a significant step toward the integration of national interests or policies among a wide range of countries.

The limits of a global society were revealed early in the 1990s. The genocide committed in Rwanda in 1994, which was the subject of widespread international media attention, did not prompt the United States to intervene in the critical phases of the slaughter. American hesitation to get involved stemmed in part from public and official perceptions that events in Rwanda were remote from American interests.[6] Debates in international forums about the ethical imperative of the larger powers to protect innocent civilians against wholesale aggression raged on even as the United States vacillated.[7] Americans were made aware of the human suffering in Rwanda when the images were broadcast in real time, made possible by portable satellite hookups, but this did not necessarily lead to the sense of affinity or empathy with the victims that many experts would posit as an inevitable by-product of advanced global communications.

The concept of progressive global economic integration promoted by some theorists is similarly overblown.[8] The opening of trade opportunities to new countries is inherently limited by disparities in levels of development and relative wealth. Even the Internet has to contend with the reality of the digital divide; commodities cannot in reality be shared instantly across borders regardless of Internet connectivity, much to the detriment of many e-commerce firms that had hoped to eclipse their brick-and-mortar rivals. Indeed, the degree of abstraction and imprecision characterizing many discussions of globalization has left the concept almost devoid of content, certainly not very useful as a basis for formulating policies.

A comprehensive study sponsored by the Department of the Navy in 1999 that focused on globalization and national security produced a definition of greater nuance and utility, terming globalization "a dynamic process of change characterized by growing cross-border flows of trade, investments, finances, technology, ideas, cultures, values, and people."[9] This wording focuses helpfully not on the distant prospect of global integration but on the gradual erosion of physical borders that have long defined nation-states and provided the foundation for the political-military entities on which traditional concepts of national and international security have relied. Globalization may be less about cultural, social, and economic integration as such than about the growing importance of transnational and subnational phenomena in influencing international political and economic relations.

The navy study does not posit the idea that global integration is an inevitable outcome of twenty-first-century information technology. To the contrary, the consensus view contained in the study is that globalizing trends brought about by exogenous forces such as advances in communications will prove uneven in their application internationally, will be concentrated in the advanced industrial states, and will remain politically controversial for the foreseeable future. This is sharply at odds with the depiction contained in the Defense Science Board study, in which globalization is presented as a fait accompli to which U.S. national security and defense industrial policy must adapt.[10] In this view, unrestricted cross-border commerce in technology, including military technology, is an epiphenomenon of globalization and no longer open for discussion or political consideration.

The problem with using globalization as a central concept in security or economic studies is that it is not precise, is very abstract, and generally lacks a specific context. It also carries excess baggage, particularly the implication—rarely questioned—that states and policymakers are somehow being subordinated to a larger and irresistible set of supranational processes and institutions, one that encompasses multinational corporations and multilateral economic and political organizations. The task, therefore, is to delimit the concept of globalization in such a way as to minimize ideological components and economic or special interests, so that national security, nonproliferation, and the public interest can prevail.

For purposes of clarity and analysis, what many call globalization can readily be rendered as an incremental process; it can be demystified if thought of simply as an *intensification of international commerce, communications,* and *multilateral organization.* The dramatic expansion over the past two decades of international finance, commerce (including technology transfer), multinational production, economic governance, and the conduct of electronic business would all fit this construction. The consequences for nonproliferation are easier to examine by adopting this process-based definition. At the turn of the millennium, security, commerce, nonproliferation, and liberty are at a crossroads.

IMPLICATIONS OF GLOBALIZATION FOR NONPROLIFERATION POLICY

There is a debate that needs to take place regarding the critical importance of nonproliferation policy on one hand and the degree to which the U.S. government and its allies should intentionally integrate their respective military industrial assets and markets on the other. A policy that favors nonproliferation is hostile to multinational research and development and production of weapons systems precisely because international collaboration in military technology and armaments is a form of conventional proliferation. It is premature to state, as does the Defense Science

Board report, that "globalization" has created an international military-industrial sector to which the United States and allied governments must increasingly look for their military equipment. Efforts at interallied cooperation and integration have been a stated goal of U.S. defense policy for several decades, a goal that continues to remain elusive. The situation is unlikely to change markedly in the near term.

In a climate in which the United States is deemed the "sole super-power" (or "hyperpower," as French commentators have sometimes characterized it), the disparity between U.S. military technological innovation and that of its allies in NATO has led to increasing friction. Europeans complain bitterly that U.S. national security export controls are in fact trade barriers, making it impossible for most European arms companies to sell weapons to the U.S. government.[11] The Europeans would like to establish freer and more open transatlantic military-industrial cooperation and competition. They view unilateral U.S. export controls as a signal impediment to this grand ambition. American rhetoric about globalization notwithstanding, the reality is that the Pentagon and Congress continue to promote protectionist policies, such as "buy America" legislative provisions.

Conventional Proliferation

The intensification of international commerce, advances in communications, and the ascendance of multilateral organizations have broad implications for the production and proliferation of conventional weapons and technology. But these are not inexorable forces. The rate at which military technology proliferates depends, at least in part, on the conscious decisions of policymakers. These policy decisions should be tied closely to national security and defense of the nation. But all too often they pander instead to the defense industrial interests and their lobbyists, whose overriding interest most decidedly is the bottom line. To understand the nature of conventional weapons and technology proliferation, it is important to disaggregate the underlying forces and policies that have shaped the arms trade and international armaments production historically and that continue to exert influence today.

Beginning the 1970s and 1980s, the objective of the major arms producers—the United States, the European powers, and the Soviet Union—was to disseminate military equipment and production technology widely, a practice that deepened in the 1990s and remains in effect today on a reduced scale. During the early parts of the cold war, the superpowers sought to build up the military-industrial bases of their allies and surrogates, while the Europeans sought to achieve economies of scale through licensed production and foreign sales of major military equipment. The traditional rationale that had aided sales of weapons in the past—to herald or cement an alliance or to provide self-defense capabilities to close friends—gave way by the 1970s to a policy characterized by former Senator William Proxmire as "sell anything, anywhere, anytime."

The twin imperatives of securing access to strategic resources (petroleum) and the need to offset the cost of increasingly expensive military innovations encouraged the traditional supplier countries to expand their circle of arms recipients. The effect was to accelerate the proliferation of nationally based military-industrial infrastructures in many parts of the world, as more states achieved the leverage to demand access to design data and production technology. This laissez-faire approach to arms trade forms the backdrop against which subsequent events unfolded. The one U.S. president who opposed a permissive arms sales policy was Jimmy Carter. He took a resolute stand against global proliferation of conventional weapons, a position that he was unable to sustain in the face of Soviet rivalry and aggressiveness and the deeply entrenched dependency of the arms sector on export revenues—as well as a determined, resistant bureaucracy and arms lobby at home.[12]

The winding down of the cold war transformed the global military market, reducing arms exports overall. Significant overcapacity in weapons production helped promote increasing consolidation in the arms industries around the world. As procurement budgets in most of the major arms-producing states declined precipitously after the dissolution of the Soviet Union, so too did the demand for weapons imports. In the United States, arms firms shed hundreds of thousands of workers as they reduced their activities and attempted to diversify into civilian markets. The Defense Department's prime contractors, the largest companies, then set about eliminating or acquiring their subcontractors, both "upstream" with respect to research and development and "downstream," buying firms involved in the whole spectrum of military production from prototyping to manufacturing.

This process led to rapid consolidation in the U.S. armaments sector in the middle and late 1990s. Under considerable pressure from the federal government, some twenty major arms manufacturers merged into four military conglomerates: Boeing, Lockheed Martin, Northrop Grumman,

and Raytheon. In Europe, a similar process gained momentum in the closing years of the 1990s but with a different outcome. European integration
was a multinational process, combining dozens of British, French, German,
Italian and other European arms makers in three megamergers—BAE
Systems, EADS, and Thomson-CSF. This has accorded European firms
sufficient scale and scope to compete worldwide. These mergers have significant implications for proliferation of conventional weapons, a subject
that will be addressed later in this chapter.

A second force shaping conventional proliferation was the onset in
1990 of a buyers' market that lasted more than a decade.[13] This was particularly apparent in international arms deals, where buyers—who did not
have the capability to produce the weapons themselves—pitted one company (or country) against another, driving down the price of materiel and
influencing the conditions under which the sale would take place.
Numerous countries in East Asia, the Middle East, and elsewhere were
and still are able to extract concessions from major arms firms—in terms
of coproduction arrangements, technology transfer, and access to the ever-
increasing sophistication of a wide array of armaments and electronic
components.[14]

In effect, overcapacity in the arms sectors of the major weapons-
producing states spurred the transfer to the buyer of production know-how
and military technologies, a process that had been escalating for the preceding two decades. The difference was one of motivation, particularly in
the case of the United States. In the 1970s and 1980s, Washington transferred military technology and equipment to strengthen alliance relations, enhance interoperability, and build up the armed forces and
indigenous military-industrial capabilities of friends and allies. But after
the end of the cold war, with the demise of the Soviet threat, U.S. arms
companies transferred production and technology to the buyer not for
reasons of state but more often as a condition of closing the deal. And
they did it with the blessings and encouragement of the Pentagon and the
White House.

The extent and composition of the international arms market also
changed markedly. By the mid-1990s, the volume of sales fell to about
40–50 percent of cold war levels, averaging approximately $30 billion a
year, with a significant increase over the last three years of the decade,
reaching $36.9 billion in 2000.[15] But paradoxically, even as the volume of
arms exports fell, what remained became increasingly important to arms
manufacturers. This is because overall demand for weapons and defense
services diminished, and export sales tended to generate higher profit

margins than domestic ones, particularly for U.S. companies. At the same time, the United States took a commanding lead in export markets, on average gaining more than 50 percent of such business, as compared to less than 12 percent for the nearest competitors—Russia, France, and the United Kingdom.

I have written elsewhere about the forms of conventional proliferation and about the global spread of military industry and technology throughout Europe, East Asia, and parts of the less developed world.[16] As budget considerations and domestic concerns about the health of the military sector supplanted foreign policy objectives, export controls were relaxed considerably. Even the armed services came to see foreign sales as a means of achieving economies of scale and strengthening their prime contractors at home. In any case, throughout the 1990s licenses were not required for the export of military equipment conducted under the U.S. Foreign Military Sales program (as opposed to direct commercial sales), which constituted the vast majority of arms exports. Buying nations contracted with the Defense Security Assistance Agency, which then typically worked with the "buying commands" of the army, navy, and air force to procure and deliver the equipment. Foreign buyers also had access to stock and excess equipment through U.S. government programs.

As domestic procurement fell throughout the 1990s and foreign sales assumed a larger portion of the arms market, to some, the United States began to look more like its European allies. Since the 1970s, the Europeans had sold as much as 40 percent of their armaments globally in order to attain economies of scale, to enable domestic production, and to fund research and development for the next generation of weapons. This led France into many questionable arms deals; it was in fact a major supplier of arms to Iraq in the years leading up to the Persian Gulf War. As one French commentator characterized the process, "French arms sales policy might be deemed distasteful, but it is nearly always a policy, most often conducted with the full knowledge and support of the state."[17]

Along these lines, some analysts contend that the United States should offset pressures to sell to questionable recipients by joining with the Europeans, permitting freer and more open competition and cooperation for military procurement on both sides of the Atlantic. This would be a big step, but they believe it is a necessary one because the United States is no longer able to generate sufficient demand internally to "go it alone." This argument is sometimes applied to "force modernization" programs associated with cutting-edge, advanced technology clustered, in the parlance of the Pentagon, as C^4/ISR systems, sometimes referred to as the "revolution in military affairs."[18] But collaboration of this sort with the Europeans would be costly and largely counterproductive because the nature of military equipment—and the technological, industrial, and economic underpinnings that support its development—has undergone radical change. The Europeans cannot compete and would make poor collaborators because they lack the military technological acumen, the financial resources, and the political will of their American counterparts. The transformation of the U.S. military is closely linked with the increasing suitability and performance in military systems of technologies and products initially developed for global business and consumer markets.

The end of the cold war and the collapse of the Soviet Union overlapped considerably with the advent of the information age and the transition to a more digital economy. Over several decades, starting in the 1970s, computers and communications ushered in the potential for new efficiencies and greater productivity, changing the way that hundreds of millions of people work, think, and entertain themselves. It was only a matter of time before commercially developed technologies would be applied to military systems on a massive scale.

The pursuit of the Persian Gulf War, as the first major post–cold war conflict, must be seen against the backdrop of a rapidly maturing multinational corporate presence in all sectors of the global economy. The increase in multinational activity included large-scale foreign direct investment, international mergers and acquisitions, increased trade, the expansion of markets worldwide for new goods and services, and transnational phenomena such as extensive technology transfer, footloose capital, and the sudden, wide availability of information technology. "Moore's Law" seemed to ensure that unlimited memory and processing power would continue to be available.[19] If weapons were destined to become increasingly information-intensive, the technology was already in the pipeline and surging forward, even for real-time military applications.

Gordon Moore and his friends were military-friendly, but they soon learned that the innovative power, the driving force behind late-twentieth-century technology, would come not from government research projects but from consumer demand on a global scale. The financial integration of the advanced and newly industrialized economies and the commercialization of new information technologies had enormous repercussions for military organizations as well as businesses the world over. These processes have eroded the effectiveness of export controls and will do so increasingly in the future unless new multilateral mechanisms, perhaps among them private sector initiatives, can be found.

During the years of the Reagan military spend-up, a wide range of information and other technologies became available for military applications, many of which were combat tested in the Persian Gulf War. New technologies were made possible in part by the transnational production networks of multinational corporations. These circumstances ensured that after 1990 the United States could never "go it alone" again, primarily because parts and components in complex electronic systems are manufactured in many parts of the world. Moreover, it is very difficult, if not impossible, to track the national origins of equipment that is provided by the second or third tiers in the Pentagon's vast contracting system.[20]

By the late 1980s, the U.S. military—which had championed the development of semiconductors and computers—found itself far outpaced by the commercial sectors of the U.S. and international economies. As the United States prepared to attack Iraq in 1991, two large-scale trends that would change forever the face of American and global military power were gathering momentum. These involved the commercialization of military procurement, or "civil-military integration" as it came to be called, and, more significant, the aforementioned expansion and interdependence of the advanced industrial economies. This was signaled by a tremendous rise in foreign direct investment among the advanced industrial nations and the rapidly increasing market presence and technological prowess of a variety of newly industrialized states.

Many of these rising industrial powers were the recipients of generations of advanced American, Soviet, and European military technology and weapons.[21] Some, like Taiwan and Singapore, welcomed inbound foreign direct investment in the commercial sector, especially in semiconductors and other information technology industries, as a means of gaining manufacturing skill and know-how.[22] Several emerging industrial countries targeted U.S. institutions of higher learning, sending their best and brightest students to the great American research universities—the envy of the world. These talented, U.S.-trained scientists and engineers often worked for high-technology companies in the United States for several years following graduation. Most were Asians.[23] When they went home, they took with them knowledge of the latest innovations. Approximately three thousand American-schooled scientists and engineers, for example, returned in the 1990s to take jobs in the Hsinchu Science-Based Industrial Park in Taiwan.[24]

This amounted to a transparent yet highly effective form of technology transfer. It is very much in the U.S. academic tradition of openness, a tradition that fosters innovation and the international diffusion of technical understanding. It also is, unfortunately, a custom that has come under scrutiny and approbation in the wake of the terrorist attacks on New York and Washington on September 11, 2001. As important to academic freedom and scientific advancement as this openness is, it tends to undercut most forms of export control. If a new technology has multiple applications, and a young scientist or engineer is trained in its intricacies, it will be possible to develop it along either civil or military lines when the student goes home to become a professor or technician.

A parallel process unfolded in the United States as a result of the pursuit of civil-military integration. Civil-military integration refers to the effort, originating in the 1980s and championed by the Clinton administration in the 1990s, to break down barriers between the military and various commercial sectors of the U.S. technology and industrial base.[25] Following the Second World War, the Department of Defense cultivated an array of contractors to meet its military procurement needs. As the defense sector became more highly regulated, it became increasingly inefficient, driving up the cost of military equipment to unacceptable and unsustainable levels. Concurrently, the Defense Department funded the development of a range of new technologies, eventually making them available to the wider economy in a spin-off process.

At some point in the late 1980s or early 1990s, various commercial industries, driven by trade and consumer demand, began to outdistance the military contractors, producing far better technology at a fraction of the cost. Essentially, the Defense Department previously had created a separate military command economy (not unlike that of the Soviet Union) that catered almost exclusively to the armed services' "buying commands." Civil-military integration was the culmination of a process in which Defense Department officials, particularly appointees of Bill Clinton, moved to unshackle the military contractors, which had previously been required to develop most technology and materiel in-house to government specifications. As they had been hoping to do for many years, William Perry, John Deutch, and Jacques Gansler all took steps from inside the Pentagon to open the procurement contest to companies predominantly doing business in the commercial sectors of the economy.[26]

In retrospect, it is easy enough to see that there is an inherent tension between effective implementation of export controls and the policy of civil-military integration, primarily because the latter requires that dual-use technologies originally intended for consumer markets flow freely into the design and production of complex weapon systems. This is especially true in military applications of digital information technologies and software programs that were developed for business-to-business or retail sales. The conflict occurs when the military user adopts a civilian technical standard, and the proof of principle is thereby established. From that point, the military application is carried forward by commercial or global economies of scale, and it is therefore automatically disseminated widely on an international basis. Anyone who thinks that the South Koreans or Taiwanese cannot make state-of-the-art semiconductors with military applications is living in the past century.

PROLIFERATION AND WEAPONIZATION

One sometimes hears the argument that it is one thing to have access to a given technology but quite another to develop military applications from it, a process referred to as "weaponization." But from the preceding discussion, it ought to be apparent that the gap between acquisition and weaponization is not so wide or difficult to cross. The United States, its allies, and even its adversaries pursued a decades-long policy of transferring military production know-how to many countries around the world. The cumulative results have been impressive, as countries like Israel, India, South Africa, Brazil, South Korea, and others have developed substantial military-industrial sectors with export potential. In July 2001, for example, South Korea announced a deal worth approximately $1 billion to sell artillery components to Turkey. As one commentator noted, "It is quite clear their defense manufacturers have been aggressively trying to break into the export market. Their extravagant efforts obviously have borne fruit."[27]

At the same time, there has been a leveling of technology on a worldwide basis and in a wide variety of sectors. Although the United States will retain a commanding lead in military high technology and innovation for the foreseeable future, it would simply be American hubris to assume that other countries will be unable to absorb emerging commercial innovations and derive military applications, even if at a slower pace. This applies to all but the most complex and intricate technologies requiring elaborate processes of systems integration and, to a lesser degree, those that are most closely controlled through so-called black or compartmented programs.

There is a significant temporal dimension as well. Highly sophisticated technologies that are top secret today may be commonplace in a decade or two. This is certainly the case with nuclear weapons technology, which most industrialized countries could readily develop but for decades was considered to be out of the range of developing countries. Most nations have not pursued nuclear weapons, however, because they have entered instead into nonproliferation agreements. But, as recent developments on the Korean Peninsula attest, here as in so many other cases the issue is not a technical or economic one. Other nations in the region may feel the need to follow North Korea's stated intention to withdraw from the Treaty on the Non-Proliferation of Nuclear Weapons (NPT) and begin to pursue a technology, now globally distributed, whose devastating effectiveness was demonstrated more than fifty years ago. It is well to recall that the quid pro quo for countries forgoing the development of nuclear weapons was assistance in acquiring nuclear power for peaceful purposes. Even though non-nuclear state parties to the NPT are subject to full-scope safeguards, which forestall or prevent their developing nuclear weapons, in many cases it is only the lack of political will that keeps them from doing so.

The process by which U.S. and European arms companies transfer production technology to other countries naturally facilitates communication between the military and commercial sectors of the domestic economy. When the United States offered F-15J fighter technology to Japan, for example, scores of companies were involved at the subcontractor level, transferring parts, components, and subsystem technologies to their Japanese counterpart companies, which would be responsible for producing the fighter plane in question. Most of the Japanese companies involved, including Tokyo Instruments, Ishikawajima-Harima Heavy Industries, Mitsubishi Electric, and Hitachi, conduct the vast majority of their business in the nonmilitary sectors of the Japanese and global economies.[28]

But these companies certainly have the ability to derive additional applications of the technologies received from the United States and can incorporate them into a range of products with minimal outside technical assistance. Mitsubishi Electric, for example, was able to produce phased-array radars using gallium arsenide substrate technology that had been developed for commercial purposes inside the company for twenty years. Historically, both European and Asian companies have tended not to distinguish military from civilian technology as rigorously as companies based in the United States. The absence of this distinction—and a set of strictures such as the Defense Federal Acquisition Regulations to enforce it—meant that technology flowed more freely both within and among foreign firms.

There also is a well-defined hierarchy in the kinds of collaboration in military technology that can take place. When the arms industry in the receiving country is relatively primitive, the transfer may take the form of "knock-down kits" or "screwdriver plants." As more experience is gained and military-industrial infrastructure is built up, it becomes possible for the receiving company or nation to build individual parts, components, or even subsystems. In time, starting with the Europeans in the late 1960s, many countries were able to climb to higher rungs on the ladder of technology transfer and sophistication. If military-industrial relations deepen sufficiently, companies of different nations can enter into joint research and development projects for weapon systems that have not been produced in the past. It is here that the specialized learning and technology transfer is the most robust.

This is the arrangement that is now sought by the major European and U.S. arms manufacturers. They would like to be able to combine their technical, financial, and other assets to produce weapons for a variety of different nations. Most important, the European companies are seeking greater access to what they see as the most lucrative arms market of all, the United States. Transatlantic cooperation in the development of new military technology, complete with "rationalization, standardization, and interoperability," has long been an elusive goal. But now arms lobbyists on both sides of the Atlantic argue that a window has opened (one of uncertain duration) through which joint international "private sector" development of weapons systems can be accomplished. Such arrangements, they claim, would decrease the cost of new armaments by increasing efficiency and scale of operations. The new "defense products" would be sold to governments around the world, starting in Europe and North America. For some European states, though, military-industrial relations may be set back by disagreements over the way in which the United States is handling the so-called war on terrorism. German and French leaders, in particular, have evinced a grave reluctance to assist the Bush administration in its use of preventive military intervention to depose Iraqi president Saddam Hussein and search Iraq for elusive weapons of mass destruction.

Today some arms companies aspire to become multinational corporations. The European conglomerate BAE Systems is among the most aggressive in this respect. It claims to have a significant industrial presence in nine different countries—"significant" as measured by numbers of employees, ranging from 25,000 in North America to 5,400 in Saudi Arabia and 3,000 in Australia. These figures should be interpreted with care, however, because the foreign holdings of the company may not be under European control. In the United States, for example, the subsidiaries of BAE Systems are controlled by proxy boards of American citizens that oversee the day-to-day operations of the company's U.S. investments, a situation that is greatly lamented by European arms makers and their consultants.[29] Contrary to their protestations, cross-border integration of the military-industrial base at the prime contractor level would be an unwelcome development for arms control. It would transform the environment for arms production and dissemination and would likely become a major driver in the proliferation of conventional weapons.

The companies in question are mainly in the business of manufacturing weapon systems and providing associated maintenance and construction services. As noted earlier, they have in recent years consolidated on both sides of the Atlantic. Among such companies, there is a long history of transatlantic and inter-European collaboration in military technology and industry, although it has not always been successful. This has taken the form of teaming arrangements, joint ventures, mergers and acquisitions, foreign direct investment, and strategic alliances. Fundamental to these arrangements is the erroneous perception that the military sector is very much like other high-technology sectors of the global economy, notwithstanding that it is more strictly regulated for reasons of national and international security. If for no other reason, the military sector stands apart because the introduction of new weapons to a region can invite military adventurism and conquest on the part of unprincipled leaders.

The emergence of multinational corporations that conduct business primarily in the arms sector under contract to a number of different governments is a legitimate concern. To the extent that arms manufacturers act as free agents in the international economy, their relationship to their country of origin and its military security becomes attenuated. There is a high likelihood of a conflict of interests with grave consequences. Given enough latitude, military multinationals could change the balance of power among nations by making advanced weapons available according to free market opportunities. It has long been the policy of France and French arms companies to seek exports not on security grounds but because foreign sales are necessary to bring down unit costs in the development and fielding of new weapon systems.

A NEW WORLD WITH NEW DANGERS?

So far this discussion has focused on commercial forces, the weaponization of technologies, and the proliferation of conventional arms. The question naturally arises as to how globalization—that is, the intensification of international commerce, communications, and multilateral organization, in both its military and commercial aspects—reaches beyond conventional weapons to so-called weapons of mass destruction.

The end of the cold war and the brief Persian Gulf War combined to produce a sea change in the U.S. strategic agenda and the way in which we think about foreign and military policy, including export controls. Iraq was an oil-rich nation with an ambitious leader who sought to acquire nuclear, chemical, and biological weapons capabilities and missiles. The fact that a minor power could amass so many weapons, including weapons of mass destruction, was deeply disconcerting to the U.S. political leadership and the American people. To many observers, this kind of proliferation constituted a heretofore largely unexamined threat to the security of the United States.

By selling tens of billions of dollars in conventional weapons to Iraq, the arms-producing nations gave Saddam Hussein the ability to cause mischief on a grand scale. He probably thought the Iraqi army was invincible. But the willing sellers, with a wink and a nod from their respective governments, did not stop with sales of conventional weapons. European companies sold chemical precursors and built chemical production sites in Iraq, and many have today admitted that there was a general awareness that the volume and types of such exports exceeded requirements for commercial uses. More than eighty German technicians worked in Iraqi missile labs.[30] When intelligence officers at Los Alamos National Laboratory reported to Washington an ominous pattern of nuclear exports to Iraq, their concerns went unheeded.[31] In hindsight, as incredible as it may seem today, it is clear that many governments and companies pursued reckless policies when they made powerful conventional weapons and the technologies that underlie nuclear, chemical, and biological weapons readily available to the Iraqi regime.[32]

That Western countries supplied "unconventional" weapons technology to Iraq, even if unwittingly (and this is the charitable interpretation), signaled a failure in export controls, both those unilaterally imposed by the United States and those that were applied through various other national and the several multilateral arrangements. Had such countries possessed the political will to exercise proper vigilance, the companies that provided weapons and military technology of all kinds to Iraq would not have been permitted to do so. But in the waning years of the cold war, ideological and economic motivations mixed to foster unwise policies with catastrophic consequences. These ultimately led to war, to the devastation of Kuwait and Iraq, and to a decade of economic deprivation of the Iraqi people.

The arming of Iraq in the 1980s showed that policymakers misunderstood the significance of exports of weapons and their associated technologies at nearly every level. It demonstrated how ineffective both U.S. unilateral and multilateral export controls had become by the end of the cold war. This failure is all the more ominous today because it presaged efforts of business and government, beginning in the Clinton administration, to loosen controls on high-technology items in the interest of increasing exports and the higher-paying jobs that went along with them.[33] This sets the interests of legitimate business against the inexorable harm that universal diffusion of industrial processes and techniques with dangerous applications poses.

TYING ARMS AND EXPORT CONTROLS TO THE THREAT

If controls are to be real and effective, they must certainly include, and perhaps must begin with, the arena of conventional weapons and advanced dual-use technologies for which applications are primarily military. This is where there is the greatest confusion about means and ends and about the overall purpose of technology and arms transfers, the Wassenaar Arrangement notwithstanding. The Wassenaar Arrangement is an agreement among thirty-three arms-exporting nations, whose stated purpose is to "contribute to regional and international security and stability, by promoting transparency and greater responsibility in transfers of conventional arms and dual-use goods and technologies, preventing destabilizing accumulations."[34] In reality, however, Wassenaar is a weak arrangement that has languished owing to lack of effective enforcement provisions and involvement by high-level government officials.

By the end of the twentieth century, it should have become obvious that unless conducted for reasons of foreign policy and in the interests of the national security, the transfer of weapons and associated technology itself becomes part of the threat. It places powerful weapons in the hands of countries and leaders who should not have them. Just as important, it builds up industrial armaments capacity in many parts of the world, generally making sporadic militarism a more likely possibility and decreasing the chances for meaningful nonproliferation.

The Treaty on Conventional Armed Forces in Europe (CFE) is perhaps instructive in this regard. Signed in Paris on November 19, 1990, by twenty-two members of NATO and the former Warsaw Pact, the CFE Treaty established parity in major conventional weapons between the East and West from the Atlantic to the Urals. Those systems included main battle tanks, armored combat vehicles, artillery pieces, combat aircraft (except for naval air support), and attack helicopters. The treaty is responsible for large-scale reductions of major military equipment in Europe and for creating an enduring balance of power in the European theater. It constituted a clear recognition that Russia and the other former Soviet states posed a reduced conventional threat to Western Europe, all the more so if the levels of weapons could be reduced on all sides. This concept—linking the nature of the threat to permissible levels of weaponry—might be applied broadly to the arms trade and then incorporated in a range of nonproliferation instruments, for which there is already broad agreement among signatories that greater controls are necessary.

Ten years after the end of the cold war, there is almost universal agreement that the United States possesses undisputed conventional military superiority. Its dominance in this sphere means that U.S. unilateral restraints on the arms trade can be a singularly effective complement to multilateral nonproliferation pacts. If the United States can get its own house in order—identifying and articulating the kinds of restrictions that can and should be imposed on the development of military multinational corporations—it can then assume a leadership position in developing real multilateral controls, controls that extend far beyond the fragile and ephemeral efforts of the Wassenaar Arrangement.

As a first step, the United States would have to act to restore its credibility and authority, which are suffering precisely because it is the world's leading arms merchant, a dubious credential that it has retained even beyond the cold war. After the Persian Gulf War, moreover, the administration of George H. W. Bush engaged in a policy of bold duplicity, offering a "new world order" in which the permanent five members of the UN Security Council would curtail "destabilizing" arms transfers while it simultaneously negotiated record levels of American arms sales to Saudi Arabia and other states in the Middle East and East Asia.[35]

This unsavory legacy cannot be allowed to compromise nonproliferation efforts in the future. But the United States will have to engage in serious and transparent reform of its arms and technology transfer policies. There is a precedent in the cold war arms transfer policy of the Carter administration, which was formalized in Presidential Directive 13 (PD13).

PD13 envisaged "arms transfers as an exceptional foreign policy implement, to be used only in instances where it can be clearly demonstrated that the transfer contributes to our national security interests." It put a cap on the "dollar volume . . . of new commitments under the Foreign Military Sales" program and asserted that the United States would not be the first nation to transfer advanced weapons into a region "which would create a new or significantly higher combat capability." It also sought to prohibit the export of U.S. military technology through international coproduction agreements.[36]

Such a policy would fly in the face of the efforts of later administrations to increase "defense industrial cooperation" with close allies and to "reform defense trade." The objective of recent U.S. policy on arms and technology transfers has been to create efficiencies by realizing economies of scale and to lower unit costs, often through multinational production. But a revived Carter policy could nevertheless form the basis of a grand bargain. At the center of such a bargain would be a compromise in which strict multilateral controls would be imposed on explicit military items and technologies in exchange for a greater liberalization and flexibility of unilateral U.S. controls on dual-use and commercial technologies. Such a policy would place commercial sales above military sales. This makes sense because the volume of commercial trade in dual-use commodities far exceeds the value of the trade in military products and technology.

If such schemes were to have any staying power, the United States would have to lead, devising a new policy on arms transfers, perhaps in concert with the several other major arms-producing nations. A two-step policy, beginning with disciplined restraint in arms exports on the part of the United States, would be in order. U.S. leadership in this area could be tied to a second phase of negotiated principles and practices on a multilateral basis. If additional countries failed to follow suit, the United States could revert to its former policies with little or no degradation of the present state of affairs.

The initial focus would be on conventional weapons, bringing the transfer of weapons in line with the actual nature of present-day threats to U.S. national and, more broadly, international security. After all, the major arms-exporting countries in North America and Western Europe do not face significant conventional military threats. For these states, transferring large amounts of conventional weaponry and associated production technology has the perverse effect of arming potential adversaries or, at the very least, creating a higher level of armaments in regions where stability and peace are very much in the interests of the arms-exporting states—regions such as the Middle East and East Asia.

It would be important to resolve the "dual-use" issue, simplifying matters considerably in two ways. First, the process of identifying and designating armaments, platforms, and other weapons-related items is straightforward, whereas it is more difficult to specify commercially available goods and technologies that also have military applications. Second, as mentioned earlier, the magnitude of the traffic in arms is economically insignificant (less than 0.7 percent of GDP) compared to that of commercial trade that might be useful for military purposes.

Several studies have advanced our understanding of the need to simplify and harmonize export controls, most notably one commissioned by Congress and carried out by the Study Group on Enhancing Multilateral Export Controls for U.S. National Security. It made three principal recommendations. The first is to merge existing multilateral export control regimes into a single body. The second seeks to establish a new interim framework to coordinate multilateral export controls. It would harmonize policies among close allies in exchange for enhanced military-industrial cooperation. The third recommendation is to overhaul the U.S. systems of export controls.

There can be little doubt that the preponderance of these recommendations would be beneficial, particularly simplifying existing multilateral export regimes and harmonizing controls among the states involved. Moreover, U.S. export control laws, bureaucracies, and regulations are outmoded and in need of substantial modification to reflect international developments since the end of the cold war. But the notion of permitting "enhanced defense cooperation" and "freer access to arms-related and dual-use technologies" among participating nations is a recipe for further proliferation of weapons of all kinds. In this aspect, the study relies directly and too heavily on a 1999 Defense Science Board report that was both ill considered and dominated by military-industrial interests.[37] Considering the advanced state of U.S. conventional military production capabilities, it would be better to set controls on military trade and technology at the national level and then to extend them by mutual consent to close allies and other friendly states.

It is clear that commercial industry, and here the arms sector is specifically excluded, is in need of relief from obsolete and burdensome export controls. By and large, companies can be trusted to protect sensitive technologies when they are informed that it is a matter of national security, especially when the guidelines are well understood, equitable, and universally applied. It would be necessary to disaggregate weapons systems and other specifically military end-use items from dual-use items that have

legitimate, nonmilitary commercial applications. In this way, the manufacturers of dual-use items could be held responsible for ensuring that their
products were not destined for military purposes, except in cases where
the military application was explicit. In those cases, export licenses would
be mandatory.

IS CONTROL STILL POSSIBLE?

In highly competitive global markets, where standards are not yet established, or even cases in which one company is trying to impose its standard, a great deal of control can be exerted over technology. The whole
phenomenon of "foundry" production of high-end semiconductors, for
example, rests on the premise that the foundries can segregate the intellectual property of their customers, even when very similar products are
mass-produced using the same fabrication facility in back-to-back runs.

Companies have learned to control the dissemination of technologies in, for example, trade networks among firms and their wholly owned
foreign subsidiaries, or in instances when they have mutually beneficial
supplier-buyer or affiliate relations. For this reason, the mechanisms that the
private sector uses to maintain secrecy and control the dissemination of
proprietary technology could become part of an export control regime. But
companies also have learned to reverse-engineer one another's products, to
purloin intellectual property, to hire away top technical talent, and to
obtain secrets through various forms of industrial espionage. Still, if they are
given a voice in the implementation of reasonable controls and are held to
strict accountability through harsh sanctions, few companies will run the
risk of distributing proscribed technologies and goods.

PROLIFERATION, COUNTERPROLIFERATION, AND CIVIL LIBERTIES

In light of the "war on terrorism," the occupation of Iraq, and increased
attention to the elimination of North Korea's weapons of mass destruction,
the cause of nonproliferation will continue to acquire greater salience,
both horizontally with known weapons and in new dimensions with as
yet undeveloped weapons of mass destruction. This will complicate efforts

to maintain or establish regimes to contain the diffusion of dangerous technologies. Military action to preempt or counter terrorism is very likely to generate unintended consequences, including "blowback" (further terrorism) and the displacement of a wide range of budget priorities associated with protecting the environment, health, and human welfare. But, perhaps more important, countering terrorism, asymmetric threats from hostile powers, and emerging weapons of mass destruction will inevitably pose a direct challenge to the civil liberties of people everywhere.

As the Deutch Commission (Commission to Assess the Organization of the Federal Government to Combat the Proliferation of Weapons of Mass Destruction) made plain several years ago, there are dozens of agencies spread throughout the government that have embraced counterproliferation (aggressive measures to stem proliferation) as a cause célèbre. One of the greatest assets in the counterproliferation arsenal is intelligence and, in the extreme, counterintelligence. The intelligence community, after all, has the responsibility of informing and advising political authorities of the status of proliferation in antagonistic states or of likely terrorist attacks against the United States and its citizens and military assets abroad. The effort to fend off potential terrorist attacks will inevitably involve significant foreign and domestic counterintelligence activities. To civil libertarians, the new internal security responsibilities of the intelligence community and the Department of Defense, carried out in conjunction with the Office of the Attorney General and the nascent Department of Homeland Security, give pause for reflection.

The relationship between international security threats and internal security does not have to be particularly empirical or strong to provoke a massive reaction from intelligence and law enforcement authorities, a reaction that has historically led to diminution of liberty. This was demonstrated in the era of McCarthyism in the 1950s, taking the form of a witch-hunt against largely impotent domestic communism. New powers were institutionalized for twenty-five years thereafter in the Federal Bureau of Investigation, which conducted numerous domestic counterintelligence programs, or "cointelpros," that illegally targeted thousands of American citizens.[38] Terrorism and the threat of weapons of mass destruction appear to have catalyzed a similar response today. It would seem that the majority of Americans are willing to give up a measure of their constitutional rights and civil liberties in the name of securing the homeland from foreign and domestic terrorism.

In the mid-1970s, it was possible for a group of senators, led by Senator Frank Church (D.-Ida.), to publish secret documents and to dismantle the threat to liberty posed by rogue intelligence agencies operating domestically outside of the rule of law. They could do this because the threat in question, a virtually nonexistent communist presence in the United States, did not resonate with public fear and perceptions. But the fear of international terrorists armed with weapons of mass destruction takes hold at peaks several orders of magnitude higher than the fear of domestic communism. We can blame the paranoia of J. Edgar Hoover and his cronies for the latter, but it all pales in comparison to the very real threat demonstrated by Osama bin Laden's al Qaeda operatives on September 11, 2001.

Since that time, the Bush administration has mounted the most severe challenge to our civil liberties since the mass internment of Japanese Americans in 1942, risking the undermining of basic institutions that have sustained such liberties since the founding of the Republic. In response to the threat of terrorism, the federal government is in the midst of its most far-reaching reorganization since the New Deal. New powers were conferred upon the executive branch by Congress in the passage of the Iraq war powers resolution, the USA Patriot Act, and the creation of the Department of Homeland Security.

These powers have been used to extend the reach of internal security as well, by executive order, by secret tribunals, by clandestine interrogations, by harsh imprisonment, and by the arrest of thousands of immigrants based on racial and national profiling. Many of these actions were authorized by an overzealous attorney general, John Ashcroft, whose conduct is reminiscent of another attorney general, A. Mitchell Palmer, the perpetrator, together with his first lieutenant, J. Edgar Hoover, of the infamous "slacker" raids in 1920. Today, American citizens can be classified as "enemy combatants" and held without being charged with a crime and without access to counsel in military prisons for indefinite periods.

Moreover, the Bush administration has gone to great lengths to create and sustain a state of permanent emergency. The president claims the power to strike preemptively against presumed enemies, foreign and domestic, on the ground that they may be seeking weapons of mass destruction or may be engaged in plotting terrorist activities. The White House engaged in a public affairs offensive to link the regime of former Iraqi leader Saddam Hussein to the al Qaeda terrorist network—a connection that it has so far been unable to substantiate. The United States invaded Iraq, ostensibly to prevent the Iraqi government from providing weapons of mass destruction to terrorists who might use them against the United States. But to date, even with Iraq under U.S. occupation, few if any such weapons have been found. While the intelligence activity and the logic associated with these claims are deeply flawed, the executive branch has nevertheless been imbued with extraordinary powers.

The theoretical drawback in the concept of nonproliferation was that it was almost exclusively applied to known weapons of mass destruction and to a limited number of delivery vehicles. This is reflected in the names of the principal control regimes themselves—the Treaty on the Nonproliferation of Nuclear Weapons, the Chemical Weapons Convention, the Biological and Toxin Weapons Convention, and the Missile Technology Control Regime. Far less strict standards have been applied to conventional weapon systems and tactical missiles, which are routinely traded among the major weapons-producing states and the developing nations that have become major customers.

But the artificial distinctions between various weapons of mass destruction and conventional ones become increasingly difficult to maintain as new technologies and derivative weapons evolve and proliferate. We are now at a crossroads, contemplating new governmental and international societal norms and practices based on the possibility that weapons of mass destruction might fall into the hands of terrorists who would not hesitate to use them against innocent populations. This is indeed a daunting challenge to nonproliferation and to the maintenance of an open society, but it is one with which we must come to terms, even as we face vast uncertainties in the months and years to come.

8

ORGANIZING FOR INTERNATIONAL COUNTERPROLIFERATION NATO AND U.S. NONPROLIFERATION POLICY

Joanna Spear

Since the end of the cold war, the United States has relied heavily on international coalitions to support its foreign policy objectives.[1] Although this preference for coalitions does not necessarily imply multilateralism in the sense of genuine consultative process, it does highlight the U.S. understanding that many of its policy preferences can only be accomplished with the cooperation of other nations. Among those, the industrialized democracies of Western Europe are clearly the most important with regard to nonproliferation policy. Just as the division of nonproliferation policy between several departments and agencies within the United States creates problems of policy coordination and programmatic coherence, so does the reliance on European allies to take concerted action. Indeed, since America's allies are sovereign states, the difficulties are more intractable than are those caused simply by bureaucratic infighting and intransigence. As noted in the chapter by David Kay elsewhere in this volume, the erosion of support in Europe for sanctions against Baghdad significantly affected the inspection regime in Iraq. This skepticism about U.S. policy is deep-rooted and could be seen even in European ambivalence toward the

Coordinating Committee on Export Controls (CoCom), which sought to control high-technology exports to the Soviet Union.[2]

European states view the proliferation problem differently than the United States. Although they recognize that proliferation has worsened since the end of the cold war, they do not share the United States' pessimism about the threats and are therefore generally happy to rely on a range of "traditional" nonproliferation approaches, eschewing more coercive measures. European activism on proliferation issues (such as it is) is directed toward improving the performance of the various arms control regimes rather than finding substitutes for them. This chapter examines European assessments of the proliferation threats, the tools they use to deal with them, and the reasons why their thinking and their tactics are frequently at odds with U.S. approaches. Understanding—and respecting—where Europe "comes from" on these issues will be helpful in shaping more effective U.S. nonproliferation policies.

Other chapters in this volume have identified two driving forces that have led to new directions in U.S. nonproliferation policies: first, structural changes in the international system and, second, organizational changes to meet the challenges of the new international environment. The latter involved assigning a much larger role for nonproliferation to the Department of Defense. Whereas the United States has fundamentally reorganized to confront proliferation as its number-one strategic challenge, European states have not undergone such a strategic or institutional revolution. Europe has not truly moved to a counterproliferation policy. This is because as medium-sized international players the Europeans are less exposed to proliferation threats than is the United States. Consequently, Europeans have seen no need for a strategic overhaul or a reordering of priorities to tackle the problem. Although there has been some evolution in European conceptions of nonproliferation, there is a lot of continuity in institutional arrangements and policy approaches.

Two consequences flow from this continuity. First, U.S. policymakers have implicitly assumed that the European states have undertaken similar organizational changes as they have. They have as a result privileged NATO—primarily a military institution—as the key route for selling U.S. ideas on how to treat proliferation. However, even if the European delegations to NATO were to go along with the U.S. threat assessments and remedies for proliferation—which, it will be shown later, they do not—these cut little ice with those really in charge of policy on proliferation across the Atlantic, who generally reside in foreign ministries. Second, given the differences in who on each side is responsible for making the critical decisions, European nonproliferation policies are increasingly at odds with those of the United States, to the frustration of both. This widening gap has the potential to undermine concerted international action toward proliferators. Unless remedial steps are taken, U.S. initiatives to engage its European allies on proliferation will bring diminishing returns.

This chapter is divided into four sections. The first part answers the question of how the European states regard the proliferation problem. After examining the collective nature of decisionmaking on security affairs in Europe, it looks in some detail at the policies and attitudes of the three most significant European players: Britain, France, and Germany. This is followed by section analyzing European views of the range of tools available for dealing with the threats. The third section examines why there are such divergent approaches in the United States and Europe, suggesting that differing geostrategic realities, strategic cultures, and the influence of institutional arrangements all play a part. The final section of the chapter examines the implications of these different approaches for international cooperation on proliferation and for the ability of the United States to implement its chosen nonproliferation strategies.

HOW EUROPEANS SEE THE PROBLEM

Just as there are divisions between the United States and Europe, there is no united Europe on proliferation issues. The states of the European Union (EU) have different geostrategic outlooks and preoccupations. Although there are some common concerns, perceptions of the severity of the various proliferation threats differ. The most extreme cleavage is between neutral states and nuclear states. Ireland and Sweden are members of the New Agenda coalition attempting to move beyond arms control to nuclear disarmament. This is in clear contrast to Britain and France, which regard their nuclear weapons as Europe's ultimate protection against weapons of mass destruction (WMD) threats.[3]

Just as there is no united Europe on proliferation, there is no formal, integrated European threat assessment to draw upon. One must therefore use a variety of sources in order to discuss European security perceptions. Threat assessments are regularly conducted by NATO, but there are differences between those of NATO (into which the United States has a strong input) and those emanating from national capitals. The failure of the Europeans to produce an integrated threat assessment in part reflects a desire to avoid opening up an explicit chasm between the United States and Europe over proliferation.

European states do not currently regard the proliferation of weapons of mass destruction as the preeminent threat to their security. The problem that most commands their attention is intrastate conflict on the borders of Europe.[4] It is this difficulty—spurred by the experience of clashing with Yugoslavia and contending with Albanian rebels in Kosovo—that has given a fillip to attempts to establish a common European approach to security and a rapid reaction force.[5]

Fundamentally, for Europeans the crux of the proliferation issue is the health of the various nonproliferation regimes, as opposed to the problem of "rogue states" as such.[6] This has implications for where the Europeans choose to target their resources. European efforts primarily go into reducing threats by making the multilateral regimes function more effectively, rejecting the apparent U.S. assumption that such regimes are beyond repair.

Although not the primary security concern for Europe, proliferation is higher on its agenda than it was during the cold war. While acknowledging the threats, the Europeans assign far less credibility to them than does the United States. The Europeans believe that a theoretical ability to produce weapons of mass destruction does not necessarily mean that they will be produced and used. Europeans also see a longer time frame before long-range missiles become a real threat.[7] Europe doubts the technological ability of rogue states to mount nuclear warheads on long-range missiles (an acid test in European threat assessments),[8] a judgment informed by the negative British experiences of trying to do just that in the abortive Blue Streak ballistic missile project, which ran between 1954 and 1960 and cost £60 million but did not even yield a prototype.[9] Consequently, there have been running disputes within NATO between the Europeans and the United States over the extent of the WMD proliferation threat. In particular, there has been European resistance to the U.S. attempt to introduce an equivalent to the Defense Counterproliferation Initiative into NATO. At the 1994 NATO summit, there was a long debate over whether the proliferation of weapons was a potential or an actual threat.[10] The United States, arguing that these represented an imminent threat, won that battle but not the war, which still rages through diplomatic skirmishing over counterproliferation within key committees of NATO. This means that less has been achieved in terms of agreed policy development and implementation than the United States had intended.

Whereas the United States has been keen to name and blame rogue states there is a singular unwillingness to follow suit in Europe, in part motivated by a fear that doing so would issue a self-fulfilling prophecy. Lawrence Freedman has commented that in Europe there is a nervousness about the concept of rogue states: "It risks stereotyping and, by suggesting that some states are beyond reasonable hope, precludes political measures designed to blunt their aggressiveness and bring them in out of the cold."[11] As Robert Litwak notes elsewhere in this volume, a similar reassessment occurred in the United States toward the end of the Clinton administration, only to be reversed when George W. Bush took office.

The European states acknowledge that the threat of chemical and biological weapons has increased.[12] Indeed, according to Wyn Bowen, this is one reason for European skepticism about investing in missile defense when there are far easier ways than ballistic missiles to deliver a WMD payload.[13] However, the expectation in Europe seems to be that the threat of the use of chemical and biological weapons is more likely to come from internal terrorist groups than from rogue states. This expectation has only been heightened by the events of September 11 and beyond. Unlike the United States, many European states have long experience in dealing with persistent terrorist threats (the violent campaigns of the competing factions in Northern Ireland, the Basques in Spain, Algerian Muslims in France, etc.). Therefore, Europeans place these threats within a domestic political context and adopt existing antiterrorist measures to deal with threats from terrorist groups both new and old. Much European effort has been directed into improving civil defenses. The EU is taking steps to counter the threat of WMD terrorism, particularly bioterrorism. It has taken a proactive stance, utilizing its existing public health networks as a launchpad for new measures. For example, the EU-wide communicable disease network is being expanded and is creating a rapid-alert system.[14] In May 2002, a Task Force on Bio-Terrorism was created to coordinate activities between member states and implement the security measures such as the rapid-alert system. In addition, the EU departments dealing with health and consumer protection and enterprise will be working with the pharmaceutical industry to develop new vaccines to combat communicable diseases that may have been caused by deliberate attack.[15]

BRITAIN

In terms of threat assessment and responses, the British approach to proliferation is certainly the closest to that of the United States, as demonstrated by their joint actions against Iraq. This closeness has come about in part because of Britain's nuclear weapons status and hegemonic imperial legacy, which gives it wider geostrategic interests than many of its European allies. However, even in Britain proliferation is not regarded as a preeminent threat. For example, the chief of defense staff, General Sir Charles Guthrie, in assessing the geopolitical environment the British armed forces would face over the next decade, gave proliferation minimal attention, focusing primarily on the need for peacekeeping and the rehabilitation of failed states.[16] Britain does regard the proliferation problem as increasingly serious, though. An August 2000 parliamentary Foreign Affairs Committee report on WMD proliferation noted a range of complications and problem states. Included in the report alongside "the usual suspects" were Syria for its refusal to sign the Biological and Toxin Weapons and Chemical Weapons conventions; Russia because of its failure to destroy chemical weapon stocks; Israel for failing to join the Comprehensive Test Ban Treaty; and the United States, cited by some witnesses for its failure to submit the required declarations to the Organization for the Prohibition of Chemical Weapons.[17] Thus, for Parliament, a major concern was the effects of these states' actions in weakening the arms control regimes.

The British take a regime-based approach to dealing with the proliferation problem. As the 1993 defense white paper affirmed, it was no longer necessary to plan military responses to the threats that were now being effectively addressed by arms control agreements.[18] Arms control and disarmament was endorsed by the 1998 *Strategic Defence Review* as the preferred policy option for contending with proliferation threats.[19] The Ministry of Defence is nevertheless increasingly concerned about diffusion of lethal weaponry, as illustrated by a gloomy prognosis for the chances of stemming proliferation from the ministry's director of the Proliferation and Arms Control Secretariat.[20] This is leading to schisms within and between departments over U.S. plans for a national missile defense. Less controversial are plans for theater missile defense, for there is increasing recognition of the vulnerability of British expeditionary forces to chemical and biological weapons in the field.[21] In May 2000, the National Health Service and other emergency services began planning responses to a possible biological weapons attack by terrorists.[22] In March 2002, £5 million ($7.5 million) was provided for resources to respond to WMD attacks. However, a November report from the National Audit Office concluded that Britain was ill-prepared to respond to WMD terrorism, particularly bacteriological and radiological attacks.[23]

Additionally, Britain has instituted a Civil Contingencies Secretariat, which will provide early warning of disasters and a strategy for handling them.[24] The secretariat serves the Civil Contingencies Committee, chaired by the home secretary and located in the Cabinet Office.[25] The immediate spurs for the development of this unit were two purely domestic events: fuel price protests that swiftly brought the country to a standstill and the foot-and-mouth disease crisis that closed vast areas of the countryside for months on end. Nevertheless, heightened concerns about domestic terrorism have helped propel this initiative. The new system is called UK Resilience.[26] Already these antiterrorism measures have had positive effects; in August 2002 an outbreak of Legionnaire's Disease was successfully contained using strategies developed to deal with chemical or biological attacks.[27]

The Terrorism Act of 2000, which allows the establishment of cordons to assist in the investigation of terrorist incidents, is soon to be joined by a civil contingencies bill that will allow the establishment of health cordons (a form of quarantine) to prevent people in areas hit by biological attack from spreading deadly infections across Britain.[28] In order to implement these measures, a civil contingencies force of 7,000 volunteer reservists also is planned, as is an expanded role for the Territorial Army (the British reserve force).[29]

FRANCE

The French government has an interest in the proliferation problems posed by the states of North Africa and the Middle East.[30] Nevertheless, French foreign minister Hubert Vedrine stated in May 2000 that he did not regard the missile threat as dire enough to justify deploying missile defenses.[31] This opinion was endorsed by a recent parliamentary report that expressed doubts about the political consequences of missile defense development.[32]

France believes that the *force de frappe* is a valuable deterrent against rogue states and therefore has no intention to disarm, much to the chagrin of some of its neutral allies in the EU. Despite continuing to rely on deterrence, French nonproliferation policy has undergone significant change in the past decade, coming to greater acceptance of cooperative approaches as signaled by the 1991 decision to join the Treaty on the Non-Proliferation of Nuclear Weapons (NPT). As Camille Grand noted in 1998, "Concerns about proliferation are fairly new in French strategic thinking." Grand qualified this by saying, "Not long ago limited proliferation was often seen as acceptable in many regional contexts. Although now fully committed

to the NPT regime, France is not really anxious about further WMD proliferation."[33] The French want to strengthen existing nonproliferation
regimes and verification procedures within a multilateral framework and
have "always been reluctant to support unilateral policies (e.g., U.S. vs.
North Korea) . . ."[34]

The 1994 *Livre Blanc sur la Défense* was not radically different from
previous Ministry of Defense white papers, although it did give greater
attention to the problem of WMD proliferation, and there has been no
subsequent strategic upheaval.[35] On the whole, growing concerns have
not led to a French counterproliferation doctrine, and the spread of dev-
astatingly powerful armaments remains a challenge to be dealt with by
the classic tools of nonproliferation and deterrence.[36] This sentiment was
made plain by Prime Minister Jean-Pierre Raffarin in October 2002: "The
United States is still suffering from the shock of the terrorist attacks, which
is today leading her to base her strategic doctrine more on the quest for
security than that for peace. America seems tempted to go it alone and
anxious to legitimize the unilateral and preventive use of force. We can
appreciate the traumatic experience she has suffered, but we are determined to reiterate the pre-eminence of the law."[37]

Despite its commitment to nonproliferation, actions taken by France
on occasion undermine multilateral arms limitation regimes. For example,
French decisions on arms sales are sometimes challenged by other members
of the Missile Technology Control Regime (MTCR). France's sense of its
national interest at times brings it into conflict with its EU allies, most significantly over the series of nuclear tests it conducted in 1995–96.[38] The
same is true with regard to policy toward Iraq (a valued potential trading
partner for the French), which has brought France into conflict with
Britain and the United States.[39] For example, in the spring of 1998, France
helped the United Nations to avert British-American attacks on Iraq in
response to Iraqi defiance of the United Nations Special Commission
(UNSCOM), set up to oversee and monitor its disarmament. President
Jacques Chirac saw this as a success for French diplomacy.[40]

GERMANY

German proliferation concerns focus largely on Russia and other former Soviet states. A priority for Berlin is preventing the leakage of fissile
materials from the region.[41] It is drawing on the former East German
intelligence networks and is working with the Russian government and the

United States to prevent diffusion of deadly substances and dangerous technologies. Germany also is preoccupied with Iranian behavior, but even in this case the key aspect of their concern is the relationship between Russia and Iran and the technology transfers this may involve. In the 1990s the Germans pursued a policy of "active influence" (*aktive Einwirkung*) with Iran. This engagement was seen as the best way to deal with the risk of unconstrained technology flows.[42]

During the most recent decade, Germany has continued to advocate a response to nonproliferation problems based on treaties and international agreements. This was most robustly set out in Foreign Minister Klaus Kinkel's ten-point nonproliferation initiative of 1993.[43] In addition to asserting the importance of the NPT and other nonproliferation regimes, the initiative made it clear that Germany wanted disarmament to include the existing arsenals of the declared nuclear states through multilateral arms control.[44]

Germany has been working within NATO to try to move the organization away from a first-use doctrine.[45] This has caused significant friction within the alliance, and its proposal has now been handed to a NATO working group to consider—a surefire bureaucratic route to burying the idea. Germany has fought within NATO to ensure that the alliance remains strongly supportive of the various WMD nonproliferation regimes, and it opposes any resort to use of force. These initiatives reflect a German attempt to square the circle in terms of being both a leading nonnuclear state and part of a nuclear-based alliance. Berlin faces similar dilemmas because of its close relationship with France, its principal ally in the drive for European integration. Although publicly silent about the French resumption of nuclear testing in 1995, in private the German government protested to Paris.[46]

INTRA-EUROPEAN COOPERATION

Aside from discussions routed through NATO and occasional EU Joint Actions, there is currently very little deliberation on proliferation issues. One exception to this is the increasing dialogue between the ministries of defense of Britain and France. It seems that the French Ministry of Defense is increasingly aware of the dangers of proliferation. However, the utility of this dialogue is somewhat blunted—in the eyes of the British at least—by the fact that the making of nonproliferation policy is firmly in the hands of the Quai d'Orsay, the foreign ministry, which takes a solely political outlook.[47]

HOW DO EUROPEANS ASSESS THE UTILITY OF VARIOUS POLICY INSTRUMENTS?

It is clear from this review that there are marked discrepancies between the United States and Europe in the degree of credibility given to various threats. This leads to profoundly different conclusions about the range of tools necessary and sufficient to deal with proliferation perils and the institutions best able to handle nonproliferation policies. This section discusses four types of policy instruments, in order of their acceptability to Europe: cooperative approaches; economic approaches; ballistic missile defenses; and use of force.

COOPERATIVE APPROACHES

European policy on proliferation is largely reactive. The only area where the Europeans have been proactive is in shoring up arms control regimes. They are aware that these regimes are not without flaws and have attempted to increase their efficacy. For example:

- The European states played prominent roles in reinforcing the arms control regimes shown by the UNSCOM experience to have serious shortcomings. They participated in revamping the NPT and the International Atomic Energy Agency (IAEA), strengthening and extending export control measures (especially those pertaining to problematic dual-use goods), and stiffening various forms of enforcement and compliance mechanisms aimed at proliferators.[48] Within the European Community (as the EU was then called), measures were taken to coordinate and intensify nonproliferation policy in the wake of the Persian Gulf War.[49]

- The first ever Common Foreign and Security Policy (CFSP) Joint Action related to the 1995 NPT review conference. The EU formulated and implemented a diplomatic strategy designed to ensure the success of the campaign for indefinite and unconditional extension of the NPT. This unity was impressive given that NPT extension had not been favored by members such as Italy, Belgium, Germany, and Ireland, which feared that it would lead to maintenance of the status quo rather than real nuclear disarmament.[50] The Joint Action "underlined that the EU considered the NPT as a cornerstone for the international legal order, for the international non-proliferation regime and for its European security interest."[51]

♦   In June 1996, the EU adopted a CFSP position seeking to conclude in a satisfactory manner talks aimed at reinforcing the Biological and Toxin Weapons Convention (BTWC) with a legally binding and effective verification system. The EU as a whole and key European countries individually have played an important role in the negotiations over the additional protocols designed to strengthen the BTWC. The Bush administration's subsequent decision to reject the protocols caused anger in Europe, most particularly in Britain, which had worked hard to shore up the BTWC.[52]

♦   Another CFSP Joint Action concerned North Korea. At the instigation of the European Commission, the EU and its atomic energy agency, EURATOM, have participated in the Korean Peninsular Energy Development Organization (KEDO) alongside Japan, South Korea, and the United States.[53] When the new Bush administration signaled that it would adopt a tougher stance toward Pyongyang, the EU stepped in and sent a high-level delegation to North Korea to open up a dialogue on issues such as "human rights, missiles and economic co-operation," thus helping to keep the nonproliferation deal the Clinton administration negotiated (the 1994 Agreed Framework) with North Korea from falling off the table, at least in the short term.[54]

♦   Most recently, Europe has gathered support for a strengthened MTCR (with a code of conduct) to deal with the ballistic missile problem.[55]

With many of these initiatives, the Europeans have contributed more rhetoric than solid activity. Such actions as have been conducted have been of a diplomatic nature and relatively cost free. On the other hand, in their opinion at least, the Europeans do less harm to existing regimes than does the United States.

ECONOMIC APPROACHES

Although the Europeans favor cooperative approaches to tackling the proliferation problem, their collective record of implementing export controls agreed in regimes such as MTCR, the Australia Group, and the

Wassenaar Arrangement, is far from showing perfect faith.[56] European export controls have generally only been tightened up in the aftermath of scandals, as in the case of West German reforms after the Rabta chemical weapons plant scandal (in which it was revealed that a West German company was selling equipment to help Libya build such a facility in the desert southeast of Tripoli).[57] Following the Gulf War, several supplier states altered their control policies and practices. In February 1991, the Federal Republic of Germany announced that it had tightened export controls relating to nuclear weapons materials.[58] This was followed in January 1992 by the adoption of new legislation that further stiffened export controls and imposed heavy penalties for violations.[59] The speed with which the revised law was introduced was attributed to disclosures about German nuclear-usable exports to Iraq and the seizure in Germany of American nuclear-usable equipment supplied by a Dutch firm and intended for Libya.[60] Despite the evidence of European government complicity in many of these transfers (through, for example, the granting of export licenses and the extension of trade credits), there has been minimal political fallout from these revelations. In Britain the five-volume Scott Report into British trade with Iraq was a media issue for less than a week after its publication.[61]

Economic tools in support of nonproliferation have been used reluctantly and sparingly by the Europeans. They have broadly complied with multilateral export control regimes but have showed little appetite for improving them, except when the evidence of their limitations is public and overwhelming. Interestingly, despite the pervasive desire to avoid economic pain, in the wake of renewed U.S. interest in missile defenses, the European states within the MTCR have showed themselves willing to tighten up significantly the regime's export controls. France (without a trace of irony) has led the way in developing a "code of conduct" to cover MTCR exports and hopes the initiative will soon be adopted.[62] This indicates their great unease about the concept of missile defense and their anxiousness to head off U.S. plans.

Many of the European states would prefer to rule out the use of economic sanctions, primarily because many of them have potential or actual trade relations with target states that they are unwilling to place at risk. Many continental Europeans were unhappy about the idea of sanctions on Iran—proposed by the United States but rejected by the EU—because of their economic links and their general preference for engagement. The U.S. response to this rebuff was to pass the 1996 Iran-Libya Sanctions Act (ILSA). The act sought to contain those two countries economically and therefore ran up against European sensibilities that favor trade and other forms of exchange. ILSA aggravated U.S. relations with the EU because its imposition of "extraterritoriality" (claiming jurisdiction over activities abroad that affect the United States in some manner),[63] and in retaliation Brussels passed legislation that made it difficult for EU members to comply with the U.S. sanctions.[64]

This case illustrates the differing attitudes of the United States and Europe about using economics as a means to deal with WMD issues and problem states. As the EU is principally an economic alliance, it is reluctant to curb trade and investment, even in the cause of halting weapons proliferation.

BALLISTIC MISSILE DEFENSES

Although they were clearly unified in opposition to a plan for the unilateral American abrogation of the 1972 Anti-Ballistic Missile (ABM) Treaty and were unhappy about the U.S. decision to withdraw formally from the treaty, there are nevertheless divisions within and between the European states over American plans for missile defense.[65] At the negative end of the scale, a study by the Mountbatten Center found that European leaders did not think the missile threat serious enough to warrant constructing complex defensive systems. Indeed, they investigated the level of European interest in creating its own ballistic missile defense and found it negligible.[66] President Chirac declared that he regarded U.S. defense plans as "a fantastic incentive to proliferate" weapons of mass destruction, undermining rather than reinforcing security.[67] This perception is shared across the English Channel, among the British public, 70 percent of whom think that U.S. missile defense will encourage other states to build more advanced nuclear weapons, according to a MORI (Market and Opinion Research International) poll conducted in July 2001 on behalf of arms control groups.[68]

Even in Britain, seen as the most receptive in Europe to U.S. missile defense plans, there are deep divisions over the issue. British territory would play an important role in the system's global architecture, and there is a political desire to please the United States, particularly on the part of Prime Minister Tony Blair, but elsewhere there are doubts; ". . . senior Whitehall officials and military advisers adopt a much more skeptical view than ministers."[69] The Foreign and Commonwealth Office is firmly opposed to American plans, but the foreign secretary, Jack Straw, declared his support.[70] Within the Ministry of Defence there are those who think that missile defense is necessary; however, key officials remain concerned about the technological feasibility of the scheme and are extremely concerned about the costs of British involvement in an elaborate defensive shield program. Admiral Sir Michael Boyce, chief of the defense staff, although noting the growing problem of missile proliferation, contended, "There is no point in completely impoverishing ourselves in order to provide ourselves with a defense against one particular system and not being able to do anything else."[71] The divisions within the government are a mirror of divisions in Parliament and across the whole country.[72] Opposition to British cooperation with the United States on missile defense has been coalescing, and, uncomfortably for the government, many traditional Labour Party supporters are drawn to these dissenting groups.[73] Opposition was slightly muted out of sympathy for the United States in the aftermath of the September 11 attacks but has grown steadily since the Bush administration's May 2002 announcement that the United States may choose to preempt a potential WMD attack on itself or its allies using "overwhelming force" that could include nuclear weapons.[74] Ian Davis, an opponent of British involvement in missile defenses, noted, "Having sought to reassure its allies that the proposed missile defence system is limited and purely protective in nature, the new policy of sanctioning first-strike attacks against terrorists and hostile states suspected of possessing weapons of mass destruction suggests completely the opposite: missile defence as a tool of offensive power projection."[75] Despite objections at home and across Europe to British-American cooperation in this area—pointedly, the French attempt to portray the British decision as the "acid test" of its commitment to Europe—Britain has fallen into line and agreed to the American use of Fylingdales and Menwith Hill bases as part of the missile defense architecture.

USE OF FORCE

There is a gulf between the Americans and Europeans over the use of force to tackle the problem of WMD proliferation, best shown by the fate of the United States' attempt in the 1990s to bring a version of its counterproliferation policy into NATO. Freedman has remarked that counterproliferation strategies are "normally interpreted as forms of pre-emption."[76] They were designed to address two scenarios: threats to the territories of NATO members and threats to NATO forces acting in regional theaters. However, as Joachim Krause made clear, these were not necessarily the proliferation threats that would have the greatest effect on NATO in the longer run.[77] "Of greater relevance strategically are cases in which proliferation of weapons of mass destruction— nuclear weapons especially—might lead to shifts in regional power balances with negative consequences for the military and economic security of the West.[78]

Before the European members were prepared to accept fully the concept of counterproliferation and to begin work on the strategic planning, they sought from the United States reassurances that are telling about European concerns. The first dealt with the relationship between counterproliferation and nonproliferation. The majority of European allies sought strong assurances that NATO would still give primary emphasis to nonproliferation (regime-based and cooperative approaches) over counterproliferation. The second sensitive issue was the relationship between counterproliferation and international law.[79] Most NATO members sought assurances that military action would only be contemplated if the UN had given a mandate or if an unambiguous case of self-defense presented itself.[80]

The battle over the definition and substance of counterproliferation was never settled to American satisfaction. The very term counterproliferation proved such a lightning rod for the allies' anxiety that it increasingly fell into disuse. As late as 1997, Jeffrey Larsen could report that "French and German officials continue to insist that 'counterproliferation' is not an acceptable NATO term and that the U.S. focus on retaliation and pre-emptive strikes could seriously undermine nonproliferation efforts."[81] Six years on from formal acceptance of the policy, it remains clear that it has not been implemented as U.S. policymakers had hoped. Indeed, as Kori Schake makes clear, the United States has actually lost ground, with U.S. diplomats conceding that the 1999 Strategic Concept (NATO's guiding strategy doctrine) is "probably weaker than the 1996 NATO endorsement of counterproliferation."[82] The Bush administration's 2002 doctrine of preemption has caused consternation in the EU and great concern among NATO's European members. There is evidence as well that the issue of Iraq is leading to divisions within NATO between the secretary-general, George Robertson—who has pledged NATO support for the United States in the event of a war with Iraq—and continental European member states, who are much cooler about involvement in any such conflict.[83]

WHY DO EUROPEANS SEE THINGS DIFFERENTLY FROM AMERICANS?

Geostrategy, strategic culture, and institutional arrangements explain why the Europeans are wedded to international regimes and cooperation as the preferred way of dealing with the proliferation problem and are hostile to forceful responses and schemes such as national missile defenses. Each of these points of departure is examined in turn.

GEOSTRATEGY

Five points can be made here. First, the Europeans feel less threatened by proliferation because they do not consider themselves a likely target. The United States, as an activist global hegemon, is a target. For many of the "rogue states," the United States is the primary threat that they face, and there is always the temptation to strike at that threat preemptively. This is not true for Europe. "Europe is geographically more exposed than the US, but strategically considerably less so."[84]

Second, there is a difference in the context within which WMD proliferation is viewed by the United States and the European states. The United States tends to view the problems caused by individual states in a global framework. Thus, issues are extracted from their regional setting, and both the problem and possible solutions are decided at an abstract global level. The Clinton administration's Defense Counterproliferation Initiative is a prime example of this global approach, as is the tendency to identify a class of rogue states or to describe an "axis of evil," either of which categorization actually includes very different types of countries and regional conflicts.[85] By contrast, the European countries view the issue of proliferation primarily in the context of regional security and do not necessarily single out the question of weapons of mass destruction for special attention. This difference of approaches is well illustrated by the case of EU and U.S. attitudes toward Ukraine in the early 1990s. The United States concentrated entirely on the issue of Ukraine's nuclear weapons and the status of its pending NPT membership. By contrast, the EU assembled a package for Ukraine that dealt with a whole spectrum of economic and political interests but made implementation of the proposal contingent on renunciation of nuclear weapons and joining the NPT.[86]

Third, the United States—as the nearest the international system has to a hegemon—has responsibilities for regional security, which means that it puts a premium on power projection capabilities and minimizing threats to them. The European states, by contrast, have traditionally had less involvement in regional power projection and therefore place less emphasis on this issue. The exceptions have been Britain and France, both of which have wider geostrategic interests and have been involved alongside the United States in far-flung activities. They have therefore been more closely aligned with the United States in terms of their interest in protecting troops engaged in regional security operations from WMD threats.

Europeans, because they nowadays have more limited regional interests, grant only cursory attention to some episodes of proliferation, for instance, the problem of North Korea's nuclear weapons program. Absent the global role of the United States, they look on some proliferation issues in a more dispassionate light. For example, European states generally have a much less benign view of Israeli weapons proliferation than does Washington.

Fourth, it is often noted that the intelligence resources that the Europeans are able to devote to tracking global WMD proliferation are considerably fewer than those the United States can employ. This means that Europeans are often unable to verify independently the intelligence provided by the United States, which breeds a certain skepticism.[87] As Joachim Krause has commented, "Risks associated with the proliferation of weapons of mass destruction have usually been defined by U.S. authors or by U.S. authorities. Some of these analyses are excellent, some are not."[88] This skepticism is increased by the Europeans' judgment that the United States is particularly poor at combining human intelligence with electronic and signals intelligence (leading to some spectacular errors).[89]

The Europeans do have access to human intelligence—on a par with the United States, if not better—in part because of continuing relationships with so-called rogue states. Moreover, over the past decade the French in particular have sought to increase their intelligence resources, in part so that they can verify U.S. conclusions. As Prime Minister Raffarin concluded in 2002, "In several theatres recently we have seen the huge importance for our armed forces of having our own autonomous intelligence assets."[90] This capacity will be further enhanced when the second-generation Hélios satellites are launched in 2004 and 2008. The Central and East European states, with their excellent human intelligence capabilities (particularly in the Middle East), are a new asset for NATO and the EU. As a start in solving intra-alliance intelligence problems, the newly inaugurated NATO WMD Center in Brussels is designed to increase information exchanges between the allies.[91] Within the EU, strengthening intelligence services is a CFSP priority.

Fifth, the economic positions of Europe and the United States play a role in determining how each side approaches the problem of proliferation. Some of the individual states the United States has identified as warranting concern (and therefore to be subject to sanctions or tight export controls on dual-use goods) are regarded as important actual or potential trading partners by the Europeans. France regards both Iran and Iraq as vital markets, and this affects the French attitude toward nonproliferation policies directed against them.[92] Another dimension of economic relations concerns leverage. European countries have had to adjust to the loss of control over other parts of the world where they once held sway. Their expectations of being able to hold back the diffusion of power globally are lower. As European states have few cards to play, they play them warily and are reluctant to start taking positions that they will find impossible to back up in practice. Further, European states both compete and cooperate with each other. Within the EU they are partners, but in seeking trade abroad they are often rivals. This means that they are often reluctant to accept export controls (particularly over dual-use technologies and systems) that could damage their competitive position unless there is strong evidence of the dangers to security in making the sales.

STRATEGIC CULTURE

The concept of strategic culture is much disputed and necessarily subjective.[93] Dichotomies in approach between Europe and the United States offer plenty of scope for transatlantic misapprehensions and disagreements over grand strategy: multilateralism versus unilateralism, engagement versus containment, focusing on intentions versus concentrating on capabilities, relying on diplomacy versus putting stress on technology.

What Americans find hard to understand about European attitudes to nonproliferation is their willingness to accept multilateral, regime-based approaches as all that is necessary for dealing with the problem. Within the terms of the U.S. debate this was encapsulated by Senator Jon Kyl's question, "Which would you trust, a missile or a piece of paper?" To many Americans the answer seems to be self-evident.[94] Not so for the Europeans. What Americans often fail to acknowledge is that European security has long rested on pieces of paper—such as the Washington Treaty (which established NATO)—and that these have yielded good outcomes for Europe. Thus, cooperative approaches to security have a positive resonance across the Atlantic.

Multilateralism involves a lot of diplomatic interaction and activity, an area where Europeans pride themselves on their smooth confidence and performance. Their positive attitude to diplomacy is in stark contrast to that of the United States, for which, as François Heisbourg noted, "the complexities of diplomacy and, particularly, multilateral diplomacy are seen as inevitable but secondary at best, needlessly burdensome and constraining at worst."[95] In addition to favoring multilateralism, the European strategic culture is averse to unilateralism; better the posse than the Lone Ranger. Europeans express another concern about U.S. unilateralism, articulated by Heisbourg: "Such a perception of a militarily activist U.S. may have adverse strategic consequences by providing certain countries with a politically convenient and effective packaging for their attempts to acquire weapons of mass destruction."[96]

Europeans believe that the way forward is to engage problem states, not merely to contain them and freeze the situation into a hostile status quo. For example, during the cold war the West Germans pursued a policy of *Ostpolitik*, trying to get Communist East Germany to open up.[97] European diplomats have adopted a "critical dialogue" with Iran. They believe this has yielded benefits such as a decrease in Iranian terrorism in Europe, although the United States is of a different mind.[98] There have been positive results, too, from Italy's "critical dialogue" with Libya, its one-time colony.[99] In accordance with this approach, the British chief of staff, Admiral Boyce, believes that Britain should engage in talks with the rogue states whose alleged threat provides the rationale for America's missile defense project. He advocates Western diplomatic engagement with Iraq, declaring that "there is rarely, if ever, a military solution" to problems.[100]

The argument that the Europeans consider both a state's strategic aims and capabilities but that the United States only considers the latter is shown to be overplayed by Robert Litwak's piece in this volume. The perception is nevertheless a concern in Europe, as voiced by the British Parliamentary Foreign Affairs Committee: "We are concerned that the U.S. over-emphasizes the capability component of the threat equation, when it comes to assessing the extent of the threat it faces, and attaches too little importance to intention."[101]

Finally, Andréani observed that there developed in the late 1990s a U.S. mind-set that increasingly tends to emphasize military, technological, and unilateral solutions to international problems, possibly at the expense of cooperative and political ones.[102] Clearly, for their part, the Europeans favor diplomatic and political solutions over intrusive and coercive ones.[103] However, European attachment to diplomacy also may represent a pragmatic acknowledgment that costs put advanced technological means largely beyond them.

INSTITUTIONAL ARRANGEMENTS

A number of features of the U.S. political process are either absent or muted in Europe. These institutional differences, when combined with the others just detailed, can have a significant impact on nonproliferation policies, leading the United States to be much more proactive.

Although the European states broadly perceive the same threat environment as Washington (caveats noted), this has not resulted in the fundamental reorientation of bureaucracies dealing with proliferation in Europe as it has in the United States, where the making of nonproliferation policy has become largely the province of the Department of Defense, with the Pentagon taking the lead in initiatives such as the Defense Counterproliferation Initiative. The institution in charge of a policy stamps its own approach and preferences on it. Accordingly, nonproliferation policies emanating from the Pentagon are now oriented more toward active military measures such as prevention, protection, preemption, and missile defenses and away from the diplomatic and cooperative engagement traditionally employed by the State Department and the governmental arms control community. Although European military organizations are playing a role in preparing to counter WMD threats, this tends to be limited to traditional defense planning. In stark contrast to the situation in the United States, in Europe there has been no shift of responsibility toward the armed forces. In the case of France, "In spite of the new emphasis placed upon non-proliferation issues in French foreign and security policy, there have been no major changes in governmental structures involved in non-proliferation."[104] Admittedly, the French Ministry of Defense is now taking greater interest in proliferation issues, but its influence is limited, as nonproliferation policy is firmly under the control of the Quai d'Orsay. In Britain, nonproliferation decisionmaking remains in the hands of the diplomats. The Ministry of Defence underwent some internal change and expansion in 1992 in response to the increase in volume and scope of its nonproliferation work resulting from the dissolution of the Soviet Union, but this has not changed the balance of power that remains in favor of the Foreign and Commonwealth Office on questions of weapons of mass destruction.[105] A similar story is told in other European capitals.[106] The institutional locus for nonproliferation decisionmaking obviously has some influence over the policies that result, with bureaucrats and policymakers favoring the tools with which they are most familiar, those that preserve their organizational turf. Thus, Europeans' tendency to favor diplomatic and cooperative solutions to proliferation problems is reinforced.

Another difference in institutional arrangements lies in the weakness of European legislatures. As noted elsewhere, the institutional locus for the development of policy on WMD issues varies greatly between Europe and America.[107] Whereas in Europe the presumption is that such policy should emanate from the executive, in the United States the legislature also takes part.[108] This forces the administration into an active role, either fulfilling a mandate from Congress or designing a plan intended to preempt congressional policymaking. In Washington, legislative activism can sometimes undermine executive branch regional policies. For example, the Senate and House conditioned funding of KEDO on confirmation by the president that North Korea had respected its nuclear obligations under the framework agreement that set up the energy consortium and had not transferred missiles to countries considered by the United States to engage in terrorism.[109] This limited the hand that the president could play in the region. The 1996 ILSA similarly has limited White House room to maneuver. Gideon Rose's comment regarding the effects of this act was, "By forcing the issue and binding the administration's hands, Congress deliberately tried to disrupt the status quo and turn transatlantic relations on this issue into a game of chicken."[110] Similarly, the 1985 Pressler amendment (cutting off aid to Pakistan if the president failed to certify that Islamabad was not pursuing a nuclear program) later came to be seen as a straitjacket.

European governments are generally not subject to this legislative pressure. In Europe there is very little evidence of parliamentary activity on the nonproliferation issue, and where there is, it is generally at the behest of the executive, which controls the legislative agenda (aided by much tighter party discipline in Europe). Thus, deliberative chambers in Europe are not initiating, amending, or blocking nonproliferation policies in the way that occurs regularly in the United States. Even if they were to try, their constitutional weakness would permit the executive branch to ignore them. In Britain in 2001, a rare note of discord was struck over missile defense. The Foreign Affairs Select Committee, reflecting the "very strong concerns that have been expressed about NMD [national missile defense] within the UK," expressed skepticism about U.S. plans to deploy an antimissile system.[111] It is perhaps not unconnected that the Labour government subsequently attempted to depose the (Labour) chair of the Foreign Affairs Committee, Donald Anderson, and to change the membership of what was seen as an "over-critical" committee.[112]

In contrast to the U.S. system, the majority of European officials dealing with nonproliferation are not political appointees but civil servants. There is no "revolving door" in and out of European governments. This means that there is more continuity of tenure among defense and foreign policy officials and therefore fewer lurches in nonproliferation policy as a new team comes in and sets about trying to make an impact. More than that, though, European political environments do not provide career incentives to talking up the nonproliferation problem in the way that can be observed in the United States. Would-be U.S. policymakers position themselves for jobs in a future administration by staking out claims of expertise in an area and producing a new spin on it.[113] The best such claims for a job are based on "sexy" issues like the recognition of a new threat or concern, precisely as exemplified by identifying new aspects of the proliferation problem. In Europe, to put it baldly, no civil servant regards nonproliferation as a dynamic, career-making springboard in this way.

CONCLUSIONS
IMPLICATIONS OF THESE DIFFERENT VIEWS

It is clear from the review of European nonproliferation policies that the United States has tended to underestimate the degree of difference between itself and European states in a number of respects. Europeans do not attribute the same credibility and immediacy to proliferation threats as the United States does. As a consequence, there has not been the same urgency in confronting the problem nor the need felt to engineer organizational changes to face an overwhelming strategic challenge. Indeed, the one area where Europe has refashioned its institutional architecture to confront a security challenge is in the development of CFSP, motivated by the need to confront conflict within states, primarily on the periphery of Europe, that could destabilize the region.

To date, American attempts to convince the Europeans of the immediate threat from proliferation have not succeeded, leading Washington to toy with unilateral policy tools. If the United States goes down this route, however, it imperils transatlantic harmony and could make unbridgeable the divide between itself and Europe. Moreover, it is not clear that unilateral action would be a successful response; it might actually create more problems (with allies and with potential enemies elsewhere) than it solves. In the words of Gilles Andréani, "Along with ballistic-missile defenses, counter-proliferation risks creating the illusion that the U.S. can solve the proliferation problem on its own, which it obviously cannot."[114]

IMPLICATIONS FOR THE SUCCESS OF NONPROLIFERATION INITIATIVES

Americans and Europeans, far from coordinating their positions, seem on occasion to be working at cross-purposes on nonproliferation policy. This is leading to tensions on both sides. For example, in 1999, in the run-up to the Senate vote on the Comprehensive Test Ban Treaty, President Chirac, Prime Minister Blair, and Chancellor Gerhard Schroeder of Germany warned that a U.S. failure to ratify would "expose a fundamental divergence within NATO."[115] When the treaty was ultimately rejected by the Senate, this was viewed as a slap in the face to the European leaders who had very publicly laid their credibility on the line in its support. There are similar concerns about the July 2001 American "torpedoing" of the efforts to negotiate verification protocols to the Biological and Toxin Weapons Convention of 1972. This is an effort that several of the European states invested in heavily, and there is a sense of betrayal as a result of the U.S. stance.[116]

The policy with the greatest potential to undermine the efficacy of other nonproliferation initiatives is the U.S. plan for antimissile systems. There are concerns in Europe that the United States' proceeding with missile defense signals abandonment of the various nonproliferation regimes, creating a self-fulfilling prophecy whereby such regimes become ineffective because the United States assumed that they were. According to Schake, "Europeans are concerned that the U.S. approach is destabilizing to the status quo that is so beneficial to their security."[117] This fear is increasingly bringing them into conflict with a United States enamored of unilateralism.

The Bush administration has been presenting missile defense to the European allies as inevitable in an attempt to make them accept it and be grateful for any minor concessions made to arms control along the way.

This is a political gambit that the Europeans are alert to and a logic they are unimpressed by. Given that the central European concern is the effect of missile defense development on existing nonproliferation regimes (which the United States has already weakened by its actions), the only way to mollify the Europeans would be for Washington to start making a parallel political investment in the surviving regimes. If the United States moved from being a block on these regimes to supporting what they are trying to achieve (and recognizing their role as one element in a web of deterrence), it would reap some further security benefits and would ease tensions with its transatlantic partners. The U.S. government need not regard the situation as zero-sum; it can, for example, get some advantage from a strengthened BTWC while continuing through unilateral action (intelligence gathering, etc.) to be vigilant in tracking the spread of bioweapons. Signing on to a regime does not have to mean that the United States must drop its guard and fall victim to a false sense of security.

Implications for U.S.-European Cooperation

The U.S.-European relationship is exhibiting increasing strain over nonproliferation. Europeans fret about the increasing tendency toward unilateral action by the United States. There is strong U.S. concern that European backpedaling is allowing the proliferation problem to worsen. However, it is worth reiterating for both sides' sake that neither is the other's biggest problem; states that flout regime rules they signed up to and the rogue states themselves are actually where energy should be focused.

Ivo Daalder has suggested that the transatlantic relationship will drift while the Europeans undertake a lot of institution building. He regards it as a sufficiently serious setback for the relationship that some opportunities for cooperation will be lost.[118] Nonproliferation may be one of the areas to suffer in the interim. In a sense, continental drifting does not matter if the European threat assessments remain sharply at odds with U.S. views. However, for those who believe a compromise between the two sides' outlooks is needed—more activism but not to the point of imposing unilateral solutions—a prolonged period of indecision and mutual suspicion is the worst of all worlds.

The United States needs to learn from its attempt to introduce a parallel to the Defense Counterproliferation Initiative into NATO and to bring the Europeans toward forceful responses to proliferation; they are not currently prepared to adopt those types of policy tools. For Europeans, the problem does not merit such a drastic response. However, the Europeans may be amenable to more activism—in terms of employing economic tools in support of nonproliferation—if it staves off American use of policies they find counterproductive. Clearly, the Europeans need to increase the attention they devote to nonproliferation and must move beyond rhetoric to greater action. There has been free riding in the past. For the United States, which would benefit from European willingness to cooperate on economic restraints, there is a need to offer the EU incentive by moving away from unilateralism.

It is worth noting that within the United States there are those who are more sympathetic to the European, regime-based approach to the proliferation problem. However, they are currently beleaguered and find themselves up against tough opposition as they make arguments in support of cooperative responses. Their task became even more difficult following the terrorist attacks of September 11, 2001, which served to heighten Americans' sense of vulnerability. Still, Europe's clear voicing of objections to unilateralism can empower and reinforce these dissenting voices, enabling the arms control community to speak with more authority. Conversely, knowledge that they have sympathizers in the United States can embolden Europeans to express their opposition (often subdued for fear of antagonizing their main ally). European disillusionment with Washington's go-it-alone tendencies ought to be communicated to various parts of the executive branch (not just the State Department), so as to be filtered into the internal U.S. government debate.

IMPLICATIONS FOR INSTITUTIONAL DEVELOPMENT

One of the problems in the European-American relationship is that there does not appear to be sufficient discussion, even within NATO forums, between members regarding the security implications of proliferation and how best to proceed. As Christoph Bertram has noted, many of the rogue states are outside of the NATO region and beyond its scope of operations (particularly North Korea). In these cases, the United States has little practice, and perhaps little inclination, of consulting Europe.[119]

However, consultation with Europe on these issues is important. The initial unilateralist rhetoric of the Bush administration has been replaced by a pledge to consult with allies before action. Both President Bush and National Security Adviser Condoleezza Rice have said that they thought

European allies would appreciate their candor. But that will only be so if the "consultation" is not just for show and involves real dialogue and some compromise. Uta Zapf, a Social Democratic member of the German Bundestag (legislature), recounted at the 2001 Carnegie International Non-Proliferation Conference her experience of one such consultation with a senior Bush appointee. She and fellow Bundestag members were allowed an hour with the official; however, virtually all of that time was taken up by him talking to them (or at them). There was no real discussion.[120] This is obviously unsatisfactory: the Bush team's approach was resented and its message given less attention because of the peremptory manner of its delivery.

Just who gets consulted needs to be reconsidered as well. The United States has for a long time primarily been using NATO to cajole its allies into greater activism on the issue of WMD proliferation, particularly through the Defense Counterproliferation Initiative. This is not likely to be the most fruitful route for a dialogue with Europe, given that the European governments tend to conduct nonproliferation policy through foreign ministries as opposed to ministries of defense. Washington also should increasingly cultivate the European Union and its burgeoning CFSP for serious discussions about future nonproliferation activity.

One of the more ironic consequences of U.S. support for the CFSP in nonproliferation is that it would force the Europeans actually to hammer out a common policy, in a forum within which intra-European tensions (for example, concerns about noncompliance with export control regimes) could be aired and dealt with. An institutionalized CFSP would provide the United States and Europe together with a much more effective means for deliberation and working out differences in approach. As has been shown in this chapter, in order for U.S. nonproliferation policy to bear more influence on the other side of the Atlantic, there must be more contact with the real policymakers, namely, diplomats, not soldiers.

PART THREE
CONCLUSION

CONCLUSION
MODIFYING AMERICA'S NONPROLIFERATION POLICY FOR AN UNCERTAIN FUTURE

Janne E. Nolan, Bernard I. Finel, and Brian D. Finlay

The past decade has brought about dramatic changes in the international security system—the end of the cold war, the coalition wars waged against Iraq in 1991 and again in 2003, the ascendance of new nuclear-capable states such as North Korea, and a series of terrorist strikes, first against American territory on September 11, 2001, and, less than two years later, against Western interests in Saudi Arabia and Morocco. These events have radically reoriented American perceptions of the world order. New international schisms have emerged, testing the ability of governments to organize responses against unfamiliar adversaries. The ascendance of transnational terrorist movements and groups engaging in illicit trafficking in weapons technologies are frustrating states' attempts to exert control. There is a deepening sense of susceptibility in the United States to unpredictable risks arising from global political, military, economic, and even public health crises.

This book has addressed these issues in context of American nonproliferation policy. After five decades of a military strategy preoccupied with defeating a rival nuclear superpower, American security planning increasingly is focused on the threat of smaller states and terrorist organizations seeking to disrupt established regimes, to challenge American power projection, or to cause mass destruction on a regional or global scale. The prominence that is now accorded to the global diffusion of technical and military capabilities in the calculus of national security threats has made sweeping structural and budgetary reordering essential.

The new conceptions of urgent security problems suggest that even small states aspiring to become regional powers and nonstate agents have the means to menace and perhaps to undercut the superior military capabilities of the advanced states. Organizational and financial resources have shifted accordingly, accompanied by a vast and rapid increase in counterproliferation and "homeland security" agencies, bureaus, and special task forces, each with its own stake in the campaign against the spread of weapons of mass destruction.[1] Formerly the preoccupation of a few diplomats and arms control specialists, proliferation has become a genuine, national cause célèbre.

The new strategic thinking posits that the diffusion of lethal technologies to high-risk states not only is far more problematic in the twenty-first century but is a virtual inevitability. Director of Central Intelligence George Tenet articulated this view to Congress in February 2003, "We have entered a new world of proliferation. In the vanguard of this new world are knowledgeable non-state purveyors of WMD materials and technology. . . . This is taking place side by side with the continued weakening of the international nonproliferation consensus. Control regimes like the Non-Proliferation Treaty are being battered by [these] developments." Tenet went on to suggest that the "domino theory" of the twenty-first century could take the form of a rapid escalation of the number of states with nuclear capabilities.

In a world made up of states that perceive nuclear status as the sine qua non of power and sovereignty, the logic underlying long-standing patterns of the distribution of military power in the international system becomes far less compelling. The belief that there is an escalating global competition for nuclear and other WMD capabilities undermines the viability of multinational agreements such as the Treaty on the Non-Proliferation of Nuclear Weapons. At the same time, to view proliferation as an inexorable trend is to discount the record of progress toward denuclearization in the states of the former Soviet Union, as well among as smaller states such as South Korea, Brazil, Argentina, and South Africa, which abjured nuclear weapons programs in favor of more pressing domestic priorities.

Nuclear weapons were for decades the exclusive domain of a handful of powerful states, all of which pledged to reduce and eventually to eliminate these arsenals as part of the global nonproliferation bargain. According to Bush administration officials, however, nuclear forces have reemerged as the currency of choice in international relations. Even small states with limited technical capacity, they argue, are striving to level the playing field by acquiring nuclear capabilities, however rudimentary. As

Tenet remarked, "The example of new nuclear states that seem able to deter threats from more powerful states, simply by brandishing nuclear weaponry will resonate deeply among other countries that want to enter the nuclear weapons club."

Reflecting its skepticism about the value of nonproliferation agreements and treaties, the current administration has redefined proliferation as a problem of regimes with aggressive ambitions. As such, the traditional focus of policy instruments—to seek restrictions on the sale and acquisition of illicit weapon technologies on global basis—has given way to a new realpolitik. It is not the global spread of weapons per se that imperils security, according to this calculation, but their possession by states vividly described by Bush officials as outliers, rogues, or members of "the axis of evil," a reference to Iran, Iraq, and North Korea from President Bush's State of the Union speech in 2002.

Disarmament efforts, from the Non-Proliferation Treaty to the Missile Technology Control Regime, have always relied on identifying and targeting specific military capabilities whose possession, development, or use poses undue risks to regional and global stability. The core objective of nonproliferation efforts has been to stigmatize weapons whose capabilities are regarded as violating basic tenets of international law—by endangering noncombatants, for example. Although existing agreements are rife with exceptions, this approach aspires to legitimacy by affirming international, if not universal, acceptance of common values. Rather than targeting specific states or regimes, whose character can after all change over time, the body of nonproliferation agreements seeks to undercut the prerogative of all countries to deploy or use weapons that the global community has defined as out of bounds. The principle of universality defines the challenge of proliferation as an intrinsically international problem, to be redressed by multinational instruments and a collectively shared set of norms.

The approach of the current American administration thrusts these issues squarely into the arena of sovereign prerogative. Some states legitimately possess nuclear weapons, it is argued, because they are law-abiding and would contemplate their use only in self-defense (or as part of a collective security alliance). States seen as criminal, by contrast, forfeit the right to acquire or possess weapons of mass destruction, not so much because of international strictures but because of their belligerence toward the West. This formulation accords wider latitude to the United States to tailor nonproliferation policies according to its perception of a particular government's intentions and capacities. Some argue that this approach weakens the fabric of the nonproliferation regime by allowing nationally determined strategies, such as preemption, to overshadow the quest for internationally accepted codes of conduct.

THE EMERGING "UNDETERRABLES"

Much of the attention to proliferation during the cold war revolved around concerns about "vertical" proliferation—the progressive buildup of new weapons and weapons designs by the major powers. Even the threat of "horizontal" proliferation—the expansion in the number of states possessing the atomic secret—focused on established regional powers or advanced industrial states, such as China, South Korea, Taiwan, Brazil, Argentina, India, Pakistan, and Sweden. Since the mid-1980s, but particularly over the past decade, the locus of concern has shifted to smaller, less stable states such as Iran, Iraq, and North Korea. The political and military motivations of such states in seeking unconventional weapons are characterized as inherently aggressive but are still not well understood.

Overshadowed by the rhetoric about "rogue" states are the perils facing successor states of the former Soviet Union, which are, without exception, weaker and less stable than the communist regime that preceded them. As Rose Gottemoeller discussed earlier in this book, many of these states could present proliferation dangers of far greater magnitude should they experience lapses in the security of their nuclear, chemical, or biological production facilities. Proliferation risks also arise from the rampant under- or unemployment among highly trained and specialized weapons scientists throughout the former Soviet Union or as a result of the poorly secured fissile material in Russia itself.[2] The risk of operational weapons falling into the wrong hands is often overstated, but the export of materials and expertise from states that made up the former Soviet Union is a genuinely sobering prospect and is far more pressing than is commonly acknowledged in the heated debate about undeterrable rogue states.

The past decade has revealed an increased interest among terrorist groups, some of them believed to be increasingly independent of state sponsorship and control, in acquiring unconventional capabilities.[3] In the wake of the attacks on the World Trade Center and the Pentagon in

2001 and several subsequent incidents of terrorist attacks against civilian installations in the Middle East and North Africa, many believe that terrorist groups are now more willing to participate in "mass casualty events" as a form of political warfare—a distinct escalation in the scale of violence compared to previous terrorist operations. The hijackings of the 1970s evolved in 2001 to the use of civilian airliners as guided missiles. Similarly, as testimony from the trials of the Japanese doomsday cult Aum Shinrikyo revealed, at least one terrorist group was determined to acquire and use chemical and biological weapons less for political influence than for the express intent of inflicting a high number of casualties.[4]

Arms traffickers and terrorist groups are largely immune to the regulations or diplomatic pressures imposed by nonproliferation instruments, which were designed to influence governments. That said, these groups are not easily targeted and defeated by military or intelligence operations either, as is evident from the failure of U.S.-led forces, despite large-scale deployments of advanced technologies and personnel, to eradicate al Qaeda or to uncover clandestine weapons programs in Iraq.

Detecting, preventing, and responding to terrorism or illegal arms exports is hindered by domestic political and jurisdictional constraints, which stem in part from the competing mandates of various agencies seeking to set their stamp on national strategy. This is particularly evident within the law enforcement and intelligence communities. For decades, terrorist acts against American citizens at home or abroad were seen as a law enforcement problem, prompting criminal investigations to identify and indict individuals involved in carrying out these operations. Traditional police methods, such as publicly announcing indictments of individuals involved or removing evidence from a terrorist site for forensic evaluation, have compromised intelligence operations on more that one occasion.

Despite significant efforts to deepen cooperation between law enforcement and intelligence agencies in recent years, policymakers and intelligence analysts are still struggling to gain access to the kind of information needed to analyze the origins, motivations, and behavioral patterns of terrorist groups. The establishment of the Department of Homeland Security and the implementation of associated counterterrorist measures are welcome steps but are still are a long way from resolving these kinds of institutional impediments.

The critical weakness of American policymaking is the failure to invest sufficiently in the kinds of expertise and analysis needed to understand the motivations of emerging regional powers and terrorist movements. Caricatured images of "rogues" operating outside of any recognized rules of behavior are not helping officials or intelligence analysts to come to grips with the real dynamics that lead states or individuals to embrace violence. Without this knowledge, it is virtually impossible to craft appropriate strategies for the long term to prevent or even to contain effectively new security dangers.

TECHNOLOGY AND NONPROLIFERATION

The management of new proliferation dangers also has become more difficult because technological innovations have altered both what needs to be controlled and how it is disseminated. This is in large measure the result of an accelerating convergence between civilian and military technology, particularly in areas such as computing and communications.

The problem of dual-use technologies is certainly not a new phenomenon, as it was recognized in the Treaty on the Non-Proliferation of Nuclear Weapons regime back in 1968. The diffusion of nuclear technologies seemed to be tolerable in the past because of the very small number of states that had access to the materials and technologies needed for weapons production and the capacity to exploit them. Peaceful applications of nuclear science and energy could plausibly be segregated from activities relating to the development of weapons without interfering with legitimate commerce. Even in the conventional realm, export controls could target items of clear strategic value that had limited commercial applications, such as guidance systems, as long as the advanced powers enjoyed a monopoly in production and possession of them.[5]

Today the dual-use problem is far more intractable. Entire areas of industry are engaged in the development of goods and services that have broad military and commercial applications. In the 1990s, for example, manufacturers of chemical goods discovered that they would be subject to treaty-related verification inspections because a large part of chemical production relies on what are known as "precursor materials," which are useful for developing weapons. Biotechnological advances and genetic engineering techniques pose similar dilemmas, as was discussed in Jessica Stern's chapter here. More recently, Pentagon and intelligence planners have been struggling to find ways to protect global information networks from potentially debilitating information warfare. There is no easy answer to these dilemmas, but, as William Keller has articulated, there are a number of important steps that need to be taken, beginning with the involvement of private industry in crafting security regulations for the commerce in sensitive technologies.

ORGANIZATIONAL CHALLENGES

The reorganization, augmentation, and consolidation of domestic agencies to combat proliferation has been thoroughgoing in recent years, ostensibly in response to international events. More often than not, however, the design of these entities, as shown in the analysis by Amy Zegart in the first chapter, has been subject to parochial political pressures and compromises, resulting in piecemeal and poorly coordinated initiatives.

During the cold war, nonproliferation policy was the purview of career professionals in the State Department and the Arms Control and Disarmament Agency and, to a lesser degree, among agencies in the Departments of Defense and Commerce that had oversight authority for military exports. Congressional interest was quite limited and White House attention sporadic, at best.

The agencies participating in some fashion today are numerous and heterogeneous. The Commerce Department has found itself much more deeply involved. Often it is at odds with the Pentagon over what is perceived at Commerce to be injurious export controls on American products such as satellite technology.[6] The Department of the Treasury has been mobilized to aid in the tracking of financial flows that may be pertinent to proliferation activities and terrorism. The Environmental Protection Agency has become concerned with the development of weapons targeting our air, water, and soil. The Agriculture Department is similarly concerned about "designer pests" that might attack U.S. crops. States and localities have taken on a role as "first responders" in the event of use of weapons of mass destruction on American territory.

Most significantly, the progressive integration of nonproliferation into Pentagon and intelligence planning greatly increased the level of political and bureaucratic interest in the issue just in the past few years. According to one estimate, more than one hundred different agencies and bureaus are currently involved in some fashion in the development and execution of nonproliferation.[7] This situation can be attributed to several changes in outlook, including the elevation of the perceived nature of the threat and concerns about weaknesses in existing nonpro-liferation arrangements, but it is obvious that bureaucratic competition for a stake in an emerging national security priority has been the most important impetus.

By 1998 the Arms Control and Disarmament Agency, a longtime target of conservatives in Congress, had been folded into the Department of State. As that department's authority over nonproliferation policy waned, the Department of Defense became the principal policy voice in the Bush administration, a trend that actually began during the Clinton administration. Nonproliferation objectives are informing a variety of Pentagon initiatives: transformation of the military to take advantage of advanced technologies; modernization of the nuclear posture; plans to deploy national missile defenses; and the "war on terror," which has been espoused by the White House and spearheaded by the secretary of defense and director of central intelligence.

While this all presages major increases in budget outlays to enhance and modernize interventionary capabilities, beef up deterrence forces, increase covert operations, and seek ways to limit damage to the United States in the event of attack, one casualty of this institutional realign-ment is a focus on the prevention of proliferation, at least in any tradi-tional sense. Preventing states from acquiring weapons of mass destruction, according to the new security logic, will best be achieved by demonstrat-ing that the U.S. military can fight and win conflicts even if opponents use unconventional weapons. In the familiar rationale of deterrence, adver-saries will be less likely to seek such weapons to counter the United States once they realize that they are likely to be defeated through overwhelm-ing force. The political ramifications of this strategy for encouraging states to comply voluntarily with international norms, however, are another matter. That is definitely not a high-priority concern in the Pentagon.

It has long been a complaint among the more vocal states that make up the 158 nonnuclear signatories to the Non-Proliferation Treaty (and some new nuclear states, such as India) that the United States and the four other traditional nuclear powers have failed to live up to their treaty commitments, particularly with regard to the pledge to de-emphasize and eventually eliminate nuclear forces in return for other signatories' agreement not to seek nuclear weapons of their own. Ongoing and high-ly publicized calls for the development of new generations of U.S. nuclear weapons to counter both nuclear and nonnuclear WMD facili-ties have exacerbated these tensions, to say nothing of their effect on states the United States relies on for support in critical ways, such as

Russia and China.[8] As Robert Litwak has argued, there are numerous proliferation challenges that are not likely to be responsive to the threat of coercion and in some cases could be adversely affected by an excessive emphasis on military options.

POLICY RECOMMENDATIONS

The current debate indicates clearly that the United States does not have a nonproliferation strategy that is supported by the president and his senior appointees. At least there is no evidence of an articulated strategy that explains how military, political, and economic instruments need to be harmonized to serve the national interest. At the bureaucratic level, similarly, the vast increase in the number of participating agencies has not been accompanied by a sufficient effort to prioritize and coordinate their activities. Notwithstanding the impressive work that has gone into establishing a Department of Homeland Security, the evident patterns of institutional fragmentation bear out Zegart's analysis that the failure to create coherent organizational alignments can eviscerate policy.

It is past time for the White House to conduct a strategic review of nonproliferation mechanisms, going beyond its fixation on military countermeasures and seeking instead to lay out the continuum of proliferation policy instruments that can be brought to bear in different contingencies. It seems premature, Joseph Cirincione persuasively argues, to declare that the international nonproliferation regime has outlived its usefulness.

This is not the first time an administration has discounted the importance of diplomacy to resolve security dilemmas. Incoming Reagan administration officials declared that strategic arms control negotiations were a failed legacy of the past, only to discover their vital role in managing the U.S.-Soviet relationship later on. The case can certainly be made that the weaknesses and flaws of nonproliferation arrangements stem in large measure from a failure of presidential commitment and the political discipline needed to make them more effective. Even compared to strategic arms control, interest in and support for nonproliferation issues in the executive branch and the Congress have been extremely limited, and White House attention has been sporadic at best.

It took almost an entire decade to establish the Non-Proliferation Treaty regime, for example, while the treaties banning chemical and biological weapons were signed but left to languish for decades without enforcement or verification mechanisms. The shortcomings of international bodies like the IAEA or UNSCOM, or of cooperative disarmament ventures such as the threat reduction programs in the former Soviet Union, are as much a reflection of Washington's reluctance to mobilize the requisite resources and grant sufficient enforcement authority as a pointer to any substantive failings of these agencies' missions. Gottemoeller and David Kay have stressed this point convincingly in their chapters.

Without a national nonproliferation strategy to impose discipline on the bureaucracy, it is inevitable that policymaking will be dominated by the most powerful agencies—to the detriment of initiatives taking into account the intricacies of the challenges and the myriad interests involved. Measures boosting the capabilities of the intelligence agencies to predict and prevent new security risks, for example, have been hobbled by the exaggerated emphasis on military countermeasures as displayed in the war on terrorism. Complicated phenomena like terrorism and proliferation require sustained attention and multidisciplinary expertise. The United States needs to draw on the full range of technical, regional, and political professionals, especially in the intelligence community, to analyze and explain what motivates adversaries, as well as to identify the levers in particular societies that prod governments to move in a different direction. These conundrums are not subject to quick fixes or papering over with catchy slogans.

The increasing incursion of partisan interests influencing national security and intelligence priorities over the past decade has added to temptations for the executive branch to design policy initiatives that appeal to salient constituencies. The controversies that raged in Congress in the 1990s about intelligence assessments of the ballistic missile threat from rogue states, for example, imposed enormous pressures on intelligence professionals to demonstrate that their analysis was informed and impartial—not the result of ideological opposition to missile defense programs favored by certain members of Congress. The decline of mechanisms to harness congressional expertise in bipartisan panels—like the Senate Arms Control Observer Group of the 1980s—has made it more difficult to elicit durable congressional consensus for sensitive national security issues. Reviving expert panels of this kind could help attenuate the hard sell for policies that may be politically expedient but are not optimal for security.

As Joanna Spear points out, American leadership in multinational agencies has been on a path of steady decline for some time, not just as a result of the opposition engendered by the recent war against Iraq. The national interest would be better served if officials spent more time highlighting the successful diplomatic efforts that the United States has spear-headed to reduce global proliferation. There is very little discussion of the vital role played by the United States in persuading states like Argentina and Brazil to abandon their nuclear and missile programs, for example. The successes of the cooperative threat reduction programs, similarly, are rarely mentioned by administration officials. If the goal is ultimately to devalue the currency of weapons of mass destruction, it would make sense to promote international understanding of the benefits that have accrued from cooperation and to engage other countries in projects that help solid-ify their appreciation of the advantages of compliance to nonprolifera-tion norms. Focusing on countries that are success stories seems a better strategy for eliciting international support than sponsoring weapons research and programs that effectively concede the inevitability of a renewed worldwide nuclear arms race.

A global nonproliferation strategy, like the war on terrorism, clear-ly needs the strong backing of allies and pro-Western states. The two Persian Gulf wars have shown that international legitimacy is a vital ingredient of the success of ventures like disarmament inspections or, as in Iraq currently, nation building. For all of the resentment engendered in the United States by the opposition of France and Germany to military operations in Iraq, the American government needs to reestablish the habits of consultation and cooperation with allies in order to craft suc-cessful nonproliferation policies. Spear observes that consultations that were perceived to be perfunctory and ad hoc failed to convince influen-tial states of the nature and gravity of the threat in Iraq, abetting the criticism of American objectives.

Containing the diffusion of biological weapons and advanced delivery systems, as discussed in the chapters by Stern and Keller, also requires that more stakeholders be brought in to help articulate and support control regimes. Obviously there is a need for more robust intelligence operations to detect illicit weapons programs and exports. But it is as important for the private sector to be involved. Companies need to be made much more aware of the enormous security implications of some of their activities—the consequences of the spread of pathogens, for example. The ongoing diffi-culties in eliciting support from the American pharmaceutical industry for verification measures associated with the biological weapons convention are partly attributable to failures of communication and consultation.

It should be apparent to industry leaders that they are better served by participating in the design of control mechanisms than by simply express-ing opposition. As the international technology trading system moves toward full commercialization, governments cannot hope to contain the spread of lethal biological agents or advanced weapons production technologies without full cooperation and assistance from the private sector. At a minimum, business interests have an incentive to get involved to discourage the kind of draconian measures on commerce governments might impose in the absence of expert guidance.

It is essential to give caution about the message that the United States is transmitting to other countries concerning the challenges of proliferation. The implicit assumption that nuclear proliferation is virtually a given, in particular, could have the effect of infusing a sense of cynicism internationally about the seriousness and endurance of the nonproliferation regime. In so doing, this could become a self-fulfilling prophecy. Realism is not a pretext for fatalism. As the chapters in this volume demonstrate, there are many instruments the United States can bring to bear to contain and even to reverse the pace of proliferation if it is willing to commit the leadership, political skill, and sustained attention that is required to bring about a more stable world order.

NOTES

INTRODUCTION

1. "National Security Strategy to Combat Weapons of Mass Destruction," White House, December 2002, available online at http://www.whitehouse.gov/news/releases/2002/12/WMDStrategy.pdf.

2. "National Strategy For Homeland Security," Office of Homeland Security, White House, July 2002, pp. 41-46, available online at http://www.whitehouse.gov/homeland/book/nat_strat_hls.pdf.

3. Ceci Connolly, "A Smallpox Vaccine Program Readied: Inoculations May Surpass 500,000 under U.S. Plan," *Washington Post*, July 8, 2002, p. A-1.

4. Joseph Cirincione, with Jon B. Wolfsthal and Miriam Rajkumar, *Deadly Arsenals: Tracking Weapons of Mass Destruction* (Washington, D.C.: Carnegie Endowment for International Peace, 2002), pp. 107-18 (figures for Russia) and 316-24 (for Ukraine, Kazakhstan, and Belarus).

5. Matthew Bunn, "The Next Wave: Urgently Needed New Steps to Control Warheads and Fissile Material," Non-Proliferation Working Papers no. 7, Carnegie Endowment for International Peace, Washington, D.C., copublished with the Project on Managing the Atom, Belfer Center for Science and International Affairs, John F. Kennedy School of Government, Harvard University, March 2000, p. 10, available online at http://www.ceip.org/programs/npp/nextwave.htm.

6. Jon Brook Wolfsthal, Cristina Astrid-Chuen, and Emily Ewell Daughtry, eds., *Nuclear Status Report: Nuclear Weapons, Fissile Material, and Export Controls in the Former Soviet Union*, report no. 6., Non-Proliferation Project, Carnegie Endowment for International Peace, Washington, D.C., and Center for Nonproliferation Studies, Monterey Institute of International Studies, Monterey, Calif., June 2001, p. ix, available online at http://www.ceip.org/files/pdf/Status.pdf.

7. "Cooperative Threat Reduction Scorecard," Defense Threat Reduction Agency, U.S. Department of Defense, updated March 19, 2003, available online at http://www.dtra.mil/ctr/ctr_score.html.

CHAPTER ONE

1. Letter to Lyndon B. Johnson, President of the Senate, June 29, 1961. Reprinted in U.S. Congress, Senate, Committee on Foreign Relations, *Hearings on S. 2180, a Bill to Establish a United States Disarmament Agency for World Peace and Security*, 87th Cong., 1st sess., August 14–16, 1961, p. 9.

2. *Combating Proliferation of Weapons of Mass Destruction*, Report of the Commission to Assess the Organization of the Federal Government to Combat the Proliferation of Weapons of Mass Destruction (hereafter referred to as *Deutch Commission Report*), July 14, 1999, pp. 9, 13, available online at www.fas.org/spp/starwars/program/deutch/11910book.pdf.

3. The term "weapons of mass destruction" includes nuclear, chemical, and biological weapons as well as their means of delivery.

4. In a November 2001 interview, bin Laden publicly claimed for the first time to possess nuclear and chemical weapons and said he reserved "the right to use them." Tim Weiner, "Bin Laden Asserts He Has Nuclear Arms," *New York Times*, November 10, 2001, p. B4. Although bin Laden presented no proof that he had such weapons in hand, his al Qaeda network is known to have sought WMD components as early as 1993. For more, see "Public Statements on Potential Terrorist Use of Chemical, Biological, Radiological, and Nuclear (CBRN) Agents since July 1997," Central Intelligence Agency, updated April 12, 2002, available online at http://www.cia.gov/terrorism/pub_statements_cbrn.html; Kimberly McCloud and Matthew Osborne, "WMD Terrorism and Usama bin Laden," *CNS Reports*, Center for Nonproliferation Studies, Monterey Institute for International Studies, rev. ed. November 20, 2001, available online at http://cns.miis.edu/pubs/reports/binladen.htm.

5. Sam Nunn, "Moving Away from Doomsday and Other Dangers: The Need to Think Anew," speech at the National Press Club, Washington, D.C., March 29, 2001, text available online at http://www.ransac.org/new-web-site/related/govt/testimony/final_npc_speech.html.

6. ACDA was an independent agency charged with developing, advocating, and implementing arms control agreements. Before the merger, the State Department's nonproliferation efforts were scattered and underemphasized, a product of the department's strong regional orientation.

The merger consolidated all nonproliferation operations of both organizations into three State Department bureaus—the Bureau of Nonproliferation, the Bureau of Arms Control, and the Bureau of Political-Military Affairs—and placed them under the direction of the undersecretary for arms control and international security.

7. In 1993, Secretary of Defense Les Aspin launched the Defense Counterproliferation Initiative (CPI) to elevate WMD issues within the military and to establish the Pentagon's bureaucratic primacy in nonproliferation policy across the U.S. government. Aspin called for a review of WMD defense technologies, established a new assistant secretary position for nuclear security and counterproliferation, and charged the armed services with identifying specific research and acquisition programs to be funded. The CPI did not get far. The services, facing overall budget cuts, resisted shifting budgets and priorities to new WMD programs; the new assistant secretary position was soon abolished; and the program encountered opposition from the State Department and other civilian agencies that feared Pentagon primacy would downgrade nonmilitary aspects of nonproliferation policy. The 1997 Defense Reform Initiative brought together five different agencies that dealt with proliferation-related technology acquisition programs into a single Defense Threat Reduction Agency; it consolidated a number of policy areas in the Office of the Secretary of Defense under a single assistant secretary for strategy and threat reduction; and it cut support business costs. Again, however, these reform efforts fell short of expectations. In 1999, the Deutch Commission found that, even after the Defense Reform Initiative, the Pentagon still lacked the managerial direction to set broad programmatic goals and to integrate all of the department's programs in pursuit of those goals. The commission concluded that responsibility for proliferation-related issues was "so diffused as to make it impossible to determine who—below the Deputy Secretary—has the authority and the responsibility to integrate plans, policy requirements, and programs." *Deutch Commission Report*, p. 53.

8. For an overview of this debate, see Michael Moodie and Amy Sands, "New Approaches to Compliance with Arms Control and Nonproliferation Agreements," *Nonproliferation Review* (Center for Nonproliferation Studies, Monterey Institute for International Studies) 8, no. 1 (Spring 2001): 1–9.

9. The commissions are: The Commission to Assess the Organization of the Federal Government to Combat the Proliferation of Weapons of Mass Destruction (Deutch Commission); The U.S. Commission on National Security/21st Century (Hart-Rudman Commission); The National Commission on Terrorism (Bremer Commission); and the Advisory Panel

to Assess Domestic Response Capabilities for Terrorism Involving Weapons of Mass Destruction (Gilmore Panel).

10. U.S. Congress, Senate, *Report to Accompany H.R. 4690 on the Departments of Commerce, Justice, and State, the Judiciary, and Related Agencies Appropriation Bill 2001*, 106th Cong., 2nd sess., S. Rpt. 106-404, September 8, 2000.

11. Russia Task Force (Cutler-Baker Task Force), *A Report Card on the Department of Energy's Nonproliferation Programs with Russia*, Secretary of Energy Advisory Board, U.S. Department of Energy, January 10, 2001, available online at http://www.seab.energy.gov/publications/rusrpt.pdf.

12. I include both reports and testimony officially submitted to Congress by the U.S. General Accounting Office (GAO): "Nuclear Nonproliferation: Coordination of U.S. Programs Designed to Reduce the Threat Posed by Weapons of Mass Destruction," testimony of Gary L. Jones, director, Natural Resources and Environment, GAO, before U.S. Congress, Senate, Committee on Governmental Affairs, Subcommittee on International Security, Proliferation, and Federal Services, GAO-02-180T, November 14, 2001, available online at http://www.gao.gov/new.items/d02180t.pdf; "Combating Terrorism: Observations on Options to Improve the Federal Response," testimony of Raymond J. Decker, director, Defense Capabilities and Management, GAO, before U.S. Congress, House, Committee on Transportation and Infrastructure, Subcommittee on Economic Development, Public Buildings, and Emergency Management, and Committee on Government Reform, Subcommittee on National Security, Veterans Affairs, and International Relations, GAO-01-660T, April 24, 2001, available online at http://www.gao.gov/new.items/d01660t.pdf; "Combating Terrorism: Comments on Counterterrorism Leadership and National Strategy," testimony of Raymond J. Decker, director, Defense Capabilities and Management, GAO, before U.S. Congress, House, Committee on Government Reform, Subcommittee on National Security, Veterans Affairs, and International Relations, GAO-01-556T, March 27, 2001, available online at http://www.gao.gov/new.items/d01556t.pdf; *Combating Terrorism: FEMA Continues to Make Progress in Coordinating Preparedness and Response*, GAO-01-15, March 2001, available online at http://www.gao.gov/new.items/d0115.pdf; *Combating Terrorism: Federal Response Teams Provide Varied Capabilities; Opportunities Remain to Improve Coordination*, GAO 01-14, November 2000, available online at http://www.gao.gov/new.items/d0114.pdf; "Combating Terrorism: Linking Threats to Strategies and Resources," testimony of Norman J. Rabkin, director, National Security Preparedness Issues, National Security and International Affairs Division, GAO, before U.S. Congress, House, Committee on Government Reform, Subcommittee on National Security, Veterans Affairs, and

International Relations, GAO/T-NSIAD-00-218, July 26, 2000, available online at http://www.gao.gov/new.items/ns00218t.pdf; "Combating Terrorism: Comments on Bill H.R. 4210 to Manage Selected Counterterrorist Programs," testimony of Norman J. Rabkin, director, National Security Preparedness Issues, National Security and International Affairs Division, GAO, before U.S. Congress, House, Committee on Transportation and Infrastructure, Subcommittee on Oversight, Investigations, and Emergency Management, GAO/T-NSIAD-00-172, May 4, 2000, available online at http://www.gao.gov/new.items/ns00172t.pdf; *Combating Terrorism: How Five Foreign Countries Are Organized to Combat Terrorism*, GAO/NSIAD-00-85, April 2000, available online at http://www.gao.gov/new.items/ns00085.pdf; "Combating Terrorism: Issues in Managing Counterterrorist Programs," testimony of Norman J. Rabkin, director, National Security Preparedness Issues, National Security and International Affairs Division, GAO, before U.S. Congress, House, Committee on Transportation and Infrastructure, Subcommittee on Oversight, Investigations, and Emergency Management, GAO/T-NSIAD-00-145, April 6, 2000, available online at http://www.gao.gov/new.items/ns00145t.pdf; *Combating Terrorism: Need to Eliminate Duplicate Federal Weapons of Mass Destruction Training*, GAO/NSIAD-00-64, March 2000, available online at http://www.gao.gov/new.items/ns00064.pdf; *Critical Infrastructure Protection: Comprehensive Strategy Can Draw on Year 2000 Experiences*, GAO/AIMD-00-1, October 1999, available online at http://www.gao.gov/archive/2000/ai00001.pdf; *Combating Terrorism: Need for Comprehensive Threat and Risk Assessments of Chemical and Biological Attack*, GAO/NSIAD-99-163, September 7, 1999; *Combating Terrorism: Observations on Growth in Federal Programs*, GAO/T-NSIAD-99-181, June 9, 1999; *Combating Terrorism: Issues to Be Resolved to Improve Counterterrorist Operations*, GAO/NSIAD-99-135, May 13, 1999; *Combating Terrorism: Observations on Federal Spending to Combat Terrorism*, GAO/T-NSIAD/GGD-99-107, March 11, 1999.

13. I am grateful to Ashton Carter for originally suggesting this distinction.

14. Unfortunately, organization theory offers no ideal-type organizational design. Incomplete information, imperfect monitoring, and the uncertainties of human interaction make all organizational arrangements prone to problems. See Paul Milgrom and John Roberts, *Economics, Organization and Management* (Englewood Cliffs, N.J.: Prentice-Hall, 1992).

15. John McClaughry, "The United States Arms Control and Disarmament Agency: A Legislative History," Ph.D. diss., University of California, Berkeley, 1963, p. 52.

16. Hubert Humphrey, speech in U.S. Senate, March 8, 1960, reprinted in *Congressional Record*, 86th Cong., 2d sess., vol. 106, p. 4915.

17. U.S. Congress, Senate, *Hearings on S. 2180*, August 14–16, 1961, pp. 62, 112.

18. When asked to elaborate about the difficulties and delays he experienced in getting his negotiating instructions, Lodge replied that he would go into the details at the committee's executive session. See ibid., p. 120.

19. Ibid., pp. 116–17.

20. Senator John F. Kennedy, remarks at the University of New Hampshire, March 7, 1960, reprinted in *Congressional Record*, 86th Cong., 2nd sess., March 7, 1960, vol. 106, pp. 4707–9.

21. McClaughry, "United States Arms Control and Disarmament Agency," p. 44.

22. Dianne Feinstein, U.S. Congress, Senate, Judiciary Committee, Subcommittee on Technology, Terrorism, and Government Information, *Hearings on the Hart-Rudman Report*, 107th Cong., 1st sess., April 3, 2001; Sam Nunn, former U.S. senator, testimony before U.S. Congress, House, Government Reform Committee, Subcommittee on National Security, Veterans Affairs, and International Relations, *Hearing on Terrorism Prevention*, 107th Cong., 1st sess., July 23, 2001.

23. Andrea Stone, "United States is Open to Attacks by Terrorists, Report Warns," *USA Today*, July 9, 1999, p. 11A.

24. *Deutch Commission Report*, p. 9.

25. Robert P. Bongiovi, acting director, Defense Threat Reduction Agency, testimony before U.S. Congress, Senate, Armed Services Committee, Subcommittee on Emerging Threats and Capabilities, 107th Cong., 1st sess., July 12, 2001.

26. Suzanne E. Spaulding, "The Deutch Commission Report: An Overview," *Nonproliferation Review* (Center for Nonproliferation Studies, Monterey Institute for International Studies) 6, no. 4 (Fall 1999): 170–71.

27. Ashton B. Carter and William J. Perry, *Preventive Defense: A New Security Strategy for America* (Washington, D.C.: Brookings Institution Press, 1999), pp. 75–76.

28. Author's confidential telephone interview with administration official, March 21, 2001.

29. See in particular: U.S. Congress, Senate, *Hearings on the Hart-Rudman Report*, April 3, 2001; U.S. Congress, Senate, Armed Services Committee, Subcommittee on Emerging Threats and Capabilities, *Hearings*, 107th Cong., 1st sess., July 12, 2001; U.S. Congress, House, *Hearing on Terrorism Prevention*, July 23, 2001; U.S. Congress, Senate, Government Reform Committee, Subcommittee on International Security, Proliferation, and Federal Service, *Hearing on Handling Bioterrorist*

Attacks, 107th Cong., 1st sess., July 23, 2001; U.S. Congress, Senate, Foreign Relations Committee, *Hearing on the Department of Energy's Nonproliferation Programs with Russia*, 107th Cong., 1st sess., July 24, 2001.

30. U.S. General Accounting Office, *Combating Terrorism: Comments on Counterterrorist Leadership*.

31. Feinstein, *Hearings on the Hart-Rudman Report*, April 3, 2001.

32. *First Annual Report to the President and the Congress of the Advisory Panel to Assess Domestic Response Capabilities for Terrorism Involving Weapons of Mass Destruction*, December 15, 1999, p. 59, available online at http://www.rand.org/nsrd/terrpanel/terror.pdf.

33. Russia Task Force, *Report Card on the Department of Energy's Nonproliferation Programs with Russia*.

34. Kennedy, remarks at the University of New Hampshire, March 7, 1960.

35. Trevor Gardner, "Organizing for Peace," *Bulletin of the Atomic Scientists* 16, no. 7 (September 1960): 299.

36. Arthur M. Schlesinger, Jr., *A Thousand Days: John F. Kennedy in the White House* (Boston: Houghton Mifflin, 1965), p. 472.

37. U.S. Congress, Senate, *Hearings on S. 2180*, August 14–16, 1961, pp. 8–9.

38. U.S. Congress, Senate, Foreign Relations Committee, Subcommittee on Disarmament, Control, and Reduction of Arms, *Hearings*, Part II, 85th Cong., 1st sess., January 9–10, 1957, p. 1085.

39. Thomas E. Murray, *Nuclear Policy for War and Peace* (Cleveland: World Publishing, 1960), p. 202.

40. Kennedy, remarks at the University of New Hampshire, March 7, 1960.

41. Gardner, "Organizing for Peace."

42. U.S. Congress, Senate, *Hearings on S. 2180*, August 14–16, 1961, p. 9.

43. Ibid., p. 62.

44. Hart-Rudman Commission, *Road Map for National Security: Imperative for Change*, Phase III Report, February 15, 2001, p. x, available online at http://www.nssg.gov/PhaseIIIFR.pdf.

45. Ibid., p. 10. The emphasis is the commission's.

46. *Toward a National Strategy for Combating Terrorism: Second Annual Report of the Advisory Panel to Assess Domestic Response Capabilities for Terrorism Involving Weapons of Mass Destruction*, December 15, 2000, p. iii, available online at http://www.rand.org/nsrd/terrpanel/terror2.pdf.

47. *Deutch Commission Report*, p. 5.

48. Ibid., pp. 5–6.

49. Ibid., p. 4.

50. U.S. General Accounting Office, *Nuclear Nonproliferation: Coordination of U.S. Programs*, p. 7.

51. *Deutch Commission Report*, p. 9.

52. For a side-by-side analysis of proposals in this area, see U.S. General Accounting Office, *Combating Terrorism: Observations on Options to Improve the Federal Response*.

53. *Toward a National Strategy for Combating Terrorism*, p. v.

54. Jason Peckenpaugh, "Building a Behemoth," *Government Executive*, September 1, 2002, available online at http://www.govexec.com/features/0902/0902mag.htm.

55. *Deutch Commission Report*, p. 19.

56. Spaulding, "Deutch Commission Report," p. 171.

57. U.S. Congress, Senate, *Hearings on S. 2180*, August 14–16, 1961, pp. 39–40.

58. President John F. Kennedy, speech to the United Nations General Assembly, September 15, 1961, reprinted in Disarmament Document Series no. 29 (mimeograph), U.S. Arms Control and Disarmament Agency, 1962, p. 1.

59. *Deutch Commission Report*, p. 4.

60. For a good analysis of ACDA's troubled history, see Barry M. Blechman and Janne E. Nolan, "Reorganizing for More Effective Arms Negotiations," *Foreign Affairs* 61, no. 5 (Summer 1983): 1157–82; Duncan L. Clarke, *Politics of Arms Control: The Role and Effectiveness of the U.S. Arms Control and Disarmament Agency* (New York: Free Press, 1979).

61. Richard E. Neustadt, *Presidential Power and the Modern Presidents: The Politics of Leadership from Roosevelt to Reagan*, rev. ed. (New York: Free Press, 1990), pp. 128–51.

62. Terry M. Moe, "The Politics of Bureaucratic Structure," in John E. Chubb and Paul E. Peterson, eds., *Can the Government Govern?* (Washington, D.C.: Brookings Institution, 1989), pp. 267–329; James Q. Wilson, *Bureaucracy: What Government Agencies Do and Why They Do It*, rev. ed. (New York: Basic Books, 2000), pp. 257–76.

63. As Terry Moe concludes, "in the political system, public bureaucracies are designed in no small measure by participants who explicitly want them to fail." Terry M. Moe, "The Politics of Structural Choice: Toward a Theory of Public Bureaucracy," in Oliver E. Williamson, ed., *Organization Theory: From Chester Barnard to the Present and Beyond*, expanded ed. (New York: Oxford University Press, 1995), p. 127.

64. Neustadt, *Presidential Power and the Modern Presidents*, p. ix.

65. Author's confidential telephone interview with a former senior official, March 20, 2001.

66. Herbert A. Simon, "Public Administration in Today's World of Organizations and Markets," John Gaus Lecture, American Political Science Association annual meeting, Washington D.C., September 1,

2000, reprinted in *PS: Political Science and Politics* (American Political Science Association, Washington, D.C.) 33, no. 4 (December 2000): 753, available online at http://www.apsanet.org/PS/dec00/simon.cfm.

67. In July 2001, Sam Nunn provided a vivid description of the problem. Testifying before Congress, he noted that a few years ago, when the Clinton administration held a meeting to discuss supplemental funding legislation for defense against biological weapons, the presiding White House officer greeted officials from the FBI, the CIA, the National Security Council staff, and the Defense Department. But when he saw the assistant secretary for health and human services, he did a double take and asked, "What are you doing here?" As Nunn concluded, "Health officials should not need to be given directions to the White House Situation Room." Nunn, testimony before U.S. Congress, House, July 23, 2001.

68. Clarke, *Politics of Arms Control*, p. 19.

69. U.S. Congress, House, Committee on Foreign Affairs, Subcommittee on National Security Policy and Scientific Developments, *Arms Control and Disarmament Agency Hearings*, 93rd Cong., 2nd sess., September 24, 1974, p. 3.

70. McClaughry, "United States Arms Control and Disarmament Agency," pp. 177–81.

71. Author's confidential telephone interview with a former administration official, March 21, 2001.

72. Kennedy, remarks at the University of New Hampshire, March 7, 1960.

73. Clarke, *Politics of Arms Control*, p. 19.

74. McClaughry, "United States Arms Control and Disarmament Agency," p. 147.

75. Text of S. 2180, U.S. Congress, Senate, *Hearings on S. 2180*, August 14–16, 1961, p. 2.

76. *United States Statutes at Large*, vol. 75 (Washington, D.C.: U.S. Government Printing Office, 1961), p. 632.

77. Text of S. 2180, U.S. Congress, Senate, *Hearings on S. 2180*, August 14–16, 1961, p. 2.

78. *United States Statutes at Large*, vol. 75.

79. Text of S. 2180, U.S. Congress, Senate, *Hearings on S. 2180*, August 14–16, 1961, p. 4.

80. *United States Statutes at Large*, vol. 75, p. 635.

81. Text of S. 2180, U.S. Congress, Senate, *Hearings on S. 2180*, August 14–16, 1961, p. 4.

CHAPTER TWO

1. "Proliferation: Threat and Response," Office of the Secretary of Defense, U.S. Department of Defense, January 2001, p. 1.

2. Resolution of the United Nations General Assembly, January 24, 1946; see also "General Findings and Recommendations Approved by the Atomic Energy Commission and Incorporated in Its First Report to the Security Council, December 31, 1946," UN Atomic Energy Commission, available online at http://www.yale.edu/lawweb/avalon/decade/decad240.htm.

3. See Henry D. Sokolski, *Best of Intentions: America's Campaign against Strategic Weapons Proliferation* (Westport, Conn.: Praeger, 2001), pp. 6–8.

4. "Joint Declaration by the Heads of Government of the United States, the United Kingdom, and Canada," November 15, 1945, cited in ibid., p. 7.

5. "The Baruch Plan, Presented to the United Nations Atomic Energy Commission, June 14, 1946," cited in U.S. Congress, Senate, Committee on Governmental Affairs, *Nuclear Proliferation Factbook*, S.Prt. 103-111, December 1994, p. 2.

6. See Sokolski, *Best of Intentions*, pp. 13–24, for a good, brief history of the Baruch Plan.

7. Dwight D. Eisenhower, "Address before the General Assembly of the United Nations on the Peaceful Uses of Nuclear Energy," December 8, 1953, cited in U.S. Congress, *Nuclear Proliferation Factbook*, p. 15.

8. Ibid.

9. "Face to Face, Nixon-Kennedy," third presidential debate between Vice President Richard M. Nixon and Senator John F. Kennedy, October 13, 1960, text available through the John F. Kennedy Library and Museum, Boston, and online at http://www.cs.umb.edu/jfklibrary/60-3rd.htm.

10. President John F. Kennedy, address before the UN General Assembly, September 25, 1961, text available through the John F. Kennedy Library and Museum, Boston, and online at http://www.cs.umb.edu/jfklibrary/j092561.htm.

11. "Remarks of President Nixon at a Ceremony Marking the Ratification and Entry into Force of the Treaty on Non-Proliferation of Nuclear Weapons," *Public Papers of the Presidents: Richard Nixon, 1970* (Washington, D.C.: U.S. Government Printing Office, 1971), p. 241.

12. Cited in Joseph Cirincione, "The Non-Proliferation Treaty and the Nuclear Balance," *Current History*, May 1995, p. 202.

13. David Fischer, *Stopping the Spread of Nuclear Weapons: The Past and the Prospects* (London: Routledge, 1992), pp. 6–7.

14. Lewis A. Dunn, *Controlling the Bomb: Nuclear Proliferation in the 1980s* (New Haven: Yale University Press, 1982), p. 1.

15. Ibid.

16. Leonard S. Spector, *Nuclear Ambitions: The Spread of Nuclear Weapons* (Boulder, Colo.: Westview Press, 1990), pp. 6–9.

17. Ibid., p. 8.

18. Regional approaches to nonproliferation are an important part of the overall regime. Treaties that have established nuclear-weapon-free zones include the Antarctic Treaty of 1959, the Treaty for the Prohibition of Nuclear Weapons in Latin America (the Tlatelolco Treaty) of 1967, the South Pacific Nuclear Free Zone (Rarotonga Treaty) of 1985, and the Africa Nuclear-Weapon-Free Zone (Pelindaba Treaty) of 1998.

19. Thomas W. Graham, "Proliferation Threats: Growing, Shrinking or Changing?" paper presented to the Carnegie International Non-Proliferation Conference 2001, Carnegie Endowment for International Peace, Washington, D.C., June 18–19, 2001, available online at www.ceip.org/files/projects/npp/resources/nppconf2001.htm.

20. Ibid.

21. Ibid.

22. George W. Bush, "Defense Policy Speech at the Citadel," September 23, 1999, available online at www.ceip.org/programs/npp/bush923.htm.

23. Samuel P. Huntington, "The Clash of Civilizations?" *Foreign Affairs* 72, no. 3 (Summer 1993): 22.

24. See Joseph Cirincione, "Non-Proliferation Paralysis: The Decline and Stall of US Policy," *Disarmament Diplomacy* (Acronym Institute for Disarmament Diplomacy, London), no. 30, September 1998, available online at http://www.acronym.org.uk/dd/dd30/30usnon.htm.

25. Statement of Jeane Kirkpatrick, professor of government, Georgetown University, and senior fellow, American Enterprise Institute, before U.S. Congress, Senate, Foreign Relations Committee, hearing on the Comprehensive Test Ban Treaty, 106th Cong., 1st sess., October 7, 1999, text available online at http://www.fas.org/nuke/control/ctbt/text/100799kirkpatrick.htm.

26. "Rumsfeld Adviser: Bomb N. Korea if Necessary," *Atlanta Journal-Constitution*, June 12, 2003.

27. The IAEA provided North Korea with the wrong forms for completing its safeguards agreement, and the country was granted an eighteen-month extension. This delay, however, did not release North Korea from its obligations under the treaty not to pursue nuclear weapons development.

28. K. Subrahmanyam, "Indian Nuclear Policy—1964–68: A Personal Recollection," in Jasjit Singh, ed., *Nuclear India* (New Delhi: Institute for Defense Studies and Analysis, 1998).

29. Jaswant Singh, interview with *Time* magazine, November 25, 1999.

30. George Perkovich, in conversation at a Carnegie Proliferation Roundtable, Carnegie Endowment for International Peace, Washington, D.C., November 16, 1999.

31. George Perkovich, *India's Nuclear Bomb: The Impact on Proliferation* (Berkeley, Calif.: University of California Press, 1999), pp. 455–59.

32. C. Raja Mohan, "India Joins the NPT Debate," *The Hindu* (Madras), May 11, 2000.

33. Scott D. Sagan, "Why Do States Build Nuclear Weapons?" *International Security* 21, no. 3 (Winter 1996/97): 55.

34. Ibid., pp. 85–86.

35. Quoted in the *Washington Post*, August 2, 1999.

36. Kent E. Calder, *Pacific Defense: Arms, Energy, and America's Future in Asia* (New York: William Morrow and Company, 1996), p. 79.

37. Final communiqué, ministerial meeting of the North Atlantic Council, Budapest, May 29, 2001, paragraphs 76–77.

38. Richard G. Lugar, keynote address to the Carnegie International Non-Proliferation Conference 2001, Carnegie Endowment for International Peace, Washington, D.C., June 18, 2001, available online at www.ceip.org/files/projects/npp/resources/nppconf2001.htm.

39. Geoffrey Kemp, "Imaginative Diplomacy, Not Hardline Rhetoric: Dealing with Iran's Nuclear Program," *National Interest*, June 11, 2003.

40. Ibid.

41. James Ceasar, "The Great Divide: American Internationalism and Its Opponents," in Robert Kagan and William Kristol, eds., *Present Dangers: Crisis and Opportunity in American Foreign and Defense Policy* (San Francisco: Encounter Books, 2000), p. 27.

42. James Kitfield, "Is Arms Control Dead?" *National Journal*, July 14, 2001, p. 2223.

CHAPTER THREE

1. The author gratefully acknowledges the following individuals for their comments on the initial draft of this chapter: Janne Nolan, Bernard Finel, Victor Utgoff, Michael Brown, Daniel Poneman, Gary Samore, Paul Stares, Zachary Davis, Mitchell Reiss, Joseph Pilat, and Michael Glennon.

2. The term "preemption" is analytically distinct from "prevention." Prevention is forestalling the acquisition of WMD capabilities by the target state. Preemption is the anticipatory use of force to neutralize existing WMD capabilities before they can be employed. In the current policy debate, preemption is often used interchangeably to describe both missions.

3. See Alexander L. George, *Bridging the Gap: Theory and Practice in Foreign Policy* (Washington, D.C.: United States Institute of Peace Press, 1993), especially Chapter 4, "Reforming Outlaw States and Rogue Leaders," pp. 45–60.

4. Coercive nonproliferation also includes some nonmilitary tools, of course, such as economic sanctions, but this chapter focuses exclusively on military instruments and the use of force.

5. There are few cases in which force was used or considered against WMD-related facilities. The ones selected in this chapter are those for which reliable documentary evidence exists. One must distinguish between these cases and those that are in the realm of military contingency planning and rumor. Other cases include an unsuccessful Iranian raid on the Iraqi Osiraq reactor construction site in September 1980 and several Iraqi attacks on Iran's Bushehr reactor construction site between 1984 and 1988; whether these missions were conducted explicitly to forestall proliferation is not clear. In addition, an Indian source reports the rumor that Israel sounded out the New Delhi government about the possibility of providing landing rights for Israeli aircraft if they were to undertake an Osriaq-type raid against Pakistan's Kahuta nuclear reactor. See Barry R. Schneider, *Future War and Counterproliferation: U.S. Military Responses to NBC Proliferation Threats* (Westport, Conn.: Praeger, 1999), pp. 151–54. Perhaps the best-known additional case is the report that Soviet diplomats sounded out their American counterparts in 1969 regarding a possible Soviet attack on Chinese nuclear facilities. No information is available yet from the Russian archives as to how seriously the Soviet regime considered this option or whether the threat was floated to coerce China to enter into negotiations on their border dispute that had flared into open military skirmishes early that year. The pertinent U.S. documents have been declassified and are available with commentary by historian William Burr on the National Security Archive Web site, available online at www.gwu.edu/~nsarchiv/NSAEBB.

6. Alexander George, "Case Studies: The Method of 'Structured, Focused Comparison,'" in Paul Gordon Lauren, ed., *Diplomacy: New Approaches in History, Theory, and Policy* (New York: Free Press, 1979).

7. See Philip Zelikow, "Offensive Military Options," in Robert D. Blackwill and Albert Carnesale, eds., *New Nuclear Nations: Consequences for U.S. Policy* (New York: Council on Foreign Relations Press, 1993), pp. 162–63;

Michèle A. Flournoy, "Implications for U.S. Military Strategy" in Blackwill and Carnesale, *New Nuclear Nations*, pp. 148–52; Schneider, *Future War and Counterproliferation*, pp. 157–62.

8. Wyn Q. Bowen and David H. Dunn, *American Security Policy in the 1990s: Beyond Containment* (Aldershot, U.K.: Dartmouth Publishing Co., 1996), p. 119.

9. Quoted in Michael Klare, *Rogue States and Nuclear Outlaws: America's Search for a New Foreign Policy* (New York: Hill and Wang, 1995), pp. 26–27.

10. A literature survey reveals that, prior to 1980, "pariah" or "outlaw" status was primarily reserved for states such as Idi Amin's Uganda or Pol Pot's Cambodia on the basis of their regimes' objectionable internal behavior (i.e., how they treated their own people). During the 1980s, as concern focused on international terrorism and WMD acquisition, the criteria shifted from internal to external behavioral criteria, a trend strongly reinforced by the Persian Gulf War. See Robert S. Litwak, *Rogue States and U.S. Foreign Policy: Containment after the Cold War* (Washington, D.C.: Woodrow Wilson Center Press, 2000), pp. 49–56.

11. Richard A. Melanson, *American Foreign Policy since the Vietnam War: The Search for Consensus from Nixon to Clinton* (Armonk, N.Y.: M. E. Sharpe, 1996), pp. 236, 245.

12. Michael Nacht, "Weapons Proliferation and Missile Defense: New Patterns, Tough Choices," in Robert J. Lieber, *Eagle Rules? Foreign Policy and American Primacy in the Twenty-first Century* (Englewood Cliffs, N.J.: Prentice Hall, 2002).

13. "Weapons of Mass Destruction in the Middle East," Center for Nonproliferation Studies, Monterey Institute of International Studies, Monterey, Calif., available online at http://cns.miis.edu/research/wmdme/iraq.htm#fnB2.

14. Anthony Lake, "Confronting Backlash States," *Foreign Affairs* 73, no. 2 (March/April 1994): 45–46.

15. Secretary of State Madeleine K. Albright, address and question-and-answer session before the Council on Foreign Relations, New York, September 30, 1997, available online at http://secretary.state.gov/www/statements/970930.html.

16. The administration established a separate Nonproliferation and Export Controls directorate within the National Security Council, which oversaw an intensive interagency review process that yielded Presidential Decision Directive 13 (PDD-13). That framework did not specifically mention counterproliferation but did say that the administration would "ensure that our own force structure and defense planning address the

potential threat from weapons of mass destruction and missiles." See "Nonproliferation and Export Control: Fact Sheet," Office of the Press Secretary, White House, September 27, 1993.

17. *Report on the Bottom-up Review*, Department of Defense, October 1993, pp. 1, 19.

18. Remarks by Secretary of Defense Les Aspin at the National Academy of Sciences Committee on International Security and Arms Control, Washington, D.C., December 7, 1993, published in U.S. Congress, Senate, Committee on Governmental Affairs, *Nuclear Proliferation Factbook*, 103d Cong., 2d sess., December 1994, S. Prt. 103-111, pp. 198, 203 (emphasis added). See also Zachary S. Davis and Mitchell Reiss, "U.S. Counterproliferation Doctrine: Issues for Congress," Report for Congress no. 94-734 ENR, Congressional Research Service, September 21, 1994.

19. "1998 CPRC Report to Congress," Counterproliferation Program Review Committee, Office of the Deputy Secretary of Defense, May 1998, p. ES-3, available online at http://www.acq.osd.mil/cp/es98.pdf.

20. Daniel Poneman, "National Security Council Memorandum: Agreed Definitions," February 18, 1994, published in U.S. Congress, Senate, Committee on Governmental Affairs, *Nuclear Proliferation Factbook*, p. 205.

21. "Report on Activities and Programs for Countering Proliferation" (also known as the Deutch Report), Counterproliferation Program Review Committee, Office of the Deputy Secretary of Defense, May 1995.

22. See Mitchell Reiss and Harold Müller, eds., *International Perspectives on Counterproliferaton*, Working Paper no. 99, Division of International Studies, Woodrow Wilson Center, Washington, D.C., January 1995.

23. Charles Krauthammer, "The Unipolar Moment," *Foreign Affairs* 70, no. 1 (America and the World 1990/91): 25, 33.

24. Thomas W. Lippman, "If Nonproliferation Fails, Pentagon Wants 'Counterproliferation' in Place," *Washington Post*, May 15, 1994, p. A11.

25. "DoD News Briefing," Office of the Assistant Secretary of Defense (Public Affairs), January 20, 1999, available online at http://www.defenselink.mil/news/Jan1999/t01201999_t0120md.html.

26. "Remarks of Secretary of Defense William Perry at George Washington University," Federal News Service transcript, April 25, 1996, p. 1.

27. The issue of "undeterrable" states is discussed in Janne Nolan and Mark Strauss, "The Rogues' Gallery," *Brown Journal of World Affairs* 4, no. 1 (Winter/Spring 1997): 32–36.

28. Senate Minority Leader Robert Dole (R.-Kan.) said, "It is always possible to get an agreement when you give enough away." Cited in Leon V.

Sigal, *Disarming Strangers: Nuclear Diplomacy with North Korea* (Princeton, N.J.: Princeton University Press, 1998), p. 192.

29. "Address of the President to the Joint Session of Congress," February 27, 2001.

30. Jeffrey A. Larsen, "NATO Counterproliferation Policy: A Case Study in Alliance Politics," Occasional Paper no. 17, Institute for National Security Studies, Air Force Academy, November 1997, p. 3.

31. The general language of NATO's "strategic concept," approved by heads of state and government at the April 1999 North Atlantic Council meeting, provides little guidance: "The Alliance's defence posture must have the capability to address appropriately and effectively the risks associated with the proliferation of NBC weapons and their means of delivery, which also pose a potential threat to the Allies' populations, territory, and forces. A balanced mix of forces, response capabilities and strengthened defences is needed." See "The Alliance's Strategic Concept," press release NAC-S(99)65, North Atlantic Treaty Organization, Brussels, April 24, 1999, available online at http://www.nato.int/docu/pr/1999/p99-065e.htm. A separate, thorny issue, beyond the scope of this paper, is whether the Alliance should threaten a nuclear response to the use of chemical or biological agents by a WMD-armed adversary.

32. Gilles Andréani, "The Disarray of US Non-Proliferation Policy," *Survival* 41, no. 4 (Winter 1999–2000): 43.

33. Speech by Secretary of State Colin Powell to the U.S. business community in China during the Asia-Pacific Economic Cooperation Summit in Shanghai, October 18, 2001, text available online at http://www.state.gov/secretary/rm/2001/5441.htm.

34. "President Speaks on War Effort to Citadel Cadets," Office of the Press Secretary, White House, December 11, 2001, text available online at http://www.whitehouse.gov/news/releases/2001/12/20011211-6.html.

35. "President Delivers State of the Union Address," Office of the Press Secretary, White House, January 29, 2002, text available online at http://www.whitehouse.gov/news/releases/2002/01/print/20020129-11.html.

36. "President Bush Delivers Graduation Speech at West Point," Office of the Press Secretary, White House, June 1, 2002, text available online at http://www.whitehouse.gov/news/releases/2002/06/20020601-3.html.

37. "The National Security Strategy of the United States of America," White House, September 2002, p. 15, available online at http://www.whitehouse.gov/nsc/nss.pdf.

38. Elements of this criticism emerged after the West Point speech; see "Dealing with the 'Axis of Evil': The US and the 'Perilous Crossroads,'"

Strategic Comments (International Institute of Strategic Studies, London) 8, no. 5 (June 2002), available online at http://www.iiss.org/showfreepdfs. php?scID=222&type=iiss.pdf.

39. Statement of Secretary of State Colin Powell before the Foreign Relations Committee, U.S. Congress, Senate, "The Administration's Position with Regard to Iraq," 107th Cong., 2d sess., September 26, 2002, text available online at http://www.state.gov/secretary/rm/2002/13765.htm.

40. Peter Slevin, "Analysts: New Strategy Courts Unseen Dangers," *Washington Post*, September 22, 2002, p. A1.

41. "Dealing with the 'Axis of Evil.'"

42. This case summary is drawn from William Burr and Jeffrey T. Richelson, "Whether to 'Strangle the Baby in the Cradle': The United States and the Chinese Nuclear Program, 1960–64," *International Security* 25, no. 3 (Winter 2000–2001): 54–99. This outstanding article is based upon oral history interviews and declassified U.S. documents.

43. Ibid., p. 67.

44. Ibid., pp. 76–77.

45. Ibid., p. 88.

46. Shai Feldman, "The Bombing of Osiraq—Revisited," *International Security* 7, no. 2 (Fall 1982): 115–16.

47. Angus Deming, Ron Moreau, and David C. Marin, "Two Minutes over Baghdad," *Newsweek*, June 22, 1981, p. 22.

48. Feldman, "Bombing of Osiraq," p. 136. The United States accepted this UN Security Council language after threatening to veto punitive economic and political sanctions against Israel advocated by Iraq.

49. Thomas A. Keaney and Eliot A. Cohen, *Revolution in Warfare? Air Power in the Persian Gulf*, repr. ed. (Annapolis, Md.: Naval Institute Press, 1995), pp. 70–71. This volume is a revised and expanded version of Thomas A. Keaney and Eliot A. Cohen, *Gulf War Air Power Survey*, Summary Report (Washington, D.C.: U.S. Government Printing Office, 1993).

50. Department of Defense, *Proliferation: Threat and Response* (Washington, D.C.: U.S. Government Printing Office, April 1996), pp. 20–21, available online at http://www.defenselink.mil/pubs/prolif97/.

51. Keaney and Cohen, *Revolution in Warfare?* p. 72.

52. Amatzia Baram, *Building toward Crisis: Saddam Husayn's Strategy for Survival*, Washington Institute for Near East Policy, Washington, D.C., July 1998, pp. 80–82.

53. Bradley Graham and Dana Priest, "U.S. Details Strategy, Damage," *Washington Post*, December 18, 1998, p. A1.

54. Warren P. Strobel et al., "Sticking It to Saddam," *U.S. News & World Report*, January 11, 1999, p. 38. The following exchange with a reporter is from Secretary of Defense William S. Cohen's press briefing on December 19, 1998 (transcript available online at www.defenselink.mil/news/Dec1998/t12191998_t1219fox.html):

"Q: [A]re you not going after those facilities that are dual use capable because of the concern that we have for the amount of damage to innocent civilians?

Secretary Cohen: I indicated yesterday that we did not target those facilities that are dual use capable because of the concern that we have for amount of damage to innocent civilians.

Q: Mr. Secretary, if you target them at night, why would they have anybody there?

Secretary Cohen: People don't have to be in the facility in order to do damage to the area itself. We took that into account. We were not going to engage in acts which could result in many, many deaths to innocent people."

55. See Litwak, *Rogue States and U.S. Foreign Policy*, Chapter 6, for an overview, as well as following books that trace the United States' nuclear diplomacy with North Korea leading to the conclusion of the Agreed Framework in October 1994: Mitchell Reiss, "North Korea: Living with Uncertainty," in Mitchell Reiss, *Bridled Ambition: Why Countries Constrain Their Nuclear Capabilities* (Washington, D.C.: Woodrow Wilson Center Press, 1995), pp. 231–319; Michael J. Mazarr, *North Korea and the Bomb: A Case Study in Nonproliferation* (New York: St. Martin's Press, 1995); Sigal, *Disarming Strangers*; and Don Oberdorfer, *The Two Koreas: A Contemporary History* (Reading, Mass.: Addison-Wesley, 1997), Chapters 11–14.

56. Ashton B. Carter and William J. Perry, *Preventive Defense: A New Security Strategy for America* (Washington, D.C.: Brookings Institution Press, 1999), pp. 128–29. An op-ed by former Bush national security adviser Brent Scowcroft and undersecretary of state Arnold Kanter, "Korea: Time for Action," *Washington Post*, June 15, 1994, p. A25, advocated a military strike to destroy the reprocessing plant at Yongbyon if North Korea continued to reject IAEA monitoring. Scowcroft and Kanter wrote, "The stakes could hardly be higher. The time for temporizing is over."

57. Indeed, one of the political objectives of the operation was to respond to the bin Laden attacks in kind by striking two geographically distinct targets, thereby underscoring the United States' global reach.

58. "Key Quotes on U.S. Strikes against Terrorism," USIS Washington File, U.S. Information Agency, August 28, 1998, p. 2, text available online at http://usembassy-australia.state.gov/hyper/WF980828/epf502.htm.

59. Ibid., p. 19.

60. Seymour M. Hersh, "The Missiles of August," *New Yorker*, October 12, 1998, p. 40.

61. Gregory Koblenz, "Countering Dual-Use Facilities: Lessons from Iraq and Sudan," *Jane's Intelligence Review* 11, no. 3 (March 1, 1999): 48.

62. Ibid.

63. Daniel Benjamin and Steven Simon, "A Failure of Intelligence?" *New York Review of Books*, December 20, 2001, p. 76.

64. The United States and Britain used force against Iraq—a hostile proliferator—in December 1998 during Operation Desert Fox. By contrast, as Ian Anthony and Elisabeth French observe: "In the case of India and Pakistan, there is little evidence that coercive measures (whether the use of force or sanctions) were seen as central instruments to prevent the development of nuclear weapons arsenals. Although some economic sanctions were introduced, the preferred approach appeared to be a combination of diplomacy (intended to persuade India and Pakistan to join cooperative arms control and disarmament processes) along with enhanced export controls (intended to make weapon development as difficult and costly as possible for India and Pakistan)." See Ian Anthony and Elisabeth M. French, "Non-Cooperative Responses to Proliferation: Multilateral Dimensions," *SIPRI Yearbook 1999* (New York: Oxford University Press, 1999), p. 691, available online at http://projects.sipri.se/expcon/expconpubs/yb9915.pdf.

65. James A. Baker III, with Thomas M. DeFrank, *The Politics of Diplomacy: Revolution, War and Peace, 1989–1992* (New York: G. P. Putnam's Sons, 1995), p. 359.

66. Cited in *Strategic Assessment 1996: Instruments of U.S. Power*, Institute for National Strategic Studies, National Defense University, 1996, p. 203, available online at http://www.ndu.edu/ndu/inss/sa96/sa96cont.html.

67. Flournoy, "Implications for U.S. Military Strategy," p. 144. This particular phrase is that of Ashton B. Carter and Robert D. Blackwill in their chapter on "The Role of Intelligence" in that same edited volume, Blackwill and Carnesale, *New Nuclear Nations*, p. 217. According to Caroline F. Ziemke, Philippe Loustaunau, and Amy Alrich, strategic personality "focuses on broad historical and cultural patterns that evolve over the whole course of a state's history (its historical plot) and identifies the fundamental consistencies in its long-term strategic conduct in order to shed light on how they might shape its current and future strategic decisions. The methodology is not deterministic and, hence, not precisely predictive." See Caroline F. Ziemke, Philippe Loustaunau, and Amy Alrich,

Strategic Personality and the Effectiveness of Nuclear Deterrence, Institute for Defense Analyses, Alexandria, Va., November 2000, p. ES-1, available online at http://www.dtra.mil/about/organization/d2537dtra.pdf.

68. Secretary of State Daniel Webster originally formulated this limitation on the scope of anticipatory self-defense in the landmark *Caroline* case of 1837, cited in Davis and Reiss, "U.S. Counterproliferation Doctrine," p. 19.

69. David Fischer, "Forcible Counterproliferation: Necessary? Feasible?" in Reiss and Müller, *International Perspectives on Counterproliferaton*, pp. 17–20.

70. Stephen M. Walt, "Containing Rogues and Renegades: Coalition Strategies and Counterproliferation" in Victor A. Utgoff, ed., *The Coming Crisis: Nuclear Proliferation, U.S. Interests, and World Order* (Cambridge, Mass.: MIT Press, 1999), p. 217.

71. James Risen and Judith Miller, "Al Qaeda Sites Point to Tests of Chemicals," *New York Times*, November 11, 2001, pp. B1, B3.

72. See John Pike, "Agent Defeat Warhead (ADW)," Military Analysis Network, Federation of American Scientists, Washington, D.C., updated November 29, 1999, available online at http://www.fas.org/man/dod-101/sys/smart/adw.htm.

73. For excellent analyses of the motivations to acquire or give up nuclear weapons see Scott D. Sagan, "Rethinking the Causes of Nuclear Proliferation: Three Bomb Models in Search of a Bomb" in Utgoff, *Coming Crisis*, pp. 17–50; and Reiss, *Bridled Ambition*.

74. Timothy V. McCarthy and Jonathan B. Tucker, "Saddam's Toxic Arsenal: Chemical and Biological Weapons in the Gulf Wars," in Peter R. Lavoy, Scott D. Sagan, and James J. Wirtz, *Planning the Unthinkable: How New Powers Will Use Nuclear, Biological, and Chemical Weapons* (Ithaca, N.Y.: Cornell University Press, 2000), p. 73.

75. Richard N. Haass and Meghan L. O'Sullivan, eds., *Honey and Vinegar: Incentives, Sanctions, and Foreign Policy* (Washington, D.C.: Brookings Institution, 2000), p. 175.

76. During the 2003 war in Iraq, concern over collateral damage remained a significant military constraint. The United States reportedly deployed specialized munitions to attack suspect Iraqi WMD sites but refrained from using them because of the danger of releasing deadly toxins into the atmosphere. See David E. Sanger and Thom Shanker, "Allies Say They Took Iraqi Posts Early to Prevent Use of Chemical and Biological Arms," *New York Times*, March 23, 2003, p. B5.

77. Prepared testimony of William J. Perry before the Foreign Relations Committee, U.S. Congress, Senate, 107th Cong., 1st sess., July 24, 2001.

Perry's testimony is cited by Michael J. Glennon, "The Fog of Law: Self-Defense, Inherence, and Incoherence in the United Nations Charter," 25 *Harvard Journal of Law and Public Policy* 539–40 (2002).

78. "President Delivers State of the Union Address," January 29, 2002.

79. "President's Remarks at the United Nations General Assembly," Office of the Press Secretary, White House, September 12, 2002, text available online at http://www.whitehouse.gov/news/releases/2002/09/20020912-1.html.

CHAPTER FOUR

1. The forceful reversal of national programs to acquire weapons of mass destruction has few parallels in modern times, and the closest parallel is more of a warning than a success. The Peace Treaty of Versailles marked the first modern effort to achieve the involuntary reversal of a major nation's military capability through a tough, coercive regime based on intrusive on-site inspections. The Inter-Allied Commissions of Control established under the treaty were given sweeping rights of access, "anytime, anywhere, with anything," and carried out inspections designed to collect information on the location and amounts of treaty-restricted items, to compile baseline information to verify information provided by Germany, to take possession of surplus or prohibited items, to supervise the destruction of these items, to identify military factories permitted to continue production, to supervise the destruction or conversion of all other military production facilities, and to provide for the long-term monitoring of Germany's military activities. Between 1919 and 1927, almost 34,000 on-site inspections were carried out by 400 Allied officers and 1,000 additional support personnel. It needs to be remembered, however, that Germany began rebuilding its military capabilities even while the arms limitation regime was in place, and after renouncing the restrictions imposed by the Versailles regime it quickly acquired a military more powerful than the one it had been deprived of, indeed, stronger than those of the nations that had been imposing the controls.

2. United Nations Security Council Resolution 687, April 3, 1991, para. 8: Decides that Iraq shall unconditionally accept the destruction, removal, or rendering harmless, under international supervision, of:

> (a) All chemical and biological weapons and all stocks of agents and all related subsystems and components and all research, development, support and manufacturing facilities;

(b) All ballistic missiles with a range greater than 150 kilometres and related major parts, and repair and production facilities.

UNSCR 687, para. 12:

Decides that Iraq shall unconditionally agree not to acquire or develop nuclear weapons or nuclear-weapons-usable material or any subsystems or components or any research, development, support or manufacturing facilities related to the above; to submit to the Secretary-General and the Director-General of the International Atomic Energy Agency within fifteen days of the adoption of the present resolution a declaration of the locations, amounts, and types of all items specified above; to place all of its nuclear-weapons-usable materials under the exclusive control, for custody and removal, of the International Atomic Energy Agency, with the assistance and cooperation of the Special Commission as provided for in the plan of the Secretary-General discussed in paragraph 9 (b) above; to accept, in accordance with the arrangements provided for in paragraph 13 below, urgent on-site inspection and the destruction, removal or rendering harmless as appropriate of all items specified above; and to accept the plan discussed in paragraph 13 below for the future ongoing monitoring and verification of its compliance with these undertakings.

3. There is a striking parallel here with the Versailles regime that lends support to the argument that this is a product of the process of coercive arms control. A somewhat more optimistic interpretation would be that coercive disarmament buys time but in and of itself does not constitute fundamental political change. Post–World War II actions with regard to both Germany and Japan put a far greater emphasis on political reform than had been the case after 1919.

4. See Michael R. Gordon and Bernard E. Trainor, *The Generals' War: The Inside Story of the Conflict in the Gulf* (New York: Little, Brown and Company, 1995).

5. United Nations Document S/22456, April 6, 1991, pp. 1–7.

6. Agence France-Presse, Baghdad, June 21, 1997.

7. A broad exception to this generalization applies to the bilateral arms control arrangements negotiated during the cold war by the United States and the Soviet Union. These arrangements, such as the SALT and START treaties, drew heavily on national technical means for their operation and verification. This was certainly not true in the case of multilateral arms control arrangements like the nuclear safeguard system run by the International Atomic Energy Agency.

8. United Nations Security Council Resolution 1284, December 17, 1999.

9. Butler's account of the demise of UNSCOM can be found in Richard

Butler, *Saddam Defiant: The Threat of Weapons of Mass Destruction and the Crisis of Global Security* (London: Weidenfeld and Nicolson, 2000).

10. Rolf Ekeus stepped down at the end of June 1997 to become Swedish ambassador to the United States.

11. The technical impact of this discovery is detailed in Jay C. Davis and David A. Kay, "Iraq's Secret Nuclear Weapons Program," *Physics Today*, July 1992, pp. 21–27. For a fuller account of the events of that mission, see Tim Trevan, *Saddam's Secrets: The Hunt for Iraq's Hidden Weapons* (London: HarperCollins, 1999); Shyam Bhatia and Daniel McGrory, *Brighter than the Baghdad Sun: Saddam Hussein's Nuclear Threat to the United States* (London: Little, Brown and Company, 1999).

12. Informal summary of Rolf Ekeus's luncheon speech to the Conference on Nuclear Non-Proliferation, Carnegie Endowment for International Peace, Washington, D.C., June 10, 1997.

13. The failure of UNSCOM and the IAEA to pay attention to operational security and the active measures taken by Iraq and other hostile intelligence services against them was a major obstacle in developing a high level of trust with the nations supplying those two organizations with information, and it limited that sharing. The UN diplomatic culture never really understood the capabilities of a modern intelligence service, and this benefited Iraq and its friends.

14. For example, Benon Sevan, the head of the UN's oil-for-food program in Iraq, according to the BBC World Service, "urged the UN Security Council to put politics aside and focus on improving the humanitarian situation of the Iraqi people." BBC News Online, May 30, 2001.

15. It is not widely understood that the decision to conduct coercive disarmament and verification actions in Iraq sprang from the Security Council upon a United Nations almost completely unprepared for collecting and analyzing the type and volume of information necessary to support intrusive inspections under hostile conditions. Even in the nuclear area, where the IAEA had more than twenty years of inspection experience, its nuclear safeguard role under the Treaty on the Non-Proliferation of Nuclear Weapons had narrowly focused on nuclear facilities that countries had declared to the IAEA, and the methods and instruments used in inspections had to be approved in advance by the states being inspected. The IAEA's inspection methods had been selected with a view to answering only the most narrow verification question: "Was a state party to the NPT diverting any of its declared nuclear materials from approved peaceful uses?" In Iraq, the IAEA and UNSCOM had to answer the much tougher *proliferation* question: "What was Iraq doing in its clandestine

weapons programs?" In answering this question the UN faced the daunting challenge of not only unraveling a clandestine program but unraveling
a clandestine program that Iraq had invested considerable effort to hide
from outside eyes and that it was continuing to try to protect even while
the inspections continued. This basic fact made establishing collaboration with national intelligence organizations an early requirement if
UNSCOM was to be effective it carrying out the obligations placed upon
it by the Security Council.

16. A full discussion of the extent of Iraq's tactics of deception in the
early phases of UNSCOM can be found in David A. Kay, "Denial and
Deception Practices of WMD Proliferators: Iraq and Beyond," *Washington
Quarterly* 18, no. 1 (Winter 1995): 85–105.

17. UNSCOM Report, S/1995, 17 December 1995.

18. Since my last report, the Government of Iraq has continued to flout its
obligations under UNSC Resolutions. Under the terms of relevant UNSC
Resolutions, Iraq must grant the U.N. Special Commission on Iraq
(UNSCOM) inspectors immediate, unconditional, and unrestricted access
to any location in Iraq that they wish to examine, and access to any Iraqi
official whom they may wish to interview, so that UNSCOM may fully
discharge its mandate to ensure that Iraq's weapons of mass destruction
(WMD) program has been eliminated. Iraq continues, as it has for the past
six years, to fail to live up to either the letter or the spirit of the commitment. Of particular concern is UNSCOM's June report to the Security
Council of serious incidents involving Iraqi escort helicopters flying dan-
gerously close to the Commission's aircraft to force it to change direction
and multiple cases of Iraqi personnel aboard UNSCOM helicopters
attempting to wrest control of aircraft from their pilots.
"In his June report, UNSCOM Chairman Rolf Ekeus also indicated that
UNSCOM had found new indications that Iraq has not fulfilled its
requirement to destroy its WMD. Chairman Ekeus told the Security
Council that on June 10 and 12, Iraqi officials totally blocked UNSCOM
inspectors from access to three sites suspected of containing hidden information about its prohibited weapons programs. Chairman Ekeus singled
out Iraq's leadership as having hindered several attempts by UNSCOM
inspectors to inspect areas that are suspected of being hiding places for
chemical or biological weapons or technology used to manufacture those
weapons." (Presidential Report to Congress on Iraq, July 10, 1997.)

19. See for example, Paul William Roberts, *The Demonic Comedy: Some
Detours in the Baghdad of Saddam Hussein* (New York: Farrar, Straus and
Giroux, 1997).

20. It needs to be emphasized again that UNSCOM sought national intelligence help only because of the failure of Iraq to honor its obligations under Security Council Resolution 687 to give a full disclosure of all of its prohibited weapons systems. Lacking the voluntary cooperation of Iraq, UNSCOM had only two choices: Report to the Security Council that Iraq was in breach of its obligations; therefore, UNSCOM was ceasing operations and leaving it up to the Council to decide whether to let Iraq off or to resume the war. Alternatively, the choice UNSCOM actually took, seek ways to negate Iraq's noncompliance and carry out the tasks set forth in Resolution 687.

21. "Remarks by President Bush and Prime Minister Tony Blair in Joint Press Availability" (Crawford, Texas), Office of the Press Secretary, White House, April 6, 2002, available online at http://www.whitehouse.gov/news/releases/2002/04/20020406-3.html.

22. There were serious discussions inside the secretariat and the board of governors during which a strong case was made that UN Security Council Resolution 687 embarked on a coercive process that was incompatible with the cooperative, voluntary approach of IAEA safeguards and was only a cover for continued political efforts of the United States in the United Nations. Some staff members of the agency's safeguards inspectorate refused to participate in UNSCOM inspections, and others argued that the confrontational approaches that UNSCOM was forced into by Iraqi intransigence endangered their safety in carrying out their normal functions.

23. The authoritative *Strategic Survey 2000/2001* produced by the International Institute for Strategic Studies reported that "the marginal improvements of the IAEA's 93+2 safeguards system—aimed at facilitating the discovery of undeclared nuclear activities—will not be in widespread operation for some years." International Institute for Strategic Studies, *Strategic Survey 2000/2001* (Oxford: Oxford University Press, 2001), p. 43.

24. The parallel is the demand for unconditional surrender at the conclusion of World War II as a way to avoid the "failure" of Versailles.

CHAPTER FIVE

1. Joseph Cirincione, with Jon B. Wolfsthal and Miriam Rajkumar, *Deadly Arsenals: Tracking Weapons of Mass Destruction* (Washington, D.C.: Carnegie Endowment for International Peace, 2002), pp. 107–18 (Russia) and 316–24 (Ukraine, Kazakhstan, Belarus).

2. Ibid., p. 115.

3. The U.S. government counts only about 3,000–5,000 people as "highly trained" designers; the rest know some part of the process, but not all—nevertheless, they would be valuable to a weapon program and are considered part of the "brain drain" problem.

4. For a concise discussion of the conceptual underpinnings of the threat reduction programs, see Ashton B. Carter, William J. Perry, and John D. Steinbruner, A New Concept of Cooperative Security, Brookings Occasional Papers (Washington, D.C.: Brookings Institution, 1992).

5. A useful listing of General Accounting Office reports on the Energy Department threat reduction programs is contained in "A Report Card on the Department of Energy's Nonproliferation Programs with Russia," Russia Task Force, Secretary of Energy Advisory Board, U.S. Department of Energy, January 10, 2000, Appendix H, available online at http://www.hr.doe.gov/seab/rpt.pdf. The most recent such reports are U.S. General Accounting Office, "Nuclear Nonproliferation: Security of Russia's Nuclear Material Improving; Further Enhancements Needed," GAO-01-312, February 2001, available online at http://www.gao.gov/new.items/d01312.pdf; U.S. General Accounting Office, "Nuclear Nonproliferation: DOE's Efforts to Assist Weapons Scientists in Russia's Nuclear Cities Face Challenges," GAO-01-429, May 2001 available online at http://www.ceip.org/files/projects/npp/pdf/ncichallenges.pdf.

6. Quoted in Peter Eisler, "Plan to Destroy Weapons in Russia Nears Collapse," USA Today, October 1, 2002, p. 1.

7. Prohibitions on the use of funds for specified purposes were first attached to the FY97 National Defense Authorization Act, Public Law 201, 1048. Cong., 2nd sess., September 23, 1996, sec. 1503, and have been included every year since then.

8. A useful summary of such incidents is contained in Graham Allison et al., "Avoiding Nuclear Anarchy," Washington Quarterly 20, no. 3 (Summer 1997): 185–98.

9. Judith Miller, "Russia Asks U.S. to Expand Nuclear Cleanup, Even to Secret Sites," New York Times, September 30, 1999, p. A9.

10. For the budget history of the programs in the FY02–FY03 period, see William Hoehn, "Analysis of the Bush Administration's Fiscal Year 2003 Budget Requests for U.S.-Former Soviet Union Nonproliferation Programs," Russian American Nuclear Security Advisory Council, Washington, D.C., April 2002, available online at http://www.ransac.org/new-web-site/index.html. For a useful brief summary of threat reduction funding from 1994 to 2000, see "U.S. Programs Face Growing Russian Threat," Proliferation Brief, vol. 2, no. 4, Carnegie Endowment for International Peace,

Washington, D.C., March 4, 1999, available online at http://www.ceip.org/ files/nonprolif/templates/Publications.asp?p=8&PublicationID=100.

11. The Department of Energy and the Bush administration will dispose of thirty-four metric tons of surplus weapons-grade plutonium by turning the material into mixed oxide fuel (MOX) for use in nuclear reactors. The MOX conversion process is expected to cost $3.8 billion over twenty years, including the construction of two new conversion facilities at the Energy Department's Savannah River site in South Carolina. See "Secretary Abraham Announces Administration Plan to Proceed with Plutonium Disposition and Reduce Proliferation Concerns," press release no. PR-02-007, U.S. Department of Energy, January 23, 2002, available online at http://www.energy.gov/HQPress/releases02/janpr/pr02007.htm.

12. As explained in "A Report Card on the Department of Energy's Nonproliferation Programs with Russia," p. 12, "the HEU agreement represents a challenge to the worldwide nuclear fuel market because it brings to market material representing 15 percent of world demand. Tension between the commercial interests of entities in the nuclear fuel market, and the international security interest of rendering this fissile material impotent as rapidly as possible, are inevitable." For a more thorough discussion of the mechanics of the HEU deal, see Thomas L. Neff, "Privatizing U.S. National Security: The U.S.-Russian HEU Deal at Risk," *Arms Control Today*, August/September 1998, available online at http://www.armscontrol.org/act/1998_08-09/tnas98.asp.

13. For a brief history to the U.S.-China "lab-to-lab" program, see Nancy Prindle, "The U.S.-China Lab-to-Lab Technical Exchange Program," *Nonproliferation Review* 5, no. 3 (Spring/Summer 1998): 111–18, available online at http://cns.miis.edu/pubs/npr/vol05/53/prindl53.pdf.

14. In response to allegations of Chinese espionage and poor security at several U.S. national laboratories, in the spring of 1999 Representative Jim Ryun (R.-Kan.) introduced in the House H.R. 1348, the *Department of Energy Foreign Visitors Program Moratorium Act of 1999*. In late April 1999, Senator Richard Shelby (R.-Ala.) introduced similar legislation in the Senate (S. 887). Both of these bills would have prohibited visits by scientists and officials from sensitive countries to U.S. nuclear labs, with the consequence not only of halting the early program with China but also of stopping the cooperative lab-to-lab program with Russia and other former Soviet states. Although the bills were eventually moderated, they did have an impact, increasing greatly the number of bureaucratic procedures that have to be completed before foreign visitors can enter U.S. nuclear facilities.

15. U.S. General Accounting Office, "Nuclear Nonproliferation: DOE's Efforts to Assist Weapons Scientists."

16. Russian survey data on this question are contained in Valentin Tikhonov, *Russia's Nuclear and Missile Complex: The Human Factor in Proliferation*, report of the Non-Proliferation Project, Carnegie Endowment for International Peace, Washington, D.C., April 2001, available online at http://www.ceip.org/files/Publications/NPPDemoStudytoc.asp?from=pubtitle.

17. Keynote address made by Lev Ryabev at "Russian Scientific Talents: Economic Opportunities and Challenges," Sam Nunn Bank of America Policy Forum, Sam Nunn School for International Affairs, Georgia Institute of Technology, March 26, 2001.

CHAPTER SIX

1. I would like to thank Nicole Simon and Jason Sanchez for research assistance, and Marie Chevrier, Eileen Choffnes, Audrey Cronin, Jeanne Guillemin, Victor Utgoff, Raymond Zilinskas, and the editors of this volume for their comments.

2. See, for example, Brian Jenkins, "The Future Course of International Terrorism," *Futurist* (World Future Society, Bethesda, Md.) 21, no. 4 (July–August 1987): 8; Jeffrey D. Simon, *Terrorists and the Potential Use of Biological Weapons: A Discussion of Possibilities* (Santa Monica, Calif.: Rand Corporation, 1989); W. Seth Carus, *Bioterrorism and Biocrimes: The Illicit Use of Biological Agents in the 20th Century*, working paper, Center for Counterproliferation Research, National Defense University, August 1998, rev. ed. (February 2001) available online at http://www.ndu.edu/center-counter/Full_Doc.pdf; W. Seth Carus, "The Poor Man's Atomic Bomb? Biological Weapons in the Middle East," Policy Papers no. 23, Washington Institute for Near East Policy, Washington, D.C., June 1991; Jessica Stern, "Will Terrorists Turn to Poison?" *Orbis* 37, no. 3 (Summer 1993): 393–410; Ron Purver, "The Threat of Chemical/Biological Terrorism," *Commentary* (Canadian Security Intelligence Service), no. 60 (August 1995), available online at http://www.csis-scrs.gc.ca/eng/comment/com60_e.html; Jonathan B. Tucker, "Chemical/Biological Terrorism: Coping with a New Threat," *Politics and the Life Sciences* 15, no. 2 (September 1996): 167-83; Leonard A. Cole, "The Specter of Biological Weapons," *Scientific American*, December 1996, pp. 60–65; Brad Roberts, ed., *Terrorism with Chemical and Biological Weapons: Calibrating Risks and Responses* (Alexandria, Va.: Chemical and Biological Arms Control Institute, 1997), pp. 71–90; Richard A.

Falkenrath, Robert D. Newman, and Bradley A. Thayer, *America's Achilles' Heel: Nuclear, Biological, and Chemical Terrorism and Covert Attack* (Cambridge, Mass.: MIT Press, 1998); Philip B. Heymann, *Terrorism and America: A Commonsense Strategy for a Democratic Society* (Cambridge, Mass.: MIT Press, 1998); Ashton B. Carter, John Deutch, and Philip Zelikow, "Catastrophic Terrorism: Tackling the New Danger," *Foreign Affairs* 77, no. 6 (November/December 1998): 80–94; Gavin Cameron, *Nuclear Terrorism: A Threat Assessment for the 21st Century* (New York: Palgrave Press, 1999); Joshua Lederberg, ed., *Biological Weapons: Limiting the Threat* (Cambridge, Mass.: MIT Press, 1999); Raymond A. Zilinskas, ed., *Biological Warfare: Modern Offense and Defense* (Boulder, Colo.: Lynne Rienner, 1999); Jonathan B. Tucker, *Toxic Terror: Assessing Terrorist Use of Chemical and Biological Weapons* (Cambridge, Mass.: MIT Press, 2000); Amy Smithson and Leslie-Anne Levy, *Ataxia: The Chemical and Biological Terrorism Threat and the US Response*, Report no. 35, Henry L. Stimson Center, Washington, D.C., October 2000, available online at http://www.stimson.org/cbw/pubs.cfm?id=12; Ashton B. Carter and William J. Perry with David Aidekman, "Countering Asymmetric Threats," in Ashton B. Carter and John P. White, eds., *Keeping the Edge: Managing Defense for the Future* (Cambridge, Mass.: MIT Press, 2001), pp. 119–28.

3. As of December 5, 2001, eleven cases of inhalation anthrax and seven cases of cutaneous anthrax had been confirmed. There were four additional suspected cases of cutaneous anthrax. "Update: Investigation of Bioterrorism-Related Anthrax—Connecticut, 2001," *MMWR: Morbidity and Mortality Weekly Report* (Centers for Disease Control and Prevention) 50, no. 48 (December 7, 2001): 1077–79, available online at http://www.cdc.gov/mmwr/preview/mmwrhtml/mm5048a1.htm. The fatalities included a ninety-four-year-old woman from rural Connecticut and a hospital employee in New York City, both whom are suspected to have contracted the disease from contaminated mail, two Washington-area postal workers, and a newspaper picture editor in Florida.

4. In a survey conducted by the Harvard School of Public Health/Robert Wood Johnson Foundation, Survey Project on Americans' Response to Biological Terrorism on November 8, 2001, 57 percent of those surveyed stated that they had taken one or more precautions in response to reports of bioterrorism.

5. Ibid.

6. U.S. Congress, *Report of the Commission to Assess the Ballistic Missile Threat to the United States*, 104th Cong., 2d sess., July 15, 1998, executive summary, available online at http://www.fas.org/irp/threat/bm-threat.htm.

7. Rick Weiss, "Germ Tests Point away from Iraq; Hill, N.Y. Post Spores Lack Telltale Compound," *Washington Post*, October 30, 2001, p. A9.

8. Kournikakis et al., "Risk Assessment of Anthrax Threat Letters," Technical Report, DRES TR-2001-048, Defence Research Establishment Suffield, Department of National Defence, Canada, September 2001, available online at http://hs.cupw.ca/pdfs/anthrax_threat_letter_eng.pdf.

9. For example, on the positive side, it was discovered that antibiotics may be effective even after symptoms appear; on the negative side, there is no "safe" dose of inhaled spores. David Brown, "New Questions Raised on Anthrax Perils; Study Finds Spores in Daschle Office Easily Stirred Up, Complicating Risk Analysis," *Washington Post*, December 11, 2001, p. A15. The U.S. military offered the information from its monkey studies that LD50 (the dose at which half a population dies of infection) was 8,000–10,000 spores. In miscommunications to the public, the federal government promoted the idea that a dose below 8,000 spores would not lead to infection. Yet a lesser number of spores, in theory even one germinating spore, could be infective. Some ten thousand people were prescribed antibiotics. At the military's recommendation, ciprofloxin (which can have severe side effects) was prescribed; later the less controversial doxycycline was substituted, as recommended in the open literature. For treatment recommendations, see Terry C. Dixon et al., "*Bacillus Anthracis*: Infection Revisited," *New England Journal of Medicine* 341, no. 11 (September 9, 1999): 815–26, available online at http://content.nejm.org/cgi/content/full/341/11/815. Those thought exposed to anthrax spores were advised to take antibiotics for several weeks to sixty days. Data from the largest recorded outbreak of inhalation anthrax, in 1979 in Sverdlovsk, U.S.S.R., showed for the first time that anthrax spores could remain dormant in the human lung as long as six weeks after exposure, then could germinate and cause fatal illness. See Matthew Meselson et al., "The Sverdlovsk Anthrax Outbreak of 1979," *Science* 266, no. 5188 (November 18, 1994): 1202–8. Unpublished military research on monkeys supported this finding.

10. Testimony of James T. Caruso, acting assistant director, counterterrorism division, Federal Bureau of Investigation, before U.S. Congress, Senate, Judiciary Committee, Subcommittee on Technology, Terrorism, and Government Information, 107th Cong., 1st sess., November 6, 2001.

11. Susan Candiotti, "Breakthrough May Be Close in Anthrax Probe," CNN Report, January 21, 2002, available online at http://www.cnn.com/2002/US/01/21/anthrax.probe/index.html. As the investigation proceeded, authorities learned of more laboratories, including nonmilitary ones, that had the Ames strain of anthrax used in the attacks. Such laboratories were

identified in at least five foreign countries, and investigators expected to continue to find more. Scott Shane, "FBI Scrutinizes Biodefense Labs in Anthrax Probe," *Baltimore Sun*, February 22, 2002.

12. Thus, when Larry Wayne Harris bought three vials of the bacterium that causes bubonic plague, he was not breaking the law. He was convicted of misrepresenting himself in his purchase order—not of possessing an illegal agent. Moreover, as Harris explained, no law prevented him from isolating the bacteria that cause anthrax, brucellosis, or tularemia, which he claims to have done. Author's interview with Larry Wayne Harris, January 23, 1998.

13. *Uniting and Strengthening America by Providing Appropriate Tools Required to Intercept and Obstruct Terrorism Act of 2001*, 107th Cong., 1st sess., H.R. 3162, Title 18, Section 175B.

14. *Bioterrorism Preparedness Act of 2001*, 107th Cong., 1st sess., S. 1765.

15. Combined official figures from the World Trade Center, Pentagon, and Pennsylvania airline crashes.

16. Survey by Harvard University School of Public Health/Robert Wood Johnson Foundation, Survey Project on Americans' Response to Biological Terrorism, November 8, 2001. Fifty-seven percent of those surveyed stated that they had taken one or more precautions in response to reports of bioterrorism.

17. John D. Graham and Jonathan Baert Wiener, eds., *Risk vs. Risk: Tradeoffs in Protecting Health and the Environment* (Cambridge, Mass.: Harvard University Press, 1995).

18. In a survey comparing expert and lay judgment, experts ranked nuclear power number twenty on a list of thirty dangerous technologies and activities, whereas most lay respondents ranked it first. Paul Slovic, "Perception of Risk," *Science* 236, no. 4799 (April 17, 1987): 280–81; Paul Slovic, Baruch Fischoff, and Sarah Lichtenstein, "Facts and Fears: Understanding Perceived Risk," in Richard C. Schwing and Walter A. Albers, eds., *Societal Risk Assessment: How Safe Is Safe Enough?* (New York: Plenum, 1980), pp. 181–216. There are drawbacks to this approach. While "experts" may consider fecal matter in breakfast cereal to be medically acceptable provided the quantity is kept relatively low, the "expert" is likely to become a "layperson" if informed that the particular bowl of cereal his child is about to eat is contaminated with the maximally acceptable amount. Author's interview with Sheila Jasanoff, June 25, 2001. See also Jonathan Baert Wiener, "Risk in the Republic," *Duke Environmental Law and Policy Forum* 8, no. 1 (Fall 1997): 1–22, as well as the entire Part III of that same issue, available online at http://www.law.duke.edu/journals/delpf/delpftoc8n1.htm.

19. Graham and Wiener, *Risk vs. Risk*, p. 232. Interestingly, there are a number of risk-coincident strategies for counterterrorism, although not

necessarily regarding bioterror. Efforts to assist failed or failing states and removal of import quotas on commodities produced in countries where terrorists thrive are but two examples. Raising the opportunity cost of young men's time and improving governance in developing countries are likely to reduce the appeal of terrorism for terror groups' prospective foot soldiers. Graham and Wiener use the term "risk-coincident" rather than "dual-use" policies.

20. Slovic, Fischoff, and Lichtenstein, "Facts and Fears"; Slovic, "Perception of Risk," pp. 280–85.

21. N. D. Weinstein, "Optimistic Biases about Personal Risks," *Science* 246, no. 4935 (December 8, 1989): 1232–33; Frank P. McKenna, "It Won't Happen to Me: Unrealistic Optimism or the Illusion of Control?" *British Journal of Psychology* 84 (1993): 39–50, cited in Lynn J. Frewer et al., "Methodological Approaches to Assessing Risk Perceptions Associated with Food-Related Hazards," *Risk Analysis* 18, no. 1 (February 1998): 95–102. According to Frewer and her colleagues, the more individuals feel they know about food-borne health hazards, the more they feel they have control over exposure. Food deliberately contaminated with unknown biological agents could be expected to fall into the category of less controllable hazards.

22. The National Center for Statistics and Analysis (which reports to the National Highway Traffic Safety Administration) estimates there were 41,800 car accident fatalities in the year 2000, an average of 115 per day. Figures available online at http://www.nhtsa.gov/.

23. James Hammitt, a Harvard professor of environmental economics, points out that, in fact, much of the risk associated with driving is imposed by other drivers and by the manufacturer of one's own car and the cars of others. For this and a discussion of the problems in defining voluntary versus involuntary risks, see J. K. Hammitt, "Evaluating Risk Communication: In Search of a Gold Standard," in Martin P. Cottam et al., eds., *Foresight and Precaution*, proceedings of ESREL [European Safety and Reliability Conference] 2000, SaRS [Safety and Reliability Society] and SRA-Europe [Society of Risk Analysis] Annual Conference, Edinburgh, May 14–17, 2000 (Rotterdam: A. A. Balkema, 2000), pp. 15–19. See also Cass Sunstein, "A Note on 'Voluntary' versus 'Involuntary' Risks," *Duke Environmental Law and Policy Forum* 8, no. 1 (Fall 1997): 173–80, available online at http://www.law.duke.edu/journals/delpf/delpftoc8n1.htm.

24. The word "fear" is used colloquially here to describe a judgment-based, general concern—that is, to mean risk perception, not an emotionally

based fear of a specific thing. For a discussion of this distinction, see Pamela Wilcox Rountree and Kenneth C. Land, "Perceived Risk versus Fear of Crime: Empirical Evidence of Conceptually Distinct Reactions in Survey Data," *Social Forces* 74, no. 4 (June 1996): 1353–77.

25. In the first six months of 1993 there were 11 terrorist killings in Belfast but 230 murders in Washington, D.C. "Degrees of Terror," *Economist*, July 10, 1993, p. 24.

26. People are more willing to pay for risk reduction when they believe zero risk is attainable, according to Kazuya Nakayachi, "How Do People Evaluate Risk Reduction when They Are Told Zero Risk Is Impossible?" *Risk Analysis* 18, no. 3 (June 1998): 235–42. Nakayachi explains that although "the actual difficulty involved in achieving zero risk is obvious, studies of human judgment and decision-making report that the allure of zero risk is, for the general populace, essentially irresistible."

27. Amos Tversky and Daniel Kahneman, "Judgment under Uncertainty: Heuristics and Biases," *Science* 185, no. 4157 (September 27, 1974): 1124–31; Slovic, Fischoff, and Lichtenstein, "Facts and Fears." Other biases include the fact that people tend to be overconfident in the accuracy of their assessments, even when those assessments are based on nothing more than guesses. Moreover, people seem to desire certainty: they respond to the anxiety of uncertainty by blithely ignoring uncertain risks and by believing that although others may be vulnerable (to, for example, being involved in an automobile accident), they are not.

28. For a detailed explanation, see Anand Pandya, "Coping with Disaster—Aftermath of September 11," Ask the Doctor column, NAMI-NYC Metro [National Alliance for the Mentally Ill], New York, n.d., available online at http://naminyc.nami.org/askthedoctor/ask10.htm.

29. Stephen Breyer, *Breaking the Vicious Circle: Toward Effective Risk Regulation* (Cambridge, Mass.: Harvard University Press, 1993), p. 35.

30. William Ian Miller, *The Anatomy of Disgust* (Cambridge, Mass.: Harvard University Press, 1997), p. 26; Susan Miller, "Disgust: Conceptualization, Development and Dynamics," *International Review of Psychoanalysis* 13 (1986): 295–307.

31. Miller, *Anatomy of Disgust*, p. 26.

32. Ibid.

33. Donald G. MacGregor, Paul Slovic, and Torbjorn Malmfors, "'How Exposed Is Exposed Enough?' Lay Inferences about Chemical Exposure," *Risk Analysis* 19, no. 4 (August 1999): 649–59.

34. Ibid.

35. Ibid., p. 649.

36. According to Centers for Disease Control and Prevention statistics, available online at http://www.cdc.gov/ncidod/dvrd/spb/mnpages/dispages/ebotabl.htm.

37. National biological weapons programs have included work on Ebola and antibiotic-resistant bacteria. If terrorists do try to spread disease, they are probably more likely to choose more ordinary diseases. Still, the very idea of deliberately disseminated disease—whether ordinary or rare—is terrifying. Audrey Cronin points out that diseases for which there is no cure elicit particular dread, even if they are rare. Author's personal communication with Audrey Cronin, April 24, 2001.

38. Laurie Garrett, *Betrayal of Trust: The Collapse of Global Public Health* (New York: Hyperion, 2000); Philip M. Boffey, "Lessons of the Plague," *New York Times*, November 14, 1994, p. A16. The response to the foot-and-mouth disease epidemic in the United Kingdom is perhaps a counterexample, in that there seems to have been little panic. Foot-and-mouth is a fairly common disease that affects humans only very rarely. Perhaps this knowledge, together with the (possibly false) perception that the government was in control, fed into the public's response. This issue requires further study.

39. U.S. Congress, Office of Technology Assessment, *The Regulatory Environment for Science: A Technical Memorandum*, OTA-TM-SET-34 (Washington, D.C.: Government Printing Office, February 1986), pp. 130–32, cited in Charles Piller, *The Fail-Safe Society: Community Defiance and the End of American Technological Optimism* (New York: Basic Books, 1991), p. 5.

40. Ibid.

41. Piller, *Fail-Safe Society*.

42. Kristin Shrader-Frechette, "Science versus Educated Guessing: Risk Assessment, Nuclear Waste, and Public Policy," *BioScience* 46, no. 7 (July–August 1996): 498, available online at http://www.nd.edu/~kshrader/pubs/biosci_46_488_science_educated.pdf.

43. See Sheila Jasanoff, "Civilization and Madness: The Great BSE Scare of 1996," *Public Understanding of Science* 6, no. 3 (July 1997): 221–32. For discussion of the impact of risk communication, see, for example, Nakayachi, "How Do People Evaluate Risk Reduction?"; MacGregor, Slovic, and Malmfors, "'How Exposed Is Exposed Enough?'"

44. The following variables would probably indicate the need for further study: an outbreak at an unusual time of year, an outbreak affecting a surprising number of healthy adults (as opposed to immune-compromised or aged populations), unusually rapid spread of disease, or (as was the case for

West Nile) the appearance of a disease in a new area. Jeanne Guillemin argues that that nongovernmental teams of experts are the best means for getting to causes of suspicious outbreaks. See J. Guillemin, "The 1979 Anthrax Outbreak in the USSR: Applied Science and Political Controversy," *Proceedings of the American Philosophical Society* 146, no. 1 (March 2002): 18–36.

45. Richard Preston, "West Nile Mystery: How Did It Get Here? The CIA Would Like to Know," *New Yorker*, October 18–25, 1999, pp. 90–108. The virus was originally misdiagnosed as St. Louis encephalitis, which is commonly seen during the late summer months in the northeastern United States as a mosquito-borne disease.

46. The West Nile incident was not the first time that biological terrorism has been suspected when an unfamiliar or dangerous disease breaks out unexpectedly. When foot-and-mouth disease struck Taiwan's pigs in 1997 for the first time in eighty-three years, the Taiwanese government was forced to slaughter more than four million hogs. Taiwanese farmers suspected that China had deliberately introduced the disease to damage the island's economy. After Cuba suffered an epidemic of dengue hemorrhagic fever in 1981, it accused the United States of biological aggression. In 1997, Cuba made another allegation of biological warfare, charging that the United States had dropped crop-eating pests from a low-flying plane. See Raymond A. Zilinskas, "Cuban Allegations of Biological Warfare by the United States: Assessing the Evidence," *Critical Reviews in Microbiology* 25, no. 3 (September 1999): 173–227. When plague broke out in India in 1994, authorities accused a rebel group of deliberately spreading the disease, although there was little evidence to support that claim. *Contagion and Conflict: Health as a Global Security Challenge*, Report of the Chemical and Biological Arms Control Institute and Center for Strategic and International Studies International Security Program, Washington, D.C., January 2000, pp. 11, 58.

47. Jeanne Guillemin, *Anthrax: The Investigation of a Deadly Outbreak* (Berkeley, Calif.: University of California Press, 1999).

48. Thomas J. Tórk et al., "A Large Community Outbreak of Salmonellosis Caused by Intentional Contamination of Restaurant Salad Bars," in Lederberg, *Biological Weapons*, pp. 167–84.

49. "The Last 12 Days," *St. Petersburg Times*, October 14, 2001, p. 13A.

50. See discussion in Lennart Sjöberg, "Worry and Risk Perception," *Risk Analysis* 18, no. 1 (February 1998): 92.

51. There are problems with the terrorism data in general. See Jessica Stern, *The Ultimate Terrorists* (Cambridge, Mass.: Harvard University Press,

1999). The Monterey Institute of International Studies maintains the best unclassified database of unconventional terrorist crimes.

52. Raymond A. Zilinskas, "Iraq's Biological Warfare Program: The Past as Future," in Lederberg, *Biological Weapons*, pp. 137–58; Stephen Black, "Investigating Iraq's Biological Weapons Program," in Lederberg, *Biological Weapons*, pp. 159–64.

53. Purported intelligence findings include evidence of recent inoculations against smallpox in the blood of North Korean defectors and Iraqi prisoners of war, evidence that Iraq had recently produced smallpox vaccine, and the word "smallpox" on a freeze-drying vessel that UNSCOM discovered in Iraq. William J. Broad, "Smallpox: The Once and Future Scourge?" *New York Times*, June 15, 1999, p. F1. The article was researched by Lawrence K. Altman, William J. Broad, and Judith Miller.

54. The United States stopped routine vaccinations in 1972, meaning that most people under the age of thirty—more than 40 percent of the population—are completely unprotected. Experts believe that immunity is minimal ten years after the vaccine is administered. Thus, only those who have been vaccinated relatively recently (military and medical personnel working with smallpox) can expect to be immune.

55. Although only about seven hundred people were hospitalized for injury, thousands of people showed up at hospitals in the belief they might have been injured.

56. Statement (as prepared for delivery) by George J. Tenet, director of central intelligence, before U.S. Congress, Senate, Foreign Relations Committee, "The Worldwide Threat in 2000: Global Realities of Our National Security," 106th Cong., 2d sess., March 21, 2000, text available online at http://www.cia.gov/cia/public_affairs/speeches/archives/2000/dci_speech_032100.html.

57. Ibid.

58. "Britain Cites Iraqi Threat," *New York Times*, March 11, 1998, p. A11.

59. See Louis R. Beam, "Leaderless Resistance: An Essay by L. R. Beam," Mo-Net, Inc., Mount Vernon, Mo., n.d., available online at http://www2.mo-net.com/~mlindste/ledrless.html.

60. Experts claim that schizophrenics and sociopaths may *want* to commit acts of mass destruction, but they are probably the least likely to succeed because of their difficulty functioning in groups. B. J. Berkowitz et al., *Superviolence: The Civil Threat of Mass Destruction Weapons*, Report no. A72-034-10, ADCON (Advance Concepts Research) Corporation, Santa Barbara, Calif., September 29, 1972, pp. 3-9, 4-4.

61. Osama bin Laden's support of a number of anti-Western organizations is an example of this phenomenon.

62. Statement by Tenet, "Worldwide Threat in 2000."

63. For an excellent assessment of the entire government program for responding to biological weapons, see Smithson and Levy, *Ataxia*.

64. For an excellent analysis of a comprehensive recent exercise, see Tara O'Toole, Michael Mair, and Thomas V. Inglesby, "Shining Light on Dark Winter," *Clinical Infectious Diseases* 34, no. 7 (April 1, 2002): 972–83.

65. Al J. Venter, "Elements Loyal to Bin Laden Acquire Biological Agents 'Through the Mail,'" *Jane's Intelligence Review* 11, no. 8 (August 1999): 5.

66. See for example, Ehud Sprinzak, "The Great Superterrorism Scare," *Foreign Policy*, no. 112 (Fall 1998): 110–24, available online at http://www.foreignpolicy.com/issue_SeptOct_2001/sprinzaksuperterrorism.html; Milton Leitenberg, "False Alarm," *Washington Post*, August 14, 1999; Leonard Cole, "A Plague of Publicity," *Washington Post*, August 16, 1999. An alternative explanation for the disagreements among experts about the significance of the threat is that terrorism studies scholars tend to focus exclusively on the risks posed by terrorists, while national security analysts tend to focus on the kinds of probabilities and consequences among a variety of threats. See Richard Falkenrath, "Analytic Models and Policy Prescription: Understanding Recent Innovation in U.S. Counterterrorism," *Studies in Conflict and Terrorism* 24, no. 3 (May 2001): 159–81.

67. For more discussion of the myriad difficulties in defining terrorism and references to the literature, Bruce Hoffman, *Inside Terrorism* (New York, Columbia University Press, 1998), pp. 13–44; Stern, *Ultimate Terrorists*, pp. 15–19.

68. For some policy options it does make a difference, for example, in the area of deterrence.

69. See Lederberg, *Biological Warfare*.

70. Statement by Robert Burnham, section chief, Domestic Terrorism, National Security Division, Federal Bureau of Investigation, before U.S. Congress, House, Committee on Commerce, Subcommittee on Oversight and Investigations, "The Threat of Bioterrorism in America: Assessing the Adequacy of the Federal Law Relating to Dangerous Biological Agents," 106th Cong., 1st sess., May 20, 1999, available online at http://comnotes.house.gov/cchear/hearings106.nsf/768df0faa6d9ddab852564f1004886 c0/a9e73f86ea1cb7c185256777005f1c5f ?OpenDocument.

71. For an excellent bibliography of the growing literature on this subject and for an assessment based on extensive interviews with experts, see *Bioterrorism in the United States: Threat, Preparedness, and Response*, Final Report, Chemical and Biological Arms Control Institute, Washington, D.C., November 2000, available online at http://www.cbaci.org/PDFCDCFinalReport.pdf.

72. Russia still has not opened its military biological weapons facilities to inspection, according to a former director of the program. See Ken Alibek, "Russia's Deadly Expertise," *New York Times*, March 27, 1998, p. A23.

73. See *CBW Conventions Bulletin* (quarterly journal of the Harvard Sussex Program on CBW Armament and Arms Limitation, Harvard University), no. 42, December 1998, available online at http://www.fas.harvard.edu/~hsp/bulletin/crimconv.pdf.

74. Judith Miller, Stephen Engelberg, and William J. Broad, "U.S. Germ Warfare Research Pushes Treaty Limits," *New York Times*, September 4, 2001, p. A1; Judith Miller, "When Is Bomb Not a Bomb? Germ Experts Confront U.S.," *New York Times*, September 5, 2001, p. A5.

75. Testimony of Caruso, U.S. Congress, Senate, November 6, 2001.

76. Part 72 of Title 42 of *Code of Federal Regulations*. The list is divided into three categories. Category A, "critical biological agents," encompasses those that can be easily disseminated or transmitted person to person, can result in high mortality, might cause public panic, or might require special action for public health preparedness. They include *Bacillus anthracis* (anthrax), *Yersinia pestis* (plague), *Clostridium botulinum* toxin (botulism), *Francisella tularensis* (tularemia), filoviruses such as Ebola and Marburg hemorrhagic fever, and arenaviruses such as Lassa and Junin fever. Category B agents include *Coxiella burnetti* (Q fever), *Brucella* species (brucellosis), ricin toxin, and others. Category C includes Nipah virus, hantaviruses, yellow fever virus, multidrug-resistant tuberculosis, and others. See "Biological and Chemical Terrorism: Strategic Plan for Preparedness and Response," recommendations of the CDC Strategic Planning Workgroup, *Morbidity and Mortality Weekly Report* (Centers for Disease Control and Prevention) 49, no. RR-4 (April 21, 2000), available online at http://www.cdc.gov/mmwr/PDF/RR/RR4904.pdf.

77. Statement by Burnham, "Threat of Terrorism in America."

78. Statement by Congressman Fred Upton of Michigan before U.S. Congress, House, Committee on Commerce, Subcommittee on Oversight and Investigations, "The Threat of Bioterrorism in America: Assessing the Adequacy of the Federal Law Relating to Dangerous Biological Agents," 106th Cong., 1st sess., May 20, 1999.

79. Ibid.

80. Ibid.

81. Author's interview with a Department of Justice official, April 12, 2001.

82. Statement by Congressman Tom Bliley of Virginia before U.S. Congress, House, Committee on Commerce, Subcommittee on Oversight

and Investigations, "The Threat of Bioterrorism in America: Assessing the Adequacy of the Federal Law Relating to Dangerous Biological Agents," 106th Cong., 1st sess., May 20, 1999.

83. *Biological Weapons Act of 1989*, 101st Cong., 1st sess., H.R. 237, amended Title 18, Sec. 817 (C) b.

84. In December 2001, a graduate student at the University of Connecticut stashed two vials of anthrax bacteria in his private freezer, claiming he was saving them for epidemiological research or future study. In July 2002, he was charged with possessing a biological agent but was told he would not be prosecuted if he completed a pretrial community service program. Dave Altimari and Grace Merritt, "Patriot Law May Be Used in UConn Anthrax Case: Grad Student with Lab Vials Would Be First Charged," *Hartford Courant*, December 13, 2001, p. A1; David Malakoff, "Student Charged with Possessing Anthrax," *Science Now* (American Association for the Advancement of Science), July 30, 2002, p. 3.

85. *Biological Weapons Act of 1989*, amended Title 18, Section 175B.

86. International Traffic in Arms Regulations, Subchapter M, Part 120: Purpose and Definitions (22 CFR 120-130), revised April 1, 2002, §120.9, text available online at http://pmdtc.org/docs/ITAR/22cfr120_Part_120.pdf.

87. Eugene Skolnikoff, "Research Universities and National Security: Can Traditional Values Survive?" in Albert H. Teich et al., eds., *Science and Technology in a Vulnerable World: Supplement to AAAS Science and Technology Policy Yearbook 2003*, American Association for the Advancement of Science, Washington, D.C., 2002, p. 67, available online at http://www.aaas.org/spp/yearbook/2003/stvwch6.pdf.

88. Ibid., p. 68.

89. See "Biological and Chemical Terrorism: Strategic Plan for Preparedness and Response."

90. Kevin Merida and John Mintz, "Rockville Firm Shipped Germ Agents to Iraq, Riegle Says," *Washington Post*, February 10, 1994, p. A8.

91. Draft: West Nile Virus Strain, New York, 1999," CDC Media Relations, Centers for Disease Control and Prevention, April 2000, in files, contact (404) 639-3286 for copies.

92. See website of the Australia Group, Paris, available online at http://www.australiagroup.net/index.html.

93. William J. Broad, "When a Cult Turns to Germ Warfare," *New York Times*, May 26, 1998. The article was researched by Sheryl WuDunn, Judith Miller, and William J. Broad.

94. See "The Culture Collection in This World," available on the Web site of WFCC-MIRCEN (World Federation for Culture Collections

Microbial Resources Centres) World Data Centre for Microorganisms, National Institute of Genetics, Mishima, Japan, November 27, 2001, available online at http://wdcm.nig.ac.jp/statistics2001.html.

95. Broad, "When a Cult Turns to Germ Warfare."

96. Barry Kellman, "Biological Terrorism: Legal Measures for Preventing Catastrophe," *Harvard Journal of Law and Public Policy* 24, no. 2 (Spring 2001): 417–88.

97. Statement by Ronald M. Atlas, president-elect, American Society of Microbiology, before U.S. Congress, Senate, Judiciary Committee, Subcommittee on Technology, Terrorism, and Government Information, "Germs, Toxins, and Terror: The New Threat to America," 107th Cong., 1st sess., November 6, 2001, text available online at http://judiciary.senate.gov/testimony.cfm?id=123&wit_id=49.

98. Statement by Stephen Ostroff, associate director for Epidemiologic Science, National Center for Infectious Diseases, Centers for Disease Control and Prevention, before U.S. Congress, House, Committee on Commerce, Subcommittee on Oversight and Investigations, "The Threat of Bioterrorism in America: Assessing the Adequacy of the Federal Law Relating to Dangerous Biological Agents," 106th Cong., 1st sess., May 20, 1999, text available online at http://com-notes.house.gov/cchear/hearings106.nsf/768df0faa6d9ddab852564f1004886c0/696a4988bb607c7985256777005f7f2 6?OpenDocument. Another possibility is that increased funding for research on threat agents and budget cuts in the area of infectious diseases could induce some scientists who would otherwise work on more common diseases to work on more unusual ones that might be used as warfare agents.

99. Statement by David Gordon, national intelligence officer for economics and global issues, National Intelligence Council, before U.S. Congress, House, International Relations Committee, "Infectious Diseases: A Growing Threat to America's Health and Security," 106th Cong., 2d sess., June 29, 2000, p. 35, text available online at http://frwebgate.access.gpo.gov/cgi-bin/getdoc.cgi?IPaddress=wais.access.gpo.gov&dbname=106_house_hearings&docid=f:67067.pdf

100. Statement by Atlas before U.S. Congress, Senate, November 6, 2001.

101. "Infectious Disease—A Global Health Threat," Report of the Working Group on Emerging and Re-emerging Infectious Diseases, Committee on International Science, Engineering, and Technology, National Science and Technology Council, September 1995, available online at http://www.ostp.gov/CISET/html/toc.html.

102. Leonard A. Cole, *The Eleventh Plague: The Politics of Biological and Chemical Warfare* (New York: W. H. Freeman and Co., 1996), p. 214.

103. John E. van Courtland Moon, "Controlling Chemical and Biological Weapons through World War II," in Richard Dean Burns, ed., *Encyclopedia of Arms Control and Disarmament* (New York: Charles Scribner's Sons, 1993), vol. 2, pp. 657–74

CHAPTER SEVEN

1. U.S. Congress, House, *Report of the Select Committee on U.S. National Security and Military/Commercial Concerns with the People's Republic of China*, 106th Cong., 1st sess., declassified May 25, 1999, H. Rept. 105-851, available online at http://www.gpo.gov/congress/house/hr105851-html.

2. "A National Security Strategy for a New Century," White House, December 1999, p. 1, available online at http://www.dtic.mil/doctrine/jel/other_pubs/nssr99.pdf.

3. "Study Group on Enhancing Multilateral Export Controls for US National Security: Final Report," Henry L. Stimson Center, Washington, D.C., April 2001, p. 45, note 3, available online at http://www.stimson.org/exportcontrol/pdf/finalreport.pdf.

4. "The National Security Strategy of the United States of America," White House, September 2002, p. 31, available online at http://www.whitehouse.gov/nsc/nss.pdf.

5. Craig Hoyle and Andrew Koch, "Yemen Drone Strike: Just the Start?" *Jane's Defence Weekly*, November 8, 2002, p. 1, abbreviated version available online at http://www.janes.com/aerospace/military/news/jdw/jdw021108_1_n.shtml; "Predator Drone Kills Six Al Qaeda Suspects: Sources Say CIA Operation Targeted *USS Cole* Bomb Suspect," ABC *World News Tonight*, November 5, 2002, text version available online at http://abcnews.go.com/sections/wnt/DailyNews/yemen021105.html.

6. "The Triumph of Evil: How the West Ignored Warnings of the 1994 Rwanda Genocide and Turned Its Back on the Victims," PBS and WGBH *Frontline*, 1999, associated materials available online at http://www.pbs.org/wgbh/pages/frontline/shows/evil/.

7. For an analysis of UN Resolutions and U.S. refusal to agree to the word "genocide," see Samantha Power, *A Problem from Hell: America and the Age of Genocide* (New York: Basic Books, 2002), pp. 329–90.

8. See Paul N. Doremus et al., *The Myth of the Global Corporation* (Princeton, N.J.: Princeton University Press, 1998), pp. 4–10.

9. Richard L. Kugler and Ellen L. Frost, eds., *The Global Century: Globalization and National Security*, 2 vols. (Washington, D.C.: National Defense University Press, 2001), vol. 1, p. 4.

10. "More importantly, globalization is largely irresistible. Thus, globalization is not a policy option, but a fact to which policymakers must adapt." *Final Report of the Defense Science Board Task Force on Globalization and Security*, Office of the Under Secretary of Defense for Acquisition and Technology, December 1999, p. i, available online at http://www.acq.osd.mil/dsb/globalization.pdf.

11. See for example, François Heisbourg, "From European Defense Industrial Restructuring to Transatlantic Deal?" working paper no. 4, CSIS Study Group on Enhancing Multilateral Export Controls for US National Security, Center for Strategic and International Studies and Henry L. Stimson Center, Washington, D.C., February 2001, p. 22, available online at http://www.stimson.org/exportcontrol/pdf/paper4.pdf; Alexandra Ashbourne, "The United States and Multilateral Export Controls: The British Perspective," working paper no. 6, CSIS Study Group on Enhancing Multilateral Export Controls for US National Security, Center for Strategic and International Studies and Henry L. Stimson Center, Washington, D.C., April 2001, pp. vi, 4, available online at http://www.stimson.org/export-control/pdf/paper6.pdf.

12. Andrew J. Pierre, *The Global Politics of Arms Sales* (Princeton, N.J.: Princeton University Press, 1982), pp. 285–90, 292–98.

13. U.S. Congress, Office of Technology Assessment, *Global Arms Trade: Commerce in Advanced Military Technology and Weapons*, OTA-ISC-460 (Washington, D.C.: U.S. Government Printing Office, June 1991), pp. 12–13, available online at http://www.wws.princeton.edu/~ota/disk1/1991/9122.html.

14. For examples, see William W. Keller and Janne E. Nolan, "Mortgaging Security for Economic Gain: U.S. Arms Policy in an Insecure World," *International Studies Perspectives* 2, no. 2 (May 2002): 182–83.

15. "Global Arms Sales Rise Again, and the U.S. Leads the Pack," *New York Times*, August 20, 2001, p. A 1. This article is based on an annual report of the Congressional Research Service, Richard F. Grimmett, "Conventional Arms Transfers to Developing Nations, 1993–2000," CRS Report for Congress, August 16, 2001, available online at http://www.fas.org/asmp/resources/govern/crs2000.pdf.

16. Keller and Nolan, "Mortgaging Security for Economic Gain," pp. 181–87; William W. Keller, *Arm in Arm: The Political Economy of the Global Arms Trade* (New York: Basic Books, 1995), pp. 97–145.

17. Heisbourg, "From European Defense Industrial Restructuring to Transatlantic Deal?" p. 7.

18. C^4/ISR is the acronym for command, control, communications, and computers/intelligence, surveillance, and reconnaissance.

19. "Moore's Law," coined by the founder of the Intel Corporation, Gordon Moore, is the observation that the logic density of silicon integrated circuits closely follows the curve bits per square inch $= 2^{(t-1962)}$, where t is time measured in calendar years. That is, the amount of information that can be stored on a given area of silicon has roughly doubled every year since the technology was invented.

20. For example, see "National Security Assessment of the Domestic and Foreign Subcontractor Base: A Study of Three U.S. Navy Weapon Systems," Strategic Analysis Division, Office of Industrial Resource Administration, Bureau of Export Administration, U.S. Department of Commerce, March 1992, pp. ii–iii.

21. Keller, *Arm in Arm*, pp. 125–45.

22. William W. Keller and Richard J. Samuels, eds., *Crisis and Innovation in Asian Technology* (Cambridge: Cambridge University Press, 2003), chapter 1.

23. Special tabulation by R. Lehming, Survey of Earned Doctorates, Division of Science Resources Studies, National Science Foundation, January 29, 2000.

24. William W. Keller and Louis W. Pauly, "Crisis and Adaptation in East Asian Innovation Systems: The Case of the Semiconductor Industry in Taiwan and South Korea," *Business and Politics* 2, no. 3 (December 2000): 347, figure 10.

25. U.S. Congress, Office of Technology Assessment, *Assessing the Potential for Civil-Military Integration: Technologies, Processes, and Practices*, OTA-ISS-611 (Washington, D.C.: U.S. Government Printing Office, September 1994), pp. 1–3.

26. Keller, *Arm in Arm*, pp. 152–58.

27. *Defense News*, July 30–August 5, 2001, pp. 1, 4.

28. Richard J. Samuels, *"Rich Nation, Strong Army": National Security and the Technological Transformation of Japan* (Ithaca, N.Y.: Cornell University Press, 1994), p. 232 and table 7.3.

29. Ashbourne, "United States and Multilateral Export Controls," pp. v–vi.

30. Author's interview with staff at the U.S. Defense Technology Security Agency, Department of Defense, July 1991.

31. Author's interview with intelligence officials at Los Alamos National Laboratory, September 1992.

32. "Over 80 German firms, including such respected enterprises as MBB and Karl Zeiss, have been implicated as suppliers for Iraqi unconventional weapons capability. The Karl Kolb firm has been identified as the principal contractor for the Iraqi nerve gas plant at Samara, perhaps the largest

in the world." U.S. Congress, Office of Technology Assessment, *Global Arms Trade*, p. 69.

33. "Average real wages in the U.S. economy have grown 6.3% under President Clinton, and grew by 2.7% in 1998—the fastest annual growth in over 20 years. From 1992 to 1998, export-related jobs paid 15% more on average than non-export-related jobs." From "President Clinton Participates in 'National Dialogue on Jobs and Trade Day' Building a New American Consensus on Trade," November 10, 1999, fact sheet, Third WTO [World Trade Organization] Ministerial Conference, Seattle, November 30–December 3, 1999, available online at http://clinton3.nara.gov/WH/New/WTO-Conf-1999/factsheets/fs003.html.

34. "Welcome to the Wassenaar Arrangement," Wassenaar Arrangement on Export Controls for Conventional Arms and Dual-Use Goods and Technologies, available online at http://www.wassenaar.org/welcomepage.html.

35. DSAA (Facts Book), *Foreign Military Sales, Foreign Military Construction Sales and Military Assistance Facts*, FMS Control and Reports Division, Comptroller, Defense Security Assistance Agency, Department of Defense, September 30, 1993, p. 3.

36. "Conventional Arms Transfer Policy," statement by the president, May 19, 1977, *Presidential Documents—Jimmy Carter*, vol. 13, no. 21, pp. 756–57.

37. *Final Report of the Defense Science Board Task Force on Globalization and Security*, passim.

38. William W. Keller, *The Liberals and J. Edgar Hoover: Rise and Fall of a Domestic Intelligence State* (Princeton, N.J.: Princeton University Press, 1989), passim.

CHAPTER EIGHT

1. In the course of preparing this chapter I benefited from several background briefings by European government officials, and I wish to thank them for their insights. I also would like to thank the participants and particularly the commentators who attended the two Century Foundation/Georgetown project conferences and the B-WIIS members (British chapter of Women in International Security) who attended a seminar I gave on this topic. In addition, I would like to thank Emma Reade for her impressive research assistance.

2. Michael Mastanduno, *Economic Containment: CoCom and the Politics of East-West Trade* (Ithaca, N.Y.: Cornell University Press, 1992), pp. 228–33.

3. Sean Howard, "Moderation in Excess: NATO's Arms Control Review and the NPT Action Plan," *Disarmament Diplomacy* (Acronym Institute for Disarmament Diplomacy, London), no. 54 (February 2001): 14, available online at http://www.acronym.org.uk/dd/dd54/54sean.htm.

4. As a 1996 report into the new security agenda for Europe concluded, "The most serious threats to security in Europe after the cold war no longer arise from conflicts *between* states but from conflicts *within* states." Report of the Independent Working Group established by SIPRI, "A Future Security Agenda for Europe," Stockholm International Peace Research Institute, Stockholm, October 1996, available online at http://editors.sipri.se/pubs/iwg/text.html.

5. Paul Cornish and Geoffrey Edwards, "Beyond the EU/NATO Dichotomy: The Beginnings of a European Strategic Culture," *International Affairs* 77, no. 3 (July 2001): 587–603.

6. Harald Müller, ed., *A European Non-Proliferation Policy: Prospects and Problems* (Oxford: Clarendon Press, 1987).

7. Stephen Cambone et al., "European Views of National Missile Defense," policy paper, Atlantic Council of the United States, Washington, D.C., September 2000, p. 6, available online at http://www.acus.org/Publications/policypapers/TransatlanticRelations/EuropeNMD.pdf.

8. Camille Grand, "Missile Defence: The View from the Other Side of the Atlantic," *Arms Control Today* 30, no. 7 (September 2000): 13.

9. For more on the Blue Streak project, see Nicholas Hill, "Blue Streak— Its Brief Life as a Weapon," available online at http://members.aol.com/nicolashl/ukspace/bs/bs_weapon.htm.

10. Natalie J. Goldring, "Skittish on Counterproliferation," *Bulletin of the Atomic Scientists* 50, no. 2 (March/April 1994): 12–13, available online at http://www.thebulletin.org/issues/1994/ma94/ma94reports.html.

11. Lawrence Freedman, "Europe and Deterrence," in Burkard Schmitt, ed., *Nuclear Weapons: A New Great Debate*, Chaillot Paper no. 48, Institute for Security Studies, Western European Union, Paris, July 2001, p. 100, available online at http://www.iss-eu.org/chaillot/chai48e.pdf.

12. British Medical Association, *Biotechnology Weapons and Humanity* (Amsterdam: Harwood Academic Publishers, January 1999), especially pp. 45–51.

13. Wyn Q. Bowen, "Missile Defence and the Transatlantic Security Relationship," *International Affairs* 77, no. 3 (July 2001): 494.

14. Statement of David Byrne, European commissioner for health and consumer protection, "Global Health Security Initiative Strengthens Preparedness and Response to Bioterrorist Threats," December 10, 2002,

available online at http://europa.eu.int/rapid/start/cgi/guesten.ksh?p_action. gettxt=gt&doc=IP/02/1833 | 0 | RAPID&lg=EN&display.

15. See the European Commission's public health web page on bioterrorism, available online at http://europa.ed.int/comm/health/ph/programmes/ bio-terrorism/index_en.html.

16. Charles Guthrie, "British Defence: The Chief of the Defence Staff's Lecture 2000," *Royal United Service Institute Journal* 146, no. 1 (February 2001): 1–7.

17. U.K. House of Commons, Foreign Affairs Committee, Eighth Report, *Weapons of Mass Destruction*, HC 407 of 1999–2000, July 25, 2000, available online at http://www.publications.parliament.uk/pa/cm199900/ cmselect/cmfaff/407/40702.htm.

18. "Defending Our Future: Statement on the Defence Estimates 1993," cited in Darryl Howlett and John Simpson, "The United Kingdom," in Harald Müller, ed., *European Non-Proliferation Policy 1993–1995* (Brussels: European Interuniversity Press, 1996), p. 98.

19. U.K. Ministry of Defence, *Strategic Defence Review*, July 1998, available online at http://www.mod.uk/issues/sdr/wp_contents.htm.

20. Paul Schulte, "Intelligence and Weapons Proliferation in a Changing World," in Harold Shukman, ed., *Agents for Change: Intelligence Services in the 21st Century* (London: St Ermin's Press, 2001), pp. 203–21.

21. "Defence Policy 2001" (brochure), U.K. Ministry of Defence, February 2001, p. 8.

22. Jeremy Laurance, "Hospitals Told to Make Emergency Plans to Cope with Biological Terrorism Attacks," *Independent* (London), May 1, 2000, available online at http://www.independent.co.uk/story.jsp?story=2300.

23. Sarah Boseley, "'Protect and Survive' Posters on the Streets," *Guardian* (Manchester), November 15, 2002, p. 7.

24. Rachel Sylvester, "Blair Forms National Emergency Crisis Unit," *Daily Telegraph* (London) July 11, 2001.

25. David Walker, "Cobra, the Whitehall Secret that Never Was," *Guardian* (Manchester), October 22, 2002, available online at http:// www.guardian.co.uk/guardianpolitics/story/0,3605,816486,00.html.

26. See the UK Resilience Web site, available online at http://www. ukresilience.info/home.htm.

27. Nicholas Pyke, "How Legionnaire's Toll Was Restricted," *Guardian* (Manchester), December 27, 2002, p. 9.

28. Patrick Wintour and Richard Norton-Taylor, "Ministers Draw Up Terror Cordon and Evacuation Plans," *Guardian* (Manchester), December 30, 2002.

29. "TA Poised for New Terror Role," BBC News Web site, February 14, 2002, available online at http://news.bbc.co.uk/2/hi/uk_news/politics/1819698.stm.

30. See in particular the French Ministry of Defense, *Livre Blanc sur la Défense, 1994* (Paris: Service d'Information et de Relations Publiques des Armées, Ministère de la Défense, 1994).

31. Ian Kenyon et al., "Prospects for a European Ballistic Missile Defence System," *Southampton Papers in International Policy* (Mountbatten Centre for International Studies, University of Southampton), no. 4 (June 2001): 8.

32. Xavier de Villepin, "La Défense Antimissiles du Territoire (NMD) aux Etats-Unis," rapport d'information no. 417, French Senate, Foreign Affairs, Defense and Armed Forces Committee, June 14, 2000, available online at http://www.senat.fr/rap/r99-417/r99-417.html, cited in Grand, "Missile Defence," p. 14.

33. Camille Grand, "Drivers of Nuclear Weapons Policies: France," paper presented at a conference titled "Alternative Strategies for Nuclear Policies," Programme for Promoting Nuclear Non-Proliferation, Mountbatten Centre for International Studies, University of Southampton, June 5, 1998, p. 8.

34. Camille Grand and Philippe Richard, "France," in Müller, *European Non-Proliferation Policy 1993–1995*, p. 66.

35. French Ministry of Defense, *Livre Blanc sur la Défense, 1994*.

36. Grand and Richard, "France," p. 69.

37. "National Defense," excerpts of a speech by Jean-Pierre Raffarin to the fifty-fifth session of the Institute of National Defense Studies (IHEDN), Paris, October 14, 2002, text available online at http://www.info-france-usa.org/news/statmnts/2002/raffarin_ihedn.asp.

38. Alain Michel and Harald Müller, "The European Union," in Müller, *European Non-Proliferation Policy 1993–1995*, p. 37.

39. For an explanation of the roots of French policy towards Iraq and a fairly robust defense of it, see Dominique Moïsi, "Iraq," in Richard N. Haass, ed., *Transatlantic Tensions: The United States, Europe, and Problem Countries* (Washington, D.C.: Brookings Institution Press, 1999), pp. 124–39.

40. William Shawcross, *Deliver Us from Evil: Warlords and Peacekeepers in a World of Endless Conflict* (London: Bloomsbury Publishing, 2000), p. 245.

41. Karl Kaiser, "Challenges and Contingencies for European Defence Policy," in Laurence Martin and John Roper, eds., *Towards a Common Defence Policy* (Paris: Institute for Security Studies, Western European Union, 1995), p. 35.

42. Peter Rudolf, "Managing Strategic Divergence: German-American Conflict over Policy Towards Iran," in Peter Rudolf and Geoffrey Kemp, eds., *The Iranian Dilemma: Challenges for German and American Foreign*

Policy, Conference Report, American Institute for Contemporary German Studies, Johns Hopkins University, April 21, 1997, pp. 1–10, available online at http://www.aicgs.org/publications/PDF/iran.pdf.

43. "'Ten Point-initiative' on Non-Proliferation," in *Deutscher Bundestag, Drucksache 12/6985*, p. 85ff., cited in Henning Riecke, "NATO's Non-Proliferation and Deterrence Policies: Mixed Signals and the Norm of WMD Non-Use," in Eric Herring, ed., *Preventing the Use of Weapons of Mass Destruction* (London: Frank Cass, 2000), p. 50, n. 35.

44. Alexander Kelle and Harald Müller, "Germany," in Müller, *European Non-Proliferation Policy 1993–1995*, p. 119.

45. Riecke, "NATO's Non-Proliferation and Deterrence Policies," pp. 25-51; William Drozdiak, "Bonn Proposes that NATO Pledge No-First-Use of Nuclear Weapons," *Washington Post* (foreign service), November 23, 1998, p. A16, available online at http://tms.physics.lsa.umich.edu/214/other/news/no_first_use.html.

46. Kelle and Müller, "Germany," pp. 120, 127.

47. Grand and Richard, "France," p. 65.

48. Joseph F. Pilat and Walter L. Kirchner, "The Technological Promise of Counterproliferation," *Washington Quarterly*, 18, no. 1 (Winter 1995): 154; David Fischer et al., *A New Nuclear Triad: The Non-Proliferation of Nuclear Weapons, International Verification and the IAEA*, PPNN Study no. 3, Programme for Promoting Non-Proliferation, Mountbatten Centre for International Studies, Southampton University, September 1992.

49. Stockholm International Peace Research Institute, *SIPRI Yearbook 1992: World Armaments and Disarmament* (Oxford: Oxford University Press, 1992), pp. 98–99.

50. Michel and Müller, "European Union," pp. 38–46.

51. Pablo Benavides "Safeguards and Non-Proliferation in the EU: Reflections on 40 Years of EURATOM Safeguards and Some Thoughts Concerning Future Developments," European Commission, 1997, formerly available (no longer available) online at http://europa.eu.int/en/comm/dg17/s97005pb.htm.

52. Background interview with a British government official, London, February 2002.

53. Ibid., section 3.3.

54. Stephen Castle, "EU Visit to Pyongyang Challenges Bush Stance," *Independent* (London), March 26, 2001, available online at http://news.independent.co.uk/europe/story.jsp?story=62794.

55. "MTCR Draft Code of Conduct," *Disarmament Diplomacy* (Acronym Institute for Disarmament Diplomacy, London), no. 57 (May 2001): 2–4,

available online at http://www.acronym.org.uk/dd/dd57/57note.htm; Brooks Tigner, "EU Hopes Code of Conduct Will Cool Missile Proliferation," *Defense News*, July 9–15, 2001, pp. 1, 4.

56. For a discussion of the problems with these regimes, see Peter van Ham, *Managing Non-Proliferation Regimes in the 1990s: Power, Politics and Policies* (London: Royal Institute of International Affairs/Pinter Publishers, 1994).

57. Dan Charles, "Exporting Trouble: West Germany's Freewheeling Nuclear Business," *Bulletin of the Atomic Scientists* 45, no. 3 (April 1989): 21–27.

58. *Die Welt* (Berlin), February 7, 1991; *Frankfurter Rundschau* (Frankfurt), February 7,1991; *Frankfurter Allgemeine* (Frankfurt), February 9, 1991; all cited in Newsbrief no. 13, Programme for Promoting Nuclear Non-Proliferation, Mountbatten Centre for International Studies, Southampton University, Spring 1991, p. 2, available online at http://www.ppnn.soton.ac.uk/nb13.pdf.

59. Release from the German Federal Ministry for Economic Cooperation, December 4, 1990, cited in Newsbrief no. 12, Programme for Promoting Nuclear Non-Proliferation, Mountbatten Centre for International Studies, Southampton University, Winter 1990/1991, p. 2, available online at http://www.ppnn.soton.ac.uk/nb12.pdf.

60. *Guardian* (Manchester), January 24, 1992, cited in Newsbrief no. 17, Programme for Promoting Nuclear Non-Proliferation, Mountbatten Centre for International Studies, Southampton University, Spring 1992, p. 3, available online at http://www.ppnn.soton.ac.uk/nb17.pdf.

61. Davina Miller, *Export or Die: Britain's Defence Trade with Iran and Iraq* (London: Cassell, 1996).

62. "National Defense," excerpts of a speech by Jean-Pierre Raffarin.

63. *Report on United States Barriers to Trade and Investments*, European Commission, Brussels, 1996, formerly available (no longer accessible) online at http://europa.eu.int/en/comm/c9500/comm9500.html.

64. Raymond Tanter, *Rogue Regimes: Terrorism and Proliferation* (New York: St. Martin's Press, 1999), p. 175.

65. As Camille Grand noted, preservation of the ABM Treaty seems to be the lowest common denominator in European opinion. Grand, "Missile Defence," p. 13.

66. Kenyon et al., "Prospects for a European Ballistic Missile Defence System," p. 8.

67. Frank Bruni, "France and Germany Caution Bush on Missile Defense Plan," *New York Times*, June 14, 2001.

68. "70% of Britain Fears US-Driven Arms Race," BASIC press release, British American Security Information Council, London, July 18, 2001, available online at http://www.basicint.org/pubs/Press/2001july-NMDpoll.htm.

69. Richard Norton-Taylor, "Europe Resigned While Britain Clicks Its Heels," *Guardian* (Manchester), December 14, 2001, p. 17.

70. Kevin Maguire, "Straw Backs Bush's Son of Star Wars," *Guardian* (Manchester), July 27, 2001, p. 7.

71. Richard Norton-Taylor, "Military Chief Casts Doubts on Star Wars," *Guardian* (Manchester), July 28, 2001, p. 1.

72. Nicola Butler, "Missile Defence Divergence: Britain Debates NMD," *Disarmament Diplomacy* (Acronym Institute for Disarmament Diplomacy, London), no. 48 (July 2000): 19–24, available online at http://www. acronym.org.uk/dd/dd48/48ukparl.htm.

73. Hugo Young, "This Anti-American Stunt in Yorkshire is a Perfect Gesture," *Guardian* (Manchester), July 5, 2001, p. 20.

74. See the unclassified version of National Security Presidential Directive 17, "National Strategy to Combat Weapons of Mass Destruction," December 2002, available online at http://www.whitehouse.gov/news/ releases/2002/12/WMDStrategy.pdf; Mike Allen and Barton Gellman, "Preemptive Strikes Part of U.S. Strategic Doctrine," *Washington Post,* December 11, 2002, p. A1.

75. Ian Davis, "Beware Bush's Summer Charm Offensive, *Observer* (Manchester), July 14, 2002, available online at http://www.observer. co.uk/Print/0,3858,4460958,00.html.

76. Freedman, "Europe and Deterrence," p. 90.

77. Joachim Krause, "Proliferation Risks and Their Strategic Relevance: What Role for NATO?" *Survival* 37, no. 2 (Summer 1995): 135–48.

78. Ibid., p. 140.

79. Pilat and Kirchner, "Technological Promise of Counterproliferation," p. 163.

80. Harald Müller and Mitchell Reiss, "Counterproliferation: Putting New Wine in Old Bottles," *Washington Quarterly* 18, no. 2 (Spring 1995): 145.

81. Jeffrey A. Larsen, "NATO Counterproliferation Policy: A Case Study in Alliance Politics," Occasional Paper no. 17, Institute for National Security Studies, U.S. Air Force Academy, November 1997, available online at http://www.usafa.af.mil/inss/ocp17.htm.

82. Kori Schake, "NATO's 'Fundamental Divergence' over Proliferation," in Ted Galen Carpenter, ed., *NATO Enters the 21st Century* (London: Frank Cass, 2000), p. 119.

83. Nicholas Watt, "Nato Chief Says Alliance Has Moral Duty to Back Washington's Line," *Guardian* (Manchester), December 27, 2002,

available online at http://www.guardian.co.uk/international/story/0,3604,865356,00.html.

84. Gilles Andréani, "The Disarray of US Non-Proliferation Policy," *Survival* 41, no. 4 (Winter 1999–2000): 56.

85. Office of the Secretary of Defense, *Proliferation: Threat and Response* (Washington, D.C.: U.S. Government Printing Office, January 1996), pp. 1–42; President's State of the Union Address, January 30, 2002, text available online at http://www.whitehouse.gov/news/releases/2002/01/20020129-11.html.

86. Harald Müller, "European Nuclear Non-Proliferation after the NPT Extension: Achievements, Shortcomings and Needs," in Paul Cornish, Peter van Ham, and Joachim Krause, eds., *Europe and the Challenge of Proliferation*, Challiot Paper no. 24, Institute for Security Studies, Western European Union, Paris, May 1996, pp. 45–46, available online at http://www.iss-eu.org/chaillot/chai24e.html.

87. Kori N. Schake and Jeffrey Simon, "Europe," in *Strategic Challenges for the Bush Administration: Perspectives from the Institute for National Strategic Studies* (Washington, D.C.: National Defense University Press, 2001), p. 17, available online at http://www.ndu.edu/inss/press/BUSH.HTML#ch2.

88. Joachim Krause, "The Proliferation of Weapons of Mass Destruction: The Risks for Europe," in Cornish, van Ham, and Krause, *Europe and the Challenge of Proliferation*, p. 5.

89. Personal interview with source requesting anonymity.

90. "National Defense," excerpts of a speech by Jean-Pierre Raffarin.

91. Crispin Hain-Cole, "The Summit Initiative on Weapons of Mass Destruction: Rationale and Aims," *NATO Review* 47, no. 2 (Summer 1999): 34, available online at http://www.nato.int/docu/review/1999/9902-08.htm.

92. Moïsi, "Iraq," pp. 124–37.

93. See Keith R. Krause, ed., *Culture and Security: Multilateralism, Arms Control and Security Building* (London: Frank Cass, 1999), especially Chapter 1.

94. As quoted by Dean Robert Gallucci to participants at the first Georgetown/Century Foundation Project Conference in Washington, D.C., October 9, 2000.

95. François Heisbourg, "American Hegemony? Perceptions of the US Abroad," *Survival* 41, no. 4 (Winter 1999–2000): 10.

96. Ibid., p. 13.

97. Catherine M. Kelleher, *Germany and the Politics of Nuclear Weapons* (New York: Columbia University Press, 1975).

98. Robert S. Litwak, *Rogue States and U.S. Foreign Policy: Containment after the Cold War* (Washington, D.C.: Woodrow Wilson Center Press, 2000), p. 4.

99. Comments by Alessandro Politi, consultant to the Italian Ministry of Defense, participating in the BASIC Forum at the Carnegie Endowment for International Peace, Washington, D.C., September 18, 2000, full transcript available at http://www.ceip.org/files/events/IntlPerspecsNMD. asp?EventID=199.

100. Richard Norton-Taylor, "Military Chief in Search of Peace," *Guardian* (Manchester), July 28, 2001, p. 8.

101. U.K. House of Commons, Foreign Affairs Committee, *Weapons of Mass Destruction.*

102. Andréani, "Disarray of U.S. Non-Proliferation Policy," p. 51.

103. Bowen, "Missile Defence and the Transatlantic Security Relationship," p. 495.

104. Grand and Richard, "France," p. 65.

105. Howlett and Simpson, "United Kingdom," p. 92.

106. Müller, *European Non-Proliferation Policy 1993–1995.*

107. Joanna Spear, "Weapons of Mass Destruction," in Robert D. Blackwill and Michael Stürmer, eds., *Allies Divided: Transatlantic Policies for the Greater Middle East* (Cambridge, Mass.: MIT Press, 1997), p. 247.

108. See also Bertrand Goldschmidt, "Proliferation and Non-Proliferation in Western Europe: A Historical Survey," in Müller, *European Non-Proliferation Policy: Prospects and Problems*, p. 28.

109. See "North Korea's Birthday Fireworks," *Strategic Comments* (International Institute for Strategic Studies, London) 4, no. 8 (October 1998): 1–8.

110. Gideon Rose, "The United States and Libya," in Haass, *Transatlantic Tensions*, pp. 155–56.

111. U.K. House of Commons, Foreign Affairs Committee, *Weapons of Mass Destruction.*

112. This led to the first parliamentary rebellion against the government since Labour came to power in 1997. The House of Commons voted to reinstate Anderson by an unprecedented 301 to 232 vote, with several junior members of the government joining the rebellion. Michael White, "Rebels Give Blair a Bloody Nose," *Guardian* (Manchester), July 17, 2001, p. 1.

113. Robert E. Hunter, "Think Tanks: Helping to Shape U.S. Foreign and Security Policy," *U.S. Foreign Policy Agenda* (an electronic journal of the U.S. Department of State) 5, no. 1 (March 2000), available online at http://usinfo.state.gov/journals/itps/0300/ijpe/pj51hunt.htm.

114. Andréani, "Disarray of U.S. Non-Proliferation Policy," p. 51.

115. Jacques Chirac, Tony Blair, and Gerhard Schröder, "A Treaty We All Need," full-page advertisement, *New York Times*, October 8, 1999.

116. Peter Capella and Ewen MacAskill, "US Thwarts Deal on Biological Weapons," *Guardian* (Manchester), July 26, 2001, p. 14.

117. Schake, "NATO's 'Fundamental Divergence' over Proliferation," p. 118.

118. Ivo Daalder, "Are the United States and Europe Heading for Divorce?" *International Affairs* 77, no. 3 (July 2001): 553–568, available online at http://www.brook.edu/dybdocroot/views/articles/daalder/divorce.pdf.

119. Christoph Bertram, "The Transatlantic Link Today: Starting Over Again," *NATO Review* 49, no. 1 (Spring 2001): 12–14, available online at http://www.nato.int/docu/review/2001/0101-03.htm.

120. For a more diplomatic summary of Zapf's remarks, see "Uta Zapf: Plenary Remarks from the 2001 Carnegie International Non-Proliferation Conference," Washington, D.C., June 18, 2001," text available online at http://www.ceip.org/files/nonprolif/prolif2001/assets/tranzap.html.

CONCLUSION

1. In the Report of the Commission to Assess the Organization of the Federal Government to Combat the Proliferation of Weapons of Mass Destruction (hereafter referred to as *Deutch Commission Report*), *Combating Proliferation of Weapons of Mass Destruction*, July 14, 1999, p. 2, available online at http://www.fas.org/spp/starwars/program/deutch/11910book.pdf, it was estimated that more than five dozen federal agencies have jurisdiction over some aspect of proliferation policy. Despite efforts to consolidate some of these missions under the Department of Homeland Security, the number has actually grown in the past three years.

2. Graham T. Allison et al., eds., *Avoiding Nuclear Anarchy: Containing the Threat of Loose Russian Nuclear Weapons and Fissile Material* (Cambridge, Mass.: MIT Press, 1996), pp. 23–28, 61–62; Valentin Tikhonov, *Russia's Nuclear and Missile Complex: The Human Factor in Proliferation* (Washington, D.C.: Carnegie Endowment for International Peace, April 2001), pp. 7–16.

3. The terrorist attacks of September 11, 2001, confirmed the fears of many. See Laurie Garrett, "The Nightmare of Bioterrorism," *Foreign Affairs* 80, no. 1 (January/February 2001): 76–89; Richard K. Betts, "The New Threat of Mass Destruction," *Foreign Affairs* 77, no. 1 (January/February 1998): 26–41.

4. Testimony of Kyle Olson before U.S. Congress, Senate, Committee on Government Affairs, Permanent Subcommittee on Investigations, "Global Proliferation of Weapons of Mass Destruction: Case Study on Aum Shinrikyo," Part I, 104th Cong., 1st sess., October 31, 1995.

5. Although, even then, the definition of strategic items could often be quite contentious. Michael Mastanduno, *Economic Containment: CoCom and the Politics of East-West Trade* (Ithaca, N.Y.: Cornell University Press, 1992).

6. See Shirley A. Kan, "China: Possible Missile Technology Transfers from U.S. Satellite Export Policy—Actions and Chronology," CRS Report for Congress, Congressional Research Service, updated September 5, 2001, available online at: http://www.fas.org/spp/starwars/crs/98-485.pdf.

7. For a comprehensive discussion, see the *Deutch Commission Report,* pp. 7–12, 43–93.

8. A recent congressionally mandated report on the defeat of hard and deeply buried targets noted that while there is no current requirement for miniaturized nuclear weapons, there is a current mission need. The Air Force, STRATCOM, and the Department of Energy are working to fill that necessity. See "Report to Congress on the Defeat of Hard and Deeply Buried Targets," submitted to the secretary of defense in conjunction with the secretary of energy, July 2001, unclassified version available online at http://www.nukewatch.org/facts/nwd/HiRes_Report_to_Congress_on_the_Defeat.pdf.

INDEX

ABM Treaty. *See* Anti-Ballistic Missile Treaty
Abu Ali (Qaed Senyan al-Harthi), 179
ACDA. *See* Arms Control and Disarmament Agency
AEC. *See* Atomic Energy Commission
Africa, nuclear programs in, 61
Agencies, U.S.: in biological weapons control, 159, 170–71; in national security, 5–6; number responsible for nonproliferation, 24, 37, 237; role in policy organization, 36–37 (*See also* Organization); self-interest in, 36; trade controls by, 178
Agreed Framework (1994), 57*t*, 65, 94–95
Agreements. *See* Multilateral agreements
Agriculture Department, U.S., 237
Aktau chemical combine (Kazakstan), 138
Albright, Madeleine: on Operation Desert Fox, 93; on rogue states, 80
The Anatomy of Disgust (Miller), 161
Anderson, Donald, 224, 294n112
Andréani, Gilles, 85, 221, 225
Annan, Kofi, 124
Anthony, Ian, 261n64
Anthrax: scientific understanding of, 157, 272n9; in Soviet Union (1979), 164, 169; in U.S. mail (2001), 155–58, 164–65, 170, 271n3
Anti-Ballistic Missile (ABM) Treaty (1972): European support for, 215; U.S. involvement in, 54; U.S. withdrawal from, 85, 215
Antibiotics, for biological attacks, 272n9
Anticholinesterase agents, 52
Antiterrorism and Effective Death Penalty Act (1996), 170
Argentina, nuclear program of, 61

Arms Control and Disarmament Act (1961), 19–20, 28
Arms Control and Disarmament Agency (ACDA): creation of, 19–20; Kennedy's proposal for, 26, 28, 38–40; limitations of, 9, 33, 39–40; merger with State Department, 18, 238, 244–45n6
Ashcroft, John, 200
Aspin, Les, 80, 82, 245n7
Asymmetrical forces, 5
Atlas, Ronald, 174
Atomic Energy Commission (AEC), 49
Auburn Endeavor, Operation, 25
Aum Shinrikyo cult, biological attack by, 155, 166, 235
Australia Group, 174
"Axis of evil," 86, 102, 233
Aziz, Tariq, 97

BAE Systems, 184, 191
Baker, Howard, 62
Baker, James: meeting with Iraqi leaders, 97–98; on rogue nations, 79
Ballistic missile(s): assessment of threat, 82–83, 156, 206; British attempt to create, 206; and counterproliferation, 82, 104; multilateral agreements on, 4, 54, 55, 57*t*, 214, 215; rogue nations with, 82–83, 84
Ballistic missile defense: British participation in, 215–16, 223–24; European resistance to, 215–16, 225–26; U.S. perception of need for, 72, 82–83, 84
Baruch, Bernard, 49
Begin, Menachem, 90
Belarus: nuclear program of, 61, 128; threat reduction in, 128, 134

Page numbers followed by letters *f*, *n*, and *t* refer to figures, notes, and tables, respectively.

ABOUT THE CONTRIBUTORS

JOSEPH CIRINCIONE is the director of the Non-Proliferation Project at the Carnegie Endowment for International Peace. He is a frequent commentator on proliferation and security issues and is widely quoted in the media. He served for nine years as a national security specialist in the U.S. House of Representatives on the professional staff of the Committee on Armed Services and the Committee on Government Operations. He is the author of numerous books and articles, including *Deadly Arsenals: Tracking Weapons of Mass Destruction* (Carnegie Endowment, 2002).

BERNARD I. FINEL is executive director of the Security Studies Program and the Center for Peace and Security Studies at Georgetown University. He served as associate director of the program from 1997 to 2001 and was a member of the Security Studies Program core faculty from 1997 to 2002. His research has focused on the links between changes in relative power, domestic coalition structure, and foreign policy choices. He also has written extensively on democratic peace theory, transparency, and the revolution in military affairs. Finel's work has been published in numerous journals including *International Studies Quarterly*, *Security Studies*, and *International Security*. He is coeditor of *Power and Conflict in the Age of Transparency* (Palgrave/Macmillan, 2000) as well as the author of several book chapters.

BRIAN D. FINLAY is the director of the Nuclear Threat Reduction Campaign, an initiative of the Vietnam Veterans of America Foundation. Most recently, he was a program officer at The Century Foundation. He is author of numerous articles on global security policy, arms control, and the nonproliferation of weapons of mass destruction. Before joining The Century Foundation, he was a senior researcher at the Brookings

Institution in Washington, D.C. He also has served as project manager at the Laboratory Center for Disease Control (Health Canada) in Ottawa and as a consultant to Canada's Department of Foreign Affairs and International Trade.

ROSE GOTTEMOELLER is a senior associate at the Carnegie Endowment for International Peace. A specialist in arms control issues in Russia and the other former Soviet states, her research focuses on issues of nuclear security and stability resulting from the breakup of the Soviet Union. Before joining the Carnegie Endowment, Gottemoeller was deputy undersecretary for defense nuclear nonproliferation in the U.S. Department of Energy. Previously, she served as the department's assistant secretary for nonproliferation and national security. From 1993 to 1994, she worked at the National Security Council as director for Russia, Ukraine, and Eurasia affairs.

DAVID A. KAY is a senior fellow at the Potomac Institute for Policy Studies concentrating on issues of counterterrorism and homeland security. At present he is working for the CIA as special adviser for strategy regarding Iraqi weapons of mass destruction. Previously, he served as corporate senior vice president of Science Applications International Corporation (SAIC). Formerly the UN's chief nuclear weapons inspector, he led numerous inspections into Iraq following the end of the Gulf War. Kay has testified frequently before Congress, and his opinion pieces and articles have appeared in the *New York Times*, the *Washington Post*, the *Christian Science Monitor*, the *Washington Quarterly*, and the *New Republic*.

WILLIAM W. KELLER is the director of the Matthew B. Ridgway Center for International Security Studies at the University of Pittsburgh. Previously, he was executive director of the Center for International Studies at MIT. His research interests include proliferation, East Asian economic and security issues, the political economy of multinational corporations, and internal security. From 1987 to 1995, he directed international projects at the Office of Technology Assessment under the auspices of various committees of Congress, including the Senate Committee on Armed Services and the Senate Committee on Commerce. Keller is the author and editor of numerous publications, including *Crisis and Innovation in Asian Technology* (Cambridge University Press, 2002), which he coedited.

ROBERT S. LITWAK is director of the Division of International Studies at the Woodrow Wilson International Center for Scholars of the Smithsonian Institution and an adjunct professor at Georgetown University's School of Foreign Service. He served on the National Security Council staff as director for nonproliferation and export controls during President Clinton's first term. Litwak's most recent book is *Rogue States and U.S. Foreign Policy: Containment after the Cold War* (Johns Hopkins University Press, 2000).

JANNE E. NOLAN serves on the faculty of the international security program at Georgetown University and is working on a book about dissent and national security for The Century Foundation. Nolan has held several senior positions in the private sector, including director of international programs at the Eisenhower Institute for Global Affairs, foreign policy director at The Century Foundation, senior fellow in foreign policy at the Brookings Institution, and senior international security consultant at the Science Applications International Corporation (SAIC). In her public sector career, she served as a foreign affairs officer in the Department of State, a senior representative to the Senate Armed Services Committee for Senator Gary Hart (D.-Colo.), and a member of the National Defense Panel and the U.S. Defense Policy Board. She is the author of numerous books and articles, including *An Elusive Consensus: Nuclear Weapons and American Security after the Cold War* (Brookings Institution Press, 1999).

JOANNA SPEAR is a senior lecturer and director of the postgraduate research program in the Department of War Studies, King's College London, University of London. Between 1993 and 1995 she conducted postdoctoral work at the Center for Science and International Affairs at Harvard University. She is the author of *Carter and Arms Sales: Implementing the Carter Administration's Arms Transfer Restraint Policy* (St. Martin's Press, 1995) and coeditor of *The Changing Labour Party* (Routledge, 1992). Her research interests include problems of weapons proliferation, U.S. foreign and defense policy, the defense trade, and disarmament and demobilization after civil wars. She is currently completing a book on the changing political economy of the defense trade in the post–cold war period, to be published by the Brookings Institution Press.

JESSICA STERN is a lecturer on terrorism at Harvard University's Kennedy School of Government. She is the author of *Terror in the Name*

ULTIMATE SECURITY: COMBATING WEAPONS OF MASS DESTRUCTION

of God: Why Religious Militants Kill (Ecco, 2003) and *The Ultimate Terrorists* (Harvard University Press, 1999) as well as numerous articles on terrorism and weapons of mass destruction. She served on President Clinton's National Security Council staff in 1994–95 and earlier worked at the Lawrence Livermore National Laboratory.

AMY B. ZEGART is an assistant professor of policy studies at the University of California, Los Angeles. Before coming to UCLA, she served as a consultant to the presidential campaign of George W. Bush (2000), worked on the National Security Council staff (1993), and spent three years at McKinsey & Company, a management consulting firm. She is the author of *Flawed by Design: The Evolution of the CIA, JCS, and NSC* (Stanford University Press, 2000) and is currently writing a book about why American national security agencies adapted poorly to terrorism before September 11.

Cases and Materials on the Theft Acts

Janet M Dine, LLB, PhD, AKC, Barrister

First published in Great Britain 1985 by Financial Training Publications Limited,
Avenue House, 131 Holland Park Avenue, London W11 4UT

© Dr. J. M. Dine, 1985

ISBN: 0 906322 80 4

Typeset by LKM Typesetting Ltd, Paddock Wood, Nr Tonbridge
Printed in Great Britain by Biddles Ltd, Guildford

CONTENTS

INTRODUCTION

In this book the more common offences in the Theft Acts 1968 and 1978 are examined. The problems of interpretation raised by the Acts are examined by looking at the case law they have generated. The author's comments have been kept to a minimum in the expectation that reference to the original material will be considerably more illuminating.

Each offence is dealt with by examining the elements of the actus reus first and separately from those of the mens rea. Because this is an artificial division, occasional overlap and cross-reference is unavoidable.

At the beginning of each section there is a summary of the main problems of interpretation. It is hoped that this will provide a method of quickly finding material relevant to any particular question in the mind of the reader.

Where the more difficult problems of interpretation arise, I am most grateful for permission to reproduce discussion on those issues by the learned authors whose work is to be found herein.

TABLE OF CASES CITED

TABLE OF CASES FROM WHICH EXTRACTS ARE TAKEN

TABLE OF STATUTES

ACKNOWLEDGEMENTS

I am grateful to the following for their permission to use copyright material: Butterworths (extracts from the *All England Law Reports* and Smith, *The Law of Theft,* 5th ed.), Her Majesty's Stationery Office (extracts from the 8th report of the Criminal Law Revision Committee (Cmnd 2977)), Incorporated Council of Law Reporting for England and Wales (extracts from the *Law Reports*), the publishers of the *Road Traffic Reports*, Sweet & Maxwell (extracts from Benjamin, *Sale of Goods*, articles in the *Criminal Law Review*, and extracts from Cases and Commentaries in the *Criminal Law Review*, which are by Professor J. C. Smith of Nottingham unless otherwise stated at the end of the commentary), *The Times* (extracts from its law reports).

1 THE ACTUS REUS OF THEFT

Section 1 Theft Act 1968

(1) A person is guilty of theft if he dishonestly appropriates property belonging to another with the intention of permanently depriving the other of it; and 'thief' and 'steal' shall be construed accordingly.

(2) It is immaterial whether the appropriation is made with a view to gain, or is made for the thief's own benefit.

(3) The five following sections of this Act shall have effect as regards the interpretation and operation of this section (and, except as otherwise provided by this Act, shall apply only for purposes of this section).

THE ACTUS REUS OF THEFT

The actus reus of theft, contrary to s. 1 of the Theft Act 1968, is made up of three elements. These elements are themselves explained by other sections of the Theft Act 1968 and the case law. The following is an outline of the relevant sections.

(1) APPROPRIATION

Section 3 Theft Act 1968

Section 3(1) includes innocent acquisition but subsequent assumption of rights.
Section 3(2): bona fide purchaser for value may act in accordance with rights he believes himself to be acquiring.

The definition of appropriation raises the question of whether appropriation must be an act in relation to the property which the owner has in no sense consented to.

(2) PROPERTY

Section 4 Theft Act 1968

Section 4(2): land is not property unless within the stated exceptions.

Section 4(3): wild flowers which are picked are not property unless defendant has commercial purpose.
Section 4(4): wild animals are not property unless another person has or is about to get possession.

(3) BELONGING TO ANOTHER

Section 5 Theft Act 1968

Section 5(1): ownership includes possession and control. The property belongs to another when that other has ownership or possession or control.
Section 5(3) extends the concept to cover the situation where an obligation to return property arises.
Section 5(4) includes property got by another's mistake.

(1) APPROPRIATION

The exact ambit of the concept of appropriation has troubled the courts. Six main problem situations can be identified:

(a)   Where the defendant is innocently in possession of the goods at the outset, but then forms a dishonest intent.
(b)   Where the defendant assumes the rights of an owner without being in possession of the goods.
(c)   Where the defendant's acts are consented to by the owner, especially if the owner's consent is obtained by deception.
(d)   Where not all the rights of the owner are assumed by the defendant.
(e)   Where title to the goods passes immediately before or at the time of the appropriation.
(f)   Where the defendant was a bona-fide purchaser of the property but subsequently discovers that he has no title to the goods.

(a) Original innocent possession

Section 3(1) Any assumption by a person of the rights of an owner amounts to an appropriation, and this includes, where he has come by the property (innocently or not) without stealing it, any later assumption of a right to it by keeping or dealing with it as owner.

The operation of s. 3(1) of the 1968 Act is illustrated by the following case:

Pilgram v *Rice-Smith* [1977] 1 WLR 671   Court of Appeal

The first defendant, who was employed as a shop assistant, served her friend, the second defendant, with corned beef valued at 61p and bacon valued at 80½p. She marked the wrappings at 20p and 38p respectively. At the check out, the second defendant paid the marked price of the goods. They were both convicted by the justices of the theft of corned beef and bacon together valued at 83½p, contrary to sections 1 (1) and 7 of the Theft Act 1968. They appealed to the Crown Court and, on a defence submission, the judge ruled that, since the defendants were not charged with theft of the whole of the corned beef and bacon and the prosecution could not point to any particular part of the articles as having been appropriated, there was no case to answer.

On appeal by the prosecutor:—

Held, that, on the presumption that the defendants' transaction so far as it related to the corned beef and the bacon was fraudulent from the start, the first defendant did not have her employers' authority to supply the second defendant with the goods and the sale or the purported sale was a nullity from the beginning and, in those circumstances, there could have been a conviction for theft of all the corned beef and bacon supplied; and, that, since it was established that, where goods had been proved to have been stolen and a defendant was charged only with theft of part, a conviction could be entered in respect of the goods charged, the judge had wrongly ruled that there was no case to answer; but that no order would be made on the appeal on the prosecutor's undertaking to withdraw it.

The Court of Appeal found it perfectly proper to convict the shop assistant of theft. The whole of the corned beef and bacon had been stolen by her despite the fact that when she was honestly doing her job she was innocently in possession of all the articles at her counter.

(b) Assumption of the rights of an owner while not in possession of the goods

If a defendant offered to sell property belonging to another, whether or not he was in possession of that property, he could be considered to have committed an appropriation. He would have assumed the right of an owner to sell his goods. The defendant would commit theft whether or not he intended to deliver the goods. The intention to permanently deprive the owner would be present by virtue of s. 6(1) which provides that this requirement will be satisfied by an intention 'to treat the thing as his own to dispose of' even where the defendant does not mean the 'other permanently to lose the thing itself'.

R v *Pitham and Hehl* (1976) 65 Cr App Rep 45   Court of Appeal

One M., who knew an acquaintance X was in prison, decided to take advantage of X's incarceration to steal his furniture and sell it. M. offered the furniture to the appellants for sale and they both went individually to X's house to look at the furniture and agreed to buy it, paying M. a sum which they knew to be considerably under the true value. M. and the appellants were later seen to enter X's house after arriving there in a furniture van. M was arrested, but the appellants escaped, but both were later interviewed by the police. They insisted that "they had not screwed the place". All three were charged on counts of burglary, the appellants additionally each on an individual count of handling stolen goods. M. was convicted on two counts of burglary and the appellants only on the individual handling counts. They appealed on the ground that their handling of the furniture was "in the course of stealing" and, therefore, outside the scope of section 22 (1) of the Theft Act 1968.

Held, that the definition of theft in section 1 (1) of the Theft Act 1968 comprised a dishonest appropriation, "appropriation" being defined in section 3 (1), the final words of that subsection being words of inclusion, and the general words at the beginning of that subsection being wide enough to cover *any* assumption by a person of the rights of an owner; and in the instant case M. had assumed the rights of the owner within section 3 (1) when he took the appellants to X's house and showed them the furniture and invited them to buy what they wanted, and at that moment he appropriated X's goods to himself; thus there was no question of the appellants dealing with the goods, *i.e.* the furniture, "in the course of the stealing," it followed that they had rightly been convicted under section 22 (1) on the individual counts of handling, and the appeal would be dimissed.

Situations (c), (d), and (e) above have caused great difficulty and deserve particular attention. A summary of the problems and the various relevant cases is set out below.

(c) Does a defendant assume the rights of an owner only when acting outside the ambit of the owner's consent?

Is the answer the same when the consent of the owner is implied consent or consent obtained by deception? Meech, Skipp, Eddy v Niman and Morris all seem to lead to an affirmative answer. Can Lawrence, however, be reconciled by the idea that consent was only given to the taking of the correct fare?

(d) Do all the rights of the owner need to be assumed before an appropriation takes place? No — even if the defendant offers to buy an article at a lower price than that at which the owner displayed it for sale (thus acknowledging that the owner still has rights in the goods) the defendant has still appropriated the goods by assuming the right to name the price at which the article is displayed for sale. (Anderton v Wish, and Morris).

(e) Must the property belong to another at the time of appropriation?

Court of Appeal in Lawrence say no but in Kaur, Edward v Ddin, and Hircock the courts all assume that the property must belong to another, and the words of the section make no sense otherwise.

Situations (c), (d), and (e) are now examined in detail.

(c) Appropriation and consent

R v *Meech* [1974] QB 549   Court of Appeal

ROSKILL LJ — A man named McCord had obtained a cheque for £1,450 from a hire-purchase finance company by means of a forged instrument. The cheque itself was a perfectly valid document. McCord, who was an undischarged bankrupt, feared that were he to cash this cheque himself his crime would be more likely to be discovered than if he persuaded a friend to cash it for him. McCord, therefore, asked Meech (to whom McCord owed £40) to cash the cheque for him and Meech agreed so to do. At the time he agreed so to do Meech was wholly unaware of the dishonest means whereby McCord had become possessed of the cheque. Meech paid the cheque into his own account at a branch of Lloyds Bank Ltd. at High Wycombe on September 11, 1972. The bank was seemingly unwilling to allow him to cash the cheque until it had been cleared. On September 13, 1972, Meech drew his own cheque for £1,410 on his own account at that branch and that cheque was duly cashed by the bank on that day. The difference between the two sums was represented by McCord's £40 debt to Meech. By the time this cheque was cashed, the original cheque had been cleared. Between the paying in of the original cheque on September 11 and the obtaining of the cash on September 13, Meech became aware that McCord had acquired the original cheque dishonestly.

We were told by counsel that Meech, following legal argument at the end of the evidence, was allowed by the judge to be re-called. Meech then told the jury that not only did he find out about McCord's dishonesty but that he then honestly believed that if he cashed the cheque he would commit an offence. In view of the direction given by the judge to which we refer later, we think it clear that the jury must be taken to have rejected this story of honest belief on Meech's part.

Before the cheque was cashed but after Meech discovered its dishonest origin. Meech agreed with Parslow and Jolliffe that after the cheque was cashed Meech would take the money to a prearranged destination. The two other men were to join him there. A fake robbery, with Meech as the victim was to be staged and indeed was staged, the purpose clearly being to provide some explanation to McCord of Meech's inability to hand over the money of McCord.

This was done; Parslow and Jolliffe between them removed the money after leaving Meech as the apparent victim. The bogus robbery was reported to the police, who being less credulous than the three men imagined McCord might be, investigated the matter and soon became convinced that the robbery story was bogus, as indeed it was soon shown to be. It is clear that Meech was influenced by the thought that even if the bogus nature of the robbery were suspected by McCord, McCord would never dare to go to the police and complain for that would involve revealing his own dishonesty.

All the defendants alleged in evidence that the "robbery" was honest in its purpose in that it was designed to enable the money to be returned to the hire-purchase finance company whom McCord had defrauded. Not surprisingly this story was rejected by the jury.

. . . it was argued for Parslow and Jolliffe that there was a misdirection in relation to appropriation. The judge said:

"As I direct you in law, the time of the appropriation was the time of the fake robbery. Up to that moment, although Meech had drawn the money from the bank, it was still open to him to honour the agreement which he had made with McCord and to pay it over, in due course, to McCord; but once the fake robbery had taken place, that was no longer possible."

It was argued that Meech alone had dishonestly misappropriated the proceeds of the cheque when he drew the money from the bank and that thereafter Parslow and Jolliffe were not guilty of dishonest misappropriation since Meech had already dishonestly misappropriated that money once and for all. It was said that Parslow and Jolliffe were thereafter only liable to be convicted, if at all, of dishonest handling, an offence with which neither was charged.

We think that the judge's direction when he said that the time of the appropriation was the time of the fake robbery was right. A dishonest intention had been formed before the money was withdrawn but the misappropriation only took place when the three men divided up the money at the scene of the fake robbery. It was then that the performance of the obligation by Meech finally became impossible by the dishonest act of these three men acting in concert together.

The convictions must all be affirmed and the appeals dismissed. Meech's application for leave to appeal against sentence is formally refused.

Here the Court of Appeal held that it was only when there was a clear departure from the wishes of the owner (when the fake robbery took place) that the appropriation happened. This was despite the fact that Meech intended to keep the money for himself at the time when he withdrew it from the bank.

R v Skipp [1975] Crim LR 114   Court of Appeal

S was convicted on a count which charged the theft of 450 boxes of oranges and 50 bags of onions. Posing as a genuine haulage contractor he obtained instructions to collect two loads of oranges and one load of onions from three different places in London and deliver them to customers in Leicester. Having collected the goods he made off with them. It was submitted that as S had the intention to steal the goods from the outset the count was bad for duplicity in that there were three separate appropriations.

Held, dismissing the appeal, whether one looked at the matter in the light of cases such as *Jemmison* v *Priddle* [1972] 1 QB 489 and considered if the different acts constituted parts of one activity, or the wording of the Theft Act, the three loads were properly included in the one count. An aussmption [sic] of the rights of an owner over property did not necessarily take place at the same time as an intent permanently to deprive the owner of it. There might be many cases in which a person having formed the intent was lawfully in possession of the goods and could not be said to have assumed the rights of an owner because he had not done something inconsistent with those rights. In the present case it was proper to take the view that up to the point when all the goods were loaded, and probably up to the point when the goods were diverted from their true destination, there had been no assumption of rights, and so there was only one appropriation. There was no conceivable prejudice to S.

Eddy v *Niman* [1981] Crim LR 502   Queen's Bench Divisional Court

The defendant and a friend, having spent some time drinking in public houses, entered a self-service supermarket with the intention of stealing goods from the store. The defendant then changed his mind and informed his friend that the idea was stupid. He left the goods with the friend and went out of the store. The defendant was later arrested, having accepted the facts in full, he was charged with theft contrary to section 1 of the Theft Act 1968. The justices found that, although the defendant had a dishonest intention, there had been no appropriation by him because the public at large were authorised by self-service stores to take goods from the shelves and place them in a receptacle provided by them. Accordingly the defendant could not be guilty of theft. The prosecutor appealed.

Held, dismissing the appeal, that for the prosecution to prove theft, in addition to a dishonest intention they must show that the defendant assumed the rights of an owner. The placing of goods in a receptacle provided by the store was acting within the store's implied consent, so that such an action could not amount to an appropriation.

Commentary. Although it is established that section 1 of the Theft Act is not to be read as if it contained the words, "without the consent of the owner," (*Lawrence* v *M.P.C.* [1972] AC 626) the consent of the owner is a relevant fact in determining (*inter alia*) whether there has been an appropriation. A person who is authorised by the owner of property to exercise certain rights over it does not "assume" those rights when he does so. *Cf.* Smith, *Law of Theft* (4th ed.), paras. 28-32. The result, it is submitted, accords with common sense. The defendant had not yet done anything wrong. Putting the goods in the wire basket was a lawful act, although preparatory to a proposed theft.

The more difficult case is that of the customer at the self-service petrol station who, not intending to pay, fills his tank and drives off without doing so. Common sense here (it is submitted) suggests that this is theft, the practical difference, obviously, being that the owner has lost his petrol whereas, in a case like the present the owner of the supermarket has lost nothing. Common sense is an uncertain guide in the law of theft but it is desirable that the law should coincide with it. If we look at the conduct of the motorist without reference to his state of mind he too has done nothing unlawful, no "overt act inconsistent with the owner's rights," until he gets into the car and drives off. Until then he appears to be doing exactly what the owner has invited him to do. In *McHugh* (1976) 64 Cr App R 92 the Court of Appeal assumed without argument that this was theft.

When the motorist drives off without paying he certainly acts without the consent and against the will of the garage proprietor but the difficulty now is that the ownership in the petrol appears to have passed to the motorist — *Edwards* v *Ddin* [1973] 3 All ER 705 — so there is nothing for him to steal.

Anderton v *Burnside, R* v *Morris* [1983] 3 WLR 697   House of Lords

In the first case, the defendant removed a price label from a joint of pork in a supermarket and attached it to a second, more expensive, joint. His action was detected at the check-out point before he had paid for the joint. He was arrested and charged with theft contrary to section 1(1) of the Act of 1968. He was

R. v Morris

convicted by the justices, and his appeal against conviction was dismissed by the Divisional Court of the Queen's Bench Division. In the second case, the defendant took goods from the shelves of a supermarket and replaced the price labels attached to them with labels showing lesser prices. At the check-out point he was asked for and paid the lesser prices. He was arrested and subsequently tried in the Crown Court on two counts of theft contrary to section 1(1) of the Act of 1968 and one of obtaining property by deception contrary to section 15. The jury convicted him on the counts of theft. The assistant recorder did not take a verdict from them on the third count, ordering it to lie on the file. The defendant's appeal against conviction was dismissed by the Court of Appeal (Criminal Division).

On appeal by the defendants by leave of the House of Lords:—

Held, dismissing the appeals, that on the true construction of sections 1(1) and 3(1) of the Theft Act 1968 it was sufficient, to establish an appropriation, for the prosecution to prove an assumption by the defendant of any of the rights of the owner of the goods; that the concept of appropriation involved adverse interference with, or usurpation of, some right of the owner, which interference or usurpation might be evidenced by one act or by the combination of acts, which need not be overt, the precise moment when the appropriation occurred varying according to the circumstances of the case; that the defendants, by removing the goods in question from the shelves and switching the labels, had adversely interfered with or usurped the rights of the owners of the goods to ensure that they were sold and paid for at the proper prices, it being immaterial in which order those acts had taken place; and that those acts had constituted an appropriation within section 1(1) of the Act of 1968 and the defendants had rightly been convicted.

LORD ROSKILL — My Lords, Mr. Jeffreys sought to argue that any removal from the shelves of the supermarket, even if unaccompanied by label switching, was without more an appropriation. In one passage in his judgment in *Morris's* case, the learned Lord Chief Justice appears to have accepted the submission, for he said [1983] QB 587, 596:

"it seems to us that in taking the article from the shelf the customer is indeed assuming one of the rights of the owner — the right to move the article from its position on the shelf to carry it to the check-out."

With the utmost respect, I cannot accept this statement as correct. If one postulates an honest customer taking goods from a shelf to put in his or her trolley to take to the checkpoint there to pay the proper price, I am unable to see that any of these actions involves any assumption by the shopper of the rights of the supermarket. In the context of section 3(1), the concept of appropriation in my view involves not an act expressly or impliedly authorised by the owner but an act by way of adverse interference with or usurpation of those rights. When the honest shopper acts as I have just described, he or she is acting with the implied authority of the owner of the supermarket to take the goods from the shelf, put them in the trolley, take them to the checkpoint and there pay the correct price, at which moment the property in the goods will pass to the shopper for the first time. It is with the consent of the owners of the supermarket, be that consent express or implied, that the shopper does these acts and thus obtains at least control if not actual possession of the goods preparatory, at a later stage, to obtaining the property in them upon payment of the proper amount at the checkpoint. I do not think that section 3(1) envisages any such act as an "appropriation," whatever may be the meaning of that word in other fields such as contract or sale of goods law. . . .

If, as I understand all of your Lordships to agree, the concept of appropriation in section 3(1) involves an element of adverse interference with or usurpation of some right of the owner, it is necessary next to consider whether that requirement is satisfied in either of these cases. As I have already said, in my view mere removal from the shelves without more is not an appropriation. Further, if a shopper with some perverted sense of humour, intending only to create confusion and nothing more, both for the supermarket and for other shoppers, switches labels, I do not think that that act of label switching alone is without more an appropriation, though it is not difficult to envisage some cases of dishonest label-switching which could be. In cases such as the present, it is in truth a combination of these actions, the removal from the shelf and the switching of the labels, which evidences adverse interference with or usurpation of the right of the owner. Those acts, therefore, amount to an appropriation and if they are accompanied by proof of the other three elements to which I have referred, the offence of theft is established. Further if they are accompanied by other acts such as putting the goods so removed and relabelled into a receptacle, whether a trolley or the shopper's own bag or basket, proof of appropriation within section 3(1) becomes overwhelming. It is the doing of one or more acts which individually or collectively amount to such adverse interference with or usurpation of the owner's rights which constitute appropriation under section 3(1) and I do not think it matters where there is more than one such act in which order the successive acts take place, or whether there is any interval of time between them. To suggest that it matters whether the mislabelling precedes or succeeds removal from the shelves is to reduce this branch of the law to an absurdity.

My Lords, it will have been observed that I have endeavoured so far to resolve the question for determination in these appeals without reference to any decided cases except *R* v *Lawrence (Alan)* [1972] AC 626 which alone of the many cases cited in argument is a decision of this House. If your Lordships accept as correct the analysis which I have endeavoured to express by reference to the construction of the relevant sections of the Theft Act; a trail through a forest of decisions, many briefly and indeed inadequately reported, will tend to confuse rather than to enlighten. There are however some to which brief reference should perhaps be made.

First, *R* v *McPherson* [1973] Crim LR 191. Your Lordships have had the benefit of a transcript of the judgment of Lord Widgery CJ. I quote from page 3 of the transcript:

"Reducing this case to its bare essentials we have this: Mrs. McPherson in common design with the others takes two bottles of whisky from the stand, puts them in her shopping bag; at the time she intends to take them out without paying for them, in other words she intends to steal them from the very beginning. She acts dishonestly as the jury found, and the sole question is whether that is an appropriation of the bottles within the meaning of section 1. We have no hesitation whatever in saying that it is such an appropriation and indeed we content ourselves with a judgment of this brevity because we have been unable to accept or to find any argument to the contrary, to suggest that an appropriation is not effective in those simple circumstances."

That was not, of course, a label switching case, but it is a plain case of appropriation effected by the combination of the acts of removing the goods from the shelf and of concealing them in the shopping bag. *R* v *McPherson* is to my mind clearly correctly decided as are all the cases which have followed it. It is wholly consistent with the principles which I have endeavoured to state in this speech.

It has been suggested that *R* v *Meech* [1974] QB 549, *R* v *Skipp* [1975] Crim LR 114 — your Lordships also have a transcript of the judgment in this case — and certain other cases are inconsistent with *R* v *McPherson*. I do not propose to examine these or other cases in detail. Suffice it to say that I am far from convinced that there is any inconsistency between them and other cases as has been suggested once it is appreciated that facts will vary infinitely. The precise moment when dishonest acts, not of themselves amounting to an appropriation within section 3(1) will necessarily vary according to the particular case in which the question arises.

Of all other cases referred to, I understand all your Lordships to agree that *Anderton* v *Wish (Note)* (1980) 72 Cr App R 23 was rightly decided for the reasons given. I need not therefore refer to it further. *Eddy* v *Niman* (1981) 73 Cr App R 237 was in my view also correctly decided on its somewhat unusual facts. I think that Webster J, giving the first judgment, asked the right question at p. 241, though, with respect, I think that the phrase "some overt act . . . inconsistent with the true owner's rights" is too narrow. I think that the act need not necessarily be "overt."

Kaur (Dip) v *Chief Constable for Hampshire* [1981] 1 WLR 578 is a difficult case. I am disposed to agree with the learned Lord Chief Justice that it was wrongly decided but without going into further detail I respectfully suggest that it is on any view wrong to introduce into this branch of the criminal law questions whether particular contracts are void or voidable on the ground of mistake or fraud or whether any mistake is sufficiently fundamental to vitiate a contract. These difficult questions should so far as possible be confined to those fields of law to which they are immediately relevant and I do not regard them as relevant questions under the Theft Act 1968.

I would answer the certified questions in this way:

"There is a dishonest appropriation for the purposes of the Theft Act 1968 where by the substitution of a price label showing a lesser price on goods for one showing a greater price, a defendant either by that act alone or by that act in conjunction with another act or other acts (whether done before or after the substitution of the labels) adversely interferes with or usurps the right of the owner to ensure that the goods concerned are sold and paid for at that greater price."

I would dismiss these appeals.

One thing to be noted about Lord Roskill's definition of appropriation is that he said: ' "some overt act . . . inconsistent with the true owner's rights" is too narrow.

I think that the act need not necessarily be "overt." ' Does this mean that an appropriation takes place when the defendant does an act by which he seeks to usurp the owner's rights, even when the owner is unaware of this because the defendant's dishonesty is known only to himself? If so, how can it be reconciled with the cases mentioned by Lord Roskill with approval? In *R v Meech, R v Skipp* and *Eddy v Niman* the decisions all turned on the fact that the appropriation did *not* take place until the defendant overtly and clearly stepped outside the authority granted by the owner. Of course, if a secret dishonest intent is enough to turn an act which would appear innocent to a bystander into an appropriation, this would provide an explanation of the ease with which Lord Roskill reconciled his definition of appropriation with *R v Lawrence*. In *R v Morris* Lord Roskill said:

> The starting point of any consideration of Mr. Denison's submissions must, I think, be the decision of this House in *R v Lawrence (Alan)* [1972] AC 626. In the leading speech, Viscount Dilhorne expressly accepted the view of the Court of Appeal (Criminal Division) in that case that the offence of theft involved four elements, (1) a dishonest (2) appropriation (3) of property belonging to another, (4) with the intention of permanently depriving the owner of it. Viscount Dilhorne also rejected the argument that even if these four elements were all present there could not be theft within the section if the owner of the property in question had consented to the acts which were done by the defendant. That there was in that case a dishonest appropriation was beyond question and the House did not have to consider the precise meaning of that word in section 3(1).

> It is, however, very far from clear that in *R v Lawrence* there was an act done by the defendant which was an act adverse to the owner's rights. The only act which could be considered an appropriation (the taking of the money) took place when the defendant himself had become the owner of that money under a contract voidable for fraud. Perhaps the situation in *R v Lawrence* is an example of the situations Lord Roskill spoke of in *R v Morris* where the civil law as to the passing of property is to be ignored. If so, what is to take its place?

R v Lawrence [1972] AC 626   House of Lords

> An Italian student arrived in London at Victoria Station. The defendant, a taxi driver, was waiting outside the station. The student showed the defendant a piece of paper on which was written an address in Ladbroke Grove. The defendant said it was a long and expensive journey. The student got into the taxi and tendered the defendant a £1 note. The defendant said it was not enough and he proceeded to take a further £1 note and a £5 note from the student's open wallet. He then drove the student to his destination. The correct lawful fare for that journey was approximately 10s. 6d.
> The defendant was convicted of theft under section 1 (1) of the Theft Act 1968. The Court of Appeal (Criminal Division) affirmed the conviction.
> On the defendant's appeal:—

Held that the defendant was rightly charged and convicted under section 1 (1), since there were present the four elements required by section 1 (1) of the Act: (i) a dishonest, (ii) appropriation, (iii) of property belonging to another, (iv) with the intention of permanently depriving the owner of it. Section 1 (1) was not to be construed as though it contained the words "without the consent of the owner" and accordingly it was not necessary for the prosecution to prove that the taking was without his consent.

VISCOUNT DILHORNE — Prior to the passage of the Theft Act 1968, which made radical changes in and greatly simplified the law relating to theft and some other offences, it was necessary to prove that the property alleged to have been stolen was taken "without the consent of the owner" (Larceny Act 1916, section 1 (1)).

These words are not included in section 1 (1) of the Theft Act, but the appellant contended that the subsection should be construed as if they were, as if they appeared after the word "appropriates." Section 1 (1) reads as follows:

"A person is guilty of theft if he dishonestly appropriates property belonging to another with the intention of permanently depriving the other of it; and 'thief' and 'steal' shall be construed accordingly."

I see no ground for concluding that the omission of the words "without the consent of the owner" was inadvertent and not deliberate, and to read the subsection as if they were included is, in my opinion, wholly unwarranted. Parliament by the omission of these words has relieved the prosecution of the burden of establishing that the taking was without the owner's consent. That is no longer an ingredient of the offence.

Megaw LJ, delivering the judgment of the Court of Appeal, said [1971] 1 QB 373, 376 that the offence created by section 1 (1) involved four elements: "(i) a dishonest (ii) appropriation (iii) of property belonging to another (iv) with the intention of permanently depriving the owner of it."

I agree. That there was appropriation in this case is clear. Section 3 (1) states that any assumption by a person of the rights of an owner amounts to an appropriation. Here there was clearly such an assumption.

With respect to Lord Dilhorne, if there was an assumption of the owner's rights, this would not, according to R v *Morris* amount to an appropriation, unless the assumption was outside the ambit of the owner's consent. If the defendant had become owner of the property under a contract, the victim's consent would not be relevant. This point seems to have been overlooked by Viscount Dilhorne when he said in R v *Lawrence*:

My Lords, in cross-examination, Mr. Occhi, when asked whether he had consented to the money being taken, said that he had "permitted." He gave evidence through an interpreter and it does not appear that he was asked to explain what he meant by the use of that word. He had not objected when the £6 was taken. He had not asked for the return of any of it. It may well be that when he used the word "permitted," he meant no more than that he had allowed the money to be taken. It certainly was not established at the trial that he had agreed to pay to the appellant a sum far in excess of the legal fare for the journey and so had consented to the acquisition by the appellant of the £6.

The main contention of the appellant in this House and in the Court of Appeal was that Mr. Occhi had consented to the taking of the £6 and that, consequently, his conviction could not stand. In my opinion, the facts of this case to which I have referred fall far short of establishing that Mr. Occhi had so consented.

In fact any consent that Lawrence gained to take any of the money was consent obtained by fraud. The difficulty is that consents obtained by fraud were held in both *R* v *Meech* and *R* v *Skipp* to be sufficient to prevent an appropriation taking place at the time of removing the money from the bank and the time of picking up the oranges respectively. Neither owner would have consented to the acts of the defendants in those cases had they known the true facts.

Although *R* v *Lawrence* decided that 'without the consent of the owner' should not be imported into s. 1(1) of the Theft Act 1968, in fact the *R* v *Morris* definition of appropriation imports just those words.

(d) Do all the rights of the owner need to be assumed?

In *R* v *Morris* the House of Lords decided this question unequivocally in the negative.

R v *Morris* [1983] 3 WLR 697   House of Lords

LORD ROSKILL — Mr. Denison submitted that the phrase in section 3(1) "any assumption by a person of *the rights*" (my emphasis) "of an owner amounts to an appropriation" must mean any assumption of "*all* the rights of an owner." Since neither respondent had at the time of the removal of the goods from the shelves and of the label switching assumed *all* the rights of the owner, there was no appropriation and therefore no theft. Mr Jeffreys for the prosecution, on the other hand, contended that *the* rights in this context only meant *any* of the rights. An owner of goods has many rights — they have been described as "a bundle or package of rights." Mr. Jeffreys contended that on a fair reading of the subsection it cannot have been the intention that every one of an owner's rights had to be assumed by the alleged thief before an appropriation was proved and that essential ingredient of the offence of theft established.

My Lords, if one reads the words "the rights" at the opening of section 3(1) literally and in isolation from the rest of the section, Mr. Denison's submission undoubtedly has force. But the later words "any later assumption of a right" in subsection (1) and the words in subsection (2) "no later assumption by him of rights" seem to me to militate strongly against the correctness of the submission. Moreover the provisions of section 2(1)(*a*) also seem to point in the same direction. It follows therefore that it is enough for the prosecution if they have proved in these cases the assumption by the respondents of *any* of the rights of the owner of the goods in question, that is to say, the supermarket concerned. . . .

(e) Must the property belong to another at the time of the appropriation?

In *R* v *Lawrence* Lord Donovan dismissed this problem very briefly:

R v *Lawrence* [1972] AC 626   House of Lords

LORD DONOVAN — I now turn to the third element "property belonging to another." Mr. Back QC, for the appellant, contended that if Mr. Occhi consented to the appellant taking the £6, he consented to the property in the money passing from him to the appellant and that the appellant had not, therefore, appropriatd property belonging to another. He argued that the old distinction between the offence of false pretences and larceny had been preserved. I am unable to agree with this. The new offence of obtaining property by deception created by section 15 (1) of the Theft Act also contains the words "belonging to another." "A person who by any deception dishonestly obtains property belonging to another, with the intention of permanently depriving the other of it" commits that offence. "Belonging to another" in section 1 (1) and in section 15 (1) in my view signifies no more than that, at the time of the appropriation or the obtaining, the property belonged to another, with the words "belonging to another" having the extended meaning given by section 5. The short answer to this contention on behalf of the appellant is that the money in the wallet which he appropriated belonged to another, to Mr. Occhi.

If this means that title to the money did not pass then the case is clearly reconcilable with *Kaur, Edwards* v *Ddin* and *Walker* (see below pages 30-32). It may be, however, that in *Lawrence,* the question of title was not decided according to the complicated civil law, and that that law was regarded as irrelevant as Lord Morris suggested when giving judgment in *R* v *Morris*. In neither case was any alternative to the civil law suggested and the courts have continued to struggle with and apply the civil law despite its complexities.

(f) The bona-fide purchaser

This problem is specifically dealt with by s. 3(2) of the 1968 Theft Act:

Where property or a right or interest in property is or purports to be transferred for value to a person acting in good faith, no later assumption by him of rights which he believed himself to be acquiring shall, by reason of any defect in the transferor's title, amount to theft of the property.

(2) PROPERTY — WHAT IS CAPABLE OF BEING STOLEN

Section 4(1) Theft Act 1968

'Property' includes money and all other property, real or personal, including things in action and other intangible property.

Real property includes land and houses.
Personal property includes all moveable things which may be owned.
Things in action are rights of action which are protected by law but cannot be seen. Examples are copyrights, trade marks and contractual rights (including the right to sue a bank which arises between a customer and his bank when an ordinary bank account is opened). If a defendant dishonestly pays his debts with money from another's account (e.g. by using a forged cheque) he steals not only the cheque but also part of the debt (the thing in action) owed by the bank to the other.
Other intangible property includes patents which, by the Patents Act 1977 s. 30, are not things in action but are personal property. Information is not included:

Oxford v *Moss* [1979] Crim LR 119   Queen's Bench Division

In 1976, M was an engineering student at Liverpool University. He acquired the proof of an examination paper for a Civil Engineering examination at the University: An information was preferred against him by O, alleging that he stole certain intangible property, *i.e.* confidential information, being property of the Senate of the University. It was agreed that he never intended to permanently deprive the owner of the piece of paper on which the questions were printed.
Held, by the stipendiary at Liverpool: on the facts of the case, confidential information is not a form of intangible property as opposed to property in the paper itself, and that confidence consisted in the right to control the publication of the proof paper and was a right over property other than a form of intangible property. The owner had not been permanently deprived of any intangible property. The charge was dismissed.
On appeal by the prosecutor, as to whether confidential information can amount to property within the meaning of section 4 of the Theft Act 1968.
Held: there was no property in the information capable of being the subject of a charge of theft, *i.e.* it was not intangible property within the meaning of section 4.
Appeal dismissed.
Commentary. The case is of some importance in making clear that confidential information is not property within the meaning of section 4 of the Theft Act 1968. There is no difference in principle between trade secrets and the examination questions and the decision may be taken to settle that trade secrets cannot be stolen.
If more than one person had been involved the case might have been dealt with as a conspiracy to defraud: ". . . an agreement by two or more by dishonesty to injure some proprietary right of [another] suffices to constitute the offence

of conspiracy to defraud": *Scott* v *Metropolitan Police Commissioner* [1975] AC 819 at p. 840 *per* Viscount Dilhorne. The defendant injured the proprietary right of the University in the examination paper by borrowing it (a trespass) and either copying it (a breach of copyright) or memorising it. In either case the University's proprietary interest in the question paper was injured in a very real sense. It is true that they retained unimpaired ownership in the piece of paper throughout; but as a *question* paper it was rendered quite useless.

Section 4(2) Theft Act 1968

A person cannot steal land, or things forming part of land and severed from it by him or by his directions, except in the following cases, that is to say—

(a)   when he is a trustee or personal representative, or is authorised by power of attorney, or as liquidator of a company, or otherwise, to sell or dispose of land belonging to another, and he appropriates the land or anything forming part of it by dealing with it in breach of the confidence reposed in him; or

(b)   when he is not in possession of the land and he appropriates anything forming part of the land by severing it or causing it to be severed, or after it has been severed; or

(c)   when, being in possession of the land under a tenancy, he appropriates the whole or part of any fixture or structure let to be used with the land.

For purposes of this subsection 'land' does not include incorporeal hereditaments; 'tenancy' means a tenancy for years or any less period and includes an agreement for such a tenancy, but a person who after the end of a tenancy remains in possession under the tenancy, and 'let' shall be construed accordingly.

A basic distinction is made between property which is 'on' the land and other property which 'forms part of the land'. The latter can only be stolen in the circumstances specified in s. 4(2) (a), (b) and (c).

The same distinction was made in the Larceny Act 1916. It was explained in *Billing* v *Pill*:

Billing v *Pill* [1954] 1 QB 70   Queen's Bench Division

By section 1 (3) of the Larceny Act, 1916: "Everything which has value . . . and if adhering to the realty then after severance therefrom, shall be capable of being stolen: Provided that − . . . anything attached to or forming part of the realty shall not be capable of being stolen by the person who severs the same from the realty, unless after severance he has abandoned possession thereof."

Any army hut, which was constructed in seven sections, rested on a concrete foundation, the floor of the hut being secured to the foundation by bolts let into the concrete. The hut was one of a number erected by the War Office during the war on land used as a gun emplacement. In 1946 the army vacated the huts, and in 1947 the local authority was instructed to demolish them. In 1951 the appellant, without lawful authority, dismantled the hut in question, removed it from the site and re-erected it on his own land. He was convicted by justices of stealing the hut. On appeal, on the grounds that the justices were wrong in law in convicting as the hut was attached to or formed part of the realty within the meaning of the proviso to section 1 (3) of the Larceny Act, 1916, and was not capable of being stolen since the appellant had not abandoned possession after severing it:—

Held, that the Larceny Act, 1916 was a consolidating Act not intended to alter the law; that the proviso to section 1 (3) was intended to preserve the old common law position; that the words "anything attached to or forming part" of the realty in it should be read as meaning "anything attached so as to form part" of the realty; and that when something in the nature of a chattel was affixed to land the true test was whether it was meant to be a temporary fixture not intended to form part of the realty. The hut was a chattel erected for a purely temporary purpose and did not become attached to or form part of the realty merely because, in order to steady it, it was bolted to the concrete foundation. It remained a chattel capable of being stolen and the appellant had been rightly convicted.

LORD GODDARD CJ — The construction which I put upon that section is this: it starts by saying that things which adhere to the realty can be stolen after they have been severed, but a person who actually severs them, subject to the provisions of section 8 of the Larceny Act, and one or two other sections with which we are not concerned, cannot be convicted of larceny unless after the severance he has left the thing on the land and then returned, on what one may call a separate excursion, and taken the thing because, when he has taken it, it has reverted to the possession of the person on whose land it was. Therefore, the whole of this case depends on the meaning of the words "anything attached to or forming part of the realty." Those words might be read as meaning "attached so as to form part."

The matter is summed up admirably by du Parcq LJ in the Laws of England, Hailsham ed., vol. 20, para. 107: "Whether a chattel has been so affixed to the land or buildings as to become a fixture depends on the object and purpose of the annexation, and if the chattel can be removed without doing irreparable damage to the premises, neither the method nor the degree of annexation, nor the quantum of damage that would be done to the chattel or to the premises by the removal, affect the question save in so far as they throw a light upon the object and purpose of the annexation. If the object and purpose was for the permanent and substantial improvement of the land or building, the article will be deemed to be a fixture, but if it was attached to the premises merely for a temporary purpose or for the more complete enjoyment and use of it as a chattel, then it will not lose its chattel character and it does not become part of the realty." That is a useful exposition of the law, and if one requires authority to support it, there is a very good instance in *Holland* v *Hodgson*.[1] Blackburn J,[2] than whom there was no higher authority on these matters, giving his judgment in that case, emphasized that one must look at the circumstances; and that is also pointed out in the paragraph I have read from the Laws of England.

Can anybody doubt that the hut in question was erected for a temporary purpose? It can be removed without doing any damage to the freehold at all. It rests upon a concrete bed which is let into the land. I should say that there is no question but that the concrete bed has become part of the land, but the hut which stands upon it has not become part of the land merely because some bolts have been put through the floor of the hut to stabilise or steady it. It was erected merely for a temporary purpose so that the Army personnel who were going to the site for a presumed temporary purpose, to man a gun emplacement during the war, would have somewhere to sleep.

[1] (1872) LR 7 CP 328.   [2] Ibid. 335.

Thus, the more difficult the 'thing' is to remove from the ground, the more likely it is that it will be regarded as 'land' or a 'thing forming part of land'.

If something comes within this category, s. 4 of the 1968 Act must be consulted. That section sets out the only three instances in which 'land' or 'things forming part of land' can be stolen. The following is a summary of the effects of that section:

(a)   If the defendant is in a position of trust then, according to s. 4(2)(a), he can steal land (or things forming part of it) to which his position of trust relates.

(b)   When the defendant is not in possession of land he can steal anything forming part of the land (but not the land itself) (s. 4(2)(b)).

(c)   When the defendant is in possession of the land under a tenancy he can steal a fixture or structure (e.g. a bath or a greenhouse: if a greenhouse is a structure – it is not a fixture (Dean v Andrews and another, The Times, 25th May 1985)).

None of the subsections specifically cover a person who has permission to be on the land but who has no lease. It is not clear whether such a person would be considered to be 'in possession' of the land. If he were, the curious situation would be that he would be in a better position than a person in possession of land under a tenancy.

Incorporeal hereditaments can be stolen. Examples would be rights of way and rent charges. The occasions on which this type of theft will occur will be very rare.

Tenancy includes a statutory tenancy. A statutory tenancy arises most frequently when an ordinary lease comes to an end and yet the tenant remains in possession and continues to pay rent to the landlord.

Section 4(3) Theft Act 1968

There is some difficulty in determining the borderline between s. 4(2) and s. 4(3). Severance of plants growing wild by a person not in possession of the land where they are growing might be theft. However, 'picking' of wild flowers by a person not in possession of that land will not be theft unless the picking is done for a commercial purpose.

Section 4(3) Theft Act 1968

A person who picks mushrooms growing wild on any land, or who picks flowers, fruit or foliage from a plant growing wild on any land, does not (although not in possession of the land) steal what he picks, unless he does it for reward or for sale or other commercial purpose.

For purposes of this subsection 'mushroom' includes any fungus, and 'plant' includes any shrub or tree.

Thus:

(a)   Taking a whole plant will probably be theft (if the other elements of the offence are present). This will be so either because there was severance of a thing 'forming part of land' (s. 4(2)), or because the defendant's action could not be described as 'picking from' a plant within s. 4(3).

(b)   There is as yet no case law on the definition of 'picking' in s. 4(3), but it seems a misuse of language to speak of a branch of a tree removed with a chainsaw as having been 'picked'. If all the other elements of s. 1 were present, such behaviour would be theft.

(c)   It will be theft if all the other elements of s. 1 are present and the picking is done 'for sale or other commercial purpose'. It would seem that the commercial intent must be formed at the time of the picking. This is because the subsection reads 'unless he does it [i.e. the picking] for reward' etc.

Section 4(4) Theft Act 1968

Wild creatures, tamed or untamed, shall be regarded as property; but a person cannot steal a wild creature not tamed nor ordinarily kept in captivity, or the carcase of any such creature, unless either it has been reduced into possession by or on behalf of another person and possession of it has not since been lost or abandoned, or another person is in course of reducing it into possession.

'Wild' refers to the way of life of the creature rather than its disposition:

R v Howlett [1968] Crim LR 222   Court of Appeal

H. was convicted of stealing, in 1965, mussels from a mussel bed on the foreshore. The foreshore was alleged to belong to S. who had granted to L. the exclusive right of taking shellfish from it. L. had tended the bed in order to try to preserve and improve it but it remained subject to the action of the sea. H. appealed on the grounds, *inter alia*, that the mussels were not capable of being stolen since they adhered to the realty, alternatively they were animals *ferae naturae* and not capable of being stolen until reduced into possession.

Held, allowing the appeal, it was not necessary to decide the first question because there was not sufficient evidence that the mussels had been reduced into possession. The most that could be said to have been done was that the bed was tended with a view to improving the growth and edible qualities of the mussels until they were removed from the bed. The mere act of raking over an existing natural bed, and occasionally moving some mussels from a place where they were growing too thickly to a place where they were growing too thinly, and where they would again come to rest and adhere to the soil, did not amount to the reduction into possession of the mussels, particularly since in 1966 the majority of the mussels had disappeared as the result of the action of the sea.

Commentary. Wild creatures at large are incapable of being stolen since they are not the property of any person until reduced into possession. Though the terms 'wild' and 'at large' seem singularly inappropriate when applied to a creature so immobile as the mussel, the decision seems, with respect, to be clearly correct.

Although *R* v *Howlett* was a decision under the Larceny Act 1916, there seems to be no reason why the position should be any different under the 1968 Theft Act. Thus, a wild creature can only be stolen if:

(i)   It is tamed or ordinarily kept in captivity.

(ii)   It is in the course of being reduced into another's possession (e.g. it has been shot and is about to be collected by a gun dog), or has been reduced into and remained in another's possession.

There are some things which cannot be stolen because no one has a sufficient proprietary interest in them. They are:

(i)   Electricity – which is dealt with by s. 13 of the 1968 Theft Act.

(ii)   A human corpse.

R v *Sharpe* (1857) Dears & B 160   Court of Criminal Appeal

The following case was reserved and stated for the consideration and decision of the Court of Criminal Appeal by Erle J.

The indictment in the first count charged that the defendant a certain burial ground belonging to a certain meeting house of a congregation of Protestants, dissenting from the Church of England, unlawfully and wilfully did break and enter; a certain grave there, in which the body of one Louisa Sharpe had before then been interred, with force and arms unlawfully, wilfully, and indecently did dig open, and the said body of the said Louisa Sharpe out of the said grave unlawfully, wilfully, and indecently did take and carry away.

And there were other counts varying the charge which may be resorted to, if necessary.

The evidence was as follows.

That the defendant's family had belonged to a congregation of dissenters at Hitchin, and his mother, with some others of his relatives, had been buried in one grave in the burying ground of that congregation there, with the consent of those who were interested. That the father of the defendant had recently died. That the defendant prevailed on the wife of the person to whom the key of the burying ground was entrusted to allow him to cause the grave above mentioned to be opened, under the pretext that he wished to bury his father in the same grave, and in order thereto to examine whether the size of the grave would admit his father's coffin. That he caused the coffins of his step mother and two children to be taken out, and so came to the coffin of his mother, which was under them, and was much decomposed, and that he caused the remains of this coffin, with the corpse therein, to be placed in a shell and carried to a cart near the burying ground, and driven therein some miles away towards a churchyard, where he intended to bury his father's corpse with the remains of his mother.

These acts were done without the knowledge or consent of the congregation to whom the burying ground belonged, or of the trustees having the legal estate therein. The person having the keys of the ground was induced to admit the defendant into the ground and to the grave by reason of the pretext that the defendant intended to bury his father there, and the jury found that this was only a pretext, and that his real intention from the beginning was to remove his mother's corpse. But the defendant acted throughout without intentional disrespect to any one, being actuated by motives of affection to his mother and of religious duty.

I directed the jury to convict, if they believed these facts to be true, and reserved for the decision of this Court the question whether the conviction could be sustained.

Accordingly a verdict of guilty was entered, and the defendant was discharged on his recognizances to appear if called on.

This case was considered on Saturday, 15th of November, 1856, by Pollock CB, Erle J, Willes J, Bramwell B and Watson B.

The defendant appeared in person, and contended that the conviction was wrong. No one appeared for the Crown.

The judgment of the Court was delivered on the 31st of January, 1857, by

Erle J — We are of opinion that the conviction ought to be affirmed. The defendant was wrongfully in the burial ground, and wrongfully opened the grave, and took out several corpses, and carried away one. We say he did this wrongfully, that is to say, by trespass; for the licence which he obtained to enter and open, from the person who had the care of the place, was not given or intended for the purpose to which he applied it, and was, as to that purpose, no licence at all. The evidence for the prosecution proved the misdemeanor, unless there was a defence. We have considered the grounds relied on in that behalf, and, although we are fully sensible of the estimable motives on which the defendant acted, namely, filial affection and religious duty, still neither authority nor principle would justify the position that the wrongful removal of a corpse was no misdemeanor if the motive for the act deserved approbation. A purpose of anatomical science would fall within that category. Neither does our law recognise the right of any one child to the corpse of its parent as claimed by the defendant. Our law recognises no property in a corpse, and the protection of the grave at common law, as contradistinguished from ecclesiastical protection to consecrated ground, depends upon this form of indictment; and there is no authority for saying that relationship will justify the taking a corpse away from the grave where it has been buried.

Stealing the body and its parts [1976] Crim LR 622   A. T. H. Smith

How far the non-property rule extends even in the criminal law is a matter of conjecture. After a period of time, a body may acquire attributes that differentiate it from a corpse awaiting burial, especially where work has been expended on it by reducing it to a skeleton or mummifying it.[15] Nor does there seem to be authority dealing with severed parts of the body or its products, although magistrates have held it to be theft to cut another's hair against his (more commonly perhaps her) will.[17] Since the person taking from a live human being will invariably be guilty of some form of assault, the addition of a charge of theft in such circumstances would seem to be rather pointless. In any case, it would seem logically to follow from the no-property rule that severed parts of the body are not the proper subject-matter of theft, but in the absence of authority the point is approachable in terms of principle.

Nobody acquainted with modern jurisprudence would quarrel with the opening words of *Crosley Vaines on Personal Property* that "property is a word of different meanings" (p. 3). It may be used to mean different things in different contexts, and the courts are free to (and should) examine the policy behind the rule in which the word appears. There are two principal reasons why the non-property rule should be confined within narrow limits. As a purely legal matter, it is anomalous. Even if it is true that the corpse is *res nullius* at the moment of death, there is no reason why it should not become property by *occupation*.[18] If the civil law recognises and protects rights to possession, there is no reason why the criminal law should not do likewise. Similar arguments apply to parts of the body which, like the corpse itself, might lose their character as such, as when human hair is manufactured into wigs. But irrespective of whether this ever happens, there are in purely practical terms strong grounds for refusing to extend the no-property rule to the parts and products of the human body. As a result of advances in medical science, many parts of the body have a usefulness unimaginable to our forbears. Use can now be made of the eyes, bones and skin and, provided they can be utilised with sufficient speed to prevent anoxic damage, the heart, liver and kidneys. Although the point might rarely arise in practice, it would seem absurd that these valuable objects (for they are when severed nothing more) should continue to be treated as *res nullius*. There is no reason why blood, eye or sperm banks should be denied the protection of the criminal law. Nor should it matter that the limb is eventually useless or that, like the urine sample in *Welsh*[19], the thing taken is of little commercial value. The value rule is not reproduced in the Act, and since the Act makes no special provision excluding parts of the body, it is submitted that they fall under the general rule relating to the theft of property.

Perhaps the strongest argument against a reappraisal of the no-property rule at this stage is that the medical profession is in practice the group most likely to fall foul of it. It has recently been held that it is an offence under section 1 (4) of the Human Tissue Act 1961, punishable by unlimited fine or imprisonment, for a person other than a full registered medical practitioner to remove part of a dead body.[20] It could be argued that this provides ample protection against unauthorised tampering with therapeutically useful corpses without at the same time jeopardising the medical profession. Indeed doctors might be forgiven for thinking that the law has already proved itself hopelessly slow in responding to urgent medical problems. That a fresh obstacle should be raised at this stage is but a further example of an unnecessarily legalistic and obstructive approach.

In reply, the following points could be made. It is precisely the advance in medical knowledge, which has added a new dimension to the usefulness of the deceased human body, that necessitates a fresh look at the law. A rule premised on medical knowledge not much more advanced than that of Harvey scarcely commands much respect. As has been pointed out, the rule is in any case an anomaly of uncertain ambit, and although a prosecution for theft is unlikely, it cannot be ruled out altogether. It is in just such emotively charged areas that a private prosecution is an ever present possibility.

[15] *Cp. Doodeward* v *Spence* (1908) 6 CLR 406.
[17] *Herbert* (1960) 25 J Cr L 163. *Quaere* whether, even where this is done with the intention of selling the locks, the conduct is really dishonest.
[18] As in the case, for example, of wild animals, which are expressly dealt with in the Theft Act (s 4(4)).
[19] [1974] RTR 478.
[20] *Lennox-Wright* [1973] Crim LR 529.

That fluids taken from a living body can be stolen was confirmed in *R* v *Rothery:*

R v *Rothery* [1976] RTR 550   Court of Appeal

By section 9 (3) of the Road Traffic Act 1972. "A person who, without reasonable excuse, fails to supply a specimen for a laboratory test in pursuance of a requirement imposed under this section shall be guilty of an offence."

A motorist who has complied with the provisions of sections 8 and 9 of the Road Traffic Act 1972 and provides a specimen of blood when requested to do so by a constable at a police station and later steals the police part specimen, though guilty of the theft, is not guilty of the statutory offence under section 9 (3) of the Act of 1972, for the theft was a subsequent and distinct event from the provision of the specimen.

(3) THE PROPERTY MUST BELONG TO ANOTHER

Here five major problems can be identified:

(a)   How wide is the extended definition of ownership? In what circumstances can a defendant be convicted of stealing his own property? s. 5(1)

(b)   Can there be theft when the defendant obtains ownership by fraud? Should all the complexities of the civil law apply to determine when title passes?

(c)   To whom does trust property belong? s. 5(2)

(d)   s. 5(3). When does an obligation to retain and deal with another's property arise? Must it be a legal obligation?

(e)   s. 5(4) When does an obligation to restore property got by another's mistake arise? Must it be a legal obligation?

(a) The extended definition of ownership

Section 5(1) Theft Act 1968

Property shall be regarded as belonging to any person having possession or control of it, or having in it any proprietary right or interest (not being an equitable interest arising only from an agreement to transfer or grant an interest).

(i)   Equitable interests arising from an agreement to transfer or grant an interest.

These will arise in at least two situations. Where there is a contract to sell land or to sell shares, the transaction is in two stages. The conclusion of an agreement to sell gives the buyer a right to have the sale completed. This right is the equitable interest referred to in s. 5(1). It is excluded from the interests which are protected by the Theft Act 1968.

(ii)   Sufficient possession or control.

An owner of land owns the things on that land if he intends to exclude trespassers. This is so even when the owner is unaware of the presence of those things on his land.

R v Woodman [1974] QB 758

Court of Appeal

The defendant was charged with the theft of scrap metal remnants from a disused factory site. The occupier of the site had no knowledge of the existence of the scrap, although a barbed-wire fence had been erected around the site to exclude trespassers. The defendant submitted that there was no case to answer on the ground that the scrap did not belong to another within the meaning of section 5 (1) of the Theft Act 1968. The recorder allowed the case to go to the jury on the question whether the occupier was in control of the scrap, and the defendant was convicted.

On appeal against conviction:—

Held, dismissing the appeal, that a person in control of a site, by excluding others from it, was prima facie also in control of articles on that site within the meaning of section 5 (1) of the Theft Act 1968, it being immaterial that he was unconcious [sic] of their existence; and accordingly the case had been rightly allowed to go to the jury.

Per curiam. If articles of serious criminal consequence, such as explosives or drugs, were placed within the barbed-wire fence by some third person in circumstances in which the occupier had no means of knowledge, it might produce a different result from that which arose under the general presumption. . . .

One partner has a sufficient interest in partnership property so that another partner can steal that property from him:

R v Bonner [1970] 1 WLR 838   Court of Appeal

EDMUND DAVIES LJ — The facts which gave rise to this complicated trial were that on May 16, 1969, Bonner and the other three appellants called at the house of a Mr. Webb. Putting it quite neutrally for the moment, Bonner and Webb were business associates. The defence was, in fact, that they were partners and, therefore, co-owners of all the property with which the trial was concerned. Having called with a van at Webb's house in the afternoon at a time when Webb was out, they broke the lock of a garage and splintered the door and, having gained access that way, they loaded some metal from inside the garage on to the van and Anthony Town and Michael Town claimed that they were moving it for Bonner, who they thought had a right to do what he had asked them to do. Bonner's defence was that he honestly thought he had a right to take the lead as it was partnership property owned by himself and Webb, and, in any event, he did not intend to deprive Webb of it permanently.

Webb's case at first was that there was no partnership at all, and then that it was not what he called "a true partnership." During his evidence he specifically denied that he had ever applied for registration in the Business Names Register of himself and Bonner as partners. But this court has been furnished with a document, which unhappily was not before the lower court. It is a certified copy of an application made on March 8, 1966, for registration by a firm, and the business name is "J. Webb, Excavation & Demolition Co.," the partners are described as "Joseph Webb" and "George Andrew Bonner," and it was signed by each of them.

I said a little earlier that the object of the Theft Act, 1968, was to get rid of the subtleties and, indeed, in many cases the absurd anomalies of the pre-existing law. The view of this court is that in relation to partnership property the provisions in the Theft Act, 1968, have the following result: provided there is the basic ingredient of dishonesty, provided there be no question of there being a claim of right made in good faith, provided there be an intent permanently to deprive, one partner can commit theft of partnership property just as much as one person can commit the theft of the property of another to whom he is a complete stranger.

Early though these days are, this matter has not gone without comment by learned writers. Professor Smith in his valuable work on the Theft Act, 1968, expresses his own view quite clearly in paragraph 80 under the heading "Co-owners and partners" in this way:

"D and P are co-owners of a car. D sells the car without P's consent. Since P has a proprietary right in the car, it belongs to him under section 5 (1). The position is precisely the same where a partner appropriates the partnership property."

In the joint work of Professor Smith and Professor Hogan, the matter is thus dealt with (*Smith and Hogan's 'Criminal Law,'* 2nd ed. (1969), p. 361):

". . . D and P . . . may . . . be joint owners of property. Obviously, there is no reason in principle why D should not be treated as a thief if he dishonestly appropriates P's share, and he is so treated under the Theft Act."

We thus have no doubt that there may be an "appropriation" by a partner within the meaning of the Act, and that in a proper case there is nothing in law to prevent his being convicted of the theft of partnership property.

(iii) Theft of the defendant's own property

This may occur where another person has a right to the property which the owner violates:

R v *Turner (No. 2)* [1971] 1 WLR 901   Court of Appeal

The defendant took the car of which he was the registered owner to a garage to have it repaired. Those repairs having been practically completed, the car was left in the road outside the garage. The defendant called at the garage and told the proprietor that he would return the following day, pay him and take the car: instead, he took the car away several hours later without paying for the repairs.

He was charged on indictment with theft of the car contrary to section 1 of the Theft Act 1968. The defendant submitted that the car did not "belong" to the proprietor within the meaning of section 5 (1) of the Theft Act 1968 and that the appropriation was not dishonest within the meaning of section 2 (1) (*a*) of the Act.

On the defendant's appeal against conviction:—

Held, dismissing the appeal, (1) that property belonged to a person if at the time of the appropriation that person was in fact in possession or control of it, and that the words "possession or control" in section 5 (1) did not require to be qualified in any way.

(2) That the test of dishonesty was the mental element of belief and on the facts, the jury having been properly directed on a claim of right, there was no ground for saying that there was any error of law.

LORD PARKER CJ — This court is quite satisfied that there is no ground whatever for qualifying the words "possession or control" in any way. It is sufficient if it is found that the person from whom the property is taken, or to use the words of the Act, appropriated, was at the time in fact in possession or control. At the trial there was a long argument as to whether that possession or control must be lawful, it being said that by reason of the fact that this car was subject to a hire purchase agreement, Mr. Brown could never even as against the defendant obtain lawful possession or control. As I have said, this court is quite satisfied that the judge was quite correct in telling the jury they need not bother about lien, and that they need not bother about hire purchase agreements. The only question was whether Mr. Brown was in fact in possession or control.

J. C. Smith "The Law of Theft" 5th edition para. 60:

It looks more than a little odd that, where D has a better right to possession than P, he can nevertheless commit theft by the exercise (however dishonestly) of that "right". It might have been thought that a thing does *not* belong to a possessor, P, as against D who has an immediate right to take possession from him. Possibly *Turner* (*No. 2*) may be explained by holding that a bailor has no right, even in the civil law, to take back the chattel bailed, without notice to the bailee at will.

Suppose D's car is stolen by P, and D later finds the car standing outside P's house (or the house of a *bona fide* purchaser, P). D has, of course, a right to take it back. But suppose he does not know this, and thinks that a court order is necessary to enable him lawfully to resume possession. Believing that he has no right in law to do so (i.e. dishonestly), he takes the car. According to *Turner* (*No. 2*), he is guilty of theft. If he were convicted and the court asked to exercise its power to order the car to be restored to the person entitled to it, the incongruous result would be that the car should be given to the convicted thief, who was and always had been the person entitled to it. Perhaps the decision in *Turner* (*No. 2*) would not be pressed so far.

The strange thing about the decision in *R* v *Turner* (*No. 2*) (above) is that the garage almost certainly had a better right to possession of the car than the owner at the time it was taken by the defendant. This is because the garage would have had a repairer's lien on the car − a right to keep the car until the bill was paid. However the judge told the jury that they were not concerned with liens and the Court of Appeal upheld this direction.

(b) Where the defendant gets ownership by fraud

The issues surrounding the requirement in s. 1 that the property must belong to another have caused more confusion than any other in the interpretation of s. 1.

It is now at last clear that an appropriation is an act contrary to the owner's rights (*R* v *Morris* above). The wording of s. 1 requires that the appropriation must be of property 'belonging to another', i.e. at the time of the appropriation ownership must be vested in a person other than the alleged thief. Therefore, if the act alleged to be the appropriation takes place after or at the time of transfer of ownership to the alleged thief, no one can be said to have acted adversely to the owner's rights. The original owner has caused all his rights to be transferred to the new owner who has simply assumed those rights.

The next question is whether fraud or trickery should prevent the passing of property? If it does the original owner will (unknown to him) retain ownership and the alleged thief will clearly be appropriating property belonging to another.

Strangely, the two issues of what constitutes an appropriation and whether that appropriation must be of property 'belonging to another' have been regarded by the courts as separate and distinct issues. This may be one of the reasons for the resultant confusion. Now that *R* v *Morris* (above) has clarified the fact that, built into the definition of appropriation is the element of violating the owner's rights, it becomes plain that theft cannot take place where ownership passes before or at the time of the appropriation.

The final question to answer is — should the criminal law follow all the complexities of the civil law and determine questions of passing of title according to those rules, or should it invent rules of its own to determine those issues?

It is submitted that it would be invidious to allow the two systems to diverge and such a divergence might lead to absurdities such as a defendant rightly asserting a civil claim over property he was rightly convicted of stealing. However, the court accepted this position in *R* v *Turner* (above). There are also dicta to the effect that the criminal law should take its own course and not import the complexities of civil law to determine issues of ownership under s. 1 of the Theft Act 1968 (see especially Lord Roskill in *R* v *Morris* below).

R v *Lawrence* (1970) 55 Cr App Rep 73   Court of Appeal

The facts are set out above (page 11)

MEGAW LJ — Theft, under the terms of section 1 (1), involves four elements: (i) a dishonest (ii) appropriation (iii) of property belonging to another (iv) with the intention of permanently depriving the owner of it. On the facts, no question could possibly arise as regards any of these elements. No one could possibly doubt the dishonesty of the appellant's conduct. Nor, in view of the words of section 3 (1) and section 4 (1) already quoted, could there be any serious argument that there was not an "appropriation," and an appropriation of "property." As we understand the argument, counsel for the appellant did not dispute any of these matters. He did, however, contend that there must be implied into the subsection a requirement that the dishonest appropriation must be without the consent of the owner of the property.

In our view, no such implication is justified. The words contained in the former definition of larceny, in section 1 of the Larceny Act 1916, "without the consent of the owner," have been omitted, and, we have no doubt, deliberately omitted, from the definition of theft in the new Act. If the owner does not resist the taking of his property, or actually hands it over, because of, for example, threats of violence, in one sense it could be said that there is "consent": yet the offence of robbery as defined in section 8 (1) of the Act involves, as one of its elements, theft. Again, the former offences of larceny by a trick and obtaining property by false pretences, though technically distinct offences under the old law, both involved what in one sense could be described as "consent" by the victim. It was conceded by counsel for the appellant, necessarily and rightly, that the old offence of larceny by a trick is covered by section 1 (1) of the 1968 Act, as well as by section 15 (1) to which we shall refer later, despite what may be called the apparent consent of the victim.

Of course, where there is true consent by the owner of property to the appropriation of it by another, a charge of theft under section 1 (1) must fail. This is not, however, because the words "without consent" have to be implied in the new definition of theft. It is simply because, if there is such true consent, the essential element of dishonesty is not established. If, however, the apparent consent is brought about by dishonesty, there is nothing in the words of section 1 (1), or by reason of any implication that can properly be read into those words, to make such apparent consent relevant as providing a defence. The prosecution have to prove the four elements already mentioned, and no more.

It should be noted that nowhere in the Court of Appeal's judgments is there any consideration of the requirement that the property must belong to another at the time of the appropriation. However, in this case, title to the student's money would have passed to the defendant under a voidable contract. A contract voidable for fraud is effective to pass title unless and until it is avoided by the victim of the fraud. Despite this both the Court of Appeal and the House of Lords upheld the conviction of the defendant.

In the House of Lords the issue was dealt with by Viscount Dilhorne. Strictly, all he said on this matter is obiter. This is because the questions that the House of Lords were asked to consider did not include this problem.

When granting leave to appeal, the Court of Appeal certified the following questions as involving points of law of general public importance:

(i)   Whether section 1(1) of the Theft Act 1968 is to be construed as though it contained the words 'without the consent of the owner' or words to that effect?

(ii)   Whether the provisions of section 15(1) and of section 1(1) of the Theft Act 1968 are mutually exclusive in the sense that if the facts proved would justify a conviction under section 15(1) there cannot lawfully be a conviction under section 1(1) on those facts?

Both those questions were answered in the negative, but no answer to the question of passing of property is obviously forthcoming from the judgments.

R v Lawrence (Alan) [1972] AC 626   House of Lords

VISCOUNT DILHORNE — "I now turn to the third element 'property belonging to another'. Mr. Back QC for the appellant submitted that Mr. Occhi, in consenting to the appellant taking the £6, he consented to the property in the money passing from him to the appellant and that the appellant had not, therefore, appropriated property belonging to another . . . I am unable to agree with this . . . The new offence of obtaining property by deception credited by s. 15(1) of the Theft Act also contains the words 'belonging to another'. . . Belonging to another in section 1(1) and in section 15(1) in my view signifies no more than at the time of the appropriation or the obtaining, the property belonged to another . . . The short answer to this contention on behalf of the appellant is that the money in the wallet which he appropriated belonged to another, to Mr. Occhi."

This ignores the fact that the s. 15 obtaining in these circumstances could be the obtaining of title to the money. Thus it would ante-date the s. 1 appropriation. This could only have happened when the money was actually taken. By that time, if title did pass to the defendant it would already have done so. Presumably Viscount

Dilhorne was deciding that ownership of the money did not pass to the defendant. If this is so the criminal law has clearly diverged from the civil law.

It seems that there are two possible explanations of the fact that Lawrence remained convicted of theft;

(i)   That the property does not need to belong to another at the moment of appropriation — only at a time immediately before that appropriation. This, with respect, is inconsistent with the wording of s. 1(1) of the 1968 Theft Act.

(ii)   That ownership in the money involved in Lawrence did not pass to the defendant. If that is the case the criminal law and the civil law have different rules about the passing of title to property.

The second viewpoint has enjoyed various degrees of success since the decision in *R* v *Lawrence*.

In the following two cases the court thought that the civil law concerning the passing of title should be followed where similar issues arose under the Theft Act.

Edwards v *Ddin* [1976] 1 WLR 942   Queen's Bench

The defendant drove his car into a garage and requested the attendant to fill up the tank with petrol and put two pints of oil into the engine. After the attendant had done so, the defendant drove off without paying. He was charged with theft, contrary to section 1 of the Theft Act 1968. The justices dismissed the information holding that the ownership of the petrol and oil had been transferred to the defendant when the attendant put them into his car and, therefore, as the sale was not conditional on payment, the defendant had not appropriated the property of another when he drove away from the garage premises.

On appeal by the prosecutor:—

Held, dismissing the appeal, that a garage owner selling petrol and oil to a motorist did not retain the right to dispose of the petrol and oil once it had been put in the motorist's car and mixed with the petrol or oil already there; that the delivery of the petrol and oil was an unconditional appropriation of the goods to the contract and, under rule 5 (2) in section 18 of the goods to the contract and, under rule 5 (2) in section 18 of the Sale of Goods Act 1893, the property passed to the defendant when they were placed in his car; that, since section 5 (3) of the Theft Act 1968 did not apply to a case of an outright sale, the property could not be regarded as belonging to the owner of the garage until payment and, accordingly, the defendant had not appropriated the goods of another at the time he drove away from the garage.

Kaur v *Chief Constable for Hampshire* [1981] 1 WLR 578   Queen's Bench Division

Shoes were displayed in a store on two racks, shoes on one rack being priced at £6.99 and on the other at £4.99. The defendant selected a pair of shoes from the £6.99 rack and noticed that one shoe bore a price label to that effect and the other had a £4.99 label. Without concealing either label, she took the shoes to the cashier with the intention of obtaining the advantage of the lower price, and on being asked for £4.99 she paid and left the store with the shoes. Outside the store she was stopped and later charged with theft contrary to section 1 (1) of the Theft Act 1968. The justices held that the cashier had no authority to accept an offer to pay £4.99 and that, since the defendant knew that that was not the correct price, the contract was void and the defendant had appropriated property belonging to the store and was guilty of theft.

On appeal by the defendant:—

Held, allowing the appeal, that the cashier had authority to charge the price marked on the shoes, and the fact that she chose the lower of two prices so marked did not mean that she was acting without authority; that a mistake as to the price induced by wrong marking was not so fundamental as to destroy the validity of the contract of sale, but merely rendered it voidable, and, accordingly, since the contract had not been avoided by the time that the defendant left the store, property in the shoes passed on payment and the defendant had not appropriated property belonging to another.

LORD LANE CJ — There is ample authority for the proposition that, so far as supermarkets, at any rate, are concerned, and in so far as an ordinary transaction in a supermarket is concerned, the intention of the parties, under section 18 of the Sale of Goods Act 1979, is that the ownership of the goods should pass on payment by the customer of the price to the cashier. It also seems to accord with good sense, and if any authority is needed for that, it is to be found in *Lacis* v *Cashmarts* [1969] 2 QB 400.

Prima facie, then, when the defendant picked up the shoes to take them home, she was already the owner of the shoes. They did not then belong to somebody else, and she was not intending to deprive the owner of them.

In the later case of *R* v *Morris* (C.A. below) Lord Lane decided that *Kaur* was wrongly decided. This was not because he believed any less emphasis should be laid on when title passed under the civil law, but because in *R* v *Morris* the Court of Appeal decided that an appropriation would take place even where an honest customer took an item from a shelf with the intention of paying for it. Consequently in *Kaur* the defendant would have appropriated the property before there could be any question of ownership passing to her and while the property clearly still belonged to the store. This view of appropriation was subsequently overruled by the House of Lords.

R v *Morris* [1983] 1 QB 587   Court of Appeal

LORD LANE CJ — As far as *Kaur (Dip)* v *Chief Constable for Hampshire* [1981] 1 WLR 578 is concerned, a decision for which I was at least partly responsible, on the facts as found by the justices theft was plainly made out and our decision was wrong. There was an appropriation when the shoes were taken from the shelf, dishonesty was found as a fact by the justices, the property then belonged to another and the intent to deprive was obvious. In retrospect the real answer to *Kaur* was that what the appellant did was probably not rightly categorised as dishonest.

In view of the definition of appropriation subsequently adopted by the House of Lords in *R* v *Morris*, this analysis of *Kaur* is plainly wrong. No act amounting to a usurpation of the owner's rights took place in that case unless title to the goods did not pass at the checkout. This may be the explanation that Lord Roskill is advancing in the following, rather curious, part of his judgment in the House of Lords:

R v Morris [1983] 3 WLR 697   House of Lords

LORD ROSKILL — *Kaur (Dip)* v *Chief Constable for Hampshire* [1981] 1 WLR 578 is a difficult case. I am disposed to agree with the learned Lord Chief Justice that it was wrongly decided but without going into further detail I respectfully suggest that it is on any view wrong to introduce into this branch of the criminal law questions whether particular contracts are void or voidable on the ground of mistake or fraud or whether any mistake is sufficiently fundamental to vitiate a contract. These difficult questions should so far as possible be confined to those fields of law to which they are immediately relevant and I do not regard them as relevant questions under the Theft Act 1968.

It is respectfully suggested that such a sweeping exclusion of the civil law in this area leaves a large vacuum. Lord Roskill gives no clues as to how the issue of when property is to be regarded as 'belonging to another' is to be determined.

Even if fraud and mistake are the only areas of the civil law to be disregarded in future, this could have a significant impact on a number of cases under the Theft Acts.

According to the civil law a contract which is affected by a fundamental mistake (e.g. as to the identity of the parties) is of no effect at all and cannot pass title. Non-fundamental mistakes and fraud will make a contract voidable. A voidable contract will pass title and that title will only revert to the victim of the fraud if and when the victim takes steps to avoid that contract. (See Russell Heaton, 'Belonging to another' [1973] Crim LR 736.)

Where other complicated issues of ownership have arisen, the courts have insisted that the jury should be directed on the effect of the civil law to determine who owned the property in question for the purpose of applying the 1968 Theft Act:

R v Walker [1984] Crim LR 112   Court of Appeal

The appellant sold an unsatisfactory video recorder, which was returned to him for repair. After some time the purchaser issued a summons claiming the price of the video as the "return of money paid for defective goods." Two days after the summons was served on him the appellant sold the video to another.

The judge directed the jury that it was for them to decide on the evidence whether the property belonged to the original purchaser when it was sold by the appellant to another. The appellant was convicted of theft and obtaining property by deception. He appealed on the ground, *inter alia*, that the trial judge had failed adequately to direct the jury on the defences.

Held, allowing the appeal, that the onus was on the prosecution to prove as a matter of law that the video did not belong to the appellant when he sold it to another. In effect the trial judge had withdrawn the issue of the law from the jury. The relevant law, which was contained in the Sale of Goods Act 1979 was complicated but the judge had made no attempt to explain it. For centuries juries had decided civil actions on points arising under the law of sale of goods. There was no reason why this jury should not have had the relevant law explained to them and in the absence of such an explanation it was impossible for them, to do justice in the case.

Commentary. It was stated in the House of Lords in *Morris* [1983] 3 All ER 288 at 294, [1983] Crim LR and commentary, that "it is on any view wrong to introduce into this branch of the criminal law [*sc.*, the law of theft] questions whether particular contracts are void or voidable on the ground of mistake or fraud or whether any mistake is sufficiently fundamental to vitiate a contract." As the present case shows, when a question arises whether property belongs to another, recourse to the civil law is inevitable and it must be the whole of the civil law, including that part of it which determines whether contracts are void or merely voidable when that is relevant, as it may be, to determine whether property belongs to another.

In the present case, it is clear that, after the sale, the video belonged to the purchaser and that it continued to do so when it was returned to the appellant for repair. The appellant was at that stage a bailee of the recorder. It may well be, however, that the service of the summons claiming the return of the price amounted to a rescission of the contract of sale. In that case, the parties would be restored to the position they were in before the contract. Ownership in the recorder would be re-vested in the appellant. If that were so, since the appellant was already in possession, he would hold the entire proprietary interest, the property would no longer belong to the purchaser, and theft would be an impossibility.

See also Glanville Williams, 'Theft and Voidable Title' [1981] Crim LR 666 and J. C. Smith, 'Theft and Voidable Title: A Reply' [1981] Crim LR 677.

When Title Passes

Benjamin: Sale of Goods (2nd ed.)

Intention of the parties. Section 17 (1) of the 1979 Act provides that, where there is a contract for the sale of specific goods the property in them is transferred to the buyer at such time as the parties to the contract intend it to be transferred. By section 17 (2), for the purpose of ascertaining the intention of the parties regard is to be had to the terms of the contract, the conduct of the parties and the circumstances of the case. In *Varley* v *Whipp*,[44] Channell J. commented: "It is impossible to imagine a clause more vague than this, but I think it correctly represents the state of the authorities when the [1893] Act was passed." In order, however, to assist in ascertaining the intention of the parties, the Act of 1979 lays down three rules in section 18 which govern the time at which property passes in specific goods unless a different intention appears. But these rules are only presumptions: "the law permits [the parties] to settle the point for themselves by any intelligible expression of their intention."

Section 18, rule 1. The first rule set out in section 18 of the 1979 Act relates to "an unconditional contract for the sale of specific goods in a deliverable state." In this case, unless a different intention appears, the property in the goods passes to the buyer when the contract is made, and it is immaterial whether the time of payment or the time of delivery, or both, be postponed. This rule codifies the common law at the date of the passing of the 1893 Act.

Postponement of delivery or payment. Under English law, as distinct from the civil law, the property in a specific chattel may pass under a contract of sale without delivery.

Specific goods. Section 18, rule 1, will not apply unless the goods are "specific goods" as defined in section 61 (1) of the Act. In *Kursell* v *Timber Operators and Contractors Ltd.*[79] a contract was entered into for the sale and purchase of all timber of a certain height in a designated Latvian forest, the buyer being given 15 years to cut the timber. Shortly afterwards the forest was expropriated by the Latvian State. It was held that the property in the timber had not passed to the buyer under the rule. Sargant and Scrutton LJJ were of the opinion that the timber was not specific goods. The contract was ambiguous. The more probable construction was that the buyer was entitled to cut such timber as would have attained the requisite height when it came to be felled within the 15-year period. If this was so, the goods were not specific as the timber to be sold depended on the trees' rate of growth. But even if the contract was construed to mean timber which had attained that height at the time the contract was made, Sargant L.J. considered that it was not specific goods since, though identifiable, it was not "identified" at that time.

Section 18, rule 4. The fourth rule set out in section 18 of the Sale of Goods Act 1979 provides that, unless a different intention appears, "when goods are delivered to the buyer on approval or on sale or return or other similar terms the property in the goods passes to the buyer: (*a*) when he signifies his approval or acceptance to the seller or does any other act adopting the transaction; (*b*) if he does not signify his approval or acceptance to the seller but retains the goods without giving notice of rejection, then, if a time has been fixed for the return of the goods, on the expiration of that time, and, if no time has been fixed, on the expiration of a reasonable time". This rule codifies in substance the common law before the 1893 Act.

Goods must be ascertained. Section 16 of the Sale of Goods Act 1979 provides that "where there is a contract for the sale of unascertained goods no property in the goods is transferred to the buyer unless and until the goods are ascertained." It is to be noted that this section does not state that property will pass if and when the goods are ascertained. Property in ascertained goods passes when the parties intend it to pass. But the section lays down in clear terms that no property can pass in unascertained goods.

Unascertained goods. A contract for the sale of unascertained goods is not a sale, but an agreement to sell. The Act does not define "unascertained goods," but it would appear that three categories of goods are included. The first is that of generic goods, that is to say, of a certain quantity of goods in general, without any specific identification of them, such as "50 hogsheads of sugar." The second is certain types of future goods. The third is that of an unidentified part of a larger quantity of ascertained goods, such as "500 tons of wheat out of a cargo of 1,000 tons" on board a certain ship. The common characteristic seems to be that the goods cannot presently be identified and can be referred to by description only.

Separation from bulk. It follows that no property can pass in goods which have still to be separated from a larger gulk, where the identity of the portion sold is uncertain. In *Gillett* v *Hill*[54] Bayley B. said: "Where there is a bargain for a certain quantity *ex* a greater quantity, and there is a power of selection in the vendor to deliver which he thinks fit, then the right to [the goods] does not pass to the vendee until the vendor has made his selection, and trover is not maintainable before that is done. If I agree to deliver a certain quantity of oil as ten out of eighteen tons, no one can say which part of the whole quantity I have agreed to deliver until a selection is made. There is no individuality until it has been divided." Thus, where the identification of the goods depends upon their being severed, weighed, measured or in some other way separated by the seller from bulk, no property can pass until this be done.

[44] [1900] 1 QB 513, 517
[79] [1927] 1 KB 298
[54] *Gillett* v *Hill* (1834) 2 C & M 530, 535

Russell Heaton: Belonging to Another [1973] Crim LR 736

Does the ownership pass?

The generally accepted rule is that ownership passes if and when the parties to a transaction intend it to pass. Where the transaction is a sale of goods this rule has statutory force in respect of the transfer of ownership in the goods. The position is exactly the same with regard to the passing of the ownership in money.[3] So the intention of the parties and particularly of the transferor governs the matter. How far will such an intention be negatived by a mistake on the part of the transferor? Only where the mistake is "of such a nature that it can be properly described as a mistake in respect of the underlying assumption of the contract or transaction or as being fundamental or basic."[4] Statements such as this abound in the cases although they do not give much practical guidance in deciding the question posed. But it is suggested that as a matter of principle only the kind of mistakes which would make a contract void would be sufficiently "fundamental or basic" to vitiate the apparent intention to pass ownership.

Mistake can be relevant not only at the (attempted) formation of a contract but also in the performance of a contract.

It is the former situation which the law of mistake in contract deals with. Certain kinds of mistake make the contract void. These seem to be limited to mistakes as to the existence of the subject-matter or the underlying assumption of the contract,[5] the identity of the subject-matter,[6] the identity of the offeree[7] and *non est factum*,[8] though of course not every mistake in these categories would make the contract void. Recently the courts have been active in civil cases in limiting the occasions when a mistake will make the contract void because they quite rightly feel that innocent third parties ought to be protected.[9]

[3] See, *e.g. Norwich Fire Insurance Society Ltd.* v *William H. Price Ltd.* [1934] AC 455 *per* Lord Wright at p. 462.
[4] *Ibid.* at p. 463.
[5] *e.g. Scott* v *Coulson* [1903] 2 Ch 249.
[6] *e.g. Scriven* v *Hindley* [1913] 3 KB 564.
[7] *e.g. Cundy* v *Lindsay* (1878) 3 App Cas 459.
[8] *e.g. Carlisle and Cumberland Banking Company* v *Bragg* [1911] 1 KB 489.
[9] *Magee* v *Pennine Insurance Co. Ltd.* [1969] 2 All ER 891 (though possibly *contra* Edmund Davies LJ); *Saunders* v *Anglia Building Society* [1970] 3 All ER 961; *Lewis* v *Averay* [1971] 3 All ER 907.

(c) To whom does trust property belong?

Section 5(2) Theft Act 1968

Where property is subject to a trust, the persons to whom it belongs shall be regarded as including any person having a right to enforce the trust, and an intention to defeat the trust shall be regarded accordingly as an intention to deprive of the property any person having that right.

Any beneficiary of a trust has a right to enforce a trust. A charitable trust, which may or may not have particular individuals as beneficiaries, is enforceable by the Attorney-General so that property which is the subject of such a trust would be regarded as belonging to him. Any non-charitable trust without human beneficiaries would be regarded as belonging to the person entitled to the residue. This subsection makes it impossible for anyone dishonestly taking trust funds to argue that the funds belonged to no one.

(d) When does an obligation to retain and deal with another's property arise? Must it be a legal obligation?

Section 5(3) Theft Act 1968

Where a person receives property from or on account of another, and is under an obligation to the other to retain and deal with that property or its proceeds in a particular way, the property or proceeds shall be regarded (as against him) as belonging to the other.

Two problems arise in the interpretation of this subsection:

(i)   To what extent must the 'obligation' attach to the particular property which has changed hands?

(ii)   Must the 'obligation to retain and deal' be a legal obligation or will a moral obligation suffice?

(i) R v Hall [1973] 1 QB 126   Court of Appeal

The defendant, who carried on the business of a travel agent, received money as deposits and payments for air trips to America. No flights were provided for the defendant's clients and no money was refunded. He was charged with seven counts of theft, contrary to section 1 of the Theft Act 1968.[1] The defendant claimed that the money received had become his property which he had applied in the conduct of the firm's business and that he had not been guilty of theft merely because the firm had failed and no money remained. He was convicted.

The defendant appealed on the ground, inter alia, that the moneys belonged to him and not to his clients as he was under no obligation, under section 5 (3) of the Theft Act 1968, to retain and deal with the money or its proceeds in a particular way:—

Held, allowing the appeal, that, although a client, in return for his money, expected a travel agent to provide tickets and other documents for the journey, and travel agents were under an obligation to perform their part of the contract, there was no evidence that the defendant's clients expected him to retain and deal with their money or its proceeds in a particular way, and, there being no obligation undertaken by the defendant to do so, the money, under section 5 (3) of the Act, could not be considered as belonging to the clients and, accordingly, the defendant had not committed the offence of theft.

EDMUND DAVIES LJ – Point (1) turns on the application of section 5 (3) of the Theft Act 1968, which provides that:

"Where a person receives property from or on account of another, and is under an obligation to the other to retain and deal with that property or its proceeds in a particular way, the property or proceeds shall be regarded (as against him) as belonging to the other."

Mr. Jolly submitted that in the circumstances arising in [previous] cases there arose no such "obligation" upon the defendant. He referred us to a passage in the eighth report of the Criminal Law Revision Committee (1966) (Cmnd. 2977), at p. 127, which reads:

"Subsection (3) provides for the special case where property is transferred to a person to retain and deal with for a particular purpose and he misapplies it or its proceeds. An example would be the treasurer of a holiday fund. The person in question is in law the owner of the property; but the subsection treats the property, as against him, as belonging to the persons to whom he owes the duty to retain and deal with the property as agreed. He will therefore be guilty of stealing from them if he misapplies the property or its proceeds."

Mr. Jolly submitted that the example there given is, for all practical purposes, identical with the actual facts in *R* v *Pulham* (unreported) June 15, 1971, where, incidentally, section 5 (3) was not discussed, the convictions there being quashed, as we have already indicated, owing to the lack of a proper direction as to the accused's state of mind at the time he appropriated. But he submits that the position of a treasurer of a solitary fund is quite different from that of a person like the defendant, who was in general, and genuine, business as a travel agent, and to whom people pay money in order to achieve a certain object – in the present cases, to obtain charter flights to America. It is true, he concedes, that thereby the travel agent undertakes a contractual obligation in relation to arranging flights and at the proper time paying the air line and any other expenses. Indeed, the defendant throughout acknowledged that this was so, though contending that in some of the seven cases it was the other party who was in breach. But what Mr. Jolly resists is that in such circumstances the travel agent "is under an obligation" to the client "to retain and deal with . . . in a particular way" sums paid to him in such circumstances.

What cannot of itself be decisive of the matter is the fact that the defendant paid the money into the firm's general trading account. As Widgery J said in *R* v *Yule* [1964] 1 QB 5, decided under section 20 (1) (iv) of the Larceny Act 1916, at p. 10:

> "The fact that a particular sum is paid into a particular banking account, . . . does not affect the right of persons interested in that sum or any duty of the solicitor either towards his client or towards third parties with regard to disposal of that sum."

Nevertheless, when a client goes to a firm carrying on the business of travel agents and pays them money, he expects that in return he will, in due course, receive the tickets and other documents necessary for him to accomplish the trip for which he is paying, and the firm are "under an obligation" to perform their part to fulfil his expectation and are liable to pay him damages if they do not. But, in our judgment, what was not here established was that these clients expected them "to retain and deal with that property or its proceeds in a particular way," and that an "obligation" to do this was undertaken by the defendant.

We must make clear, however, that each case turns on its own facts. Cases could, we suppose, conceivably arise where by some special arrangement (preferably evidenced by documents), the client could impose upon the travel agent an "obligation" falling within section 5 (3). But no such special arrangement was made in any of the seven cases here being considered. It is true that in some of them documents were signed by the parties; thus, in respect of the counts 1 and 3 incidents there was a clause to the effect that the "People to People" organisation did not guarantee to refund deposits if withdrawals were made later than a certain date; and in respect of counts 6, 7 and 8 the defendant wrote promising "a full refund" after the flights paid for failed to materialise. But neither in those nor in the remaining two cases (in relation to which there was no documentary evidence of any kind) was there, in our judgment, such a special arrangement as would give rise to an "obligation" within section 5 (3).

It follows from this that, despite what on any view must be condemned as scandalous conduct by the defendant, in our judgment upon this ground alone this appeal must be allowed and the convictions quashed.

R v *Hayes* (1977) 64 Cr App Rep 82   Court of Appeal

The appellant started trading with another man as estate agents. He received money from clients as deposits on account of sales or purchase of houses. He was charged, *inter alia*, on 11 counts alleging theft contrary to section 1 of the Theft Act 1968. In summing-up the judge, *inter alia*, failed to invite the jury to consider whether there was an obligation on the appellant to deal with the clients' money within section 5 (3) of the Act of 1968; nor did he direct them that there was an obligation on the prosecution to prove that at the time when the misappropriation took place there was already an intention to be dishonest. The appellant was convicted, *inter alia*, of theft. On appeal.

Held that in view of the aforesaid misdirections the convictions of theft were unsafe and unsatisfactory; accordingly, the appeals on those counts would be allowed.

Hall (1972) 56 Cr App R 547; [1973] 1 QB 126 applied.

THE LORD CHIEF JUSTICE — The case really revolved around section 5 (3) because, as will be understood from the brief extracts I have already given of the facts, the real issue which arose between the prosecution and the defence was whether the appellant was appropriating and therefore stealing property of another which would amount to an offence under the Theft Act 1968, or whether the true position was that he was apparently appropriating or stealing money which had become his because it had become his property according to this argument when the payment was made.

The circumstances which gave rise to count 1 form a useful illustration of the working of those principles. In the transaction on October 23, 1970 the appellant through Blake gave a receipt to a Mr. Newman for £300, which was described as being a deposit and part-payment of a dwelling house at Sheppart Street, Stoke, the purchase price being £600. That money was paid over in cash. It was not paid into the bank, the bank at that time having only a credit balance of £13 in it. It was entered in a book kept by the appellant which was intended to disclose cash in hand, and it was entered in that book at a time in October 1970 when, according to the book, there was cash in hand to the tune of £6,480. The prosecution sought, not without some success, to show that this record of cash in hand was itself bogus and that the money referred to as being in hand never was in hand. But conclusions of that sort were not necessarily obtained on the directions which were given to the jury in this case, and I cite those facts merely to disclose the oddities of the transaction upon which count 1 is based, the other counts being based on similar oddities.

It is important, we think, to compare the situation in *Hall* (*supra*) with the situation in our present case. In *Hall* (*supra*) the argument on the one side was that the ticket agent receiving the money for the tickets was obliged to use that money in a particular way and to go and buy tickets with it. On the other side it was argued that he was not bound to use the particular money in a particular way. All that happened on his receiving the money was that he incurred a civil responsibility to carry out his side of the bargain. Edmund Davies LJ is taking the point there that in the absence of some special term in the contract the second view is the right one.

Convictions quashed.

Davidge v *Bunnett* [1984] Crim LR 296   Queen's Bench Division

In July 1982 D shared a flat with two other young women, C and McF. In September 1982 they were joined by H. There was an oral agreement to share the costs of gas, electricity and telephone. The gas account was in C's name. In October 1982 C received a gas bill for £159.75. D, C and McF each agreed to pay £50, and H the balance of £9.75. D did not have a bank account. The others all did, and gave D cheques in the appropriate sums, made payable to P, D's employer. They thought that D would either encash the cheques with P, add her own £50 and pay the gas bill, or that P would write out a cheque for the Gas Board on receipt of funds totalling £159.75. They did not expect D to apply any actual banknotes received from P to the discharge of the bill. On November 18, 1982, £59.75 was paid to the Gas Board. The balance of £100 was carried over to the next account in December. In January 1983 C received a final demand. C asked D to look into the matter, to which D agreed. D then left the flat without giving notice or leaving a forwarding address. C and McF later discovered that their cheques for £50 had been cashed on November 1, 1982. When interviewed by the police, D admitted "I spent the £100 on Christmas presents but intended to pay it back." The magistrates convicted D of theft, finding that D was under a legal obligation to apply the proceeds of C and McF's cheques to the payment of the gas bill. They also found that the proceeds of the cheques were property belonging to another within the meaning of the Theft Act 1968, and that there was evidence of an appropriation of two sums of £50, notwithstanding the payment of £59.75.

Held, dismissing the appeal, that the position was simple. D was under an obligation to use the cheques or their proceeds in whatever way she saw fit so long as they were applied *pro tanto* to the discharge of the gas bill. This could have been achieved by one cheque from her employer, or a banker's draft, or her own cheque had so opened her own bank account, or by endorsing the other cheques. Hence the magistrates' finding that she was not obliged to use the actual banknotes. Using the proceeds of the cheques on presents amounted to a very negation of her obligation to discharge the bill. She was under an obligation to deal with the proceeds in a particular way. As against D, the proceeds of the cheques were property belonging to another within section 5(3) of the Act.

Commentary. Domestic arrangements are frequently not intended to give rise to legal relations: *Balfour* v *Balfour* [1919] 2 KB 571. Where money is paid in pursuance of such an arrangement section 5(3) can have no application since it is well settled that it is concerned only with legal obligations. In *Cullen* (Unreported, No. 968/C/74 of 1974, Smith, *Law of Theft,* 36) a man gave the defendant, his mistress, money to buy food for their household and to pay certain debts. She made off, spending the money on herself. The Court of Appeal upheld her conviction for theft, holding that there was plainly a legal obligation on her to use the money as directed; but does a wife really commit theft, if contrary to her husband's instructions, she spends the housekeeping money on a new hat?

In the present case, the parties were not members of the same family. Their agreement to share the flat and to share the costs of the gas, etc., would seem clearly to have been intended to create legal relationships. When D cashed the cheques with her employer she no doubt became the legal owner of the money she received, because the employer gave it to her intending to make her the owner of it; but, quite clearly, her flat-mates did not intend that the money should be hers to do as she liked with. She was under no obligation to use the particular notes and coins because, if she had had a pocket full of money of her own, she could have used some of that to pay the bill and spent some of the money received from her employer for her own purposes, without committing any wrong. Her obligation would seem to be one of keeping in existence a fund sufficient to pay the bill and to pay within a reasonable time.

It seems from the above cases that the 'obligation to retain and deal' with property in a particular way will arise when the contractual relationship between the parties obliges the defendant to keep in existence a fund sufficient to fulfil the purpose for which the money was given within a reasonable time.

(ii)   Must the 'obligation' be a legally enforceable one?

It is clear from *R* v *Mainwaring* (below) that the obligation must be a legal one, and also that it is for the judge to direct the jury on when such an obligation arises:

R v *Mainwaring* (1982) 74 Cr App Rep 99   Court of Appeal

LAWTON LJ — The prosecution case was that when Mainwaring and Madders received money from prospective purchasers they did so knowing that it was in part payment of villas purchased from Frenchmen or Spaniards, that they were under an obligation to hand that money over to the developers in France or Spain, as the case might be, and that it would have been, and in fact was, dishonest of them to appropriate the money there and then for their own purposes.

Clearly there was some confusion in the mind of the learned judge about the operation of section 5 (3) of the Theft Act 1968.

We think that it may help judges if we make this comment about that section of the Act. Whether or not an obligation arises is a matter of law, because an obligation must be a legal obligation. But a legal obligation arises only in certain circumstances, and in many cases the circumstances cannot be known until the facts have been established. It is for the jury, not the judge, to establish the facts, if they are in dispute.

What, in our judgment, a judge ought to do is this: if the facts relied upon by the prosecution are in dispute he should direct the jury to make their findings on the facts, and then say to them: "If you find the facts to be such-and-such, then I direct you as a matter of law that a legal obligation arose to which section 5 (3) applies."

Must the obligation actually be enforceable?

R v *Meech* [1974] QB 549   Court of Appeal

McC obtained a cheque for £1,450 from a hire-purchase finance company by means of a forged instrument. He asked M (to whom he owed £40) to cash the cheque for him. M agreed, not knowing of the fraud, and paid the cheque into

his own account. Two days later, after he had become aware that the cheque had
been acquired dishonestly, he drew his own cheque for £1,410 (representing the
£1,450 less the £40 owed to him). Before obtaining the cash from the bank he
arranged with the defendants, P and J, to stage a fake robbery. They took the
£1,410, leaving M as the apparent victim. M, P and J were charged with theft.
The judge directed the jury, inter alia, that M was under an obligation for the
purposes of section 5 (3) of the Theft Act 1968 to pay the money to McC unless
the jury found that M's refusal to pay was caused by his belief that such payment
would implicate him in a criminal offence. The defendants were convicted.

On appeal against conviction:—

Held, dismissing the appeals, (1) that when the defendant M agreed to cash
the cheque for McC, not knowing that it was a dishonest transaction, he accepted
the obligation to pay McC £1,410 and, whether or not the obligation could be
legally performed or enforced by McC, an obligation was created within the
meaning of section 5 (3) of the Theft Act 1968 and, under that subsection, the
money was deemed to belong to McC (post, pp. 554F—555A).

(2) That, although M would be excused performance of the obligation if he
acted honestly and had an honest reason for not performing his obligation and
for claiming relief from performance, a dishonest misappropriation would be
theft by reason of section 5 (3) as the money was deemed to belong to McC,
and, since the time of the appropriation was the time when the defendants had
divided the money at the scene of the fake robbery, and the jury after a proper
direction had found that they had acted dishonestly, the defendants had been
rightly convicted of theft. . . .

ROSKILL LJ — Counsel for all the defendants relied strongly on the series of
recent decisions that "obligation" means "legal obligation." The judge so directed
the jury. In giving this direction he no doubt had in mind the successive decisions
of this court in *R* v *Hall* [1973] QB 126; *R* v *Gilks* [1972] 1 WLR 1341 and
R v *Pearce* (unreported), November 21, 1972 (both the court and counsel were
supplied with copies of the judgment). Reliance was also placed on paragraph 76
of Professor Smith's *The Law of Theft*, 2nd ed. (1972) — a passage written just
before the decisions referred to. Since the judge so directed the jury, we do not
find it necessary further to consider those decisions beyond observing that the
facts of those cases were vastly different from those of the present case.

Starting from this premise — that "obligation" means "legal obligation" — it
was argued that even at the time when Meech was ignorant of the dishonest
origin of the cheque, as he was at the time when he agreed to cash the cheque
and hand the proceeds less the £40 to McCord, McCord could never have enforced
that obligation because McCord had acquired the cheque illegally. In our view
this submission is unsound in principle. The question has to be looked at from
Meech's point of view, not McCord's.

Meech plainly assumed an "obligation" to McCord which, on the facts then
known to him, he remained obliged to fulfil and, on the facts as found, he must
be taken at that time honestly to have intended to fulfil. The fact that on the
true facts if known McCord might not and indeed would not subsequently have
been permitted to enforce that obligation in a civil court does not prevent that
"obligation" on Meech having arisen. The argument confuses the creation of the
obligation with the subsequent discharge of that obligation either by performance
or otherwise. That the obligation might have become impossible of performance

by Meech or of enforcement by McCord on grounds of illegality or for reasons of public policy is irrelevant. The opening words of section 5 (3) clearly look to the time of the creation of or the acceptance of the obligation by the bailee and not to the time of performance by him of the obligation so created and accepted by him.

Lord Roskill's judgment in *R* v *Meech* (above) looks not at whether the obligation was legally enforceable, but at whether the defendant believed the obligation to be enforceable. In fact no legally enforceable obligation ever arose between Meech and McCord. It seems strange that if the defendant believes such an obligation to exist, this should cause s. 5(3) to operate. The subsection refers to a situation where the defendant *is* 'under an obligation' – not where he believes himself to be so.

A possible way out of the difficulty would be to hold that a legal obligation did arise but it was not such a one as could be enforced by the dishonest McCord. This raises the whole question of whether there is such a thing as an 'unenforceable obligation'. Such a thing would, of course, be quite useless to its owner. Further, this explanation of the result in Meech strains the words of Roskill LJ to the limit.

Whether s. 5(3) operates where no legally enforceable obligation has in fact arisen but the defendant believes himself to be under such an obligation must remain doubtful.

Where the section does operate, ownership of the property concerned, by a fiction, remains with the person who has given the property to the defendant. The property therefore 'belongs to another' within the definition of theft in s. 1 of the Theft Act 1968.

A duty to account for secret profits in an employer-employee or principal-agent relationship will not bring s. 5(3) into operation:

Powell v *MacRae* [1977] Crim LR 571   Queen's Bench Division

While employed as a turnstile operator at Wembley Stadium when admission was by ticket only, the defendant was given £2 by a member of the public who knew that he ought not to give the money, and the defendant allowed him to enter the stadium without a ticket through the turnstile. The defendant was charged that he stole £2 cash, the property of his employers, contrary to section 1 of the Theft Act 1968. The justices, who found that the defendant had acted dishonestly, were of the opinion that as the money was received in the course of employment, it belonged to the employers for the purposes of the Act. The defendant was convicted. He appealed by case stated to the Queen's Bench Divisional Court.

Held, allowing the appeal, that the defendant was no more than the recipient of a bribe; that by no stretch of language could it be said that the money "belonged to" the employers; that, therefore, the definition of theft in section 1 of the Theft Act 1968 was not satisfied and, accordingly, the conviction would be quashed.

Commentary. The defendant's employers have the right in civil law to recover £2 from the defendant. They have no proprietary right in the particular notes received by the defendant. The money did not belong to the employer for the purposes of the Theft Act. It belonged to the defendant and to him alone. There could, therefore be no theft.

(e) When does an obligation to restore property got by another's mistake arise? Must it be a legal obligation?

Section 5(4) Theft Act 1968

Where a person gets property by another's mistake, and is under an obligation to make restoration (in whole or in part) of the property or its proceeds or of the value thereof, then to the extent of that obligation the property or proceeds shall be regarded (as against him) as belonging to the person entitled to restoration, and an intention not to make restoration shall be regarded accordingly as an intention to deprive that person of the property or proceeds.

As with s. 5(3) above, this subsection allows the courts to regard a person who has parted with property as retaining title to it, although the civil law would normally consider that title had passed to the defendant.

There are two main problems raised by this subsection:

(i)   How wide is the subsection? Is its scope limited by the definition of appropriation in *R* v *Morris*?

(ii)   Must the 'obligation' be a legal one?

(i)   The subsection was designed to alter the pre-Act decision in *Moynes* v *Coopper* (below). It has clearly done so. It may be so wide that it encompasses the situation where a debtor avoids paying a debt even where the opportunity to do so has been thrust upon the debtor by the mistake of the creditor (*Attorney-General's Reference (No. 1 of 1983)*) (below). It may be questioned whether this is too wide.

Moynes v *Coopper* [1956] 1 QB 439   Queen's Bench Division

A wages clerk, by mistake, put £6 19s. 6½d. more money than was in fact due to an employee into a pay packet which he handed to the employee, thinking that the whole amount was due to him and intending that the employee should receive the whole of the contents. At the time when he received the pay packet the employee did not know that it contained more than was due to him, and he first discovered what it contained when he opened it later the same day at his home. When he opened the packet the employee knew that he had been over-paid £6 19s. 6½d. by mistake and dishonestly decided to, and did, appropriate to his own use the whole of the contents of the packet. The employee was charged with stealing £6 19s. 6½d., the property of his employers, contrary to section 2 of the Larceny Act, 1916:—

Held (Stable J dissenting), that the definition of "takes" in section (2) (i) (*c*) of the Larceny Act, 1916, affirmed the common law that to constitute the offence of larceny the taker must have animus furandi at the time when he took the property and that, since at the time when he took the packet the employee did not know of the mistake on the part of the wages clerk, the taking was not animo furandi and, therefore, was not a taking within the section. Accordingly, although the employee had been guilty of grave dishonesty, he was not guilty of larceny or of any criminal offence.

Attorney-General's Reference (No 1 of 1983) [1984] Crim LR 570   Court of Appeal

The respondent, a woman police officer, was paid by the Receiver of the Metropolitan Police and, owing to an error in his department, she was credited with £74.74 for wages and overtime in respect of a day on which she had not been at work. The amount (together with other amounts properly due to her) was credited to her account at a bank by means of direct debit operation of the Receiver's bank. She knew nothing of the error until later; he made no demand for repayment. She was tried on a count charging that she stole £74 belonging to the Receiver, contrary to section 1(1) of the Theft Act 1968. There was some evidence that she decided to say nothing about the excess credit and to take no action about it after she discovered the error, and it was assumed that her account was in credit throughout. At the close of prosecution evidence the judge stopped the case and directed an acquittal. The Attorney-General referred a question on a point of law for the court's opinion under section 36 of the Criminal Justice Act 1972.

Held, considering *Davenport* [1954] 1 WLR 569 and *Kohn* (1979) 69 Cr App R 395, that the respondent's account being in credit, the debt due to her from her own bank was a chose in action, *i.e.* a thing in action within section 4(1) of the Act of 1968 and was, therefore, property within section 1(1) capable of being stolen. At first blush the debt belonged to no one but her. However, she had got property by another's mistake within section 5(4) and, albeit she was not under an obligation to restore the property and there were no proceeds of the chose in action to restore, "restoration" having the same meaning as restitution, she was obliged to restore to the Receiver the value of the thing in action when she found that the mistake had been made: *Norwich Union Fire Insurance Society* v *Price* [1934] AC 455; the thing in action had to be regarded as belonging to the Receiver, so that the prosecution had proved that the property belonged to another within section 1(1) from the moment when she became aware that the mistake had been made and her account credited and thereupon became subject to the obligation to restore. Furthermore, by the final words of section 5(4), proof that she intended not to make restoration was notionally to be regarded as an intention to deprive the Receiver of that property which notionally belonged to him. Under section 1(1) there remained for proof by the prosecution that there was an appropriation, unless it was already established by virtue of section 3(1), and that she had acted dishonestly. Such cases should normally be resolved without resort to the criminal courts.

Commentary. The case is indistinguishable in principle from *Moynes* v *Cooper* [sic] [1956] 1 QB 439, DC, the case with which section 5(4) of the Theft Act was intended to deal. Moynes was overpaid in cash whereas the respondent was overpaid by the creation of additional credit at her bank. When Moynes received the overpayment the money belonged to no one but him. In the absence of some special provision he could not therefore be convicted of stealing it. The special provision is now section 5(4) which provides that "Where a person gets property by another's mistake, and is under an obligation to make restoration (in whole or in part) of the property or its proceeds or of the value thereof, then to the extent of that obligation the property or proceeds shall be regarded as belonging to the person entitled to restoration. . . ." Whether property "belongs" to a person is a question of civil law; and in the cases the overpayment does not belong to the payer but to the payee. It shall however, for the purposes of the law of theft, be regarded as belonging to the payer if the conditions of section 5(4) are satisfied.

Where money is paid under a mistake of fact it belongs to the payee but he is under a quasi-contractual obligation to repay a sum equivalent to the overpayment. From the moment the money is received the payee is indebted to the payer. He is therefore under an obligation to restore, not the property or its proceeds, but *the value* of the overpayment.

Section 5(4) does not create an offence. It remains necessary to prove an appropriation. In a case like *Moynes's* case there would be no difficulty about this because, after he had learned of the mistake, he disposed of the overpaid money which would now be regarded as property belonging to the payer. It seems that it is not necessary, however, to prove any actual disposition. Section 5(4) concludes: ". . . and an intention not to make restoration shall be regarded accordingly as an intention to deprive that person of the property or proceeds." If an intention not to make restoration is an intention to deprive, the omission to make restoration is a deprivation and presumably a sufficient appropriation. It is moreover, a case within section 3(1) where the defendant has "come by the property . . . without stealing it" in which case "any later assumption of a right to it by *keeping* or dealing with it as owner" is a sufficient appropriation.

It is of course necessary to establish dishonesty as in every other case of theft — the jury would have to be satisfied (i) that the retention of an overpayment in these circumstances was dishonest according to the ordinary standards of reasonable and honest people; and (ii) that the defendant knew that it would be so regarded by reasonable and honest people.

It is very exceptional for the law to allow a criminal conviction in the case of a dishonest debtor who has avoided paying a debt. Another example is provided by section 3 (making off without payment) of the Theft Act 1978 which was designed to provide for a prevalent and increasing type of fraud for which civil remedies will not usually be available. Section 5(4) deals with an exceptional case where, moreover, the opportunity for dishonesty is thrust upon the defendant instead of resulting from his initiative and where civil remedies will usually be available (even if, because of the defendant's impecuniosity) not worth pursuing. It is doubtful whether the law of theft was wisely extended to such cases. Hence, no doubt, the court's concluding remark.

The difficulty in showing that there was an appropriation here is that, as title to the money did in fact pass to the defendant, it is not possible to prove an act which interferes with the true owner's rights. Smith suggests a solution:

Smith: The Law of Theft (5th ed. para 81)

> *Morris* presents a difficulty. Since P, by mistake, has parted with his entire proprietary interest in the property, nothing that D does with it can be done without his authority or be a usurpation of or interference with P's rights, since he has none. Unless s. 5(4) is to be wholly ineffective, this must be one instance where the normal conditions for appropriation are inapplicable. Since P's proprietary interest is fictional, the appropriation of it must also be to some extent a fiction. The fiction is that P has not parted with his proprietary interest and, if he had not parted with it, he would not have consented to D's assuming his rights.

It remains to be seen whether the solution suggested by Smith will be adopted by the courts.

(ii)   Must the 'obligation' be a legal one?

R v Gilks [1972] 3 All ER 280   Court of Appeal

CAIRNS LJ — An alternative ground on which the deputy chairman held that the money should be regarded as belonging to Ladbrokes was that 'obligation' in s 5 (4) meant an obligation whether a legal one or not. In the opinion of this court that was an incorrect ruling. In a criminal statute, where a person's criminal liability is made dependent on his having an obligation, it would be quite wrong to construe that word so as to cover a moral or social obligation as distinct from a legal one.

(f) Corporations sole

For the sake of completeness the provisions of s. 5(5) should be noted:

Section 5(5) Theft Act 1968

Property of a corporation sole shall be regarded as belonging to the corporation notwithstanding a vacancy in the corporation.

2 THE MENS REA OF THEFT

Section 1(1) Theft Act 1968

A person is guilty of theft if he dishonestly appropriates property belonging to another with the intention of permanently depriving the other of it; and 'thief' and 'steal' shall be construed accordingly.

See also s. 1(2) and s. 1(3) above, page 1.

The two elements of the mens rea of theft are:

(1)   dishonesty,
(2)   intention to permanently deprive.

(1) DISHONESTY

Two issues have to be examined here:

(a)   *The application of s. 2 of the 1968 Act – an honest belief is enough.*
(b)   *What test should the jury apply to determine dishonesty? Should the test be subjective or objective?*

(a) An honest belief is enough

Section 2 Theft Act 1968

(1) A person's appropriation of property belonging to another is not to be regarded as dishonest–

(a)   *if he appropriates property in the belief that he has in law the right to deprive the other of it, on behalf of himself or of a third person; or*
(b)   *if he appropriates the property in the belief that he would have the other's consent if the other knew of the appropriation and the circumstances of it; or*

(c)   (except where the property came to him as trustee or personal representative) if he appropriates the property in the belief that the person to whom the property belongs cannot be discovered by taking reasonable steps.

(2) A person's appropriation of property belonging to another may be dishonest notwithstanding that he is willing to pay for the property.

The belief required under s. 2 is an honest belief, i.e., one actually held by the defendant. There is no requirement that the belief should be reasonable (*R* v *Kell* [1985] Crim LR 240). If the defendant's conduct is not covered by s. 2 then we have to consider the question set out in (b) above:

(b) What test should the jury apply to determine dishonesty? Should the test be subjective or objective?

It is now clear that the jury must be directed to consider this question in the light of the model direction set out in *R* v *Ghosh* (below). It has now been held that a full 'Ghosh' direction absolves a judge from the necessity of giving a direction under s. 2(1)(a) of the 1968 Act because such a full direction was said to include consideration of all the elements in s. 2(1)(a) (*R* v *Kell* [1985] Crim LR 240). *R* v *Ghosh* represents a reconciliation (which at present seems to be working quite well) between two previous lines of authority. One of these sought to impose a subjective test of dishonesty (i.e., did the defendant believe he had been acting dishonestly?). The other line of authority put forward a wholly objective test (i.e., would the jury consider such behaviour dishonest?).

R v *Feely* [1973] 1 QB 530   Court of Appeal

In September 1971, branch managers employed by a firm of bookmakers were sent by their employers a circular stating that the practice of borrowing from the branch tills by employees was to stop. On October 4, the defendant, a branch manager, took about £30 from his branch safe. On October 8, he was transferred to another branch. The defendant said to his successor, who had found a shortage of about £40, "before you go to check, here is an IOU," and gave him an IOU for £40. The following day, in reply to questions by a member of his employers' security staff, he said that he had paid out £10.92 bets to punters and that he himself had taken £29.89, the rest of his missing money, as he had been "stuck for cash." He made a written statement at a police station that he had borrowed about £30 and intended paying it back, that his employers owed him about £70, from which he wanted them to deduct the money which he had taken. He was charged under section 1 (1) of the Theft Act 1968 with the theft of £29.89. The trial judge directed the jury that if the defendant had taken the money it was no defence for him to say that he had intended to repay it and that his employers owed him enough to cover what he had taken.

On the defendant's appeal against his conviction:—

Held, allowing the appeal, that "dishonestly" in section 1 (1) of the Theft Act 1968 related only to the state of mind of the person who did the act amounting to appropriation; that that, being a question of fact, should have been left to the jury; that the judge should not have defined "dishonestly," since it was a word in common use, but should have left it to the jury to apply the current standards of ordinary decent people; that, since the question whether the defendant acted "dishonestly" was not left to the jury, the conviction would be quashed. . . .

LAWTON LJ — We do not agree that judges should define what "dishonestly" means. This word is in common use whereas the word "fraudulently" which was used in section 1 (1) of the Larceny Act 1916 had acquired as a result of case law a special meaning. Jurors, when deciding whether an appropriation was dishonest can be reasonably expected to, and should, apply the current standards of ordinary decent people. In their own lives they have to decide what is and what is not dishonest. We can see no reason why, when in a jury box, they should require the help of a judge to tell them what amounts to dishonesty.

R v Gilks [1972] 3 All ER 280   Court of Appeal

The defendant placed a bet on a horse with a bookmaker. The horse was unplaced. The bookmaker however paid the defendant a sum of £106 in the mistaken belief that he had backed the winner. The defendant knew that the bookmaker had made a mistake and that he was not entitled to the money but he kept it. On a charge of theft under s. 1 of the Theft Act 1968 the defendant contended that in paying the money the bookmaker did not suppose, since the bet was a gaming transaction, that he was discharging a legal liability; he was in fact simply making a gift; accordingly at the moment of payment the money was not money 'belonging to another' within s. 1 (1) of the 1968 Act, for at that very moment the ownership was transferred; furthermore s. 5 (4) of the 1968 Act had no application because the defendant had no obligation to repay the money.

Held — The defendant was guilty of theft.

CAIRNS LJ — The other main branch of the appellant's case is the contention that the deputy chairman misdirected the jury on the meaning of 'dishonestly' in s. 1 (1) of the Theft Act. The relevant part of the appellant's evidence is set out in the summing-up in a passage of which no complaint is made:

'Now, what [the appellant] says is that he did not act dishonestly. He says in his view bookmakers and punters are a race apart and that when you are dealing with your bookmaker different rules apply. He agreed it would be dishonest if his grocer gave him too much change and he knew it and kept the change; he agreed it would be dishonest but he says bookmakers are different and if your bookmaker makes a mistake and pays you too much there is nothing dishonest about keeping it.'

The deputy chairman, having referred to this evidence, and to evidence that the appellant had not hurried away from the betting shop after receiving this large sum, said:

'Well, it is a matter for you to consider, members of the jury, but try and place yourselves in [the appellant's] position at that time and answer the question whether in your view he thought he was acting honestly or dishonestly.'

In our view that was in the circumstances of this case a proper and sufficient direction on the matter of dishonesty. On the face of it the appellant's conduct was dishonest; the only possible basis on which the jury could find that the prosecution had not established dishonesty would be if they thought it possible that the appellant did have the belief which he claimed to have.

R v *Greenstein* [1976] 1 All ER 1   Court of Appeal

During the years 1971 and 1972 most public issues of shares were greatly oversubscribed. In order to improve their chances of obtaining the full number of shares they wanted the appellants made a practice of applying for very large quantities of shares which they did not have funds to pay for, in the knowledge that, when an issue was over-subscribed, it was the practice of the issuing houses to allot shares to applicants in proportion to the quantity applied for. In most cases the appellants were required to send a cheque for the full amount of the price of the shares applied for. In each case the appellants drew cheques for the amount in question although at the time when the cheques were drawn they did not have sufficient funds in their bank accounts to meet the cheques on presentation. The appellants had no authority from their banks to overdraw but relied on the fact that, when the shares were issued to them, they would receive a 'return cheque' from the issuing house for the amount of the difference between the price of the shares applied for and the price of those allotted. On most occasions, the cheques drawn by the appellants were honoured on first presentation, the return cheques having previously been cleared. On some occasions, however, the appellants' cheques were dishonoured on first presentation. The appellants were charged on a number of counts with obtaining or attempting to obtain property by deception, contrary to s. 15(1) of the Theft Act 1968. The charges alleged that the appellants had dishonestly obtained, or attempted to obtain, a letter of acceptance in respect of shares and a return cheque belonging to an issuing house with the intention of permanently depriving the issuing house of the shares and cheque by deception.

   Held – The appeals would be dismissed for the following reasons–

   (i)   The question whether the appellants had been guilty of dishonesty was a question of fact for the jury. From the evidence the jury were entitled to conclude that the appellants had made a dishonest representation to the issuing houses that there were, or would be, sufficient funds in their bank accounts to meet the cheques on first presentation apart from the funds supplied by the issuing houses themselves by means of the return cheques.

STEPHENSON LJ — The learned judge ruled that the case was not difficult to understand nor one of real complexity and that the question whether what the appellants were alleged to have done was dishonest was essentially a question to be decided by a jury. 'There are facts', he said, 'which can point in both directions in this case, and in the circumstances I could not conscientiously say that there was no evidence fit to be left to the jury.' We need only say, without enumerating the undisputed facts which point to dishonesty, that we agree with him.

In summing up the case to the jury the judge laid down the law in a way which is beyond criticism. He told the jury:

'. . . there is nothing illegal in stagging. The question you have to decide and what this case is all about is whether these defendants, or either of them, carried out their stagging operations in a dishonest way. To that question you apply your own standards of dishonesty. It is no good, you see, applying the standards of anyone accused of dishonesty otherwise everybody accused of dishonesty, if he were to be tested by his own standards, would be acquitted automatically, you may think. The question is essentially one for a jury to decide and it is essentially one which the jury must decide by applying its own standards.'

That was correct: see *R* v *Feely*, and he repeated it more than once.

R v *Ghosh* [1982] 1 QB 1053 {: .left} Court of Appeal

The appellant, while a surgeon acting as a locum tenens consultant at a hospital, claimed fees for carrying out operations or fees payable for an anaesthetist in circumstances where either another surgeon had performed the operation or the operation had been carried out under the National Health Service. He was tried on an indictment containing one count alleging that he had attempted to procure the execution of a valuable security by deception, contrary to section 20 (2) of the Theft Act 1968, and three counts alleging that he had obtained or attempted to obtain money by deception, contrary to section 15 (1) of the Act. The appellant denied that he had been dishonest and stated that the sums were legitimately payable to him for consultation fees. The judge directed the jury that it was for them to decide whether the appellant had been dishonest by applying contemporary standards of honesty and dishonesty in the context of all that they had heard in the case. The jury found the appellant guilty on all four counts.

On appeal against conviction:—

Held, dismissing the appeal, that "dishonestly" in section 1 of the Theft Act 1968 described the state of mind and not the conduct of the person accused and, therefore, the test of dishonesty was subjective but the standard of honesty to be applied was the standard of reasonable and honest men and not that of the accused; that, accordingly, the jury, in determining whether the appellant had acted dishonestly for the purposes of sections 15 (1) and 20 (2) of the Act, should have first considered whether the appellant had acted dishonestly by the standards of ordinary and honest people and, if they found that he had, then they had to consider whether the appellant himself must have realised that what he was doing was by those standards dishonest; and that, since on the jury's finding they would have convicted the appellant on such a direction, it was a proper case for applying the proviso to section 2 (1) of the Criminal Appeal Act 1968. . . .

LORD LANE CJ — . . . Is "dishonestly" in section 1 of the Theft Act 1968 intended to characterise a course of conduct? Or is it intended to describe a state of mind? If the former, then we can well understand that it could be established independently of the knowledge or belief of the accused. But if, as we think, it is the latter, then the knowledge and belief of the accused are at the root of the problem.

Take for example a man who comes from a country where public transport is free. On his first day here he travels on a bus. He gets off without paying. He never had any intention of paying. His mind is clearly honest; but his conduct, judged objectively by what he has done, is dishonest. It seems to us that in using the word "dishonestly" in the Theft Act 1968, Parliament cannot have intended to catch dishonest conduct in that sense, that is to say conduct to which no moral obloquy could possibly attach. This is sufficiently established by the partial definition in section 2 of the Theft Act itself. All the matters covered by section 2 (1) relate to the belief of the accused. Section 2 (2) relates to his willingness to pay. A man's belief and his willingness to pay are things which can only be established subjectively. It is difficult to see how a partially subjective definition can be made to work in harness with the test which in all other respects is wholly objective.

If we are right that dishonesty is something in the mind of the accused (what Professor Glanville Williams calls "a special mental state"), then if the mind of the accused is honest, it cannot be deemed dishonest merely because members of the jury would have regarded it as dishonest to embark on that course of conduct.

So we would reject the simple uncomplicated approach that the test is purely objective, however attractive from the practical point of view that solution may be.

There remains the objection that to adopt a subjective test is to abandon all standards but that of the accused himself, and to bring about a state of affairs in which "Robin Hood would be no robber": R v Greenstein [1975] 1 WLR 1353. This objection misunderstands the nature of the subjective test. It is no defence for a man to say "I knew that what I was doing is generally regarded as dishonest; but I do not regard it as dishonest myself. Therefore I am not guilty." What he is however entitled to say is "I did not know that anybody would regard what I was doing as dishonest." He may not be believed; just as he may not be believed if he sets up "a claim of right" under section 2 (1) of the Theft Act 1968, or asserts that he believed in the truth of a misrepresentation under section 15 of the Act of 1968. But if he is believed, or raises a real doubt about the matter, the jury cannot be sure that he was dishonest.

In determining whether the prosecution has proved that the defendant was acting dishonestly, a jury must first of all decide whether according to the ordinary standards of reasonable and honest people what was done was dishonest. If it was not dishonest by those standards, that is the end of the matter and the prosecution fails.

If it was dishonest by those standards, then the jury must consider whether the defendant himself must have realised that what he was doing was by those standards dishonest. In most cases, where the actions are obviously dishonest by ordinary standards, there will be no doubt about it. It will be obvious that the defendant himself knew that he was acting dishonestly. It is dishonest for a defendant to act in a way which he knows ordinary people consider to be dishonest, even if he asserts or genuinely believes that he is morally justified in acting as he did. For example, Robin Hood or those ardent anti-vivisectionists who remove animals from vivisection laboratories are acting dishonestly, even though they may consider themselves to be morally justified in doing what they do, because they know that ordinary people would consider these actions to be dishonest.

(2) INTENTION TO PERMANENTLY DEPRIVE

The intention of the defendant must be to deprive the loser of the whole of his interest. If this is a limited interest, then, so long as an intention to deprive him of all of that interest can be shown, the requisite intent will be present.

An example would be where the legitimate hirer of a car for a day is deprived of the whole of his interest by the defendant who takes the car for the whole day, knowing that the hirer will lose the whole of his interest in that car.

Three main issues arise in determining when there is an intention to permanently deprive:

(a)   Is there an intention to permanently deprive if the defendant intends to return the goods but puts himself in a position where he may not be able to do so?

(b)   In what circumstances can an intended borrowing amount to an intention to permanently deprive?

(c)   Can a 'conditional intention' be sufficient mens rea?

(a) Intention to return the goods but inability to do so

Section 6(2) Theft Act 1968

Without predudice to the generality of subsection (1) above, where a person, having possession or control (lawfully or not) of property belonging to another, parts with the property under a condition as to its return which he may not be able to perform, this (if done for purposes of his own and without the other's authority) amounts to treating the property as his own to dispose of regardless of the other's rights.

Section 6(2) was specifically designed to cover the case where the defendant pawns another's property without authority. The condition which he 'may not be able to perform' is the condition imposed by the pawnbroker that the property will not be returned unless payment is first forthcoming.

The subsection is not in terms confined to pawning situations and there may be other cases which fall within its ambit.

(b) In what circumstances can an intended borrowing amount to an intention to permanently deprive?

Section 6(1) Theft Act 1968

A person appropriating property belonging to another without meaning the other permanently to lose the thing itself is nevertheless to be regarded as having the intention of permanently depriving the other of it if his intention is to treat the thing as his own to dispose of regardless of the other's rights; and a borrowing or lending of it may amount to so treating it if, but only if, the borrowing or lending is for a period and in circumstances making it equivalent to an outright taking or disposal.

One situation in which s. 6(1) applies is where the thing which the defendant intends to return to the owner is so changed in nature as to have lost all its value so far as the owner is concerned. It is not clear whether the subsection is satisfied where the item has lost nearly all its value — e.g., a season ticket which has almost expired.

R v *Duru* [1973] 3 All ER 715   Court of Appeal

The accused, D, A and K, collaborated together to assist certain prospective house buyers to obtain mortgages from the Greater London Council. D was at the time employed by the council in the department which dealt with such applications. The applications in question, to the knowledge of each of the accused, contained false information about the applicants' income and employment. On the basis of that information, the applications, which were dealt with by D on behalf of the council, were granted. The council's cheques representing the mortgage loans were sent to solicitors who acted both for the council and for the respective applicants. Those cheques were in due course cashed and on completion of the house purchases the moneys represented by them were paid as mortgage moneys to the person who thereupon became mortgagors. The accused were convicted of obtaining property, i.e. the cheques, 'with the intention of permanently depriving' the council of them, contrary to s. 15 (1) of the Theft Act 1968. D and A appealed against their convictions contending (i) that they had no intention of depriving the council permanently either of the cheques, since the cheques themselves would ultimately, after they had been paid by the council's bank on presentation, go back to the council, or of the moneys represented by the cheques, since the mortgage transactions involved a loan of the moneys which would in due course be repaid; and (ii) that, even if the accused had such an intention, they had not themselves 'obtained' the property in question, nor had they enabled another to obtain or retain it, within s. 15 (2) of the 1968 Act, because the cheques went into the hands of solicitors who were acting for both the council and the applicants with the result that neither ownership, possession nor control of the property had passed to anybody for whom it had been obtained.

Held — The appeals would be dismissed for the following reasons—

(i)   The accused had obtained the property, within s. 15 (2) of the 1968 Act, since by their conduct they had enabled the solicitors concerned to obtain possession and control of the cheques. It was irrelevant that the solicitors themselves had not been guilty of, or party to, any kind of deception.

(ii)   A cheque was a thing in action which changed its character once it had been paid. It was the intention of the accused, dishonestly and by deception, not only that the cheques should be handed over but also that they should be presented and paid, thereby permanently depriving the council of them in their substance as things in action. The fact that the mortgagors were under an obligation to repay the mortgage loans did not affect the accused's intention permanently to deprive the council of the cheques. . ..

MEGAW LJ — . . . In the view of this court there can be no doubt that the intention of both of these appellants, as would necessarily have been found by the jury if the matter had been left to the jury on a proper direction of law (a direction which would no doubt have been given if the pleas of guilty had not been entered), was permanently to deprive the Greater London Council of that thing in action, that cheque; that piece of paper, in the sense of a piece of paper carrying with it the right to receive payment of the sum of £6,002.50, which is the amount concerned in count 3.

So far as the cheque itself is concerned, true it is a piece of paper. But it is a piece of paper which changes its character completely once it is paid, because then it receives a rubber stamp on it saying it has been paid and it ceases to be a thing in action, or at any rate it ceases to be, in its substance, the same thing as it was before: that is, an instrument on which payment falls to be made. It was the intention of the appellants, dishonestly and by deception, not only that the cheques should be made out and handed over, but also that they should be presented and paid, thereby permanently depriving the Greater London Council of the cheque in substance as their things in action. The fact that the mortgagors were under an obligation to repay the mortgage loans does not affect the appellants' intention permanently to deprive the council of these cheques.

If it were necessary to look to s. 6 (1) of the Theft Act 1968, this court would have no hesitation in saying that that subsection, brought in by the terms of s. 15 (3), would also be relevant, since it is plain that the appellants each had the intention of causing to cheque to be treated as the property of the person by whom it was to be obtained, to dispose of, regardless of the rights of the true owner.

For those reasons the grounds of appeal which have been put forward in respect of conviction are unsound and the appeals of Duru and Asghar in respect of conviction are both dismissed.

R v *Pick* [1982] Crim LR 238   Knightsbridge Crown Court

The defendant was indicted for theft of gaming chips the property of the Curzon House Club. The evidence was that the defendant was seen on a video film taking from a roulette table chips which had been placed by another punter. The evidence further showed that on each occasion the defendant took a chip, it was before "no more bets" had been called. The defence conceded appropriation but would have contended that he had a claim of right as the other punter had wrongly taken the defendant's chips earlier in the game.

At the close of the prosecution case the defence submitted that there was no case to answer on the indictment as laid because the defendant had always intended to return the actual chips to the casino (and indeed the evidence showed he had done so) and thus there was no intention to permanently deprive the casino of the chips.

Held, that the indictment as laid was wrong in that before the game commenced the "value" of the chips belonged to the punter, not to the casino. The casino acted merely as stakeholders and at this stage the only interest they had in the "chip" was its value as a plastic token, which acknowledge their position as stakeholder.

Further, that having regard to the fact that no efforts had been made to identify the punter due to the prosecution's misconception as to the relevant charge, and having regard to all the merits of the case, it would be unjust at this stage to allow the indictment to be amended to read theft from a person unknown.

Commentary. There seems to be no doubt that the chips belonged to the Club. If so, they were capable of being stolen from the Club and it was immaterial how small their value might be. The difficulty lies in finding an intention permanently to deprive. The problem is considered in correspondence, arising out of the case of *Charles* [1976] Crim LR 198, at [1976] Crim LR 329-331. It was well settled at common law that a person who took another's property intending to sell it back to him had a sufficient intention permanently to deprive. The same principle probably applies under the Theft Act: Smith, *Law of Theft* (4th ed.), para. 120. The defendant took the chips intending to return them to the Club only in return for being allowed to play — that is, for the value of the chips. If the defendant, claiming to be the rightful holder of the chips, were prevented from playing, he would naturally expect to receive back the money paid for the chips. It is submitted that there are good grounds for argument that he had a sufficient intention permanently to deprive the Club.

R v Johnstone, Comerford and Jalil [1982] Crim LR 454

Newcastle-Upon-Tyne Crown Court

D1 and D2 were employed by a bottling company as draymen to deliver supplies of bottled soft drinks, cider and beer to, and to collect the empties and crates from, retail outlets. They were required to note down on a separate delivery sheet for each outlet the amount of empties collected so that the retailer could be credited with the deposit upon them on D1 and D2's return to the bottling company. Evidence was adduced by the prosecution that on the day in question D1 and D2 collected 28 more bottles and crates than they credited to the outlets, thereby creating a surplus of empties upon the lorry. Instead of delivering the surplus directly to their employers they dishonestly delivered it to D3, a retailer who was also a customer of the employers, with the intention of receiving a part of the deposit which D3 would himself dishonestly obtain. The Recorder accepted that this scheme only made sense if the surplus bottles were returned to the bottling company either directly or via a bottle exchange with only a short delay, since it was only in such circumstances that D3 would be able to obtain credit for the deposit. It was thus intended by D1 and D2 that the bottling company would receive their bottles back and would have to pay no more than one deposit, albeit to the wrong person.

D1 and D2 were charged with theft of the surplus bottles from the bottling company (it not being possible for the prosecution to prove from which individual retail outlet(s) the surplus had been obtained). D3 was charged with handling the surplus.

On a submission at the end of the prosecution case of no case to answer upon the argument that D1 and D2 did not intend permanently to deprive their employers of the surplus bottles the prosecution sought to rely upon the provisions of section 6 (1) of the Theft Act upon the basis that D1 and D2 had treated the bottles as their own to dispose of regardless of the others rights:

Held.

That since on the above facts D1 and D2 contemplated and intended that the bottles should be returned to the true owners, albeit with some delay and since the object of the scheme was merely to manipulate the bottles in order to obtain the deposit, it could not be said that D1 and D2 were treating the bottles as their own to dispose of. A disposal which negates an intention permanently to deprive cannot be capable of providing what can be regarded as an intent permanently to deprive under section 6 (1) of the Theft Act.

In the above case the court held that the defendants always treated the bottles as belonging to the bottling company — an intention to return the bottles and collect the deposits would not be consistent with any other attitude. The bottling company would not, in any event, be entitled to the return of the bottles unless they paid the deposits. It was not, therefore, a case of taking the company's property intending to sell it back to them (i.e., to extract money which would not have been due to anyone). The defendants were diverting the deposit rather than claiming extra money from the company.

Thus, although 'selling back' situations are probably covered by s. 6(1), as are situations where the whole of the value of the property is lost, the courts seem reluctant to extend s. 6(1) any further. The subsection is rightly strictly construed.

(c) Can a 'conditional intention' be sufficient mens rea?

This problem arises where the defendant only intends to permanently keep anything which he finds to be valuable after he has examined the property. In *R v Easom* such an intention was held not to be sufficient for theft. Whether it can be attempted theft turns on the way the indictment is framed. According to the court in *Re Attorney-General's References (Nos. 1 & 2 of 1979)* the defendant in *R v Easom* could now be convicted if he were charged with 'attempting to steal some or all of the contents of the handbag'. This dictum was of doubtful validity at the time of the decision in the *A.-G.'s References* (below). It was not then an offence to attempt to steal an article which was not in fact there (but c.f. *R* v *Bayley and Easterbrook* (below)). Since *Easom* rejected the actual contents of the bag he could only have been attempting to steal items which were not in fact there. This particular problem has been solved by the Criminal Attempts Act 1981 whereby it is now an offence to attempt a theft even where the full offence would be physically impossible. An example would be where the defendant attempts to steal from an empty pocket.

Anderton v *Ryan The Times*, 13 May 1985 [1985] 2 WLR 968   House of Lords

LORD ROSKILL – The 1981 [Criminal Attempts] Act did not create an offence where only *mens rea* existed and there was no *actus reus* and it was still no offence to attempt to do that which if done was not in law an offence.

That submission depended solely on subsections (1) and (4) of section 1 of the 1981 Act. It ignored subsections (2) and (3).

Subsection (2) was seemingly aimed at cases such as that of the pickpocket who put his hand into an empty pocket. Because he was attempting to do that which was factually impossible it had been said that he must be acquitted.

That happily was now a matter of past controversy. Subsection (2) had at least removed the viability of the "pickpocket's defence." It might cover more, but his Lordship did not find it necessary to consider its precise scope.

He found great difficulty in determining the precise ambit of subsection (3). He agreed with Lord Bridge of Harwich that subsections (2) and (3) were complementary and must be considered together.

Lord Bridge instanced the case of a thief who stole a suitcase that was in fact full of strips of newspaper but that he believed to contain £10,000 in cash. On the law as laid down in *Smith*[1] and, indeed, under the 1981 Act if section 1 (1) and (4) stood alone, he was only guilty of stealing the strips of newspaper. Subsection (3), however, enabled him to be convicted of attempting to steal £10,000 in cash.

[1] *R* v *Smith (Roger)* [1975] 3 AC 747

The indictment must still be framed with care:

J. C. Smith: The Law of Theft (5th ed., para. 130)

A person looking for money in an empty handbag might now be convicted of attempting to steal money. The only problem in cases of this kind is one of the form of the indictment. The formula approved in the *A-G's References* is not satisfactory because, in these cases, the defendant did not intend (or it was not proved that he intended) to steal any of the contents. But he undoubtedly intended to steal something – something which was *not* "all or any of the contents". The indictment would be accurate if it alleged simply that D attempted to steal from the handbag, or holdall. This is so whether or not there is anything there that D would have stolen. D's intention to steal anything he finds which he thinks worth stealing is a present intention to steal, at least so far as the law of attempts is concerned. The failure to specify any subject matter cannot be an objection since the 1981 [Attempts] Act.[5]

[5] Similarly with the law of burglary. Below, para [357]. It is different where the charge is theft. A lorry driver is not guilty of theft of the goods loaded on his lorry when he drives off intending to steal the load "if and when the circumstances were favourable": *Grundy (Teddington) Ltd* v *Fulton* [1983] 1 Lloyd's Rep 16, CA.

R v *Easom* [1971] 2 QB 315

Court of Appeal

The appellant took a handbag, searched through it, found nothing to interest him and left it with contents intact near the owner, who repossessed it. The appellant was charged with theft of the bag and its detailed contents. The jury were directed that, if they were satisfied on the issue of identity, they must convict the appellant of theft and not of attempted theft. They convicted him of theft as charged.

On appeal against conviction:—

Held, allowing the appeal, that, since every case of theft had to be accompanied by the intention of permanently depriving the owner of his property, an appropriator did not steal if at the time of appropriation he intended merely to deprive the owner of such of his property as might prove valuable to the appropriator on examination and subsequently, on finding that the appropriated property was valueless to him, left it ready to hand for repossession by the owner; and that, since the jury had not been directed to consider the appellant's state of mind when he had taken the handbag and the facts indicated that his intention then had been merely to determine whether it contained property of interest to him, the conviction for theft could not stand.

R v *Stark* (unreported), October 5, 1967, CA applied.

Held, further, that the appellant could not be convicted of attempted theft on the indictment against him, for the jury's verdict did not establish that he had intended permanently to deprive the owner of the particular goods detailed therein. . ..

EDMUND DAVIES LJ — This is an appeal by the appellant against his conviction at the Inner London Quarter Sessions last October on an indictment charging him with theft, the particulars of the charge being that, on December 27, 1969, he "stole one handbag, one purse, one notebook, a quantity of tissues, a quantity of cosmetics and one pen, the property of Joyce Crooks."

The circumstances giving rise to the charge may be shortly stated. In the evening of December 27, 1969, woman Police Sergeant Crooks and other plain-clothes officers went to the metropole cinema in Victoria. Sergeant Crooks sat in an aisle seat and put her handbag (containing the articles enumerated in the charge) alongside her on the floor. It was attached to her right wrist by a piece of black cotton. Police Constable Hensman sat next to her on the inside seat. When the house lights came on during an interval, it was seen that the appellant was occupying the aisle seat in the row immediately behind Sergeant Crooks and that the seat next to him was vacant. Within a few minutes of the lights being put out, Sergeant Crooks felt the cotton attached to her wrist tighten. She thereupon gave Police Constable Hensman a pre-arranged signal. The cotton was again pulled, this time so strongly that she broke it off. Moments later the officers could hear the rustle of tissues and the sound of her handbag being closed. Very shortly afterwards the appellant left his seat and went to the lavatory. The officers then turned round and found Sergeant Crook's handbag on the floor behind her seat and in front of that which the appellant had vacated. Its contents were intact. When the appellant emerged from the lavatory and seated himself in another part of the cinema, he was approached by the police officers. When the offence of theft was put to him, he denied it. In every case of theft the appropriation must be accompanied by the intention of permanently depriving the owner of his property. What may be loosely described as a "conditional" appropriation will not do. If the appropriator has it in mind merely to deprive the owner of such of his property as, on examination, proves worth taking and then, finding that the booty is valueless to the appropriator, leaves it ready to hand to be repossessed by the owner, the appropriator has not stolen. If a dishonest postal sorter picks up a pile of letters, intending to steal any which are registered, but, on finding that none of them are, replaces them, he has stolen nothing, and this is so notwithstanding the provisions of section 6 (1) of the Theft Act 1968. In the present case the jury were never invited to consider the possibility that such was the appellant's state of mind or the legal consequences flowing therefrom. Yet the facts are strongly indicative that this was exactly how his mind was working, for he left the handbag and its contents entirely intact and to hand, once he had carried out his exploration. For this reason we hold that conviction of the full offence of theft cannot stand. . . . Furthermore, it is implicit in the concept of an attempt that the person acting intends to do the act attempted, so that the mens rea of an attempt is essentially that of the complete crime (see Smith and Hogan, *Criminal Law*, 2nd ed. (1969), p. 163). That being so, there could be no valid conviction of the appellant of attempted theft on the present indictment unless it were established that he was animated by the same intention permanently to deprive Sergeant Crooks of the goods enumerated in the particulars of the charge as would be necessary to establish the full offence. We hope that we have already made sufficiently clear why we consider that, in the light of the evidence and of the direction given, it is impossible to uphold the verdict on the basis that such intention was established in this case.

For these reasons, we are compelled to allow the appeal and quash the conviction.

R v Husseyn (1978) 67 Cr App Rep 131   Court of Appeal

On February 14 at Middlesex Crown Court (Judge Solomon) the appellant and one Demetriou, were convicted of attempted theft. On that day Demetriou was sentenced to three months' detention, and on March 7, 1977, the appellant was also sentenced to three months' detention.

The following facts are taken from the judgment:

In the early hours of the morning of February 27, 1976, police officers observed in a London Street a parked van. They saw the appellant standing in the middle of the road, looking up and down and, as they saw him in the middle of the road, they heard an alarm go off. One of the officers then noticed that another young man appeared to be tampering with the back door of the van. As the officer approached, the young man who was tampering with the back door appeared to attempt to close it and both young men, who proved to be Hussein [sic] and Demetriou, made off at a fast pace.

The van belonged to a Mr. Johnson, and it was correctly described by the learned judge, in the course of the summing up, as a van with certain eccentric features. The interior of the van was covered with white rabbit fur. This fur even extended to the decoration of the dashboard. Inside the door, with which one of these men was tampering, was a holdall which, according to the evidence of Mr. Johnson, contained some valuable sub-aqua equipment.

The case came before the court as an application, but during the hearing was treated as the appeal.

LORD SCARMAN − . . . The learned judge said that the jury could infer that what the young men were about was to look into the holdall and, if its contents were valuable, to steal it. In the view of this Court that was a misdirection. What has to be established is an intention to steal at the time when the step is taken, which constitutes, or which is alleged to constitute, the attempt. Edmund Davies LJ put the point in *Easom* (1971) 55 Cr App R 410; [1971] 2 QB 315, in a passage which begins at p. 413 and p. 319 of the respective reports: "In every case of theft the appropriation must be accompanied by the intention of permanently depriving the owner of his property. What may be *loosely* described as a 'conditional' appropriation will not do. If the appropriator has it in mind merely to deprive the owner of such of his property as, on examination, proves worth taking and then, finding that the booty is valueless to the appropriator, leaves it ready to hand to be repossessed by the owner, the appropriator has not stolen."

The direction of the learned judge in this case is exactly the contrary. It must be wrong, for it cannot be said that one who has it in mind to steal only if what he finds is worth stealing has a present intention to steal.

In the course of his judgment at pp. 414, 415 and p. 320 of the respective reports Edmund Davies LJ referred to the unreported case of *Stark* October 5, 1967, which Mr. Bartlett said, correctly, is very close on its facts to the present case. In that case the Court of Appeal quashed the conviction of larceny of a man caught in the act of lifting a tool-kit from the boot of a car, the judge having misdirected the jury by telling them: "Was Stark intending, if he could get away with it, and if it was worthwhile, to take that tool-kit when he lifted it out? If he picked up something, saying 'I am sticking to this − if it is worthwhile,' then he would be guilty."

We have come to the conclusion that there was here a misdirection on an essential part of the case for the Crown. In the light of that misdirection the verdict must be quashed.

Accordingly the appeal will be allowed and the conviction quashed.

Attorney-General's References (Nos. 1 & 2 of 1979) [1979] 2 WLR 578

Court of Appeal

In the first reference a grocer who lived above his shop heard the backdoor open and close late one night and intercepted the defendant who was ascending the stairs. The police were called and arrested the defendant. They asked him why he had entered the house and he replied "To rob £2,000" and on being asked why he thought there was £2,000 there he said "I don't know, I was just going to take something." The indictment before the Crown Court averred that he had entered the grocer's premises as a trespasser "with intent to steal therein." The trial judge withdrew the case from the jury at the close of the prosecution case and directed an acquittal. The Attorney-General referred to the court for opinion the question whether a man who had entered a house as a trespasser with the intention of stealing money therein was entitled to be acquitted of an offence against section 9 (1) (*a*) of the Theft Act 1968 on the ground that his intention to steal was conditional upon his finding money in the house.

In the second reference a householder heard a sound at the French windows at the rear of her house. She called the police who went to the rear of the house and found the defendant holding and turning the handle of the French windows and inserting a long thin stick between the door and the doorframe. Later at the police station the defendant made a written statement in which he said "I wasn't going to do any damage in the house, only see if there was anything lying around." The indictment averred that the defendant had attempted to enter the dwelling house concerned "with intent to steal therein." At the close of the prosecution case the judge directed the jury to return a verdict of not guilty upon the ground that the evidence did not disclose a present intention to steal but merely a conditional intention. The Attorney-General referred to the court for opinion the question whether a man who was attempting to enter a house as a trespasser with the intention of stealing anything of value which he might find therein was entitled to be acquitted of the offence of attempted burglary on the ground that at the time of the attempt his intention was insufficient to amount to "the intention of stealing anything" necessary for conviction under section 9 of the Theft Act 1968.

On the hearing of both references:—

Held, (1) that, under section 9 (1) (*a*) of the Theft Act 1968, the offence of burglary was committed if a person entered a building as a trespasser with an intention to steal; that, where a person was charged with burglary, it was no defence to show that he did not intend to steal any specific objects, and, accordingly, the fact that the intention to steal was conditional on finding money in the house did not entitle a person to be acquitted on a charge of entering premises as a trespasser with intent to steal therein; and that the question asked in the first reference was to be answered in the negative . . ..

(2) that both principle and logic required the same answer whether the charge were burglary, attempted burglary, theft or attempted theft, or loitering with intent to commit an arrestable offence; that, accordingly, the second question referred was also to be answered in the negative.

Per curiam. Plainly it may be undesirable in some cases to frame indictments by reference to the theft or attempted theft of specific objects. There is no reason in principle against more imprecise pleading, if the justice of the case requires it, as for example, attempting to steal some or all the contents of a car or some or all the contents of a handbag . . ..

ROSKILL LJ – The question referred in Reference No. 1 is:

"Whether a man who has entered a house as a trespasser with the intention of stealing money therein is entitled to be acquitted of an offence against section 9 (1) (*a*) of the Theft Act 1968 on the grounds that his intention to steal is conditional upon his finding money in the house."

The answer of this court to this question is "No." In the second reference the question is:

"Whether a man who is attempting to enter a house as a trespasser with the intention of stealing anything of value which he may find therein is entitled to be acquitted of the offence of attempted burglary on the ground that at the time of the attempt his said intention was insufficient to amount to 'the intention of stealing anything' necessary for conviction under section 9 of the Theft Act 1968."

The answer of this court to this question is also "No."

We had an interesting discussion, with the help of Mr. Tudor Price and Mr. Simon Brown, how, in these cases of burglary or theft or attempted burglary or theft, it is in future desirable to frame indictments. Plainly it may be undesirable in some cases to frame indictments by reference to the theft or attempted theft of specific objects. Obviously draftsmen of indictments require the maximum latitude to adapt the particulars charged to the facts of the particular case, but we see no reason in principle why what was described in argument as a more imprecise method of criminal pleading should not be adopted, if the justice of the case requires it, as for example, attempting to steal some or all the contents of a car or some or all of the contents of a handbag. . . .

Taking as an example the facts in *R v Easom* [1971] 2 QB 315, plainly what the accused intended was to steal some or all of the contents of the handbag if and when he got them into his possession. It seems clear from the latter part of Edmund Davies LJ's judgment that, if he had been charged with an attempt to steal some or all the contents of that handbag, he could properly have been convicted, subject of course to a proper direction to the jury.

R v Bayley and Easterbrook [1980] Crim LR 503   Court of Appeal

Two defendants, who by direction were found not guilty of theft, were charged additionally with jointly attempting to steal the contents of a box belonging to the British Railways Board. The jury was directed that the defendants were guilty of that charge if they removed the box from the railway line dishonestly and with the already-formed intention of keeping its contents, whatever they might be, if of value to them. They were both convicted and appealed on the ground that the judge had erred in his direction to the jury.

Held, dismissing the appeal, that the jury had been correctly directed. In *Attorney-General's References (Nos. 1 and 2 of 1979)* [1979] 3 WLR 577, the Court of Appeal held that the offence of burglary was committed if a person entered a building as a trespasser with an intention to steal and it was no defence to show that he did not intend to steal any specific objects. At p. 590 Roskill LJ said that it was impossible to justify different answers for burglary or attempted burglary, theft or attempted theft. A case of attempted theft, *Scudder v Barrett* [1979] 3 WLR 591, was heard immediately afterwards by the same court reconstituted as a Divisional court and the *Attorney-General's References* were followed. Strictly *Scudder* was not binding on this court, but clearly was right. Professor Glanville Williams, in his article "Three Rogues' Charters" [1980] Crim LR 263 at p. 267 had suggested questions for a jury in this class of case, but a complicated direction of that kind was more likely to confuse a jury than to help it.

Commentary. When the defendants opened the box they found that it contained "a Pammex Model 60 rail and flange lubricator." These were valuable articles but the defendants did not want them so they returned the box with its contents to British Rail, saying that they had disturbed youngsters with it on the railway line and removed it before an accident was caused. They later admitted that this story was untrue.

As originally drawn the indictment charged the defendants "that on April 8, 1979, they stole a Pammex Model 60 rail and flange lubricator belonging to the British Railways Board." At the instance of counsel for the prosecution a further count was added alleging that the defendants "attempted to steal the contents of a box belonging to the British Railways Board." The Court of Appeal held that the defendants were rightly acquitted on the first count because they "did not know of the existence of the two pieces of railway equipment and had no intention of stealing them." They were rightly convicted on count 2 because they "did intend to steal whatever was in the box; whether they would keep the contents or any of them would depend on what they were."

It is clear then that the defendants were convicted of attempting to steal not the actual contents but something, unidentified, that was not in the box. The difficulty about this is the decision of the House of Lords in *Haughton* v *Smith* [1975] AC 476. The House said that there can be no conviction for an attempt to steal from a place, such as a pocket or a room, which is empty.

The difficulty with regard to attempts has now largely been removed by the terms of the Criminal Attempts Act 1981 (see *Anderton* v *Ryan*, above page 59 and below page 129). But as Professor Smith points out in his commentary on *R* v *Bayley and Easterbrook* (below) the problem of *Easom* and conditional intent remains where the allegation is one of the full offence of theft:

The court repeats the dictum in *Attorney-General's References* that the same rule must apply to theft. It does not explain how this is possible. The charge of burglary or attempted theft is good because it leaves the property unspecified; but how can a charge of theft leave the property unspecified? It is submitted that it is simply not possible to apply the rule to theft.

3 ROBBERY

Six problem areas can be identified here:

(a)   At whom must the force of threat be directed?
(b)   When is force used 'in order to steal'?
(c)   When does the theft take place?

  (i)   When is an appropriation complete?
  (ii) When does the stealing stop?

(d)   For how long does a 'threat of force' remain effective?
(e)   Will a defence to a charge of theft defeat a robbery charge?
(f)   Who determines what amounts to force?

Section 8 Theft Act 1968

(1) A person is guilty of robbery if he steals, and immediately before or at the time of doing so, and in order to do so, he uses force on any person or puts or seeks to put any person in fear of being then and there subjected to force.
(2) Any person guilty of robbery, or of an assault with intent to rob, shall on conviction on indictment be liable to imprisonment for life.

(a) At whom must the force or threat be directed?

The section clearly specifies that 'any person' may be the victim of the force or threat of force — not just the victim of the theft.

(b) When is force used 'in order to steal'?

The force or threat must be used for the purpose of stealing;

R v *Shendley* [1970] Crim LR 49   Court of Appeal

S was convicted of robbery, contrary to section 8 of the Theft Act 1968. The complainant said that S attacked him, took some of his property and forced him to sign receipts purporting to show that S had bought the property from him. S said that he had purchased the property. The judge directed the jury: "robbery is stealing property in the presence of the owner . . . the allegation is that immediately before taking the property, or at the time of taking it, or immediately after, force was used towards [the complainant] to put him in fear . . . if you came to the conclusion that the violence was unconnected with the stealing but you were satisfied there was a stealing it does not mean that is an acquittal because it would be open to you to find [him] guilty of robbery, that is, robbery without violence."

Held, the directions were wrong. The judge must have had in mind section 23 of the Larceny Act 1916 and overlooked the fact that the definition of robbery in the Theft Act is different. There is no such thing as robbery without violence. What the judge no doubt intended to say was that if the jury were satisfied that S stole the property but not satisfied that he used violence for the purpose of stealing they should find him not guilty of robbery but guilty of theft (the court substituted a conviction for theft).

(c) When does the theft take place?

(i) When is an appropriation complete?

Full control of the article is not necessary:

Corcoran v *Anderton* [1980] Crim LR 385   Queen's Bench Division

Two youths, the defendant and his co-accused, saw a woman in the street, and agreed together to steal her handbag. The co-accused hit her in the back and tugged at her bag to release it, while the defendant participated. She released her bag, screamed, and fell to the ground. The two youths ran away empty-handed, and the woman recovered her bag, neither youth having had sole control of the bag at any time. The defendant was later convicted of robbery under section 8 of the Theft Act 1968, which provided that a person was guilty of robbery if he stole, using force. "Steal" was defined in section 1 (1) of the Act as being the dishonest "appropriation" of another's property with the intention of depriving him or her of it permanently, and "appropriation" was defined in section 3 (1) as "an assumption by a person of the rights of an owner."

The defendant appealed against conviction on the ground that neither he nor the co-accused had sole control of the bag at any time.

Held, dismissing the appeal, that an appropriation took place at the moment when the youths, acting with an intention to deprive the woman of the bag, snatched it from her grasp so that she no longer had physical control of it. In doing so each accused was trying to exclude the woman from her exclusive claim to the bag, and was trying to treat the bag as his. Such an action was an unlawful assumption of the rights of the owner and accordingly the defendant was properly convicted by the justices.

(ii) When does the stealing stop?

According to s. 8 the force or threat of force must be immediately before or at the time of the stealing. If the theft is complete when the violence is used there will be no robbery. It seems that for the purposes of robbery (as for burglary — see *R* v *Gregory* (below) — appropriation can be a continuing act:

R v *Robert Angus Hale* (1978) 68 Cr App Rep 415   Court of Appeal

The appellant was charged with robbery. The prosecution case was that he and one M, both wearing stocking masks, had forced their way into the house of a Mrs C who had answered the door to their knock. The appellant had then put his hand over Mrs C's mouth to stop her screaming while M went upstairs and returned carrying a jewellery box and had asked Mrs C "where the rest was." A neighbour who had heard Mrs C's scream had then rung up to ask if she was all right. Under threats from the appellant and M she replied that she was. They again asked Mrs C where she kept her money and before leaving the house tied her up and threatened what would happen to her young boy if she informed the police within five minutes of their leaving.

The trial judge read the definition of robbery in section 8 of the Theft Act 1968 to the jury and the meaning of "steal" in section 1 of that Act. He directed them that the question they had to decide was whether they felt sure that the appellant by use of force or putting Mrs C in fear got hold of her property without her consent and without believing that he had her consent and intending to appropriate that property to himself without giving it back to her afterwards. The jury convicted. On appeal that the jury had been misdirected in that the judge's direction could indicate to the jury that if an accused used force in order to effect his escape with the stolen goods that would be sufficient to constitute robbery and that on the facts of the present case it was submitted that the theft was completed as soon as the jewellery box was seized.

Held, that for the purposes of section 1 (1) of the Theft Act 1968 the act of appropriation — the intention to deprive the owner permanently, which accompanied the assumption of the owner's rights — was a continuing one at all material times; and in the instant case the appellant, as a matter of common sense, was in the course of committing theft: he was stealing; further, the jury were quite entitled to find the appellant guilty of robbery relying on the force used by him when he put his hand over Mrs C's mouth to restrain her from calling for help. They were also entitled to rely on the fact of tying Mrs C up provided they were satisfied that the force so used was to enable the appellant and M. to steal. Accordingly, the appeal would be dismissed as there was no misdirection taking the summing-up as a whole.

EVELEIGH LJ — . . . In so far as the facts of the present case are concerned, counsel submitted that the theft was completed when the jewellery box was first seized and any force thereafter could not have been "immediately before or at the time of stealing" and certainly not "in order to steal." The essence of the submission was that the theft was completed as soon as the jewellery box was seized.

Section 8 of the Theft Act 1968 begins: "A person is guilty of robbery if he steals. . . ." He steals when he acts in accordance with the basic definition of theft in section 1 of the Theft Act; that is to say when he dishonestly appropriates property belonging to another with the intention of permanently depriving the other of it. It thus becomes necessary to consider what is "appropriation" or, according to section 3, "any assumption by a person of the rights of an owner." An assumption of the rights of an owner describes the conduct of a person towards a particular article. It is conduct which usurps the rights of the owner. To say that the conduct is over and done with as soon as he lays hands upon the property, or when he first manifests an intention to deal with it as his, is contrary to common-sense and to the natural meaning of words. A thief who steals a motor car first opens the door. It is to be said that the act of starting up the motor is no more a part of the theft?

In the present case there can be little doubt that if the appellant had been interrupted after the seizure of the jewellery box the jury would have been entitled to find that the appellant and his accomplice were assuming the rights of an owner at the time when the jewellery box was seized. However, the act of appropriation does not suddenly cease. It is a continuous act and it is a matter for the jury to decide whether or not the act of appropriation has finished. Moreover, it is quite clear that the intention to deprive the owner permanently, which accompanied the assumption of the owner's rights was a continuing one at all material times. This Court therefore rejects the contention that the theft had ceased by the time the lady was tied up. As a matter of common-sense the appellant was in the course of committing theft; he was stealing.

There remains the question whether there was robbery. Quite clearly the jury were at liberty to find the appellant guilty of robbery relying upon the force used when he put his hand over Mrs. Carrett's mouth to restrain her from calling for help. We also think that they were also entitled to rely upon the act of tying her up provided they were satisfied (and it is difficult to see how they could not be satisfied) that the force so used was to enable them to steal. If they were still engaged in the act of stealing the force was clearly used to enable them to continue to assume the rights of the owner and permanently to deprive Mrs. Carrett of her box, which is what they began to do when they first seized it.

(d) For how long does a 'threat of force' remain effective?

R v Donaghy and Marshall [1981] Crim LR 644   Snaresbrook Crown Court

D and M stopped a mini-cab in Newmarket. They asked the driver to take them to a local public house, but when they got there demanded that he drive them to London. The driver protested but complied with the demand after threats to his life were made, the prosecution alleging, *inter alia*, that D, who was sitting in the rear of the cab, poked his finger into the driver's back so as to simulate a gun. Once at London it was agreed that M stole £22 from the driver. There was no evidence, however, of any further specific threats being made at the time of or immediately prior to the theft.

Quaere, whether the latter act of M amounted to robbery since the threats to the driver's life were not made in order to force the driver to hand over his money but rather to force the driver to drive to London?

Stated by his Honour Judge Chavasse in summing-up, that the case could be treated as one of joint enterprise, and that before the jury could convict the defendants of robbery they had to be satisfied of five things: .

(I)   that there had been threats made by the defendants;
(II)   that the effect of the threats was continuing;
(III) that the defendants knew that the effect of the threats was continuing;
(IV)   that the defendants deliberately made use of the effect of these threats in order to obtain the money;
(V)   that by their manner the defendants gave the impression that they were continuing the threats at the time the theft occurred.

The jury acquitted both defendants of robbery.

Commentary. See *Hale* [1979] Crim LR 596 and commentary where it was held that an appropriation within the crime of robbery could be a continuing as distinct from an instantaneous act, and that if as a matter of common sense the jury found that D was still in the process of committing theft when the force or threat of force was employed they could find that robbery was committed at that point.

This case seems to be the other side of the coin from *Hale,* except that the difficulties of finding a continuing threat are not as great as those involved in holding that an appropriation may continue.

. . . Where a threat of force is made at a point in time well before the alleged appropriation it is submitted that the same principles should apply. Provided the jury are satisfied in a case such as the present that the threat was intended to continue in effect and was still present to the mind of the victim when the £20 [sic] was taken it matters not that it was not reiterated immediately before the appropriation itself. (Even if the fear initially created in the driver's mind had evaporated once the taxi arrived in London a conviction could still follow if D was still seeking to put him in fear of being subjected to force when the money was taken − section 8 (1).) The situation is in many ways similar to cases of duress where the fear must be of immediate force − *cf.* for example *Hudson* [1971] 2 QB 202.

Of course the jury must also be satisfied that the force or threat of force was employed *in order to* steal. If the taxi was "hi-jacked" in order to serve the dual purpose of procuring a ride to London and relieving the driver of his takings at the end of the trip the fact that stealing was not the sole purpose could hardly absolve DD [sic] of liability. But the result would be different if their purpose was solely to procure the ride. Suppose that D accidentally parks his car on a policeman's foot. When his attention is drawn to the officer's predicament he switches off the engine, gets out and walks round the car in some glee to inspect his victim. For the first time he notices that the officer is wearing an attractive watch, which he then decides to steal, and does so. Robbery? Taking advantage of the vulnerability of the victim of ones [sic] own continuing threatening or forceful behaviour in order to steal from him might be thought in principle to be robbery, and it would seem that this was the case at common law (see *e.g.* *Blackham* (1787) 2 East PC 711) but this view may not easily be reconciled with the wording of the Theft Act and it would seem that no robbery is committed. (see Smith, *Theft* (4th ed. p. 74.) Could a charge of blackmail have succeeded in

respect of the original "hi-jacking"? It is submitted that it could.
(Commentary by D. J. Birch.)

(e) Will a defence to a charge of theft defeat a robbery charge?

The answer here must be affirmative. Section 8 requires all elements of theft to be proved by the prosecution:

R v *Robinson* [1977] Crim LR 173   Court of Appeal

R ran a clothing club. He was charged (with others) with robbing and assault-ing I, who, with his wife, was a contributor to the club. I's wife owed £7. It was the prosecution case that R and two others had approached him in the street late at night, R brandishing a knife, and that a fight ensued during the course of which a £5 note fell from I's pocket. R had snatched the note and asked if I had any more money as he was still owed £2. R's defence to robbery, reduced by the jury to theft, was that I gave him the money and he had received it willingly as repayment of the debt and that it was not dishonestly appropriated. R appealed on the ground of misdirection to the jury that an honest belief by the defendant that he was entitled in law to get his money in a particular way was necessary before he could avail himself of the defence under section 2 (1) (*a*) of the Theft Act 1968.

Held, allowing the appeal, that the law as laid down in *Skivington* [1968] 1 QB 166 had not been altered by section 2 (1) (*a*) of the Theft Act 1968, and that it was unnecessary for a defendant to show that he had an honest belief not only that he was entitled to take the money but also that he was entitled to take it in the way that he did.

Commentary: . . . If then R believed that he had the right in law to deprive I of the money, he could not be guilty of stealing it even though he knew very well that he was not entitled to use a knife in order to get it. If he was not guilty of theft, it follows necessarily that he was not guilty of robbery either, because robbery is an aggravated form of theft.

R might perhaps have been convicted of blackmail. Even if he did believe that he had reasonable grounds for making the demand, he was guilty of that offence if he knew that the use of the knife was not a proper means of reinforcing the demand.

(f) Who determines what amounts to force?

R v *Dawson* [1976] Crim LR 692   Court of Appeal

D was convicted of robbery. He and two others approached a man in the street and two of them stood either side of him and the third behind him. One of them nudged the man so that he lost his balance and whilst he was thus unbalanced another stole his wallet. It was submitted that what D and his accomplices did could not amount to the use of force, relying on cases prior to the Theft Act 1968.

Held, dismissing the appeal, what counted now was the words of the Act, the object of which was to get rid of the old technicalities. The choice of the word force was not without interest because the Larceny Act 1916 used violence. Whether there was any difference between the words was not relevant to the case. Force was a word in ordinary use which juries understood. The judge left it to the jury to decide whether jostling to an extent which caused a person to have difficulty in keeping his balance amounted to the use of force. In deference to the submissions he said that the force must be substantial. It was not necessary to consider whether he was right to apply an adjective to the word of the Act. It was a matter for the jury and it could not be said that they were wrong. It had also been canvassed whether the force had been used for distracting the victim's attention or for overcoming resistance. That sort of refinement might have been relevant under the old law: the sole question under the new was whether force had been used in order to steal.

Commentary. The decision does not answer, as a matter of law, the question posed in the headnote. It decides such a nudge is capable of being "force." Whether it is force or not is a question for the individual jury. . . .

4 BURGLARY

Section 9 Theft Act 1968

(1) A person is guilty of burglary if—

(a)   he enters any building or part of a building as a trespasser and with intent to commit any such offence as is mentioned in subsection (2) below; or

(b)   having entered any building or part of a building as a trespasser he steals or attempts to steal anything in the building or that part of it or inflicts or attempts to inflict on any person therein any grievous bodily harm.

(2) The offences referred to in subsection (1)(a) above are offences of stealing anything in the building or part of a building in question, of inflicting on any person therein any grievous bodily harm or raping any woman therein, and of doing unlawful damage to the building or anything therein.

(3) References in subsections (1) and (2) above to a building shall apply also to an inhabited vehicle or vessel, and shall apply to any such vehicle or vessel at times when the person having a habitation in it is not there as well as at times when he is.

(4) A person guilty of burglary shall on conviction on indictment be liable to imprisonment for a term not exceeding fourteen years.

(1) THE ACTUS REUS OF BURGLARY

Section 9 creates two quite distinct offences. Both require proof of entry by the defendant as a trespasser. If the requisite intent is present, a s. 9(1)(a) offence is committed at the moment of entry whereas a s. 9(1)(b) offence is committed at the time that the ulterior offence is complete.

The actus reus of burglary presents the following problems;

(a)   What constitutes a sufficient entry?

(b)   When is a defendant trespassing?

(c)   How are 'building' and 'part of a building' defined?

(d)   For s. 9(1)(b) only, when can the ulterior offence be considered to have been committed?

(a) What constitutes a sufficient entry?

Many of the problems encountered in proving burglary were discussed in the following case:

R v Collins [1972] 2 All ER 1105   Court of Appeal

The appellant was a young man of 19 and the complainant a girl of 18. One evening the appellant had had a good deal to drink and was desirous of having sexual intercourse. Passing the complainant's house he saw a light on in an upstairs room which he knew was the complainant's bedroom. He fetched a ladder, put it up against the window and climbed up. He saw the complainant lying on her bed, which was just under the window, naked and asleep. He descended the ladder, stripped off his clothes, climbed back up and pulled himself on to the window sill. As he did so the complainant awoke and saw a naked male form outlined against the window. She jumped to the conclusion that it was her boyfriend, with whom she was on terms of regular and frequent sexual intimacy. Assuming that he had come to pay her an ardent nocturnal visit she beckoned him in. In response the appellant descended from the sill and joined her in bed where they had full sexual intercourse. After the lapse of some time the complainant became aware of features of her companion which roused her suspicions. Switching on the bed-side light she discovered that he was not her boyfriend but the appellant. She thereupon slapped him and went into the bathroom. The appellant promptly vanished. He was subsequently charged with burglary with intent to commit rape contrary to s 9 (1) (a) of the Theft Act 1968. The complainant stated that she would not have agreed to intercourse if she had known that the intruder was not her boyfriend. In the course of his testimony the appellant stated that he would not have entered the room if the complainant had not beckoned him in. There was no clear evidence whether, when the complainant beckoned him, he was still outside the window or had entered the room and was kneeling on the inner sill. The judge directed the jury that they had to be satisfied that the appellant had entered the room as a trespasser with the intent to commit rape and that the issue of entry as a trespasser depended on the question: was the entry intentional or reckless? The appellant was convicted and appealed.

Held — (1) There could not be a conviction for entering premises 'as a trespasser: within s. 9 of the 1968 Act unless the person entering did so knowing that he was a trespasser and nevertheless deliberately entered or was reckless whether or not he was entering the premises of another without the other party's consent (see p 1110 c, post).

(2) The crucial question for the jury, therefore, was whether the Crown had established that, at the moment that he entered the bedroom, the appellant knew that he was not welcome there or, being reckless whether or not he was welcome, was nevertheless determined to enter. That in turn involved considera-

tion whether he was inside or outside the window at the moment when the complainant beckoned him in.

(3) It followed that the appeal would be allowed since the jury had not been invited to consider the vital question whether the appellant had entered the premises as a trespasser.

Per Curiam. The common law doctrine of trespass ab initio has no application to burglary under the Theft Act 1968.

EDMUND DAVIES LJ — Delivered the judgment of the court. This is about as extraordinary a case as my brethren and I have ever heard either on the Bench or while at the Bar. Stephen William George Collins was convicted on 29th October 1971 at Essex Assizes of burglary with intent to commit rape and he was sentenced to 21 months' imprisonment. He is a 19 year old youth, and he appeals against that conviction by the certificate of the trial judge. The terms in which that certificate is expressed reveals that the judge was clearly troubled about the case and the conviction.

Let me relate the facts. Were they put into a novel or portrayed on the stage, they would be regarded as being so improbable as to be unworthy of serious consideration and as verging at times on farce. At about two o'clock in the early morning of Saturday, 24th July 1971, a young lady of 18 went to bed at her mother's home in Colchester. She had spent the evening with her boyfriend. She had taken a certain amount of drink, and it may be that this fact affords some explanation of her inability to answer satisfactorily certain crucial questions put to her. She has the habit of sleeping without wearing night apparel in a bed which is very near the lattice-type window of her room. At one stage on her evidence she seemed to be saying that the bed was close up against the window which, in accordance with her practice, was wide open. In the photographs which we have before us, however, there appears to be a gap of some sort between the two, but the bed was clearly quite near the window. At about 3.30 or 4.00 a m she awoke and she then saw in the moonlight a vague form crouched in the open window. She was unable to remember, and this is important, whether the form was on the outside of the window sill or on the part of the sill which was inside the room, and for reasons which will later become clear, that seemingly narrow point is of crucial importance. The young lady then realised several things: first of all that the form in the window was that of a male; secondly that he was a naked male; and thirdly that he was a naked male with an erect penis. She also saw in the moonlight that his hair was blond. She thereupon leapt to the conclusion that her boyfriend, with whom for some time she had been on terms of regular and frequent sexual intimacy, was paying her an ardent nocturnal visit. She promptly sat up in bed, and the man descended from the sill and joined her in bed and they had full sexual intercourse. But there was something about him which made her think that things were not as they usually were between her and her boyfriend. The length of his hair, his voice as they had exchanged what was described as 'love talk', and other features led her to the conclusion that somehow there was something different. So she turned on the bed-side light, saw that her companion was not her boyfriend and slapped the face of the intruder, who was none other than the appellant. He said to her, 'Give me a good time tonight', and got hold of her arm, but she bit him and told him to go. She then went into the bathroom and he promptly vanished.

The complainant said that she would not have agreed to intercourse if she had known tht the person entering her room was not her boyfriend. But there was no suggestion of any force having been used on her, and the intercourse which took place was undoubtedly effected with no resistance on her part.

The appellant was seen by the police at about 10.30 a. m. later that same morning. According to the police, the conversation which took place then elicited these points: He was very lustful the previous night. He had taken a lot of drink, and we may here note that drink (which to him is a very real problem) had brought this young man into trouble several times before, but never for an offence of this kind. He went on to say that he knew the complainant because he had worked around her house. On this occasion, desiring sexual intercourse — and according to the police evidence he had added that he was determined to have a girl, by force if necessary, although that part of the police evidence he challenged — he went on to say that he walked around the house, saw a light in an upstairs bedroom, and he knew that this was the girl's bedroom. He found a step ladder, leaned it against the wall and climbed up and looked into the bedroom. What he could see inside through the wide open window was a girl who was naked and asleep. So he descended the ladder and stripped off all his clothes, with the exception of his socks, because apparently he took the view that if the girl's mother entered the bedroom it would be easier to effect a rapid escape if he had his socks on than if he was in his bare feet. That is a matter about which we are not called on to express any view, and would in any event find ourselves unable to express one. Having undressed, he then climbed the ladder and pulled himself up on to the window sill. His version of the matter is that he was pulling himself in when she awoke. She then got up and knelt on the bed, she put her arms around his neck and body, and she seemed to pull him into the bed. He went on:

'. . . I was rather dazed, because I didn't think she would want to know me. We kissed and cuddled for about ten or fifteen minutes and then I had it away with her but found it hard because I had had so much to drink.'

The police officer said to the appellant:

'It appears that it was your intention to have intercourse with this girl by force if necessary and it was only pure coincidence that this girl was under the impression that you were her boyfriend and apparently that is why she consented to allowing you to have sexual intercourse with her.'

It was alleged that he then said:

'Yes, I feel awful about this. It is the worst day of my life, but I know it could have been worse.'

Thereupon the officer said to him — and the appellant challenges this — 'What do you mean, you know it could have been worse?' to which he is alleged to have replied:

'Well, my trouble is drink and I got very frustrated. As I've told you I only wanted to have it away with a girl and I'm only glad I haven't really hurt her.'

Then he made a statement under caution, in the course of which he said:

> 'When I stripped off and got up the ladder I made my mind up that I was
> going to try and have it away with this girl. I feel terrible about this now, but
> I had too much to drink. I am sorry for what I have done.'

In the course of his testimony, the appellant said that he would not have gone
into the room if the girl had not knelt on the bed and beckoned him into the
room. He said that if she had objected immediately to his being there or to his
having intercourse he would not have persisted. While he was keen on having
sexual intercourse that night, it was only if he could find someone who was
willing. He strongly denied having told the police that he would, if necessary,
have pushed over some girl for the purpose of having intercourse.

There was a submission of no case to answer on the ground that the evidence
did not support the charge, particularly that ingredient of it which had reference
to entry into the house 'as a trespasser'. But the submission was overruled, and
as we have already related, he gave evidence.

Now, one feature of the case which remained at the conclusion of the evidence
in great obscurity is where exactly the appellant was at the moment when,
according to him, the girl manifested that she was welcoming him. Was he kneeling on the sill outside the window or was he already inside the room, having
climbed through the window frame, and kneeling on the inner sill? It was a
crucial matter, for there were certainly three ingredients that it was incumbent
on the Crown to establish. Under s. 9 of the Theft Act 1968, which renders a
person guilty of burglary if he enters any building or part of a building as a
trespasser and with the intention of committing rape, the entry of the appellant
into the building must first be proved. Well, there is no doubt about that, for it
is common ground that he did enter this girl's bedroom. Secondly, it must be
proved that he entered as a trespasser. We will develop that point a little later.
Thirdly it must be proved that he entered as a trespasser with intent at the time
of entry to commit rape therein.

. . . Unless the jury were entirely satisfied that the appellant made an effective
and substantial entry into the bedroom without the complainant doing or saying
anything to cause him to believe that she was consenting to his entering it, he
ought not to be convicted of the offence charged. The point is a narrow one, as
narrow maybe as the window sill which is crucial to this case. But this is a
criminal charge of gravity and, even though one may suspect that his *intention*
was to commit the offence charged, unless the facts show with clarity that he in
fact committed it he ought not to remain convicted.

The rule is, therefore, that the entry must be 'effective and substantial'. That
formula was applied in the following case:

R v Brown The Times, 31 January 1985   Court of Appeal

A person could "enter" a building for the purposes of section 9 of the Theft
Act 1968 even though the whole of his body was not within that building, the
Court of Appeal (Criminal Division) (Lord Justice Watkins, Mr Justice Peter Pain

and Sir John Thompson) held on January 18, dismissing an appeal by Vincent Brown against his conviction of burglary at Luton Crown Court (Judge Colston, QC) on May 18, 1984.

LORD JUSTICE WATKINS — said that the appellant had been seen by a witness to be half inside a broken shop window, as though he were rummaging inside it. He was later arrested and charged with burglary.

He appealed on the ground that a person could not be said to have "entered" a building if only part of his body had been in it.

The court would accept for the purposes of the present case that it might not be appropriate to look at the pre-Theft Act authorities, but questioned whether that would always be so.

The requirement in *R* v *Collins* ([1973] QB100) that entry be "substantial" and "effective" did not support the appellant's case. Although it was right that a jury should be directed that entry must be "effective", the direction in the present case was perfectly adequate. It seemed an astounding proposition that a person could break a shop window, put in his hand and steal and not be held as having entered as a trespasser.

(b) When is a defendant trespassing?

In *R* v *Collins* the Court of Appeal made it clear that not all the technicalities of the tort of trespass will be used to define the concept of trespass as an ingredient of burglary.

Three problems need consideration:

(i)   Does the defendant need to know he is trespassing?

(ii)   Is it trespass when the defendant is invited into premises but, unknown to the person issuing the invitation, he has a secret unlawful intent?

(iii)   Will the doctrine of trespass ab initio apply?

(i) Does the defendant need to know he is trespassing?

R v *Collins* (above)

EDMUND DAVIES LJ — . . . The second ingredient of the offence — the entry must be as a trespasser — is one which has not, to the best of our knowledge, been previously canvassed in the courts. Views as to its ambit have naturally been canvassed by the textbook writers, and it is perhaps not wholly irrelevant to recall that those who were advising the Home Secretary before the Theft Bill was presented to Parliament had it in mind to get rid of some of the frequently absurd technical rules which had been built up in relation to the old requirement in burglary of a 'breaking and entering'. The cases are legion as to what this did or did not amount to, and happily it is not now necessary for us to consider them. But it was in order to get rid of those technical rules that a new test was introduced, namely that the entry must be 'as a trespasser'.

What does that involve? According to the learned editors of Archbold:

> 'Any intentional, reckless or negligent entry into a building will, it would appear, constitute a trespass if the building is in the possession of another person who does not consent to the entry. Nor will it make any difference that the entry was the result of a reasonable mistake on the part of the defendant, so far as trespass is concerned.'

If that be right, then it would be no defence for this man to say (and even were he believed in saying), 'Well, I honestly thought that this girl was welcoming me into the room and I therefore entered, fully believing that I had her consent to go in'. If Archbold is right, he would nevertheless be a trespasser, since the apparent consent of the girl was unreal, she being mistaken as to who was at her window. We disagree. We hold that, for the purposes of s. 9 of the Theft Act 1968, a person entering a building is not guilty of trespass if he enters without knowledge that he is trespassing or at least without acting recklessly as to whether or not he is unlawfully entering.

A view contrary to that of the learned editors of Archbold was expressed in Professor J C Smith's book on The Law of Theft, where, having given an illustration of an entry into premises, the learned author comments:

> 'It is submitted that . . . D should be acquitted on the ground of lack of *mens rea*. Though, under the civil law, he entered as a trespasser, it is submitted that he cannot be convicted of the criminal offence unless he knew of the facts which caused him to be a trespasser or, at least, was reckless.'

The matter has also been dealt with by Professor Griew who in his work on the Theft Act 1968 has this passage:

> 'What if D wrongly believes that he is not trespassing? His belief may rest on facts which, if true, would mean that he was not trespassing: for instance, he may enter a building by mistake, thinking that it is the one he has been invited to enter. Or his belief may be based on a false view of the legal effect of the known facts: for instance, he may misunderstand the effect of a contract granting him a right of passage through a building. Neither kind of mistake will protect him from tort liability for trespass. In either case, then, D satisfies the literal terms of section 9 (1): he "enters . . . as a trespasser." But for the purposes of criminal liability a man should be judged on the basis of the facts as he believed them to be, and this should include making allowances for a mistake as to rights under the civil law. This is another way of saying that a serious offence like burglary should be held to require *mens rea* in the fullest sense of the phrase: D should be liable for burglary only if he knowingly trespasses or is reckless as to whether he trespasses or not. Unhappily it is common for Parliament to omit to make clear whether *mens rea* is intended to be an element in a statutory offence. It is also, though not equally, common for the courts to supply the mental element by construction of the statute.'

We prefer the view expressed by Professor Smith and Professor Griew to that of the learned editors of Archbold. In the judgment of this court, there cannot be a conviction for entering premises 'as a trespasser' within the meaning of s 9 of the Theft Act 1968 unless the person entering does so knowing that he is a trespasser and nevertheless deliberately enters, or, at the very least, is reckless whether or not he is entering the premises of another without the other party's consent.

We have to say that this appeal must be allowed on the basis that the jury were never invited to consider the vital question whether this young man did enter the premises as a trespasser, that is to say knowing perfectly well that he had no invitation to enter or reckless of whether or not his entry was with permission.

(ii) Is it trespass when the defendant is invited into premises but, unknown to the person issuing the invitation, he has a secret unlawful intent?

This would seem to be trespass as is the case where an invitation is exceeded:

R v *Christopher Smith and John Jones* [1976] 3 All ER 54   Court of Appeal

For the purposes of section 9 (1) (b) of the Theft Act 1968 a person is a trespasser if the facts are such that he realises that he enters the premises in question in excess of the permission that has been given to him, or he is reckless as to whether he is entering in excess of that permission.

The following facts are taken from the judgment.

The facts of the matter which gave rise to the charge of burglary were these. Christopher Smith's father, Alfred Smith, lived at 72 Chapel Lane, Farnborough. He was in the course of negotiating a move from the house to other premises. At the material time, in May 1975, in that house were two television sets; one owned by Mr. Alfred Smith, the other owned by another person but lawfully in the possession of Mr. Alfred Smith. Christopher Smith lived with his own family at Aberfield. The appellant Jones lived in the opposite direction from Chapel Lane, Farnborough to Aberfield, namely in Lakeside Road, Ashvale.

In the early hours of May 10, 1975, a police officer in Ashvale saw a motor car with the two appellants inside and a television set protruding from the boot of the car. Having regard to that which he saw and the time of the morning he followed the car which turned into a side road where eventually it was stopped by a gate being in its way. The officer called for further officers to attend and when another officer went to the car he saw the appellant Jones sitting on the back seat with a second television set behind him. In the front of the car was Smith. They were told that the police believed that the television sets were stolen and that they were being arrested. Smith responded with the question: "Are they bent?" and Jones made the observation: "You cannot arrest me for just having a ride in a car."

At the trial both of the appellants gave evidence. It was the case for Smith that he had permission from his father to go into the house of his father. With that permission was a general licence to go there at any time he wanted to. It was the case for Jones at the trial that, contrary to what he had said to the police, he had gone into the house, he had gone purely as a passenger with Smith and gone in in the belief, honestly held, that Smith had permission to take the television sets from his father and that in taking them Smith was not stealing them or acting in any dishonest way. He himself, in so far as he was concerned with the matter, was not acting in any dishonest way.

JAMES LJ — . . . Mr. Rose argues that a person who had a general permission to enter premises of another person cannot be a trespasser. His submission is as short and as simple as that. Related to this case he says that a son to whom a father has given permission generally to enter the father's house cannot be a trespasser if he enters it even though he had decided in his mind before making the entry to commit a criminal offence of theft against the father once he had got into the house and had entered the house solely for the purpose of committing that theft. It is a bold submission. Mr. Rose frankly accepts that there has been no decision of the Court since this statute was passed which governs particularly this point. He has reminded us of the decision in *Byrne* v *Kinematograph Renters Society Ltd.* [1958] 2 All ER 579, which he prays in aid of his argument. In that case persons had entered a cinema by producing tickets not for the purpose of seeing the show, but for an ulterior purpose. It was held in the action, which sought to show that they entered as trespassers pursuant to a conspiracy to trespass, that in fact they were not trespassers. The important words in the judgment of Harman J at p. 593D are "They did nothing that they were not invited to do, . . ." That provides a distinction between that case and what we consider the position to be in this case.

Mr. Rose has also referred us to one of the trickery cases, a case of *Boyle* (1954) 38 Cr App R 111; [1954] 2 QB 293, and in particular the passage on pp. 112-113, 295 of the respective reports. He accepts that the trickery cases can be distinguished from such a case as the present because in the trickery cases it can be said that that which would otherwise have been consent to enter was negatived by the fact that consent was obtained by a trick. We do not gain any help in the particular case from that decision.

We were also referred to *Collins* (1972) 56 Cr App R 554; [1973] QB 100 and in particular to the long passage of Edmund Davies LJ, as he then was, commencing at pp. 559 and 104 of the respective reports where the learned Lord Justice commenced the consideration of what is involved by the words ". . . the entry must be 'as a trespasser'." At p. 561 and pp. 104-105 — again it is unnecessary to cite the long passage in full, suffice it to say that this Court on that occasion expressly approved the view expressed in Professor Smith's book on the *Law of Theft* (1968) (1st ed.) para. 462, and also the view of Professor Griew in his book on the *Theft Act* (1968) (1st ed.) para. 4-05 upon this aspect of what is involved in being a trespasser.

In our view the passage there referred to is consonant with the passage in the well known case of *Hillen and Pettigrew* v *I.C.I (Alkali) Ltd.* [1936] AC 65 where, in the speech of Lord Atkin these words appear at p. 69: "My Lords, in my opinion this duty to an invitee only extends so long as and so far as the invitee is making what can reasonably be contemplated as an ordinary and reasonable use of the premises by the invitee for the purpose for which he has been invited. He is not invited to use any part of the premises for purposes which he knows are wrongfully dangerous and constitute an improper use. As Scrutton LJ has pointedly said [in *The Calgarth* [1926] P. 93 at p. 110] 'When you invite a person into your house to use the staircase you do not invite him to slide down the banisters.'" that case of course was a civil case in which it was sought to make the defendant liable for a tort.

The decision in *Collins* (*supra*) in this Court, a decision upon the criminal law, added to the concept of trespass as a civil wrong only the mental element of *mens rea*, which is essential to the criminal offence. Taking the law as expressed in *Hillen and Pettigrew* v *I.C.I. Ltd.* (*supra*) and in the case of *Collins* (*supra*) it is our view that a person is a trespasser for the purpose of section 9 (1) (*b*) of the Theft Act 1968, if he enters premises of another knowing that he is entering in excess of the permission that has been given to him, or being reckless as to whether he is entering in excess of the permission that has been given to him to enter, providing the facts are known to the accused which enable him to realise that he is acting in excess of the permission given or that he is acting recklessly as to whether he exceeds that permission, then that is sufficient for the jury to decide that he is in fact a trespasser.

In this particular case it was a matter for the jury to consider whether, on all the facts, it was shown by the prosecution that the appellants entered with the knowledge that entry was being effected against the consent or in excess of the consent that had been given by Mr. Smith senior to his son Christopher. The jury were, by their verdict satisfied of that. It was a novel argument that we heard, interesting but one without, in our view, any foundation.

Finally, before parting with the matter, we would refer to a passage at p. 25 of the transcript of the summing-up to the jury. In particular the passage which I think one must read in full (from p. 25B to 26B). In the course of that the learned recorder said this: "I have read out the conversations they had with Detective-Sergeant Tarrant and in essence Smith said, 'My father gave me leave to take these sets and Jones was invited along to help.' If that account may be true, that is an end of the case, but if you are convinced that that night they went to the house and entered as trespassers and had no leave or licence to go there for that purpose and they intended to steal these sets and keep them permanently themselves, acting dishonestly, then you will convict them. Learned counsel for the prosecution did mention the possibility that you might come to the conclusion that they had gone into the house with leave or licence of the father and it would be possible for you to bring in a verdict simply of theft but, members of the jury, of course it is open to you to do that if you felt that the entry to the house was as a consequence of the father's leave or licence, but what counts of course for the crime of burglary to be made out is the frame of mind of each person when they go into the property. If you go in intending to steal, then your entry is burglarious, it is to trespass because no-one gave you permission to go in and steal in the house." Then the learned recorder gave an illustration of the example of a person who is invited to go into a house to make a cup of tea and that person goes in and steals the silver and he goes on: "I hope that illustrates the matter sensibly. Therefore you may find it difficult not to say, if they went in there they must have gone in order to steal because they took elaborate precautions, going there at the dead of night, you really cannot say that under any circumstances their entry to the house could have been other than trespass."

In that passage that I have just read the learned recorder put the matter properly to the jury in relation to the aspect of trespass and on this ground of appeal as upon the others we find that the case is not made out, that there was no misdirection, as I have already indicated early in the judgment, and in those circumstances the appeal will be dismissed in the case of each of the appellants.

It seems likely that the same principles will apply where the invitation to enter is an implied one — e.g., an invitation to enter a shop to purchase goods. If the defendant enters the shop intending to steal and knowing that the shopkeeper would not want him there, he should be considered a burglar.

(iii) Will the doctrine of trespass ab initio apply?

It was made clear in *R* v *Collins* that the doctrine of trespass ab initio is not part of the criminal law:

R v *Collins* (above)

EDMUND DAVIES LJ — Some question arose whether or not the appellant can be regarded as a trespasser ab initio. But we are entirely in agreement with the view expressed in Archbold that the common law doctrine of trespass ab initio has no application to burglary under the Theft Act 1968. One further matter that was canvassed ought perhaps to be mentioned. The point was raised that, the complainant not being the tenant or occupier of the dwelling-house and her mother being apparently in occupation, this girl herself could not in any event have extended an effective invitation to enter, so that even if she had expressly and with full knowledge of all material facts invited the appellant in, he would nevertheless be a trespasser. Whatever be the position in the law of tort, to regard such a proposition as acceptable in the criminal law would be unthinkable.

(c) How are 'building' and 'part of a building' defined?

Some degree of permanence will be required:

Stevens v *Gourley* (1859) 7 CBNS 99   Court of Common Pleas

A contract for the erection of a building in contravention of the provisions of the Metropolitan Building Act, 18 & 19 Vict. c. 122 (2), cannot be enforced.

A structure of wood, of considerable size (16 feet by 13), and intended to be permanently used as a shop, is a "building" within the 18 & 19 Vict. c. 122, although not let into the ground, but merely laid upon timbers upon the surface.

'Part of a building' includes any part into which the defendant has no authority to go. There need be no physical barrier between the 'part' into which the defendant is invited and the 'part' in which he is trespassing:

R v *Walkington* (1979) 68 Cr App Rep 427   Court of Appeal

At 5.40 p.m. one evening the appellant entered a department store at a time when the assistants were "cashing-up" their tills, the store closing at 6 p.m. A store detective and two colleagues noticed that the appellant only appeared to be interested in the tills in the menswear department; but he was seen to ascend an escalator to the first floor to the dress display part where there was an un-attached till in the centre of a three-sided counter, the till being left partially open and, unknown to the appellant but appreciated by the staff, empty. That drawer was located at least four yards inside the private area of the store restricted to the sales staff. The appellant moved into the opening of that counter, looked around him, and bent down and opened the drawer of the partially open till. After looking inside it, he slammed it shut and left the store when he was detained for questioning and later charged with burglary contrary to section 9 (1) (*a*) and (2) of the Theft Act 1968. The particulars of the offence alleged that he had entered the store in question as a trespasser with intent to steal therein. At the end of the prosecution case the appellant submitted that he had no case to answer in that there had been no trespass. The trial judge overruled that sub-mission and directed that jury to consider first, so far as the store was concerned, whether the area where the half-opened till was situated was a prohibited area; secondly, if so, did the appellant realise when he crossed the limit that that area was prohibited; thirdly, at the time when he crossed that limit, the first two questions being decided against the appellant, did he have the intention to steal? The jury convicted. On appeal it was contended that the judge had erred in refusing to withdraw the case from the jury in that it was wrong to divide the store artificially and the appellant could not be said to have trespassed behind the counter, alternatively, that the appellant's intention to steal was conditional, and a conditional intention fell short of the required *mens rea* for theft.

Held, that (1) whether the physical partition was sufficient to amount to an area from which the public was plainly excluded was a question of fact for the jury — the trial judge had left the issue fairly and clearly to them and there was ample evidence on which they could come to the conclusion (a) that the manage-ment had impliedly prohibited customers entering that area and (b) that the appellant knew of that prohibition; accordingly, (2) the appellant was, when he entered the prohibited area, a trespasser and the mere fact that the till in question was empty did not destroy his undoubted intention to steal the contents of it, *i.e.* any cash found therein — the fact that the till was empty was immaterial, thus the offence charged was proved and the appeal would be dismissed.

GEOFFREY LANE LJ — . . . The first question really arising out of this, which you have to consider is the use of the words 'part of a building.' The case for the prosecution is that the defendant formed an intent to steal while within this Debenhams, but before he entered the cash desk area, so that the prosecution are alleging that when he entered that area he was entering part of a building. Now, it is for you to decide whether on this section of the Theft Act that area was part of a building. Now, if you take the case of an ordinary shop, at the ordinary shop, which comprises a room with one part of it separated off by a counter, you might find little difficulty in deciding that the part of the room behind the counter was a separate part of the building from the shop area, and one which the public were not allowed to enter unless invited to do so. On the other hand, if you have the case of a large store, such as Debenhams, and there is a till placed on a table situated in the middle of the shop area, you might find it difficult, or even impossible, to say that any particular area, definable area, round that table was a separate part of the building. So that in approaching the problem you are entitled, of course, to use your own experience. You have been round shops, so you know the sort of layout you find in shops, so you may find it helpful to ask yourselves whether a shopper coming into a store and seeing the area with which you are concerned in this case would realise that that is an area to which the public were not entitled to go, and separate from the rest of the shopping area where they were entitled to go. It is a matter for you to decide. It is for you to decide whether that is the case. Coming back to the question of the definition of trespass, that is to say, of entering any part of a building as a trespasser, you now have to consider the next part of the definition, that is to say, 'with intent to steal.' Now in order to convict under this part of the section, section 9 of the Theft Act, the intent to steal must have been formed before the defendant entered that part of the area which was a separate part of the building. In other words, if, having gone into that area with some other intention, . . . he then formed the intention to steal, that would not be burglary. Likewise it would not be burglary if you were of the opinion and decide that the cash till area was not a separate part of the building but was like the rest of the shopping area, in other words, did not form a separate part of a building. So these are the two questions which you have to decide."

Finally, when considering the defintiion of 'building', the extended definition in s. 9(3) should be noted:

References in subsections (1) and (2) above to a building shall apply also to an inhabited vehicle or vessel, and shall apply to any such vehicle or vessel at times when the person having a habitation in it is not there as well as when he is.

Some difficulty may be experienced in deciding when a vehicle or vessel is 'inhabited'. For example, is a caravan 'inhabited' during the week if it is kept fully ready to be used, but only used at weekends? There is as yet no authority on this point.

(d) For s. 9(1)(b) only, when can the ulterior offence be considered to have been committed?

Two authorities have been decided in this area and they make the following points clear:

(i) For the purpose of burglary the 'appropriation' in stealing is a continuing act (as with robbery c.f. *R* v *Hale* above, page 68).

(ii) For the purpose of s. 9(1)(b) the infliction of grievous bodily harm on any person need not amount to an offence.

(i) The appropriation in stealing is a continuing act

R v Gregory (1972) 56 Cr App Rep 441   Court of Appeal.

The question whether, when or by whom there has been an appropriation of property within section 3(1) of the Theft Act 1968 has always to be determined by the jury having regard to the circumstances of the case. The length of time involved, the manner in which it came about and the number of people who can properly be said to have taken part in an appropriation will vary according to those circumstances. In the case of burglary of a dwelling-house contrary to section 9 of the Act of 1968 and before any property is removed from it, it may consist of a continuing process and involve either a single appropriation by one or more persons or a number of appropriations of the property in the house by several persons at different times during the same incident. Thus a person who may have more the appearance of a handler than a thief can nevertheless be convicted of theft, and thus of burglary, if the jury is satisfied that with the requisite dishonest intent he appropriates, or took part in the appropriation, of another person's goods.

WATKINS LJ — '. . . The applicant, when giving evidence, had said that he was innocent both of burglary and of handling stolen property. The day before the burglary had taken place he had met a man called Tony and another man called Barry in Ramsgate. Tony knew that he, the applicant, was a general dealer and he told him that one of his (Tony's) parents had died and that he was clearing out their bungalow. Thereupon it was agreed between them that the applicant should, on the following day, go to the bungalow in order to see whether there was anything there he would like to purchase. The following day he and Tony went to the bungalow. Barry opened the door to them. He went in and examined what was there for sale. He singled out the jewellery for further examination and paid a deposit on it. He left the bungalow with Tony taking the jewellery with him. He left through the back door, the damage to which he failed to observe. He had no reason to, and did not, suspect that he was involved in a dishonest transaction until the moment when he and Tony parted, when Tony warned him not to say anything if he were asked any questions about the property which came from the bungalow. He agreed that he had admitted to the police having committed burglary. This was only because they refused to allow him access to pills which he was in the habit of taking for asthma. They refused to allow him bail and falsely told him that if he admitted burglary they could influence the decision to allow him bail.

There was, therefore, but one single and uncomplicated issue between the prosecution and defence. It was, did the applicant, then intending to steal, commit burglary either by himself, or with another, by, as a trespasser, entering the bungalow and stealing the jewellery?

At the outset of his summing-up the judge confined his directions to the jury to that issue. However, towards the end of it he introduced for the jury's consideration what he called the "middle ground" circumstance, in which the jury would be entitled to convict the applicant of burglary. It was an alternative basis for a verdict of guilty which lay, so he said, in between straightforward burglary and an acquittal.

In this connection he told the jury: "So there may be that halfway house situation. If you found that he may be telling the truth in saying that his first knowledge of this was from some fellow probably called Tony, 'and I went round there to really do a bit of fencing' it would be open to you to say that he entered as a trespasser and stole therein, because he appropriated with the intention of permanently depriving the owner."

Learned counsel for the defence was surprised to hear this direction to the jury. Accordingly, during an interruption of the summing-up, he brought the judge's attention to the case of *Pitham and Hehl* (1977) 65 Cr App R 45.

In *Pitham and Hehl's* case (1977) 65 Cr App R 45, three men, namely Millman, Pitham and Hehl were charged with burglary and handling stolen goods. Millman was convicted of burglary; Pitham and Hehl were convicted of handling stolen goods. What had happened was that Millman knew that a friend of his was in prison. This friend, McGregor, had a house which contained a substantial amount of property in it. Millman, without McGregor's knowledge or consent, offered to sell this property, or some of it, to Pitham and Hehl. Pitham and Hehl agreed to buy it and either at the house, or before going there, paid Millman well below the proper price for it. The three men were seen arriving at McGregor's house in a furniture van. They entered it. Millman was arrested within it; the other two escaped, but were later also arrested. They insisted that they had not, as they put it, "Screwed the place." Nevertheless, upon being convicted of handling stolen goods, they appealed upon the ground that their handling of the furniture was in the course of stealing and therefore it was outside the scope of section 22(1) of the Theft Act 1968 — the section which contains the provisions relating to handling stolen goods. The appeal was dismissed.

In the course of his judgment Lawton LJ said at p. 49: "What was the appropriation in this case? The jury found that the two appellants had handled the property after Millman had stolen it. That is clear from their acquittal of these two appellants on count 3 of the indictment which had charged them jointly with Millman. What had Millman done? He had assumed the rights of the owner. He had done that when he took the two appellants to 20 Parry Road, showed them the property and invited them to buy what they wanted. He was then acting as the owner. He was then, in the words of the statute, 'assuming the rights of the owner.' The moment he did that he appropriated McGregor's goods to himself. The appropriation was complete. After this appropriation had been completed there was no question of these two appellants taking part, in the words of section 22, in dealing with the goods 'in the course of the stealing.' "It follows that no problem arises in this case. It may well be that some of the situations which the two learned professors" (referring to Professors Smith and Griew) "envisage and discuss in their books may have to be dealt with at some future date, but not in this case. The facts are too clear."

It was a case, therefore, of what might be called instantaneous appropriation. But not every appropriation under the Theft Act need be or indeed is instantaneous. In *Hale* (1979) 68 Cr App R 415, Eveleigh LJ, in giving the judgment of the Court, said at p. 418: "It thus becomes necessary to consider what is 'appropriation' or, according to section 3 'any assumption by a person of the rights of an owner.' An assumption of the rights of an owner describes the conduct of a person towards a particular article. It is conduct which usurps the rights of the owner. To say that that conduct is over and done with as soon as he lays hands upon the property, or when he first manifests an intention to deal with it as his, is contrary to commonsense and to the natural meaning of words. A thief who steals a motor car first opens the door. Is it to be said that the act of starting up the motor is no more a part of the theft? In the present case there can be little doubt that if the appellant had been interrupted after the seizure of the jewellery box the jury would have been entitled to find that the appellant and his accomplice were assuming the rights of an owner at the time when the jewellery box was seized. However, the act of appropriation does not suddenly cease. It is a continuous act and it is a matter for the jury to decide whether or not the act of appropriation has finished."

Nor do we think that in a given criminal enterprise involving theft there can necessarily be only one "appropriation" within section 3(1) of the Theft Act 1968. It seems to us that the question of whether, when and by whom there has been an appropriation of property has always to be determined by the jury having regard to the circumstances of the case. The length of time involved, the manner in which it came about and the number of people who can properly be said to have taken part in an appropriation will vary according to those circumstances. In a case of burglary of a dwelling-house and before any property is removed from it, it may consist of a continuing process and involve either a single appropriation by one or more person or a number of appropriations of the property in the house by several persons at different times during the same incident. If this were not a correct exposition of the law of appropriation, startling and disturbing consequences could arise out of the presence of two or more trespassers in a dwelling-house.

Thus a person who may have more the appearance of a handler than the thief can nevertheless still be convicted of theft, and thus of burglary, if the jury are satisfied that with the requisite dishonest intent he appropriated, or took part in the appropriation, of another person's goods.

This we think was the substance of Judge Streeter's final direction to the jury about the "middle ground" which I have quoted. It was, in our view, an accurate and clear explanation of factual circumstances upon which the jury were entitled to convict the applicant were they minded so to find the facts.

Accordingly if it was on the middle ground that the jury convicted, we cannot regard it as unsafe or unsatisfactory.

(ii) For the purposes of s. 9(1)(b) the infliction of grievous bodily harm on any person need not amount to an offence:

R v *Jenkins* [1983] Crim LR 386   Court of Appeal

The defendants were charged with burglary contrary to section 9 (1) (*b*) of the Theft Act 1968 the particulars of which were that they, having entered a building as trespassers, inflicted grievous bodily harm on Jeffrey Wilson therein. The recorder permitted the jury under the provisions of section 6 (3) of the Criminal Law Act 1967 to consider an alternative verdict of assault occasioning actual bodily harm. The jury returned a verdict of not guilty as charged but guilty of assault occasioning actual bodily harm. The defendants appealed against conviction on the ground that the recorder was wrong in leaving the alternative verdict to the jury.

Held, allowing the appeals, that if the majority decision in *Clarence* (1888) 22 QBD 23 was correct as was accepted in *Snewing* [1972] Crim LR 267 and *Carpenter* (unreported, July 30, 1979) the meaning of the phrase "inflict grievous bodily harm" in section 9 (1) (*b*) would not be the same as the meaning of that expression in section 20 of the Offences against the Person Act 1861. If the decision in *Salisbury* [1976] VR 452 as adopted in *Wilson* (*The Times,* February 7, 1983) was right the meaning of the phrase in section 20 held in *Wilson* would cover the meaning of the phrase in section 9 (1) (*b*). Their Lordships were bound by *Wilson* to hold that the meaning of the words in section 20 was not exclusively restricted to assaults within the meaning of assault in section 47 of the 1861 Act. The expression had the wider meaning in section 9 (1) (*b*) and therefore, for the reasons in *Wilson*, it was not open to a jury to return an alternative verdict of assault occasioning actual bodily harm. The recorder was wrong in leaving to the jury the alternative verdict.

Commentary. Section 9 (1) (*a*) of the Theft Act requires an intent "to commit any such *offence* as is mentioned in subsection (2)." Section 9 (1) (*b*), however, requires that the defendant "steals or attempts to steal . . . or inflicts or attempts to inflict on any person therein any grievous bodily harm" and does not use the word "offence." Stealing and attempting to steal are obviously offences but it is possible to inflict or attempt to inflict grievous bodily harm without committing an offence — as, for example, where it is done in self-defence. However, the absence of the word "offence" in paragraph (*b*) is an accident. Under the draft Bill proposed by the Criminal Law Revision Committee and the Bill introduced into Parliament, paragraph (*b*) read: "having entered any building or part of a building as a trespasser he commits or attempts to commit *any such offence*."

This would have included the commission or attempted commission of rape or criminal damage. The House of Lords thought the inclusion of these offences unnecessary and that the paragraph should apply only to offences of theft and the infliction of grievous bodily harm contrary to section 20 of the 1861 Act. See Smith, "Burglary under the Theft Bill" [1968] Crim LR 367. The amendment was not well drafted and does not expressly require the infliction of grievous bodily harm to be an offence. There is, however, no doubt that Parliament intended to require it to be an offence (HL Deb, Vol. 291, col. 75) and it is submitted that, reading the section as a whole, the proper interpretation so requires: Smith and Hogan, *Criminal Law* (4th ed.), p. 593.

The Court of Appeal's decision in *R* v *Jenkins* was overruled by the House of Lords ([1983] 3 All ER 448). The decision of the House was on a different ground — one which is quite compatible with the above conclusion of the Court of Appeal.

(2) THE MENS REA OF BURGLARY

There are two aspects to the mens rea of burglary;

(a) *The defendant must have the intention to enter as a trespasser, or knowledge that he has trespassed.*

(b) *The defendant must be shown to have either:*

(i)   the intention to commit the ulterior offence for a s. 9(1)(a) burglary, or
(ii)   the mens rea of the ulterior offence for a s. 9(1)(b) burglary.

In both cases conditional intention is irrelevant.

(a)   The 'intention to trespass' is dealt with above under Actus Reus, section
(b): When is a defendant trespassing? (p. 78).
(b)   (i)   The intention to commit the ulterior offence for a s. 9(1)(a) burglary.

For s. 9(1)(a) the ulterior offences are to be found in s. 9(2):

Section 9(2) Theft Act 1968

*The offences referred to in subsection (1)(a) above are offences of stealing anything
in the building or part of a building in question, of inflicting on any person therein
any grievous bodily harm or raping any woman therein, and of doing unlawful
damage to the building or anything therein.*

(b)   (ii)   The mens rea of the ulterior offence for a s. 9(1)(b) burglary.

In fact, as is shown by *R* v *Jenkins* (above), no reference to 'offence' appears in
s. 9(1)(b);

Section 9(1)(b) Theft Act 1968

*Having entered any building or part of a building as a trespasser he steals or attempts
to steal anything in the building or that part of it or inflicts or attempts to inflict
on any person therein any grievous bodily harm.*

Stealing and attempting to steal are obviously offences but, as was held in *R* v
Jenkins, it is not necessary to prove an offence under ss. 18 or 20 of the offences
Against the Person Act 1861 where the allegation is that the defendant inflicted or
attempted to inflict on any person 'any grievous bodily harm'.
    The irrelevance of 'conditional intention' where the indictment does not specify
an intention to steal specific articles was emphasised in the following case:

Attorney-General's References (Nos. 1 & 2 of 1979) [1979] 2 WLR 578
                                                                    Court of Appeal

    In the first reference a grocer who lived above his shop heard the backdoor
open and close late one night and intercepted the defendant who was ascending
the stairs. The police were called and arrested the defendant. They asked him

why he had entered the house and he replied "To rob £2,000" and on being asked why he thought there was £2,000 there he said "I don't know, I was just going to take something." The indictment before the Crown Court averred that he had entered the grocer's premises as a trespasser "with intent to steal therein." The trial judge withdrew the case from the jury at the close of the prosecution case and directed an acquittal. The Attorney-General referred to the court for opinion the question whether a man who had entered a house as a trespasser with the intention of stealing money therein was entitled to be acquitted of an offence against section 9 (1) (a) of the Theft Act 1968 on the ground that his intention to steal was conditional upon his finding money in the house.

In the second reference a householder heard a sound at the French windows at the rear of her house. She called the police who went to the rear of the house and found the defendant holding and turning the handle of the French windows and inserting a long thin stick between the door and the doorframe. Later at the police station the defendant made a written statement in which he said "I wasn't going to do any damage in the house, only see if there was anything lying around." The indictment averred that the defendant had attempted to enter the dwelling house concerned "with intent to steal therein." At the close of the prosecution case the judge directed the jury to return a verdict of not guilty upon the ground that the evidence did not disclose a present intention to steal but merely a conditional intention. The Attorney-General referred to the court for opinion the question whether a man who was attempting to enter a house as a trespasser with the intention of stealing anything of value which he might find therein was entitled to be acquitted of the offence of attempted burglary on the ground that at the time of the attempt his intention was insufficient to amount to "the intention of stealing anything" necessary for conviction under section 9 of the Theft Act 1968.

On the hearing of both references: —

Held, (1) that, under section 9 (1) (a) of the Theft Act 1968, the offence of burglary was committed if a person entered a building as a trespasser with an intention to steal; that, where a person was charged with burglary, it was no defence to show that he did not intend to steal any specific objects, and, accordingly, the fact that the intention to steal was conditional on finding money in the house did not entitle a person to be acquitted on a charge of entering premises as a trespasser with intent to steal therein; and that the question asked in the first reference was to be answered in the negative.

Dictum in *R* v *Husseyn (Note)* (1977) 67 Cr App R 131, 132, CA explained.

R v *Walkington* [1979] 1 WLR 1169, CA applied.

R v *Easom* [1971] 2 QB 315, CA distinguished.

5 AGGRAVATED BURGLARY

Two main problems arise:

(a)   What is a weapon of offence?
(b)   When is 'at the time of the burglary'?

Section 10 Theft Act 1968

(1) A person is guilty of aggravated burglary if he commits any burglary and at the time has with him any firearm or imitation firearm, any weapon of offence, or any explosive; and for this purpose—

(a)   'firearm' includes an airgun or air pistol, and 'imitation firearm' means anything which has the appearance of being a firearm, whether capable of being discharged or not; and
(b)   'weapon of offence' means any article made or adapted for use for causing injury to or incapacitating a person, or intended by the person having it with him for such use; and
(c)   'explosive' means any article manufactured for the purpose of producing a practical effect by explosion, or intended by the person having it with him for that purpose.

(2) A person guilty of aggravated burglary shall on conviction on indictment be liable to imprisonment for life.

(a) What is a weapon of offence?

'Weapon of offence' in s. 10 is wider than 'offensive weapon' in s. 1(4) of the Prevention of Crime Act 1953.

Smith: *The Law of Theft* (5th ed., para. 364)

The definition of "weapon of offence" is somewhat wider than that of "offensive weapon" in s. 1 (4) of the Prevention of Crime Act 1953. It would seem that (i) articles made for causing injury to a person, (ii) articles adapted for causing injury to a person, and (iii) articles which D has with him for that purpose are precisely the same as under the 1953 Act. Thus, (i) would include a service rifle, or bayonet, a revolver, a cosh, knuckleduster, dagger or flick-knife; (ii) would include razor blades inserted in a potato, a bottle broken for the purpose, a chair leg studded with nails; and (iii) would include anything that could cause injury to the person if so desired by the person using it — a sheath-knife, a razor, a shotgun, a sandbag, a pick-axe handle, a bicycle chain or a stone. To these categories, however, s. 10 (1) (b) adds (iv) any article made for *incapacitating* a person, (v) any article adapted for *incapacitating* a person, and (vi) any article which D has with him for that purpose. Articles *made* for incapacitating a person might include a pair of handcuffs and a gag; articles *adapted* for incapacitating a person might include a pair of socks made into a gag, and articles *intended* for incapacitating a person might include sleeping pills to put in the night-watchman's tea, a rope to tie him up, a sack to put over hs head, pepper to throw in his face, and so on.

In the cases of (i), (ii), (iv) and (v) the prosecution need prove no more than that the article was made or adapted for use for causing injury or incapacitating as the case may be. In the case of (iii) and (vi) clearly they must go further and prove that D was carrying the thing with him with the intention of using it to injure or incapacitate, not necessarily in any event, but at least if the need arose.

(b) When is 'at the time of the burglary'?

Where the burglary alleged is a s. 9(1)(a) burglary the relevant time is the time of the trespassory entry. For a s. 9(1)(b) burglary the relevant time is the time that the ulterior offence is committed:

R v *Francis and Another* [1982] Crim LR 363   Court of Appeal

The defendants, armed with sticks, demanded entry to a dwelling house by banging and kicking the door. As a result of the banging and kicking, the occupant, with whom the defendants were acquainted, allowed them to enter. Either just before entering the house, or soon after entering the house, the defendants discarded their sticks. They subsequently stole items from the house and committed other offences against the occupant. The defendants were charged, *inter alia*, with aggravated burglary, contrary to section 10 (1) of the Theft Act 1968. At their trial on indictment the judge directed the jury that the prosecution had to prove that the defendants entered the house as trespassers; that having entered they stole; and that when they entered they were armed with weapons of offence. The jury returned a verdict of guilty and the defendants appealed against conviction.

Held, allowing the appeal and substituting convictions for burglary, that having regard to the provisions of sections 9 and 10 of the Theft Act 1968 it was clear that if a person entered a building as a trespasser with intent to steal, he was guilty of burglary under section 9 (1) (*a*) and if at the time of entry he had with him a weapon of offence, he was guilty of aggravated burglary; and that if a person entered a building as a trespasser and stole under section 9 (1) (*b*) he committed burglary at the moment when he stole and he committed aggravated burglary only if he had with him a weapon of offence at the time when he stole; that, accordingly, the judge misdirected the jury that all the prosecution were required to prove was that the defendants were armed when they entered the house as trespassers.

Commentary. If the defendants, being armed with weapons of offence, entered as trespassers but without any intention to steal, they were not at that time guilty of burglary, aggravated or otherwise. If, having so entered and being armed, they stole, they thereupon committed aggravated burglary. If, however, they had discarded the weapons before committing the theft, they were guilty only of simple burglary. The direction wrongly instructed the jury to convict of aggravated burglary in this last situation.

6   TAKING A CONVEYANCE

Section 12 of the 1968 Act creates three or possibly four offences. The major problems encountered in interpretation are as follows:

(1) TAKING A CONVEYANCE WITHOUT AUTHORITY

(a)   *ACTUS REUS*

(i)   What is a conveyance?
(ii)   What constitutes a 'taking'?
(iii)   When is the taking 'for his own or another's use'?
(iv)   To what extent will the consent of the owner prevent the commission of the offence?
(v)   What constitutes 'other lawful authority'?

(b)   *MENS REA*

Must the defendant know he is taking the vehicle without consent?

(2) & (3) DRIVING OR ALLOWING ONESELF TO BE CARRIED

(a)   *ACTUS REUS*

(i)   Is actual movement necessary?
(ii)   The vehicle must actually have been taken without consent, but must an offence of 'taking' actually have been committed?
(iii)   Can a 'taker' also commit this offence when driving the vehicle he has 'taken'?

(b)   *MENS REA*

Must the defendant know he is taking the vehicle without consent?

(4) TAKING A PEDAL CYCLE WITHOUT AUTHORITY

The problems of interpretation are similar to those encountered in interpreting offences (1), (2) and (3) above.

Section 12 Theft Act 1968

(1) Subject to subsections (5) and (6) below, a person shall be guilty of an offence if, without having the consent of the owner or other lawful authority, he takes any conveyance for his own or another's use or, knowing that any conveyance has been taken without such authority, drives it or allows himself to be carried in or on it.

(2) A person guilty of an offence under subsection (1) above shall on conviction on indictment be liable to imprisonment for a term not exceeding three years.

(3) Offences under subsection (1) above and attempts to commit them shall be deemed for all purposes to be arrestable offences within the meaning of section 2 of the Criminal Law Act 1967.

(4) If on the trial of an indictment for theft the jury are not satisfied that the accused committed theft, but it is proved that the accused committed an offence under subsection (1) above, the jury may find him guilty of the offence under subsection (1).

(5) Subsection (1) above shall not apply in relation to pedal cycles; but, subject to subsection (6) below, a person who, without having the consent of the owner or other lawful authority, takes a pedal cycle for his own or another's use, or rides a pedal cycle knowing it to have been taken without such authority, shall on summary conviction be liable to a fine not exceeding fifty pounds.

(6) A person does not commit an offence under this section by anything done in the belief that he has lawful authority to do it or that he would have the owner's consent if the owner knew of his doing it and the circumstances of it.

(7) For purposes of this section—

(a)   'conveyance' means any conveyance constructed or adapted for the carriage of a person or persons whether by land, water or air, except that it does not include a conveyance constructed or adapted for use only under the control of a person not carried in or on it, and 'drive' shall be construed accordingly; and

(b)   'owner', in relation to a conveyance which is the subject of a hiring agreement or hire-purchase agreement, means the person in possession of the conveyance under that agreement.

(1) TAKING A CONVEYANCE WITHOUT AUTHORITY

(a) Actus reus

The offence under s. 12 was specifically created to deal with the problem of temporary use of a car which did not belong to the defendant. The police efficiency at returning such cars to the owners means that a 'joy-rider' who abandons a car can expect the owner to get it back. It is thus very difficult to prove 'an intention to permanently deprive' for the purpose of obtaining a conviction under s. 1 of the 1968 Theft Act. The essence of a s. 12 offence is temporary deprivation. Where it is possible to prove that the defendant did intend permanent deprivation the more serious charge under s. 1 will lie. This might be the case where professional car thieves take several vehicles and swap the parts of them around with a view to resale of the 'new' vehicles to the unsuspecting public.

(i) What is a conveyance?

See s. 12(7)(a) above. This subsection fell to be interpreted in *Neal* v *Gribble:*

Neal v Gribble [1978] RTR 409   Queen's Bench Division

> The defendants, who went to a field where horses were grazing, attached ropes to three of them including a Palamino stallion for use as bridles, and rode them away. The defendants were jointly charged with taking a conveyance, namely a Palamino stallion, without the consent of the owner or other lawful authority, contrary to section 12(1) of the Theft Act 1968. The justices were of opinion that a horse was not a 'conveyance' for the purpose of the section and that attaching a bridle to a horse did not constitute 'adapting' it for the carriage of a person, and they dismissed the information.
>
> On appeal by the prosecutor:
>
> **Held**, dismissing the appeal, that since the word 'conveyance' in its ordinary meaning did not include a horse, and section 12 was directed towards artefacts rather than animals, a horse was not a conveyance in the meaning of the section; and that, even if that were wrong, putting a bridle on a horse did not 'adapt' it, but simply made it easier to ride.

Excluded from the operation of the section are vehicles with no space for anyone to ride on them, e.g., a cart which is pushed along. Boats and aircraft are, however, included.

(ii) What constitutes a 'taking'?

It seems that two elements must be shown. There must be an unauthorised taking of possession and control and some movement of the vehicle, however small:

R v Bogacki [1973] QB 832   Court of Appeal

The three defendants boarded a bus in a garage late at night and one of them attempted to start the engine but the bus did not move, and the defendants left the garage. They were charged on indictment with attempting to take a motor vehicle without authority. At the trial the judge directed the jury that the complete offence of taking a conveyance without authority, contrary to section 12 (1) of the Theft Act, 1968, was committed if there was an unauthorised use of the conveyance, and that movement of the conveyance was not an essential part of the offence. All the defendants were convicted.

On the defendants' appeals against conviction:—

Held, allowing the appeals, that the judge's direction was wrong because although the offence under section 12 of the Theft Act 1968 had replaced the old offence of taking and driving away, the concept of movement was still built into the word "takes," and that before there could be a conviction of the completed offence it had to be shown that there had been an unauthorised taking of possession or control followed by some movement of the conveyance, however small, and that therefore the convictions had to be quashed although in fact there was ample evidence to justify convictions of attempt.

(iii) When is the taking 'for his own or another's use'?

Does the conveyance actually have to be used 'as a conveyance'?

R v Pearce [1973] Crim LR 321   Court of Appeal

P was convicted of taking a conveyance contrary to section 12, Theft Act 1968. He took an inflatable rubber dinghy from outside a life-boat depot, putting it on a trailer and driving it away. He appealed on the ground that on a proper construction of section 12 the taking must be the removal of the conveyance by propelling it in some way or removing it in some way in its own element *e.g.* in the case of a boat removing it in some way along water.

Held, dismissing the appeal, the section given its ordinary and natural meaning covered what P did. Whether intentionally or accidentally the element of driving away had been omitted from the section.

If this case were to be followed there would seem to be no requirement that the vehicle must be used 'as a conveyance'. This is so unless the court inferred, as Smith suggests (J. C. Smith, *The Law of Theft*, 5th ed. para 284), that 'D intended to use the dinghy for its normal purposes'. There is certainly no indication that the court enquired into the use to which the boat would be put in the future. The emphasis in the case is on the omission of the word 'driving' from s. 12. This seems to indicate that the court believed that nothing beyond a 'taking for the defendant's own purposes' was required. What the defendant intended to do with the dinghy did not seem important to the court. That was not the view taken in *R v Bow:*

R v *Bow* (1976) 64 Cr App Rep 54   Court of Appeal

The appellant, his brother and father were in his brother's car when stopped on the narrow road of a private estate by gamekeepers who suspected them of poaching. One gamekeeper blocked the road with his Land Rover. On the game-keeper refusing to move the Land Rover, a scuffle ensued and during it the appellant got into the Land Rover, sat in the driving seat, did not start the engine, but released the handbrake causing the Land Rover to coast downhill some 200 yards, thereby to enable his brother's car to be driven off. The appellant was convicted of taking a conveyance without authority contrary to section 12 (1) of the Theft Act 1968. He appealed against conviction on the ground that the moving of an obstructing vehicle only so far as necessary could not amount to an offence under section 12 (1) since his purpose was not to use it as a conveyance but to remove it as an obstruction.

Held, that the taking of a vehicle by a person "for his own or another's use" within section 12 (1) of the Theft Act 1968 meant that the vehicle must be used as a conveyance, *i.e.* as a means of transport, and whether the moving of an obstructing vehicle involved using it as a conveyance depended on the facts of each particular case; and in the present case as the appellant had driven the Land Rover some 200 yards, albeit without using its engine, that necessarily involved its use as a conveyance, and the appellant had been rightly convicted for he could not be heard to say that the taking was not for that use.

BRIDGE LJ – The interpretation of the phrase "for his own or another's use" as meaning "for his own or another's use as a conveyance" would fall into line, we think, with the discriminations suggested in *Smith and Hogan's Criminal Law,* 3rd ed. (1973) at p. 462, where the following passage occurs: "But subject to the requirement of taking, the offence does seem, in essence, to consist in steal-ing a ride. This seems implicit in the requirement that the taking be for 'his own or another's use.' Thus if D releases the handbrake of a car so that it runs down an incline, or releases a boat from its moorings so that it is carried off by the tide this would not as such be an offence within the section."

Pausing at that point in the quotation from the textbook, the reason why neither of those examples would constitute an offence within the section would be that in neither case, although the conveyance had been moved, would it have been used as a conveyance.

The quotation from the textbook goes on: "The taking must be for D's use or the use of another and if he intends to make no use of the car or boat there would be no offence under section 12. But it would be enough if D were to release the boat from its moorings so that he would be carried downstream in the boat." In that case, since he would be carried downstream in the boat there would be a use of the boat as a conveyance, as a means of transporting him downstream.

So far the court is in agreement with Mr. Toulson's submissions. But then the next step has to be taken. The next step is, as Mr. Toulson submits, that merely to move a vehicle which constitutes an obstruction so that it shall be an obstruc-tion no more cannot involve use of the vehicle as a conveyance. It is at this point that the submission requires to be carefully analysed.

Clearly one can envisage instances in which an obstructing vehicle was merely pushed out of the way a yard or two which would not involve any use of it as a conveyance. But the facts involved in the removal of the obstructing vehicle must be examined in each case.

Mr. Matheson, for the Crown, meets this submission squarely by pointing to the circumstance that here the Land Rover was in the ordinary sense of the English language driven for 200 yards. Attention has already been drawn to the fact that no distinction was relied upon by Mr. Toulson between a vehicle driven under its own power and a vehicle driven by being allowed to coast down hill. Mr. Matheson says that again, as a matter of ordinary use of English, in the course of driving the vehicle a distance of 200 yards the appellant was inevitably using it as a conveyance and that his motive for so doing is immaterial. This submission for the Crown, it is pointed out to us, is in line with another suggestion by Professor Smith in his textbook on the *Law of Theft*, 2nd ed. (1972), paragraph 317, where he says: "Probably driving, whatever the motive, would be held to be 'use.'"

In reply, Mr. Toulson submits that even if it be right that the appellant had in the ordinary sense of the word to drive the Land Rover for 200 yards, and even if that did involve its use as a conveyance, nevertheless the offence was still not made out because the purpose of the taking was not to use the conveyance as a conveyance but merely to remove it as an obstruction. He emphasises that the words of the section are: "takes for his own use," not "takes and uses." This is in our judgment a very subtle and refined distinction and if it were admitted it would open a very wide door to persons who take conveyances without authority and use them as such to dispute their guilt on the ground that the motive of the taking was something other than the use of the conveyance as such.

The short answer, we think, is that where as here, a conveyance is taken and moved in a way which necessarily involves its use as a conveyance, the taker cannot be heard to say that the taking was not for that use. If he has in fact taken the conveyance and used it as such, his motive in so doing is, as Mr. Matheson submits, quite immaterial. It follows, in our judgment, that the trial judge was right, not only to reject the submission of no case, but also to direct the jury, as he did, that on the undisputed facts the appellant had taken the Land Rover for his own use. Accordingly the appeal will be dismissed.

Appeal dismissed.

R v *Pearce* was not cited in *R* v *Bow*. It may well be that the only way to reconcile the two cases is to accept that an intention to use the vehicle as a conveyance in the future would be sufficient. It may well be, however, that in a future case on facts similar to those in *R* v *Pearce* a court would find that no s. 12 offence had been committed until the vehicle was actually used as a conveyance at a later date.

The defendant's argument in *R* v *Bow* that he did not 'intend' to use the vehicle as a conveyance confuses 'intention' (in the sense usually used in the criminal law) with 'motive'.

In *R* v *Bow* the defendant used the conveyance knowing that it was certain that he would be conveyed in it. He therefore intended to use it as a conveyance (*see R* v *Belfon* [1976] 3 All ER 46 and *R* v *Moloney* [1985] 2 WLR 648 (HL)).

Use for the conveyance of persons was held to be necessary in *R* v *Stokes;*

R v Stokes [1982] Crim LR 695   Court of Appeal

   The appellant and two friends were driving past the home of a former girl
friend of one of them. The girl's car was parked outside. As a practical joke the
men moved it round the corner so that she would think it had been stolen. The
appellant was charged, *inter alia,* with taking a vehicle for his/another's use,
contrary to section 12 of the Theft Act 1968. At his trial there was a conflict
of evidence as to whether anyone was in the car when it was being moved. The
appellant was convicted and sentenced to seven days' imprisonment and his
licence was endorsed. He appealed on the ground, *inter alia,* that there was no
evidence that the vehicle had been taken for his own or another's use.
   Held, allowing the appeal and quashing the conviction, that on the authority
of *Bow* (1977) 64 Cr App R 54 "use" of a vehicle necessarily involved use as a
conveyance. The trial judge had failed specifically to emphasise the importance
of establishing that someone was being conveyed inside the car or riding in it as
an element of its use as a conveyance, and there was a danger that the jury had
convicted on an interpretation of section 12 of the Theft Act 1968 which
involved the use of the car as a conveyance even if no-one was inside it but
merely if one or other of the men involved was pushing it from outside.

R v Stokes was followed in *R v Dunn and Derby.*

R v Dunn and Derby [1984] Crim LR 367   Snaresbrook Crown Court

   The two defendants were seen by police officers at about 7.15 p.m. holding a
motor bike and apparently tampering with it. On being questioned they allegedly
denied touching it, but later admitted to having wheeled the bike a distance of
about 40 yards to look at it by a porch light. At the close of the prosecution
case it was submitted on behalf of the defendants that there was no case to
answer. It was submitted that, takes any conveyance "for his own or another's
use" meant for use as a conveyance, *i.e.* as a means of transport. The mischief
aimed at was stealing a ride. *Bow* (1977) 64 Cr App R 54 cited. Although the
defendants had taken unauthorised possession of the conveyance, and wheeled it
40 yards, it had not been used as a means of transport. To move it from A to B,
to look at it out of curiosity was no offence. The Crown conceded these submissions, and accordingly the learned judge directed the jury to enter a verdict
of not guilty.
   Commentary. It is a common fallacy to say that the mischief at which the
section is aimed is stealing a ride. If it were so, *Pearce* [1973] Crim LR 321, CA
(taking inflatable rubber dinghy away on a trailer) would be wrongly decided.
Assuming that *Pearce* is right, the defendants in the present case would have been
guilty if it had been their intention to use the bike at some later time as a means
of transport. It must be assumed that in *Pearce* the court was satisfied that the
defendant was carrying off the dinghy with the intention of using it to sail in
and not merely, for example, as a paddling pool for his children.
   If the defendants took the bike to the light merely to admire it, they were
certainly not guilty. If they took it there so that they could see how to start it
and then ride away on it, it is submitted that they were guilty, not merely of an

attempt but, following *Pearce*, of the full offence. If they took it to the light to examine it in order to decide whether or not it was a machine worth taking for a ride, we have a problem similar to that in *Husseyn* (1978) 67 Cr App R 131 — is a conditional intention to use the thing as a conveyance enough?

(iv) To what extent will the consent of the owner prevent the commission of the offence?

The answer to this question is contained in two lines of authority. They are reconcilable, but combined, could lead to undesirable results. The first line is represented by *R v Phipps and McGill* (below) and *McKnight v Davies* [1974] RTR 4:

R v Phipps and McGill [1970] RTR 209   Court of Appeal

M, with the consent of the car's owner, borrowed it for a particular purpose on one evening, the owner having agreed to lend the car only on the express condition that it was returned directly afterwards. M did not return the car directly afterwards, and subsequently drove it for a different purpose, the car not being returned until later. He was charged with contravening section 217(1) of the Road Traffic Act 1960, as amended, in taking and driving away the car without the owner's consent or other lawful authority, and he raised a defence under section 217(2), but there was evidence that he had no reason to think that the owner would approve of the subsequent use of the car. The jury were directed that, as from the time M decided not to return the car on the evening and drove it off, then as a matter of law and common sense, if he did not have the owner's permission, M took and drove it away in contravention of section 217(1), but that he was not guilty if he reasonably believed that, if he had asked, the owner would have agreed in all the circumstances to the car being kept for the extra period until it was returned. M was convicted.

On appeal, on the contention that, the original taking and use being with consent, the subsequent failure to return and continued use of the car without consent could not amount to taking and driving away contrary to section 217:

Held, rejecting the contention, that the jury had been properly and accurately directed; and that, there being ample evidence to support the conviction, the appeal should be dismissed.

FENTON ATKINSON LJ — . . . The question which was raised in the notice of appeal and on which the court gave leave was this: the original taking and using of the car being with the permission of Mr Larking, could it be said that McGill was guilty of the offence of taking and driving away the car because afterwards he failed to return it at the appropriate time and continued using it without consent or authority? The same point arose, of course, in the case of Phipps who was a passenger being carried in that vehicle.

The point that Miss Pearlman takes on their behalf is that so long as the original taking and driving away was with the consent of the owner it really does not matter for how long they kept it thereafter, or what they did with it short of actually stealing it, and that if they decided the next day to drive off or to take it to the continent on a holiday, they could not have been taking and driving away without consent or authority, even though they knew perfectly well that the owner would object strongly to what they were doing. In our view, that is an impossible submission, with respect to Miss Pearlman, who said everything possible in support of this appeal.

R v Phipps and McGill was decided on the old law but the defendant still had to be shown to have acted 'without the consent of the owner'. There is no reason to believe that the 1968 Theft Act changed the law in that respect. Indeed, *R v Phipps and McGill* was followed in *McKnight v Davies:*

McKnight v Davies [1974] RTR 4   Queen's Bench Division

. . . The defendant was employed as a lorry driver. His duty was to deliver goods from his employer's depot to shops and on completion of deliveries to return the lorry to the depot. He was not permitted to use the employer's vehicle for his own purposes. At about 6 pm on 30 November 1972, the defendant, having completed his deliveries, was driving his employer's four-ton lorry back to the depot when the roof of the lorry struck a low bridge. When the defendant saw the damage to the lorry he was scared. He drove the lorry to a public house and had a drink. After that he drove three men to their homes on the outskirts of Cardiff, drove back to the centre of the city and had a drink at another public house and then drove to the area where he lived and parked the lorry near his home. He drove the lorry to his employer's depot at 6.20am on 1 December 1972. The defendant concocted a story which he later admitted was not true, that he had left the lorry at the depot at 7pm and that someone must have broken into it during the night. The tripometer of the lorry had recorded about 30 miles in excess of the defendant's delivery route for 30 November 1972.
It was contended by the defendant that the facts did not disclose an offence in that he had been lawfully in possession of the lorry and had not 'taken' it within the meaning of section 12 of the Act of 1968.
It was contended by the prosecutor that the defendant 'took' the lorry when he drove it away from the first public house he visited.
The justices were of opinion that, when the defendant decided not to return the lorry immediately to the depot, he ceased to control it for his employer's purposes and that his use of the lorry for his own purposes constituted an unlawful taking; and, accordingly, they convicted the defendant. . . .

LORD WIDGERY CJ — . . . I have no hesitation in saying that we should follow the decision of the Court of Appeal in *R v Phipps* [1970] RTR 209. It is, therefore, not in itself an answer in the present case for the defendant to say that he was lawfully put in control of the vehicle by his employers. The difficulty which I feel is in defining the kind of unauthorised activity on the part of the driver, whose original control of the vehicle is lawful, which will amount to an unlawful taking for the purpose of section 12. Not every brief, unauthorised diversion from his proper route by an employed driver in the course of his working day will necessarily involve a 'taking' of the vehicle for his own use. If, however, as in *R v Wibberley* [1966] 2 QB 214 he returns to the vehicle after he has parked it for the night and drives if off on an unauthorised errand, he is clearly guilty of the offence. Similarly, if in the course of his working day, or otherwise while his authority to use the vehicle is unexpired, he appropriates it to his own use in a manner which repudiates the rights of the true owner, and shows that he has assumed control of the vehicle for his own purposes, he can properly be regarded as having taken the vehicle within section 12.

As Professor Smith puts it (in *Smith's Law of Theft* 2nd ed (1972) p 113) he has

'. . . altered the character of his control over the vehicle, so that he no longer held as servant but assumed possession of it in the legal sense.'

In the present case I think that the defendant took the vehicle when he left the first public house. At that point he assumed control for his own purposes in a manner which was inconsistent with his duty to his employer to finish his round and drive the vehicle to the depot. I think that the justices reached the correct conclusion and I would dismiss the appeal.

In both *R* v *Phipps and McGill* and *McKnight* v *Davies* the court used the phrase 'for his own or another's use' to mean 'for the defendant's or another's purposes'. However, as we have already seen, in *R* v *Bow* and *R* v *Stokes* the words 'for his own or another's use' were used to mean 'for the defendant's use *as a conveyance*'.

The courts have thus given the phrase two separate and distinct meanings. It seems unlikely that the legislature meant the same phrase to signify two such different things simultaneously, and the courts may in future prefer one interpretation to the other. This may particularly be so because there is a line of cases which are difficult to reconcile with *R* v *Phipps and McGill* and *McKnight* v *Davies*. The following cases establish that a consent to take a vehicle, obtained from the owner of that vehicle, if operative at the time of taking, is valid and no offence is committed under s. 12 even if the consent is obtained by fundamental fraud.

The combined effect of *R* v *Phipps and McGill* and *McKnight* v *Davies* if followed together with *R* v *Peart* and *Whittaker* v *Campbell* (below) is most curious. It seems that the man who is honest at the outset but goes beyond the bounds of the authority given to him is liable to be convicted, but the expert confidence trickster who obtains the owner's consent to the taking by fraud cannot be convicted thereafter, whatever he does with the vehicle:

R v *Peart* [1970] 2 QB 672   Court of Appeal

The defendant was tried and convicted of taking a motor vehicle for his own use without having the consent of the owner contrary to section 12 (1) of the Theft Act, 1968. He had made false representations to the owner of a motor vehicle, saying that he urgently needed to borrow a car for the afternoon to drive to the nearby town of Alnwick to sign a contract. The owner consented in those circumstances to lend his vehicle provided it was returned that evening. The defendant drove the vehicle not to Alnwick but to Burnley and failed to return it that day. The deputy chairman directed the jury that consent induced by dishonest statements was not real consent.

On appeal on the ground, inter alia, that the deputy chairman had misdirected the jury by ruling that a consent induced by dishonest statements could not be a true consent for the purposes of the offence charged:—

Held, allowing the appeal, that section 12 (1) of the Theft Act, 1968, did not extend to cases where consent was obtained by such fraudulent representations and, accordingly, the defendant was not guilty of an offence under the subsection as the owner's consent was not vitiated by his false statements.

SACHS LJ — . . . whilst, however, reserving the point as to whether in regard to section 12 (1) of the Theft Act, 1968, a fundamental misrepresentation can vitiate consent, this court has today to deal with a false pretence of the most usual category, no different in principle to the false pretences which come before the courts on a very great variety of occasions. If this court acceded to the submission put forward by the Crown, it would have some far-reaching consequences which can hardly have been within the intention of the legislature. If, for instance, the false representation induced someone to enter into a hiring agreement or a hire-purchase agreement by reason of which alone the representor obtained possession of and licence to take away a vehicle, that would then result in an offence which falls within the ambit of section 12 (1). That does not, however, appear to this court to be the mischief aimed at by the legislature. So to hold would in effect be inventing a fresh crime of obtaining possession by false pretences, an offence unknown to the law except when accompanied by intent to deprive the owner permanently of possession. It is a feature of the law of this country that unless there is an intent permanently to deprive of possession, temporary deprivation of an owner of his property is in general no offence. It may perhaps be apposite to refer to what the Eighth Report of the Criminal Law Revision Committee on Theft and Related Offences (May 1966) said, at p. 27, when considering whether such temporary deprivation should in general be made a crime:

"Quarrelling neighbours and families would be able to threaten one another with prosecution; students and young people sharing accommodation who might be tempted to borrow one another's property in disregard of a prohibition by the owner would be in danger of acquiring a criminal record. Further it would be difficult for the police to avoid being involved in wasteful and undesirable investigation into alleged offences which had no social importance."

To introduce the offence of obtaining possession by false pretences as regards motor vehicles would obviously tend to produce disadvantages of the types recited and to induce considerable confusion into what has so far been an uncomplicated crime. For those reasons this court is not prepared to hold that section 12 (1) extends to cases where consent is obtained by the category of misrepresentation here under review.

There is some suggestion here that a fundamental fraud will be sufficient to vitiate consent. However, *Whittaker* v *Campbell* seems to lead to the opposite conclusion;

Whittaker v *Campbell* [1983] 3 WLR 676   Queen's Bench Division

   The defendants, neither of whom held a full driving licence, represented to a
director of a vehicle-hire firm that the first defendant was D., the holder of a full
driving licence, and produced D.'s licence. Acting upon that misrepresentation,
the director agreed to their hiring a van, and the first defendant signed D.'s name
on the hire agreement. The director would not have agreed to the hire had he
known that neither defendant held a full driving licence and that they would
consequently not be insured to drive the van. The defendants were convicted
before justices of taking the van without the owner's consent or other lawful
authority, contrary to section 12(1) of the Theft Act 1968. Their appeals to
the Crown Court were dismissed on the ground that the director of the hire
firm had not consented to their taking the van since the deception as to the first
defendant's identity had vitiated his de facto consent.
   On appeal to the Divisional Court by way of case stated:—
   Held, allowing the appeal, that there was no general principle of law that
fraud vitiated consent; that on the true construction of section 12(1) of the
Theft Act 1968, and in view of the mischief to which it was directed, where a
person had given de facto consent to another to drive a conveyance owned by
him, that consent was not vitiated by reason of its having been obtained by
means of a fraudulent deception perpetrated by the other and that, accordingly,
the defendants were not guilty of an offence under the subsection. . . .

ROBERT GOFF LJ . . . There being no general principle that fraud vitiates
consent, we see the problem simply as this: can a person be said to have taken
a conveyance for his own or another's use "without having the consent of the
owner or other lawful authority" within those words as used in section 12(1)
of the Theft Act 1968, if he induces the owner to part with possession of the
conveyance by a fraudulent misrepresentation of the kind employed by the
defendants in the present case? Now there is no doubt about the mischief
towards which this provision (like its predecessors, sections 28(1) and 217(1) of
the Road Traffic Acts 1930 and 1960, respectively) is directed. It is directed
against persons simply taking other persons' vehicles for their own purposes, for
example, for use in the commission of a crime, or for a joyride, or just to get
home, without troubling to obtain the consent of the owner, but without having
the animus furandi necessary for theft. In the vast majority of circumstances, no
approach is made to the owner at all; the vehicle is just taken. But is the crime
committed when the owner is approached, and when he is compelled to part
with his possession by force, or when he is induced to part with his possession
by fraud?
   Now it may be that, if the owner is induced by force to part with possession
of his vehicle, the offence is committed, because a sensible distinction may be
drawn between consent on the one hand and submission to force on the other.
This is a point which, however, we do not have to decide, though we comment
that, in the generality of such cases, the accused is likely to have committed
one or more other offences with which he could perhaps be more appropriately
charged. But where the owner is induced by fraud to part with the possession of
his vehicle, no such sensible distinction can be drawn. In common sense terms,
he has consented to part with the possession of his vehicle, but his consent has

been obtained by the fraud. In such a case no offence under this subsection will have been committed unless, on a true construction, a different meaning is to be placed upon the word "consent" in the subsection. We do not however consider that any such construction is required.

It is to be observed, in the first instance, that the presence or absence of consent would be as much affected by innocent as by fraudulent misrepresentation. We do not however regard this point as persuasive, for the answer may lie in the fact that, where the misrepresentation is innocent, the accused would lack the mens rea which, on the principle in *R* v *Tolson* (1889) 23 QBD 168, may well be required as a matter of implication (a point which, once again, we do not have to decide). It is also to be observed that the owner's consent may, to the knowledge of the accused, have been self-induced, without any misrepresentation, fraudulent or innocent, on the part of the accused. More compelling, however, is the fact that it does not appear sensible to us that, in cases of fraud, the commission of the offence should depend not upon the simple question whether possession of the vehicle had been obtained by fraud, but upon the intricate question whether the effect of the fraud had been such that it precluded the existence of objective agreement to part with possession of the car, as might for example be the case where the owner was only willing to part with possession to a third party, and the accused fraudulently induced him to do so by impersonating that third party.

We find it very difficult to accept that the commission of an offence under this subsection should depend upon the drawing of such a line which, having regard to the mischief to which this subsection is directed, appears to us to be irrelevant. The judge in the Crown Court felt it necessary to inquire, on the appeal before him, whether this line had been crossed before he could hold that the defendants had committed the offence. An inquiry of this kind is by no means an easy one, as is demonstrated by, for example, the disagreement on a similar point among the members of the Court of Appeal in *Ingram* v *Little* [1961] 1 QB 31, and by the subsequent preference by the Court of Appeal in *Lewis* v *Averay* [1972] 1 QB 198 for the dissenting judgment of Devlin LJ in the earlier case. Indeed, we would (had we thought it necessary to do so) have reached a different conclusion on the point from that reached by the judge in the Crown Court in the present case, considering that the effect of the defendants' fraud was not that the owner parted with possession of his vehicle to a different person from the one to whom he intended to give possession, but that the owner believed that the person to whom he gave possession had the attribute, albeit a very important attribute, of holding a driving licence. However, on our view of the subsection, the point does not arise.

In circumstances such as those of the present case, the criminality (if any) of the act would appear to rest rather in the fact of the deception, inducing the person to part with the possession of his vehicle, rather than in the fact (if it be the case) that the fraud has the effect of inducing a mistake as to, for example, "identity" rather than "attributes" of the deceiver. It would be very strange if fraudulent conduct of this kind has only to be punished if it happened to induce a fundamental mistake; and it would be even more strange if such fraudulent conduct has only to be punished where the chattel in question happened to be a vehicle. If such fraudulent conduct is to be the subject of prosecution, the crime should surely be classified as one of obtaining by deception, rather than an offence under section 12(1) of the Act of 1968, which appears to us to be directed to the prohibition and punishment of a different form of activity. It was suggested to us in argument that, in the present case, the defendants could have been accused of dishonestly obtaining services by deception contrary to section 1(1) of the Theft Act 1978; the submission was that, having regard to the broad definition of "services" inherent in section 1(2) of the Act of 1978, the hiring of a vehicle could, untypically, be regarded as a form of services. Since we did not hear full argument upon the point, we express no opinion upon it, commenting only that, in a comprehensive law of theft and related offences, a decision of policy has to be made whether a fraudulent obtaining of temporary possession of a vehicle or other goods should be punishable, irrespective of any of the nice distinctions which the Crown Court felt required to consider in the present case.

We are fortified in our conclusion by the opinion expressed by Sachs LJ in *R v Peart* [1970] 2 QB 672. In that case, on comparable facts, the Court of Appeal held that no offence had been committed under section 12(1) of the Act of 1968, because the fraudulent misrepresentation did not relate to a fact which was sufficiently fundamental. But Sachs LJ, in delivering the judgment of the court, at p. 676, expressly reserved the question whether, in any case where consent had been induced by fraud, an offence would be committed under the subsection; and it is plain from his comments that he had serious misgivings whether any such offence would be committed in those circumstances. These misgivings we share in full measure, and it is our conclusion that the subsection on its true construction contemplates no such offence.

We wish to add that our judgment is confined to the construction of section 12(1) of the Theft Act 1968. We are not to be understood to be expressing any opinion upon the meaning to be attached to the word "consent" in other parts of the criminal law, where the word must be construed in its own particular context.

It is clear, then, that however fundamental the misrepresentation used by the defendant, it will not prevent a consent given by the owner being effective. If the vehicle is in fact driven away with the owner's agreement no offence is committed.

If the defendant in *McKnight v Davies* had been sufficiently dishonest to return to his employer's depot and, by a misrepresentation, get his employer to allow him to keep the lorry overnight, he would have been acquitted. His moral guilt might be considered greater in those circumstances as an element of cold calculation would be involved.

For other issues involving consent in the Theft Acts see *Lawrence v M.P.C.* [1972] AC 626 (above, page 11), *R v Morris* [1983] 3 WLR 697 (above page 7), *R v Smith and Jones* [1976] 3 All ER 54 (above, page 80), *R v Hammond* [1982] Crim LR 611 (below, page 190).

(v) What constitutes 'other lawful authority'?

This would cover removal of a vehicle by a person exercising any common law or statutory power.

(b) Mens rea

Must the defendant know he is taking the vehicle without consent?

Section 12(6) Theft Act 1968

A person does not commit an offence under this section by anything done in the belief that he has lawful authority to do it or that he would have the owner's consent if the owner knew of his doing it and the circumstances of it.

R v Clotworthy [1981] Crim LR 501   Court of Appeal

The appellant worked in a garage to which a customer had brought his car for repair. In order to expedite the repair and ensure that the car was undercover at night it had to be driven to an associated garage, and the garage owner asked a mechanic to drive the car, but he had a prior appointment and asked the appellant to drive the car to the other garage. The appellant, who held no driving licence and was uninsured to drive, while driving the car was stopped by police. He was tried on a charge of contravening section 12 (1) of the Theft Act 1968 by taking a conveyance without authority. His defence was that, within section 12 (6), he believed that he had lawful authority to drive the car since it was common practice for garage employees to drive in the course of business whether or not they were insured and he had often done so with the garage owner's knowledge and approval. The prosecutor submitted that the appellant had no defence as the car owner would not have given consent to an unlicensed or uninsured driver, it was contrary to the garage owner's terms of bailment to allow such a person to drive and, therefore, the appellant could not rely on section 12 (6) since he knew that he had no licence or insurance. The trial judge upheld that submission, the appellant thereupon changed his plea and was convicted and sentenced. He appealed against conviction.

Held, allowing the appeal, that the submission was invalid. It was for the jury to decide what the appellant's state of mind was, whether they thought that his defence might be acceptable to them or whether they were sure that he had no genuine belief. Clearly a car owner (albeit thereby committing an offence) could authorise an unlicensed and uninsured person to drive it. Accordingly it was open to any defendant to assert his reasonable belief in having authority or consent of the owner. Whether or not such an assertion carried weight with a jury would depend on the circumstances of the case. The judge erred and the conviction would be quashed.

Commentary. Notwithstanding the use of the word "reasonable" in the report, a wholly unreasonable belief by the defendant that the owner had, or would have, consented to his driving the car, is a defence to the charge. Once the defendant has stated that he held such a belief the onus is on the prosecution to prove that he did not; and the unreasonableness of the belief is a matter to be taken into account by the jury in deciding whether they are satisfied that he is not speaking the truth. Though the judge might properly express an opinion about it, the question was clearly one which could be decided only by the jury.

J. C. Smith: The Law of Theft (5th ed., para. 289)

It is clear then that the prosecution must prove that D knew that he was taking the vehicle without the owner's consent and did not believe that the owner would have consented if asked. If an unlicensed and uninsured garage employee who has driven a customer's car asserts that he believed he had lawful authority to do so, it must be left to the jury to decide whether they are satisfied that he had no genuine belief that the owner had consented, or would have consented, to his doing so.[1] The more unreasonable the alleged belief, the more likely is the jury to be satisfied that it was not really held.

[1] *Clotworthy* [1981] RTR 126, [1981] Crim LR 501. CA.

(2) & (3) DRIVING OR ALLOWING ONESELF TO BE CARRIED

(a) Actus reus

J. C. Smith: The Law of Theft (5th ed., para. 290)

. . . It seems clear that at least one offence, separate and distinct from taking a conveyance, is created; and there are two such offences if *driving* and *allowing oneself to be carried* cannot be regarded as alternative modes of commission of a single offence. If, when D allows himself to be carried, he is aiding and abetting the driver of the taken conveyance, he may be convicted of "driving" as a secondary party. But "allow" is probably a word of wider ambit than "aid, abet, counsel or procure". If D allows himself to be driven by a person who, as he knows, would drive the car whether D was there or not, he may neither assist or encourage, nor intend to assist or encourage, the driver. He is not aiding and abetting the driving but he is allowing himself to be carried. The fact that D allows himself to be carried is some evidence of secondary participation in the driving offence, but no more.

(i) Is actual movement necessary?

R v Miller [1976] Crim LR 147   Court of Appeal

Some persons took a motor launch without authority, moving it from one wharf to another. Thereafter M, knowing this, boarded the launch in anticipation of going for a journey on it. However, it was not moved whilst he was on it. He was convicted of allowing himself to be carried in the launch contrary to section 12 (1) of the Theft Act 1968. M submitted that carried implied some movement. The Crown submitted that movement was not necessary, and carried included being supported in or on a conveyance.

Held, allowing the appeal, the court agreed with M's submission: considering *Bogacki,* 57 Cr App R 593; *Pearce* [1973] Crim LR 321. An argument which influenced the court was that if Parliament had intended that mere presence in or on a conveyance was sufficient this could have been done by leaving out the word carried.

Commentary. Bogacki decides that some movement of the conveyance, however small, is necessary to constitute "taking." The present case applies a similar principle to the related offence of allowing oneself to be carried in or on the conveyance.

R v *Diggin* [1980] Crim LR 656   Court of Appeal

The appellant was charged with allowing himself to be carried in a car taken without consent, contrary to section 12 (1) of the Theft Act 1968. The car had been taken in the early hours of June 18, 1978 by D's brother, Edward Diggin, and one Subal, from an address in Northampton. They had pleaded guilty at magistrate's court to taking the car without consent. They collected D, having taken the car. It was his case that he was in drink at the time and thought he was in Z's car, which was of the same make and year of manufacture. The three drove to Newport Pagnel [sic] service area on the M1 and stopped for refreshments. They were then seen getting into the car by police officers, and were arrested before the vehicle moved. D asserted that it was only when the police approached that he learnt the car had been taken without consent.

At the trial, the judge directed the jury that such an assertion revealed no defence because the offence was committed by "allowing" oneself to be carried and not by "being carried," so the offence was committed before the ignition switch was turned.

The Court of Appeal held that this decision was wrong, and the conviction was quashed. There must be some movement for someone to be carried. They applied the decision in *Miller* [1976] Crim LR 147 (CA) which related to a motor boat which never left its moorings.

Any movement of the vehicle with the consent of the passenger will make that passenger liable to conviction of the offence of 'allowing himself to be carried'. As soon as a defendant is aware that the vehicle has been 'taken' contrary to s. 12, he is under a duty to get out of it:

Boldizsar v *Knight* [1980] Crim LR 653   Queen's Bench Division

The defendant met a man who gave him a lift in a van. During the course of the drive the conversation revealed that the man was driving the van without the owner's consent. The defendant remained in the van because he did not want to walk home. There was no valid insurance policy in force in respect of the vehicle. The defendant pleaded guilty to a charge of allowing himself to be carried in a van without the consent of the owner or other lawful authority contrary to section 12 (1) of the Theft Act 1968. He pleaded not guilty to using a motorvehicle without insurance contrary to section 143 of the Road Traffic Act 1972. The justices convicted the defendant and remitted the case to the juvenile court for sentence. The defendant appealed by way of case stated to the Divisional Court.

Held, allowing the appeal, that the defendant was merely given a lift during the course of the driver's use of the vehicle. The defendant was not using the vehicle within section 143 of the Act of 1972. There was no question of joint enterprise so the conviction should be set aside.

Commentary. It would seem that the defendant was under a duty, created by section 12 (1) of the Theft Act 1968, to require the driver of the van to put him down as soon as he discovered that the van was being driven without consent. It might be interesting to speculate whether this duty applies in all circumstances — for example where the passenger is a young woman and she discovers the facts late at night while driving across a lonely moor.

(ii) The vehicle must actually have been taken without consent, but must an offence of 'taking' actually have been committed?

The defendant's belief that an offence of 'taking' has been committed is not enough:

R v Ronald Francis [1982] Crim LR 694   Knightsbridge Crown Court

F was seen in the West End of London by three police officers. He was with another young man. They were observed walking up to a parked Ford Consul motorcar where, having looked up and down the street, they got into the car. F's companion sat in the driver's seat. F, in the passenger seat, was stopped and questioned. He said twice that his companion had told him that he had "nicked" the car. F also said that he thought that his friend was 15 years old. There was evidence from the police that the friend looked "rather young."

F was indicted for attempting to allow himself to be carried in a motor-vehicle taken without the consent of the owner.

At the close of the prosecution case, it was submitted that, in the absence of evidence from the owner of the motor car, neither the verbal admissions of F nor the surrounding circumstances were sufficient to prove that the motorcar had, in fact, been taken without the owner's consent.

Held, that the principles in *Hulbert* (1979) 69 Cr App R 243 were applicable to the case. The fact that the accused had said that the driver of the motorcar had told him that he had "nicked it" was not evidence upon which the prosecution could rely to prove that the motorcar had been taken without consent. Equally, the surrounding circumstances were not such that the jury could properly infer that the owner had not, as a matter of fact, consented to the taking of the car.

The case would be withdrawn from the jury.

The defendant was, in due course, acquitted.

The result in *R v Ronald Francis* would be the same now despite the provisions of the Criminal Attempts Act 1981. In *Anderton v Ryan* (above, page 59 and below, page 120) the House of Lords held that where it was not possible to prove that goods had been stolen no offence of attempted handling could be proved. This was so despite the belief of the defendant in that case that the goods were stolen goods.

For s. 12 a belief that the vehicle had been taken without consent would not be enough to secure a conviction for an attempt to commit a s. 12 offence.

(iii) Can a 'taker' also commit this offence when driving the vehicle he has 'taken'?

J. C. Smith: The Law of Theft (5th ed., para. 292)

> The vehicle must actually have been taken; one cannot know a thing to be so, unless it is so.
> The provision is intended to deal with persons other than the original taker, but is not limited to such persons. The taker would appear to commit another offence on each subsequent occasion when he drives the vehicle or allows himself to be carried in or on it.

This proposition seems unarguably right, but Smith continues:

> Where the original taking is not an offence because of lack of *mens rea*, a subsequent driving of it may make the taker liable. For example, D takes P's car, wrongly supposing that P consents to his doing so. The car has been taken without P's consent but no offence has been committed. Having learnt that P does not consent to his having the car, D continues to drive it. He appears to commit the offence though it is arguable that a "taken" conveyance is one taken with *mens rea*.

This raises the difficult question of whether the vehicle becomes a 'taken' conveyance if it is taken in circumstances where an offence is committed, or if it is also 'taken' in any case where the owner has not in fact consented. If the analogy of s. 22 were to be followed, an offence would actually have to have been committed before a vehicle became a 'taken' vehicle. For the purposes of achieving a conviction under s. 22 (handling) the goods must actually have been stolen.

Whether or not an offence is necessary was left open by the decision in *R* v *Ronald Francis* (above). That case made it clear that where more than one person was involved in the 'taking' and the subsequent 'driving or allowing oneself to be carried', there must be proof that the car was actually taken without the consent of the owner. The court made no reference to a necessity to prove that an offence had been committed.

There should be no difference between a situation involving a separate 'taker' and 'driver', and the situation involving only one defendant.

(b) Mens rea

Must the defendant know he is taking the vehicle without consent?

Section 12(6) applies equally to this offence as it applies to a 'taking' offence. Thus it must be proved that the defendant knew that the conveyance had been taken without authority when he drove it or allowed himself to be carried in or on it.

(4) TAKING A PEDAL CYCLE WITHOUT AUTHORITY

See s. 12(5) (above).

There is a dearth of authority on the interpretation of this subsection. It may, however, be safely assumed that the cases concerning the interpretation of s. 12(1) will be closely followed when s. 12(5) falls to be construed.

For further discussion of the issues raised by s. 12 see 'Taking the Joy out of Joy-Riding: The Mental Element of Taking a Conveyance Without Authority,' by Stephen White [1980] Crim LR 609.

7 BLACKMAIL

(1) THE ACTUS REUS

The actus reus of blackmail consists of the two elements 'demand' and 'menaces'. The answers given to the problems that have arisen for the consideration of the courts can be summarised as follows:

(a) Demand

(i) It is irrelevant what act is demanded provided economic gain or loss are involved.
(ii) A demand made by post is made where the letter is posted.
(iii) What constitutes a 'demand' depends on what an ordinary literate person would consider as a demand.

(b) Menaces

(i) A menace is threats of any action detrimental to or unpleasant to the person addressed.
(ii) There is no menace unless an ordinary person of normal stability and courage would be influenced.
(iii) It is irrelevant that, unknown to the defendant, the threats will have no effect on the victim.

Section 21 Theft Act 1968

(1) A person is guilty of blackmail if, with a view to gain for himself or another or with intent to cause loss to another, he makes any unwarranted demand with menaces; and for this purpose a demand with menaces is unwarranted unless the person making it does so in the belief:—

(a) that he has reasonable grounds for making the demand; and
(b) that the use of the menaces is a proper means of reinforcing the demand.

(2) The nature of the act or omission demanded is immaterial, and it is also immaterial whether the menaces relate to action to be taken by the person making the demand.

(3) A person guilty of blackmail shall on conviction on indictment be liable to imprisonment for a term not exceeding fourteen years.

(a) Demand

(i) It is irrelevant what act is demanded provided economic gain or loss are involved.

See s. 21(1) and (2) and s. 34(2)(a).

Section 34(2)(a) Theft Act 1968

For purposes of this Act—

(a)   'gain' and 'loss' are to be construed as extending only to gain or loss in money or other property, but as extending to any such gain or loss whether temporary or permanent; and—

(i)   'gain' includes a gain by keeping what one has, as well as a gain by getting what one has not; and
(ii)   'loss' includes a loss by not getting what one might get, as well as a loss by parting with what one has.

Gain may include the acquisition of money or other property even if that money or property is legally due to the defendant. In *R* v *Lawrence* (below) the defendant believed that the debt was in fact due from the victim. He was nevertheless held by the Court of Appeal to have been rightly convicted of blackmail.

(ii) A demand made by post is made where the letter is posted:

Treacy v *DPP* [1971] AC 537   House of Lords

The appellant posted in the Isle of Wight a letter written by him and addressed to a Mrs. X in West Germany demanding money with menaces. The letter was received by Mrs. X in West Germany. The appellant was charged with blackmail contrary to section 21 of the Theft Act 1968. At the trial, he pleaded not guilty and objected that the court had no jurisdiction to try the case because the offence had been committed outside England. His objection was overruled and he changed his plea to one of guilty, preserving his objection. The Court of Appeal dismissed his appeal against conviction.

On appeal by the appellant, contending, inter alia, that no demand had been made by him within the meaning of section 21 of the Act of 1968 until the letter had been received by Mrs. X in Germany:—

Held, dismissing the appeal (Lord Reid and Lord Morris of Borth-y-Gest dissenting), that the offence of blackmail had been committed by the appellant in that he had made a demand when he had written and posted the letter to Mrs. X. . . .

LORD DIPLOCK — My Lords, I too think that the Court of Appeal were right as to the construction of the section and that the appeal could be dismissed on this alternative ground. Arguments as to the meaning of ordinary everyday phrases are not susceptible of much elaboration. The Theft Act 1968 makes a welcome departure from the former style of drafting in criminal statutes. It is expressed in simple language as used and understood by ordinary literate men and women. It avoids so far as possible those terms of art which have acquired a special meaning understood only by lawyers in which many of the penal enactments which it supersedes were couched. So the question which has to be answered is: Would a man say in ordinary conversation: "I have made a demand" when he had written a letter containing a demand and posted it to the person to whom the demand was addressed? Or would he not use those words until the letter had been received and read by the addressee?

My answer to that question is that it would be natural for him to say "I have made a demand" as soon as he had posted the letter, for he would have done all that was in his power to make the demand. He might add, if it were the fact: "but it has not reached X yet," or: "I made a demand but it got lost in the post." What, at any rate, he would not say is: "I shall make a demand when X receives my letter," unless he contemplated making some further demand after the letter had been received.

I see nothing in the context or in the purpose of the section to indicate that the words bear any other meaning than that which I have suggested they would bear in ordinary conversation.

The Court of Appeal discussed in more detail when they consider other types of demand were made:

Treacy v DPP [1971] AC 537   Court of Appeal

JOHN STEPHENSON J — . . . When the demand is made by word of mouth it is usually made at one time and place. If the intended victim is too deaf to hear it or unable to understand it, it is nonetheless made. Or a demand may be made orally over the telephone. In that case it is made and received simultaneously and it may be right to regard it as made at one time but in two places, as counsel for the Crown suggested. When the demand is made in writing, as in this case, it will usually be made at one time and place and received at another time and place. If the intended victim is blind or illiterate, the demand is nonetheless made and first made, in our opinion, not with it reaches the victim but when it leaves the demander beyond recall on its way to the intended victim whom it will reach in the ordinary course of things.

We say "first made," because it may be right to regard the demand as continuing until it is received, or as repeated when received. On that view the defendant's demand was made both in England and in Germany, but he would still be triable for the offence in England although he might also be triable for an offence in Germany. The demand is not made when the threatening letter is written because it may never be sent and the writer may have no firm intention to gain anything by it or to cause any loss by it. But once the letter is posted the demand is completed and the offence of blackmail is committed. The blackmailer has then made his demand, whether or not the letter goes astray or is read by the intended recipient. To make a demand is not the same thing as to make it known.

(iii) What constitutes a 'demand' depends on what an ordinary literate person would consider to be a demand:

Treacy v *DPP* [1971] AC 537   House of Lords

LORD DIPLOCK — . . . As respects the purpose of the section. I see no reason for supposing that Parliament did not intend to punish conduct which was anti-social or wicked — if that word is still in current use — unless the person guilty of the conduct achieved his intended object of gain to himself or loss caused to another. The fact that what a reasonable man would regard as an unwarranted demand with menaces after being posted by its author goes astray and never reaches the addressee, or reaches him but is not understood by him, or because of his unusual fortitude fails to disturb his equanimity, as was the case in *R* v *Clear* [1968] 1 QB 670, may be a relevant factor in considering what punishment is appropriate but does not make the conduct of the author himself any less wicked or anti-social or less meet to be deterred.

My Lords, all that has to be decided upon this aspect of the instant appeal is whether the appellant "made a demand" when he posted his letter to the addressee. In the course of the argument many other and ingenious ways in which a blackmailer might choose to send his demand to his victim have been canvassed, and many possible, even though unlikely, events which might intervene between the sending of the demand by the blackmailer and its receipt and comprehension by the victim have been discussed. These cases which so far are only imaginary may fall to be decided if they ever should occur in real life. But unless the purpose of the new style of drafting used in the Theft Act 1968 is to be defeated they, too, should be decided by answering the question: "Are the circumstances of this case such as would prompt a man in ordinary conversation to say: 'I have made a demand'?"

(b) Menaces

(i) A menace is threats of any action detrimental to or unpleasant to the person addressed:

Criminal Law Revision Committee (Eight report, Cmnd. 2977 para. 123)

We have chosen the word 'menaces' instead of 'threats' because, notwithstanding the wide meaning given to 'menaces' in *Thorne* v *Motor Trade Association* . . . we regard that word as stronger than 'threats', and the consequent slight restriction of the scope of the offence seems to us right.

Thorne v *Motor Trade Association* [1937] AC 797   House of Lords

A trade association which by its constitution is entitled to put on a Stop List the name of a member or other person who has infringed its rule forbidding the sale of articles at other than the list prices relevant thereto, may, instead of putting the name of that member or other person on the Stop List, require him, in furtherance of its trade interests, to pay a sum of money within reasonable limits. To ask for such payment in those circumstances is not in itself a demand of money with menaces and without reasonable or probable cause within s. 29, sub-s. I (*i*), of the Larceny Act, 1916:—

Held, that in a criminal charge under s. 29, sub-s. I, of the Larceny Act, 1916, the absence of reasonable or probable cause is a question of fact for the jury; but, if the cause is reasonably capable of being associated with the promotion of lawful business interests, the judge should not allow the case to go to the jury if there is no evidence of the accused's intention going beyond such lawful business interests.

LORD WRIGHT — . . . I think the word "menace" is to be liberally construed and not as limited to threats of violence but as including threats of any action detrimental to or unpleasant to the person addressed. It may also include a warning that in certain events such action is intended. Thus it might ordinarily include such a threat as the threat to place on the Stop List, which for a motor trader has serious consequences.

(ii) There is no menace unless an ordinary person of normal stability and courage would be influenced.

R v *Clear* [1968] 1 QB 670   Court of Appeal

In 1963 a lorry of which the appellant, an employee of a company, was the driver, and its load were stolen. The appellant reported to the managing director that he had left the loaded lorry for a short time near his home, having set the alarm system and having taken with him the ignition key and the key of the alarm system. The company claimed against their insurers. In 1966 the appellant was served with a subpoena to give evidence in an action by the owners of the goods against the company. The appellant then visited the managing director on several occasions and, in effect, made demand for £300 threatening to withhold or change his evidence that care had been taken of the lorry and its contents by setting the burglar alarm. There was no evidence that the managing director had any interest in the company other than as managing director. After the appellant's third visit the managing director communicated with the police concerning the appellant's conduct. On appeal by the appellant against conviction of demanding money with menaces contrary to s. 30 of the Larceny Act, 1916,

Held: (i) words or conduct were menaces for the purposes of s. 30 of the Larceny Act, 1916, if they were such as were likely to operate on the mind of a person of ordinary courage and firmness so as to make him accede unwillingly to the demand. . . .

R v Harry [1974] Crim LR 32   Chelmsford Crown Court

H was indicated on two counts of blackmail. As treasurer of a college rag committee he sent letters to 115 local shopkeepers asking them to buy indemnity posters for amounts between £1 and £5, the money to go to charity. The purchase of a poster was to "protect you from any Rag Activity which could in any way cause you inconvenience." The letter continued: "The Committee sincerely hope that you will contribute, as we are sure you will agree that these charities are worthy causes which demand the support of all the community." The poster read "These premises are immune from all rag '73 activities whatever they may be." Fewer than six traders complained about the letter. None who complained had paid. One witness said in evidence that his objection was to the veiled threat contained in the words "protect you from . . . inconvenience." The President of the local Chamber of Trade said that he thought the letter was ill-conceived but that he took no serious view about it; because it was so loosely worded it was apt to be misconstrued.

The prosecution submitted that the letter contained "the clearest threat or menace however nicely it was couched, and that there was no need for direct evidence that anyone thought it was a threat.

Defence counsel submitted that there was no or no sufficient evidence to leave the jury. Not every threat, veiled or otherwise, was within the section but only if it satisfied the test in *R v Clear* [1968] 2 WLR 122, 130 of being "of such a nature and extent that the mind of an ordinary person of normal stability and courage might be influenced or made apprehensive so as to accede unwillingly to the demand." There was no evidence from any victim or possible victim that the letter had that effect at all.

The judge ruled that he was not satisfied there were any menaces within the definition in *Clear*. That case had stiffened the law as previously laid down in *Thorne v Motor Trade Association* [1937] AC 797, 817. Normally a demand with menaces was made to one person; in this case it was made to over 100 people. To some extent one could be guided by their reaction. Exercising a broad general judgment commonsense indicated that no menaces had been proved such as fell within the Act. In directing the jury to return verdicts of not guilty on both counts, Judge Petre said: "Menaces is a strong word. You may think that menaces must be of a fairly stern nature to fall within the definition." [*Report and commentary by D. J. Lamming, Barrister.*]

Commentary. The mere fact that no evidence was given that anyone acceded unwillingly to the demand was not in itself conclusive that the letter contained no menaces: *Clear*. However, since it was not suggested that any shopkeeper was unduly phlegmatic it is submitted that the judge was right in having regard to the reactions of the recipients. "Words or conduct which would not intimidate or influence anyone to respond to the demand would not be menaces": *Clear*. It is not blackmail merely to induce a response of annoyance. However, had the judge thought that the letter could reasonably have been construed as containing a menace it would not have been necessary for him to spell out the meaning of the word for "menaces" is an "ordinary English word that a jury can be expected to understand": *R* v *Lawrence and Pomroy* (1971) 55 Cr App R 64, 72.

Defence counsel made two further submissions which were not dealt with by the judge:

1. That there was no demand but only an invitation or request. Stress was laid on the words "hope you will contribute." However, the whole of the letter must be looked at for the addition of a menace may show that what is couched in terms of request is in reality a demand: *R* v *Robinson* (1796) 168 ER 475, 483.

2. That the prosecution had failed to show that the demand was unwarranted. In an interview with the police when H was being "co-operative, frank and helpful" H had said that he thought there was nothing wrong with the letter. This had been raised evidentially in cross-examination of the detective constable who had conducted the interview and the prosecution had not started to prove that H did not honestly believe this.

For a case dealing with submission 2 above see *R* v *Harvey and Others* (1981) 72 Cr App Rep 139 (below)

(iii) It is irrelevant that, unknown to the defendant, the threats will have no effect on the victim.

In *R* v *Clear* (above) the victim had no interest in the outcome of the litigation and therefore was not likely to be influenced by the threats. This fact was not appreciated by the defendant and was therefore held to be irrelevant.

R v *Clear* (above)

SELLERS LJ — . . . There may be special circumstances unknown to an accused which would make the threats innocuous and unavailing for the accused's demand, but such circumstances would have no bearing on the accused's state of mind and of his intention. If an accused knew that what he threatened would have no effect on the victim it might be different.

Smith: The Law of Theft (5th ed., para. 307)

It is submitted, therefore, that there is a sufficient menace if, in the circumstances known to the accused, the threat might:

(i) influence the mind of an ordinary person or normal stability and courage, whether or not it in fact influences the person addressed; or

(ii) influence the mind of the person addressed, though it would not influence an ordinary person.

It is assumed, of course, that in both cases there is an intention to influence the person addressed to accede to the demand by means of the threat.

While (i) above is clearly correct following *R* v *Clear* and *R* v *Harry*, there is no authority for (ii), and whether it correctly represents the law is a matter of pure speculation. The emphasis in *R* v *Clear* was placed firmly on the objective test: would a person of ordinary firmness be influenced?

(2) THE MENS REA

(a)   There must be a demand with menaces.
(b)   The defendant must have a view to gain for himself or another or intent to cause loss to another.
(c)   The demand must be unwarranted, i.e.

(i)   the defendant had no belief that he had reasonable grounds for making the demand, or
(ii)   the defendant had no belief that the use of the menaces was a proper means of reinforcing the demand.

(a) There must be a demand with menaces

This aspect of the mens rea is dealt with above – see the case of *R* v *Clear* and discussion thereon.

(b) The defendant must have a view to gain for himself or another or intent to cause loss to another

The definitions of 'gain' and 'loss' are set out in s. 34(2)(a) (see above, page 116).

The major problem is whether it should be regarded as a 'gain' where the defendant uses menaces to secure the payment of money due to him, i.e., does 'gain' mean profit or acquisition? It seems that acquisition is the correct interpretation.

Criminal Law Revision Committee (Eighth Report Comnd. 2977, para. 119)

'. . . there are some threats which should make the demand amount to blackmail even if there is a valid claim to the thing demanded. For example, we believe that most people would say that it should be blackmail to threaten to denounce a person, however truly, as a homosexual unless he paid a debt. It does not seem to follow from the existence of a debt that the creditor should be entitled to resort to any method, otherwise non-criminal, to obtain payment.'

It is clear, therefore, that the Criminal Law Revision Committee envisaged 'gain' as meaning acquisition. It could be blackmail even when the money demanded was legally due to the defendant.

That interpretation was also applied in *R* v *Lawrence* (below)

R v *Lawrence* (1957) 57 Cr App Rep 64   Court of Appeal

CAIRNS LJ − . . . Next, should the judge have directed the jury on the proviso to section 21 (1) (*b*) of the Theft Act: that is to say, as to whether the accused believed that what they did was a proper way of enforcing the debt? Neither of them suggested at the trial that, if menaces were used by them, it was a proper means of enforcement. It is true that the police evidence was that when Pomroy's statement was read to him, Lawrence said: "That's about it, what's wrong with that?" but he repudiated that in his evidence and said that his reaction had been "It's a lot of nonsense."

Where on the face of it the means adopted to obtain payment of a debt is not the proper way of enforcing it and where the accused does not at his trial set up the case that he believed it to be, there is no need for any direction to be given on the proviso.

R v *Parkes* [1973] Crim LR 358   Sheffield Crown Court

D was charged with blackmail (*inter alia*). The evidence adduced by the prosecution showed that in one instance the money demanded was undoubtedly money owed to D by the complainant and, indeed, long overdue. In the other instance there was some issue as to whether or not the money demanded was a debt but the submission was made and ruled upon the basis that it *was* a debt owing by the complainant to D.

It was submitted that to demand [that] what is lawfully owing to you was not a demand "with a view to gain" within the meaning of section 21 (1) of the Theft Act 1968, as interpreted by section 34 (2) (*a*) of that Act.

The Circuit Judge ruled that by demanding money lawfully owing to him D did have a view to "gain." Section 34 (2) (*a*) (i) defines gain as including "getting what one has not"; by intending to obtain hard cash as opposed to a mere right of action in respect of the debt D *was* getting more than he already had and accordingly the submission failed. [Note: D was acquitted on both these counts, so that the opportunity to ventilate the issue in the Court of Appeal did not arise.]

Commentary. The question is whether "gain" in the section means "profit" or "acquisition." It is submitted that it means acquisition, whether at a profit or not. There is no doubt that this is what the Criminal Law Revision Committee intended: Cmnd. 2977, para. 119; and section 34 (2) (a) (i) suggests that this is the right construction of the Act. It appears to have been assumed without discussion in *Lawrence and Pomroy* [1971] Crim LR 645 that an unwarranted demand with menaces for a debt believed to be due was blackmail. *Cf.* Smith, *Law of Theft* (2nd ed.), paras. 347-352.

(c) The demand must be unwarranted

That is to say:

(i)   the defendant had no belief that he had reasonable grounds for making the demand, or,

(ii)   the defendant had no belief that the use of the menaces was a proper means of reinforcing the demand.

It is for the jury to decide whether the particular defendant held the belief in question. Reasonableness of the belief is not relevant:

R v *Harvey and Others* (1981) 72 Cr App Rep 139   Court of Appeal

On a charge of blackmail contrary to section 21 (1) of the Theft Act 1968, the subsection is concerned with the belief of the individual defendant in the particular case. It matters not what the reasonable man, or any man other than the defendant, would believe save in so far as that may throw light on what the defendant in fact believed. Thus the factual question of the defendant's belief should be left to the jury. Further, in order to exonerate a defendant from liability under section 21 (1) his belief must be that the use of the menaces is a "proper" means of reinforcing the demand, *i.e.* lawful not criminal.

. . . The appellants had entered into a supposed transaction with a rogue named Scott, the basis of that transaction being that Scott would procure a large quantity of cannabis for a sum in excess of £20,000. He had no intention of supplying it, but produced to them a purported sample, which was in fact cannabis, following that up with what turned out to be a load of rubbish. The appellants were accountable to others who had made their contributions to the price of over £20,000 and were much enraged. They then kidnapped Scott's wife and small child and detained them against their will for some four days until they were released by the police. The appellants had also kidnapped Scott and subjected him to threats of what would happen to his wife and child if he did not give them their money back, and subjected him to violence forming the subject matter of count 4. After four days' "enforced detention" he was finally released by the intervention of the police and all the appellants were arrested.

BINGHAM J — For the appellants it was submitted that the learned judge's direction, was incorrect in law because it took away from the jury a question properly falling within their province of decision, namely, what the accused in fact believed. He was wrong to rule as a matter of law that a threat to perform a serious criminal act could never be thought by the person making it to be a proper means. While free to comment on the unlikelihood of a defendant believing threats such as were made in this case to be a proper means, the judge should nonetheless (it was submitted) have left the question to the jury. For the Crown it was submitted that a threat to perform a criminal act can never as a matter of law be a proper means within the subsection, and that the learned judge's direction was accordingly correct. Support for both these approaches is to be found in academic works helpfully brought to the attention of the Court.

The answer to this problem must be found in the language of the subsection, from which in our judgment two points emerge with clarity: (1) The subsection is concerned with the belief of the individual defendant in the particular case: ". . . a demand with menaces is unwarranted unless *the person making it* does so in the belief . . ." (added emphasis). It matters not what the reasonable man, or any man other than the defendant, would believe save in so far as that may throw light on what the defendant in fact believed. Thus the factual question of the defendant's belief should be left to the jury. To that extent the subsection is subjective in approach, as is generally desirable in a criminal statute. (2) in order to exonerate a defendant from liability his belief must be that the use of the menaces is a "proper" means of reinforcing the demand. "Proper" is an unusual expression to find in a criminal statute. It is not defined in the Act, and no definition need be attempted here. It is, however, plainly a word of wide meaning, certainly wider than (for example) "lawful." But the greater includes the less and no act which was not believed to be lawful could be believed to be proper within the meaning of the subsection. Thus no assistance is given to any defendant, even a fanatic or a deranged idealist, who knows or suspects that his threat, or the act threatened, is criminal, but believes it to be justified by his end or his peculiar circumstances. The test is not what he regards as justified, but what he believes to be proper. And where, as here, the threats were to do acts which any sane man knows to be against the laws of every civilised country no jury would hesitate long before dismissing the contention that the defendant genuinely believed the threats to be a proper means of reinforcing even a legitimate demand.

It is accordingly our conclusion that the direction of the learned judge was not strictly correct. If it was necessary to give a direction on this aspect of the case at all (and in the absence of any evidence by the defendants as to their belief we cannot think that there was in reality any live issue concerning it) the jury should have been directed that the demand with menaces was not to be regarded as unwarranted unless the Crown satisfied them in respect of each defendant that the defendant did not make the demand with menaces in the genuine belief both — (a) that he had had reasonable grounds for making the demand; and (b) that the use of the menaces was in the circumstances a proper (meaning for present purposes a lawful, and not a criminal) means of reinforcing the demand.

The learned judge could, of course, make appropriate comment on the unlikelihood of the defendants believing murder and rape or threats to commit those acts to be lawful or other than criminal.

8 HANDLING STOLEN GOODS

(1) THE ACTUS REUS

The actus reus of handling presents seven particular problems:

(a) When are goods considered to be 'stolen goods'?
(b) When do goods cease to be 'stolen goods'?
(c) When are goods representing stolen goods themselves considered to be 'stolen goods'?
(d) In what ways can 'handling' be committed?
(e) Can this offence be committed by omission?
(f) When is an act considered to be 'otherwise than in the course of the stealing'?
(g) When is the handling 'by or for the benefit of another person'?

Section 22 Theft Act 1968

(1) A person handles stolen goods if (otherwise than in the course of the stealing) knowing or believing them to be stolen goods he dishonestly receives the goods, or dishonestly undertakes or assists in their retention, removal, disposal or realisation by or for the benefit of another person, or if he arranges to do so.
(2) A person guilty of handling stolen goods shall on conviction on indictment be liable to imprisonment for a term not exceeding fourteen years.

(a) When are goods considered to be 'stolen goods'?

(i)   What are goods?
(ii) What constitutes 'stealing' so that goods become 'stolen'?
(iii) Is the defendant's belief that the goods are stolen sufficient to make them 'stolen goods'?

(i) What are goods?

Section 34(2)(b) Theft Act 1968

'Goods', except in so far as the context otherwise requires, includes money and every other description of property except land, and includes things severed from the land by stealing.

Things in action can be 'stolen goods' so as to form the basis of a s. 22 conviction:

Attorney-General's Reference (No 4 of 1979) (1980) 71 Cr App Rep 341
Court of Appeal

THE LORD CHIEF JUSTICE – Two points were taken on behalf of the defendand by counsel. First, that the offence of handling stolen goods could not be committed with reference to a stolen thing in action, or to a thing in action representing stolen goods; secondly, that on the evidence before the court the offence of handling stolen goods could not be proved.
As to the first point, the judge rejected the submission.

The Court of Appeal confirmed that the judge was right to do so.

(ii) What constitutes 'stealing' so that goods become 'stolen'?

Section 24(4) Theft Act 1968

For purposes of the provisions of this Act relating to goods which have been stolen (including subsections (1) to (3) above) goods obtained in England and Wales or elsewhere either by blackmail or in the circumstances described in section 15(1) of this Act shall be regarded as stolen; and 'steal', 'theft' and 'thief' shall be construed accordingly.

Section 24(1) Theft Act 1968

The provisions of this Act relating to goods which have been stolen shall apply whether the stealing occurred in England or Wales or elsewhere, and whether it occurred before or after the commencement of this Act, provided that the stealing (if not an offence under this Act) amounted to an offence where and at the time when the goods were stolen; and references to stolen goods shall be construed accordingly.

J. C. Smith: The Law of Theft (5th ed., para. 382)

Thus goods are "stolen" for the purposes of the Act if:

(i)   they have been stolen contrary to s. 1;
(ii)   they have been obtained by blackmail contrary to s. 21;
(iii) they have been obtained by deception contrary to s. 15(1);
(iv) they have been the subject of an act done in a foreign country which was (a) a crime by the law of that country and which (b), had it been done in England, would have been theft, blackmail or obtaining by deception contrary to s. 1 or s. 21 or s. 15 (1) respectively.

(iii) Is the defendant's belief that the goods are stolen sufficient to make them 'stolen goods'?

The defendant's belief that the goods are stolen is not by itself sufficient for a conviction either of handling or attempting to handle.

R v *Porter* [1976] Crim LR 58   Middlesex Crown Court

Porter was charged with dishonestly handling stolen goods. He was questioned by two police officers who told him that they were investigating the theft of oil from a nearby refinery. Porter admitted that he had bought oil and that he believed it to have been stolen. There was no other evidence before the court.

It was argued for Porter that the prosecution had failed to adduce any evidence of theft or of any circumstances from which the jury could infer that.

For the Crown it was argued that the state of the defendant's mind at the time of the handling of the goods was a circumstance of such handling. Accordingly *Fuschillo* (1940) 27 Cr App R 193 should be applied and the jury invited to infer theft from the circumstances.

Held, upholding the defence submission that there was no case to answer, that the belief of the defendant that the oil had been stolen was not a circumstance from which that inference could be drawn. *Fuschillo* should not be extended so that a defendant's belief that goods were stolen became evidence of the theft of those goods. A defendant might be mistaken in his belief that the goods which he received were stolen.

Commentary. The accused's admissions are evidence against him where it appears that he had personal knowledge of the facts admitted. If, however, he has no personal knowledge of the facts admitted but is reporting the statement of another, that statement appears to be inadmissible.

It would seem to follow that the admission of an alleged handler, "I knew the goods were stolen," while evidence of *mens rea,* is not evidence of the fact that the goods were actually stolen if it was derived entirely from the statement of the thief or another. In *Bird* v *Adams* [1972] Crim LR 174, Lawson J. said "In many cases it is not possible for those responsible for prosecutions to prove that goods are in fact stolen goods. It may not be known from what source they emanate but if the person charged has made some statement relating to the circumstances in which he acquired possession of these goods, it is quite legitimate and proper for inferences to be drawn from the evidence of that statement that the goods are in fact stolen. This is in fact a common situation. . . ."

It is one thing for the accused to admit facts of which he has personal knowledge and for an inference to be drawn from those facts that the goods are stolen. It is another thing for the accused to "admit" facts of which he has no personal knowledge.

Anderton v *Ryan The Times,* 13 May 1985 [1985] 2 WLR 968   House of Lords

Where a person dishonestly handled goods in the belief that they were stolen goods, but they were not in fact stolen, that person was not liable to be convicted of attempting dishonestly to handle stolen goods contrary to section 1 of the Criminal Attempts Act 1981.

LORD ROSKILL said that a police officer had visited the appellant at her request to investigate an alleged burglary. In the course of conversation, she had admitted to him that she had bought the video recorder for £110 from an unnamed person. Later, she had said: "I may as well be honest, it was a stolen one I bought."

The prosecution had invited the justices to convict the appellant on the second charge on the basis that, even though they could not prove that the recorder had been stolen, she could by reason of section 1 (1) of the 1981 Act be convicted of dishonestly attempting to handle it since she had known or believed that it was stolen.

The justices had found that at the time of the receipt of the recorder into the appellant's possession she had been of the belief that it was stolen. . . .

Mr Hytner had argued that dishonest handling of goods that were not stolen was not an indictable offence triable in England and Wales. The video recorder had not by concession been stolen. Therefore, the appellant had not been guilty of attempting to handle stolen goods, whatever her belief.

[Considering the provisions of the Criminal Attempts Act 1981] The Crown had argued that those provisions involved that a defendant was liable to conviction for an attempt even where his actions were innocent but he erroneously believed facts that, if true, would make those actions criminal, and further, that he was liable to such conviction whether or not in the event his intended course of action was completed.

The question was whether the language used by the draftsman in subsection (3) compelled the result. After long consideration of the difficulties to which the drafting gave rise, his Lordship had come to the conclusion that it did not.

He respectfully agreed with Lord Bridge that, if the action was innocent and the defendant did everything he intended to do subsection (3) did not compel the conclusion that erroneous belief in the existence of facts which, if true, would have made his completed act a crime, made him guilty of an attempt to commit that crime.

His Lordship also thought that, likewise, a defendant who was possessed of a like erroneous belief and who after doing innocent acts that were more than merely preparatory to fulfilling his intention, for some reason subsequently failed to achieve that which he intended, was not liable to be convicted of an attempt to commit a crime.

If the contrary proposition were correct, some remarkable results followed. To take one example, a young gentleman was determined on sexual intercourse with a young lady whom he erroneously believed to be under 16. She was in fact 18. He succeeded in his ambition.

Before subsection (3) had been enacted, he had clearly not been guilty of any offence. Since the enactment of subsection (3) his completed act was still itself not a completed offence. His Lordship found it impossible to believe that it had been intended by subsection (3) that he should be liable to be found guilty of attempting to have unlawful sexual intercourse with a girl under 16 merely because of his erroneous belief.

He found it equally impossible to believe that in those circumstances Parliament had intended that he should be liable to conviction for an attempt to commit that offence in a case where, for some reason, he had failed at the last moment to achieve his ambition.

His Lordship did not stop to speculate what Lord Reid might have thought, or, indeed, have said, about legislation that led to such a result.

In his Lordship's view, much clearer and, one might say, much more drastic language would be required to achieve that last result.

To conclude: subsection (3) covered the case of a defendant possessed of a specific criminal intent which he erroneously believed to be possible of achievement but which in fact was not possible of achievement. It did not, however, make a defendant liable to conviction for an attempt to commit an offence when, whatever his belief, on the true facts he could never have committed an offence had he gone beyond his attempt so as to achieve fruition.

His Lordship would, therefore, allow the appeal and set aside the order of the Divisional Court. The justices had reached a correct conclusion.

(b) When do goods cease to be 'stolen goods'?

Section 24(3) Theft Act 1968

But no goods shall be regarded as having continued to be stolen goods after they have been restored to the person from whom they were stolen or to other lawful possession or custody, or after that person and any other person claiming through him have otherwise ceased as regards those goods to have any right to restitution in respect of the theft.

Whether the goods have been reduced into lawful possession or custody is a matter for the jury to decide:

Attorney-General's Reference (No. 1 of 1974) [1974] 1 QB 744   Court of Appeal

A police officer found an unlocked and unattended car containing packages of new clothing which he suspected had been stolen, as was subsequently proved to be the case. He immobilised the car and kept observation. The respondent appeared and attempted to start the car. When questioned by the officer he gave an implausible explanation and was arrested.

At the respondent's trial on the charge of handling stolen goods by receiving them knowing them to have been stolen, the judge accepted the submission that since the goods had been restored to the "lawful possession or custody" of the police officer within the meaning of section 24 (3) of the Theft Act 1968 there was no case to answer. The jury acquitted the respondent on the judge's direction.

On the Attorney-General's reference to the Court of Appeal under section 36 of the Criminal Justice Act 1972 on the point of law as to whether stolen goods were restored to lawful custody when a police officer, suspecting them to be stolen, examined and kept observation on them with a view to tracing the thief or handler: —

Held, that in the opinion of the court the issue as to whether the goods had been reduced into the "lawful possession or custody" of the police officer so as to provide a defence under section 24 (3) of the Act of 1968 was a question of fact which depended upon the intentions of the officer as to whether or not he had decided to take the goods into custody and that since the judge was not entitled as a matter of law to conclude from the facts that the goods had been reduced into the possession of the police officer he was wrong in withdrawing that issue from the jury. . . .

. . . The effect of section 24 (3) of the Act of 1968 is to enable a defendant to plead that the goods had ceased to be stolen goods if they were taken by a police officer in the course of his duty and reduced into possession by him. . . .

LORD WIDGERY CJ — . . . did the conduct of the police officer, as already briefly recounted, amount to a taking of possession of the woollen goods in the back seat of the motor car? What he did, to repeat the essential facts, was: that seeing these goods in the car and being suspicious of them because they were brand new goods and in an unlikely position, he removed the rotor arm and stood by in cover to interrogate any driver of the car who might subsequently appear. Did that amount to a taking possession of the goods in the back of the car? In our judgment it depended primarily on the intentions of the police officer. If the police officer seeing these goods in the back of the car had made up his mind that he would take them into custody, that he would reduce them into his possession or control, take charge of them so that they could not be removed and so that he would have the disposal of them, then it would be a perfectly proper conclusion to say that he had taken possession of the goods. On the other hand, if the truth of the matter is that he was of an entirely open mind at that stage as to whether the goods were to be seized or not and was of an entirely open mind as to whether he should take possession of them or not, but merely stood by so that when the driver of the car appeared he could ask certain questions of that driver as to the nature of the goods and why they were there, then there is no reason whatever to suggest that he had taken the goods into his possession or control. It may be, of course, that he had both objects in mind. It is possible in a case like this that the police officer may have intended by removing the rotor arm both to prevent the car from being driven away and to enable him to assert control over the woollen goods as such. But if the jury came to the conclusion that the proper explanation of what had happened was that the police officer had not intended at that stage to reduce the goods into his possession or to assume the control of them, and at that stage was merely concerned to ensure tht the driver, if he appeared, could not get away without answering questions, then in that case the proper conclusion of the jury would have been to the effect that the goods had not been reduced into the possession of the police and therefore a defence under section 24 (3) of the Theft Act 1968 would not be of use to this particular defendant.

In the light of those considerations it has become quite obvious that the trial judge was wrong in withdrawing the issue from the jury. As a matter of law he was not entitled to conclude from the facts which I have set out more than once that these goods were reduced into the possession of the police officer. What he should have done in our opinion would have been to have left that issue to the jury for decision, directing the jury that they should find that the prosecution case was without substance if they thought that the police officer had assumed control of the goods as such and reduced them into his possession. Whereas on the other hand, they should have found the case proved, assuming that they were satisfied about its other elements, if they were of the opinion that the police officer in removing the rotor arm and standing by and watching was doing no more than ensure that the driver should not get away without interrogation and was not at that stage seeking to assume possession of the goods as such at all. That is our opinion.

The "right to restitution" referred to in s. 24(3) of the 1968 Act probably includes a right to damages and/or restitution at the court's discretion in accordance with the Torts (Interference with Goods) Act 1977. It also probably includes a potential right to restitution or damages where title passes to the defendant under a contract voidable for fraud. The Criminal Law Revision Committee explained s. 24(2) in their eighth report (Cmnd. 2977) at para. 139:

'... this is because, if the person who owned the goods when they were stolen no longer has any title to them, there will be no reason why the goods should continue to have the taint of being stolen goods. For example, the offence of handling stolen goods will ... apply also to goods obtained by criminal deception under [s. 15]. If the owner of the goods who has been deceived chooses on discovering the deception to ratify his disposal of the goods he will cease to have any title to them.'

(c) When are goods representing stolen goods themselves considered to be 'stolen goods'?

Section 24(2) Theft Act 1968

For purposes of those provisions references to stolen goods shall include, in addition to the goods originally stolen and parts of them (whether in their original state or not), –

(a)   any other goods which directly or indirectly represent or have at any time represented the stolen goods in the hands of the thief as being the proceeds

of any disposal or realisation of the whole or part of the goods stolen or of goods so representing the stolen goods; and

(b)   any other goods which directly or indirectly represent or have at any time represented the stolen goods in the hands of a handler of the stolen goods or any part of them as being the proceeds of any disposal or realisation of the whole or part of the stolen goods handled by him or of goods so representing them.

J. C. Smith: The Law of Theft (5th ed., para. 392)

The effect of the interpretation put upon the corresponding provision in the Larceny Act 1916 (s. 46 (1)) was that anything into or for which the stolen goods were converted or exchanged, whether immediately or otherwise, acquired the character of stolen goods. Thus if A stole an Austin motor car from P and exchanged it with B for a Bentley; B exchanged the Austin with C for a Citroen; and exchanged the Bentley with D for a Daimler, all four cars would now be stolen goods even though B, C and D might be innocent. And if A, B, C and D each sold the car he had in his possession, the proceeds of each sale (as well as the cars) would be stolen, as would any property purchased with the proceeds. Thus the stolen goods might be multiplied to an alarming extent. The provision did not seem to give rise to any difficulty in practice and it seems that it was very rarely invoked; but it was clearly undesirable to re-enact a provision with such far-reaching theoretical possibilities. Section 24 (2) imposes a limitation upon the possible multiplication of stolen goods.

[393] The Criminal Law Revision Committee stated of this provision [Eighth Report Cmnd. 2977, para. 139]:

"It may seem technical; but the effect will be that the goods which the accused is charged with handling must, at the time of the handling or at some previous time, (i) have been in the hands of the thief or of a handler, and (ii) have represented the original stolen goods in the sense of being the proceeds, direct or indirect, of a sale or other realisation of the original goods."

Thus, in the example above, if B, C and D were innocent (i) the Austin would continue to be stolen throughout unless P ceased to have any right to restitution of it in respect of the theft; (ii) the Bentley would be stolen goods since it directly represented the goods originally stolen in the hands of the thief as the proceeds of a disposition of them; (iii) the Citroen would not be stolen since B was neither a thief nor a handler; (iv) the Daimler would be stolen since it indirectly represented the stolen goods in the hands of the thief; and the proceeds of sale of the Daimler would also be stolen goods; but the proceeds of sale of the Austin, the Bentley and the Citroen would not, since they came into the hands of C, D and B respectively, none of whom was a thief or a handler.

The difference between the old law and the new is, of course, that a disposition or realisation of the stolen goods by a person who is neither a thief nor a handler (i.e., by one who is in fact appropriating or handling the goods but who has no *mens rea*) no longer causes the proceeds to be stolen. So if D innocently receives stolen goods and converts them into another form — for example, he buys a car with stolen money, or pays stolen money into a bank — the property in the changed form is not stolen; and the dishonest retention of it by D is not handling, nor is it theft if value was given for the goods.

Where the goods were stolen contrary to s. 1 (1), s. 24 (2) probably makes little difference. In almost every case where goods are notionally stolen by virtue of that subsection they are probably also "stolen" by virtue of other provisions in the Act together with the rules of common law and equity under which an owner can trace his property when it is converted into another form. Where the goods are "stolen" because they were obtained by deception or blackmail, the subsection has a potentially wider area of operation. The reasons for this are examined in earlier editions of this work.

(d) In what ways can 'handling' be committed?

It is not clear whether or not s. 22 creates more than one offence:

R v *Nicklin* [1977] 2 All ER 444   Court of Appeal

The appellant was charged in a count of an indictment with handling stolen goods by dishonestly receiving them, contrary to s. 22(1) of the Theft Act 1968. He pleaded not guilty to that charge but guilty to handling the goods by dishonestly assisting in their removal. Because the Crown did not wish to accept that latter charge, they did not amend the indictment to add a count charging handling the goods by assisting in their removal. The judge directed the jury that even though the indictment charged the appellant only with handling by dishonestly receiving, they could convict him of handling by dishonestly assisting in the removal of the goods. The jury returned a verdict accordingly and the appellant was convicted of handling the goods by dishonestly assisting in their removal. He appealed against the conviction on the ground that he had never been charged with that offence and therefore the verdict should be quashed.

Held – Section 22(1) of the 1968 Act created a single offence of handling stolen goods, and therefore an indictment which charged handling stolen goods simpliciter, without particularising the species of handling, would not be defective. On such a general indictment the defendant could be convicted of a particular type of handling provided that the general form of the indictment had not led to injustice or confusion. Where, however, the Crown had particularised the species of handling, the defendant could be convicted only of that species of handling. Accordingly, as the indictment had particularised the species of handling by charging the appellant with handling goods by dishonestly receiving them, it was not open to the jury to convict him of handling the goods by dishonestly assisting in their removal. The appeal would therefore be allowed. . . .

Per Curiam. The handling charged should be particularised in the indictment and, if necessary, should be particularised in more than one way. As a general rule, however, the indictment need contain only two counts, one count for the first limb of the offence, charging handling by dishonestly receiving goods and a second count for the second limb of the offence, charging handling by dishonestly undertaking or assisting in the retention, removal, disposal or realisation of the goods. The second count covering all those alternatives, would not be bad for duplicity. . . .

R v *Bloxham* [1982] 1 All ER 582   House of Lords

(Facts set out below, page 141.)

> LORD BRIDGE − . . . It is, I think, now well settled that this subsection creates
> two distinct offences, but no more than two. The first is equivalent to the old
> offence of receiving under s. 33 of the Larceny Act 1916. The second is a new
> offence designed to remedy defects in the old law and can be committed in any
> of the various ways indicated by the words from 'undertakes' to the end of the
> subsection. It follows that the new offence may and should be charged in a
> single count embodying in the particulars as much of the relevant language of
> the subsection, including alternatives, as may be appropriate to the circumstances
> of the particular case, and that such a count will not be bad for duplicity. It
> was so held by Geoffrey Lane J delivering the judgment of the Court of Appeal
> in *R* v *Willis, R* v *Syme* [1972] 3 All ER 797, [1972] 1 WLR 1605 and approved
> by the court in *R* v *Deakin* [1972] 3 All ER 803, [1972] 1 WLR 1618. So far
> as I am aware, this practice has been generally followed ever since.

It seems that, whether as a matter of practice or as a matter of law, an allegation
of receiving must be made in a different count from an allegation that the defendant
handled goods in any of the other possible ways.

The ways in which an offence of handling can be committed are by:

(i)   receiving the goods,
(ii)   undertaking the retention, removal, disposal or realisation of the goods for
the benefit of another person,
(iii)   assisting in the retention, removal, disposal or realisation of the goods by
another person.
(iv)   Arranging to do (i), (ii) or (iii).

Only receiving or arranging to receive can be committed without the acts being
done 'by or for the benefit of another person'. (See *R* v *Bloxham*, below.)

(e) Can this offence be committed by omission?

How active must the defendant be? It seems unlikely that an omission to act could
amount to 'receiving', 'undertaking' or 'arranging', but assistance can be given to
another by inactivity. Because of the rule that criminal liability should only be
imposed for failure to act where a clear duty is imposed on the defendant to do
something positive, a s. 22 conviction for an omission to act should be rare. However the courts have been somewhat inconsistent in this area. It appears that permitting goods to remain on one's premises will be a sufficiently positive act whereas,
perhaps surprisingly, using the goods may not be:

R v Brown [1970] 1 QB 105   Court of Appeal

The defendant was tried on an indictment containing three counts charging him (1) with burglary, (2) with handling stolen goods contrary to section 22 (1) of the Theft Act, 1968, in that he dishonestly received them, and (3) in that he dishonestly assisted in their retention. In January, 1969, a cafe was broken into and food and cigarettes were stolen. A quantity of the stolen food was found at the defendant's flat. The defendant denied any knowledge of the theft and told the police to "Get lost." Subsequently the cigarettes were found in the flat. At the trial, evidence was given by the prosecution that the defendant knew that the stolen goods were in the flat before the police arrived. The chairman directed the jury that "the matter for you to consider is whether, assuming that you are satisfied that [the defendant] knew that the stolen cigarettes were in the wardrobe . . . he was dishonestly assisting in their retention by not telling the constable they were there." The defendant was acquitted on the first two counts and convicted on count 3. On appeal against conviction on the ground that the chairman had misdirected the jury in that mere failure to reveal the presence of stolen property was incapable of amounting to assistance in their retention within the meaning of section 22 (1) of the Theft Act, 1968:—

Held, dismissing the appeal, that failure to reveal the presence of goods did not of itself amount to dishonestly assisting in the retention of goods within section 22 (1) but the fact that there was strong evidence to show that the defendant knew that the goods had been stolen and nevertheless permitted them to remain there was sufficient for the jury to infer that the offence had been committed. Accordingly, although the direction to the jury was incomplete, in all the circumstances the only inference which the jury could have drawn was that the defendant was assisting in the retention of the stolen goods by housing them and the proviso to section 4 of the Criminal Appeal Act, 1907, would be applied.

LORD PARKER CJ − . . . It is urged here that the mere failure to reveal the presence of the cigarettes, with or without the addition of the spoken words "Get lost," was incapable in itself of amounting to an assisting in the retention of the goods within the meaning of section 22 (1). The court has come to the conclusion that that is right. It does not seem to this court that the mere failure to tell the police, coupled if you like with the words "Get lost," amounts in itself to an assisting in their retention. On the other hand, those matters did accord strong evidence of what was the real basis of the charge here, namely that, knowing that they had been stolen, he permitted them to remain there or, as it has been put, provided accommodation for these stolen goods in order to assist Holden to retain them. To that extent, it seems to this court, that the direction was incomplete. The chairman should have gone on to say:

"But the fact that he did not tell the constable that they were there and said 'Get lost' is evidence from which you can infer if you think right that this man was permitting the goods to remain in his flat, and to that extent assisting in their retention by Holden."

It may be thought to be a matter of words, but in the opinion of the court some further direction was needed. On the other hand it is a plain case in which the proviso should be applied. It seems to the court that the only possible inference in these circumstances, once Holden was believed, is that the defendant was assisting in their retention by housing the goods and providing accommodation for them, by permitting them to remain there. In those circumstances the court is satisfied that the appeal fails and should be dismissed.

R v Pitchley (1972) Cr App Rep 30   Court of Appeal

The appellant's son handed the appellant £150 and the appellant paid the amount into his post office savings bank book.

Held, that the appellant was properly convicted under section 22 of the Theft Act 1968, as he had assisted in the retention of the money for the benefit of his son. "Retain" in the section means "keep possession of, not lose, continue to have."

CAIRNS LJ – . . . The main point that has been taken by Mr. Kalisher, who is appearing for the appellant in this Court, is that, assuming that the jury were not satisfied that the appellant received the money knowing it to have been stolen, and that is an assumption which clearly it is right to make, then there was no evidence after that, that from the time when the money was put into the savings bank, that the appellant had done any act in relation to it. His evidence was, and there is no reason to suppose that the jury did not believe it, that at the time when he put the money into the savings bank he still did not know or believe that the money had been stolen – it was only at a later stage that he did. That was on the Saturday according to his evidence, and the position was that the money had simply remained in the savings bank from the Saturday, to the Wednesday when the police approached the appellant.

In this present case there was no question on the evidence of the appellant himself, that he was permitting the money to remain under his control in his savings bank book, and it is clear that this Court in the case of *Brown (supra)* regarded such permitting as sufficient to constitute retention within the meaning of retention. . . .

In the course of the argument, Nield J. cited the dictionary meaning of the word "retain" – keep possession of, not lose, continue to have. In view of this Court, that is the meaning of the word "retain" in this section. It was submitted by Mr. Kalisher that, at any rate, it was ultimately for the jury to decide whether there was retention or not and that even assuming that what the appellant did was of such a character that it could constitute retention, the jury ought to have been directed that it was for them to determine as a matter of fact, whether that was so or not. The Court cannot agree with that submission. The meaning of the word "retention" in the section is a matter of law in so far as the construction of the word is necessary. It is hardly a difficult question of construction because it is an ordinary English word and in the view of this Court, it was no more necessary for the Deputy Chairman to leave to the jury the question of whether or not what was done amounted to retention, than it would be necessary for a judge in a case where goods had been handed to a person who knew that they had been stolen for him to direct the jury it was for them to decide whether or not that constituted receiving.

R v *Sanders* (1982) 75 Cr App Rep 84   Court of Appeal

A garage was burgled and a fan heater and a battery charger stolen. The fan heater was found by the police in a garage owned by the appellant's father, where he, the appellant was employed. The battery charger was found in a nearby garage. When interviewed by the police the appellant admitted using both stolen items while working in his father's garage.

The father was charged with dishonestly handling stolen goods by receiving them and the appellant with assisting in their retention. In respect of the appellant the jury were directed that if they were satisfied that the appellant had used the goods, knowing or believing them to be stolen, then he would be guilty of the offence charged because the goods were in his control or possession. The jury convicted both the appellant and his father. On appeal by the appellant on the ground that the jury had been misdirected.

Held, that the question whether or not stolen goods were in the control or possession of an accused person, though relevant to a charge of handling by receiving, was not relevant to a charge of handling by assisting in their retention for the benefit of another for the purposes of section 22 (1) of the Theft Act 1968; thus, for the above reasons, the jury had been misdirected, for although the criminal transaction was complete when the father received the goods, as all the appellant had done was to use them thereafter he was not guilty of assisting in their retention, and the appeal would be allowed and his conviction quashed.

DUNN LJ — . . . It is accepted in this Court that the question whether or not the goods are in the control or possession of the accused, though relevant to a charge of handling by receiving, is not relevant to a charge of handling by assisting in their retention for the benefit of another. The deputy judge left the case to the jury simply on the basis that if they were satisfied that the appellant had used the goods, knowing or believing them to be stolen, then he would be guilty of the offence as charged. . . .

The mere use of goods knowing them to be stolen is not enough. It must be proved that in some way the accused was assisting in the retention of the goods by concealing them, or making them more difficult to identify, or by holding them pending their ultimate disposal, or by some other act that was part of the chain of the dishonest handling. As Mr. Pearse Wheatley said, this criminal transaction was complete when the father received the goods. All that the appellant did was to use them thereafter. In the view of this Court the judge was wrong in the particular circumstances of this case to direct the jury that if they were satisfied of that, then the appellant was guilty. Accordingly this appeal must be allowed and the conviction quashed.

R v *Kanwar* [1982] Crim LR 532   Court of Appeal

The police searched the appellant's house in her absence and found property which had been brought there by her husband and which was later identified as the proceeds of burglaries. During a second police search the appellant entered the house, said that there was no stolen property there, and when questioned about specific articles told lies to persuade the police that they were lawfully hers. She was charged with handling stolen goods contrary to section 22 (1) of the Theft Act 1968 by dishonestly assisting in their retention for the benefit of her husband. On conviction she appealed on the ground that the verdict was unsafe and unsatisfactory.

Held, dismissing the appeal, that verbal representations, whether oral or in writing, made to conceal the identity of stolen goods, if made dishonestly and for another's benefit, might amount to handling stolen goods by assisting in their retention within the meaning of section 22 of the Theft Act 1968. It was not enough merely to use stolen goods in the possession of another. Something must be done intentionally, dishonestly, knowing or believing the goods to be stolen, for the purpose of enabling the goods to be retained for the benefit of another. There was no reason, however, why that assistance should be restricted to physical acts, nor need it be successful in its object. The appellant lied to protect her husband, but nonetheless she was dishonestly assisting in the retention of the stolen property.

Commentary. If the appellant had been believed by the police and they had gone away, leaving her husband in possession of the stolen property, her conduct would plainly have amounted to assistance in the retention of the goods by another person in the ordinary meaning of the words used in the section. A refusal to answer questions might also, in fact, have assisted the husband to retain possession but it would not have amounted to an offence: *Brown* [1970] 1 QB 105. This depends however on the fact that an omission to act does not constitute an offence unless the criminal law recognises a duty to act; and it does not recognise any general duty to answer questions put by the police or anyone else: *Rice* v *Connolly* [1966] 2 QB 414. The positive act of deception is entirely different. Merely to use the stolen goods does not in itself constitute an offence for the obvious reason that it does not necessarily amount to assistance in the retention of the goods.

(f) When is an act considered to be 'otherwise than in the course of the stealing'?

How long does the stealing last?

R v *Pitham and Hehl* (1976) 65 Cr App Rep 45   Court of Appeal

(See also above, page 3, for a fuller report of this case.)

LAWTON LJ — . . . What was the appropriation in this case? The jury found that the two appellants had handled the property *after* Millman had stolen it. That is clear from their acquittal of these two appellants on count 3 of the indictment which had charged them jointly with Millman. What had Millman done? He had assumed the rights of the owner. He had done that when he took the two appellants to 20 Parry Road, showed them the property and invited them to buy what they wanted. He was then acting as the owner. He was then, in the words of the statute, "assuming the rights of the owner." The moment he did that he appropriated McGregor's goods to himself. The appropriation was complete. After this appropriation had been completed there was no question of these two appellants taking part, in the words of section 22, in dealing with the goods "in the course of the stealing."

For a different view of appropriation, i.e., that it can be a continuing act, see *R* v *Hale* (robbery, above page 68) and *R* v *Gregory* (burglary, above page 86). J. C. Smith suggests (*The Law of Theft*, 5th ed., para. 410) that in the light of *R* v *Hale*, *R* v *Pitham and Hehl* is wrongly decided, but it is uncertain what view the courts will take if the point arises for decision again. It does seem anomalous to have different views of appropriation for the purposes of defining different offences under the same statute.

What does seem to be clear is that 'otherwise than in the course of the stealing' gives only the 'first thief' immunity from a handling charge:

R v *Sainthouse* [1980] Crim LR 506   Court of Appeal

The appellant was present while another man stole from the boot of an unattended car a box full of tools, a can of petrol and a brief-case. The appellant, who was admittedly dishonest, sold the box and tools, forced open the brief-case and took some part in putting the petrol from the can into the vehicle used by him and the other man. Later on the same day the appellant put the brief-case inside a suitcase stolen by the other man, which the appellant knew was to be thrown away. The appellant was arraigned at the Crown Court on two counts of theft of the property, contrary to section 1 (1) of the Theft Act 1968. He offered to plead guilty to handling but the prosecution would not accept the plea and he pleaded not guilty as charged. The recorder questioned the appellant when giving evidence in chief and then ruled that, on the appellant's own account in the witness box, he was guilty; the jury were directed to return verdicts of guilty, which they did. He appealed on the grounds, *inter alia*, that the recorder was wrong in ruling that the appellant could be said to have appropriated the property at a time when the property had already been appropriated by the other man and the legislature could not have intended to provide that a person might (subject to the exception in s. 22) be guilty of both stealing and handling goods by the same actions.

Held, allowing the appeal, that the legislature's intention was to be sought from the words used in the statute. There was no need to go further than section 1 (1) and section 3 (1), from which it followed that, when the actions of the handler amounted to a dishonest assumption by him of the rights of an owner with the intent permanently to deprive, the handler would also be guilty of theft; e.g. *Stapylton* v *O'Callaghan* [1973] 2 All ER 782, DC. Nothing in section 22, apart from the words in parenthesis ("otherwise than in the course of the stealing") indicated that handling was to be treated as an offence separate and apart from theft. Difficult questions might arise as to what was or was not done "in the course of stealing" e.g. *Pitham and Hehl* (1976) 65 Cr App R 45, but they were irrelevant, for the use of "the" made clear that the reference was to the previous stealing, namely, the theft by the other man. The recorder was technically correct in deciding that the appellant's handling actions were capable of amounting to the dishonest appropriation necessary for establishing theft; it would have been better to have left the matter to the jury. However, he had taken too active a part in the prosecution of the case, the convictions were unsatisfactory and they had to be quashed.

Commentary. A person who dishonestly receives stolen goods will, in the great majority of cases, dishonestly appropriate property belonging to another (*i.e.* the true owner) with the intention of permanently depriving the other of it; so he will be guilty of theft. A person who dishonestly undertakes or assists in the retention, removal, disposal or realisation of the stolen goods by or for the benefit of another person will, in the great majority of cases, either dishonestly appropriate, or aid, abet, counsel or procure the appropriation of, property belonging to another with the intention of permanently depriving the other of it; so he too will be guilty of theft. Thus almost all handlers are also thieves. Some may not be because section 22 does not require an intention permanently to deprive; but there will be few handlers who do not in fact have such an intention.

The words, "otherwise than in the course of the stealing," which govern all types of handling clearly relate to the stealing which results in the goods being stolen at the instant before the defendant receives them or otherwise handles them.

R v Dolan (1976) 62 Cr App Rep 36   Court of Appeal

A defendant may be convicted both of theft and of handling the same goods, if the evidence warrants such a conclusion. If the handling of the goods occurred only in the course of the theft, he cannot be found guilty of handling, by reason of section 22 (1) of the Theft Act 1968, but if he handles the goods later than the occasion of the theft, he may be convicted both of theft and handling.

It is now settled that the prosecution do not have a positive duty to prove that the handling is 'otherwise than in the course of the stealing' (*R v Cash* [1985] Crim LR 311).

(g) When is the handling 'by or for the benefit of another person'?

If the type of handling charged is other than receiving or arranging to receive it must be done 'by or for the benefit of another person' (s. 22(1)).

The defendant's action is not done 'for the benefit of another person' if the only other person involved in the transaction is a bona-fide purchaser for value without notice:

R v Bloxham [1982] 1 All ER 582   House of Lords

In January 1977 the defendant agreed to buy a car for £1,300 not knowing that it had been stolen and fitted with false number plates. He paid £500 on account, the balance to be paid on receipt of registration documents, which were never produced. In December he sold it for £200 to a man he did not know, who was prepared to buy it without documents. He admitted to the police that by May 1977 he suspected that the car had been stolen. He was charged with handling stolen goods contrary to section 22 (1) of the Theft Act 1968, in that he had dishonestly undertaken or assisted in the disposal or realisation of the stolen vehicle by or for the benefit of the unknown purchaser. The trial judge rejected a submission that the charge did not, in the light of the facts, reveal an offence known to the law and ruled that the realisation was for the benefit of the unknown buyer. The defendant thereupon pleaded guilty to the charge.

On the defendant's appeal against conviction, the Court of Appeal dismissed the appeal.

On appeal by the defendant:—

Held, allowing the appeal, (1) that the single offence created by the second half of section 22 (1) of the Theft Act 1968 contemplated its committal by the activities there specified in one or other of two ways, namely, either the offender might himself undertake the activity *for the benefit of another person*, or the activity might be undertaken *by* another person and the offender might assist him, and it followed that the category of other persons contemplated by the subsection was subject to the same limitations whichever way the offence was committed . . . that, accordingly, a purchaser, as such, of stolen goods could not be "another person" within the subsection since his act of purchase could not sensibly be described as a disposal or realisation of the goods *by* him, and, equally, therefore, albeit the sale to him could be described as a disposal or realisation for his benefit, the transaction was not within the ambit of the subsection. . . .

LORD BRIDGE OF HARWICH – . . . The judge ruled that the purchaser derived a benefit from the transaction, in that, although he got no title, he had the use of the car; that there was no reason to give any restricted construction to the words "another person" in the subsection; that, accordingly, on the undisputed facts, the appellant had undertaken the disposal or realisation of the car for the benefit of another person within the meaning of section 22 (1). In face of this ruling the appellant entered a plea of guilty, thereby, it may be noted, confessing both his guilty knowledge and his dishonesty in relation to the December transaction.

On appeal against conviction to the Court of Appeal, the court affirmed the trial judge's ruling and dismissed the appeal. The court certified the following point of law of general public importance as involved in their decision:

"Does a bona fide purchaser for a value commit an offence of dishonestly undertaking the disposal or realisation of stolen property for the benefit of another if when he sells the goods on he knows or believes them to be stolen."

The crucial words to be construed are "undertakes . . . their . . . disposal or realisation . . . for the benefit of another person." Considering these words first in isolation, it seems to me that, if A sells his own goods to B it is a somewhat strained use of language to describe this as a disposal or realisation of the goods for the benefit of B. True it is that B obtains a benefit from the transaction, but it is surely more natural to say that the disposal or realisation is for A's benefit than for B's. It is the purchase, not the sale, that is for the benefit of B. It is only when A in selling as agent for a third party C that it would be entirely natural to describe the sale as a disposal or realisation for the benefit of another person.

But the words cannot, of course, be construed in isolation. They must be construed in their context, bearing in mind, as I have pointed out, that the second half of the subsection creates a single offence which can be committed in various ways. I can ignore for present purposes the concluding words "or if he arranges to do so," which throw no light on the point at issue. The preceding words contemplate four activities (retention, removal, disposal, realisation). The offence can be committed in relation to any one of these activities in one or other of two ways. First, the offender may himself undertake the activity *for the benefit of* another person. Secondly, the activity may be undertaken *by* another person and the offender may assist him. Of course, if the thief or an original receiver and his friend act together in, say, removing the stolen goods, the friend may be committing the offence in both ways. But this does not invalidate the analysis and if the analysis holds good, it must follow, I think, that the category of other persons contemplated by the subsection is subject to the same limitations in whichever way the offence is committed. Accordingly, a purchaser, as such, of stolen goods, cannot, in my opinion, be "another person" within the subsection, since his act of purchase could not sensibly be described as disposal or realisation of the stolen goods *by* him. Equally, therefore, even if the sale to him could be described as a disposal or realisation for his benefit, the transaction is not, in my view, within the ambit of the subsection. In forming this opinion I have not overlooked that in *R* v *Deakin* [1972] 1 WLR 1618, 1624, Phillimore LJ said of the appellant, a purchaser of stolen goods who was clearly guilty of an offence under the first half of section 22 (1) but had only been charged under the second half, that he was "involved in the realisation." If he meant to say that a purchase of goods is a realisation of those goods by the purchaser, I must express my respectful disagreement.

If the foregoing considerations do not resolve the issue of construction in favour of the appellant, at least they are, I believe, sufficient to demonstrate that there is an ambiguity. Conversely it is no doubt right to recognise that the words to be construed are capable of the meaning which commended itself to the learned trial judge and to the Court of Appeal. In these circumstances, it is proper to test the question whether the opinion I have expressed in favour of a limited construction of the phrase "for the benefit of another person" is to be preferred to the broader meaning adopted by the courts below, by any available aids to construction apt for the resolution of statutory ambiguities.

As a general rule, ambiguities in a criminal state are to be resolved in favour of the subject, sc. in favour of the narrower rather than the wider operation of an ambiguous penal provision. But here there are, in my opinion, more specific and weightier indications which point in the same direction as the general rule.

First, it is significant that the Theft Act 1968, notwithstanding the wide ambit of the definition of theft provided by sections 1 and 3 (1), specifically protects the innocent purchaser of goods who subsequently discovers that they were stolen, by section 3 (2) which provides:

"Where property or a right or interest in property is or purports to be transferred for value to a person acting in good faith, no later assumption by him of rights which he believed himself to be acquiring shall, by reason of any defect in the transferor's title, amount to theft of the property."

It follows that, though some might think that in this situation honesty would require the purchaser, once he knew the goods were stolen, to seek out the true owner and return them, the criminal law allows him to retain them with impunity for his own benefit. It hardly seems consistent with this that, if he deals with them for the benefit of a third party in some way that falls within the ambit of the activities referred to in the second half of section 22 (1), he risks prosecution for handling which carries a heavier maximum penalty (14 years) than theft (10 years). The force of this consideration is not, in my view, significantly weakened by the possibility that the innocent purchaser of stolen goods who sells them after learning they were stolen may commit the quite distinct offences of obtaining by deception (if he represents that he has a good title) or, conceivably, of aiding and abetting the commission by the purchaser of the offence of handling by receiving (if both know the goods were stolen).

Secondly, it is clear that the words in parenthesis in section 22 (1) "otherwise than in the course of the stealing" were designed to avoid subjecting thieves, in the ordinary course, to the heavier penalty provided for handlers. But most thieves realise the goods they have stolen by disposing of them to third parties. If the judge and the Court of Appeal were right, all such thieves are liable to prosecution as principals both for theft and for handling under the second half of section 22 (1).

Finally, we have the benefit of the report of the Criminal Law Revision Committee, 8th Report, Theft and Related Offences (1966) (Cmnd. 2977), which led to the passing of the Theft Act 1968 including the provisions presently under consideration in the same form as they appeared in the draft Bill annexed to the report, to assist us in ascertaining what was the mischief which the Act, and in particular the new offence created by section 22 (1), was intended to cure. We are entitled to consider the report for this purpose to assist us in resolving any ambiguity, though we are not, of course, entitled to take account of what the committee thought their draft Bill meant: *Black-Clawson International Ltd.* v *Papierwerke Waldhof-Aschaffenberg A.G.* [1975] AC 591.

There is a long section in the report headed "Handling stolen goods, etc." from paragraphs 126 to 144. The Committee, after drawing attention to the limitations of the existing offence of receiving, say in paragraph 127:

" . . . we are in favour of extending the scope of the offence to certain other kinds of meddling with stolen property. This is because the object should be to combat theft by making it more difficult and less profitable to dispose of stolen property. Since thieves may be helped not only by buying the property but also in other ways such as facilitating its disposal, it seems right that the offence should extend to these kinds of assistance."

This gives a general indication of the mischief aimed at. The ensuing paragraphs, after setting out the proposed new provision in the terms which now appear in section 22 (1) of the Act, give numerous illustrations of the activities contemplated as proper to attract the same criminal sanction as that previously attaching to the old offence of receiving. Throughout these paragraphs there is no hint that a situation in any way approximating to the circumstances of the instant case lay within the target area of the mischief which the committee intended their new provision to hit.

For these reasons I have reached the conclusion that any ambiguity in the relevant language of section 22 (1) should be resolved in favour of the narrower meaning suggested earlier in this opinion. I would accordingly answer the certified question in the negative and allow the appeal.

(2) THE MENS REA

Handling requires proof of the following two elements:

(a) dishonesty,
(b) knowledge or belief that the goods are stolen goods.

(a) Dishonesty

An intention to return the goods to the true owner or to the police would prevent an offence being committed, even if the goods had been received in the knowledge that they were stolen. The determination of the defendant's honesty or otherwise must be a matter of fact for the jury as in a s. 1 offence (see *R* v *Ghosh*, above page 52).

(b) Knowledge or belief that the goods are stolen goods

To determine whether or not the defendant knew or believed that the goods were stolen a subjective test is applied. The fact that any reasonable man would have known that the goods were stolen goods is only evidence to show the likelihood that the defendant himself believed that they were stolen:

R v *Stagg* [1978] Crim LR 227   Court of Appeal

Police searched S's house and found in her handbag jewellery which had been obtained by the use of a stolen credit card a few days previously. The police said some of the items had been in a white box, the others in a purse, which had both been in the handbag. S told the police she was looking after the jewellery for R, who had given it to her two weeks before. Told the circumstances in which the items had been obtained, she said: "All right, but I can't tell you any more." Her evidence was that all the items had been in the box, which she had not known contained jewellery until shown it by the police. She had been keeping it for E, not R, and denied telling the police it was for R. In cross-examination she said that had she opened the box she would have asked E the origin of the jewellery out of curiosity and would not have kept it had she been made suspicious by his answers. In directing the jury as to the ingredient of knowledge at the time of receipt the judge told them that the standard to be applied was an objective one.
Held, following *Atwal* v *Mussey*, 56 Cr. App R 6, *Grainge*, 59 Cr App R 3 and *Griffiths*, 60 Cr App R 14 and allowing the appeal against conviction, the test to

be applied was a subjective one. Counsel for the Crown had submitted that the summing-up as a whole was not defective and stressed that the defence put forward by S had not been that she was unaware that the goods were stolen but that she was unaware of what they were. However, the court had reached the conclusion that the jury having through inadvertence been misdirected as to the correct test to apply as regards a material consideration on a matter which had to be proved by the prosecution, even though that matter was not the first string of S's defence, the conviction must be quashed.

Belief is not to be equated with suspicion:

R v *Grainge* [1974] 1 All ER 928   Court of Appeal

The appellant and a companion, O, went into a shop where the companion stole a pocket calculator. After leaving the shop O was seen to hand the calculator to the appellant. The appellant was charged with handling stolen goods, contrary to s. 22(1) of the Theft Act 1968, the particulars of the offence being that he had received the calculator knowing or believing that it had been stolen. In evidence the appellant stated that O was a friend of his, that he had never given a second thought about the calculator, that he thought O was honest and that he had been under the impression that it was a radio which O had asked him to hold for him as he, O, had a hole in his pocket. The jury were directed that it was for them to decide whether, at the time when the goods were handled, the appellant knew, believed or suspected that the article had been stolen and further that guilty knowledge could be inferred 'from the surrounding circumstances [of] the transaction, or if a man shuts his eyes and does not make an enquiry. A person is not entitled to shut his eyes if circumstances look suspicious and from suspicion such as that you can infer guilty knowledge'. The appellant was convicted and appealed.

Held — The appeal would be allowed and the conviction quashed for the following reasons—

(i)   In order to prove the required knowledge or belief on the part of an accused it was at least necessary to show that he had suspected that the goods in question had been stolen but had deliberately shut his eyes to the consequences. However the summing-up as a whole could well have left the jury with the impression that suspicious circumstances, irrespective of whether or not the appellant appreciated that they were suspicious, imposed a duty as a matter of law to act and enquire and that a failure to do so was to be treated as knowledge or belief; *Atwal* v *Massey* [1971] 3 All ER 881 applied.

(ii)   The recorder had failed to make it plain to the jury that, where the indictment alleged receiving, it was at the moment of receipt, and not at any time during the handling thereafter, that guilty knowledge had to be proved. . . .

R v *Reader* (1978) 66 Cr App Rep 33   Court of Appeal

WALLER LJ — . . . We are clearly of opinion that to have in mind that it is more likely that they are stolen than that they are not, which is the test which the judge told the jury to apply, is not sufficient to comply with the terms of the section. To believe that the goods are probably stolen is not to believe that the goods are stolen, and in our view this was a misdirection by the learned judge and one which was not a misdirection which was in favour of the appellant but which was against him. The jury were being told to accept a lower state of guilty mind than the section actually requires.

Our attention was drawn to two cases, *Grainge* (1973) 59 Cr App R 3; [1974] 1 WLR 619, and *Griffiths* (1974) 60 Cr App R 14, where two other directions about suspicion were considered by this Court. In the case of *Grainge* (*supra*) in giving the judgment of the Court, Eveleigh J pointed out that where there are simple words it is undesirable for the judge to try to explain what those words mean, and we entirely agree with that. If the learned judge had left the word "belief" entirely alone and left the jury to decide what is belief, that is something which everybody is concerned with almost every day of their lives and they would have been able to come to a proper conclusion without any explanation being given. In his mistaken attempt to give an explanation he erred. He erred in a sense in two ways, not only by putting the degree of belief wrong, but also in confusing the jury in our view by adding balance of probabilities into the concept which they had to be satisfied about. Accordingly there was in our view a material misdirection in this case.

R v Belleni [1980] Crim LR 437   Court of Appeal

The defendant was a partner in a firm which owned two hardware and do-it-yourself shops. One of the shops was run by a manager, but the defendant visited it regularly. He and his manager were indicted in three counts of handling stolen screws and hinges. The issue for the jury was whether the defendant knew that the goods were stolen. The trial judge, when directing the jury as to the constituents of handling, said: ". . . a man must not turn a blind eye to things which would have told him — had he given the matter ordinary attention — that he was in fact taking possession of stolen property," and ". . . a man must not shut — as it were — a convenient blind eye to things which would have undoubtedly indicated to him that he ought to be on his inquiry about that property." The defendant appealed on the ground tht the judge had misdirected the jury.

Held, allowing the appeal, that knowledge or belief was the essence of the offence of handling. Suspicion was not enough, unless it amounted to belief, and that was the vice of a "blind eye" direction. Proof that a man should have been put on inquiry was not proof that he knew or believed the goods to have been stolen. If a jury were satisfied that an accused man's eyes were blind, they would have to go on to consider whether this blindness resulted from the fact that he already knew or believed that the goods were stolen, or merely from the fact that he was gullible, stupid or inattentive. In the present case the jury had been misdirected, and the conviction must be quashed.

Commentary. The courts do not seem to have faced up to the difficulties involved in their interpretation of section 22 (1). They have told us what "believing" does not mean but have given little guidance as to what it does mean.

It does not mean "thinking he knows the goods to be stolen": *Haughton* v *Smith* [1975] AC at p. 485. The goods must actually be stolen so the person who thinks he knows must in fact know. It does not mean thinking that the goods are probably stolen: *Reader* (1977) 66 Cr App R at p. 36. It does not mean suspecting that goods are stolen and wilfully turning a blind eye. What does this leave except what is already covered by "knowing"? It seems that "believing" adds nothing yet it is right to direct the jury that they must convict if they are satisfied that the defendant knew *or* believed the goods to be stolen without offering them any guidance as to what the word means: *Reader*, above. Of course the jury may well then adopt one of the meanings which the court has excluded and, if they take any notice of the disjunctive, "or," it is difficult to see how they can avoid doing so. It is not good enough to say that "belief is something which everybody is concerned with almost every day of their lives" (*Reader*, above). If the meaning of the word is not apparent to those who have long studied the matter it is unduly optimistic to expect the jury to have a clear view about it and impossible to suppose that the view will accord with the negative decisions of the courts. It is high time the Court of Appeal gave some positive guidance.

R v Lincoln [1980] Crim LR 575   Court of Appeal

The appellant was charged with handling stolen goods, contrary to section 22 (1) of the Theft Act 1968. The jury were directed that the prosecution had to prove that, at the time he received the items of stolen property dishonestly he knew or believed it to be stolen property, which could be proved in three ways: if he was aware of the theft; if he believed that the item was stolen; and "even if he suspected that it was stolen property and deliberately shut his eyes to the circumstances." He was convicted. He appealed against conviction on the ground of misdirection by too literal an application of *Atwal* v *Massey* (1971) 56 Cr App R 6, 7.

Held, allowing the appeal, that section 22 (1) did not mention suspicion. The type of direction given to the jury had previously been the cause of trouble. In *Griffiths* (1974) 60 Cr App R 14 James LJ said that there was a danger in adopting the passage from *Atwal* v *Massey*: to direct the jury that the offence was committed if the person charged, suspecting that the goods were stolen, deliberately shut his eyes to the circumstances as an alternative to knowing or believing the goods were stolen, was a misdirection; but to direct them that, in common sense and in law they might find that he knew or believed the goods to be stolen because he deliberately shut his eyes to the circumstances, was a proper direction. The court wished to draw attention to the passage in *Griffiths* and to emphasise, for courts in future, that that passage represented a proper direction but that a direction such as was given in the instant case was incorrect and would result in the conviction being quashed. In the circumstances the proviso could not be applied, and the conviction would be quashed

Commentary. . . . The present decision seems to do nothing to resolve the problem posed in the commentary on *Bellenie* [1980] Crim LR 437.

(3) PROOF AND PROCEDURE IN HANDLING CASES

(a) Proof

Proof of handling is made easier for the prosecution in three ways:

(i)   by s. 27(3) Theft Act 1968,
(ii)   by the so-called 'doctrine of recent possession',
(iii) by s. 74 of the Police and Criminal Evidence Act 1984.

(i) Section 27(3) Theft Act 1968

Where a person is being proceeded against for handling stolen goods (but not for any offence other than handling stolen goods), then at any stage of the proceedings, if evidence has been given of his having or arranging to have in his possession the goods the subject of the charge, or of his undertaking or assisting in, or arranging to undertake or assist in, their retention, removal, disposal or realisation, the following evidence shall be admissible for the purpose of proving that he knew or believed the goods to be stolen goods:—

(a)   evidence that he has had in his possession, or has undertaken or assisted in the retention, removal, disposal or realisation of, stolen goods from any theft taking place not earlier than twelve months before the offence charged; and
(b)   (provided that seven days' notice in writing has been given to him of the intention to prove the conviction) evidence that he has within the five years preceding the date of the offence charged been convicted of theft or of handling stolen goods.

(ii) The 'doctrine of recent possession'

If a defendant is found in possession of goods which have been recently stolen the jury *may* infer that he came into possession of those goods knowing or believing them to be stolen:

R v Ball and Winning (1983) 77 Cr App Rep 131   Court of Appeal

McCULLOUGH J — . . . The so called doctrine of recent possession is misnamed. It has nothing to do with goods recently possessed. It concerns possession of goods recently stolen. It is not even a doctrine. It is in fact no more than an inference which a jury may, or may not, think it right to draw about the state of mind of a defendant who is dealing in goods stolen not long beforehand. It is based on common sense.

Stolen goods frequently pass quickly from hand to hand. Many of those who deal in them knowing or believing them to be stolen tell lies when they are asked to explain how the goods came into their possession. Others prefer to give no explanation. That has been the experience of the courts for generations. So when a defendant is found to have been in possession of goods recently stolen and either gives no explanation of how he came to acquire them innocently or gives an explanation which is patently untrue, it is the practice of judges to tell juries that they may, if they think it right, infer that he acquired them knowing

or believing that they were stolen. The innocent man has nothing to fear from
this. He has no need to lie. He will, as a rule, be only too willing to give his
explanation. It is, in any event, an inference which a jury will only draw if they
think it right to do so.

(iii) Section 74 Police and Criminal Evidence Act 1984

Walters and O'Connell: A Guide to The Police and Criminal Evidence Act 1984
(page 92)

Section 74 of the 1984 Act now brings the criminal law into line with the
civil law, in that where evidence is given (providing it is relevant to the instant
case) that the person was convicted of an offence, he is deemed to have committed
that offence, subject to the proviso set out in s. 74(2) and (3), 'unless the
contrary is proved'.

So the position now is that, in cases where the guilt of the accused depends
on another person having committed an offence, the prosecution simply have to
prove that other person was convicted of the offence. It follows that the old rule
that the fact that a thief has been convicted, far from being conclusive against
the alleged handler, was not even admissible evidence that the goods were stolen,
has now gone. The prosecution may now, under s. 74 (2), if they wish, in a case
of dishonestly handling stolen goods contrary to s. 22 of the Theft Act 1968,
prove, at the trial of the alleged handler, the conviction of the thief to prove that
the goods involved are in fact stolen goods.

(b) Procedure in handling cases

Section 27(1) and (2) Theft Act 1968

*(1) Any number of persons may be charged in one indictment, with reference to
the same theft, with having at different times or at the same time handled all or
any of the stolen goods, and the persons so charged may be tried together.*

*(2) On the trial of two or more persons indicated for jointly handling any
stolen goods the jury may find any of the accused guilty if the jury are satisfied
that he handled all or any of the stolen goods, whether or not he did so jointly
with the other accused or any of them.*

R v French [1973] Crim LR 632   Court of Appeal

F was convicted of handling by receiving. He was jointly indicted with J who
was also convicted. F took the goods to J's shop were J then received them. He
appealed on the ground that at the handling by J was subsequent to the handling
by him they should have been charged in separate counts.

Held, dismissing the appeal the situation was covered by section 27 (2) of the
Theft Act 1968. It might be that the person who drafted the indictment was not

given the true facts or misunderstood them, but when they came out at the trial there was no reason why effect should not be given to the section instead of quashing the conviction on a technicality. The judge properly directed the jury that the handlings by F and J were quite separate and the case against each must be considered separately.

Commentary. Section 27 (2) re-enacts with some modifications a provision formerly contained in the Larceny Act 1916, s. 44 (5). See the Criminal Law Revision Committee's Eighth Report, Annex 2, p. 133. If there were successive handlings of the same stolen goods two separate offences, and not a single joint offence, were committed. Section 27 (2) created an exception to rule laid down in *Scaramanga* (1963) 47 Cr App R 213 and *Parker* [1969] 2 QB 248, which was overruled in *DPP* v *Merriman* [1972] 3 All ER 42. Under the rule in *Merriman* where two persons are charged with jointly committing the same act and it appears that they were not acting in concert, each may be convicted of committing that act separately. The situation envisaged by section 27 (2) goes further in that it allows conviction, not merely where there is separate participation in a single act, but where there are different acts in relation to the same stolen goods.

9 COMMON ELEMENTS IN DECEPTION OFFENCES

The Theft Acts contain a number of offences which prohibit a defendant from obtaining various advantages by deception. They are:

(a) Obtaining property: 1968 Act s. 15
(b) Obtaining a pecuniary advantage: 1968 Act s. 16
(c) Procuring the execution of a valuable security: 1968 Act s. 20(2)
(d) Obtaining services: 1978 Act s. 1
(e) Securing the remission of a liability: 1978 Act s. 2(1)(a)
(f) Inducing a creditor to wait for or to forgo payment: 1978 Act: s. 2(1)(b)
(g) Obtaining an exemption from or abatement of liability: 1978 Act s. 2(1)(c)

These offences have certain elements in common and it is convenient to deal with those elements first, reserving the particular difficulties peculiar to each of the offences for separate consideration.

The common elements can be set out as follows:

(a) There must be a causal link between the deception and the prohibited result.

(i) The deception must be operative.
(ii) Where cheque or credit cards are involved the deception will be presumed to be operative in certain circumstances.
(iii) A human mind must be deceived.
(iv) The deception must not be too remote from the prohibited result.

(b) There must be a deception, that is, an untrue 'statement'.

(i) The statement must actually be false.
(ii) The defendant must be deliberate or reckless as to the falsity of the statement.
(iii) The statement must be by words or conduct (including implied statements).

(c)   The defendant must be dishonest.

(a) There must be a causal link between the deception and the prohibited result

(i) The deception must be operative.

A. T. H. Smith: The Idea of Criminal Deception [1982] Crim LR 721

Deception defined

Deception could have been explained by the legislators in the Theft Act, but it was not. The Act confines itself to the somewhat unhelpful observation that " 'deception' means any deception,"[9] the remainder of the section being devoted to reversing certain of the old common law rules surrounding the former "false pretences." To some extent this left the courts free to apply their own gloss to the word as the need to do so arose. But "deception" already had, by the time the Theft Act became law in 1968, acquired a reasonably settled meaning, classically that stated by Buckley J in *Re London and Globe Finance Corporation.*[10] "To deceive is, I apprehend, to induce a man to believe that a thing is true which is false . . . to deceive is by falsehood to induce a state of mind." The Criminal Law Revision Committee explained its use of "deception" by saying:

> "The substitution of 'deception' for 'false pretence' is chiefly a matter of language. The word 'deception' seems to us (as to the framers of the American Law Institute's Model Penal Code) to have the advantage of directing attention to the effect that the offender deliberately produced on the mind of the person deceived, whereas 'false pretence' makes one think of what exactly the offender did in order to deceive. 'Deception' seems also more apt in relation to deception by conduct."[11]

This reinforces the suggestion in Buckley J's definition that it is essential that the representation must operate on the conscious mind of the victim and cause him to believe that the facts are otherwise than they really are.

Apart from being inherent in the very notion of deception, there is an additional reason why the motivation of the victim must be examined in deception cases. It must be shown by the prosecution that the obtaining was *caused* by the deception, since in all the deception offences it must be established that the obtaining was effected "by" the deception. As Professor Williams puts it, "an obvious consequence of the rule [as to causation] is that the deception must affect the victim's mind. Otherwise, there will be at most an attempted deception."[12] This analysis shows that, as classically understood, there are at least two links in the causal chain. It must be shown that the victim was induced into a certain affirmative belief, and that as a result of his belief, he behaved in a certain way, as a further result of which property (or a service or other protected interest) was obtained.

[9] Theft Act 1968, s. 15 (4).

10 [1903] 1 Ch. 728 at p. 732. And see Lord Denning in *Welham* v *DPP* [1961] AC 103 at
p. 133. " 'To deceive' here conveys the element of deceit, which induces a state of mind . . ."
11 8th Report, *Theft and Related Offences,* Cmnd. 2977, para. 87.
12 Williams, *Textbook of Criminal Law* (1978), p. 749. *Cp.* Smith and Hogan, *Criminal Law*
(4th ed., 1978), p. 540. "The deception must then operate on the mind of P and *cause* him
to part with the property."

The deception need not operate on the mind of the loser:

Smith v **Koumourou** [1979] Crim LR 116   Queen's Bench Division

In March 1976 a constable took possession of the defendant's car excise
licence, which was due to expire in September 1976, and gave the defendant a
police memorandum to display on his windscreen instead. The memorandum
was undated. In October 1977 another constable found the undated memorandum
still displayed on the defendant's windscreen and was misled into thinking that it
was in substitution for a current excise licence. The defendant was charged with
obtaining a pecuniary advantage by deception under section 16 of the Theft Act
1968. The justices acceded to a submission of no case, being of the view that
the person deceived should be the creditor. The prosecutor appealed by case
stated.

Held, allowing the appeal, that there was no such requirement that the person
deceived should be the creditor. The defendant had obtained the pecuniary
advantage of not being required to pay back-duty under section 9 of the Vehicle
(Excise) Act 1971, as he would have been if the constable had not been misled.
There was a clear causal connection between the deception and the evasion of
liability, and the case clearly fell within Lord Reid's formulation in *DPP* v
Turner [1974] AC 357, 365 that "An obligation is evaded if by some contrivance
the debtor avoids or gets out of fulfilling or performing his obligation." The
case must be remitted to the justices with a direction that a prima facie case has
been shown.

Commentary. The case clearly falls within the wide meaning given to "evades"
in *DPP* v *Turner.* Section 16 (2) (*a*) was, however, repealed on October 20, 1978
by the Theft Act 1978. Whether the defendant's conduct amounts to any
offence under the new Act is by no means clear.

It should be proved, if possible by direct evidence, that the deception affected
the conduct of the person to whom it was addressed:

R v **Laverty** [1970] 3 All ER 432   Court of Appeal

LORD PARKER CJ — . The facts are in a very short compass. The car bearing
number plates DUV 111C, a Hillman Imp, was bought by a Mr Bedborough from
the appellant, and a cheque was given as part of the price. In fact the car bearing
those number plates was a car originally bearing number plates JPA 945C which
had been stolen. According to the appellant when he got the car, and there was
no question of his having stolen it, it was in a bad condition, he repaired it and
he put on to it the chassis and rear number plates of DUV 111C, those plates
having been obtained from another source relating of course to another car.

The charge made in the indictment in count 3 took the form of alleging a false representation which here was by conduct. It was not a false representation that the appellant was the owner and had a good title to sell but the false representation was by purporting that a Hillman Imp motor car which the appellant sold to Roy Clinton Bedborough was the original Hillman Imp motor car, index number DUV 111C.

Although is was contested at the trial, it was conceded in this court that there was a representation by conduct that the car being sold to Mr Bedborough was the original Hillman Imp to which the chassis plate and rear plate which it bore had been assigned. It is conceded that such a representation was made by conduct; it is clear that that was false, and false to the knowledge of the appellant. The sole question was whether this false representation operated on Mr Bedborough's mind so as to cause him to hand over this cheque.

As sometimes happens, in this case Mr Bedborough did not give the answers which were helpful to the prosecution, and no leading questions could be put. The nearest answer was 'I bought this because I thought the appellant was the owner'. In other words Mr Bedborough was saying: 'What induced me to part with my money was the representation by conduct that the appellant had a title to sell.' It was in those circumstances that at the end of the prosecution's case a submission was made that there was no case to answer. The deputy chairman did not accede to that submission. The trial proceeded, and when he came to sum up to the jury, the deputy chairman said:

'There is no evidence at all that anything was said by [the appellant] to that effect, but the prosecution is entitled to say that that representation can be made by conduct, and it is a matter for you whether you feel, in the circumstances of this case, a representation was made by conduct that the motor car in question was the original Hillman Imp, bearing in mind that there had been put upon it number plates with the registration number DUV 111C, one of which indeed had come off the original car, and that in due course a log book was produced; but it does not appear in the evidence that the log book was seen or relied on by Mr. Bedborough at the time when he handed over the cash and the cheque.

'What is meant by "the original Hillman Imp" in this case? You may think that that means the car which was originally so registered, and it is a matter for you whether or not it is a necessary inference that a car offered for sale with the registration number upon it is the car for which that number was originally issued; if you think the answer to that is "yes" then you will have to consider: Is that an inference which must have been in the mind of the purchaser; is it something that must have operated on the mind of Mr. Bedborough and played its part in inducing him to hand over the cash and the cheque?'

The jury apparently were satisfied that that was the true inference and convicted the appellant.

The point really is whether there was any evidence here which enabled the jury to draw that inference. It is axiomatic that it is for the prosecution to prove that the false representation acted on the mind of the purchaser; and in the ordinary way, and the court emphasises this, the matter should be proved by direct evidence. However, it was said in *R* v *Sullivan* that the inducement need not be proved by direct evidence, and I quote from the headnote:

'If the facts are such that the alleged false pretence is the only reason that could be suggested as having been the operative inducement.'

And in the special facts of that case it was held that the prosecution had given sufficient proof, although it was made very clear that the proper way and the ordinary way of proving the matter was by direct evidence.

Counsel for the Crown submits that when the court in *R* v *Sullivan* referred to the only reason that could be suggested, it was not emphasising that it was the only reason but that it was the only inference that could be drawn. He is saying here that the only inference in this case is that the false representation did operate on Mr Bedborough's mind and the jury were fully entitled to come to the conclusion which they did.

This court is very anxious not to extend the principle in *R* v *Sullivan* more than is necessary. The proper way of proving these matters is through the mouth of the person to whom the false representation is conveyed, and further it seems to the court in the present case that no jury could say that the only inference here was that Mr Bedborough parted with his money by reason of this false representation. Mr Bedborough may well have been of the mind as he stated he was, namely that what operated on his mind was the belief that the appellant was the owner. Provided the the [sic] appellant was the owner it may well be that Mr Bedborough did not mind that the car did not bear its original number plates. At any rate as it seems to the court it cannot be said that the only possible inference here is that it actuated on Mr Bedborough's mind.

In those circumstances, although with some reluctance, this court feels that the proper course here is to allow the appeal and quash the conviction.

Etim v *Hatfield* [1975] Crim LR 234   Queen's Bench Division

The defendant applied for supplementary benefit and a local office of the Department of Health and Social Security sent him a benefit order book containing orders bearing the inscription: "To the Post Office: the person named on the first page is entitled after signing the declaration to receive the sum [£9.40] shown on this order at the authorised post office within three calendar months of the due date." The declaration was that he was entitled to the amount shown. Before receiving the book he moved his address and applied to the department's local office appropriate to his new address and was granted supplementary benefit of £10.60, which was paid by giro order for the week beginning June 4, 1973. Subsequently he received the book sent by the original office, signed the declaration on the order for the week beginning June 4, 1973, and was paid the £9.40 at the authorised post office (Cable Street). An information was preferred against him charging that he "on June 6, 1973, at the post office, Cable Street E.1. by deception dishonestly obtained £9.40 belonging to the Department of Health and Social Security with the intention of depriving the department of it, contrary to section 15 (1) of the Theft Act 1968." No post office employee gave evidence, and no evidence other than the declaration, giro order and book was adduced to show that the deception induced the loser to part with the money or that it was the department's property. He was convicted by the justices and his appeal to the Crown Court was dismissed. He appealed by case stated to the Queen's Bench Divisional Court on the grounds that the court was not entitled to find that the money paid belonged to the department or that the deception induced the post office clerk to part with the money.

Held, dismissing the appeal. . . .

It is an essential constituent of the offence that the deception is the cause of the obtaining. This constituent must be proved beyond reasonable doubt like every other constituent of the crime. Like any other fact, however, it may be proved by inference from other facts without direct evidence. In the present case it would seem that there was ample evidence that the post office clerk was deceived — a reasonable jury would have been entitled to infer that the post office clerk would not have handed over the money if the declaration had not been signed. The court seems to have decided that this was a *necessary* inference *i.e.* a reasonable jury could not have decided otherwise. In *Laverty* where there was no direct evidence, the court held that it was not a necessary inference that the deception operated on the victim's mind and therefore the conviction was quashed.

Commentary. . . . Applying *Sullivan* (1945) 30 Cr App R 132 and distinguishing *Laverty* [1971] RTR 124, there was no conceivable reason for the payment to be made other than the false statement in the order, and therefore it was unnecessary to call any person to say that he was deceived. Accordingly the appeal failed.

The courts seem to have become increasingly likely to assume that a misrepresentation operated on someone without any evidence that such was indeed the case. This tendency reaches extremes where cheque cards or credit cards are in question (see below page 159 et seq.), but a similar trend can be seen in other situations:

DPP v *Ray* [1974] AC 370   House of Lords

The defendant and four friends went to a Chinese restaurant intending to have a meal there and pay for it. After eating the main course they decided not to pay for it but they remained until the waiter went out of the room and then they ran from the restaurant. The defendant was convicted by the justices of dishonestly obtaining a pecuniary advantage by deception contrary to section 16 (1) of the Theft Act 1968. The Divisional Court of the Queen's Bench Division quashed the conviction.

On appeal to the House of Lords:—

Held, allowing the appeal (Lord Reid and Lord Hodson dissenting), that the transaction had to be regarded as a whole in that the defendant's conduct was a continuing representation of his present intention to pay and his change of mind produced a deception, the effect of which was that he was treated as an honest customer whose conduct did not call for precautions and, accordingly, the defendant had been rightly convicted of obtaining the evasion of his debt by that deception.

LORD REID (dissenting) — . . . And there is no finding that the waiter was in fact induced to believe that by anything the accused did after he changed his mind. I would infer from the case that all that he intended to do was to take advantage of the first opportunity to escape and evade his obligation to pay.

Deception is an essential ingredient of the offence. Dishonest evasion of an obligation to pay is not enough. I cannot see that there was, in fact, any more than that in this case.

I agree with the Divisional Court [1973] 1 WLR 317, 323:

"His plan was totally lacking in the subtlety of deception and to argue that his remaining in the room until the coast was clear amounted to a representation to the waiter is to introduce an artificiality which should have no place in the Act."

I would therefore dismiss this appeal.

LORD MacDERMOTT — . . . Was the respondent's evasion of the debt obtained by that deception?

I think the material before the justices was enough to show that it was. The obvious effect of the deception was that the respondent and his associates were treated as they had been previously, that is to say as ordinary, honest customers whose conduct did not excite suspicion or call for precautions. In consequence the waiter was off his guard and vanished into the kitchen. That gave the respondent the opportunity of running out without hindrance and he took it. I would therefore answer this second question in the affirmative.

I would, accordingly, allow the appeal and restore the conviction.

LORD MORRIS OF BORTH-Y-GEST — The final question which arises is whether, if there was deception and if there was pecuniary advantage, it was by the deception that the respondent obtained the pecuniary advantage. In my view, this must be a question of fact and the magistrates have found that it was by his deception that the respondent dishonestly evaded payment. It would seem to be clear that if the waiter had thought that if he left the restaurant to go to the kitchen the respondent would at once run out, he (the waiter) would not have left the restaurant and would have taken suitable action. The waiter proceeded on the basis that the implied representation made to him (i.e. of an honest intention to pay) was effective. The waiter was caused to refrain from taking certain courses of action which but for the representation he would have taken. In my view, the respondent during the whole time that he was in the restaurant made and by his continuing conduct continued to make a representation of his intention to pay before leaving. When in place of his original intention he substituted the dishonest intention of running away as soon as the waiter's back was turned, he was continuing to lead the waiter to believe that he intended to pay. He practised a deception on the waiter and by so doing he obtained for himself the pecuniary advantage of evading his obligation to pay before leaving. That he did so dishonestly was found by the magistrates who, in my opinion, rightly convicted him.

I would allow the appeal.

R v *Doukas* [1978] 1 All ER 1061   Court of Appeal

The applicant was employed as a casual wine waiter at a hotel. He was discovered on the hotel premises with six bottles of wine in his coat pockets. He
told the police that if a guest in the restaurant ordered carafe wine he would
substitute his own wine, make out a separate bill and keep the money. He was
charged with the offence under s. 25(1) of the Theft Act 1968 of going equipped
to 'cheat', which, by ss. 25(5) and 15 of the 1968 Act, meant obtaining property
by deception. He was convicted and applied for leave to appeal on the ground,
inter alia, that the prosecution evidence did not prove the necessary causal
connection between the intended deception and the obtaining of money from
the customer.

Held — It had to be assumed that the hypothetical customer against whom
the intended deception was to be practised was reasonably honest as well as
being reasonably intelligent. It could not be supposed that such a customer to
whom the true situation had been made clear would have willingly made himself
a party to what would obviously have been a fraud by the waiter on his employers.
It was therefore open to the jury to find that the obtaining of money from the
customer would have been caused by the deception practised on him. The
application would therefore be dismissed. . . .

*(ii) Where cheque or credit cards are involved the deception will be presumed to be
operative in certain circumstances*

Commissioner of Police for the Metropolis v *Charles* [1977] AC 177
                                                              House of Lords

The defendant was granted an overdraft of £100 by his bank and given a
cheque book and a cheque card on which was printed an undertaking by the
bank to honour any cheque up to £30 on certain stated conditions. Between
December 18 and 31, 1972, he used the card to back 18 cheques for £30 each.
On January 2, 1973, four of them were presented for payment so that his
account was overdrawn to an amount exceeding £100. On the same day the
manager of the bank told him that he should not cash more than one cheque for
£30 a day at a bank but gave him no further instructions as to the use of the
card. He allowed another book of 25 cheques to be issued to him. That night
the defendant used the card to back all 25 cheques for £30 each at a gambling
club.

In relation to two of the cheques he was convicted of obtaining a pecuniary
advantage by deception contrary to section 16 of the Theft Act 1962 [sic]. The
Court of Appeal (Criminal Division) upheld the conviction.

On appeal:—

Held, dismissing the appeal, that, when the drawer of a cheque accepted in
exchange for goods, services or cash used a cheque card, he made to the payee a
representation that he had the actual authority of the bank to enter on its behalf
into the contract expressed on the card that it would honour the cheque on
presentment for payment and accordingly there was evidence to convict the
defendant. . . .

LORD EDMUND-DAVIES — . . . There remains to be considered the vitally
important question of whether it was established that it was as a result of such
dishonest deception that the club's staff were induced to give chips for cheques
and so, in due course, caused the accused's bank account to become improperly
overdrawn. This point exercised the Court of Appeal, though they were not
troubled by the fact that, whereas the deception alleged was said to have induced
the club servants to accept the cheques, the pecuniary advantage was obtained
from and damnified only the bank. In that they were, in my judgment, right, for
R v Kovacks [1974] 1 WLR 370 correctly decided (as, indeed, appellant's
counsel accepted) that, in the words of Lawton LJ, at p. 373:

> "Section 16 (1) does not provide either expressly or by implication that the
> person deceived must suffer any loss arising from the deception. What does
> have to be proved is that the accused by deception obtained for himself or
> another a pecuniary advantage. What there must be is a causal connection
> between the deception used and the pecuniary advantage obtained."

What had troubled the Court of Appeal, however, was the question of inducement, and this after hearing Mr. Tabachnik, learned counsel for the accused,
submit that in a cheque card case there is no such implied representation as that
conveniently labelled "Page (2)":

> "for the simple reason that the payee is not, in the slightest degree, concerned
> with the question of the drawer's credit-worthiness. The state of the drawer's
> account at the bank, the state of the contractual relationship between the
> bank and the drawer is . . . a matter of complete indifference to the payee of
> the cheque; it is a matter to which he never needs to apply his mind. . . . where
> the recipient of the cheque has the bank's express undertaking held out in the
> form of a cheque card to rely on, there is no necessity, in order to give
> business efficacy to the transaction, that there should be any collateral
> representation implied on the part of the drawer of the cheque as to the state
> of his account with the bank or the state of his authority to draw on that
> account. Still less is there any basis for an inference that any such representa-
> tion operates on the mind of the recipient of the cheque as an inducement
> persuading him to accept it. He relies, . . . and relies exclusively, on the bank's
> undertaking embodied in the cheque card." (*per* Bridge LJ [1976] 1 WLR
> 248, 255C–F).

Whether a party was induced to act as he did because of the deception to
which he was dishonestly subjected is a question of fact to be decided on the
evidence adduced in each case. In the present case the Court of Appeal were
apparently led to reject — with some reluctance — the foregoing trenchant
submissions on behalf of the accused because in what the court regarded as the
virtually indistinguishable case of *R v Kovacks* [1974] 1 WLR 370, 373 Lawton
LJ had said:

> "The railway booking clerk and the pet shop owner had been deceived
> because the appellant in presenting the cheque card with her cheque had
> represented that she was entitled to be in possession of it and to use it . . .

The next question is: how did she obtain this pecuniary advantage? On the facts the answer is clear, namely, by inducing the railway booking clerk and the pet shop owner to believe that she was entitled to use the cheque card when she was not."

Then is there room for coming to a different conclusion on the similar, though not identical, facts of the present case? In my judgment, it again emerges clearly from the evidence of Mr. Cersell that there is not. He accepted that

"with a cheque card, so long as the conditions on the back are met, the bank will honour that card irrespective of the state of the drawer's account or the authority, or lack of it, which he has in drawing on the account,"

and that "All those matters, in fact, once there is a cheque card, are totally irrelevant." But in this context it has again to be borne in mind that the witness made clear that the accused's cheques were accepted *only* because he produced a cheque card, and he repeatedly stressed that, had he been aware that the accused was using his cheque book and cheque card "in a way in which he was not allowed or entitled to use [them]" no cheque would have been accepted. The evidence of that witness, taken as a whole, points irresistibly to the conclusions (a) that by this dishonest conduct the accused deceived Mr. Cersell in the manner averred in the particulars of the charges and (b) that Mr. Cersell was thereby induced to accept the cheques because of his belief that the representations as to both cheque and card were true. These and all other relevant matters were fully and fairly dealt with in the admirable summing up of His Honour Judge Finestein QC, the jury showed by their verdicts that they were fully alive to the nature of the issues involved, and in my judgment there was ample evidence to entitle them to arrive at their "guilty" verdicts on the two charges with which we are concerned in this appeal. I would therefore dismiss it.

Something finally needs to be said about the point of law of public importance certified as fit to be considered by this House. It was expressed in this way [1976] 1 WLR 248, 259:

"When the holder of a cheque card presents a cheque in accordance with the conditions of the card which is accepted in exchange for goods, services or cash, does this transaction provide evidence of itself from which it can or should be inferred (a) that the drawer represented that he then had authority, as between himself and the bank, to draw a cheque for that amount, and (b) that the recipient of the cheque was induced by that representation to accept the cheque?"

I have to say that (b) is not a point of law at all. It raises a question of pure fact. As such, it is unanswerable in general terms (which is the object of certifying points for consideration by this House), for whether people were induced must depend on all the circumstances and, above all, upon what the recipient of cheques in those circumstances has to say. In the vast majority of cases the recipient will be a witness, and it becomes a question for the jury who have seen and heard him to determine whether inducement has been established.

It seems, therefore, that whether the deception was operative is a matter for the jury to decide. However it also appears that the jury may infer that the deception was operative where there is little or no evidence to that effect:

R v Lambie [1981] Crim LR 712   House of Lords

The defendant possessed a Barclaycard. She had substantially exceeded her credit limit and been asked to return the card, but at the material time had not done so. She selected some items in a shop and tendered the card. The assistant checked her signature on the voucher against that on the card and ascertained that the total purchase was within the shop's "floor limit" and that the card was not on the current "stop list." She then allowed the defendant to take the goods. The defendant was subsequently charged with, *inter alia,* obtaining a pecuniary advantage by deception, contrary to section 16 (1) of the Theft Act 1968 and was convicted. She appealed against conviction, contending, *inter alia,* that the evidence had not shown that any deception had been operative, and the Court of Appeal (Criminal Division) allowed the appeal. The Crown appealed by leave of the House of Lords.

Held, allowing the appeal, that the representation arising from the presentation of the credit card had nothing to do with the defendant's credit standing at the bank but was a representation of actual authority to make the contract with, in the present case, the shop on the bank's behalf that the bank would honour the voucher on presentation: *Charles* [1977] AC 177. On that view, the existence and terms of the agreement between the bank and the shop were irrelevant, as was the fact that the shop, because of that agreement would look to the bank for payment. As to whether the shop assistant had been induced by the defendant's representation to complete the transaction and allow the defendant's representation to complete the transaction and allow the defendant to take away the goods, had she been asked whether, if she had known that the defendant was acting dishonestly and had no authority from the bank to use the card in that way, she would have completed the transaction, only one answer was possible: "no." Although that question had not been put to her at the trial, where, as in the present case, no one could reasonably be expected to remember a particular transaction in detail, and the inference of inducement might well be in all the circumstances quite irresistible, there was no reason in principle why it should not be left to the jury to decide, on the evidence as a whole, whether that inference was in truth irresistible, as it was in the present case: *Sullivan* (1945) 30 Cr App R 132, 136.

Per curiam. Had the defendant been charged with obtaining property by deception, contrary to section 15 of the Act of 1968, it is difficult to see what defence there could have been once the jury were convinced of the defendant's dishonesty.

Commentary. The point of law of general public importance certified by the Court of Appeal was: "In view of the proved differences between a cheque card transaction and a credit card transaction, were we right in distinguishing this case from that of *Commissioner of Metropolitan Police v Charles* upon the issue of inducement?"

For the reasons given in the commentary on the decision of the Court of Appeal, [1980] Crim LR 726, it is respectfully submitted that no relevant distinction can be drawn between a cheque card transaction and a credit card transaction and that the question asked was correctly answered in the negative by the House of Lords.

The question which is not, with respect, satisfactorily answered is how there can properly be held to be an offence of obtaining by deception in *either* transaction in the light of the established principles of obtaining offences (which the House does not disturb) and the evidence given by the victim of the offence in each of these particular cases.

. . . Suppose Miss Rounding had been cross-examined as

Q. Did it matter to you whether Miss Lambie was exceeding her credit limit or not?

A. No. [This is obvious from her evidence and undisputed.]

Q. You realise that if she was exceeding her credit limit she had no right to use the card?

A. Yes. [the only answer which could be expected from an intelligent witness with some slight knowledge of credit cards or even common sense.]

Q. So it did not matter to you whether she had authority to use the card or not?

A. No. [the only logical and consistent answer.]

In principle, the judge should then direct an acquittal. The witness has testified that the defendant did *not* obtain the pecuniary advantage by the only false representation stated in the indictment, namely, that she was entitled to use a Barclaycard.

Of course it is clear in both cases that if Mr. Cersell or Miss Rounding had been aware that the bearer of the card had no authority to use it, they would not have entered into the transaction. They would not have been parties to a fraud on the bank. But this is not at all to the purpose.

In their determination to convict the dishonest user of cheque and credit cards, the courts have strained the criminal law in at least two respects. (i) In the concept of obtaining – the subject of this commentary; and (ii) in *Kovacs* and *Charles*, in the concept of "being allowed to borrow by way of overdraft." The defendant certainly increased his overdraft but, since he did so without the consent and against the will of the bank, it seems, to put it mildly, an unusual use of language to say that he was *allowed* to do so. Such straining of language and of concepts has been all too common a feature of the law of stealing and related offences for at least 150 years but it has usually been directed to procuring the conviction of a rogue who clearly ought to be guilty of a crime. In the present case it is not so clear. One view is that it is the responsibility of the banks and credit companies to ensure that these cards are given only to creditworthy and responsible people and that they should not look to the criminal law to protect them from dishonest breaches of contract by their clients. They put great temptation in the way of ordinary people, often young and inexperienced, some of whom take too literally the slogan that the card "takes the waiting out of wanting." Views of this nature have recently been expressed from the bench by His Honour, Judge Sir Harold Cassel. *The Times*, July 28, 1981. The Council of Europe Committee on Crime Problems considered this problem recently: Report on Decriminalisation (1980) Chapter XIII. They found that the law of most member states covered cases where there is a false declaration, forgery or falsification of identity but, they said (p. 201) – "it is not appropriate to criminalise other forms of credit cards abuse (*e.g.* exceeding the credit allowed) since there is a civil law contract freely entered into between the credit institution and its customer for which the guarantee of civil damages seems adequate. It is up to the banks and credit institutions to look to the "morality" of their credit policy by making all necessary checks beforehand on the reliability of their customers and their financial standing, applying the necessary safeguards, moderating their advertising policy, etc.

Criminalisation in this field might have the contrary effect of encouraging banks and credit institutions to be irresponsible and hence increase credit card abuse."

As for cheques, the committee would decriminalise the use of guaranteed cheques in countries where their use is an offence.

If we followed these recommendations, neither *Charles* and *Lambie* would be guilty of an offence.

There is a good deal of force in these observations though it may be a bit unrealistic to suggest a civil remedy as a solution in the United Kingdom. The offending party would usually not be worth suing and, if he were, the cost involved would probably be uneconomic. Furthermore, while these modern methods of credit and of trading are certainly of benefit to the banks and to the traders, they are also of benefit to the public, as is apparent from the readiness of the public to take advantage of them. Most people it is thought, would regard the conduct of *Charles* and of *Lambie* as fraudulent.

(iii) A human mind must be deceived

This follows from the definition of deception to be found in *Re London and Globe Finance Corporation* (see above, page 153 as discussed by A. T. H. Smith in his article 'The Idea of Criminal Deception'). Buckley J's definition was approved by the House of Lords in *R* v *Charles* (above).

(iv) The deception must no be too remote from the prohibited result;

R v *Button* [1900] 2 QB 597   Queen's Bench Division

On the trial of an indictment for attempting to obtain property by false pretences the following facts were proved.

Entries for two handicaps were sent to the secretary of an athletic meeting, in the name of Sims, containing statements as to the recent performances of Sims, which were very moderate, and in consequence Sims was given long starts. The entries were not written by either Sims or the prisoner. At the meeting the prisoner, who was a good runner, personated Sims, who was absent, and came in first in both races. After the first race the handicapper asked the prisoner whether he was really Sims, whether the performance given in the entry form was really his, and whether he had never won a race, as stated in the entry. He answered these questions, falsely, in the affirmative.

On a case stated:—

Held, that the attempt to obtain the prizes was not too remote from the pretence, that the case was rightly left to the jury, and the prisoner was properly convicted.

R v Clucas [1949] 2 KB 226   King's Bench Division

On the trial of an indictment for conspiring to obtain, attempting to obtain and obtaining, money by false pretences the following facts were proved:

The appellant and another man, induced bookmakers to bet with them by representing that they were commission agents acting on behalf of a large number of workmen who were placing small bets on various races, whereas in fact they were making bets in considerable sums of money for themselves alone. Payment was made by the bookmaker on the horse winning.

Held, that the money paid by the bookmaker was not obtained by false pretences as the effective cause of the payment was the horse winning and not the false representations.

R v Button [1900] 2 QB 597 distinguished.

LORD GODDARD CJ − . . . In the opinion of the court it is impossible to say that there was an obtaining of the money by the false pretences which were alleged, because the money was obtained not by reason of the fact that the people falsely pretended that they were somebody else or acting in some capacity which they were not; it was obtained because they backed a winning horse and the bookmaker paid because the horse had won. No doubt the bookmaker might never have opened an account with these men if he had known the true facts, but we must distinguish in this case between one contributing cause and the effective cause which led the bookmaker to pay the money.

The effective cause which led the bookmaker to pay the money was the fact that these men had backed a winning horse.

The deception is too remote and does not cause the obtaining if it does not precede the obtaining in point of time:

R v Collis-Smith [1971] Crim LR 716   Court of Appeal

C was convicted of obtaining property by deception contrary to section 15 (1) of the Theft Act 1968 in that he obtained petrol by a false oral representation that he was authorised to draw petrol for his private motor-car on the account of his employer. He drove his car to a petrol station and asked for petrol which the attendant put in the tank of the car. The attendant then asked if he were paying for it and he said it was to be booked to his firm as he had the use of the car for business, and it was so booked. C appealed on the ground that the conviction was wrong since no false representation was made until after the petrol had been obtained.

Held, allowing the appeal, it appeared from the wording of section 15 (1) that if a conviction were to be obtained the order of events must be that there should be a deception which operated on the mind of the person to whom it was directed and that by reason of that deception the obtaining took place.

(b) There must be a deception, that is, an untrue statement

Section 15(4) Theft Act 1968

For purposes of this section 'deception' means any deception (whether deliberate or reckless) by words or conduct as to fact or as to law, including a deception as to the present intentions of the person using the deception or any other person.

(i) The statement must actually be false

The falsity of the statement is for the jury to determine:

R v *Mandry and Wooster* [1973] 3 All ER 996   Court of Appeal

M and W were street traders who worked in partnership. Acting in concert they offered bottles of scent for sale in a street in Romford. M told a crowd of by-standers that they could go down the road to the big stores and buy the scent for two guineas whereas he was offering it to them for £1. He also displayed magazines which contained advertisements offering the scent for sale at 42s a bottle. M and W were charged, inter alia, with going equipped to cheat, contrary to s. 25 of the Theft Act 1968 (count 1), and attempting to obtain £1 by decep-tion (count 2). Evidence was given for the prosecution by a constable that he had visited four shops in the area and that the scent was not sold at any of them. In cross-examination he was asked if he had visited a well-known London Department store and he replied that he had not. The fact that the advertise-ments in the magazines were spurious was not denied by the defence. The judge directed the jury that the police could not be expected to visit every shop in London in order to prove that the scent was not being sold for 42s in any shop; on the contrary, the onus was on the defence to prove something that was within their personal knowledge. M and W were convicted and appealed on the ground that the judge had misdirected the jury that the onus was on the accused to prove that the scent was sold in the shops at 42s a bottle.

Held – The onus was on the Crown to prove the falsity of M's statement. The fact that the constable had been unable to find any of the scent in the shops he visited was positive evidence, when taken in conjunction with the evidence of the false magazine advertisement and in the absence of any other evidence, that what M had said was false. Furthermore the constable's negative answer in cross-examination about the department store was not evidence to put in the scales against the positive evidence given by him. Accordingly, the criticism of the direction was unfounded and the appeal would be dismissed.

R v *Banaster* [1979] RTR 113   Court of Appeal

The appellant, a minicab driver operating from Heathrow airport, was approached there by a young foreign visitor newly arrived for the first time in the United Kingdom, who asked whether the vehicle was a taxi. The appellant replied 'Yes,

I am an airport taxi'. Thereupon the visitor entered and gave an address in Ealing where the appellant drove him and told him that the correct fare was £27.50, which he paid. The appellant was charged with obtaining property by deception, contrary to section 15 of the Theft Act 1968. The jury were directed that they might think that the appellant's reference to an airport taxi and the correct fare implied that 'it was all official', thereby envouraging the visitor to think that the appellant was a man of substance so as to be relied on, and that they had to find both deception and dishonesty if they were to convict.

The appellant was convicted.

On his appeal against conviction on the ground that there was no such thing in fact or law as an 'airport taxi' so that he could not be said to have been guilty of deception within section 15(4):

Held, dismissing the appeal, that the judge was entitled to leave to the jury the vital questions of whether the description of the vehicle as an 'airport taxi' was a deception or not and also of whether the reference to 'correct fare' was also an official fare in the circumstaces [sic] (p 115H); and that, accordingly, the case had been properly left to the jury and there was no reason to interfere with the verdict.

LORD WIDGERY CJ — The main submission made by Mr Lyon in respect of this case is that there is no such thing in fact or in law in this country as an 'airport taxi'.

It is just an animal which does not exist. Accordingly, so it is argued, if A represents that his car is an airport taxi, he cannot be responsible for any consequences which might flow because he cannot be said to have told a falsity. If there is not an airport taxi as such in existence at all, then to say you are hired as an airport taxi cannot be a deception, or so I understand the argument to go.

The judge was fully apprised of the difficulties in this case such as they were, and he put it to the jury — indeed he left it all to the jury, which was very sensible of him — that they might think that the reference to 'an airport taxi' and 'the correct fare' implied, in the judge's words, that 'it was all official'. In other words, he left it to the jury to decide whether when those words were spoken they encouraged the complainant to think that the appellant was not a fly-by-night but a man of substance, and as such he could be relied upon.

(ii) The defendant must be deliberate or reckless as to the falsity of the statement

See s. 15(4) above.

R v Staines (1974) 60 Cr App Rep 160   Court of Appeal

JAMES LJ — . . . Two points are argued before us as a basis upon which the conviction should be quashed. The first point relates to the meaning of deception for the purposes of section 15 (1) of the Theft Act 1968 and in particular the construction tht has to be placed upon the wording of subsection (4) of that section. Subsection (4) reads as follows: "For purposes of this section 'deception' means any deception (whether deliberate or reckless) by words or conduct as to fact or as to law, including a deception as to the present intentions of the person using the deception or any other person."

The important words for present purposes are "any deception (whether deliberate or reckless)." There is no dispute between the appellant and the Crown through their counsel that the word "reckless" in that subsection should be given the construction of meaning "without caring," being indifferent to whether the statement is true or false; "reckless" means something more than carelessness or negligence.

In support of his argument that that is the proper construction to be placed on the statute Mr. Forbes has referred us to the old authority in civil law of *Derry* v *Peek* (1889) 14 App Cas 337, and also invited our attention to Professor Smith's current book on the Theft Act and the law of theft in which he deals with that particular statutory provision. This Court accepts the contention put forward that in this section "reckless" does mean more than being careless, does mean more than being negligent, and does involve an indifference to or disregard of the feature of whether a statement be true or false.

It is not clear whether recklessness as defined in *R* v *Caldwell* [1982] AC 341 will apply in this context. If it did the defendant would be said to be reckless where there existed a risk obvious to a reasonable person but to which the defendant had given no thought. It is suggested that there should be no place for such a test in this context.

(iii) The statement must be by words or conduct (including implied statements).

A difficulty here is to determine how positive the behaviour of the defendant must be. It seems that an omission to tell the truth will amount to a deception where that omission gives a manifestly false impression of the true state of affairs:

R v *Kylsant* [1932] 1 KB 442   King's Bench Division

By the Larceny Act, 1861, s. 84, a director of a body corporate or public company is guilty of a misdemeanour if he makes, circulates or publishes any written statement or account which he shall know to be false in any material particular with intent to induce any person to intrust or advance property to the company.

A prospectus for the issue of debenture stock issued by a company of which the appellant was chairman was composed of statements which in themselves were perfectly true, but it omitted information about the company's affairs, with the result that the prospectus, taken as a whole, gave a false impression of the position of the company. On the trial of the appellant for an offence under s. 84 of the Larceny Act, 1861, the judge directed the jury that a written statement might be false within the meaning of the section not only because of what it stated, but also because of what it concealed, or omitted, or implied:—

Held, that this was a correct statement of the effect of the section, and that the appellant was rightly convicted of an offence under it.

DPP v *Ray* [1974] AC 370   House of Lords

LORD MORRIS OF BORTH-Y-GEST — The situation may perhaps be unusual
where a customer honestly orders a meal and therefore indicates his honest
intention to pay but thereafter forms a dishonest intention of running away
without paying if he can. Inherent in an original honest representation of an
intention to pay there must surely be a representation that such intention will
continue.

In this present case it is found as a fact that when the respondent ordered his
meal he believed that he would be able to pay. One of his companions had agreed
to lend him money. He therefore intended to pay. So far as the waiter was
concerned the original implied representation made to him by the respondent
must have been a continuing representation so long as he (the respondent)
remained in the restaurant. There was nothing to alter the representation. Just as
the waiter was led at the start to believe that he was dealing with a customer
who by all that he did in the restaurant was indicating his intention to pay in the
ordinary way, so the waiter was led to believe that that state of affairs continued.
But the moment came when the respondent decided and therefore knew that he
was not going to pay: but he also knew that the waiter still thought that he was
going to pay. By ordering his meal and by his conduct in assuming the role of an
ordinary customer the respondent had previously shown that it was his intention
to pay. By continuing in the same role and behaving just as before he was
representing that his previous intention continued. That was a deception because
his intention, unknown to the waiter, had become quite otherwise. The dishonest change of intention was not likely to produce the result that the waiter
would be told of it. The essence of the deception was that the waiter should not
know of it or be given any sort of clue that it (the change of intention) had
come about. Had the waiter suspected that by a change of intention a secret
exodus was being planned, it is obvious that he would have taken action to
prevent its being achieved.

It was said in the Divisional Court that a deception under section 16 should
not be found unless an accused has actively made a representation by words or
conduct which representation is found to be false. But if there was an original
representation (as, in my view, there was when the meal was ordered) it was
a representation that was intended to be and was a continuing representation. It
continued to operate on the mind of the waiter. It became false and it became a
deliberate deception. The prosecution do not say that the deception consisted in
not informing the waiter of the change of mind; they say that the deception
consisted in continuing to represent to the waiter that there was an intention to
pay before leaving.

In both the above cases a failure to reveal the whole truth was held to amount to
a deception. That was the case in *R* v *Kylsant* even though the statements made
were literally true. It was confirmed in *R* v *King* (below) that literally true statements could amount to deception:

R v *King* [1979] Crim LR 122   Nottingham Crown Court

    The defendant was a garage proprietor who purchased motorcars with a high mileage and then turned back the odometer to give a reading consistent with average user for the age of the car. Each of the cars had a disclaimer notice on the dashboard stating that the mileage shown "may not be correct" and should not be relied upon. The prosecution was brought indicting the defendant with two offences in relation to each car. One under section 1 (1) (*a*) of the Trades Descriptions Act 1968 and the other under section 15 (1) of the Theft Act 1968. The basic essentials of each particulars of offence were as follows:

1. Ian Robert King on a day unknown between ⸺ and ⸺ in the course of the trade or business or a motor dealer applied to a ⸺ motorcar registration number ⸺ false trade description namely an odometer reading of approximately ⸺ miles whereas the actual mileage was in excess of ⸺ miles.
2. In [sic] Robert King on the ⸺ day of ⸺ dishonestly obtained from ⸺ £⸺ with the intention of permanently depriving him of the said money by deception namely by falsely representing that he the said Ian Robert King had no reason to disbelieve the mileage shown on the odometer of the ⸺ motorcar registration number ⸺ when he knew that such reading was in fact false.

    The contention with regard to the second type of count was that although a disclaimer notice was exhibited it only said that the mileage "may be incorrect." Accordingly since in each particular instance the mileage had been reduced once the car was in the possession of the defendant the defendant knew that the reading was in fact incorrect and the inaccuracy of the odometer was not a mere possibility as indicated in the disclaimer.

    The defendant pleaded guilty to an indictment containing 12 counts in relation to six cars and was given a nine months' suspended sentence on each count and fined a total of £2,400.

    Commentary. The defendant had some reason for turning back the odometer. Clearly he thought that potential customers might attach some importance to the reading even though they were warned that it "may not be correct" and were advised not to rely on it. A statement that something *may not* be correct implies that, so far as the representor knows, it may be correct. If the representor knows that it is incorrect he is practising a dishonest deception.

    The second difficulty is to determine precisely what representations are being made when they are being made by conduct alone. In *DPP* v *Ray* (above) Lord Morris of Borth-y-Gest discusses the representations made by a person who orders a meal in a restaurant. The following cases give other examples of representations the defendant is said to make when he pursues a particular course of conduct:

Commissioner of Police for the Metropolis v *Charles* [1977] AC 177
House of Lords (see also above, page 159)

LORD EDMUND-DAVIES – . . . What representation, if any, did the accused make when he cashed each of those cheques? It was against the background of his knowledge of his limited overdraft facilities that he drew each for £30 in favour of Mr. Cersell, the club manager, and on each occasion produced his cheque card so that its number could be endorsed on the back of each cheque. The essence of the defence consists in Mr. Comyn's submissions that by such conduct the only representation made was that "This cheque, backed by the card, will be honoured without question"; that such representation was true; that there was accordingly no deception of the club staff; and that therefore no offence was committed even though as a result the accused's account became overdrawn substantially beyond the permitted limit in consequence of his bank doing precisely what he had represented they would do on presentation of each of the cheques.

Both in the Court of Appeal and before your Lordships there was considerable discussion as to what representation is to be implied by the simple act of drawing a cheque. Reference was made to *R* v *Page (Note)* [1971] 2 QB 330, where the Court of Appeal (Criminal Division) adopted with apparent approval the following passage which (citing *R* v *Hazelton* (1874) LR 2 CCR 134 in support) has appeared in *Kenny, Outlines of Criminal Law* ever since the 1st edition appeared in 1902, see pp. 246-247:

"Similarly the familiar act of drawing a cheque – a document which on the face of it is only a command of a future act – is held to imply at least three statements about the present: (1) That the drawer has an account with that bank; (2) That he has authority to draw on it for that amount; (3) That the cheque, as drawn, is a valid order for the payment of that amount (i.e. that the present state of affairs is such that, in the ordinary course of events, the cheque will on its future presentment be duly honoured). It may be well to point out, however, that it does not imply any representation that the drawer now has money in this bank to the amount drawn for; inasmuch as he may well have authority to overdraw, or may intend to pay in (before the cheque can be presented) sufficient money to meet it."

My noble and learned friend, Lord Fraser of Tullybelton, rightly pointed out that representations (1) and (2) were supererogatory in the light of representation (3), which embraced both of them. My noble and learned friend, Lord Diplock, also criticised representation (2) on the ground that the representation made by the simple act of drawing a cheque does not relate to or rest upon "authority" but is rather a representation that the drawer has contracted with his bank to honour his cheques. Notwithstanding the antiquity of the quoted passage, it accordingly appears right to restrict the representation made by the act of drawing and handing over a cheque to that which has been conveniently labelled "Page (3)." The legal position created by such an act was even more laconically described by Pollock B in *R* v *Hazelton*, LR 2 CCR 134, 140 in this way:

"I think the real representation made is that the cheque will be paid. It may be said that that is a representation as to a future event. But that is not really so. It means that the existing state of facts is such that in ordinary course the cheque will be met."

With understandable enthusiasm, Mr. Comyn submitted that this was correct and that such representation was manifestly true when made, as was demonstrated by the later honouring of all the accused's cheques. But it has to be remembered that we are presently concerned to inquire what was the *totality* of the representations; with whether they were true or false to the accused's knowledge; whether they deceived; and whether they induced the party to whom they were addressed to act in such a manner as led to the accused obtaining "increased borrowing by way of overdraft." What of the production and use of the cheque card when each of the 25 cheques in the new cheque book was drawn on the night of January 2-3, 1973? Is Mr. Comyn right in submitting that the only representation made by its production was the perfectly correct one that, "This cheque, backed by this card, will be honoured without question?" In my judgment, he is not. The accused knew perfectly well that he would not be able to get more chips at the club simply by drawing a cheque. The cheque alone would not have been accepted; it had to be backed by a cheque card. The card played a vital part, for (as my noble and learned friend, Lord Diplock, put it during counsel's submission) in order to make the bank liable to the payee there must be knowledge on the payee's part that the drawer has the bank's authority to bind it, for in the absence of such knowledge the all-important contract between payee and bank is not created; and it is the representation by the drawer's production of the card that he has that authority that creates such contractual relationship and estops the bank from refusing to honour the cheque. By drawing the cheque the accused represented that it would be met, and by producing the card so that the number thereon could be endorsed on the cheque he in effect represented, "I an authorised by the bank to show this to you and so create a direct contractual relationship between the bank and you that they will honour this cheque."

R v *Gilmartin* [1983] Crim LR 330   Court of Appeal

The defendant was charged with three counts of obtaining property by deception and one count of obtaining a pecuniary advantage by deception, contrary to sections 15 and 16 of the Theft Act 1968, after using post-dated cheques to pay for goods, which were dishonoured upon presentation. He maintained at the trial that the cheques were not intended to be presented, but that the three cheques, the subject-matter of the first three counts, would be bought back for cash and that the cheque the subject-matter of the pecuniary advantage count would be handed over for bookkeeping purposes. He was convicted on all four counts and appealed on the ground that a drawer of a post-dated cheque impliedly represented no more than the fact that he was a customer of the bank on which the cheque was drawn, and since he did have such an account, there was no case for him to answer.

Held, dismissing the appeal, that following the decision of the House of Lords in *Commissioner of Police for the Metropolis* v *Charles* [1977] AC 177, the often quoted passage in *Kenny's Outlines of Criminal Law* as to the relevant representation implied by the giving of a cheque could no longer be regarded as accurate. Of the three elements in the definition, the second element, that the drawer had authority to draw on his account for the amount specified on the cheque, had to be rejected and the first element was logically covered by the third. The third element had been expressed by Kenny in two different ways; a statement that the cheque as drawn was a valid order for the payment of the amount of the cheque and a statement that the present state of affairs was such that in the ordinary course of events the cheque would on its future presentment be duly honoured. Alhough [sic] the first statement could be read as referring to the future, it was only relevant to have regard to a representation as to existing facts. The second statement should properly be regarded as an authoritative statement of the law. Was the position any different in the case of a post-dated cheque? *Maytum-White* (1958) 42 Cr App R 165 provided no authority for the proposition in *Archbold* that the only representation about the present that could properly be said to be implied in the drawing of a post-dated cheque was that the drawer was a customer of the bank concerned. The court could see no reason why in the case of a post-dated cheque the drawer did not impliedly represent that the existing facts at the date when he gave the cheque to the payee were such that in the ordinary course of events the cheque would on presentation be met on or after the date specified in the cheque. In a case like the present, when a post-dated cheque was issued when the account was heavily overdrawn and there was, as the drawer well knew, no prospect of future funds being paid in or of the bank providing other overdraft facilities, the drawer was as much guilty of deception as he would have been in the case of a cheque not post-dated. Indeed, where a drawer gave a cheque which was not post-dated, his account may have been overdrawn but he may have had in his pocket another cheque payable to him which he intended to pay into his account immediately and which would allow the cheque he had drawn to be paid on presentation; if so it was difficult to see that he had made any representation. Accordingly there was no relevant distinction between the case of a cheque which had not been post-dated and one which had.

R v Williams [1980] Crim LR 589   Court of Appeal

The appellant, a school boy aged 17, who bought some Jugoslavian dinar banknotes, which he knew were obsolete, at Stanley Gibbons, took them to the bureau de change at a department store and said to a cashier either "Will you change these notes?" or "Can I cash these in?" For notes totalling 1,100 dinars, which cost him £1.80, he received £27.39 and, two days later, for notes which cost him £5.20 he received £79.20. He went again the following day and was detained and seen by police. He agreed that he knew the notes were obsolete and said that he thought to exchange them "for a laugh" and then could not resist trying it again because it was "so easy." He was arraigned on four pairs of counts charging obtaining property by deception and, alternatively, theft. At the close of evidence for the prosecution the appellant, who admitted dishonesty, submitted that he had made no representation and the recorder ruled that there was no evidence on which a jury could safely find that the appellant had made any of the false representations alleged against him in the indictment. However, he ruled that there was a case to answer on theft. Thereupon the appellant pleaded guilty to two counts of theft and was conditionally discharged for two years and ordered to pay compensation of £107.09 — see [1979] Crim LR 736. He appealed against conviction contending that there was no evidence of guilt of theft since there had been no appropriation of money belonging to another, for the cashiers had handed over the money voluntarily and, at that moment, it was the property not of the store but the appellant.

Held, dismissing the appeal, that when a person went to the foreign exchange counter of such a concern, as opposed to the numismatic or curio counter, and proffered a banknote for exchange using words such as those used by the appellant, it was open to a jury to find that he was representing the notes to be genuine and valid as currency in the country of origin. The principle was, perhaps, slightly distinguishable from that laid down in *Charles* [1976] 1 WLR 248. The person proffering the note was, in effect, saying to the cashier "This is currency. I believe it to be valid currency in Jugoslavia. Will you please exchange it on that basis into English money." Dishonesty being admitted, an offence under section 15 of the Theft Act 1968 had been made out.

(c) The defendant must be dishonest

It appears from the following cases that there is to be no distinction between dishonesty in theft cases and dishonesty in deception cases. The direction in *R* v *Ghosh* (above, page 52) is all-important in both:

R v *Waterfall* [1970] 1 QB 148   Court of Appeal

The defendant arranged with a taxi driver to be driven from Southampton to London and back. On arrival in London the taxi driver asked for an advance. The defendant replied that he would get it later in the day when he had seen his accountant. He was driven to the accountant's address and later emerged saying that the accountant could not let him have any money. He was driven back to Southampton and tried unsuccessfully to raise money at various addresses. He was charged with dishonestly obtaining a pecuniary advantage by deception, contrary to section 16 (1) of the Theft Act, 1968. The deputy recorder directed the jury, inter alia, to the effect that they could not find that the defendant had a genuine belief that the accountant would provide the money unless he had reasonable grounds for that belief. The defendant was convicted. On appeal against conviction:—

Held, allowing the appeal, that the test of dishonesty in section 16 (1) of the Act was subjective; so that the jury had been misdirected, it being for them to decide whether ot nor this particular defendant had a genuine belief that the accountant would provide the money.

R v *Woolven* [1983] Crim LR 632   Court of Appeal

The appellant was tried on a charge of attempting to obtain property by deception. He had opened a bank account in a false name and knew that money would be transferred to it from an account belonging to his former employer, who gave evidence for the prosecution; the appellant understood that the employer could not withdraw the money in the ordinary way because, if he did so, the bank would claim it to discharge or reduce his overdraft. The appellant had a letter, false to his knowledge, purporting to establish his identity in the false name in order to induce the bank, which had refused to pay without evidence of identity, [to cash] a cheque for £16,200. He conceded that ordinary people would, on his own version, have found his behaviour to be dishonest but maintained that he at the time had not thought it to be dishonest since he thought that the money belonged to the employer. The jury were directed in accordance with *Ghosh* [1982] QB 1053 and the issue of dishonesty was left to them. The appellant was convicted. He appealed on the ground that, while section 1 (3) of the Theft Act 1968 prevented the application to section 15 of the "claim of right" defence under section 2 (1) (*a*), nevertheless its effect was to be read into the definition of obtaining by deception, so that the direction should have been to the effect that the jury should acquit if they concluded that the appellant might have attempted to obtain money from the bank in the belief that he had in law the right to deprive them of it on behalf of the employer, whom the appellant understood to be its owner.

Held, dismissing the appeal, that *Williams* (1836) 7 C & P 354; *Hamilton* (1845) 1 Cox 244; *Parker* (1910) 74 JP 208 and *Bernhard* [1938] 2 KB 264 constituted no decisive authority against the appellant's argument. The question arising for decision was whether the direction as to the element of dishonesty was adequate to do justice in the instant case. Any direction based on the concept of claim of right as set out in section 2 (1) (*a*), or otherwise, would have added nothing to what the judge had said. A direction based on *Ghosh* seemed likely to cover all occasions when a section 2 (1) (*a*) type direction might otherwise have been desirable. The direction was to be contrasted with that in *Falconer-Atlee* (1973) 58 Cr App R 349. In the present case the jury inevitably disbelieved the appellant's proposition that he had not thought his behaviour dishonest at the time, even if they believed his account otherwise. The conviction was not unsafe or unsatisfactory.

10 THE DECEPTION OFFENCES

(1) OBTAINING PROPERTY: 1968 ACT S. 15

Section 15 Theft Act 1968

(1) A person who by any deception dishonestly obtains property belonging to another, with the intention of permanently depriving the other of it, shall on conviction on indictment be liable to imprisonment for a term not exceeding ten years.

(2) For purposes of this section a person is to be treated as obtaining property if he obtains ownership, possession or control of it, and 'obtain' includes obtaining for another or enabling another to obtain or to retain.

(3) Section 6 above shall apply for the purposes of this section, with the necessary adaptation of the reference to appropriating, as it applies for purposes of section 1.

(4) For purposes of this section 'deception' means any deception (whether deliberate or reckless) by words or conduct as to fact or as to law, including a deception as to the present intentions of the person using the deception or any other person.

(a) The actus reus

The following is a summary of the elements of the actus reus of this offence. Detailed consideration of the definition of those elements is to be found elsewhere in this work.

(i) Obtaining — *must be a causal link between the deception and the obtaining (see above, page 153). The obtaining may be of ownership, possession or control (s. 1(2)).*

(ii) Property — *must obtain property — as defined in s. 4(1) (above, page 15). The limitations in s. 4(2) (land, see above, page 16) do not apply.*

(iii) Belonging to another — *s. 5(1) applies (see above, page 24) — property belongs to anyone having ownership, possession, control or a proprietary right in it.*

(iv) Deception – *There must be a false representation which has an effect on someone and which causes the obtaining.*

(b) The mens rea

This consists of four elements:

(i) Dishonesty *(see above, page 48).*
(ii) Intention to permanently deprive – *s. 6 applies (see above, page 54).*
(iii) Deliberation or recklessness in making the deception –*(see above, page 167).*
(iv) An intention to obtain property *(s. 15(1)).*

(2) OBTAINING A PECUNIARY ADVANTAGE: 1968 ACT S. 16

Section 16(2)(a) HAS BEEN ABOLISHED. The only situations in which a s. 16 offence can be committed are set out below:

Section 16 Theft Act 1968

(1) A person who by any deception dishonestly obtains for himself or another any pecuniary advantage shall on conviction on indictment be liable to imprisonment for a term not exceeding five years.

(2) The cases in which a pecuniary advantage within the meaning of this section is to be regarded as obtained for a person are cases where –

(a) [Repealed].
(b) he is allowed to borrow by way of overdraft, or to take out any policy of insurance or annuity contract, or obtains an improvement of the terms on which he is allowed to do so; or
(c) he is given the opportunity to earn remuneration or greater remuneration in an office or employment, or to win money by betting.

(3) For purposes of this section 'deception' has the same meaning as in section 15 of this Act.

The general principles of deception offences apply to s. 16 as they do to s. 15. These matters are discussed in detail in the previous chapter. Particular points to note about s. 16 are:

(a) Only one offence is created by the section although an indictment should specify the exact allegation against the defendant (*Bale* v *Rosier* [1977] 2 All ER 160).

(b)   A person is 'allowed' to borrow by way of overdraft despite the fact that the bank has expressly forbidden him to do so – *C.M.P.* v *Charles* (above, page 159).

(c)   Under s. 16(2)(b) it appears to be irrelevant that the 'contract' of insurance is invalid:

R v *Alexander (John)* [1981] Crim LR 182   Court of Appeal

The appellant, pretending that he was S, secured an insurance policy in the name of S relating to some thousands of pounds worth of goods. In respect of certain of the appellant's actions he was convicted of several offences contrary to the Theft Act 1968 and, in relation to the insurance policy, he was convicted of obtaining a pecuniary advantage by deception, contrary to section 16 (1) of the 1968 Act on the basis that within section 16 (2) (*b*) the pecuniary advantage was regarded as obtained since he was "allowed to take out any policy of insurance." He appealed on the grounds that there was no valid policy of insurance because, on the evidence, the insurers were mistaken as to the identity of the assured in thinking that he was S and he was not, and the identity of the assured was vital, so that there was no contract because of the unilateral mistake and, although there was a purported agreement, there was no agreement and, therefore, the agreement was void.

Held, dismissing the appeal on the conviction relating to the insurance policy and some other counts, that the appellant's contentions were appealing albeit they were somewhat tainted by being put forward on behalf of the man who perpetrated the fraud. However, in the circumstances, the view to be taken was that, until the validity of the policy was called into question or challenged, or until steps were taken to have the policy declared void or voidable, it remained what it purported to be, namely, a "policy of insurance" within section 16 (2) (*b*). The concern was solely with the moment of time when the appellant obtained the piece of paper, and it was to that moment of time that the proposition applied. Accordingly, the appellant's contentions could not be accepted and the appeal failed.

Commentary. It seems probable that, if the appellant had brought an action on the insurance policy a civil court would have held it to be void on the ground that the insurance company was making a material mistake of identity – it had no intention to contract with the appellant but only with S. See *Cundy* v *Lindsay* (1878) 3 App Cas 459. It does not follow, however, that if the insurance company had brought an action on the policy to recover the premiums from the appellant he could have relied on his own fraudulent conduct by way of defence. On the contrary, it is submitted that he would have had no answer to such a claim. *Cf.* Atiyah, *Introduction to the Law of Contract* (2nd ed.), pp. 53-54. If this is right, and it would therefore have been held against the appellant in the civil law that he had been allowed to take out a policy of insurance, any possible objection to such a holding in the criminal law disappears. It is respectfully submitted that the conviction was rightly upheld.

(d)   The pecuniary advantage may be obtained 'for himself or another'.

(3) PROCURING THE EXECUTION OF A VALUABLE SECURITY: 1968 ACT S. 20(2)

Section 20(2) Theft Act 1968

(2) A person who dishonestly, with a view to gain for himself or another or with intent to cause loss to another, by any deception procures the execution of a valuable security shall on conviction on indictment be liable to imprisonment for a term not exceeding seven years; and this subsection shall apply in relation to the making, acceptance, indorsement, alteration, cancellation or destruction in whole or in part of a valuable security, and in relation to the signing or sealing of any paper or other material in order that it may be made or converted into, or used or dealt with as, a valuable security, as if that were the execution of a valuable security.

(3) For purposes of this section 'deception' has the same meaning as in section 15 of this Act, and 'valuable security' means any document creating, transferring, surrendering or releasing any right to, in or over property, or authorising the payment of money or delivery of any property, or evidencing the creation, transfer, surrender or release of any such right, or the payment of money or delivery of any property, or the satisfaction of any obligation.

For the general principles relevant to the construction of this offence see the previous chapter. The use of the phrase 'by any deception procures' instead of the more familiar 'by any deception . . . obtains' (found in sections 15 and 16) makes no difference to the necessity to prove a causal connection between the deception and the bringing about of the actus reus of this offence.

(4) OBTAINING SERVICES: 1978 ACT S. 1

Section 1 Theft Act 1978

(1) A person who by any deception dishonestly obtains services from another shall be guilty of an offence.

(2) It is an obtaining of services where the other is induced to confer a benefit by doing some act, or causing or permitting some act to be done, on the understanding that the benefit has been or will be paid for.

This section raises four issues apart from those general to all deception offences which are discussed in the preceding chapter. The particular issues are:

(a)   The deception must induce the 'other' to confer the benefit. There must be a direct link between the deception and the act which causes the defendant or

'another' to receive the benefit. A secret entry to, e.g., a football stadium, would not be an offence under this section as no one would have been deceived.

(b)   There must be an understanding that the benefit has been or will be paid for.

This has the curious result that the better the 'hard-luck story' the less likely the defendant is to commit an offence under this section. If he can persuade his victim to provide the service free he will not be liable to conviction under s. 1.

However if this proviso were not there the section would be very wide and could cover favours done by members of a family or by relatives unless those requesting the favour were meticulously correct in their request for help.

(c)   Services must be obtained.

By s. 1(2) an omission is not sufficient. The precise definition of services is, however, uncertain after the surprising decision that a mortgage advance is not a service:

R v *Halai* [1983] Crim LR 624   Court of Appeal

At a time when he had £28 in his bank account H applied for a mortgage through C, the agent of a building society. He said that he had held his current job for 18 months when in fact he had held it for two months. He drew a post-dated cheque for £40 to pay for a survey by the society and opened a savings account with a post-dated cheque for £500. He was issued with a passbook showing a credit of £500 and went to a branch of the society where he dealt with R. He handed over a cheque for £250 and his account was credited with that sum. At the same time he withdrew £100 from the account, saying that the £500 had been paid in cash (it was a society rule that withdrawals could not be made against cheque credits until seven days had elapsed). All three cheques were dishonoured, as he knew they would be. He was convicted on four counts contrary to section 1 of the Theft Act 1978 and one count contrary to section 15 of the Theft Act 1968 as follows: (1) obtaining from C a service, the preparation of a surveyor's report and valuation, by representing that the cheque was good and would be honoured; (2) obtaining from C a service, the opening of a savings account, by a like representation; (3) attempting to obtain from the society a service, a mortgage advance, by representing that he had been employed for 18 months; (4) obtaining from R a service, the increase of the apparent credit balance on a savings account, by representing that the cheque was good and would be honoured; (5) obtaining from R £100 by representing that the savings account had been credited with and contained £500.

Held, count 1 (on which it was submitted that H received no benefit since the survey was for the purposes of the society, and it was not a service provided by C even as agent for the society) was made out. There was a false representation, it being immaterial that the cheque was post-dated (considering *M.P.C.* v *Charles* (1976) 63 Cr App R 252), there was a benefit from the survey to H because it was an essential step in obtaining a mortgage and C, as agent for the society, caused it to be prepared. Counts 2, 3 and 4 were bad because no service was obtained. No benefit was conferred by a building society, or a bank, on a customer when he paid money into an account. Nor was any payment made, or expected, for making the entries in the passbook or the associated office work. A mortgage advance was not a service: it was the lending of money for property. Count 5 was properly laid. He represented that the account contained £500 when he said that £500 in cash had been paid in. In fact it contained nothing despite what appeared in the passbook.

Commentary. . . . Count 1 seems to present little difficulty: the deception caused the building society to have the survey done. The survey was for the benefit of the building society but it was for H's benefit as well, since he could not obtain a mortgage without it.

The court held that count 2 was bad because the service alleged, opening of a building society savings account with a credit balance of £500, is not a service to be paid for. O'Connor LJ said: "Where a customer pays £500 into a bank, by no stretch of the use of ordinary English can anyone suggest that the bank is conferring a benefit on the customer. . . ." It is perhaps necessary to distinguish between the opening of a bank account and the payment of money into it. The banks would be very surprised, and reasonably so, to be told that they were not conferring a benefit on their customer by opening an account in his favour. People do not open banking accounts for the benefit of the bank. They do so because it is for their own advantage and it is submitted that it is clear that one who deceives a bank into opening an account in his favour induces the bank to do an act conferring a benefit on him. The more difficult question is whether the benefit is to be paid for. Banks do not make charges for opening an account. On the contrary, it is more likely at the present time that the bank will be giving the new customer a free gift of some kind. When the customer starts drawing cheques it is different because the bank will make charges unless the customer maintains a certain minimum balance. The customer is now paying for the service, either by paying the bank charges or by (in effect) making the bank an interest-free loan of the minimum balance. Since "opening an account" amounts to a contract between the customer and his bank under which the bank undertakes to meet the customer's cheques, it is arguable that the service, considered as a whole, is one which is to be paid for. The payment of money into an existing account presents a different problem. Again, however, it seems, with great respect to the court, that the bank does confer a benefit on the customer by crediting his account. It thereby extends its undertaking to meet cheques drawn by the customer and this is undoubtedly an advantage to him. It is less obvious that the benefit is to be paid for. If the bank makes a charge for crediting an account, then it is to be paid for and the offence is complete.

The present case is concerned not with a bank but with a building society. It is submitted that the opening of a building society account is also a benefit to the customer. People open building society accounts because they think, rightly, that it will be to their advantage to do so. The difficulty is to find that the service is to be paid for. Building societies do not make charges. They make their profits by lending money at a higher rate of interest than that at which they have borrowed it but it would be far-fetched and unreal to regard the member as paying for the service by allowing the building society to retain the difference between the two rates of interest. The court, with respect, rightly concluded that no payment was made or expected for the service in this case.

The decision on count 3 is much more difficult. The court says: "In our judgment, a mortgage advance cannot be described as a service." But surely it is undeniable that when a building society is induced to make a mortgage advance it "is induced to confer a benefit by doing some act . . . on the understanding that the benefit . . . will be paid for." There is clearly an act, there is no doubt that it confers a benefit and it is certainly going to be paid for by the interest charged. In that case it is an obtaining of services within the section. Of course, as the court says, this could properly be charged as an offence of obtaining property by deception, contrary to section 15 of the 1968 Act. There is however nothing to suggest that the offences are mutually exclusive. Indeed, section 1 of the 1978 Act seems to overlap both section 15 and section 16 (2) (b) of the 1968 Act.

The problem in count 5 related to the form of the indictment. It alleged that H obtained £100 "by falsely representing that a savings account in his name with the said Society had been credited with and contained £500." It was unsuccessfully argued that the alleged representation was true and that a passbook showing a credit of £500 shows that the account has been credited with and contains £500. The word "contains" seems inappropriate in this context. The £500 in question has no physical existence. It is a debt, or alleged debt, due from the society to the customer. The word "credited" is at best ambiguous and is certainly capable of bearing the meaning attributed to it by the defence — that H's account had been credited with £500 by the making of an entry to that effect in the books of the society — though it would not have been if the society's officers had known the truth. The other meaning, and that preferred by the court, is that money, or a valid order for money has been received. In the second sense, the representation was untrue. See commentary on *Ewing* [1983] Crim LR 472, where the former meaning was preferred. If the latter meaning is correct, then the court was concerned with a hearsay statement in *Ewing*.

The representation could with profit have been stated more precisely in the indictment in the present case. H falsely represented that he had paid cash into the account and this undoubted deception induced the cashier to give him £100.

(d)   There must be a benefit conferred.

Where the alleged 'benefit' is itself a criminal offence it is unlikely to be regarded as a benefit under s. 1 if either

(i)   the object of the statute making the 'benefit' illegal is to protect persons in the category to which the defendant charged with the deception offence belongs, or,

(ii)   it is an act (such as grievous bodily harm) to which the victim may not give a consent effective to prevent a criminal offence being committed.

The position with regard to acts which are immoral but not illegal (such as sexual intercourse in the course of prostitution) may be more debateable.

(5) OFFENCES UNDER S. 2 THEFT ACT 1978

Section 2 Theft Act 1978

(1) Subject to subsection (2) below, where a person by any deception –

(a)   dishonestly secures the remission of the whole or part of any existing liability to make a payment, whether his own liability or another's; or
(b)   with intent to make permanent default in whole or in part on any existing liability to make a payment, or with intent to let another do so, dishonestly induces the creditor or any person claiming payment on behalf of the creditor to wait for payment (whether or not the due date for payment is deferred) or to forgo payment; or
(c)   dishonestly obtains any exemption from or abatement of liability to make a payment;

he shall be guilty of an offence.

(2) For purposes of this section 'liability' means legally enforceable liability; and subsection (1) shall not apply in relation to a liability that has not been accepted or established to pay compensation for a wrongful act or omission.
(3) For purposes of subsection (1)(b) a person induced to take in payment a cheque or other security for money by way of conditional satisfaction of a pre-existing liability is to be treated not as being paid but as being induced to wait for payment.
(4) For purposes of subsection (1)(c) 'obtains' includes obtaining for another or enabling another to obtain.

The major problem of interpretation raised by s. 2 is to determine the degree of overlap between the three subsections. This can most conveniently be dealt with by examining the possible scope of each subsection. It should first be noted that, as with the other deception offences, the prohibited result must be obtained by reason of the operation of the defendant's deception:

R v *Andrews & Hedges* [1981] Crim LR 106   Central Criminal Court

Defendants were charged with inducing creditors to wait for payment by deception contrary to section 2 (1) (b) of the Theft Act 1978. The creditors had in the course of dealing supplied large quantities of meat to the defendants on credit terms of up to three weeks for which payments were duly made by cheques which were met. The dishonesty relied upon by the prosecution was that thereafter having obtained meat from suppliers in a later period the defendants issued cheques unsupported by funds in their bank account which were not met on presentation, and induced the creditors to wait for payment. The deception relied on in each case was the false representation that the cheque in question was a good and valid order and that in the ordinary course, the cheque would be met.

Held, there was no inducement to wait for payment where the parties had traded together previously and where credit terms had been allowed and where payment by cheque was accepted in the ordinary course of dealing between the parties; for section 2 (1) (*b*) only applied where a creditor is induced to accept a cheque instead of cash, and only then did section 2 (3) operate as a matter of law to treat the creditor as having been induced to wait for payment. There was no evidence that the creditors had asked for cash and no evidence that they had been induced to accept cheques or to wait for payment. Accordingly, there was no case to answer.

Commentary. It is a basic principle applicable to all "obtaining" offences under the Theft Acts that the obtaining, inducing, etc., must be *by deception.* The defendant's conduct must actually deceive his victim and cause him to do whatever act is appropriate to the offence charged – in the circumstances of the present case, to wait for payment.

If, without any deception, D has entered into a contract with P whereby P agrees to supply goods and to accept payment by cheque, D does not induce P to wait for payment when he gives P a cheque knowing that it will be dishonoured. P is not induced to wait for payment unless he agrees that payment may be made later than the due date. The due date is determined by the contract and here it is the date on which the cheque would, in the normal course, be honoured. P has not agreed to wait beyond that date. He will in fact have to wait beyond that date, but that makes no difference. In the present case, whatever the terms of the original contract, it seems that the effect of the course of dealing was that the buyer had the right to pay by cheque.

Even if D is dishonest from the start of the negotiations he commits no offence under section 2 (1) (*b*) if the concluded contract allows him to pay by cheque because P is induced to agree to accept a cheque before there is "any existing liability." The earliest moment at which any liability can come into existence is that of the conclusion of the contract, and P has already been induced to agree to accept a cheque. In this case, however, D would be guilty of obtaining any property or services which P delivered to him in reliance on his promise to pay with a valid cheque.

Securing the remission of a liability: 1978 Act s. 2(1)(a)

This requires the remission of an existing liability. As with the other subsections this may be widely construed in which case it overlaps very substantially with the rest of s. 2, or remission may be held to mean that the creditor must actually alter the legal liability in question, i.e., after the operation of the deception the debtor's liability would actually be less. One problem with this interpretation is that it would be very narrow. This is because a mere agreement by a creditor to accept less money in full satisfaction of a debt is not binding on him in the absence of new consideration. The Criminal Law Revision Committee thought that the section would have a wider sphere of operation than that narrow interpretation. In their thirteenth report (para. 13) the following example of the operation of s. 2 was given:

> An example would be where a man borrows £100 from a neighbour and when repayment is due, tells a false story of some family tragedy which makes it impossible for him to find the money; this deception persuades the neighbour to tell him that he need never repay.

The neighbour would not be legally bound by his agreement to forget the debt.

Inducing a creditor to wait for or to forgo payment: 1978 Act s. 2 (1)(b)

This is the only one of the three constituent subsections of s. 2 to require an intent to make permanent default. It may be that this supports the narrow construction of 'remission' which is suggested above. If remission requires that the creditor's legal liability is altered it would be superfluous to add to s. 2(1)(a) a requirement that there must be an intent to make permanent default; the creditor's liability has in any event been permanently altered by the remission.

It seems likely that s. 2(1)(b) is, of the three, the subsection most likely to be contravened. It will cover all situations where the deception is directed at inducing the creditor not to demand what is legally due to him at the due date. This type of deception may well be more common than deceptions aimed at inducing the creditor to alter the legal liability of the debtor. If s. 2(1)(a) does not require the alteration of the debtor's liability the two subsections almost wholly overlap.

The existing case law on the subject is not very illuminating:

R v Holt and Lee [1981] Crim LR 499   Court of Appeal

> The appellants ate meals costing £3.65 in a restaurant. An off-duty police officer overheard them planning to evade payment by pretending that a waitress had removed a £5 note which had been placed on the table. When presented with their bill they advanced this deception and declined payment. They were arrested and charged with attempting to evade liability by deception. They were convicted and appealed on the ground, *inter alia*, that on the facts the offence should have been charged under section 2 (1) (*a*) of the Theft Act 1978 as an attempt to secure the remission of the debt instead of under section 2 (1) (*b*) as an attempt to induce the forgoing of payment with intent to make permanent default.
>
> **Held,** dismissing the appeals, that the differences between paragraphs (*a*), (*b*) and (*c*) of section 2 (1) of the Theft Act 1978 related principally to the different situations in which the debtor-creditor relationship had arisen. Although there were substantial differences in the elements of the offences there defined they showed common features: (i) the use of deception to a creditor in relation to a liability; (ii) dishonesty in the use of deception; (iii) the use of deception to gain

some advantage in time or money. The element unique to section 2 (1) (*b*) was the intention to make permanent default on the whole or part of an existing liability. The jury concluded that the appellants' conduct was motivated by the intent to make permanent default on their supper bill. The appellants were rightly convicted as charged.

Commentary. The words of section 2 (1) (*b*) seem more appropriate to the facts than those of section 2 (1) (*a*). A creditor cannot remit, or intend to remit, a debt unless he believes there is an existing debt. The deception in the present case was intended to persuade the creditor to believe that there was no debt in existence — that it had already been paid. Remission calls for some positive action by the creditor. To forgo, on the other hand, is simply to do without — a negative thing — and the defendants were attempting to persuade the restaurateur to go without payment.

R v *Jackson* [1983] Crim LR 617   Court of Appeal

A stolen Access credit card was presented by occupants of the appellant's car at petrol stations and accepted in satisfaction of payment for petrol and other goods. The appellant was charged, *inter alia,* with handling stolen goods (count 3) and evading liability by deception by dishonestly securing the remission of an existing liability, contrary to section 2 (1) (*a*) of the Theft Act 1978 (counts 5 and 8). At the close of the prosecution evidence the defence submitted that counts 5 and 8 should have been charged under section 2 (1) (*b*), and should be withdrawn from the jury. The trial judge ruled that the case should proceed as charged. The appellant was convicted and appealed on the ground, *inter alia*, that the judge had failed properly to rule on the defence submission.

Held, dismissing the appeal, that although in *Holt* [1981] 1 WLR 1000 it was held that the element under section 2 (1) (*b*) of an intent to make permanent default on the whole or part of an existing liability was unique to sub-paragraph (*b*), that judgment was not authority for the proposition that the elements in sub-paragraphs (*a*), (*b*) and (*c*) of section 2 (1) were mutually exclusive. The transaction of tendering a stolen credit card and having it accepted by a trader who forthwith would look to the authority issuing the card for payment and not to the person tendering the card, meant that that person had dishonestly secured the remission of an existing liability. It was not necessary to consider whether a charge in respect of that transaction could be brought under section 2 (1) (*b*). In the circumstances the matter was not wrongly charged under section 2 (1) (*a*).

Commentary. On the interpretation of section 2 of the Theft Act 1978, see commentary on *Sibartie* [1983] Crim LR 471 [below].

Assuming that the signature of the defendant in the present case could reasonably pass as that of the true holder of the Access card, Access would be bound to pay the sellers of the petrol and other goods. The sellers would be right to look to Access for payment and would certainly do so in practice. If, for some reason, Access had declined to pay, no doubt the sellers could then have sued the defendant for the price. In that sense, his liability to pay continued, but it was a contingent liability and might fairly be regarded as having been remitted, even though it might revive in a certain event.

Obtaining an exemption from or abatement of liability: 1978 Act s. 2(1)(c)

This is the only one of the three subsections not requiring proof of the existence of an existing legal liability. It is suggested that this subsection should only cover the situation where the deception is directed at making the victim believe that no or less money is due from a potential or actual creditor. If the following case is correct the subsection is, however, much wider than this:

R v Sibartie [1983] Crim LR 470   Court of Appeal

The appellant, a law student who lived in Acton and attended college in Hendon, bought two season tickets on the Underground, one ticket covering the beginning of his journey on one line for two stations and the other ticket covering the end of his journey on another line for two stations; in between were 14 stations including an interchange station between the two lines. At the interchange station, on passing a ticket inspector, the appellant held aloft a wallet containing the season ticket − according to the inspector, "flashing it" so that she could not see what was on it − and on being challenged said that he was going to the first of the two stations at the end of his journey. The appellant's version was that he was going out at the interchange station and was intending to pay. He was charged on counts 1 and 2 with evasion of a liability by deception, contrary to section 2 (1) (c) of the Theft Act 1978 and on count 3 of an attempted evasion of a liability by deception. The jury acquitted him on counts 1 and 2 but convicted on count 3. He appealed against conviction.

Held, dismissing the appeal, that the correct method of approach was to ask whether, taking the words of section 2 (1) (c) in their ordinary meaning, one would say that what the appellant was attempting to do fell within the ambit of the words. The jury by their verdict must have been satisfied that the appellant dishonestly used his season tickets, which did not in fact cover the journey he was making, in an attempt to persuade the ticket inspector that they did cover the journey. Did that amount to an attempt to obtain exemption from liability to make a payment for the journey he was making or had made? He was saying, albeit tacitly, by waving the supposed season ticket in the air that he was the holder of a ticket authorising him to be making the journey without further payment and consequently he was not under any liability to pay any more. In the ordinary meaning of words that was dishonestly obtaining an exemption from the liability to pay the excess which, had he been honest, he would have had to pay. There might be a degree of overlap between section 2 (1) (a), (b) and (c), and the fact that what the appellant did might also have been an attempt to commit an offence under section 2 (1) (b) was neither here nor there.

Commentary. When the defendant "flashed" his wallet he was, it appears, attempting to avoid having to pay the proper fare for the journey which he was in fact undertaking. Payment was due at the outset of the journey and he was trying to deceive the inspector into believing that the fare had been paid by the purchase of a season ticket covering the whole journey. Section 2 (1) of the Theft Act probably creates three offences and a case may be made for saying that he was guilty of an attempt to commit all of them.

Assuming he had succeeded−

(a)   Did he secure the remission of part of an existing liability to make a payment? (s. 2 (1) (a))

(b)   Did he induce the creditor to forgo payment of part of an existing liability, with intent to make permanent default? (s. 2 (1) (b))

(c)   Did he obtain an exemption from liability to make a payment? (s. 2 (1) (c))

If he was guilty of three offences, does not this look like a case of overkill on the part of the legislator? Some overlap of offences is reasonable and to be expected; but it must surely be assumed that Parliament intended each offence to have some function. If the broadest construction is put upon each offence there seems to be nothing for paragraph (b), in so far as it relates to forgoing payment, to do.

Paragraphs (a) and (c) do not require proof of an intent to make permanent default and, if they cover cases of forgoing payment, Parliament's evident intention, that one who merely induces a creditor to forgo payment should not be guilty unless he has an intent to make permanent default, if defeated. It is no answer to this argument that there was evidence of an intent to make permanent default in the present case. Such an intent was no part of the offence of which the appellant was convicted.

There is, however, an interpretation of the section which avoids this result, and which requires nothing more extravagant than a literal reading of the words of the section. Offence (a) is not committed unless the defendant "secures the remission" of a liability. Offence (c) is not committed unless the defendant obtains an "exemption from . . . liability to make a payment." Assuming again that the defendant had succeeded in deceiving the inspector in the present case, the inspector would have had no intention to "remit" an existing liability because he would have been persuaded that there was no liability to remit, nor would he in law have remitted any liability. The defendant's liability to pay the proper fare would unquestionably have continued unimpaired. Similarly, the inspector would not have intended to exempt the defendant from any liability to make a payment, existing or otherwise, being persuaded that there was no liability, and the defendant would not have been exempted from any liability. See Smith, *Law of Theft* (4th ed.), paras. 232-241, *contra,* Griew, *The Theft Acts* (4th ed.), paras. 8-11 to 8-18.

What the defendant would have succeeded in doing if he had deceived the inspector was to induce him to forgo payment of an unremitted, still existing liability to pay the full fare, from which no one intended to exempt him and from which he was not exempted.

Though lip-service is from time to time paid to the principle that a penal statute must be construed strictly in favour of the accused, in practice that approach is out of fashion. Even where a statute is wholly unambiguous and in favour of the defendant, it may be construed to his disadvantage as in *Duncalf* [1979] 2 All ER 116. See commentary [1979] Crim LR at 452. The present case does not go so far as that. Indeed, probably the majority of those who have given thought to the matter would regard it as right, on the ground that Parliament could not have intended paragraphs (a) and (c) to have such a narrow meaning as the construction advocated above would give them. The result, then is not at all surprising; but it is submitted that a better view and one more consistent with the principles of interpretation of penal statutes would be that the appellant was guilty of an offence under paragraph (*b*) but not under paragraph (*c*), or, for that matter paragraph (*a*).

The subsection does clearly include (but is not confined to) the situation where a contract is *made* at a better rate than it would otherwise have been. An example (not covered by the other two subsections) would be where the defendant pretends to be an old-age pensioner in order to get cheap or free entry into a museum.

Finally, it should be noted that all three subsections can be committed in respect of the defendant's liability or the liability of another.

11 MAKING OFF WITHOUT PAYMENT

Section 3 Theft Act 1978

(1) Subject to subsection (3) below, a person who, knowing that payment on the spot for any goods supplied or service done is required or expected from him, dishonestly makes off without having paid as required or expected and with intent to avoid payment of the amount due shall be guilty of an offence.

(2) For purposes of this section 'payment on the spot' includes payment at the time of collecting goods on which work has been done or in respect of which service has been provided.

(3) Subsection (1) above shall not apply where the supply of the goods or the doing of the service is contrary to law, or where the service done is such that payment is not legally enforceable.

(a) The actus reus

Three elements are discernible here;

(i) The defendant must 'make off'.
(ii) The defendant must make off 'from the spot' where payment is required or expected.
(iii) There must be an enforceable debt which the defendant is avoiding.

(i) The defendant must 'make off'.

The following case seems to suggest that if the defendant is sufficiently clever at trickery to gain the victim's consent to his departure, there will be no offence:

R v Hammond [1982] Crim LR 611   Lincoln Crown Court

Philip Hammond was charged under sections 2 (1) (*b*) and 3 of the Theft Act 1978. Hammond admitted to the police that he had, between May and August 1980, gone to various garages to have repairs done to his car which he needed for his business. On each occasion when he collected the car he had offered and in fact tendered a cheque drawn on his account at the Yorkshire Bank in payment. He admitted to the police that he knew at the time of giving the cheques that he had no money in the account to meet them, but he hoped that money would be forthcoming in the future.

At the close of the prosecution the defence were invited by the judge to submit as to whether the action of the defendant amounted to an offence of making off without payment under section 3 or only to an offence of evasion of liability by deception under section 2 (1) (*b*). The prosecution conceded that the principal reason for including the count under section 3 was because of the difficulty of proving an intention never to pay which was required under section 2 (1) (*b*).

Held, there were two questions in issue. First was the tendering of a cheque, which the defendant knew would not be met in the ordinary course of banking, payment for the purposes of section 3 and, second did section 3 apply to the stalling debtor?

As to the "payment" the offer of a cheque was not the same as offering counterfeit money. A cheque without a banker's card is always taken at risk by the recipient. The defendant gave the worthless cheque and departed with the consent of the recipient and could not therefore be said to be "making off." This consent was not vitiated simply by the fact that the payee did not at that time know that the drawer had insufficient funds to his credit in his account to meet payment.

In any event it was unrealistic to look at section 3 in isolation. Sections 2 and 3 appeared in identical terms as cll. 2 and 3 of the Thirteenth Report of the Criminal Law Revision Committee in which cl. 2 (1) (*b*) is expressed to be concerned with the stalling debtor (*Archbold*, para. 1599 (*a*)), namely one "who intends to make permanent default in whole or in part of his liability to pay. . . . We recognise that the practical difficulties of proving an intention never to pay will have the consequence that there will be few prosecutions under this head, but this is consistent with our view that the criminal law should not apply to the debtor who is merely trying to delay the making of payment. . ."

If then section 2 (1) (*b*) does not apply to a debtor who is delaying payment, why should section 3 cover it since the Committee clearly wished to exclude the criminal law from cases where a debtor is merely trying to delay the making of payment?

The offence committed by the defendant, if any, was an offence under section 2 (1) (*b*) and the jury were directed to acquit of the charges under section 3.

Commentary. There seem to be three possible reasons for the decision. (i) There was no "making off" because the creditor consented to the defendant's driving away. This is the opinion of Francis Bennion: [1980] Crim LR 670. *CF*. J. R. Spencer [1979] Crim LR at p. 37. If that is the reason, then the counterfeit money case is no different. In both cases the creditor consents to the departure of the debtor because he believes he has been paid. Of course, his consent has been induced by deception. In the present case, it would appear likely that the car was obtained by deception since the repairer had a lien on it for the cost of the repairs and it therefore belonged to him for the purposes of section 15 of the Theft Act 1968. Other commentators think that a debtor who obtains consent by deception "makes off." Griew, *The Theft Acts 1968 and 1978* (4th ed.), pp. 11-12; Smith, *Law of Theft* (4th ed.), para. 242. If this is not so the law fails to provide for the case (successfully prosecuted, it is understood, in the magistrates' court) of D who, at the end of a long taxi ride, says he is just going into the house to get the fare and disappears into the night never to return.

(ii) The creditor was "paid" by the bad cheque. It was not the same as counterfeit money. Griew, pp. 11-13, is inclined to the opinion that a bad cheque is not payment. Smith, para. 246, suggests that payment has not been made "as required or expected." Syrota, *Current Law Statutes,* argues that a person who takes a cheque by way of conditional satisfaction of a pre-existing liability is to be treated as being paid. The bad cheque differs from counterfeit money in that the payee can sue on the cheque instead of suing for the existing debt; but in most cases this additional cause of action is of no value to him and he would be surprised to learn that the law regarded him as having been paid.

(iii) The section requires an intent permanently to deprive. Section 2 (1) (*b*) restricts the liability of the "stalling debtor" to one with such an intent and it would defeat the purpose of the Act, read as a whole, if section 3 applied. This is a weighty argument but Griew, 11-14, thinks the intent which must be proved is clearly only intent to avoid the on-the-spot payment known to be required; and Smith, para. 249, referring to *Corbyn* v *Saunders* [1978] 2 All ER 697; [1978] Crim LR 169, is inclined to the same view.

It is unfortunate that there is no clear answer to any of these three questions. Curiously, the prosecution would seem to have been on much stronger ground if they had relied on the more serious offence under section 15 of the Theft Act 1968 where there is no problem about consent, or "payment," and there was undoubtedly an intent to deprive the garage owner permanently of the car.

(ii) The defendant must make off 'from the spot' where payment is required or expected.

R v *McDavitt* [1981] Crim LR 843   Croydon Crown Court at Wallington

The defendant had a meal with three friends in a restaurant. At the end of the meal his friends left the restaurant and the defendant remained at the table where they had all been sitting. The bill was brought on a saucer to his table and an argument ensued between the defendant and the owner of the restaurant which ended with the defendant refusing to pay any of the bill. He went towards the door whereupon someone standing by the door advised him not to leave as the police were being called. The defendant then went to the toilet in the restaurant where he remained until the police arrived. He was arrested and taken to a police station where he later made a statement under caution in which he admitted the above facts saying that it was his intention to leave without paying for the meal but that he decided to stay on being told about the police being summoned. He was subsequently indicted under section 3 of the Theft Act 1978 with making off from the restaurant without paying for the food and wine which had been consumed. On a submission of no case to answer:

Held, "Makes off" refers to making off from the spot where payment is required or expected. What is the spot depends on the circumstances of each case. In this case the spot was the restaurant. The jury would be directed that it was not open to them to find the defendant guilty of the offence on the indictment but that it was open to them to find him guilty of an attempt to commit the offence.

R v *Brooks and Brooks* (1982) 76 Cr App Rep 66   Court of Appeal

On a charge under section 3(1) of the Theft Act 1978 of dishonestly making off without payment for goods or services the jury should be told that the words "dishonestly makes off" should be given their ordinary natural meaning and that they, the jury, should relate those words to the facts of the case in question. "Making-off" in the subsection involves a departure from the spot where payment is required.

McDavitt [1981] Crim LR 843 approved and applied.

However, in the case where the accused is stopped before passing the spot where payment is required, a jury should be directed that that may constitute an attempt to commit the offence, rather than the substantive offence, provided that the other ingredients are established.

The appellants, father and daughter, with one S. had a meal together one evening in the upstairs room of a restaurant. At 10.30 p.m. the daughter was seen leaving the premises in haste. The manager went upstairs and saw the two men were not there but found S. downstairs waiting outside the men's lavatory. Nearby was a door inside the premises which led into the yard. S. made no comment when asked about the unpaid bill but, after entering the lavatory, later made off through the outer door. The manager chased after him and asked him to come back. While they were re-entering the restaurant, the father came out of it. All three then went back inside. All the father could offer for payment for the bill of £8.52 was a cheque for £130 in his favour, which later turned out to be valueless. S. said in the father's hearing that the payment was not due from him, S. When the daughter was later interviewed by the police she maintained that S. had met them earlier that night for the first time and had generously offered to treat her and her father to a meal. Both father and daughter were charged with making off without payment contrary to section 3(1) of the Theft Act 1978. The prosecution case was that the father and daughter jointly and severally intended to avoid payment and separately made off from the spot which, it was said, was the restaurant as a whole. The recorder read out in full section 3(1) of the Act of 1978 and said the whole essence of the offence was that people left intending, if they could, to get away without paying. But he never told the jury that on the evidence the daughter had left earlier and in haste; that she said she went to the restaurant at the invitation of S. believing he would pay; and that they would have to draw the inference that at the time she left she dishonestly intended to evade payment before she could be convicted. Both father and daughter were convicted. On appeal.

Held, that (1) as to the father's appeal, the recorder had succinctly summarised the effect of section 3(1) of the Theft Act 1978 and the jury could not have been left in any doubt on the facts of the case that he had left the premises without paying the bill; accordingly, his appeal would be dismissed.

(2) as to the daughter's appeal, the recorder's failure to direct the jury as set out above meant that they had not been alerted to her defence, thus it was quite possible that they might not have been satisfied of her guilt. Her conviction was, therefore, unsafe and unsatisfactory and her appeal would be allowed and conviction quashed.

KILNER BROWN J — . . . On the facts of this case, it was not necessary to elaborate on the necessity to establish that there was a departure from the spot. The evidence of this was there. Both went outside the premises. However, in a case where the accused is stopped before passing the spot where payment is required, a jury should be directed that that may constitute an attempt to commit the offence, rather than the substantive offence, provided that the other ingredients are established.

In so far as the appellant Edward George Brooks is concerned, the appeal against conviction is dismissed. There is no appeal against the sentence of a fine of £25 and an order for compensation in the sum of £8.52.

In the case of the appellant Julie Brooks, there is a further and different consideration. It is submitted on her behalf that a clear direction was required to the effect that it must be proved that at the time she left the premises she knew that no payment was intended and that there was an intention on her part to participate in a dishonest evasion of the cost of the meal.

All that the judge said as to this was the general direction which was given in the passage previously cited and, earlier to that, he had directed the jury in these words: "There are two defendants and you will bring in separate verdicts in respect of each. You may find one guilty and one not guilty or both not guilty. Their cases must be considered separately."

That was all right as far as it went, but the jury were never told that upon the evidence that she left earlier and in haste and her defence that she went to the restaurant at the other man's invitation believing that he would pay, they would have to draw the inference that at the time she left she intended dishonestly to evade payment, before she could be convicted. If the jury had been alerted to this necessity, it is quite possible that they may not have been satisfied of her guilt.

In the opinion of this Court, this failure to direct the jury more fully in her case makes her conviction unsafe and unsatisfactory and her appeal is allowed. The conviction is quashed and the order to pay a fine of £25 is set aside.

(iii) There must be an enforceable debt which the defendant is avoiding.

This is specifically required by s. 3(3).

(b) The mens rea

Here again there are three elements:

(i)   The defendant must be dishonest.
(ii)   The defendant must know that payment on the spot is required or expected.
(iii) There must be an intent to avoid payment.

(i)   Dishonesty presumably imports the test in R v Ghosh (above, page 52). The dishonesty must be proved to have been present at the time of the making-off — see R v Brooks and Brooks (above).

(ii)   Knowledge that payment on the spot is required or expected is expressly required by s. 3(1).

(iii)   There must be an intent to avoid payment. Unlike s. 2(1)(b) there is no express requirement that the defendant should have an intention to make permanent default. If this omission is significant, a dishonest intention to avoid payment temporarily will be sufficient. The courts have yet to determine this issue.

THEFT ACT 1968

1968, c. 60. An Act to revise the law of England and Wales as to theft and similar or associated offences, and in connection therewith to make provision as to criminal proceedings by one party to a marriage against the other, and to make certain amendments extending beyond England and Wales in the Post Office Act 1953 and other enactments; and for other purposes connected therewith. [Royal assent 26 July 1968.]

Definition of 'theft'

Basic definition of theft

1.–(1) A person is guilty of theft if he dishonestly appropriates property belonging to another with the intention of permanently depriving the other of it; and 'thief' and 'steal' shall be construed accordingly.

(2) It is immaterial whether the appropriation is made with a view to gain, or is made for the thief's own benefit.

(3) The five following sections of this Act shall have effect as regards the interpretation and operation of this section (and, except as otherwise provided by this Act, shall apply only for purposes of this section).

'Dishonestly'

2.–(1) A person's appropriation of property belonging to another is not to be regarded as dishonest—

(*a*) if he appropriates the property in the belief that he has in law the right to deprive the other of it, on behalf of himself or of a third person; or

(*b*) if he appropriates the property in the belief that he would have the other's consent if the other knew of the appropriation and the circumstances of it; or

(*c*) (except where the property came to him as trustee or personal representative) if he appropriates the property in the belief that the person to whom the property belongs cannot be discovered by taking reasonable steps.

(2) A person's appropriation of property belonging to another may be dishonest notwithstanding that he is willing to pay for the property.

'Appropriates'

3.—(1) Any assumption by a person of the rights of an owner amounts to an appropriation, and this includes, where he has come by the property (innocently or not) without stealing it, any later assumption of a right to it by keeping or dealing with it as owner.

(2) Where property or a right or interest in property is or purports to be transferred for value to a person acting in good faith, no later assumption by him of rights which he believed himself to be acquiring shall, by reason of any defect in the transferor's title, amount to theft of the property.

'Property'

4.—(1) 'Property' includes money and all other property, real or personal, including things in action and other intangible property.

(2) A person cannot steal land, or things forming part of land and severed from it by him or by his directions, except in the following cases, that is to say—

(*a*)   when he is a trustee or personal representative, or is authorised by power of attorney, or as liquidator of a company, or otherwise, to sell or dispose of land belonging to another, and he appropriates the land or anything forming part of it by dealing with it in breach of the confidence reposed in him; or

(*b*)   when he is not in possession of the land and appropriates anything forming part of the land by severing it or causing it to be severed, or after it has been severed; or

(*c*)   when, being in possession of the land under a tenancy, he appropriates the whole or part of any fixture or structure let to be used with the land.

For purposes of this subsection 'land' does not include incorporeal hereditaments; 'tenancy' means a tenancy for years or any less period and includes an agreement for such a tenancy, but a person who after the end of a tenancy remains in possession as statutory tenant or otherwise is to be treated as having possession under the tenancy, and 'let' shall be construed accordingly.

(3) A person who picks mushrooms growing wild on any land, or who picks flowers, fruit or foliage from a plant growing wild on any land, does not (although not in possession of the land) steal what he picks, unless he does it for reward or for sale or other commercial purpose.

For purposes of this subsection 'mushroom' includes any fungus, and 'plant' includes any shrub or tree.

(4) Wild creatures, tamed or untamed, shall be regarded as property; but a person cannot steal a wild creature not tamed nor ordinarily kept in captivity, or the carcase of any such creature, unless either it has been reduced into possession by or on behalf of another person and possession of it has not since been lost or abandoned, or another person is in course of reducing it into possession.

'Belonging to another'

5.—(1) Property shall be regarded as belonging to any person having possession or control of it, or having in it any proprietary right or interest (not being an equitable interest arising only from an agreement to transfer or grant an interest).

(2) Where property is subject to a trust, the persons to whom it belongs shall be regarded as including any person having a right to enforce the trust, and an intention to defeat the trust shall be regarded accordingly as an intention to deprive of the property any person having that right.

(3) Where a person receives property from or on account of another, and is under an obligation to the other to retain and deal with that property or its proceeds in a particular way, the property or proceeds shall be regarded (as against him) as belonging to the other.

(4) Where a person gets property by another's mistake, and is under an obligation to make restoration (in whole or in part) of the property or its proceeds or of the value thereof, then to the extent of that obligation the property or proceeds shall be regarded (as against him) as belonging to the person entitled to restoration, and an intention not to make restoration shall be regarded accordingly as an intention to deprive that person of the property or proceeds.

(5) Property of a corporation sole shall be regarded as belonging to the corporation notwithstanding a vacancy in the corporation.

'With the intention of permanently depriving the other of it'

6.—(1) A person appropriating property belonging to another without meaning the other permanently to lose the thing itself is nevertheless to be regarded as having the intention of permanently depriving the other of it if his intention is to treat the thing as his own to dispose of regardless of the other's rights; and a borrowing or lending of it may amount to so treating it if, but only if, the borrowing or lending is for a period and in circumstances making it equivalent to an outright taking or disposal.

(2) Without prejudice to the generality of subsection (1) above, where a person, having possession or control (lawfully or not) of property belonging to another, parts with the property under a condition as to its return which he may not be able to perform, this (if done for purposes of his own and without the other's authority) amounts to treating the property as his own to dispose of regardless of the other's rights.

Theft, robbery, burglary, etc.

Theft

7. A person guilty of theft shall on conviction on indictment be liable to imprisonment for a term not exceeding ten years.

Robbery

8.—(1) A person is guilty of robbery if he steals, and immediately before or at the time of doing so, and in order to do so, he uses force on any person or puts or seeks to put any person in fear of being then and there subjected to force.

(2) A person guilty of robbery, or of an assault with intent to rob, shall on conviction on indictment be liable to imprisonment for life.

Burglary

9.—(1) A person is guilty of burglary if—

(a)   he enters any building or part of a building as a trespasser and with intent to commit any such offence as is mentioned in subsection (2) below; or

(b)   having entered any building or part of a building as a trespasser he steals or attempts to steal anything in the building or that part of it or inflicts or attempts to inflict on any person therein any grievous bodily harm.

(2) The offences referred to in subsection (1)(a) above are offences of stealing anything in the building or part of a building in question, of inflicting on any person therein any grievous bodily harm or raping any woman therein, and of doing unlawful damage to the building or anything therein.

(3) References in subsections (1) and (2) above to a building shall apply also to an inhabited vehicle or vessel, and shall apply to any such vehicle or vessel at times when the person having a habitation in it is not there as well as at times when he is.

(4) A person guilty of burglary shall on conviction on indictment be liable to imprisonment for a term not exceeding fourteen years.

Aggravated burglary

10.—(1) A person is guilty of aggravated burglary if he commits any burglary and at the time has with him any firearm or imitation firearm, any weapon of offence, or any explosive; and for this purpose—

(a)   'firearm' includes an airgun or air pistol, and 'imitation firearm' means anything which has the appearance of being a firearm, whether capable of being discharged or not; and

(b) 'weapon of offence' means any article made or adapted for use for causing injury to or incapacitating a person, or intended by the person having it with him for such use; and

(c) 'explosive' means any article manufactured for the purpose of producing a practical effect by explosion, or intended by the person having it with him for that purpose.

(2) A person guilty of aggravated burglary shall on conviction on indictment be liable to imprisonment for life.

Removal of articles from places open to the public

11.—(1) Subject to subsections (2) and (3) below, where the public have access to a building in order to view the building or part of it, or a collection or part of a collection housed in it, any person who without lawful authority removes from the building or its grounds the whole or part of any article displayed or kept for display to the public in the building or that part of it or in its grounds shall be guilty of an offence.

For this purpose 'collection' includes a collection got together for a temporary purpose, but references in this section to a collection do not apply to a collection made or exhibited for the purpose of effecting sales or other commercial dealings.

(2) It is immaterial for purposes of subsection (1) above, that the public's access to a building is limited to a particular period or particular occasion; but where anything removed from a building or its grounds is there otherwise than as forming part of, or being on loan for exhibition with, a collection intended for permanent exhibition to the public, the person removing it does not thereby commit an offence under this section unless he removes it on a day when the public have access to the building as mentioned in subsection (1) above.

(3) A person does not commit an offence under this section if he believes that he has lawful authority for the removal of the thing in question or that he would have it if the person entitled to give it knew of the removal and the circumstances of it.

(4) A person guilty of an offence under this section shall, on conviction on indictment, be liable to imprisonment for a term not exceeding five years.

Taking motor vehicle or other conveyance without authority

12.—(1) Subject to subsections (5) and (6) below, a person shall be guilty of an offence if, without having the consent of the owner or other lawful authority, he takes any conveyance for his own or another's use or, knowing that any conveyance has been taken without such authority, drives it or allows himself to be carried in or on it.

(2) A person guilty of an offence under subsection (1) above shall on conviction on indictment be liable to imprisonment for a term not exceeding three years.

[(3) Offences under subsection (1) above and attempts to commit them shall be deemed for all purposes to be arrestable offences within the meaning of section 2 of the Criminal Law Act 1967.[1]]

(4) If on the trial of an indictment for theft the jury are not satisfied that the accused committed theft, but it is proved that the accused committed an offence under subsection (1) above, the jury may find him guilty of the offence under subsection (1).

(5) Subsection (1) above shall not apply in relation to pedal cycles; but, subject to subsection (6) below, a person who, without having the consent of the owner or other lawful authority, takes a pedal cycle for his own or another's use, or rides a pedal cycle knowing it to have been taken without such authority, shall on summary conviction be liable to a fine not exceeding [level 3 on the standard scale[2]].

(6) A person does not commit an offence under this section by anything done in the belief that he has lawful authority to do it or that he would have the owner's consent if the owner knew of his doing it and the circumstances of it.

(7) For purposes of this section—

(a)   'conveyance' means any conveyance constructed or adapted for the carriage of a person or persons whether by land, water or air, except that it does not include a conveyance constructed or adapted for use only under the control of a person not carried in or on it, and 'drive' shall be construed accordingly; and

(b)   'owner', in relation to a conveyance which is the subject of a hiring agreement or hire-purchase agreement, means the person in possession of the conveyance under that agreement.

Notes

1   Section 12(3) is to be repealed by the Police and Criminal Evidence Act 1984, s. 119(2) and sch. 7, pt. 1 from a date to be appointed by the Secretary of State under s. 121(1) of that Act.
2   Words substituted by virtue of Criminal Justice Act 1982, ss. 38 and 46. Level 3 is £400 as from 1 May 1984 (SI 1984 No. 447, art. 2(4) and sch. 4).

Abstracting of electricity

13. A person who dishonestly uses without due authority, or dishonestly causes to be wasted or diverted, any electricity shall on conviction on indictment be liable to imprisonment for a term not exceeding five years.

Extension to thefts from mails outside England and Wales, and robbery etc. on such a theft

14.—(1) Where a person—

(a)   steals or attempts to steal any mail bag or postal packet in the course of transmission as such between places in different jurisdictions in the British postal area, or any of the contents of such a mail bag or postal packet; or

(b)   in stealing or with intent to steal any such mail bag or postal packet or any of its contents, commits any robbery, attempted robbery or assault with intent to rob;

then, notwithstanding that he does so outside England and Wales, he shall be guilty of committing or attempting to commit the offence against this Act as if he had done so in England or Wales, and he shall accordingly be liable to be prosecuted, tried and punished in England and Wales without proof that the offence was committed there.

(2) In subsection (1) above the reference to different jurisdictions in the British postal area is to be construed as referring to the several jurisdictions of England and Wales, of Scotland, of Northern Ireland, of the Isle of Man and of the Channel Islands.

(3) For purposes of this section 'mail bag' includes any article serving the purpose of a mail bag.

Fraud and blackmail

Obtaining property by deception

15.—(1) A person who by any deception dishonestly obtains property belonging to another, with the intention of permanently depriving the other of it, shall on conviction on indictment be liable to imprisonment for a term not exceeding ten years.

(2) For purposes of this section a person is to be treated as obtaining property if he obtains ownership, possession or control of it, and 'obtain' includes obtaining for another or enabling another to obtain or to retain.

(3) Section 6 above shall apply for purposes of this section, with the necessary adaptation of the reference to appropriating, as it applies for purposes of section 1.

(4) For purposes of this section 'deception' means any deception (whether deliberate or reckless) by words or conduct as to fact or as to law, including a deception as to the present intentions of the person using the deception or any other person.

Obtaining pecuniary advantage by deception

16.—(1) A person who by any deception dishonestly obtains for himself or another any pecuniary advantage shall on conviction on indictment be liable to imprisonment for a term not exceeding five years.

(2) The cases in which a pecuniary advantage within the meaning of this section is to be regarded as obtained for a person are cases where—

[. . .¹]
(*b*)   he is allowed to borrow by way of overdraft, or to take out any policy of
insurance or annuity contract, or obtains an improvement of the terms on
which he is allowed to do so; or
(*c*)   he is given the opportunity to earn remuneration or greater remuneration
in an office or employment, or to win money by betting.

(3) For purposes of this section 'deception' has the same meaning as in section
15 of this Act.

Note
1   Section 16(2)(*a*) repealed by Theft Act 1978, s. 5(5).

False accounting
   17.—(1) Where a person dishonestly, with a view to gain for himself or another
or with intent to cause loss to another,—

(*a*)   destroys, defaces, conceals or falsifies any account or any record or document made or required for any accounting purpose; or
(*b*)   in furnishing information for any purpose produces or makes use of any
account, or any such record or document as aforesaid, which to his knowledge is or may be misleading, false or deceptive in a material particular;

he shall, on conviction on indictment, be liable to imprisonment for a term not
exceeding seven years.
   (2) For purposes of this section a person who makes or concurs in making in an
account or other document an entry which is or may be misleading, false or deceptive
in a material particular, or who omits or concurs in omitting a material particular
from an account or other document, is to be treated as falsifying the account or
document.

Liability of company officers for certain offences by company
   18.—(1) Where an offence committed by a body corporate under section 15, 16
or 17 of this Act is proved to have been committed with the consent or connivance
of any director, manager, secretary or other similar officer of the body corporate,
or any person who was purporting to act in any such capacity, he as well as the
body corporate shall be guilty of that offence, and shall be liable to be proceeded
against and punished accordingly.
   (2) Where the affairs of a body corporate are managed by its members, this
section shall apply in relation to the acts and defaults of a member in connection
with his functions of management as if he were a director of the body corporate.

False statements by company directors, etc.

19.–(1) Where an officer of a body corporate or unincorporated association (or person purporting to act as such), with intent to deceive members or creditors of the body corporate or association about its affairs, publishes or concurs in publishing a written statement or account which to his knowledge is or may be misleading, false or deceptive in a material particular, he shall on conviction on indictment be liable to imprisonment for a term not exceeding seven years.

(2) For purposes of this section a person who has entered into a security for the benefit of a body corporate or association is to be treated as a creditor of it.

(3) Where the affairs of a body corporate or association are managed by its members, this section shall apply to any statement which a member publishes or concurs in publishing in connection with his functions of management as if he were an officer of the body corporate or association.

Suppression, etc. of documents

20.–(1) A person who dishonestly, with a view to gain for himself or another or with intent to cause loss to another, destroys, defaces or conceals any valuable security, any will or other testamentary document or any original document of or belonging to, or filed or deposited in, any court of justice or any government department shall on conviction on indictment be liable to imprisonment for a term not exceeding seven years.

(2) A person who dishonestly, with a view to gain for himself or another or with intent to cause loss to another, by any deception procures the execution of a valuable security shall on conviction on indictment be liable to imprisonment for a term not exceeding seven years; and this subsection shall apply in relation to the making, acceptance, indorsement, alteration, cancellation or destruction in whole or in part of a valuable security, and in relation to the signing or sealing of any paper or other material in order that it may be made or converted into, or used or dealt with as, a valuable security, as if that were the execution of a valuable security.

(3) For purposes of this section 'deception' has the same meaning as in section 15 of this Act, and 'valuable security' means any document creating, transferring, surrendering or releasing any right to, in or over property, or authorising the payment of money or delivery of any property, or evidencing the creation, transfer, surrender or release of any such right, or the payment of money or delivery of any property, or the satisfaction of any obligation.

Blackmail

21.–(1) A person is guilty of blackmail if, with a view to gain for himself or another, he makes any unwarranted demand with menaces; and for this purpose a demand with menaces is unwarranted unless the person making it does so in the belief–

(*a*)   that he has reasonable grounds for making the demand; and

(*b*)   that the use of the menaces is a proper means of reinforcing the demand.

(2) The nature of the act or omission demanded is immaterial, and it is also immaterial whether the menaces relate to action to be taken by the person making the demand.

(3) A person guilty of blackmail shall on conviction on indictment be liable to imprisonment for a term not exceeding fourteen years.

Offences relating to goods stolen etc.

Handling stolen goods

22.–(1) A person handles stolen goods if (otherwise than in the course of the stealing) knowing or believing them to be stolen goods he dishonestly receives the goods, or dishonestly undertakes or assists in their retention, removal, disposal or realisation by or for the benefit of another person, or if he arranges to do so.

(2) A person guilty of handling stolen goods shall on conviction on indictment be liable to imprisonment for a term not exceeding fourteen years.

Advertising rewards for return of goods stolen or lost

23. Where any public advertisement of a reward for the return of any goods which have been stolen or lost uses any words to the effect that no questions will be asked, or that the person producing the goods will be safe from apprehension or inquiry, or that any money paid for the purchase of the goods or advanced by way of loan on them will be repaid, the person advertising the reward and any person who prints or publishes the advertisement shall on summary conviction be liable to a fine not exceeding [level 3 on the standard scale[1]] .

Note

1   Words substituted by virtue of Criminal justice Act 1982, ss. 38 and 46. Level 3 is £400 as from 1 May 1984 (SI 1984 No. 447, art. 2(4) and sch. 4).

Scope of offences relating to stolen goods

24.–(1) The provisions of this Act relating to goods which have been stolen shall apply whether the stealing occurred in England and Wales or elsewhere, and whether it occurred before or after the commencement of this Act, provided that the stealing (if not an offence under this Act) amounted to an offence where and at the time when the goods were stolen; and references to stolen goods shall be construed accordingly.

(2) For purposes of those provisions references to stolen goods shall include, in addition to the goods originally stolen and parts of them (whether in their original state or not),–

(*a*) any other goods which directly or indirectly represent or have at any time represented the stolen goods in the hands of the thief as being the proceeds of any disposal or realisation of the whole or part of the goods stolen or of goods so representing the stolen goods; and

(*b*) any other goods which directly or indirectly represent or have at any time represented the stolen goods in the hands of a handler of the stolen goods or any part of them as being the proceeds of any disposal or realisation of the whole or part of the stolen goods handled by him or of goods so representing them.

(3) But no goods shall be regarded as having continued to be stolen goods after they have been restored to the person from whom they were stolen or to other lawful possession or custody, or after that person and any other person claiming through him have otherwise ceased as regards those goods to have any right to restitution in respect of the theft.

(4) For purposes of the provisions of this Act relating to goods which have been stolen (including subsections (1) to (3) above) goods obtained in England or Wales or elsewhere either by blackmail or in the circumstances described in section 15(1) of this Act shall be regarded as stolen; and 'steal', 'theft' and 'thief' shall be construed accordingly.

Possession of housebreaking implements, etc.

Going equipped for stealing, etc.

25.—(1) A person shall be guilty of an offence if, when not at his place of abode, he has with him any article for use in the course of or in connection with any burglary, theft or cheat.

(2) A person guilty of an offence under this section shall on conviction on indictment be liable to imprisonment for a term not exceeding three years.

(3) Where a person is charged with an offence under this section, proof that he had with him any article made or adapted for use in committing a burglary, theft or cheat shall be evidence that he had it with him for such use.

(4) Any person may arrest without warrant anyone who is, or whom he, with reasonable cause, suspects to be, committing an offence under this section.

(5) For purposes of this section an offence under section 12(1) of this Act of taking a conveyance shall be treated as theft, and 'cheat' means an offence under section 15 of this Act.

Enforcement and procedure

Search for stolen goods

26.—(1) If it is made to appear by information on oath before a justice of the peace that there is reasonable cause to believe that any person has in his custody or possession or on his premises any stolen goods, the justice may grant a warrant to search for and seize the same; but no warrant to search for stolen goods shall be addressed to a person other than a constable except under the authority of an enactment expressly so providing.

[(2) An officer of police not below the rank of superintendent may give a constable written authority to search any premises for stolen goods—

(a)   if the person in occupation of the premises has been convicted within the preceding five years of handling stolen goods or of any offence involving dishonesty and punishable with imprisonment; or

(b)   if a person who has been convicted within the preceding five years of handling stolen goods has within the preceding twelve months been in occupation of the premises.[1]]

(3) Where under this section a person is authorised to search premises for stolen goods, he may enter and search the premises accordingly, and may seize any goods he believes to be stolen goods.

[. . .[2]]

(5) This section is to be construed in accordance with section 24 of this Act; and in subsection (2) above the references to handling stolen goods shall include any corresponding offence committed before the commencement of this Act.

Notes

1   Section 26(2) is to be repealed by Police and Criminal Evidence Act 1984, s. 119(2) and sch. 7, pt. I, as from a date to be appointed by the Secretary of State under s. 121(1) of that Act.

2   Section 26(4) repealed by Criminal Justice Act 1972, s. 64(2) and sch. 6, pt. II.

Evidence and procedure on charge of theft or handling stolen goods

27.—(1) Any number of persons may be charged in one indictment, with reference to the same theft, with having at different times or at the same time handled all or any of the stolen goods, and the persons so charged may be tried together.

(2) On the trial of two or more persons indicted for jointly handling any stolen goods the jury may find any of the accused guilty if the jury are satisfied that he handled all or any of the stolen goods, whether or not he did so jointly with the other accused or any of them.

(3) Where a person is being proceeded against for handling stolen goods (but not for any offence other than handling stolen goods), then at any stage of the proceedings, if evidence has been given or his having or arranging to have in his possession the goods the subject of the charge, or of his undertaking or assisting in, or arranging to undertake or assist in, their retention, removal, disposal or realisation, the following evidence shall be admissible for the purpose of proving that he knew or believed the goods to be stolen goods:—

(a) evidence that he has had in his possession, or has undertaken or assisted in the retention, removal, disposal or realisation of, stolen goods from any theft taking place not earlier than twelve months before the offence charged; and

(b) (provided that seven days' notice in writing has been given to him of the intention to prove the conviction) evidence that he has within the five years preceding the date of the offence charged been convicted of theft or of handling stolen goods.

(4) In any proceedings for the theft of anything in the course of transmission (whether by post or otherwise), or for handling stolen goods from such a theft, a statutory declaration made by any person that he despatched or received or failed to receive any goods or postal packet, or that any goods or postal packet when despatched or received by him were in a particular state or condition, shall be admissible as evidence of the facts stated in the declaration, subject to the following conditions:—

(a) a statutory declaration shall only be admissible where and to the extent to which oral evidence to the like effect would have been admissible in the proceedings; and

(b) a statutory declaration shall only be admissible if at least seven days before the hearing on trial a copy of it has been given to the person charged, and he has not, at least three days before the hearing or trial or within such further time as the court may in special circumstances allow, given the prosecutor written notice requiring the attendance at the hearing or trial of the person making the declaration.

(5) This section is to be construed in accordance with section 24 of this Act; and in subsection (3)(b) above the reference to handling stolen goods shall include any corresponding offence committed before the commencement of this Act.

Orders for restitution

28.—[(1) Where goods have been stolen, and either a person is convicted of any offence with reference to the theft (whether or not the stealing is the gist of his offence) or a person is convicted of any other offence but such an offence as aforesaid is taken into consideration in determining his sentence, the court by or before which the offender is convicted may on the conviction [(whether or not the passing of sentence is in other respects deferred)[1]] exercise any of the following powers—

(a) the court may order anyone having possession or control of the goods to restore them to any person entitled to recover them from him; or

(b)   on the application of a person entitled to recover from the person convicted any other goods directly or indirectly representing the first-mentioned goods (as being the proceeds of any disposal or realisation of the whole or part of them or of goods so representing them), the court may order those other goods to be delivered or transferred to the applicant; or

(c)   the court may order that a sum not exceeding the value of the first-mentioned goods shall be paid, out of any money of the person convicted which was taken out of his possession on his apprehension, to any person who, if those goods were in the possession of the person convicted, would be entitled to recover them from him.

(2) Where under subsection (1) above the court has power on a person's conviction to make an order against him both under paragraph (b) and under paragraph (c) with reference to the stealing of the same goods, the court may make orders under both paragraphs provided that the person in whose favour the orders are made does not thereby recover more than the value of those goods.

(3) Where under subsection (1) above the court on a person's conviction makes an order under paragraph (a) for the restoration of any goods, and it appears to the court that the person convicted has sold the goods to a person acting in good faith, or has borrowed money on the security of them from a person so acting, the court may order that there shall be paid to the purchaser or lender, out of any money of the person convicted which was taken out of his possession on his apprehension, a sum not exceeding the amount paid for the purchase by the purchaser or, as the case may be, the amount owed to the lender in respect of the loan.[2]]

(4) The court shall not exercise the powers conferred by this section unless in the opinion of the court the relevant facts sufficiently appear from evidence given at the trial or the available documents, together with admissions made by or on behalf of any person in connection with any proposed exercise of the powers; and for this purpose 'the available documents' means any written statements or admissions which were made for use, and would have been admissible, as evidence at the trial, the depositions taken at any committal proceedings and any written statements or admissions used as evidence in those proceedings.

(5) Any order under this section shall be treated as an order for the restitution of property within the meaning of sections 30 and 42 of the Criminal Appeal Act 1968 (which relate to the effect on such orders of appeals).

(6) References in this section to stealing are to be construed in accordance with section 24(1) and (4) of this Act.

Notes

1   Words inserted by Criminal Law Act 1977, s. 65(4) and sch. 12.

2   New subsections (1) to (3) substituted by Criminal Justice Act 1972, s. 64(1) and sch. 5.

[. . .¹]

Note

1   Section 29(1) repealed by Courts Act 1971, s. 56(4) and sch. 11, pt IV. Section 29(2) repealed by Criminal Law Act 1977, s. 65(5) and sch. 13.

General and consequential provisions

Husband and wife

30.—(1) This Act shall apply in relation to the parties to a marriage, and to property belonging to the wife or husband whether or not by reason of an interest derived from the marriage, as it would apply if they were not married and any such interest subsisted independently of the marriage.

(2) Subject to subsection (4) below, a person shall have the same right to bring proceedings against that person's wife or husband for any offence (whether under this Act or otherwise) as if they were not married, and a person bringing any such proceedings shall be competent to give evidence for the prosecution at every stage of the proceedings.

[(3) Where a person is charged in proceedings not brought by that person's wife or husband with having committed any offence with reference to that person's wife or husband or to property belonging to the wife or husband, the wife or husband shall be competent to give evidence at every stage of the proceedings, whether for the defence or for the prosecution, and whether the accused is charged solely or jointly with any other person:

Provided that—

(*a*)   the wife or husband (unless compellable at common law) shall not be compellable either to give evidence or, in giving evidence, to disclose any communication made to her or him during the marriage by the accused; and

(*b*)   her or his failure to give evidence shall not be made the subject of any comment by the prosecution.¹]

(4) Proceedings shall not be instituted against a person for any offence of stealing or doing unlawful damage to property which at the time of the offence belongs to that person's wife or husband, or for any attempt, incitement or conspiracy to commit such an offence, unless the proceedings are instituted by or with the consent of the Director of Public Prosecutions:

Provided that—

(*a*)   this subsection shall not apply to proceedings against a person for an offence—

    (i)   if that person is charged with committing the offence jointly with the wife or husband; or

    (ii)   if by virtue of any judicial decree or order (wherever made) that person and the wife or husband are at the time of the offence under no obligation to cohabit [. . .^{2}] .

[(5) Notwithstanding [section 6 of the Prosecution of Offences Act 1979^3] subsection (4) of this section shall apply—

    (*a*)   to an arrest (if without warrant) made by the wife or husband, and

    (*b*)   to a warrant of arrest issued on an information laid by the wife or husband^4]

Notes
1   Section 30(3) is to be repealed by Police and Criminal Evidence Act 1984, s. 119(2) and sch. 7, pt V, as from a date to be appointed by the Secretary of State under s. 121(1) of that Act.
2   Remainder of subsection (4) repealed by Criminal Jurisdiction Act 1975, s. 14(4) and sch. 5, para. 2(2), and s. 14(5) and sch. 6, pt I.
3   Words substituted by Prosecution of Offences Act 1979, s. 11(1) and sch. 1.
4   New subsection (5) added by Criminal Jurisdiction Act 1975, s. 14(4) and sch. 5, para. 2(1).

Effect on civil proceedings and rights
    31.—(1) A person shall not be excused, by reason that to do so may incriminate that person or the wife or husband of that person of an offence under this Act—

    (*a*)   from answering any question put to that person in proceedings for the recovery or administration of any property, for the execution of any trust or for an account of any property or dealings with property; or

    (*b*)   from complying with any order made in any such proceedings;

but no statement or admission made by a person in answering a question put or complying with an order made as aforesaid shall, in proceedings for an offence under this Act, be admissible in evidence against that person or (unless they married after the making of the statement or admission) against the wife or husband of that person.

    (2) Notwithstanding any enactment to the contrary, where property has been stolen or obtained by fraud or other wrongful means, the title to that or any other property shall not be affected by reason only of the conviction of the offender.

Effect on existing law and construction of references to offences

32.—(1) The following offences are hereby abolished for all purposes not relating to offences committed before the commencement of this Act, that is to say—

(*a*)   any offence at common law of larceny, robbery, burglary, receiving stolen property, obtaining property by threats, extortion by colour of office or franchise, false accounting by public officers, concealment of treasure trove and, except as regards offences relating to the public revenue, cheating; and

(*b*)   any offence under an enactment mentioned in Part I of Schedule 3 to this Act, to the extent to which the offence depends on any section or part of a section included in column 3 of that Schedule;

but so that the provisions in Schedule 1 to this Act (which preserve with modifications certain offences under the Larceny Act 1861 of taking or killing deer and taking or destroying fish) shall have effect as there set out.

(2) Except as regards offences committed before the commencement of this Act, and except in so far as the context otherwise requires,—

(*a*)   references in any enactment passed before this Act to an offence abolished by this Act shall, subject to any express amendment or repeal made by this Act, have effect as references to the corresponding offence under this Act, and in any such enactment the expression 'receive' (when it relates to an offence of receiving) shall mean handle, and 'receiver' shall be construed accordingly; and

(*b*)   without prejudice to paragraph (*a*) above, references in any enactment, whenever passed, to theft or stealing (including references to stolen goods), and references to robbery, blackmail, burglary, aggravated burglary or handling stolen goods, shall be construed in accordance with the provisions of this Act, including those of section 24.

Miscellaneous and consequential amendments, and repeal

33.—(1) The Post Office Act 1953 shall have effect subject to the amendments provided for by Part I of Schedule 2 to this Act and (except in so far as the contrary intention appears) those amendments shall have effect throughout the British postal area.

(2) The enactments mentioned in Parts II and III of Schedule 2 to this Act shall have effect subject to the amendments there provided for, and (subject to subsection (4) below) the amendments made by Part II to enactments extending beyond England and Wales shall have the like extent as the enactment amended.

(3) The enactments mentioned in Schedule 3 to this Act (which include in Part II certain enactments related to the subject matter of this Act but already obsolete

or redundant apart from this Act) are hereby repealed to the extent specified in column 3 of that Schedule; and, notwithstanding that the foregoing sections of this Act do not extend to Scotland, where any enactment expressed to be repealed by Schedule 3 does so extend, the Schedule shall have effect to repeal it in its application to Scotland except in so far as the repeal is expressed not to extend to Scotland.

(4) No amendment or repeal made by this Act in Schedule 1 to the Extradition Act 1870 or in the Schedule to the Extradition Act 1873 shall affect the operation of that Schedule by reference to the law of a British possession; but the repeal made in Schedule 1 to the Extradition Act 1870 shall extend throughout the United Kingdom.

Supplementary

Interpretation

34.—(1) Sections 4(1) and 5(1) of this Act shall apply generally for purposes of this Act as they apply for purposes of section 1.

(2) For purposes of this Act—

(a) 'gain' and 'loss' are to be construed as extending only to gain or loss in money or other property, but as extending to any such gain or loss whether temporary or permanent; and—

   (i) 'gain' includes a gain by keeping what one has, as well as a gain by getting what one has not; and

   (ii) 'loss' includes a loss by not getting what one might get, as well as a loss by parting with what one has;

(b) 'goods', except in so far as the context otherwise requires, includes money and every other description of property except land, and includes things severed from the land by stealing.

Commencement and transitional provisions

35.—(1) This Act shall come into force on the 1st January 1969 and, save as otherwise provided by this Act, shall have effect only in relation to offences wholly or partly committed on or after that date.

(2) Sections 27 and 28 of this Act shall apply in relation to proceedings for an offence committed before the commencement of this Act as they would apply in relation to proceedings for a corresponding offence under this Act, and shall so apply in place of any corresponding enactment repealed by this Act.

(3) Subject to subsection (2) above, no repeal or amendment by this Act of any enactment relating to procedure or evidence, or to the jurisdiction or powers of any court, or to the effect of a conviction, shall affect the operation of the enactment in relation to offences committed before the commencement of this Act or to proceedings for any such offence.

Short title, and general provisions as to Scotland and Northern Ireland
36.—(1) This Act may be cited as the Theft Act 1968.
[. . .[1]]
(3) This Act does not extend to Scotland or [. . .[1]] to Northern Ireland, except as regards any amendment or repeal which in accordance with section 33 above is to extend to Scotland and Northern Ireland.

Note
1 Subsection (2) and words in subsection (3) repealed by Northern Ireland Constitution Act 1973, s. 41(1)(a) and sch. 6, pt I.

SCHEDULES

Schedule 1   Offences of taking, etc. Deer[1] or Fish

Note
1 The paragraph of the schedule relating to deer has been repealed.

[. . .[1]]

Note
Paragraph 1 repealed by Deer Act 1980, s. 9(2).

Taking or destroying fish
2.—(1) Subject to subparagraph (2) below, a person who unlawfully takes or destroys, or attempts to take or destroy, any fish in water which is private property or in which there is any private right of fishery shall on summary conviction be liable to a fine not exceeding fifty pounds or, for an offence committed after a previous conviction of an offence under this subparagraph, to imprisonment for a term not exceeding three months or to a fine not exceeding one hundred pounds or to both.

(2) Subparagraph (1) above shall not apply to taking or destroying fish by angling in the daytime (that is to say, in the period beginning one hour before sunrise and ending one hour after sunset); but a person who by angling in the daytime unlawfully takes or destroys, or attempts to take or destroy, any fish in water which is private property or in which there is any private right of fishery shall on summary conviction be liable to a fine not exceeding twenty pounds.

(3) The court by which a person is convicted of an offence under this paragraph may order the forfeiture of anything which, at the time of the offence, he had with him for use for taking or destroying fish.

(4) Any person may arrest without warrant anyone who is, or whom he, with reasonable cause, suspects to be, committing an offence under subparagraph (1) above, and may seize from any person who is, or whom he, with reasonable cause, suspects to be, committing any offence under this paragraph anything which on that person's conviction of the offence would be liable to be forfeited under subparagraph (3) above.

Note
Schedule 2 (miscellaneous and consequential amendments) and Schedule 3 (repeals) are omitted here.

THEFT ACT 1978

1978, c. 31. An Act to replace section 16(2)(*a*) of the Theft Act 1968 with other provision against fraudulent conduct; and for connected purposes. [Royal assent 20 July 1978.]

Obtaining services by deception
   1.–(1) A person who by any deception dishonestly obtains services from another shall be guilty of an offence.
   (2) It is an obtaining of services where the other is induced to confer a benefit by doing some act, or causing or permitting some act to be done, on the understanding that the benefit has been or will be paid for.

Evasion of liability by deception
   2.–(1) Subject to subsection (2) below, where a person by any deception–

   (*a*)   dishonestly secures the remission of the whole or part of any existing liability to make a payment, whether his own liability or another's; or
   (*b*)   with intent to make permanent default in whole or in part on any existing liability to make a payment, or
           with intent to let another do so, dishonestly induces the creditor or any person claiming payment on behalf of the creditor to wait for payment (whether or not the due date for payment is deferred) or to forgo payment; or
   (*c*)   dishonestly obtains any exemption from or abatement of liability to make a payment;

he shall be guilty of an offence.
   (2) For purposes of this section 'liability' means legally enforceable liability; and subsection (1) shall not apply in relation to a liability that has not been accepted or established to pay compensation for a wrongful act or omission.
   (3) For purposes of subsection (1)(*b*) a person induced to take in payment a cheque or other security for money by way of conditional satisfaction of a pre-

existing liability is to be treated not as being paid but as being induced to wait for payment.

(4) For purposes of subsection (1)(*c*) 'obtains' includes obtaining for another or enabling another to obtain.

Making off without payment

3.—(1) Subject to subsection (3) below, a person who knowing that payment on the spot for any goods supplied or service done is required or expected from him, dishonestly makes off without having paid as required or expected and with intent to avoid payment of the amount due shall be guilty of an offence.

(2) For purposes of this section 'payment on the spot' includes payment at the time of collecting goods on which work has been done or in respect of which service has been provided.

(3) Subsection (1) above shall not apply where the supply of the goods or the doing of the service is contrary to law, or where the service done is such that payment is not legally enforceable.

(4) Any person may arrest without warrant anyone who is, or whom he, with reasonable cause, suspects to be, committing or attempting to commit an offence under this section.

Punishments

4.—(1) Offences under this Act shall be punishable either on conviction on indictment or on summary conviction.

(2) A person convicted on indictment shall be liable—

(*a*)   for an offence under section 1 or section 2 of this Act, to imprisonment for a term not exceeding five years; and

(*b*)   for an offence under section 3 of this Act, to imprisonment for a term not exceeding two years.

(3) A person convicted summarily of an offence under this Act shall be liable—

(*a*)   to imprisonment for a term not exceeding six months; or

(*b*)   to a fine not exceeding the prescribed sum for the purposes of [section 32 of the Magistrates' Courts Act 1980[1]] (punishment on summary conviction of offences triable either way: £1,000 or other sum substituted by order under that Act),

or to both.

Note

1   Words substituted by Magistrates' Courts Act 1980, s. 154(1) and sch. 7, para.
170. The prescribed sum is £2,000 as from 1 May 1984 (SI 1984 No. 447, art. 2(1)
and sch. 1).

Supplementary

5.—(1) For purposes of sections 1 and 2 above 'deception' has the same meaning
as in section 15 of the Theft Act 1968, that is to say, it means any deception
(whether deliberate or reckless) by words or conduct as to fact or as to law, including a deception as to the present intentions of the person using the deception or
any other person; and section 18 of that Act (liability of company officers for
offences by the company) shall apply in relation to sections 1 and 2 above as it
applies in relation to section 15 of that Act.

(2) Section 30(1) (husband and wife), 31(1) (effect on civil proceedings) and 34
(interpretation) of the Theft Act 1968, so far as they are applicable in relation to
this Act, shall apply as they apply in relation to that Act.

(3) In the Schedule to the Extradition Act 1873 (additional list of extradition
crimes), after 'Theft Act 1968' there shall be inserted 'or the Theft Act 1978'; and
there shall be deemed to be included among the descriptions of offences set out in
Schedule 1 to the Fugitive Offenders Act 1967 any offence under this Act.

(4) In the Visiting Forces Act 1952, in paragraph 3 of the Schedule (which
defines for England and Wales 'offence against property' for purposes of the exclusion in certain cases of the jurisdiction of United Kingdom courts) there shall be
added at the end—

'(*j*)   the Theft Act 1978'.

(5) In the Theft Act 1968 section 16(1)(*a*) is hereby repealed.

Enactment of same provisions for Northern Ireland

6. An Order in Council under paragraph 1(1)(*b*) of Schedule 1 to the Northern
Ireland Act 1974 (legislation for Northern Ireland in the interim period) which
contains a statement that it operates only so as to make for Northern Ireland
provision corresponding to this Act—

(*a*)   shall not be subject to paragraph 1(4) and (5) of that Schedule (affirmative
          resolution of both Houses of Parliament); but
(*b*)   shall be subject to annulment by resolution of either House.

Short title, commencement and extent

7.—(1) This Act may be cited as the Theft Act 1978.

(2) This Act shall come into force at the expiration of three months beginning with the date on which it is passed.

(3) This Act except section 5(3), shall not extend to Scotland; and except for that subsection, and subject also to section 6, it shall not extend to Northern Ireland.

INDEX